HANDBOOK OF SERVICE RESEARCH

Handbook of Service Marketing Research

Edited by

Roland T. Rust

University of Maryland, USA

Ming-Hui Huang

National Taiwan University, Taiwan

Edward Elgar
Cheltenham, UK • Northampton, MA, USA

Published by
Edward Elgar Publishing Limited
The Lypiatts
15 Lansdown Road
Cheltenham
Glos GL50 2JA
UK

Edward Elgar Publishing, Inc.
William Pratt House
9 Dewey Court
Northampton
Massachusetts 01060
USA

A catalogue record for this book
is available from the British Library

Library of Congress Control Number: 2013947141

This book is available electronically in the ElgarOnline.com
Business Subject Collection, E-ISBN 978 0 85793 885 5

MIX
Paper from
responsible sources
FSC® C013056
FSC
www.fsc.org

ISBN 978 0 85793 884 8 (cased)

Typeset by Servis Filmsetting Ltd, Stockport, Cheshire
Printed and bound in Great Britain by T.J. International Ltd, Padstow

Contents

PART VII RETHINKING THE MARKETING FUNCTION

PART VIII SERVICE FOR SOCIETY

Contributors

Melissa Archpru Akaka, University of Denver, USA

Lerzan Aksoy, Fordham University, USA

Laurel Anderson, Arizona State University, USA

Tor W. Andreassen, NHH Norwegian School of Economics, Norway

Sander F.M. Beckers, University of Groningen, The Netherlands

Mary Jo Bitner, Arizona State University, USA

Ruth N. Bolton, Arizona State University, USA

Alexander Buoye, IPSOS Loyalty, USA

Jee Won (Brianna) Choi, Georgia State University, USA

Ranjit M. Christopher, Arizona State University, USA

Tuck Siong Chung, Nanyang Technological University, Singapore

Tracey S. Dagger, Monash University, Australia

Peter J. Danaher, Monash University, Australia

Arne De Keyser, Ghent University, Belgium

Chekitan S. Dev, Cornell University, USA

Bo Edvardsson, Karlstad University, Sweden

Scott Fay, Syracuse University, USA

Raymond P. Fisk, Texas State University, USA

Carly Frennea, Rice University, USA

Anders Gustafsson, Karlstad University, Sweden

Ming-Hui Huang, National Taiwan University, Taiwan

Chiharu Ishida, Illinois State University, USA

P.K. Kannan, University of Maryland, USA

Timothy L. Keiningham, IPSOS Loyalty, USA

Per Kristensson, Karlstad University, Sweden

V. Kumar, Georgia State University, USA

Stephen K. Kwan, San José State University, USA

Tom van Laer, ESCP Europe Business School, UK

Bart Larivière, Ghent University, Belgium

Robert F. Lusch, University of Arizona, USA

Daniele Mathras, Arizona State University, USA

Horace Melton, Illinois State University, USA

Vikas Mittal, Rice University, USA

Richard L. Oliver, Vanderbilt University, USA

Amy L. Ostrom, Arizona State University, USA

Paul Patterson, University of New South Wales, Australia

Werner Reinartz, University of Cologne, Germany

Hans Risselada, University of Groningen, The Netherlands

Roland T. Rust, University of Maryland, USA

Ko de Ruyter, Maastricht University, The Netherlands

Christian Schulze, Frankfurt School of Finance & Management, Germany

Steven M. Shugan, University of Florida, USA

Bernd Skiera, Goethe University Frankfurt, Germany

Jim Spohrer, IBM Almaden Research Center, USA

Sandra Streukens, Hasselt University, Belgium

Steven A. Taylor, Illinois State University, USA

Bard Tronvoll, Karlstad University, Sweden

Wolfgang Ulaga, IMD International Institute for Management Development, Switzerland

Nita Umashankar, Georgia State University, USA

Stephen L. Vargo, University of Hawai'i at Manoa, USA

Peter C. Verhoef, University of Groningen, The Netherlands

Helen Si Wang, University of Hong Kong, China

Michel Wedel, University of Maryland, USA

Robert A. Westbrook, Rice University, USA

Luke Williams, IPSOS Loyalty, USA

Lars Witell, Linköping University, Sweden

Jinhong Xie, University of Florida, USA

Ting Yu, University of New South Wales, Australia

PART I

INTRODUCTION

1 Service marketing research: emerging directions

Roland T. Rust and Ming-Hui Huang

INTRODUCTION

Prior work has advanced our thinking of how the increasingly technological world has altered service marketing, as well as the whole field of marketing (Oliver et al. 1998; Rust and Huang 2011, 2013; Rust et al. 2004, 2010; Sun 2006; Vargo and Lusch 2004). Perhaps the best way to discern the current direction of change in a discipline is to assemble an all-star team of thought leaders and see what they are thinking about now. That is exactly what we have done for this book. The most brilliant people in service research from all over the world, both from academia and business, have contributed their latest thinking. We made little attempt to shape their agenda, other than hand-selecting them as forward thinkers, and we encouraged them to pursue the topics they thought were most important. The result is that this volume looks forward as much as it looks back. The reader cannot help but come away with a transformed and enlightened viewpoint about the field.

CUSTOMER-CENTRICITY

A hallmark of service marketing is its focus on the customer. Following the introductory part, the second, third and fourth parts of the book explore this. The second part of the book, "Customer Relationships and Loyalty," investigates the most central issue in service marketing—managing and maintaining ongoing customer relationships. The Bolton and Christopher chapter, "Building long-term relationships between service organizations and customers," provides an excellent overview of this issue. The first author, Ruth Bolton, has an extensive background in business as well as academia, and is able to bring together both managerial relevance and academic rigor. To build a successful customer relationship it is essential to cultivate a loyal customer. The chapter "Loyalty: its many sources and variations" by Aksoy, Keiningham and Oliver explores the nature of loyalty, again drawing from both business experience (Keiningham) and academic theory (Aksoy and Oliver). Keiningham is arguably the leading business practitioner in the loyalty field, and Oliver is arguably the leading academic theorist in customer satisfaction and loyalty. This theoretical and conceptual piece is followed by an empirical piece by Dagger and Danaher, "A comparison of relationship marketing models," that applies necessary empirical rigor to test alternative customer relationship conceptualizations. Following that chapter is another chapter by Oliver, "Loyalty: its biogenic, psychological, and social origins – answering the question of 'Why Y?'," which delves into the underlying causes of loyalty. Finally, there is a chapter by Beckers, Risselada and Verhoef, "Customer engagement: a new frontier in customer value management," providing new insights and conceptualization into the nature of customer relationships, following seminal work by Brodie (Brodie et al. 2011) and others.

The other key aspect of customer-centricity, from a managerial standpoint, is the topic of the third part of the book, "Customer-centered Metrics." Skiera and Schulze, in their controversial but persuasive chapter, "Customer-based valuation: similarities and differences to traditional discounted cash flow models," show how customer equity is related to the value of the firm, and therefore how customer equity can be used to value companies. This provides a customer-centered alternative to existing company valuation methods that they show performs better than traditional methods. The next chapter, "CRM metrics and strategies to enhance performance in service industries," by Kumar, Umashankar and Choi, overviews methods for building metrics for measuring the success of customer relationship management (CRM). The chapter summarizes Kumar and his colleagues' extensive research stream in the area, as well as bringing in the relevant work of other researchers in the area. The next chapter results from an academic–practitioner partnership involving Keiningham and others from IPSOS Loyalty along with academic co-authors Aksoy and Larivière. They show convincingly that relative metrics (relative to competitors) are essential. The part concludes with a chapter by Frennea, Mittal and Westbrook on "The satisfaction profit chain," building on the service profit chain (Heskett et al. 1994) and return on quality (Rust et al. 1994, 1995) efforts to construct chains of effect for customer satisfaction.

The fourth and final part of the book related to customer-centricity is the "Managing Customer Contacts" part, which seeks to explore the human contact between customers and employees. The part starts with a chapter by Bitner (one of the pioneers in studying customer contacts) and Wang, "Service encounters in service marketing research." The chapter comes from academics, but with a solid understanding and experience with the managerial environment. The next chapter, by Streukens and Andreassen, focuses on the employee side of customer contact. The chapter entitled "Frontline employees and performance: optimizing the frontline, maximizing the bottom line" explores how to effectively manage frontline customer contact employees. The next chapter, "Are you (appropriately) experienced? Service–sales ambidexterity," by de Ruyter, Patterson and Yu, addresses the conundrum that many companies face, in which their customer contact people often have to divide their efforts between selling and serving customers.

MARKETING DECISION MAKING

The traditional 4 Ps have long been considered inadequate to describe service marketing, because of the greatly amplified importance of customer relationships. This is why the second, third and fourth parts of the book focus on customer-centricity and how to manage relationships with customers. Nevertheless, the traditional 4 Ps have not gone away. And three of the 4 Ps (product, price and place) have been greatly transformed by the nature of the growing service economy. Therefore it is no accident that some of our all-star author panel have chosen to focus on "Product and Pricing," which is the book's next part.

The first chapter is Shugan's "The pricing of services." Shugan is one of the deepest thinkers in service marketing and is well trained in the core discipline of economics. He shows how the pricing environment changes dramatically in the service environment. From pricing we then move to product. Xie and Fay, in their chapter, "Marketing innovation: probabilistic goods and probabilistic selling," proposes some futuristic new ways to create and sell products, based on probability theory. They show that these seemingly wild ideas are actually already being found in practice to some degree. Anyone who thinks that the service revolution is not fundamentally changing marketing should read this chapter. The next chapter is from Swedish thought leaders Edvardsson, Gustafsson, Kristensson, Tronvoll and Witell, who describe new methods of developing new service products in their chapter, "New service development from the perspective of value co-creation in a service system." Finishing the part is "Hybrid offerings: research avenues for implementing service growth strategies" by Reinartz and Ulaga. This chapter describes and motivates an increasingly common scenario—the bundling of goods and services to provide more value than either by itself—and shows how that scenario can be successfully managed.

Another of the traditional 4 Ps is place, and that has been transformed in recent years by the proliferation of the Internet, mobile communication, and social media. This motivates the next part of the book, "Digital

Service Marketing." The first chapter in this part is "Adaptive personalization of mobile information services," by Chung and Wedel. Wedel is one of the world's leading figures in recommendation systems and personalization, and he and Chung describe how instead of "recommending" products, products can be designed that can adapt themselves automatically, based on observing the behavior of a customer over time, to personalize for the customer. From personalization, the next chapter moves to social media. The chapter "It's the social, stupid! Leveraging the 4C markers of social in online service delivery," by de Ruyter and van Laer, gives guidance about how to take best advantage of the social media environment. Digital piracy is an increasing concern in many quarters, and the next chapter, "A meta-analytic investigation of the antecedents of digital piracy," by Taylor, Ishida and Melton, rigorously summarizes the existing literature about what we know about how people form their behaviors with respect to piracy.

THE BIG PICTURE—SERVICE MARKETING IN THE FIRM AND IN THE WORLD

The last two parts of the book step back to take a broader view of how the service revolution changes the marketing function, and the role service marketing plays in the society. The first part is "Rethinking the Marketing Function." Starting this part are influential marketing meta-theorists, Vargo and Lusch, along with their colleague, Akaka, with the chapter, "Rethinking the roles of marketing and operations: a service-ecosystems view." The chapter summarizes the "service-dominant logic" viewpoint of value co-creation, and how it changes the role that marketing should play in the firm. Also taking a broad view is the chapter, "Marketing: a service science and arts perspective," by IBM service science guru and evangelist Spohrer, along with noted service academics Kwan and Fisk. The chapter combines engineering/operations concepts from the service science movement with ideas from marketing, and employs metaphors from the arts. The final chapter in the part, by hospitality expert Dev, describes how the service marketing environment is changing for one particular industry, hospitality, in the chapter "Hospitality marketing and branding research: insights from a specific service context."

The final part of the book, "Service for Society," describes how service marketing can serve the needs of the society as a whole. The first chapter, "Transformative service research: an emerging subfield focused on service and well-being," by Ostrom, Mathras and Anderson, summarizes the broad topic of serving society. This conceptualization is then brought to the area of government service by Kannan, in his chapter "Creating social value through citizen co-creation," who argues that citizen co-creation can help improve government service.

WHAT WE LEARN FROM THIS BOOK

The learnings from such a stellar collection of service experts are numerous and we certainly cannot summarize all of them here. If you will grant us some editorial license, we will try to list a few of the things that we found most striking:

- The dramatically expanded emphasis on customer relationships and loyalty makes use of traditional goods marketing frameworks like the 4 Ps in service marketing woefully incomplete, if not dangerously obsolete.
- The value of the customer base, measured by customer lifetime value and customer equity, can be used to value companies, and can give better results than traditional discounted cash flow models.
- Pricing of services is completely different from the pricing of goods.
- Companies can (and do) sell a probability of receiving an offering. Not all of these companies are in Las Vegas or Macao!
- Products that change themselves to personalize for the customer can be better than recommendations or self-customization.
- New ideas from service marketing can be used to improve social well-being.

This is just a small sampling of the nuggets to be gleaned from this book. In conclusion, there are many exciting things happening in service marketing, and as service continues to expand as a proportion of every advanced economy, the marketing world will continue to evolve.

REFERENCES

Brodie, Roderick J., Linda D. Hollebeek, Biljana Jurić and Ana Ilić (2011), "Customer engagement: conceptual domain, fundamental propositions, and implications for research," *Journal of Service Research*, **14** (3), 252–71.

Heskett, James L., Thomas O. Jones, Gary W. Loveman, W. Earl Sasser and Leonard A. Schlesinger (1994), "Putting the service-profit chain to work," *Harvard Business Review*, March–April, 164–74.

Oliver, Richard W., Roland T. Rust and Sajeev Varki (1998), "Real-time marketing," *Marketing Management*, **7** (Fall–Winter), 29–37.

Rust, Roland T., Anthony J. Zahorik and Timothy L. Keiningham (1994), *Return on Quality:*

Measuring the Financial Impact of Your Company's Quest for Quality, Chicago: Probus Publishing.
Rust, Roland T., Anthony J. Zahorik and Timothy L. Keiningham (1995), "Return on quality (ROQ): making service quality financially accountable," *Journal of Marketing*, **59** (April), 58–70.
Rust, Roland T. and Ming-Hui Huang (2011), *Service Marketing: Insights and Directions*, Marketing Science Institute "Fast Forward" series.
Rust, Roland T. and Ming-Hui Huang (forthcoming), "The service revolution and the transformation of marketing science," *Marketing Science*.
Rust, Roland T., Christine Moorman and Gaurav Bhalla, (2010), "Rethinking marketing," *Harvard Business Review*, **88** (1), 94–101.
Rust, Roland T., Valarie A. Zeithaml and Katherine N. Lemon (2004), "Customer-centered brand management," *Harvard Business Review*, **82** (9), 110–18.
Sun, Baohong (2006), "Technology innovation and implications for customer relationship management," *Marketing Science*, **25** (6), 594–7.
Vargo, Stephen L. and Robert F. Lusch (2004), "Evolving to a new dominant logic for marketing," *Journal of Marketing*, **68** (January), 1–17.

PART II

CUSTOMER RELATIONSHIPS AND LOYALTY

2 Building long-term relationships between service organizations and customers

Ruth N. Bolton and Ranjit M. Christopher

Service organizations pursue long-term relationships with customers for three major reasons. First, relationships with customers are market-based assets that directly influence shareholder value by accelerating or increasing the magnitude of cash flows, lowering the volatility and vulnerability of cash flows, and increasing their residual value (Srivastava et al. 1998). Consequently, long relationships increase customer equity or the value of the customer base, as well as many other measures of financial performance (Hogan et al. 2002; Kumar and Shah 2009). Second, long relationships between a service organization and its customers imply high customer retention rates. Customer retention usually has the largest influence (vis-à-vis other components) on the value of the customer base (Gupta et al. 2004). Third, customers in long-term relationships exhibit favorable behaviors such as paying price premiums, increasing service usage, cross-buying and increasing share of customer or wallet (Bolton and Lemon 1999; Verhoef et al. 2001). These behaviors lead to better customer and employee role performance and to decreased costs to serve customers in some industries (Meuter et al. 2005).

However, long-term relationships must be managed so that they are beneficial to both the organization and its customers. Sometimes, as customers stay longer with a service organization, they may expect price discounts or better service—leading to increased costs to serve them and lower margins. Hence, customer equity may be increased by better managing individual customers' cash flows (through resource allocation decisions) or by altering the customer mix/portfolio to yield larger cash flows with the same degree of risk (Tarasi et al. 2013). For example, the budget allocation between customer acquisition and retention can be optimized by analyzing the cash flow patterns of customers (Blattberg and Deighton 1996; Rust et al. 2004; Tarasi et al. 2011).

Why do service managers and researchers study the length of the customer–organization relationship rather than studying (more broadly) relationship depth, breadth, strength or profitability? The key reason is that customer lifetime duration—and its inverse, customer churn or defection—is a significant and substantial problem for organizations in many service industries, including financial, health, utilities, telecommunications and publishing service sectors. Some service organizations face churn rates of 25–40 percent, implying that a firm's entire customer base can vanish within about five years unless these losses are offset by expensive customer acquisition efforts. Hence, there is intensive interest in how to predict and understand churn so that firms can better manage it (Neslin et al. 2006b). We do not assume that a long relationship is always a more valuable relationship (to either party). However, when all else is equal, a long relationship is preferable to a short relationship. Moreover, as this chapter will discuss, managers sometimes find customer lifetime duration a useful surrogate when estimates of customer value are difficult to make and error-prone.

Researchers have investigated how to achieve mutually beneficial long-term relationships from different theoretical perspectives, using a wide variety of research methods. This chapter reviews and synthesizes extant scholarly work by considering four broad questions:

1. What managerial and theoretical perspectives have enhanced our understanding of how to build long-term relationships between service organizations and their customers?
2. How should service researchers conceptualize and measure the duration of the relationship between a service organization and its customer?
3. What are the antecedents of long-term relationships between organizations and their customers?
4. How is the duration of the relationship between an organization and a customer linked to financial outcomes?

In this chapter, we emphasize studies that focus on customers' relationships with service organizations, as opposed to their relationships with manufacturers of goods, due to the many differences between goods and services (Vargo and Lusch 2004). For example, there is evidence to suggest that relationship marketing efforts have different effects on financial outcomes across service- and goods-based exchange (Palmatier et al. 2006). We also highlight the contextual differences between business-to-business and business-to-consumer service relationship settings. We conclude by presenting research opportunities for future research.

THEORETICAL PERSPECTIVES ON MUTUALLY BENEFICIAL LONG-TERM RELATIONSHIPS

Co-creation of Value

Service emphasizes the exchange of intangible resources between the customer and the firm, leading to the co-creation of value and relationships (Prahalad and Ramaswamy 2004; Vargo and Lusch 2004). The co-creation of value occurs in all relationships: business-to-consumer (B2C) services such as healthcare, business-to-business (B2B) services such as solution selling, and derived services, whereby customers derive value from the service provided by a tangible good such as equipment (Zeithaml et al. 2006). Managers frequently focus on the value of relationships from the firm perspective, rather than from the customer perspective, because the allocation of resources to sustain a long-term relationship necessitates financial justification. Consequently, return on marketing investment has been a key focus in the literature (Rust et al. 1995, 2004).

Value of the Relationship to the Customer

In monopoly services, such as government or regulated industries (for example, utilities), customers do not have a choice of service provider. However, in most service industries, markets are competitive and customers can switch among alternative providers seeking value (or utility) after considering switching costs and perceived risks (Jones et al. 2002; Lee et al. 2001). Customers derive value from being in a long-term relationship because the organization learns how to consistently provide customized service that matches customer needs, yielding economic, social and psychological benefits (Bendapudi and Berry 1997; Gwinner et al. 1998). Moreover, there are costs to switching such as lost performance cost (for example, loyalty rewards, volume based discounts), search costs, set-up costs, and sunk costs (Burnham et al. 2003; Jones et al. 2002). These costs can be framed in terms of service convenience, conceptualized as "consumers' time and effort perceptions related to buying or using a service" (Berry et al. 2002, p. 4). Elements of service convenience vary by industry and reflect consumers' underlying purchase and consumption activities; they include decision convenience, access convenience, transaction convenience, benefit convenience and post-benefit convenience. In sum, when a customer can terminate his/her relationship with the organization, the lifetime duration of the relationship inherently reflects the value of the relationship.

Value of the Relationship to the Organization

The value of an individual customer is usually measured by customer lifetime value (CLV)—that is, the net present value of future cash flows from an individual customer over the (forecasted) duration of the relationship. Hence, the lifetime duration of the relationship between the customer and the service organization is a key component of the value of the relationship. Customer equity (the value of the customer base) is calculated by aggregating the discounted (net) cash flows of all customers including prospects (Berger and Nasr 1998). It is directly linked to shareholder value (Gupta et al. 2004). Customer lifetime value and customer equity should be calculated by decomposing cash flows into three key underlying sources—customer acquisition, retention and margins (derived from service usage and cross-buying patterns). These calculations should be made at the customer or segment level, rather than the firm level (Gupta and Lehmann 2005, pp. 7–9). Research has highlighted that the value of an individual customer is not independent of other customers in the organization's portfolio (Dhar and Glazer 2003; Johnson and Selnes 2004). Hence, any assessment of the value of an individual customer must take into account how the customers' cash flows co-vary with other customers (Tarasi et al. 2011).

Customer Relationship Management

An organization's relationship with a customer is an asset of the organization—an asset that is valuable, hard to imitate by competition and therefore a source of competitive advantage. In studies of how the customer asset is linked to stock market performance, customer satisfaction usually serves as a mediating construct (Kumar and Shah 2009). Service research has had a long-standing focus on customer relationships and customer loyalty (Berry 1983, 1995; Grönroos 1990). Relationship marketing seeks to create bonds with customers through financial programs (for example, discounts or economic incentives), social programs (for example, meals and entertainment) and structural programs that increase the buying firm's productivity or efficiency, thereby strengthening relationships (Berry 1980, 1995).

Researchers distinguish among three dimensions of behavior in customer-organization relationships (Bolton et al. 2004): length (that is, customer lifetime duration), depth (for example, service usage) and breadth (for example, number of products). In contrast, loyalty is typically considered to be an underlying predisposition of customers—that is, an (unobserved) psychological and composite construct which includes repeat patronage—length, depth or breadth—as one of its key elements. Numerous conceptualizations of customer loyalty exist in the literature that explicate the mechanisms underlying repeat patronage behavior (Dick and Basu 1994; Oliver 1999). In sum, it is important to emphasize that the lifetime duration of the relationship between the customer and the organization—that is, customer lifetime duration—is generally considered to be a critical dimension of the customer–organization relationship and of customer loyalty.

CONCEPTUALIZATION AND MEASUREMENT OF LONG-TERM RELATIONSHIPS

Customer Lifetime Duration

From a conceptual standpoint, the duration of a customer-organization relationship is the period of time encompassing all purchase and consumption activities between the two entities. Customers may use or buy services continuously or intermittently; they may refrain from buying a product or service for a period before resuming purchases or they may defect from a relationship until the organization wins them back (Hogan et al. 2003). They can also exhibit multiple loyalties—purchasing the same product/service from different organizations either simultaneously or sequentially (Bell et al. 2002; Berger and Nasr 1998). Hence, when forecasting the customer lifetime duration, it can be misleading to assume that a customer-organization relationship has ended after a brief lull in a purchase sequence. In fact, firms make special efforts to recapture these potentially "lost customers" (Thomas et al. 2004).

Customer lifetime duration is not the same as the length of a customer-organization relationship at a given point in time. Customer lifetime duration is usually censored—that is, firms frequently do not observe the end of the relationship, it may still be ongoing.[1] In predictive models, this issue is addressed by computing a probability of whether the customer is "alive" as opposed to "gone for good" (Berger and Nasr 1998; Neslin et al. 2006b; Venkatesan and Kumar 2004). For example, customer lifetime duration can be modeled as a hazard rate—that is, the probability that the customer remains in the relationship given that he or she has not already defected (Bolton 1998).

Both CLV and customer equity are composite measures that include other elements beyond the forecasted relationship length. Note that, when a composite measure is statistically linked to an individual customer metrics (for example, customer lifetime duration) or an organization-level metric (for example, shareholder value), it is important to ensure that a '*ceteris paribus*' condition holds. The other elements that make up the CLV construct (for example, contribution margin) should remain constant or be accounted for in the statistical model.

Alternative Measures

Customer retention is closely associated with customer lifetime duration; it can be measured and modeled as the percentage of the total customer base that repurchases within a given time period or as the probability that an individual customer repurchases within a given time period (Bolton et al. 2006; Verhoef 2003). In the latter case, it can also be measured by its obverse: the likelihood of switching. While customer lifetime duration and customer retention metrics can be calculated from databases describing purchases over time (Bolton et al. 2004), it is frequently difficult to observe switching among competing service providers. Switching probabilities are sometimes obtained from survey data to calculate customer equity (Rust et al. 2004). The measurement and modeling of customer lifetime duration or retention should not be confused with methods for predicting the frequency, timing and (short-term) dollar value of customers' purchases (Reinartz and Kumar 2003; Schmittlein and Peterson 1994); the focal dependent variable and model specification are different—leading to different measures of customer value.

Many researchers use customers' self-reports of repeat purchase intentions and willingness to recommend to represent loyalty; this approach is incomplete but nevertheless useful in some circumstances (Lam et al. 2004; Sirdeshmukh et al. 2002; Zeithaml et al. 1996). For example, a combination of higher repeat purchase intentions and willingness to recommend to others may indicate that customers will be ambassadors of the service organization—so that new customer acquisition is less costly. However, self-reported intentions are only proxies for future behavior. For example, many studies have shown that purchase intentions are error prone measures of purchase behavior (Morwitz and Schmittlein 1992) and that their antecedents and consequences are quite different (for example, Mittal and Kamakura 2001; Seiders et al. 2005).

ANTECEDENTS OF LONG-TERM RELATIONSHIPS

This section describes theoretical and empirical evidence concerning the factors that influence customers' lifetime durations. These include: service design and experience quality, customer satisfaction, service brand equity and commitment, price, loyalty programs, marketing channels and communications, competitor actions, social networks and customer characteristics.

Service Design and Experience Quality

Service quality is defined to be the customer's perception of excellence or superiority in service performance (Zeithaml 1988); it encompasses the design of the service and the customer's experience with the delivery process (Grönroos 1990). Service design and experience quality directly influence customer trial and repurchase intentions (for example, Rust et al. 1999; Zeithaml et al. 1996). In addition, excellent service recovery is required to forestall customer defection after a service failure (Smith and Bolton 1998; Smith et al. 1999).

Favorable service quality perceptions increase customer retention (Bolton et al. 2006; Boulding et al. 1993). In B2C and B2B markets, the level of service quality and its consistency over time influence the lifetime duration of the organization–customer relationship. Rust et al. (1999) showed how uncertainty in service quality is directly related to repurchase likelihood in consumer markets. Bolton et al. (2006) show that service quality experience across multiple service contracts has a significant influence on a business customer's decision to renew a focal contract. They also found that customers who experienced a recent extreme and favorable change in quality tended to renew the contracts—extending the customer lifetime duration.

Customer Satisfaction

Satisfaction is a post-consumption assessment or fulfillment response and, unlike service quality, it has an emotional component. There is a large stream of research showing that more (less) satisfied customers have longer (shorter) relationships with service organizations in both B2C and B2B markets (Bolton 1998; Crosby and Stephens 1987; Lam et al. 2004). Notably, Bolton (1998) analyzed customer lifetime durations of cell phone users using a proportional hazard model and found that experienced customers weighed cumulative customer satisfaction more heavily in their decision to continue with the service relationship than did inexperienced customers. Consumers were less likely to defect from a relationship after a service failure when they had high levels of cumulative satisfaction, suggesting that service organizations should use the early stages of the relationship to build cumulative satisfaction. The influence of a service failure or a negative event decreases customer lifetime duration more than a positive event increases it. This effect is exacerbated by the presence of a contrast effect such that customer defections are higher when customers experience high quality service prior to a service failure.

The links between customers' satisfaction levels and their purchase behavior are dynamic and reciprocal over time. For example, Bolton and Lemon (1999) found empirical support for a dynamic model where prior usage levels, customer expectations and price explain customer perception of fairness (payment equity) which then influences future usage levels of the service through satisfaction. This result implies, for example, that an increase in the likelihood of patronage is likely to positively influence subsequent customer satisfaction which (in turn) influences subsequent patronage behavior. Together, these studies suggest that service organizations may reap greater benefits during the later stages of the relationship with the customer than in the early stages—justifying investments in the satisfaction programs early in the relationship.

Service Brand Equity and Commitment

Service quality perceptions help build service brand equity (Berry 2000) and brand equity has been shown to influence customer retention and profit margins (Stahl et al. 2012). Brand knowledge improves acquisition, retention and profit margin, whereas brand differentiation in high profitability markets impedes acquisition and retention. This finding suggests that the customer's service experience is vitally important, whereas differentiation vis-à-vis competitors may (ultimately) lead organizations to serve a niche market, with smaller market share.

Relationship commitment is defined as a customer's desire to continue a valued relationship with a service brand or organization into the future (Dwyer et al. 1987; Moorman et al. 1993; Morgan and Hunt 1994).[2] In contrast with satisfaction (which requires a retrospective evaluation), commitment is future oriented. Researchers frequently distinguish between customers' calculative commitment based on economic factors and affective commitment based on non-economic factors (Gustafsson et al. 2005). In both B2B and B2C markets, high calculative commitment is positively associated with high switching costs; research has consistently shown that such costs (which deter switching) are associated with high customer retention (Jones et al. 2002; Lam et al. 2004; Lee et al. 2001). Situational variables can intervene between conation and action, so that this relationship is not evident in all service industries.

Verhoef (2003) showed that affective commitment was positively related to customer retention and customer share development for customers of an insurance company. However, Gustafsson et al. (2005) did not find these relationships for customers of a telecommunications company. One reason may be that customer emotions, especially attachment, may be more important in the insurance industry—where perceived risk is important—than in the telecommunications industry (Mende et al. 2013). Moreover, discrete consumer emotions, such as regret and disappointment, explain variance in future behaviors, such as complaining, switching, word-of-mouth and customer inertia, over and above the effect of (dis) satisfaction (Inman et al. 1997; Zeelenberg and Pieters 2004).

Affect and discrete emotions are important in B2B settings as well; for example, the social bonds created between organizations (or their employees) and customers can foster a longer relationship. Bolton et al. (2003) found that social bonds had a relatively larger effect on customers' satisfaction with company representatives (employees) and perceived value, whereas structural bonds created through the exchange of economic resources (financial or operational) have a relatively larger effect on their overall satisfaction with the organization. More recently, customer gratitude (Palmatier et al. 2009) and customer relationship orientation (Palmatier 2008b) have been identified as important contributors to relationship performance.

Price

Unlike switching costs, the relationship between price and the duration of the customer-organization relationship is complex (Bolton 1998; Bolton and Lemon 1999). Clearly, price plays an important role in customer acquisition; lower prices may induce customers to try a new service. However, if the customer finds the service organization's value proposition attractive and enters into a relationship, price subsequently becomes less salient unless there is a radical discrepancy in price vis-à-vis the competition or past prices. This observation is consistent with reference price theory (Bolton et al. 2003; Mazumdar et al. 2005). For example, business customers' price sensitivity (that is, elasticity) depends on service quality dimensions and market factors (Bolton and Myers 2003). Hence, service researchers do not always find a statistically significant relationship between price and the duration of the customer–organization relationship; instead, customers modify their buying patterns so that they can continue to derive value from the relationship.

Loyalty Programs

Loyalty programs can have a positive influence on customer lifetime durations, but they operate in complex ways. One reason for their success is well recognized; many loyalty programs offer economic incentives to stay with a service provider. However, we speculate that a customer who experiences a range of service experiences over time will become more knowledgeable and demanding, thereby increasing the likelihood that he or she will defect to a competing service brand. Indeed, many marketing programs, including loyalty programs, have failed to increase customer retention, leading some managers to question the link between marketing actions and business performance (Lehman 2004). However, there is some evidence that repurchase rates increase for customers participating in a loyalty program, even after accounting for the effects of short-term promotions such as email coupons, pricing changes or discounts in shipping fees. One explanation for this finding is that loyalty programs encourage customers to take future benefits into consideration when making purchase decisions. Supporting this notion, Lewis (2004) found that a dynamic multi-period decision-making model fits customer purchase patterns better than static models in an online grocery and drugstore setting.

Using cross-sectional and time-series data from a global financial services company, Bolton et al. (2000) investigated how a loyalty rewards program influences customer evaluations, repeat purchase intentions and behavior. Their results show that members in the loyalty reward program overlook or discount negative evaluations of the company vis-à-vis competition. In other words, loyalty programs—especially programs that offer noneconomic rewards—serve to mitigate future negative experiences in an ongoing relationship. They speculate that members of the loyalty rewards program may perceive that they are getting better quality and service for their price. Of course, competing service suppliers can mimic such loyalty programs and eliminate any differential advantage quickly. Indeed, Meyer-Waarden (2007) finds a decrease in customer lifetime durations when multiple service organizations within the same geographic location have loyalty programs. Recent research suggests that service organizations should customize non-economic rewards within loyalty programs for "relationship tiers" or segments of the customer base to be successful (Drèze and Nunes 2009; Kivetz and Simonson 2003) and that they should carefully monitor subsequent purchase behavior to evaluate their effectiveness.

Marketing Channels and Communications

Channel usage patterns potentially influence customer relationship durations. For example, when the length of a customer's lifetime is conditional on customer acquisition (which varies across channels), Thomas (2001) shows that a Tobit model with selection will perform better than a standard Tobit model in predicting future purchase behavior. Customers may use different marketing channels as they progress through need recognition, information search, purchase, and after-sales service. For example, a consumer might conduct an extensive online search, purchase at the closest store and then telephone to obtain after-sales support. Or, channel preferences can be based on previous purchase experiences in the category or other categories. Thus, a service organization that lacks a customer's preferred channel may risk losing patronage.

Channel coordination requires a thorough understanding of the channel usage patterns of existing customers. Neslin et al. (2006a) suggest that complete integration of customer data across channels is not optimal based on return on investment from data integration technology and processes. Service organizations are better able to manage segment-based variation in channel usage. For example, customer role clarity, motivation, and ability influence customers' adoption and use of self-service technology (Meuter et al. 2005). Channel coordination strategies such as information-only channels aided by offline store integration can aid relationship depth (more store visits) contingent on product category and consumer segment (Montaguti et al. 2012; Pauwels et al. 2011).

The ways that marketing channels influence customer lifetime duration are not well understood, so managers tend to use proxy measures to guide the allocation of effort to customers and channels. For example, Venkatesan and Kumar (2004) use short-run forecasts of CLV to guide the allocation of customer contacts through different marketing channels to maximize profits. Channel performance is typically assessed by measuring sales growth, profitability, upgrades, cross-buying and customer lifetime duration. There is some evidence that adding new channels induces sales growth either due to increased customer loyalty, self-selection or marketing efforts (Ansari et al. 2008). There is evidence that some organizations suffer in terms of profitability, customer service, and customer retention due to duplication or cannibalization of existing channels (Godfrey et al. 2011; Lee and Grewal 2004). More research is required on the performance of channel additions to reconcile these conflicting findings.

There are many studies of how marketing communications influence purchase patterns for consumer goods, especially in a direct marketing context (for example, Thomas and Sullivan 2005; Venkatesan and Kumar 2004). However, there is substantially less research on marketing communications by service organizations. It seems likely that the effects of the organization's marketing communications on customer lifetime durations are much smaller for services than for goods because customer satisfaction and perceptions of service quality play such an important role for services. On the other hand, there are many more instances of customer-initiated contacts with service suppliers that offer opportunities to sustain and expand customer-organization relationships (Bowman and Narayandas 2001).

Competitor Actions

There is very little research on the effects of competitor actions on customer lifetime durations for service organizations (Keavney 1995). The primary reason is that most firms' databases do not capture information about competitors' actions. At best they describe the service organization's own actions over time. This omission is a handicap to forecasting customer lifetime durations and managing customer relationships because firms frequently target their competitors' customers with appeals designed to encourage switching behavior. In their "return on marketing" model, Rust et al. (2004) address this challenge by incorporating survey data that describes switching behavior over time in response to marketing actions.

Social Networks

Despite the rich literature on the role of social influence in the product diffusion and individual adoption literature, research on how social network dynamics influence customer retention is sparse. In a B2B context, Palmatier (2008a) uses social network analysis to look at the structural ties between two service organizations to predict relationship success. In a B2C context, Nitzan and Libai (2011) found that the influence of social networks on customer defection is as much as—if not higher than—its influence on adoption. Defections within close networks increase the defection hazard rate by 80 percent. Using the call database of a telecommunication services company to reconstruct personal networks of customers, they find that loyal customers tend to stay with the provider despite defection within their personal networks. Curiously, the rate of defection is not as pronounced when their network members have high connectivity.

These findings indicate that customers may not be imitating their social circle but (instead) value the decisions of their close circle of friends. This pattern of behavior is different from findings concerning the influence of highly connected network members (hubs) on new product adoption, in which hubs tend to increase the speed and volume of subsequent adoption in the network (Goldenberg et al. 2009). Also, the influence of social network effects on defection rates decreases exponentially over time, indicating that service organizations managing highly connected customers should be wary of the immediate reaction of disgruntled customers as well as long-term word-of-mouth effects (Nitzan and Libai 2011). Negative word of mouth typically has a greater influence than positive word of mouth (Goldenberg et al. 2007).

Customer Characteristics

Certain characteristics of the customer increase the odds of a relationship surviving for longer periods, including demographics (for example, age), personal characteristics (for example, attachment style) and relational preferences (for example, long-term orientation). Consumers' age is linked to the level and variation of consumption and purchases through life events (Zeithaml 1985), depending on the product category (Namias 1960). Consumers' attachment styles influence their preferences for closeness which in turn increases their propensity to be loyal to the service organization and cross-buy (Mende et al. 2013). Consumers' relational preferences are good predictors of repeat purchase intentions and consumer loyalty for B2C services (Godfrey et al. 2011; Price and Arnould 1999). For B2B services, Ganesan (1994) shows that some business customers have a long-term orientation to buyer–seller relationships that is closely related to mutual dependence and trust. He found that these two constructs are influenced by uncertainty in the business environment, the presence of transaction specific investments, service organization reputation, and satisfaction with prior business dealings. Not surprisingly, the same variables influence other aspects of customers' purchase behavior, including their cash flow levels and variability (Tarasi et al. 2013).

LINKING CUSTOMER LIFETIME DURATION TO FINANCIAL OUTCOMES

Importance of Customer Lifetime Duration to CLV and Customer Equity

In many service industries, it is more costly to acquire new customers than to retain existing customers—especially in mature markets or when discount rates are low. In these circumstances, an emphasis on customer retention (as opposed to other components of CLV) is entirely appropriate (Gupta and Lehmann 2005). For these reasons, many service organizations focus on improving customer retention (and its key antecedents, satisfaction and service quality) rather than the other sources that feed into CLV. Indeed, an emphasis on customer retention is a common feature across all approaches to managing customer equity (Kumar and George 2007). Hence, service organizations may find it useful to use market segmentation methods that take into account the forecasted length of the relationship, as well as customers' purchasing patterns (Berger et al. 2002; Tarasi et al. 2013; Wedel and Kamakura 1999)

The potential danger of focusing solely on customer lifetime duration is clear: it overlooks potential new customers. Hence, managers usually prefer to calculate CLV. This calculation requires forecasts of three components or sources of cash flows over customer lifetimes: customer acquisition, duration (or retention) and gross margin (Berger and Nasr 1998; Gupta et al. 2004). Note that gross margin reflects the effect of service usage rates and cross-buying of premium services. This approach can be used to forecast (under different scenarios) the cash flows derived from individual customers or customer segments and (ultimately) to identify the optimal allocation of resources to the customer base (Bolton et al. 2004). Berger et al. (2006) emphasize that these components must be forward-looking, rather than based on historical data. However, it can be challenging to develop forecasts of these three components for an individual customer or customer segment over a long-term time horizon. However, practical approaches exist. For example, Tirenni et al. (2007) describe Finnair's decision support system to manage CLV and customer equity. Dynamic programming algorithms are used to identify market actions that will encourage customers to repurchase and cross-buy, thereby optimizing CLV. Monte Carlo simulations are used to evaluate the financial impact of different marketing plans.

Customer acquisition, customer lifetime duration, service usage rates and cross-buying depend on firm actions, competitive behavior and market conditions (Hogan et al. 2002). Hence, there will be many different forecasts of CLV for a customer or segment generated by different assumptions about future conditions (for example, Rust et al. 2004, 2011). Nevertheless, it is not uncommon for forecasts of CLV and/or its components to be based on assumptions of fixed marketing programs, deterministic retention rates and/or stable switching patterns among competitive offerings. As discussed earlier, there is considerable evidence that customer lifetime durations depend on these antecedents—which change over time—so approaches to estimating CLV that ignore them are likely to perform poorly (except in the very short run). For the same reason, it is not appropriate to build a statistical model to predict CLV solely based on historical data unless all other components of CLV (and their antecedents) are fixed over time (which is likely to be true only in the very short term).

Customer Lifetime Durations and Resource Allocation Methods

We have emphasized that service organizations should allocate expenditures by forecasting the components of CLV of individual customers (including lifetime durations) under alternative scenarios, aggregating across customers, and identifying the scenario or set of organizational actions that optimizes shareholder value (Bolton et al. 2004; Rust et al. 1995, 2004). Recent research has emphasized that optimization of shareholder value is not the same as maximizing the CLV of an individual customer or group of customers. Instead, the service organization must manage customers' cash flow streams over time and across the entire customer portfolio to optimize risk and return (Tarasi et al. 2011, 2013). This approach seems "doable" but it can be challenging to move from forecasts of behavioral components of CLV under different scenarios to forecasting customer equity under different scenarios including characterizing risk and return rates. These challenges are especially great for service organizations because relational behaviors, including customer lifetime durations, are likely to depend on service operations, human resources and marketing decisions. See Tirenni et al. (2007) and Niraj et al. (2001) for interesting applications of these notions in practical contexts.

Instead, some service organizations segment the customer base according to estimated CLV (where forecasts of customer lifetime durations are a major component) and allocate expenditures on customer satisfaction, quality improvements, provision of loyalty instruments and so forth to more valuable customers (Kumar et al. 2009). This approach seems attractive for several reasons. First, forecasts of CLV, which incorporate customer lifetime durations, are better predictors of short-run future profitability of individual customers than other popular metrics, such as recency/frequency/monetary (RFM) or past customer value (PCV) metrics (Venkatesan and Kumar 2004). Second, estimated CLV provides a natural upper limit on expenditures allocated to a given customer (Gupta and Lehmann 2005). Third, forecasts of CLV extrapolate from past purchase behaviors, which are generally a good predictor of future purchase behavior. Fourth, relational behaviors, such as customer lifetime durations, usage and cross-buying, seem likely to be interrelated. For example, Kumar and Reinartz (2003) found that prior cross-buying and spending levels are associated with customer purchases of goods in a direct marketing context, as well as local population density and income.

Unfortunately, there are numerous difficulties in estimating CLV based on historical data (Bell et al. 2002). However, it is tempting for many firms to build predictive models of profitability or cash flows from individual customers without considering their underlying sources. Since the antecedents of these relational behaviors are quite different, these models will only perform well under *ceteris paribus* conditions. For this reason, we advise caution in utilizing these approaches.

A RESEARCH AGENDA FOR UNDERSTANDING CUSTOMER LIFETIME DURATIONS

In this section, we conclude by identifying some key research questions concerning mutually beneficial long-term relationships between customers and service organizations. They are organized under four major categories: customer engagement and social network effects, interdependence in customer relational behaviors, the implications of customer lifetime durations for customer portfolio analyses, and jointly managing service operations and long-term relationships with customers.

Customer Engagement and Social Networks

Digital and social-media use are influencing consumers' identity formation, their expectations regarding service, formation of habits, engagement with brands and firms, participation in value co-creation, brand loyalty, purchase behavior and lifetime value, and (ultimately) the value of the firm (Bolton et al. 2013). Hence, many service organizations have become interested in how customer engagement behaviors foster long-term relationships with customers. Customer engagement behaviors include non-purchase behaviors such as word-of-mouth activity, recommendations, helping other customers, blogging, writing reviews, and engaging in legal action (van Doorn et al. 2010). These behaviors may differ on the basis of valence (positive or negative), form, scope, nature of their influence, and customer goals. Researchers are only beginning to explore how customer engagement influences purchase behaviors, including customer lifetime durations (Bolton et al. 2013).

Managers' understanding of customer engagement is vital to understanding and managing long-term relationships because customers' experiences can be triggers for staying or defecting from a relationship (Gustafsson et al. 2005; Keavney 1995). There are many opportunities for service organizations to encourage positive customer engagement and forestall negative customer engagement. They can create online platforms to monitor and manage customer-to-customer and customer–organization interaction, empower frontline employees to ensure timely complaint management (for example, refunds and apologies), provide social incentives to customer support groups, and so forth (van Doorn et al. 2010). At a strategic level, service innovation in this domain is likely to influence service organizations' decisions about customization and productivity (Rust and Ming-Hui 2012), especially how resources are allocated between labor and automation. It also has implications for the design and implementation of interactive services including location-based, retail and self-service technology (Berry et al. 2010).

These observations raise several challenges. Predictions of customers' future cash-flow streams require the simulation of how dynamic events unfold over time. There is some evidence that more sophisticated dynamic models perform better than naive models based on historical data (Rust et al. 2011). However, the differential treatment of customers, who may interact with each other, brings with it unique modeling and forecasting problems. As we have noted earlier, there are (as yet) few studies that incorporate social network effects into models of customer lifetime durations or CLV or long-term cash flows.

Interdependence in Customers' Relational Behaviors

A customer's decision to stay in (or defect from) a relationship with a service organization evolves alongside his or her decisions about service usage, as well as upgrading and cross-buying products. As discussed earlier, there is statistical evidence that the channel of acquisition influences subsequent customer lifetime durations in B2C direct marketing settings. This issue is also relevant in B2B settings. For example, service organizations often highlight long-term relationships to win new contracts because long relationships signal organizational capabilities and commitment to potential and existing customers. However, little is known about this phenomenon. Since we know that relational behaviors influence each other over time, we can raise the related research question, "What is the influence of long-term relationship on the service organization's ability to acquire new customers?"

We speculate that service managers and researchers seldom use forecasts of underlying behavioral components to forecast CLV and customer equity due to a particularly vexing problem: customers' relational behaviors are likely to be correlated (for example, Reinartz and Kumar 2003, p. 94). Why? First, customer lifetime durations, service usage, and cross-buying behavior share some (but not all) of the same antecedents (for example, satisfaction), albeit operating in different ways (Bolton et al. 2004). Second, these behaviors are predicted using models estimated based on the same historical data, where the error terms are likely to be correlated due to measurement error or model specification error. For example, competitors' marketing actions are omitted from most models because they are not readily observed. Third, it is possible that relational behaviors are simultaneously determined. For example, the decision to upgrade a service contract may depend on the decision to repurchase from the same supplier (or purchase other contracts) and vice versa (Bolton et al. 2006).[3]

Future research should rigorously examine these issues by specifying and estimating a system of equations to describe customer relational behaviors that account for these complex phenomena. Instead, it is common practice for researchers to include past purchase behaviors (for example, current relationship length) as covariates in models of customer retention, usage, cross-buying and profitability that serve as surrogates for unobserved variables. These approaches are used because they make difficult problems tractable, but better models are needed. In particular, the availability of well-managed customer relationship management databases has enabled more accurate measures of CLV enabling service organizations to allocate marketing resources and treat customers differentially based on their estimated worth. Yet, the consumer response to differential treatment is not well studied and is an important area of future research.

Customer Lifetime Durations in Customer Portfolio Analysis

To optimize shareholder value, the return from an investment by a service organization must be commensurate with its risk. Up to this point, we have (usually) discussed customer lifetime duration and CLV under the implicit assumption that the goal of service organizations is to optimize returns from a customer or a group of customers over the long term. Our discussion has not considered the risk associated with these returns over the customer lifetime except that we have explicitly considered the risk of customer defection and discounted cash flows using a risk-adjusted cost of capital.

In contrast, the emerging research on customer portfolio management offers an approach to ensuring long-term profitable relationships that considers risk as well as return (Tarasi et al. 2011, 2013). It differs from earlier approaches in two ways. First, its goal is to minimize risk for a targeted level of return from a customer portfolio, thereby optimizing customer equity and shareholder value. Second, it takes into account variability in cash flows over the customer's lifetime arising from variation in customers' service consumption patterns, purchase behaviors and organizational processes that support them. Consequently, management of long-term relationships begins with targeting customers who have low cash flow variability, followed by managerial interventions to reduce cash flow variability within the extant customer base and (ultimately) optimal allocation of resources to different segments of the customer.

Tarasi et al. (2013) analyze customer data from two service organizations and find robust evidence that managerial intervention can reduce cash flow variability without adversely affecting returns. In their statistical model, variability in customers' cash flows was explained by differences in satisfaction levels, relationship characteristics (length, depth, and breadth) and demographics. Simulations showed that customer satisfaction programs increase returns and lower risk, and loyalty programs that emphasize economic rewards (as opposed to social rewards) tend to increase risk without commensurate returns. Beyond managing the cash flows of existing customers over time, firms can allocate resources to specific customers and market segments (including new customers) to yield future cash flows that complement each other and thereby decrease the variability of future cash flows derived from the entire customer base (Tarasi et al. 2011).

Note that customer lifetime durations are very important in assessing the value of the customer portfolio, just as they are for CLV. The primary reason is that the risk and return from cash flows is calculated over a time horizon that incorporates customers' lifetimes. Yet, a customer portfolio is different from a portfolio of financial assets which are bought and sold in well-defined markets. Acquiring customers and managing the mix of customers in a portfolio is not a mechanical process. Implementation of customer portfolio management—taking into account what is known about creating, maintaining and enhancing customer relationships over their lifetimes—poses many challenges.

There are many researchable issues concerning how long relationships contribute to the value of the customer portfolio. One reason is that (unlike many mature B2C markets) growth in B2B services is an important component of CLV. Consideration of the lifecycle stage of new business customers, their business model, and growth potential of their respective markets can result in significant differences in CLV computations. For example, how does a long-term B2B relationship help a service organization expand into new business areas? Small B2B service organizations that focus on expansion learn from their relationships with their large customers over time and yet, we do not have much empirical work concerning the benefits (from a customer equity standpoint) of organizational learning within these relationships. Or, how can organizations identify and persist in relationships with customers who are likely to see growth in their respective markets—despite short-term losses early in the relationship? In sum, more research is needed on customer-organization relationships in growing (as opposed to mature) markets.

Not all B2B relationships are successful. Sometimes a service organization must decide whether to make a service recovery or terminate a relationship. Such a scenario leads to the following research questions: Do long-term relationships create externalities that delay successful termination or adaptation of a relationship? Since it is not uncommon for a broad B2B service relationship to comprise numerous underlying projects that may be both functionally and administratively independent, how does structure entail complexities in the recovery/termination of a poorly performing relationship? Do long-standing relationships entail managerial inertia, path dependencies and the familiar problem of escalation of commitment?

Jointly Managing Service Operations and Long-term Relationships

Recent research on customer portfolio analysis has emphasized that variability in cash flows must be managed, as well as returns (Tarasi et al. 2011, 2013). This goal dovetails with a long-standing emphasis by experts in service operations management on reliability or consistency in service quality and service processes (Grönroos 1990, 1998). For example, service organizations must match supply and demand for perishable services, coordinate simultaneous production and consumption, and customize service to heterogeneous customers. Moreover, service organizations are more likely to be successful when they are effective in managing consumption processes so that they are less variable (and consequently cash flows are less variable).

These linkages between service operations management and customer portfolio management introduce several new questions. It has long been hypothesized that long-term customers are less costly to serve despite mixed results in empirical examinations. For example, a heavy cost is usually incurred in the initial set up of processes that ensure smooth functioning of a B2B relationship whereas the cost of relationship maintenance seems likely to go down as the relationship grows. However, more research is required to understand this notion of "relationship efficiency" and its potential enablers as well as their implications for service management and long-term relationships.

Service management includes human resource challenges, in addition to the operations and marketing challenges. There is a general belief that "internal marketing" (to employees who are linked to end-user customers) can sustain and extend customer lifetime durations. Hence, empirical examination of the effect of internal marketing efforts (that seek to modify the service employees' in-role and extra-role behavior) on customer lifetime duration could be very interesting.

CONCLUDING REMARKS

We hope this review will stimulate service researchers to identify and develop service innovations that encourage mutually beneficial relationships for consumers, organizations and society. The marketplace, the workplace and society are changing rapidly—and there are many unanswered questions about how to create, sustain and enhance relationships between customers and service organizations. We encourage service researchers to investigate the new research domains that we have identified in this article. We believe the answers can be helpful to consumers, managers, organizations and public policy makers.

NOTES

1. Service organizations should also be very careful when they investigate customer lifetime durations. Many organizations purge their databases of customers who have defected. Hence, the data do not describe a representative sample of customers' lifetime durations. Customers who defected long ago are underrepresented. Hence, statistical analyses of the purged data—intended to understand the factors that influence customer lifetime durations—must take this missing information into account.
2. In a B2B context, Palmatier et al. (2007) compare commitment–trust theory, a relational norms perspective, dependence theory, transaction cost economics and the resource-based view, using a longitudinal empirical analysis. They conclude that these approaches can be unified under the resource-based view, where the relationship can be considered an idiosyncratic asset and dependence asymmetry, interdependence, relational norms and communication predict relationship success. Relationship success is usually measured using financial performance, inter-service organization cooperation, conflict, and relationship duration.
3. This same issue arises in models of purchase incidence, brand choice and quantity (Gupta 1988).

REFERENCES

Ansari, Asim, Carl F. Mela, and Scott A. Neslin (2008), "Customer channel migration," *Journal of Marketing Research*, **45** (1), 60–76.

Bell, David, John Deighton, Werner J. Reinartz, Roland T. Rust, and Gordon Swartz (2002), "Seven barriers to customer equity management," *Journal of Service Research*, **5** (1), 77–85.

Bendapudi, Neeli and Leonard L. Berry (1997), "Customers' motivations for maintaining relationships with service providers," *Journal of Retailing*, **73** (1), 15–37.

Berger, Paul D. and Nada I. Nasr (1998), "Customer lifetime value: marketing models and applications," *Journal of Interactive Marketing*, **12** (Winter), 17–30.

Berger, Paul D., Ruth N. Bolton, Douglas Bowman, Elten Briggs, V. Kumar, A. Parasuraman and Terry Creed (2002), "Marketing actions and the value of customer assets: a framework for customer asset management," *Journal of Service Research*, **5** (1), 39–54.

Berger, Paul D., Naras Eechambadi, Morris George, and Donald R. Lehmann (2006), "From customer lifetime value to shareholder value: theory, empirical evidence and issues for future research," *Journal of Service Research*, **9** (2), 156–67.

Berry, Leonard L. (1980), "Services marketing is different," *Business*, **30** (3), 24–9.

Berry, Leonard L. (1983), "Relationship marketing," in Leonard L. Berry, G. Lynn Shostack and Gregoory Upah (eds), *Emerging Perspectives on Services Marketing*, Chicago, IL: American Marketing Association, pp. 25–8.

Berry, Leonard L. (1995), "Relationship marketing of services—growing interest, emerging perspectives," *Journal of the Academy of Marketing Science*, **23** (4), 236–45.

Berry, Leonard L. (2000), "Service brand equity," *Journal of the Academy of Marketing Science*, **28** (1), 128–37.

Berry, Leonard L., Ruth N. Bolton, Cheryl H. Bridges, Jeffrey Meyer, A. Parasuraman and

Kathleen Seiders (2010), "Opportunities for innovation in the delivery of interactive retail services," *Journal of Interactive Marketing*, **24** (2), 155–67.

Berry, Leonard L., Kathleen Seiders and Dhruv Grewal (2002), "Understanding service convenience," *Journal of Marketing*, **66** (3), 1–17.

Blattberg, Robert C. and John Deighton (1996), "Manage Marketing by the customer equity test," *Harvard Business Review*, **74** (July-August), 136–44.

Bolton, Lisa E., Luc Warlop, and Joseph W. Alba (2003), "Perceptions of price (un) fairness," *Journal of Consumer Research*, **29** (4), 474–91.

Bolton, Ruth N. (1998), "A dynamic model of the duration of the customer's relationship with a continuous service provider: the role of satisfaction," *Marketing Science*, **17** (1), 45–65.

Bolton, Ruth N. and Katherine N. Lemon (1999), "A dynamic model of customers' usage of services: usage as an antecedent and consequence of satisfaction," *Journal of Marketing Research*, **36** (2), 171–86.

Bolton, Ruth N. and Matthew B. Myers (2003), "Price-based global market segmentation for services," *Journal of Marketing*, **67** (3), 108–28.

Bolton, Ruth N., P.K. Kannan, and Matthew D. Bramlett (2000), "Implications of loyalty program membership and service experiences for customer retention and value," *Journal of the Academy of Marketing Science*, **28** (1), 95–108.

Bolton, Ruth N., Katherine N. Lemon and Matthew D. Bramlett (2006), "The effect of service experiences over time on a supplier's retention of business customers," *Management Science*, **52** (12), 1811–23.

Bolton, Ruth N., Katherine N. Lemon and Peter C. Verhoef (2004), "The Theoretical underpinnings of customer asset management: a framework and propositions for future research," *Journal of the Academy of Marketing Science*, **32** (3), 271–92.

Bolton, Ruth N., A. Parasuraman, Ankie Hoefnagels, Nanne Migchels, Sertan Kabadayi, Thorsten Gruber, Yuliya Komarova Loureiro and David Solnet (2013), "Understanding generation Y and their use of social media: a review and research agenda," *Journal of Service Management*, **24** (3), 245–67.

Bolton, Ruth N., Amy K. Smith and Janet Wagner (2003), "Striking the right balance: designing service to enhance business-to-business relationships," *Journal of Service Research*, **5** (4), 271–91.

Boulding, William, Ajay Kalra, Richard Staelin and Valarie A. Zeithaml (1993), "A dynamic process model of service quality: from expectations to behavioral intentions," *Journal of Marketing Research*, **30** (1), 7–27.

Bowman, Douglas and Das Narayandas (2001), "Managing customer-initiated contacts with manufacturers: the impact on share of category requirements and word-of-mouth behavior," *Journal of Marketing Research*, **38** (3), 281–97.

Burnham, Thomas A., Judy K. Frels and Vijay Mahajan (2003), "Consumer switching costs: a typology, antecedents, and consequences," *Journal of the Academy of Marketing Science*, **31** (2), 109–26.

Crosby, Lawrence A. and Nancy Stephens (1987), "Effects of relationship marketing on satisfaciton, retention and prices in the life insurance industry," *Journal of Marketing Rsearch*, **24** (4), 404–11.

Dhar, Ravi and Rashi Glazer (2003), "Hedging customers," *Harvard Business Review*, **81** (May), 86–92.

Dick, Alan. S. and Kunal Basu (1994), "Customer loyalty: toward an integrated conceptual framework," *Journal of the Academy of Marketing Science*, **22** (2), 99–113.

Drèze, Xavier and Joseph C. Nunes (2009), "Feeling superior: the impact of loyalty program structure on consumers' perceptions of status," *Journal of Consumer Research*, **35** (6), 890–905.

Dwyer, F. Robert, Paul H. Schurr and Sejo Oh (1987), "Developing buyer-seller relationships," *Journal of Marketing*, **51** (2), 11–27.

Ganesan, Shankar (1994), "Determinants of long-term orientation in buyer-seller relationships," *Journal of Marketing*, **58** (2), 1–19.

Godfrey, Andrea, Kathleen Seiders and Glenn B. Voss (2011), "Enough is enough! The fine line in executing multichannel relational communication," *Journal of Marketing*, **75** (4), 94–109.

Goldenberg, Jacob, Barak Libai, Sarit Moldovan and Eitan Muller (2007), "The NPV of bad news," *International Journal of Research in Marketing*, **24** (3), 186–200.

Goldenberg, Jacob, Sangman Han, Donald R Lehmann and Jae Weon Hong (2009), "The role of hubs in the adoption process," *Journal of Marketing*, **73** (2), 1–13.

Grönroos, Christian (1990), *Service Management and Marketing*, Toronto: Lexington Books.

Grönroos, Christian (1998), "Marketing services: the case of a missing product," *Journal of Business and Industrial Marketing*, **13** (4/5), 322–38.

Gupta, Sunil (1988), "Impact of sales promotions on when, what, and how much to buy," *Journal of Marketing Research*, **25**, (4), 342–55.

Gupta, Sunil and Donald Lehmann (2005), *Managing Customers as Investments: The Strategic Value of Customers in the Long Run*, Upper Saddle River, NJ: Wharton School.

Gupta, Sunil, Donald Lehmann and Jennifer Ames Stuart (2004), "Valuing Customers," *Journal of Marketing Research*, **41** (1), 7–18.

Gustafsson, Anders, Michael D. Johnson and Inger Roos (2005), "The effects of customer satisfaction, relationship commitment dimensions, and triggers on customer retention," *Journal of Marketing*, **69** (4), 210–18.

Gwinner, Kevin P., Dwayne D. Gremler and Mary Jo Bitner (1998), "Relational Benefits in services industries: the customer's perspective," *Journal of the Academy of Marketing Science*, **26** (2), 101–14.

Hogan, John E., Donald R. Lehmann, Maria Merino, Rajendra K. Srivastava, Jacquelyn S. Thomas and Peter C. Verhoef (2002), "Linking customer assets to financial performance," *Journal of Service Research*, **5** (1), 26–38.

Hogan, John E., Katherine N. Lemon and Barak Libai (2003), "What is the true value of a lost customer?," *Journal of Service Research*, **5** (3), 196–208.

Inman, J. Jeffrey, James S. Dyer and Jianmin Jia (1997), "A generalized utility model of disappointment and regret effects on post-choice valuation," *Marketing Science*, **16** (2), 97–111.

Johnson, Michael D. and Fred Selnes (2004), "Customer portfolio management: toward a dynamic theory of exchange relationships," *Journal of Marketing*, **68** (April), 1–17.

Jones, Michael A., David L. Mothersbaugh and Sharon E. Beatty (2002), "Why customers stay: measuring the underlying dimensions of services switching costs and managing their differential strategic outcomes," *Journal of Business Research*, **55** (6), 441–50.

Keavney, Susan M. (1995), "Customer switching behavior in service industries: an exploratory study," *Journal of Marketing*, **59** (2), 71–82.

Kivetz, Ran and Itamar Simonson (2003), "The idiosyncratic fit heuristic: effort advantage as a determinant of consumer response to loyalty programs," *Journal of Marketing Research*, **40** (4), 454–67.

Kumar, V. and Morris George (2007), "Measuring and maximizing customer equity: a critical analysis," *Journal of the Academy of Marketing Science*, **35**, 157–71.

Kumar, V. and Denish Shah (2009), "Expanding the role of marketing: from customer equity to market capitalization," *Journal of Marketing*, **73** (6), 119–36.

Kumar, V., Ilaria Dalla, J. Andrew Petersen and Denish Shah (2009), "Reversing the logic: the path to profitability through relationship marketing," *Journal of Interactive Marketing*, **23** (2), 147–56.

Lam, Shun Y., Venkatesh Shankar, M. Krishna Erramilli and Bvsan Murthy (2004), "Customer Value, satisfaction, loyalty, and switching costs: an illustration from a business-to-business service context," *Journal of the Academy of Marketing Science*, **32** (3), 293–311.

Lee, Jonathan, Janghyuk Lee and Lawrence Feick (2001), "The impact of switching costs on the customer satisfaction-loyalty link: mobile phone service in France," *Journal of Services Marketing*, **15** (1), 35–48.

Lee, Ruby P. and Rajdeep Grewal (2004), "Strategic responses to new technologies and their impact on service organization performance," *Journal of Marketing*, **68** (4), 157–71.

Lehmann, Donald R. (2004), "Linking marketing to financial performance and firm value," *Journal of Marketing*, **68** (4), 73–5.
Lewis, Michael (2004), "The influence of loyalty programs and short-term promotions on customer retention," *Journal of Marketing Research*, **41** (3), 281–92.
Mazumdar, Tridib, S.P. Raj and Indrajit Sinha (2005), "Reference price research: review and propositions," *Journal of Marketing*, **69** (4), 84–102.
Mende, Martin, Ruth N. Bolton and Mary Jo Bitner (2013), "Decoding customer–firm relationships: how attachment styles help explain customers' preferences for closeness, repurchase intentions, and changes in relationship breadth," *Journal of Marketing Research*, **50** (1), 25–142.
Meuter, Matthew L., Mary Jo Bitner, Amy L. Ostrom and Stephen W. Brown (2005), "Choosing among alternative service delivery modes: an investigation of customer trial of self-service technologies," *Journal of Marketing*, **69** (2), 61–83.
Meyer-Waarden, Lars (2007), "The effects of loyalty programs on customer lifetime duration and share of wallet," *Journal of Retailing*, **83** (2), 223–36.
Mittal, Vikas and Wagner A. Kamakura (2001), "Satisfaction, repurchase intent, and repurchase behavior: investigating the moderating effect of customer characteristics," *Journal of Marketing Research*, **38** (1), 131.
Montaguti, Elisa, Scott A. Neslin and Sara Valentini (2012), "Do marketing campaigns produce multichannel buying and more profitable customers? A field experiment," Marketing Science Institute report, 12–112.
Moorman, Christine, Rohit Deshpande and Gerald Zaltman (1993), "Factors affecting trust in market research relationships," *Journal of Marketing*, **57** (1), 81–101.
Morgan, Robert M. and Shelby D. Hunt (1994), "The commitment–trust theory of relationship marketing," *Journal of Marketing*, **58** (3), 20–38.
Morwitz, Vicki G. and David Schmittlein (1992), "Using segmentation to improve sales forecasts based on purchase intent: which 'intenders' actually buy," *Journal of Marketing Research*, **29** (4), 391–405.
Namias, Jean (1960), "Intentions to purchase related to consumer characteristics," *Journal of Marketing*, **25** (July), 32–6.
Neslin, Scott A., Druv Grewal, Robert Leghorn, Venkatesh Shankar, Marije L. Teerling, Jacquelyn S. Thomas and Peter C. Verhoef (2006a), "Challenges and opportunities in multichannel customer management," *Journal of Service Research*, **9** (November), 95–112.
Neslin, Scott A., Sunil Gupta, Wagner Kamakura, Junxiang Lu and Charlotte H. Mason (2006b), "Defection detection: measuring and understanding the predictive accuracy of customer churn models," *Journal of Marketing Research*, **43** (May), 204–11.
Niraj, Rakesh, Mahendra Gupta and Chakravarthi Narasimhan (2001), "Customer profitability in a supply chain," *Journal of Marketing*, **65** (3), 1–16.
Nitzan, Irit and Barak Libai (2011), "Social effects on customer retention," *Journal of Marketing*, **75** (6), 24–38.
Oliver, R.L. (1999), "Whence consumer loyalty?," *Journal of Marketing*, **63** (special issue), 33–44.
Palmatier, Robert W. (2008a), "Interfirm organization relational drivers of customer value," *Journal of Marketing*, **72** (4), 76–89.
Palmatier, Robert W. (2008b), *Relationship Marketing*, New York and Cambridge: Marketing Science Institute.
Palmatier, Robert W., Rajiv P. Dant and Dhruv Grewal (2007), "A comparative longitudinal analysis of theoretical perspectives of interorganizational relationship performance," *Journal of Marketing*, **71** (5), 172–94.
Palmatier, Robert W., Rajiv P. Dant, Dhruv Grewal and Kenneth R. Evans (2006), "Factors influencing the effectiveness of relationship marketing: a meta-analysis," *Journal of Marketing*, **70** (4), 136–53.
Palmatier, Robert W., Cheryl Burke Jarvis, Jennifer R. Bechkoff and Frank R. Kardes (2009), "The role of customer gratitude in relationship marketing," *Journal of Marketing*, **73** (5), 1–18.

Pauwels, Koen, Peter S.H. Leeflang, Marije L. Teerling and K.R. Eelko Huizingh (2011), "Does online information drive offline revenues? Only for specific products and consumer segments!," *Journal of Retailing*, **87** (1), 1–17.

Prahalad, C.K. and Venkat Ramaswamy (2004), *The Future of Competition: Co-Creating Unique Value with Customers*, Boston, MA: Harvard Business School.

Price, Linda L. and Eric J. Arnould (1999), "Commercial friendships: service provider-client relationships in context," *Journal of Marketing*, **63** (4), 38–56.

Reinartz, Werner J. and V. Kumar (2003), "The impact of customer relationship characteristics on profitable lifetime duration," *Journal of Marketing*, **67** (1), 77–99.

Rust, Roland T. and Ming-Hui Huang (2012), "Optimizing service productivity," *Journal of Marketing*, **76** (2), 47–66.

Rust, Roland T., Jeffrey J. Inman, Jianmin Jia and Anthony Zahorik (1999), "What you don't know about customer-perceived quality: the role of customer expectation distributions," *Marketing Science*, **18** (1), 77–92.

Rust, Roland T., Katherine N. Lemon and Valarie A. Zeithaml (2004), "Return on marketing: using customer equity to focus marketing strategy," *Journal of Marketing*, **68** (1), 109–27.

Rust, Roland T., V. Kumar and Rajkumar Venakesan (2011), "Will a frog change into a prince? Predicting future customer profitability," *International Journal of Research in Marketing*, **28**, 281–94.

Rust, Roland T., Anthony J. Zahorik and Timothy L. Keiningham (1995), "Return on quality (ROQ): making service quality financially accountable," *Journal of Marketing*, **59** (2), 58–70.

Schmittlein, David C. and Robert A. Peterson (1994), "Customer base analysis: an industrial purchase process application," *Marketing Science*, **13** (1), 41–67.

Seiders, Kathleen, Glenn B. Voss, Dhruv Grewal and Andrea L. Godfrey (2005), "Do satisfied customers buy more? Examining moderating influences in a retailing context," *Journal of Marketing*, **69** (4), 26–43.

Sirdeshmukh, Deepak, Jagdip Singh and Barry Sabol (2002), "Consumer trust, value, and loyalty in relational exchanges," *Journal of Marketing*, **66** (1), 15–37.

Smith, Amy K. and Ruth N. Bolton (1998), "An experimental investigation of customer reactions to service failure and recovery encounters: paradox or peril?," *Journal of Service Research*, **1** (1), 65–81.

Smith, Amy K., Ruth N. Bolton and Janet Wagner (1999), "A model of customer satisfaction with service encounters involving failure and recovery," Journal of Marketing Research, **36** (3), 1999, 356–72.

Srivastava, Rajendra K., Tasadduq A. Shervani and Liam Fahey (1998), "Market-based assets and shareholder value: a framework for analysis," *Journal of Marketing*, **62** (1), 2–18.

Stahl, Florian, Mark Heitmann, Donald R. Lehmann and Scott A. Neslin (2012), "The impact of brand equity on customer acquisition, retention, and profit margin," *Journal of Marketing*, **76** (4), 44–63.

Tarasi, Crina O., Ruth N Bolton, Michael D. Hutt and Beth A. Walker (2011), "Balancing risk and return in a customer portfolio," *Journal of Marketing*, **75** (3), 1–17.

Tarasi, Crina O., Ruth N. Bolton, Anders Gustafsson and Beth A. Walker (2013), "Relationship characteristics and cash flow variability: implications for satisfaction, loyalty, and customer portfolio management," *Journal of Service Research*, **1** (17), 1–16.

Thomas, Jacquelyn S. (2001), "A methodology for linking customer acquisition to customer retention," *Journal of Marketing Research*, **38** (2), 262–8.

Thomas, Jacquelyn S. and Ursula Y. Sullivan (2005), "Managing marketing communication with multichannel customers," *Journal of Marketing*, **69** (4), 239–51.

Thomas, Jacquelyn S., Robert C. Blattberg and Edward J. Fox (2004), "Recapturing lost customers," *Journal of Marketing Research*, **41** (1), 31–45.

Tirenni, Giuliano, Abderrahim Labbi, Cesar Berrospi, André Elisseeff, Timir Bhose, Kari Pauro and Seppo Pöyhönen (2007), "Customer equity and lifetime management (CELM) Finnair case study," *Marketing Science*, **26** (4), 553–65.

Van Doorn, Jenny, Katherine N. Lemon, Vikas Mittal, Stephan Nass, Doreén Pick, Peter

Pirner and Peter. C. Verhoef (2010), "Customer engagement behavior: theoretical foundations and research directions," *Journal of Service Research*, **13** (3), 253–66.

Vargo, Stephen L. and Robert F. Lusch (2004), "Evolving to a new dominant logic for marketing," *Journal of Marketing*, **68** (1), 1–17.

Venkatesan, Rajkumar and V. Kumar (2004), "A customer lifetime value framework for customer selection and resource allocation strategy," *Journal of Marketing*, **68** (4), 106–25.

Verhoef, Peter C. (2003), "Understanding the effect of customer relationship management efforts on customer retention and customer share development," *Journal of Marketing*, **67** (4), 30–45.

Verhoef, Peter C., Philip Hans Franses and Janny C. Hoekstra (2001), "The impact of satisfaction and payment equity on cross-buying: a dynamic model for a multi-service provider," *Journal of Retailing*, **77** (Fall), 359–78.

Wedel, Michael and Wagner A. Kamakura (1999), *Market Segmentation: Conceptual and Methodological Foundations*, Boston, MA: Kluwer Academic.

Zeelenberg, Marcel and Rik Pieters (2004), "Beyond valence in customer dissatisfaction: a review and new findings on behavioral responses to regret and disappointment in failed services", *Journal of Business Research*, **57** (4), 445–55.

Zeithaml, Valarie A. (1985), "The new demographics and market fragmentation," *Journal of Marketing*, **49** (3), 64–75.

Zeithaml, Valarie A. (1988), "Consumer perceptions of price, quality and value: a means-end model and synthesis of evidence," *Journal of Marketing*, **52** (3), 2–22.

Zeithaml, Valarie A., Leonard L. Berry, and A. Parasuraman (1996), "The behavioral consequences of service quality", *Journal of Marketing*, **60** (2), 31–46.

3 Loyalty: its many sources and variations

*Lerzan Aksoy, Timothy L. Keiningham and Richard L. Oliver**

INTRODUCTION

For most of human existence, our ability to build loyal bonds was an essential element in our survival. Today, however, loyalty is much less critical to an individual's physical existence. Yet we as human beings still feel the need to be loyal to a host of different things in our lives (for example, family, friends, country, faith, and so on).

This need to be loyal is so prevalent that some researchers have speculated that it may be an evolutionary trait (for example, Cacioppo and Hawkley 2009; Cacioppo et al. 2006). Oliver (2011) has even speculated the existence of a "molecule" (that is, genetic code) located in an unidentified brain structure that spurs our innate need for loyalty.

Given that the overwhelming majority of us demonstrate loyalty to multiple individuals and other entities, the speculation of a genetic predisposition to being loyal is plausible. Determining whether there really is a loyalty gene and/or a loyalty structure in the brain, however, will be left for future researchers as it will clearly require advances in genetic research and in functional magnetic resonance imaging (fMRI) technology to prove conclusively.

The purpose of this chapter is to explore the many facets of loyalty, and when they can be expected to appear. This differs from previous attempts from the authors in that neither forms nor variations of loyalty are specifically targeted. Rather, loyalty is approached in a loose chronological order from the earliest parental bonding to the manifestations in later life. Along the way, nontraditional exemplars of loyalty are entertained, including such topics as "loyalty" to (the concept of) disloyalty.

WHAT IS LOYALTY?

In his essay on loyalty, American author William Armstrong Fairburn (1926, p. 2) argues that the breadth of meaning associated with the word loyalty makes a definition impossible. He writes, "The word loyalty has grown beyond definition, so much so that there is no word in the English language today that can take its place . . . loyalty is impregnated with spirit that defies the limitations of description" (ibid.).

Therefore, before embarking on a discussion of the many facets of loyalty, we need a clear definition of what it means to be loyal. While the word loyalty is commonly used, definitions vary widely across scientific domains and even within the same domains, (for a review, see Aksoy et al. 2014). For example, within the marketing domain Uncles et al. (2003) report three commonly used conceptualizations of loyalty related to consumers in the literature: (1) attitudinal loyalty (for example, affective feeling of a bond), (2) behavioral loyalty (for example, repeat purchase behavior), and (3) situational/usage occasion based loyalty (for example, purchases based upon situational triggers).

Despite multiple definitions of loyalty, Aksoy et al. (2014) find four commonalities typically ascribed to the construct of loyalty across domains: "1) a perceived specialness to a relationship, 2) favorable treatment to objects of loyalty, 3) a desire to maintain the relationship even when it requires sacrifice, and 4) defense and reinforcement of the relationship (i.e., not being disloyal)." Based upon these commonalities, they go on to propose the following definition: "Loyalty is the recognition of the specialness of a relationship which results in differential and more favorable treatment towards this relationship, the creation of a bond as the result of this relationship, and the defense and reinforcement of this relationship."

This definition implies several things. First, despite colloquial expressions of being "loyal to yourself," consistent with much of the philosophical thought on loyalty (for example, Ladd 1967; Oldenquist 1982), the object of loyalty must be someone or something other than oneself. Second, loyalty requires the combination of commitment to the relationship with behaviors designed to maintain the relationship.

HIERARCHIES OF LOYALTY

We all hold some degree of loyalty to many things in our lives. Clearly, however, our different loyalties do not all carry the same level of importance to us.

Many researchers argue that our loyalties fall into a general hierarchy that can be defined primarily by the degree of abstraction from loyalty to specific individuals. Fletcher (1993, p. 154) argues that loyalties are first to people (friends, family, and so on), second to country, and third to God. This hierarchy of loyalties is virtually identical to that argued by Fairburn (1926), that is (1) loyalty to individuals (for example, family and friends),

(2) national loyalty, and (3) what he calls "universal" loyalty (specifically, "[loyalty] to the cause of one's fellows, and to that Universal Power which is the source of all that is good, real, and eternal in the world" (ibid., p. 438).

Acceptance of such hierarchies of loyalty, however, is not universal. In particular, Ladd (1967, p. 97) argues that loyalty can only exist between persons, and that loyalty to humanity or a general principle (for example, justice, democracy, and so on) is conceptually impossible. Whether or not one accepts Ladd's argument that loyalty can only exist between persons, it is clear that loyalty to specific individuals is distinct from loyalty to higher-level abstractions (for example, community, country, and so on) where the number of individuals in the group can be quite large.

Aksoy et al. (2014) found support for a classification of loyalties. In particular, their research found that loyalties can be divided into two general groups: (1) concrete loyalties (that is, loyalties to individuals), and (2) abstract loyalties (that is, loyalties to higher level abstractions). In their examination of six domains, they found that loyalties to family, friends, work colleagues, and consumer loyalty (defined as loyalty to the places where we as consumers do business) grouped with concrete loyalties, whereas loyalties to community and faith grouped with abstract loyalties. Moreover, they found that attempts to maximize both concrete and abstract loyalties simultaneously showed diminishing returns as they relate to human happiness. They speculate that this may result from the time demands necessary to nurture relationships, resulting in the need to pick and choose between competing loyalties.

THE BEGINNINGS OF LOYALTY

When can loyalty be expected to first appear? Paradoxically, while loyalty appears to be an innate trait in most human beings, we are not born loyal. We are born helpless with intense demands essential for our survival, which if exhibited in adult relationships would be considered extremely selfish. But even in infancy, there is early evidence that we possess certain "moral foundations" related to helping one another (see Bloom 2010 for a discussion of research in this area).

Parental bonding may be considered the earliest form of "loyalty" (Fletcher and Evans 1983). Outside of these familial bonds, however, it is not clear to what degree very young children are able to develop loyal bonds. For example, Isaacs (2001, p. 136) argues that young children are incapable of loyalty, stating: "How can we expect them [children] to be loyal before they reach the age of reason? The answer is simple: very young children neither are, nor can they be, loyal in the strict sense of the word."

Whether or not young children are capable of loyalty, it is clear that as children develop they will begin to enter into mutual likings and friendships with other children which will grow more complex with age. For example, if you ask a 4-year-old child what a friend is, he or she is likely to give a response regarding someone who happens to be near her or whose toys she likes. A 5- to 6-year-old child would focus on particular episodes where they interact. At ages 7, 8 and 9 children begin to realize that friendship is personal, and they may like or dislike a person due to some trait (Gurian and Goodman 2012).

As the nature of children's relationships mature, so too do children's capabilities for holding loyalty to other individuals and other entities. At this point the role of parenting may (can) be a powerful motivator of loyalty in two important and more than frequently noted areas. The first and most obvious is religion, where individuals are prone to adhere to that of their parents for lifetimes (Potvin and Sloane 1985). The second is politics, where children tend to support the same political party as their parents (for example, Maccoby et al. 1954).

Activities initiated by parents for their children also help to instill loyalty, for example the support of sports teams and other related interests including the sport itself (for example, soccer). Sports stadiums are rife with children rooting for their parents' teams, frequently wearing particular sports paraphernalia, and participating verbally in games' outcomes.

Later, this same outcome support may be transferred to the school(s) the child attends. Here one can see how the reinforcement is likely to transfer from parents to peer groups. Of course, this could be synergistic, but not necessarily so. At this point, it is safe to say that loyalty is a function of social bonding whether parental or peer (and sometimes in opposing directions).

INTERPERSONAL LOYALTY

Interpersonal loyalties are extremely intertwined with friendships and avowed relationships (for example, marriages). Loyalty is frequently cited as one of the most prominent elements of close friends (Parlee 1979). And the AskMen.com Great Male Survey and Yahoo! Shine Great Female Survey found that loyalty was the most important personality trait making a man/woman "relationship material" (Hartwell 2009).

Of course, it is hard to imagine a close friendship without loyalty—a friend without loyalty is no friend at all. An in-depth discussion on building loyal friendships is beyond the scope of this chapter. Therefore for a full discussion on the topic we direct readers to Keiningham et al. (2009, ch. 2). Similarly, for a discussion of loyalty in marriage, we direct readers to Fowers (2000) and Rusbult et al. (1982).

One aspect of friendship worth noting is that no vows are made except those of a faith nature as in "bff" (best friend forever). Marriage differs in two major aspects. First, both parties have typically agreed to an oath of "til death do us part." Second, marriage is often recognized by the court system as imparting a duty of loyalty by spouses to one another which infers legal rights not granted to loyalty in other contexts (for example friends, other family members, and so on). Regan (1995) observes: "The [spousal] loyalty that one must demonstrate represents fidelity not to the marriage itself, but acceptance of the duties that constitute the fulfillment of a specific promise" (p. 2099) ". . . By prohibiting the incrimination of one's partner, the adverse testimony privilege expresses the importance of loyalty as a regulative ideal of the spousal role" (p. 2114).

CONSUMER LOYALTY

Researchers and managers have long known that consumers can develop strong affectionate bonds with the products and services that they use (for example, Carroll and Ahuvia 2006; Fournier 1998). And the notion of brand loyalty has long been a cornerstone of marketing (for example, Chaudhuri and Holbrook 2001).

Without question, some individuals develop bonds with brands, styles, and concepts. The same can be said of musical groups. Fans will go to great lengths to attend concerts in remote cities for their favorite groups. In fact, all entertainment venues such as theater, casinos, and movies of a particular theme (for example, Harry Potter, Star Trek) or containing favorite performers have passionate fans.

But is *consumer* loyalty really loyalty, that is, does it meet the definition of loyalty across other domains? As Beer and Watson (2009, p. 286) ask, "[Is] there some common thread to all of these concepts so that one can appropriately speak of a broader, overarching construct of 'loyalty'?" The answer to that in large part depends upon how we define consumer loyalty.

Managers often think of loyalty in terms of repeat purchasing behavior. As long as repeat purchasing is used as a proxy for loyalty, any rewards program whether "locked in" or not (Yi and Jeon 2003) will give the appearance of loyalty. In fact, these programs are frequently referred to as "loyalty programs." Airlines were the first to use these loyalty programs, but they have now become abundant across many industries. "Examples of these schemes can be found in Japanese retailing, US airlines and hotels, French banks, UK grocery stores, German car companies, Australian telecommunications, Italian fashion stores, US universities, and many other areas" (Uncles et al. 2003, p. 294).

As noted earlier, Uncles et al. (2003) refer to three commonly used conceptualizations of consumer loyalty in the literature: (1) attitudinal loyalty (for example, affective feeling of a bond), (2) behavioral loyalty (for example, repeat purchase behavior), and (3) situational/usage occasion based loyalty (for example, purchases based upon situational triggers). None of these conceptualizations of loyalty, however, meet the definition of loyalty in the Aksoy et al. (2014) definition presented earlier. Attitudinal loyalty only meets the first criterion, that is, a perceived specialness to a relationship, whereas behavioral loyalty specifically lacks this same criterion. And it is unclear whether or not situational/usage occasion based loyalty meets any of the criteria.

More in line with philosophical views on loyalty, however, Oliver (2010a) argues that these conceptualizations fail to describe true consumer loyalty because they fail to capture simultaneously a customer's devotion to a product or service and the manifestations of behaviors typically associated with loyalty (for example, repeat purchase, and so on). Oliver (1999, p. 34) proposes the following definition of consumer loyalty: "[Consumer loyalty is] a deeply held commitment to re-buy or re-patronize a preferred product/service consistently in the future, thereby causing repetitive same-brand or same brand-set purchasing, *despite* situational influences and marketing efforts having the potential to cause switching behavior" (emphasis in original).

Oliver (1999, p. 36) goes on to propose four different "levels" of loyalty:

1. Cognitive loyalty—loyalty to information such as prices, features, and so on.
2. Affective loyalty—loyalty to a liking (that is, I buy it because I like it).
3. Conative loyalty—loyalty to an intention (that is, I'm committed to buying it).
4. Action loyalty—loyalty to action (that is, inertia, coupled with the overcoming of obstacles).

Oliver's definition of consumer loyalty fits well within the parameters required of loyalty in other domains. Specifically, the elements of this definition correspond well to the definition of loyalty of Aksoy et al. (2014):

1. a perceived specialness to a relationship—"deeply held commitment . . . preferred product or service;"
2. favorable treatment to objects of loyalty—"repatronize a preferred product or service consistently in the future;"

3. a desire to maintain the relationship even when it requires sacrifice—"despite situational influences;"
4. defense and reinforcement of the relationship, that is, not being disloyal—"despite . . . marketing efforts that have the potential to cause switching behavior."

Therefore, in response to the question posed by Beer and Watson (2009, p. 286)—in essence, is consumer loyalty really loyalty?—Oliver's definition provides theoretical support that consumer loyalty reflects one manifestation of an overarching loyalty construct. Additionally, as noted earlier, Aksoy et al. (2014) provide empirical support that consumer loyalty is reflective of loyalty in other domains.

HABITUAL LOYALTY

Nordhielm and Bradford (2007) argue that in consumer contexts, there are three types of brand loyalty. Nordhielm describes these as "head loyalty, which is just being interested in the features of the product; heart loyalty, which is that really strong emotional brand loyalty; and hand loyalty, which is more habitual loyalty—the consumer just grabs the same brand every time out of habit" (DeGroat 2008).

Simplistically, the head and heart loyalty designations appear to have corollaries in the three-component model of commitment introduced by Allen and Meyer (1990) (for a review of the commitment literature, see Li and Petrick 2010). In particular, affective commitment (that is, an emotional attachment representing the customer's desire to continue the relationship) appears to correspond to heart loyalty. Calculative (or continuance) commitment (that is, an attachment based on rational, economic-based dependence on product/service benefits) appears to correspond to head loyalty. Note, however, that it is unclear if normative commitment (that is, an attachment that derives from a person's sense of moral obligation) is more closely aligned with head or heart loyalty.

The loyalty classification scheme of Nordhielm and Bradford (2007) also includes the concept of habitual loyalty. While this term has been used since at least the eighteenth century to describe habit-driven behavior, it is unclear if this represents genuine loyalty or simply resistance to change.

Prior research shows that, as a consequence of habituation, repetitive exposure increases and positively influences satisfaction judgments and behavioral intentions, in part because repetitive exposure engenders positive evaluations (Wood and Neal 2009). Other streams of research related to habits reinforce this prediction. Empirical models of consumer behavior find habit or inertia to be a strong explanatory factor when modeling consumer choice (for example, Jeuland 1979).

Researchers in psychology find that habitual behavior causes individuals to infer attitudes from implications of their behavior as per self-perception theory (Bem 1967). Specifically, Wood and Neal (2009, p. 584) argue, "Because people have limited introspective access to the implicit cognitive associations that guide their habits (e.g., Beilock and Carr 2001; Foerde et al. 2006), they are forced to infer the relevant internal states from external behaviors and the contexts in which the behaviors occur (Bem 1972)." As a result, inferring from self-perception theory, habitual behavior would be expected to influence satisfaction perceptions.

These relationships may or may not represent loyalty as defined earlier. Clearly there is repeat purchasing behavior, and likely positive affect in most cases. Perhaps the lack of consideration of alternatives can be classified as both a desire to maintain the relationship and defense and reinforcement of the relationship. Or it may simply reflect what some researchers refer to as "inertia"-based behavior.

We argue that habitual loyalty may indeed exist provided that it manifests positive affect, repeat behavior, and an exclusion of competing alternatives from the consideration set, but an understanding of its prevalence and other defining characteristics cannot be ascertained until further research is conducted into this form of loyalty.

THE NEBULOUS VALENCE OF LOYALTY

Unlike satisfaction/dissatisfaction, loyalty has a nebulous valence. Disloyalty can be simply the breakdown of loyalty (that is, the relationship losing its importance to the individual giving loyalty), or it can have truly negative ramifications.

Loyalty does not have to be based upon the ideals espoused by the individual or group to whom loyalty is given. For example, in his influential work *Exit, Voice, and Loyalty*, Hirschman (1970) observes that individuals may display loyalty despite general disagreement or dissatisfaction with an entity simply to avoid personal difficulties or disruptions in group dynamics. Additionally, Oliver (2010b, p. 73) observes that loyalty bonding can simply be a desire to follow the in-crowd:

> In its pure form, the village is a social alliance whereby the primary motivation to become loyal on the part of each consumer is to be one with the group . . . the consumer becomes a willing participant because of the attention provided

> by its members . . . the product/service is not the "consumable." Rather it is the camaraderie provided by the social organization.

Because loyalty can exist absent socially beneficial ideals, it is possible for loyalty to have what society would consider negative connotations. Without question, it is possible to be a loyal Nazi, Klansman, or gang member. In fact, criminal organizations such as the Mafia, Yakuza, and Triad are all well known for their tenets of loyalty. It is no accident that the expression "thick as thieves" denotes the closest of bonds. Although exit barriers may be severe in the case of the above examples, the social glue operates nonetheless.

Moreover, individuals can be loyal to ideals that are expressly antithetical to society at large. This can manifest as disloyalty to the social norm or to authority in general. For example, the "Pirate's Code," often idealized in adventure novels and movies, represents a genuine code of conduct for governing seventeenth-century pirates which was signed by the crew. While the real pirates were a motley crew of vicious criminals, today we romanticize a pirate's life as a liberating, exhilarating fight against the constraints of society. Most of us recognize that this is a fantasy that is far better than the reality.

But there is clearly an appeal for some to be loyal to *dis*loyalty. One prominent example is the so-called "Stop Snitchin'" movement that has become widespread in many inner-city communities throughout the U.S. "Stop Snitchin'" is a popular hip-hop slogan which means "do not cooperate with the police for any reason." As CBS News's *60 Minutes* reports, "the message appears in hip-hop videos, on T-shirts, Web sites, album covers and street murals. Well-known rappers talk about it endlessly on DVDs. It is a simple message heard in African-American communities across the country: don't talk to the police" (Court and Sharman 2007).

What was once perverted loyalty to a code of silence—one that was limited to criminals who were caught by the police—"Stop Snitchin'" is now being marketed as the cultural norm in poor communities, with devastating consequences. Cold-blooded murders go unsolved because of loyalty to this disloyalty. It has become a major roadblock to stemming lawlessness in many U.S. cities.

"I don't know what frustrates me more . . . these knuckleheads killing each other, or the residents who won't cooperate with my officers," sighs one frustrated police officer. Observes another officer, "No one wants to be accused of snitching . . . these people have become so desensitized to the violence, it's almost become a way of life" (Jacobs 2007).

Clearly, the "Stop Snitchin'" movement embodies a philosophy of misguided loyalties. A pro-criminal, antisocial cultural norm is best left to the world of science fiction novels, but it permeates our inner cities nonetheless.

Fortunately, despite the existence of a genuine loyalty to disloyalty (and perhaps even an appeal of it in some cases, à la James Dean and Marlon Brando movies), it does not reflect the manifestation of the overwhelming majority of our loyalties. Rather, in general our loyalties tend to enrich our relationships with one another and to build communities. As such, they have a positive relationship with our happiness (Aksoy et al. 2014; Keiningham et al. 2009) and to society at large (Fletcher 1993; Royce 1908 [1995]).

SATISFACTION VERSUS LOYALTY

We can begin to see the (dis)similarity between satisfaction and loyalty. Satisfaction requires the formation of expectations and/or other comparative referents (Oliver 2010a). It can be based on one episode or an accumulation of episodes over time. It is necessarily comparative and involves performance compared to some referent(s). And it can be positive or with a clearly defined negative at the opposite pole.

Alternatively, loyalty is akin to social bonding (although some would not categorize product or corporate bonding as social). It occurs through either a conditioned pairing, as with parent and child, husband and wife, friends, and other potential relationships, or via long-term usage, such as with a product or firm, whereby the consumable is acquired habitually. Expectations may have no role in this process at all and performance may be taken for granted.

With regard to habitual loyalty, research indicates that it is not guided by consumer attitudes or intentions (Ji and Wood 2007; Liu-Thompkins and Tam 2010). Therefore, once a behavior has become a habit, satisfaction would not be expected to materially alter the behavior. For example, Neal et al. (2011) and Wood and Neal (2009) showed that habitual popcorn eaters ate the same amount of popcorn at a movie theater regardless of whether or not the popcorn was fresh or stale. As would be expected, however, consumers of the stale popcorn reported being less satisfied with the popcorn.

With regard to dissatisfaction versus loyalty, however, here the scenario changes. The largest threat to loyalty is dissatisfaction (Oliver 2010b), although loyalty may appear to exist on the surface, a condition Keiningham et al. (2009) refer to as "toxic loyalty," as when broken marriages stay together for reasons of convenience, children, or social norms.

Dissatisfaction is the bane of all relationships whether they are of a previously satisfactory experience or of loyalty.

ADDICTIVE LOYALTY

Are addictions loyalty behaviors? For us the decision rests on whether "wanting" will be classified as positive affect as is "liking" (Camerer 2006; Dai et al. 2010; Wyvell and Berridge 2000). If the ultimate answer to that question is yes (which the authors believe will be the case), then addictive loyalty is loyalty (albeit a potential toxic form of loyalty).

Colloquially we tend to associate wanting and liking as synonymous because we typically like the things that we want. But it is possible to want something and not like it. For example, a smoker can want a cigarette while not liking the experience. This is because wanting and liking are controlled by different circuits in the brain (Smith and Berridge 2007). Summarizing the research of Smith and Berridge (2007), *ScienceDaily* (2007) reports:

> Natural heroin-like chemicals (opioids) in a few brain "pleasure hotspots" make individuals want to eat more of a tasty sweet food, and make them like its sweet taste more when they eat it, the study says. The same thing happens with addictions to drugs, sex, gambling and other pursuits involving 'brain reward' circuits.

Craving behaviors based on wanting (for example, smoking) are not easily broken. In fact, for many it is much easier to switch political orientations or even, at one extreme, religions, than to quit smoking.

ULTIMATE LOYALTY

What is "ultimate" loyalty? To our knowledge, there is no viable definition of what constitutes "ultimate" loyalty. Oliver (1999, 2010a) provides an elementary model that may be viewed as a start for such a process. It consists of two dimensions: (1) individual fortitude and (2) community/social support. This two-by-two grid breakdown results in four cells, the weakest based on simple product superiority. When high levels of both are present, a concept of "immersed self-identity" is formed. It is unknown whether this shares elements of ultimate loyalty. Furthermore, only a small number of studies have attempted to verify its parameters (Han et al. 2008; Harris and Goode 2004; Kim et al. 2008). Clearly further work on this concept is required.

There are many examples of lifetime loyalty (for example religion, marital couples who stay together throughout their lives). But is this a demonstration of "ultimate" loyalty? Colloquially, we typically speak of "ultimate acts of loyalty" as being behaviors which manifest themselves in sacrificing reputation (for example, Reischauer 1986), freedom (for example, Shain 1989), livelihood (for example, Stoker 2005), or life (for example, Wolff 2008) in the service of another person or entity.

In the *Philosophy of Loyalty*, Josiah Royce (1908 [1995]) describes the ultimate form of loyalty as being "the willing and practical and thoroughgoing devotion of a person to a cause" (p. 16). He defined a cause as "something that unifies many human lives in one" (p. 351). For Royce, loyalty in its purest form manifests itself as "the will to believe in something eternal and to express that belief in the practical life of a human being" (p. 166).

Perhaps Royce's view of loyalty is idealistic. But our loyalties across the domains of our lives are nonetheless important. Our loyalties are signs of the types of people we choose to be. Our loyalties demonstrate what we value, what we believe, and what we want our world to be.

NOTE

* Author order is alphabetical; all contributed equally.

REFERENCES

Aksoy, Lerzan, Timothy L. Keiningham, Alexander Buoye, Bart Larivière, Luke Williams and Ian Wilson (2014), "Does loyalty span domains? Examining the relationship between consumer loyalty, other loyalties, and happiness," *Journal of Business Research* (forthcoming).

Allen, N.J. and J.P. Meyer (1990), "The measurement and antecedents of affective, continuance, and normative commitment to the organization," *Journal of Occupational Psychology*, **63** (1), 1–18.

Beer, Andrew and David Watson (2009), "Individual and group loyalty scales (IGLS): construction and preliminary validation," *Journal of Personality Assessment*, **91** (3), 277–87.

Beilock, Sian L. and Thomas H. Carr (2001), "On the fragility of skilled performance: what governs choking under pressure?" *Journal of Experimental Psychology: General*, **130** (4), 701–25.

Bem, Daryl J. (1967), "Self-perception: an alternative interpretation of cognitive dissonance phenomena," *Psychological Review*, **74** (3), 183–200.

Bem, Daryl J. (1972), "Self-perception theory," in Leonard Berkowitz (ed.), *Advances in Experimental Social Psychology*, vol. 6, New York: Academic Press, pp. 1–62.

Bloom, Paul (2010), "The moral life of babies," *New York Times Sunday Magazine*, May, MM44, accessed 24 August 2013 at www.nytimes.com/2010/05/09/magazine/09babies-t.html?pagewanted=all.

Cacioppo, John T. and Louise C. Hawkley (2009), "Loneliness," in Mark R. Leary, Rick H. Hoyle (eds), *Handbook of Individual Differences in Social Behavior*, New York: Guilford Press, pp. 227–40.
Cacioppo, John T., Louise C. Hawkley, John M. Ernst, Mary Burleson, Gary G. Berntson, Bita Nouriani and David Spiegel (2006), "Loneliness within a nomological net: an evolutionary perspective," *Journal of Research in Personality*, **40** (6), 1054–85.
Camerer, Colin F. (2006), "Wanting, liking, and learning: neuroscience and paternalism," *The University of Chicago Law Review*, **73** (1), 87–110.
Carroll, B.A. and A. Ahuvia (2006), "Some antecedents and outcomes of brand love," *Marketing Letters*, **17** (2), 79–89.
Chaudhuri, A. and M.B. Holbrook (2001), "The chain effects from brand trust and brand affect to brand performance: the role of brand loyalty," *Journal of Marketing*, **65** (April), 81–93.
Court, Andy and Keith Sharman (2007), "Stop Snitchin'," *60 Minutes* (CBS News), accessed 13 July 2007 at www.cbsnews.com/stories/2007/04/19/60minutes/printable2704565.shtml.
Dai, Xianchi, C. Miguel Brendl and Dan Ariely (2010), "Wanting, liking, and preference construction," *Emotion*, **10** (3), 324–33.
DeGroat, Bernie (2008), "Anatomy of a loyal customer," University of Michigan, Ross School of Business, News & Media, 18 August, accessed 24 August 2013 at www.bus.umich.edu/NewsRoom/ArticleDisplay.asp?news_id=13794.
Fairburn, William Armstrong (1926), *Loyalty*, New York: Nation Press Printing Company.
Fletcher, George P. (1993), *Loyalty: An Essay on the Morality of Relationships*, New York: Oxford University Press.
Fletcher, John C. and Mark I. Evans (1983), "Maternal bonding in early fetal ultrasound examinations," *New England Journal of Medicine*, **308** (February), 392–3.
Foerde, Karin, Barbara J. Knowlton and Russell A. Poldrack (2006), "Modulation of competing memory systems by distraction," *Proceedings of the National Academy of Sciences*, **103** (31), 11778–83.
Fournier, S.M. (1998), "Consumers and their brands: developing relationship theory in consumer research," *Journal of Consumer Research*, **24** (4), 343–73.
Fowers, Blaine J. (2000), *Beyond the Myth of Marital Happiness: How Embracing the Virtues of Loyalty, Generosity, Justice, and Courage Can Strengthen Your Relationship*. San Francisco, CA: Jossey-Bass.
Gurian, Anita and Robin F. Goodman (2012), "Friends and friendship", NYU Child Study Center, 1 October, accessed 20 August 2012 at www.aboutourkids.org/articles/friends_friendships.
Han, Xiaoyun, Robert J Kwortnik, Jr. and Chunxiao Wang (2008), "Service loyalty: an integrative model and examination across service contexts," *Journal of Service Research*, **11** (August), 22–42.
Harris, Lloyd C. and Mark M.H. Goode (2004), "The four levels of loyalty and the pivotal role of trust: a study of online service dynamics," *Journal of Retailing*, **80** (2), 139–58.
Hartwell, Sharalyn (2009), "Loyalty, most important personality trait to be 'relationship material'," *Generation Y Examiner*, 3 August, accessed 24 August 2013 at www.examiner.com/x-13207-Generation-Y-Examiner~y2009m8d3-Loyalty-most-important-personality-trait-to-be-relationship-material.
Hirschman, Albert O. (1970), *Exit, Voice, and Loyalty*, Cambridge, MA: Harvard University Press.
Isaacs, David (2001), *Character Building: A Guide for Parents and Teachers*, 2nd edn, Portland, OR: Four Courts Press.
Jacobs, Andrew (2007), "Newark battles murder and its accomplice, silence," *New York Times*, 27 May, sect. 1, p. 1, accessed on 13 July 2007 at NYTimes.com.
Jeuland, Abel P. (1979), "Brand choice inertia as one aspect of the notion of brand loyalty," *Management Science*, **25** (7), 671–82.
Ji, Mindy F. and Wendy Wood (2007), "Purchase and consumption habits: not necessarily what you intend," *Journal of Consumer Psychology*, **17** (4), 261–76.

Keiningham, Timothy, Lerzan Aksoy and Luke Williams (2009), *Why Loyalty Matters*, Dallas, TX: BenBella Books.
Kim, Jooyoung, Jon D. Morris and Joffre Swait (2008), "Antecedents of true brand loyalty," *Journal of Advertising*, **37** (Summer), 99–117.
Ladd, J. (1967), "Loyalty," in *Encyclopedia of Philosophy*, vol. 5, ed. Paul Edwards, New York: Macmillan and Free Press, pp. 97–8.
Li, X. and J.F. Petrick (2010), "Revisiting the commitment-loyalty distinction in a cruising context," *Journal of Leisure Research*, **42** (1), 67–90.
Liu-Thompkins, Yuping and Leona Tam (2010), "Not all repeat purchases are the same: attitudinal loyalty and habit," working paper, Old Dominion University, accessed 24 August 2013 at www.yupingliu.com/files/papers/liu_tam_loyalty_habit_acr.pdf.
Maccoby, Eleanor E., Richard E. Matthews and Anton S. Morton (1954), "Youth and political change," *Public Opinion Quarterly*, **18** (1), 23–39.
Neal, David T., Wendy Wood, Mengju Wu and David Kurlander (2011), "The pull of the past: when do habits persist despite conflict with motives?" *Personality and Social Psychology Bulletin*, **37** (11), 1428–37.
Nordhielm, Christy and Tonya Williams Bradford (2007), "Head, heart, and hand: brand loyalty," Association for Consumer Research Conference, Nashville, Tennessee, October.
Oldenquist, A. (1982), "Loyalties," *The Journal of Philosophy*, **79**, (4), 179–93.
Oliver, Richard L. (1999), "Whence consumer loyalty," *Journal of Marketing*, **63** (4), special issue, 33–44.
Oliver, Richard L. (2010a), *Satisfaction: A Behavioral Perspective on the Consumer*, 2nd edn, Armonk, NY: M.E. Sharpe.
Oliver, Richard (2010b), "Consumer brand loyalty," in Jagdish Sheth and Naresh Malhotra (eds), *Wiley International Encyclopedia of Marketing*, vol. 3: *Consumer Behavior*, Chichester: John Wiley & Sons, pp. 67–75.
Oliver, Richard L. (2011), 2011 Christopher Lovelock Career Contributions Award acceptance speech. 20th Frontiers in Service Conference, Columbus, Ohio, 2 July.
Parlee, M.B. (1979), "The friendship bond: Psychology Today's survey report on friendship in America," *Psychology Today*, **13**(4), 43–54.
Potvin, Raymond H. and Douglas M. Sloane (1985), "Parental control, age, and religious practice," *Review of Religious Research*, **27** (1), 3–14.
Regan, Milton C., Jr. (1995), "Spousal privilege and the meanings of marriage," *Virginia Law Review*, **81** (8), (November, Symposium: New Directions in Family Law), 2045–156.
Reischauer, Robert D. (1986), "Why the Reagan revolution failed: a review essay," *Political Science Quarterly*, **101** (4), 661–4.
Royce, Josiah (1908), *The Philosophy of Loyalty*, New York: Macmillan, reprinted 1995 by Vanderbilt University Press.
Rusbult, C.E., I.M. Zembrodt and L.K. Gunn (1982), "Exit, voice, loyalty, and neglect: responses to dissatisfaction in romantic involvements," *Journal of Personality and Social Psychology*, **43** (6), 1230–42.
ScienceDaily (2007), "Why 'Wanting' and 'Liking' Something Simultaneously is Overwhelming," *ScienceDaily*, 3 March, accessed 24 August 2013 at www.sciencedaily.com/releases/2007/03/070302115232.htm.
Shain, Yossi (1989), *The Frontier of Loyalty: Political Exiles in the Age of the Nation-State*, Middletown, CT: Wesleyan University Press.
Smith, Kyle S. and Kent C. Berridge (2007), "Opioid limbic circuit for reward: interaction between hedonic hotspots of nucleus accumbens and ventral pallidum," *The Journal of Neuroscience*, **27** (7), 1594–605
Stoker, K. (2005), "Loyalty in public relations: when does it cross the line between virtue and vice?" *Journal of Mass Media Ethics*, **20** (4), 269–87.
Uncles, M.D., G.R. Dowling and K. Hammond (2003), "Customer loyalty and customer loyalty programs," *Journal of Consumer Marketing*, **20**, 4, 294–316.
Wolff, David (2008), "Cultural and social history on total war's global battlefield," *The Russian Review*, **67** (January), 70–77.

Wood, Wendy and David T. Neal (2009), "The habitual consumer," *Journal of Consumer Psychology*, **19** (4), 579–92.

Wyvell, Cindy L. and Kent C. Berridge (2000), "Intra-accumbens amphetamine increases the conditioned incentive salience of sucrose reward: enhancement of reward 'wanting' without enhanced 'liking' or response reinforcement," *The Journal of Neuroscience*, **20** (21), 8122–30.

Yi, Youjae and Hoseong Jeon (2003), "Effects of loyalty programs on value perception, program loyalty, and brand loyalty," *Journal of the Academy of Marketing Science*, **31** (3), 229–40.

4 A comparison of relationship marketing models

Tracey S. Dagger and Peter J. Danaher

INTRODUCTION

As competition to win the loyalty of customers grows (Palmatier et al. 2006), relationship marketing is often suggested as a critical strategy for achieving retention (Gwinner et al. 1998) and ultimately higher sales, market share, and profits (Crosby et al. 1990; Morgan and Hunt 1994). Against this background, a substantial body of literature focused on understanding the customer–provider relationship has developed. Our knowledge of the benefits a customer derives from a relationship (Gwinner et al. 1998), of how relationship quality is evaluated (Hennig-Thurau 2000; Kumar et al. 1995), and of the factors that drive strong customer–provider relationships (De Wulf et al. 2001; Palmatier et al. 2006) has increased greatly. Importantly, viewing customer relationships as a source of loyalty has focused research attention on examining the relationship factors that drive retention, repeat purchase and recommendation (Palmatier et al. 2006).

Although the breadth of factors posited to influence customer loyalty is substantial, commitment, trust and satisfaction are seen as central to strong customer-firm relationships (De Wulf et al. 2001; Palmatier et al. 2006; Smith 1998). While these factors have been studied individually (for example, Bolton 1998; Harris and Goode 2004), they are frequently examined in subsets (for example, Aydin and Ozer 2005; Jap and Ganesan 2000; Wong and Sohal 2002) or as components of larger relationship marketing models (for example, Palmatier et al. 2006). A review of the literature offers a myriad of conflicting results about how commitment, trust and satisfaction relate to each other as well as how they relate to customer loyalty and in particular attitudinal, behavioral and word-of-mouth loyalty. Few studies offer competing models or examine these relationships across different service contexts. Indeed, virtually no effort has been made to resolve obvious incongruence in the literature.

The purpose of the current study is to examine five models of relationship quality and loyalty based on the literature. Specifically, we test a series of competing models where each model represents a plausible conceptualization of the interrelationship between commitment, trust, satisfaction, attitudinal loyalty, behavioral loyalty and word-of-mouth loyalty. We assess these models for their appropriateness and fit. To further maximize external validity nine service industries are utilized as the basis of our analysis. As no research has simultaneously compared variants of the association between these constructs, this study makes a valuable contribution to clarifying the conflicting findings presented in the literature. It also provides a solid platform for the development of more comprehensive models of relationship formation. In the remainder of this chapter we review prior theory and research relevant to commitment, trust and satisfaction as well as attitudinal, behavioral and word-of-mouth loyalty. We then draw on the literature to specify five plausible and competing relationship models. The method and analysis of the models to identify the most appropriate and valid specification of these relationships is then presented. We conclude by discussing the implications of our model testing process.

LITERATURE SYNTHESIS

The alternative models presented in our study provide a differential conceptualization of the effect that commitment, trust and satisfaction have on attitudinal, behavioral and word-of-mouth loyalty. No prior research has simultaneously examined these effects nor has past research compared alternative conceptualizations of these effects. A review of the literature suggests that confusion relative to these constructs centers on two themes. The first theme focuses on the association between commitment, trust and satisfaction as critical relationship input constructs. The second theme is concerned with relationship output constructs and in particular customer loyalty. Table 4.1 provides a summary of the key relationships posited in the literature.

Commitment, Trust and Satisfaction

Commitment, trust and satisfaction are critical relationship constructs. Commitment implies that there are mutual benefits associated with remaining in the customer–provider relationship, that both parties want the relationship to endure and are prepared to expend effort in maintaining the relationship (Morgan and Hunt 1994). Thus, we view commitment as the consumer's voluntary willingness to remain in and make efforts towards maintaining a relationship (De Wulf et al. 2001; Morgan and Hunt 1994; Palmatier et al. 2006). Trust is a fundamental building block for most relationship models (Ulaga and Eggert 2006). We view trust as

Table 4.1 Literature linking commitment, trust, satisfaction to outcomes

Author/s	Relevant paths considered	Relevant model(s)
Verhoef et al. (2002)	Trust → Referrals (word of mouth)	1, 3, 5
	Commitment → Referrals (word of mouth)	1, 3, 4, 5
	Satisfaction → Referrals (word of mouth)	1, 3, 5
	Commitment → Number of services purchased (behavioral loyalty)	1
Doney and Cannon (1997)	Trust → Anticipated future interaction (attitudinal loyalty)	1, 2, 3, 5
Cooil et al. (2007)	Satisfaction → Share of wallet (behavioral loyalty)	1
Keiningham et al. (2003)	Satisfaction → Share of wallet (behavioral loyalty)	1
Ball et al. 2004	Satisfaction → Attitudinal loyalty (behavioral loyalty)	1, 2, 3, 5
	Trust → Attitudinal loyalty	1, 2, 3, 5
Brown et al. (2005)	Satisfaction → Word of Mouth	1, 3, 5
	Satisfaction → Commitment	5
	Commitment → Word of mouth	1, 3, 4, 5
Caceres and Paparoidamis (2007)	Satisfaction → Trust	4, 5
	Satisfaction → Commitment	5
	Satisfaction → Attitudinal loyalty	1, 2, 3, 5
	Trust → Commitment	4, 5
	Trust → Attitudinal loyalty	1, 2, 3, 5
	Commitment → Attitudinal loyalty	1, 2, 3, 4, 5
Chiou and Droge (2006)	Trust → Attitudinal loyalty	1, 2, 3, 5
	Trust → Satisfaction	–
	Satisfaction → Attitudinal loyalty	1, 2, 3, 5
	Attitudinal Loyalty → Behavioral loyalty	2, 3, 4, 5

Doney et al. (2007)	Trust → Attitudinal loyalty	1, 2, 3, 5
	Trust → Share of purchase (behavioral loyalty)	1
Evanschitzky et al. (2006)	Commitment → Attitudinal loyalty	1, 2, 3, 4, 5
	Commitment → Behavioral loyalty	1
Gounaris (2005)	Trust → Commitment	4, 5
	Commitment → Maintain relationship (attitudinal loyalty)	1, 3, 4, 5
Rosenbaum et al. (2006)	Satisfaction → Future intentions (attitudinal loyalty)	1, 2, 3, 5
	Commitment → Future intentions (attitudinal loyalty)	1, 2, 3, 4, 5
Ulaga and Eggert (2006)	Satisfaction → Trust	4, 5
	Trust → Commitment	4, 5
	Satisfaction → Expansion/leave business (attitudinal loyalty)	1, 2, 3, 5
	Commitment → Expansion/leave business (attitudinal loyalty)	1, 2, 3, 4, 5
Garbarino and Johnson (1999)	Trust → Commitment	4, 5
	Commitment → Future intentions (attitudinal loyalty)	1, 2, 3, 4, 5
	Trust → Future Intentions (attitudinal loyalty)	1, 2, 3, 5
Liang and Wang 2007	Satisfaction → Trust	4, 5
	Trust → Commitment	4, 5
	Commitment → Attitudinal loyalty	1, 2, 3, 4, 5
Odekerken-Schröder et al. (2003)	Satisfaction → Trust	4, 5
	Trust → Commitment	4, 5
	Commitment → Buying behavior (behavioral loyalty)	1
Lam et al. (2004)	Satisfaction → Attitudinal loyalty	1, 2, 3, 5
Wong and Sohal (2002)	Trust → Commitment	4, 5

the consumer's confident belief in the reliability and integrity of a service provider (Crosby et al. 1990; De Wulf et al. 2001; Morgan and Hunt 1994; Palmatier et al. 2006). Without developing a reasonable degree of trust a relationship is unlikely to endure because trust between relational partners promotes efficiency, productivity and effectiveness, which are central to a strong relationship (Morgan and Hunt, 1994). We view satisfaction as a post-purchase evaluation following a consumption experience. It reflects the customer's affective appraisal of the service overall (Anderson et al. 1994; Oliver 1997; Verhoef et al. 2002). Satisfaction is essential to the exchange relationship as it represents the fulfillment of customer needs. Thus, relationship continuity depends greatly on the customer's level of satisfaction with the service (Anderson and Sullivan 1993).

The centrality of commitment, trust, and satisfaction to the notion of relationships is underscored by the sheer volume of research examining these constructs individually (for example, Bolton 1998; Harris and Goode 2004), in subsets (for example, Verhoef et al., 2002; Aydin and Ozer 2005; Jap and Ganesan, 2000; Wong and Sohal 2002) or as components of more complex relationship models (for example, Palmatier et al. 2006; Odekerken-Schröder et al. 2003). Numerous studies have specified possible relationships between commitment, trust, satisfaction and loyalty. Although the specification of these models is generally based on theory and empirical analyses, only limited consensus exists about how these constructs are related. As the degree of incongruence in conceptualizing how these constructs relate to each other is substantial, it is critical that research clarifies these relationships before more complex theoretical models can be developed and before service firms can implement relationship strategies with confidence.

A review of the literature that conceptualizes the effect of commitment, trust, and satisfaction on attitudinal, behavioral and word-of-mouth loyalty appears to be underpinned by two broad conceptual approaches. The first approach specifies commitment, trust and satisfaction as having only direct effects on outcomes, while the second views these constructs as having both direct and indirect effects on outcomes. We discuss these approaches and highlight similarities and disparities next.

Direct effect models view commitment, trust and satisfaction as directly effecting service outcomes. What differentiates these models is that interrelationships between the constructs are not specified. For example, Verhoef et al. (2002), in a study of insurance customers, specify a model in which commitment, trust and satisfaction directly influence customer referrals and the number of services purchased. Similarly, Rauyruen and Miller (2007) suggest commitment, trust and satisfaction are direct drivers of attitudinal and behavioral loyalty for business-to-business customers.

As well as the direct effect models, several researchers have specified conceptualizations that include both direct and indirect effects. These models generally fall into two categories, namely, process-based models or interactive-effect models. Process-based models incorporate both direct and indirect effects, however, their specified structure is process based where one construct influences another, which in turn drives another. Odekerken-Schröder et al. (2003) and Liang and Wang (2007) exemplify this process perspective, specifying models where satisfaction drives trust, which in turn drives commitment, which then effects behavior.

As well as these process-based models, several researchers have specified interactive models that also include both direct and indirect effects. That is, in addition to specifying the direct effect of commitment, trust and satisfaction on outcomes, the interrelationship between these constructs is also modeled. For example, Caceres and Paparoidamis (2007) suggest that satisfaction affects trust and commitment as well as loyalty, and that trust and commitment drive loyalty. Trust is further posited as driving commitment. In this model, commitment, trust and satisfaction are seen as having a direct effect on loyalty; however, satisfaction has an indirect effect via trust and commitment and trust itself indirectly influences client loyalty through commitment. Similarly, Chiou and Droge (2006) suggest that trust drives satisfaction and that both trust and satisfaction impact retail customers' attitudinal loyalty, and Garbarino and Johnson (1999) posit that trust and commitment drive the future intentions of theater customers and that trust also drives commitment to the theater.

Attitudinal, Behavioral and Word-of-mouth Loyalty

Creating a loyal customer base is not only about keeping customers over time but also about nurturing the relationship to encourage favorable attitudes toward the firm, repeat purchasing, and recommendation of the firm to other consumers (Dimitriades 2006). Numerous studies have specified relationships between commitment, trust and satisfaction and such consequences as behavioral intentions, word of mouth, willingness to pay more and loyalty. While loyalty is perhaps the most critical outcome of strong customer relationships, the facets of loyalty generally examined in the literature vary greatly. Wong and Sohal (2006), Aydin and Ozer (2005) and Rauyruen and Miller (2007), for example, examine attitudinal loyalty, Mattila (2006) and Keiningham et al. (2003) examine share-of-wallet or behavioral loyalty, and Chiou and Droge (2006) examine both attitudinal loyalty and behavioral loyalty.

A common approach in the literature is to distinguish between a customer's attitudinal loyalty and behavioral loyalty (Chaudhuri and

Holbrook 2001; Dick and Basu 1994). We make this distinction in the present study to define attitudinal loyalty as the customer's psychological attachment to the service provider/supplier and behavioral loyalty as the customer's actual repurchase behavior as exemplified by share of wallet and share of purchase (Chaudhuri and Holbrook 2001). Based on this distinction we examine the impact of commitment, trust and satisfaction on both attitudinal and behavioral loyalty. We further propose that a loyal customer will display positive word of mouth, which we view as informal communication about a product/service between private parties (Zeithaml et al. 1996). Word of mouth is considered the ultimate test of a customer's relationship with the firm (Bendapudi and Berry 1997). As suggested by Mazzarol et al. (2007), we view word-of-mouth loyalty as conceptually distinct from attitudinal loyalty.

As well as differences in the types of loyalty studied, dissimilarity also exists in regard to the effect commitment, trust and satisfaction (or a subset of these constructs) have on customer loyalty. Empirical evidence, for example, supports an antecedent link to referrals from commitment, trust and satisfaction (for example, Verhoef et al. 2002). Similarly, Rauyruen and Miller (2007) found that commitment, trust and satisfaction drove attitudinal loyalty while satisfaction also drove intentions. Trust and satisfaction were found to effect attitudinal loyalty (Chiou and Droge 2006) and satisfaction has been found to significantly impact share of wallet (for example, Mattila, 2006) as well as word-of-mouth intentions (for example, Brown et al. 2005). While it is recognized that attitudinal loyalty is intertwined with behavioral loyalty (Ball et al. 2004), only Chiou and Droge (2006) explicitly study this relationship to find that attitudinal loyalty significantly and positively influences behavioral loyalty. To date no prior study has tested a series of alternative models specifying the possible interrelationship and effect of commitment, trust and satisfaction on attitudinal, behavioral and word-of-mouth loyalty to identify the most robust specification.

ALTERNATIVE MODELS

Based on the literature reviewed we test five competing models, each offering a different specification of the relationship between commitment, trust, satisfaction and loyalty. These models, shown in Figure 4.1, exemplify the divergent approaches reported in the literature.

The first model (Model 1) positions commitment, trust and satisfaction as having a direct effect on all three loyalty constructs. This model is conceptually similar to models positioning commitment, trust and satisfaction as driving attitudinal loyalty (Rauyruen and Miller 2007), referrals

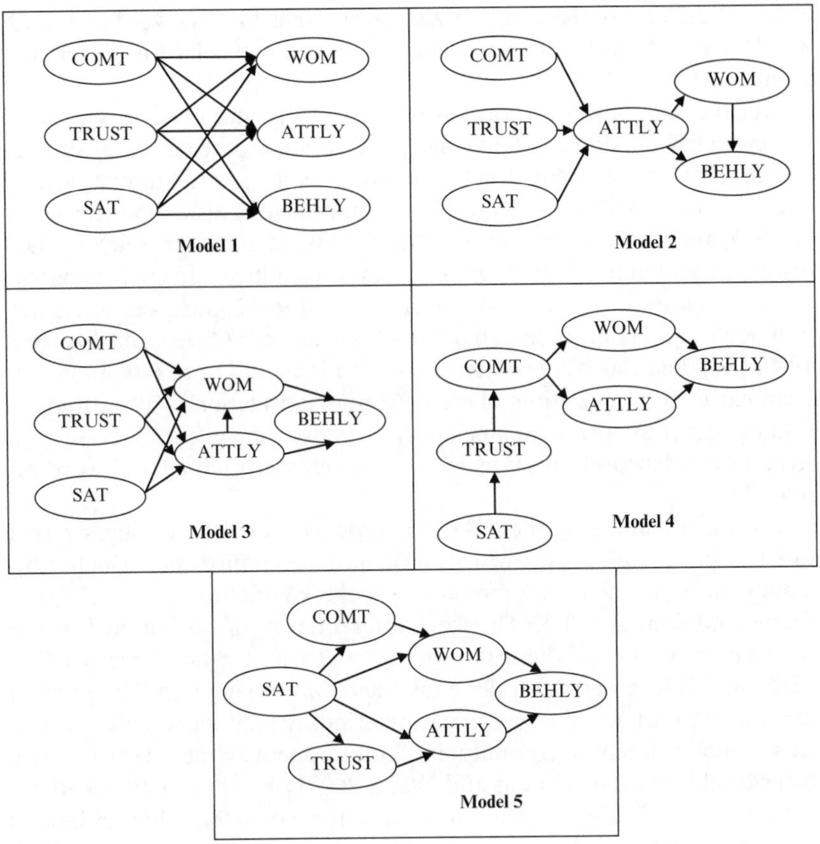

Figure 4.1 *Alternative models*

(Verhoef et al. 2002) and behavioral intentions (Rosenbaum et al. 2006). Researchers have also linked commitment, satisfaction (Brown et al. 2005) and trust (Gremler et al. 2001) directly to word of mouth. We therefore examine the direct effect of these constructs on attitudinal, word-of-mouth and behavioral loyalty in one model.

The second model (Model 2) shows commitment, trust and satisfaction as directly driving attitudinal loyalty. Attitudinal loyalty is shown as directly driving word-of-mouth and behavioral loyalty. As per Rauyruen and Miller (2007) and Verhoef et al. (2002), no interrelationships are tested between commitment, trust and satisfaction. In this model, attitudinal loyalty is posited as mediating the effect of commitment, trust and satisfaction on behavioral loyalty and word-of-mouth loyalty. Word of mouth is also shown to have a direct effect on behavioral loyalty. Attitudinal research underpins the link between attitudinal loyalty, word-of-mouth and behavioral loyalty, with attitude shown to drive behavior (Ajzen and Fishbein 1980).

Model 3 also positions both attitudinal loyalty and word of mouth as driving behavioral loyalty. This conceptualization is based on research suggesting that commitment, trust and satisfaction drive attitudinal loyalty (Rauyruen and Miller 2007) and that commitment, satisfaction (Brown et al. 2005) and trust (Gremler et al. 2001) drive word of mouth. Oliver (1997) distinguishes among four stages of loyalty: cognitive, affective, conative, and action loyalty. As noted when discussing Model 2, this assertion is well grounded in most attitude and satisfaction research (Ajzen and Fishbein 1980; Dick and Basu 1994; Oliver 1997). Chiou and Droge (2006) present a similar conceptualization where trust and satisfaction drive attitudinal loyalty, which in turn drives behavioral loyalty. The effect of these constructs on behavioral loyalty is indirect through attitudinal and word-of-mouth loyalty.

The fourth model (Model 4) is a process model and suggests that satisfaction drives trust, which influences commitment, which ultimately impacts various outcomes (Odekerken-Schröder et al. 2003; Liang and Wang 2007). The key differentiator of this model is the sequencing of effects where satisfaction and trust do not directly affect outcomes. Odekerken-Schröder et al. (2003) and Liang and Wang (2007) provide support for this specification, finding that satisfaction drives trust which influences commitment; commitment is then seen to drive behavioral intentions (Liang and Wang 2007) or behavior (Odekerken-Schröder et al. 2003). We maintain the sequencing effect that underpins each of these models but study the effect of this sequence on attitudinal, behavioral and word-of-mouth loyalty as per our rationale for Models 2 and 3.

The final model (Model 5) posits satisfaction as driving trust and commitment as well as word-of-mouth and attitudinal loyalty. Satisfaction is seen as central to this model. Caceres and Paparoidamis (2007) suggest that satisfaction affects trust and commitment as well as loyalty, and that trust and commitment drive attitudinal loyalty. Trust is further modeled as driving commitment. In this model commitment, trust and satisfaction are seen as having a direct effect on loyalty; however, satisfaction has an indirect effect via trust and commitment and trust itself indirectly influences client loyalty through commitment. Similarly, Ulaga and Eggert (2006) specify a model in which satisfaction drives trust and trust drives commitment which influences the amount of business done with a supplier and propensity to leave. Satisfaction is also seen to have a direct effect on these outcomes in the Ulaga and Eggert (2006) model.

RESEARCH METHOD

Sample

Our study involved nine service types, namely, travel agents, hairdressers, doctors, photo-printing services, general banking, pest control, cinemas, airlines and fast-food outlets. These reflect a broad spectrum of service types operating in the marketplace (Bowen 1990). We piloted the survey on a representative sample of 30 consumers. We then undertook a mail survey that involved a national sample of 3,000 consumers available through a commercially available mailing list. In total, 591 usable questionnaires were returned over the subsequent six weeks representing a response rate of 20.2 percent. This response rate is relatively high for a mail survey of consumers (Dillman 2007).

Measures

Where possible, all measures used in this study were adapted from existing scales. Commitment was measured with six items from Hennig-Thurau et al. (2002) and Smith (1998). Trust was represented by five items adapted from Morgan and Hunt (1994) and Doney and Cannon (1997), and satisfaction was measured on a six-item scale from Oliver (1997) and Hennig-Thurau et al. (2002). Word of mouth (WOM) was measured with three items adapted from Zeithaml et al. (1996). Attitudinal loyalty was measured with three items from Plank and Newell (2007) and Zeithaml et al. (1996) while behavioral loyalty comprised two items from Odekerken-Schröder et al. (2003). Scale items can be found in the appendix to this chapter.

Reliability and Validity of Measures

The measures used in the study were subjected to exploratory and confirmatory factor analyses. The result of these analyses supported the distinctions among the satisfaction, trust and commitment constructs. Cronbach's alpha values were high and analysis of the measurement model resulted in good fit with all items serving as strong measures of their respective constructs (χ^2 (445.09) = 120, p = 0.00, Comparative Fit Index (CFI) = 0.97, Increment Fit Index (IFI) = 0.97, Root Mean Square Error of Approximation (RMSEA) = 0.07). Analysis also indicated high levels of construct reliability and average variance extracted for all latent variables. Convergent and discriminant validity were also established (Fornell and Larcker 1981).

RESULTS AND DISCUSSION

After establishing the psychometric properties of our constructs, we turn attention to analyzing our five competing relationship models. In comparing the models we followed the procedures outlined by Anderson and Gerbing (1988) and Cronin et al. (2000). As our models were non-nested, model comparison was based on the Akaike's Information Criterion (AIC) (Arbuckle 1997; Bozdogan 1987) and the Bayesian Information Criterion (BIC) (Arbuckle 1997; Browne and Cudeck 1989) which penalize models as the number of parameters increase (for example, Ben-Akiva and Swait 1986; Swait and Sweeney 2000) as well as χ^2(df), χ^2/df, CFI, TLI, NFI and RMSEA. Each model comprised the same six constructs and each path in each model can be supported by the literature. The measures, sample, and testing procedure were identical for each of the five models tested. The results of model testing are reported in Table 4.2.

The model that performed best was Model 3 with a χ^2 value of 468.777 (*df* 107). This model had a lower AIC, BIC, normed χ^2/df index, and superior NFI, Tucker–Lewis Index (TLI), CFI and RMSEA indices than the alternatives. The relative ability of this model to explain variation in behavioral loyalty (as measured by the R^2 value) was 0.21. Given this support, discussion of the path results is restricted to this model. The fit indices for this model are well above the recommended threshold for good fit (Hu and Bentler 1999).

As can be seen in Table 4.2, our results indicate that commitment (β = 0.31, p<0.001) and satisfaction (β = 0.48, p<0.001) had a large and significant effect on attitudinal loyalty, suggesting that these constructs are strong drivers of a customer's intention to maintain their relationship with the service provider and remain loyal to that provider. In contrast, trust (β = 0.02, p<0.05) did not have a significant effect on attitudinal loyalty. However, trust and satisfaction did affect (β = 0.16, p<0.001; β = 0.45, p<0.001, respectively) word-of-mouth intentions with satisfaction, being a very strong driver of customers' intentions to say positive things about the service provider and to recommend the provider. Commitment had no effect (β = 0.03, p>0.05) on word-of-mouth intentions. Finally, attitudinal loyalty was found to positively drive word-of-mouth intentions and behavioral loyalty (β = 0.29, p<0.001; β = 0.33, p<0.001, respectively). This suggests that customers who intend to remain with their current service provider are more likely to recommend the firm, purchase more frequently and spend a larger portion of their wallet with that firm. Interestingly, word of mouth itself was not found to drive behavioral based loyalty (β = 0.15, p>0.05). That is, whether a customer is willing to recommend the firm or not has no effect on their spending behavior

Table 4.2 Model comparison

Fit/path	Model 1	Model 2	Model 3	Model 4	Model 5
AIC	628.084	778.185	560.777	1029.422	610.762
BIC	829.647	966.604	762.341	1204.694	807.944
χ^2(df)	536.08 (107)	692.185 (110)	468.777 (107)	949.422 (113)	520.762 (108)
χ^2/df	5.01	6.293	4.381	8.402	4.822
NFI	.952	.937	.958	.914	.953
TLI	.950	.934	.958	.908	.952
CFI	.961	.947	.967	.923	.962
RMSEA	.082	.095	.076	.112	.080
Trust→Attitudinal loyal	–.01	0.04ns	.017ns		–.007ns
Trust→Behavioral loyalty	–.06ns				
Trust→WOM	0.14ns		.156***		.139ns
Trust→Commitment				.727***	.302***
Commitment→Attitudinal loyal	.30***	.30***	.305***	.688***	.300***
Commitment→Behavioral loyalty	0.10ns				
Commitment→WOM	0.12***		.034ns	.690***	.124***

Table 4.2 (continued)

Fit/path	Model 1	Model 2	Model 3	Model 4	Model 5
Satatisfaction→Commitment					.418***
Satatisfaction →Trust				.859***	.853***
Satatisfaction→Attitudinal loyal	0.52***	.50***	.479***		.513***
Satatisfaction→Behavioral loyalty	0.41***				
Satatisfaction→WOM	0.62***		.453***		.614***
Attitudinal Loyal→Behavioral loyalty		0.38***	.336***	.335***	.337***
Attitudinal Loyal→WOM		0.76***	.287***		
WOM→Behavioral loyalty		0.10ns	.148ns	.157***	.153***
R^2Attitudinal loyal	.55				
R^2Behavioral loyal	.18	.21	.21	.19	.20
R^2WOM	.68				

Notes:
ns = not significant.
*** $p < 0.001$.

as captured through share of wallet and share of purchase (behavioral loyalty).

LIMITATIONS AND FUTURE RESEARCH

As relationships are dynamic, future research could consider how these models compare across time. Our models use cross-sectional data as this was appropriate for the comparisons we undertook and for our research question. Although our study was undertaken across nine service industries, we only considered the consumer service context. The relationship models we examine are equally relevant to business-to-business contexts and thus an extension of the present study would be to examine such a setting. An obvious avenue for future research is to examine service context as a moderator and study whether our models fit better in some contexts and not others. Despite these limitations and areas for extension, this study provides managers with a comparison of the most common relationship models proposed in the literature. A best-fitting model is identified and this provides managers with insights into the best ways to create strong customer relationships and enhance the likelihood of customers remaining with the firm, spreading positive word of mouth about the firm and its services, and ultimately spending more of their wallet with that firm.

REFERENCES

Ajzen, I. and M. Fishbein (1980), *Understanding Attitudes and Predicting Social Behaviour*, Englewood Cliffs, NJ: Prentice Hall.

Anderson, Eugene W. and Mary W. Sullivan (1993), "The antecedents and consequences of customer satisfaction for firms," *Marketing Science*, **12** (Spring), 125–43.

Anderson, Eugene W., Claes Fornell and Donald R. Lehmann (1994), "Customer satisfaction, market share, and profitability: findings from Sweden," *Journal of Marketing*, **58** (3), 53–66.

Anderson, James C. and David W. Gerbing (1988), "Structural equation modelling in practice: a review and recommended two-step approach," *Psychological Bulletin*, **103** (3), 411–23.

Arbuckle, J.L. (1997), *Amos Users' Guide Version 3.6*, Chicago, IL: Small Waters Corporation.

Aydin, S. and G. Ozer (2005), "The analysis of antecedents of customer loyalty in the Turkish mobile telecommunication market," *European Journal of Marketing*, **39** (7/8), 910–25.

Ball, Dwayne, Pedro S. Coelho and Alexandra Machas (2004), "The role of communication and trust in explaining customer loyalty," *European Journal of Marketing*, **38** (9/10), 1272–93.

Ben-Akiva, M.E. and J.D. Swait (1986), "The Akaike Likelihood Ratio Index," *Transportation Science*, **20**,133–6.

Bendapudi, N. and Berry, L. (1997), "Consumers motivations for maintaining relationships with service providers," *Journal of Retailing*, **73** (1), 15–38.

Bolton, Ruth N. (1998), "A dynamic model of the duration of the customer's relationship with a continuous service provider: the role of satisfaction," *Marketing Science*, **17** (1), 45–65.

Bowen, John (1990), "Development of a taxonomy of services to gain strategic marketing insights," *Journal of the Academy of Marketing Science*, **18** (1), 43–9.

Bozdogan, H. (1987), "Model selection and Akaike's Information Criterion (AIC): the general theory and its analytical extensions," *Psychometrika*, **52** (3), 345–70.

Brown, Tom J., Thomas E. Barry, Peter A. Dacin and Richard F. Gunst (2005), "Spreading the word: investigating antecedents of consumers' positive word-of-mouth intentions and behaviors in a retailing context," *Journal of the Academy of Marketing Science*, **33** (2), 123–38.

Browne, M.W. and R. Cudeck (1989), "Single sample cross-validation indices for covariance structures," *Multivariate Behavioral Research*, **24** (4), 445–55.

Caceres, Ruben Chumpitaz and Nicholas G. Paparoidamis (2007), "Service quality, relationship, satisfaction, trust, commitment and business-to-business loyalty," *European Journal of Marketing*, **41** (7/8), 836–67.

Chaudhuri, A. and M.B. Holbrook (2001), "The chain of effects from brand trust and brand affect to brand performance: the role of brand loyalty," *Journal of Marketing*, **65** (April), 81–93.

Chiou, Jyh-Shen and Cornelia Droge (2006), "Service quality, trust, specific asset investment, and expertise: direct and indirect effects in a satisfaction-loyalty framework," *Journal of the Academy of Marketing Science*, **34** (4), 613–27.

Cooil, Bruce, Timothy L. Keiningham, Larzan Aksoy and Michael Hsu (2007), "A longitudinal analysis of customer satisfaction and share of wallet: investigating the moderating effect of customer characteristics," *Journal of Marketing*, **71** (January), 67–83.

Cronin, J. Joseph., Michael K. Brady and G. Tomas Hult (2000), "Assessing the effects of quality, value and customer satisfaction on consumer behavioral intentions in service environments," *Journal of Retailing*, **76** (2), 193–218.

Crosby, Lawrence A., Kenneth R. Evans and Deborah Cowles (1990), "Relationship quality in services selling: an interpersonal influence perspective," *Journal of Marketing*, **54** (July), 68–81.

De Wulf, Kristof, Gaby Odekerken-Schröder and Dawn Iacobucci (2001), "Investments in consumer relationships: a cross-country and cross-industry exploration," *Journal of Marketing*, **65** (October), 33–50.

Dick, A. and Basu, K. (1994), "Customer loyalty: toward an integrated conceptual framework," *Journal of the Academy of Marketing Science*, **22** (2), 99–113.

Dillman, Donald A. (2007), *Mail and Internet Surveys: The Tailored Design Method*, 2nd edn, Hoboken, NJ: Wiley.

Dimitriades, Zoe S. (2006), "Customer satisfaction, loyalty and commitment in service organizations: some evidence from Greece," *Management Research News*, **29** (12), 782–800.

Doney, Patricia M. and Joseph P. Cannon (1997), "An examination of the nature of trust in buyer-seller relationships," *Journal of Marketing*, **61** (April), 35–51.

Doney, Patricia M., James M. Barry and Russell Abratt (2007), "Trust determinants and outcomes in global B2B services," *European Journal of Marketing*, **41** (9/10), 1096–116.

Evanschitzky, Heiner, Gopalkrishnan R. Iyer, Hilke Plassmann, Joerg Niessing and Heribert Meffert (2006), "The relative strength of affective commitment in securing loyalty in service relationships," *Journal of Business Research*, **59** (12), 1207–13.

Fornell, Claes and David F. Larcker (1981), "Evaluating structural equation models with unobserved variables and measurement error," *Journal of Marketing Research*, **28** (February), 39–50.

Garbarino, Ellen and Mark S. Johnson (1999), "The different roles of satisfaction, trust, and commitment in customer relationships," *Journal of Marketing*, **63** (April), 70–87.

Gounaris, Spiros P. (2005), "Trust and commitment influences on customer retention: insights from business-to-business services," *Journal of Business Research*, **58** (2), 126–40.

Gremler, Dwayne D., Kevin P. Gwinner and Stephen W. Brown (2001), "Generating positive

word-of-mouth communication through customer-employee relationships," *International Journal of Service Industry Management*, **12** (1), 44–59.
Gwinner, Kevin P., Dwayne D. Gremler and Mary J. Bitner (1998), "Relational benefits in services industries: the customer's perspective," *Journal of the Academy of Marketing Science*, **26** (2), 101–14.
Harris, Lloyd C. and Mark M.H. Goode (2004), "The four levels of loyalty and the pivotal role of trust: a study of online service dynamics," *Journal of Retailing*, **80** (2), 139–58.
Hennig-Thurau, Thorsten (2000), "Relationship quality and customer retention through strategic communication of customer skills," *Journal of Marketing Management*, **16** (1), 55–79.
Hennig-Thurau, Thorsten, Kevin P. Gwinner and Dwayne D. Gremler (2002), "Understanding relationship marketing outcomes: an integration of relationship benefits and relationship quality," *Journal of Service Research*, **4** (3), 230–47.
Hu, L. and P.M. Bentler (1999), "Cutoff criteria for fit indexes in covariance structure analysis: conventional criteria versus new alternatives," *Structural Equation Modeling*, **6** (1), 1–55.
Jap, Sandy D. and Shankar Ganesan (2000), "Control mechanisms and the relationship life cycle: implications for safeguarding specific investments and developing commitment," *Journal of Marketing Research*, **37** (May), 227–45.
Keiningham, Timothy L., Tiffany Perkins-Munn and Heather Evans (2003), "The impact of customer satisfaction on share-of-wallet in a business-to-business environment," *Journal of Service Research*, **6** (1), 37–50.
Kumar, Nirmalya, Lisa K. Scheer and Jan-Benedict E.M. Steenkamp (1995), "The effects of supplier fairness on vulnerable resellers," *Journal of Marketing Research*, **32** (February), 54–65.
Liang, Chiung-Ju and Wen-Hung Wang (2007), "Customer relationship management of information education services industry in Taiwan: attributes, benefits, and relationship," *The Service Industries Journal*, **27** (1), 29–46.
Mattila, A. (2006), "Affective commitment and its impact on guest loyalty and frequency reward programs," *Cornell Hotel & Restaurant Administration Quarterly*, **47** (2), 174–81.
Mazzarol, T.W., J.C. Sweeney, and G.N. Soutar (2007), "Conceptualizing word-of-mouth activity, triggers and conditions: an exploratory study," *European Journal of Marketing*, **41**, 11/12, 1475–94.
Morgan, Robert M. and Shelby D. Hunt (1994), "The commitment-trust theory of relationship marketing," *Journal of Marketing*, **58** (3), 20–38.
Oderkerken-Schröder, Gaby, Kristof De Wulf and Patrick Schumacher (2003), "Strengthening outcomes of retailer-consumer relationships: the dual impact of relationship marketing tactics and consumer personality," *Journal of Business Research*, **56** (3), 177–90.
Oliver, Richard L. (1997), *Satisfaction: A Behavioral Perspective on the Consumer*, New York: McGraw-Hill.
Palmatier, Robert W., Rajiv P. Dant, Dhruv Grewal and Kenneth R. Evans (2006), "Factors influencing the effectiveness of relationship marketing: a meta-analysis," *Journal of Marketing*, **70** (October), 136–53.
Plank, R.D. and S J. Newell (2007), "The effects of social conflict on relationship loyalty in business markets," *Industrial Marketing Management*, **36** (2), 59–67.
Rauyruen, P. and K.E. Miller (2007), "Relationship quality as a predictor of B2B customer loyalty," *Journal of Business Research*, **60** (1), 21–31.
Rosenbaum, Mark S., Carolyn Massiah and Donald W. Jackson Jr. (2006), "An investigation of trust, satisfaction, and commitment on repurchase intentions in professional services," *Services Marketing Quarterly*, **27** (3), 115–35.
Smith, J. Brock (1998), "Buyer-seller relationships: similarity, relationship management, and quality," *Psychology and Marketing*, **15** (1), 3–21.
Swait, J. and J.C. Sweeney (2000, "Perceived value and its impact on choice behavior in a retail setting," *Journal of Retailing and Consumer Services*, **7** (2), 77–88.
Ulaga, Wolfgang and Andreas Eggert (2006), "Relationship value and relationship quality:

broadening the nomological network of business-to-business relationships," *European Journal of Marketing*, **40** (3/4), 311–27.

Verhoef, Peter C., Philip H. Franses and Janny C. Hoekstra (2002), "The effect of relational constructs on customer referrals and number of services purchased from a multiservice provider: does age of relationship matter?" *Journal of the Academy of Marketing Science*, **30** (3), 202–16.

Wong, Amy and Amrik Sohal (2002), "An Examination of the relationship between trust, commitment and relationship quality," *International Journal of Retail and Distribution Management*, **30** (1), 34–50.

Zeithaml, V.A., L.L. Berry and A. Parasuraman (1996), "The behavioral consequences of service quality," *Journal of Marketing*, **60** (April), 31–46.

APPENDIX

Table 4A.1 Item measures

Construct*	Items
Commitment	My relationship with the service provider is very important to me
	My relationship with the service provider is something I really care about
	My relationship with the service provider deserves my maximum effort to maintain
Trust	This service provider can be trusted
	This service provider can be counted on to do what is right
	This service provider has high integrity
	This service provider is trustworthy
Satisfaction	I am always delighted with this service provider's service
	Overall I am satisfied with this service provider
	I feel good about using this service provider
Word of mouth	I say positive things about the service provider to other people
	I recommend the service provider to someone who seeks my advice
	I encourage friends and relatives to do business with the service provider
Attitudinal loyalty	I will continue to do business with the service provider for the next few years
	I am willing to maintain my relationship with the service provider
	I am loyal to the service provider
Behavioral loyalty	Of the 10 times you purchase from this type of service, how many times do you select the specific service provider you are thinking about?
	Think about the total amount of money you spend on this type of service. Now estimate what percent of this amount you would spend with the specific service provider you are thing about.

Note: *Scales for commitment, trust, satisfaction, word-of-mouth and attitudinal loyalty: 1 = strongly disagree, 7 = strongly agree.

5 Loyalty: its biogenic, psychological, and social origins – answering the question of "Why Y?"

Richard L. Oliver

At a recent conference, the author "speculated" that loyalty existed as a region located in an unidentified brain structure. Perhaps so; however, further reflection suggests that greater advances in functional magnetic resonance imaging (fMRI) will be required to identify where such structure may reside if it does at all. Scholars have addressed this issue previously but have not come to conclusion. For example, recent writings remain ambivalent as to the central domain of the basic emotion of pleasure (for example, Berridge and Kringelbach 2008). For instance, the authors note that electrical stimulation of hedonic "hotspots" does not discriminate between wanting and liking responses.

It is not my intention to de-emphasize the great strides being made and to be made in the field of consumer decision-making based brain region mapping. Indeed, a 2012 issue of the *Journal of Consumer Psychology* was devoted specifically to this purpose. A number of gratifying discoveries were made including some addressing loyalty (Esch et al. 2012; Plassman et al. 2012). Indeed, Plassman et al. (2007) find neural reward differences between the monetary spending frequency of high versus low groups. Similar findings are observed when familiarity is the criterion of interest (Ambler et al. 2004; Deppe et al. 2005; McClure et al. 2004; Schaefer et al. 2006).

Unfortunately, for the purposes here, Yoon et al. (2006) found that differing prefrontal brain regions were activated for judgments of person processing versus that of object (for example, brand) processing. The dilemma for students of the loyalty phenomenon is that this finding casts doubt on the intra-cranial location of a loyalty (or, for that matter, satisfaction) region. If, as Oliver (2010) suggests, satisfaction is both a cognitive and an affective construal and if loyalty is both a personal and socially mandated deeply held commitment to a cause (Oliver 1999), then satisfaction and, in a derivative sense, loyalty cannot be expected to inhabit distinct brain partitions. Rather, it appears that loyalty is learned and then "deposited" in related, but mutually accessible, neural pathways.

This problem is further exacerbated by the continuing ambivalence in the loyalty literature that exists even when "inherent" brand loyalty appears to be researched (for example, Huang and Yu 1999). These writings persist in describing the concept as conscious loyalty behavior (that is, repeat buying) and not the Holy Grail of loyalty which will be referred to as ultimate loyalty, as discussed in Oliver (1999) and referenced again in the culmination of this chapter. As presented here, it is proposed that the documented neural responses to commercial stimuli are manifestations of, and not causes or even sources of, loyalty-related expressions. The brain is merely reacting to or processing stimuli that have emotive and behavioral potential. Hopefully, the reasoning presented in this chapter will clarify the author's perspective.

Note that, unlike satisfaction/dissatisfaction, loyalty has a nebulous valence. Disloyalty can be simply the breakdown of loyalty or it can be posed in a negative frame, although this negative state appears to elude clear definition. For example, Oliver (1999, 2010) gives an example of loyalty bonding as a simple following of the crowd—the example given is one of belonging to a "village" with no more support than that. This, of course, brings up the question of "neutral," perhaps mindless, loyalty—apparent loyalty having no motivational valence. In contrast, loyalty can have what society would refer to as having negative connotations. This can manifest as disloyalty (that is, opposition) to the social norm or to authority in general. Gangs are typical examples here, although loyalty may exist within these consorts causing the social glue to operate nonetheless. Prisons are nests of such influences.

Disloyalty may have yet another and more complicating mediator. When disloyalty is imminent due to affective separation whereby one focal party can exit the relationship, the term "breakup" is frequently used and the parties are referred to as alienated or estranged. However, when exit is barred and the estranged party seeks an "out," the phrase "betrayal" is used in its stead. In the present context switching and multi-loyalty are more apt. These examples do, however, illustrate the complexity of discussing loyalty and its negative opposing pole.

As a continuation of the preceding stream, two seemingly counterintuitive topics are introduced, only to the extent that they enrich the present discussion. To this author's knowledge the first has not prominently appeared in the (consumer) literature previously, namely, loyalty to the concept of disloyalty. While one may think of this as somewhat psychopathic (and it very well may be), there are many instances of loyalty to disloyalty. Without being overly dramatic, cheating spouses come to mind, as do sports players who bet against their own team and have some influence or, at the least, inside influence over the outcome. And we should not forget that double (spy) agents have existed since medieval times (and perhaps before) as readers of espionage classics can attest. Again, returning to marketplace examples, variety seeking is one exemplar of apparent disloyalty but, as will be argued, is simply a developmental phase of learning the act of consumption in today's environment.

The second issue of note is one of self-loyalty. Here, individuals are loyal to their own self. As alluded to in more detail in the section on sociologic origins of loyalty, this is a special case of loyalty to oneself as opposed to loyalty to one "master," or loyalty to one other (spouse, "best friend forever"—BFF), or to multiple others. This and the previous discussion are mentioned simply to emphasize that loyalty may exist beyond the boundaries of present usage. This does not mean that they cannot be unraveled, just that this will require more understanding than that which is currently brought to bear. As a prelude to explanation of the subtitle of this chapter, one might ask "Why Y?" where the Y is loyalty of all persuasions.

PURPOSE

The goals of this chapter are to explore the many facets of loyalty, when they can be expected to appear and, almost parenthetically, when well-established appearances of loyalty are vulnerable to switching. This differs from previous attempts (Oliver 1999, 2010; Keiningham and Aksoy 2009) in that none discuss forms nor variations of loyalty over the life cycle, specifically as pursued in a temporal manner. Rather, loyalty will be approached here in loose chronological order from the earliest parental bonding to manifestations in later life. Along the way, the most fundamental exemplars of loyalty will be entertained including such topics as conditioned "loyalty," which most refer to under the rubric of learning.

At this point, it would be helpful for the reader *not* to anticipate "standard" traditional views. Based on a large cross-section of literature in addition to that using fMRI technology (noted previously), the substance of what is to follow is based more on evolutionary genetics and the social forces that have become encoded in the anthropologic and phylogenetic continua. In short, human individuals have been genetically programmed to embrace loyalty in its many forms, partly because of biological imperatives and partly for "survival of the species." I have put this latter phrase in quotation because the scientific literature is biased in favor of a distorted cognitive perspective to individuals' procreation activities. People (loosely consumers) do not really do anything to ensure that our species survive. Rather, *if* they do anything at all, it is for a much more shortsighted hope that their progeny inherit an advantageous profile in the next and, perhaps, future generations.

This latter argument is displayed in a number of forms. It is evident most notably in wills, artificial insemination practices (for example, fertility banks' donor criteria), "red shirting" in education (postponing the date of first schooling to allow for an extra year of intellectual/socio-emotional development), acquisition of collections or businesses to be passed on to heirs, and, at the limiting extreme, National Aeronautics and Space Administration (NASA) space explorations to find inhabitable environments for human migration when our current life sustainability is in jeopardy.

ORIGINS OF "LOYALTY"

When can loyalty be expected to first appear? It has already been alluded to that parental bonding may be considered the earliest form of "loyalty." This developmental aspect of mammalian nurturing is natural to the species and well beyond what is intended here. Interestingly, this aspect of moral sentience does present in parental infant wellbeing behaviors in the form of care, including food, clothing, and safety. And, herein lies the first of what will be referred to as misconceptions of loyal tendencies. Infants are not "loyal" to parents or caregivers; they are simply mimicking biological imperatives for survival—which cannot be a cognitive activity at this phase. Bowlby (1982), however, acknowledges that humans are equipped via evolution with a "behavioral attachment system," driving mother–infant nurturing. Later, after weaning perhaps, children "bond" to their parental objects (witness imprinting in ducklings) for security, which to the outside observer is described as protection. Such ambulatory young may not even be aware of what they should fear. This sense of derived security *is* most probably genetic and does serve to assist in survival of the species.

For an understanding of the next phase, fast-forward to the stage at which toddlers develop preferences, which at this point do not yet exhibit attitudes as we know them for there is no "good/bad for me" cognition—just pleasure. For ease of discussion, let us assume that, when children begin to respond to innate desires for consumables, even caregiver affection, they have developed preferences. Within this period, wants and needs may be indistinguishable. Like the teenager who proclaims that he or she "must have" a brand of sneaker, video game, and so on "or I will die," the want is a need (see Oliver 2010, pp. 138–40). Although this example takes us into a later developmental phase, the example makes the point. Is this loyalty? No. These preferences are merely neuronal impulses that exist at the interplay of need for the familiarly comfortable and the emergence of curiosity of the unknown (for example, Litman and Spielberger 2003).

Curiosity, then, is simply "testing the waters" for pleasurable sensations, frequently leading to avoidance cues (for example, tasting strange objects).

In the next developmental stage infants are able to express preferences and can be prompted to choose one object (most likely a toy) over another, as evidenced by simple observation. This exploratory behavior is also ingrained and cannot be explained beyond ordinary maturation phases. However, this is the beginning of the dynamic curiosity response (for example, Berlyne 1960) which grows and then retreats over the lifespan. Indeed, curiosity is one of the markers used to identify a healthy prognosis for infants and is the underlying motivation for the ubiquitous "Why?" or "But why?" or "How come?"question uttered in response to explanations given to 3- and 4-year-olds. This innate curiosity drive has been shown to permeate all phases of human development and will be posited to frustrate loyalty in early adult years and, paradoxically, sustain the semblance of loyalty in later years when this drive wanes (for example, Mikulincer 1997). One would expect to find only vestiges of loyalty at this phase, such as with the proverbial teddy bear or blanket that is held dear for security reasons. This security behavior, however, is not loyalty but is akin to the attachment styles common to all maturing young.

In later years, toddlers develop preferences for broader sets of items, particularly playthings, and friendships or mutual likings. In this sense, loyalty differs from satisfaction, particularly at this stage, because satisfaction requires expectations of a specific nature (Oliver 2010). Expectations are a necessary component of the satisfaction or fulfillment process, without which the concept degrades into mere pleasure absent intent. Once consumers are able to consciously express expectations of pleasure, then satisfaction emerges as a fulfillment response to the degree of attainment or frustration of this goal. Unfortunately, no data exists as to the developmental emergence of expectation formation (net of conditioning) and, thus, of satisfaction expression. Needs (particularly those of survival), or wants, are frequently used as expectation proxies but this does not adequately address the semantic distinctions between needs, wants, desires, and other variants or metrics against which outcomes can be judged (see Oliver 2010, ch. 3).

Whereas developmental psychology no doubt plays a role in later attachments to consumables, both innately and as a response to external stimuli, so too does sociology. As distinct from parental bonding, early maturation brings the opportunity to form bonds with others. Siblings (if present) would be naturally prepotent, followed by friends of siblings and then by less formal acquaintances (Koski and Shaver 1997). Friendship bonds are less specific than those of kinship in that they may not be inbred but likely arise from interest and physical similarities (Keiningham and Aksoy 2009;

Keller 2007). Bonding will, at first, extend to identification with other persona including those of imaginary beings (that is, heroes and heroines from children's literature such as Cinderella and Superman) and later to actual human idols including role models such as the Mouseketeers (1960s Disney performers) and the current "teen idol" craze of both genders. Is this loyalty? No, but an extension of it is as follows.

There is no doubt that familial loyalty is loyalty and dates back to the earliest of human social identification. The family ties of tribes and cave dwellers are well documented and gave rise to clans now found in the U.S. lexicon as displayed in rivalries such as that of the Hatfields and McCoys. "Brotherhood" (or sisterhood), consisting of nonfamilial bonding, goes back to the earliest accounts of human interaction when the necessity of banding together was required to present a unified force against opposition. All should be familiar with the meanings of "blood brothers," "band of brothers," and gang initiation rites signifying the trials of proving worthiness. More of this will be pursued later.

At this point the role of parenting may (can) be a powerful motivator of loyalty in three important and more than frequently noted areas specifically related to cause marketing. The first and most obvious is religion (the other two are politics and occupation) where individuals are prone to adhere to that of their parents for lifetimes. This is a complicated issue only because of the myriad of external influences on children's beliefs. Parenting is one of these influences explaining some 27 percent ($r \approx 0.5$) of the child's religious leanings (for example, Dudley and Dudley 1986; Scott 1988) and, of course, depends on the orthodoxy of the religion studied.

It is at this point that a central tenet of the present chapter is instructive. Even assuming that 27 percent or so of religion—one of the most prevalent manifestations of loyalty known—is parentally ascribed, there remains another 73 percent to be accounted for. It is argued here that some (or much) of this fraction is genetic, inherited from our ancestors. We are imbibed with an inherent "why" gene, as introduced earlier, in the form of children grasping for understanding. What follows uses the reasoning of adaptive intentional discovery (see, for example, Kelemen and DiYanni 2005; Pyysiäinen and Hauser 2010).

When we perceive a "y," we are literally obsessed with a quest for its cause—an "x" or explanation. This pun is intended, as in the ubiquitous ($x \rightarrow y$) equation found throughout science. Lower animal forms can perceive the xs and ys in their material field. Only humans have evolved to desire an understanding of the mechanism connecting the two or the arrow (the $\rightarrow$). Simple reward structures are inbred to allow conditioning to "explain" the relation between the rat's pressing of a button (the x) and receiving a food pellet (the *y*), but this is not a cognitive arrow; it is more or less a reflexive movement essential to survival instincts.

Now, what happens when *x* is not available—that is, the causal mechanism is not known? Humankind has had to grapple with this mystery from the beginnings of recorded history. What, for example, causes sunlight, fire, wind, lightning, and natural disasters? In the absence of a scientific explanation, the cause must be ascribed to an unknown entity that must exist. That entity has been, and still is, a supernatural or paranormal force. This author will not belabor discussion with the early explanations of fire (phlogiston), lightning (raining fire), or even the perception of the earth's flatness or stars in the night sky. The analogy to belief in the supernatural is direct. See the works of Bloom (2005, 2007) for greater expansion explaining this example of causality.

The second case of ascribed loyalty is politics, which is only slightly more volatile. Political preferences can change depending on numerous factors, including candidates holding office, those running for office, and a host of serendipitous events at any one time. In the main, however, the correlation between the political views of parents and that of children is also in the 0.5 range, but declines over time into their mid-twenties (Jennings et al. 2009).

Such parental preferences observed by children, much like religion, are also instilled; children are willing participants in this inculcation due to the well-known aspirational mimicry displayed when parents are viewed as emulation prototypes. This phenomenon results in two outcomes. First, it surrounds the child in a social envelope as the natural exposure of home and school is likely to conform to the parental belief system. For example, the schools the child attends are typically selected by either a public mandate or, in the case of private schooling, the parents. In the former case, urban geography assures that the child is exposed to like-minded peers (socioeconomic status, lifestyle, age and race cohorts). The second outcome is that early educational environments act, to whatever extent possible, as a reinforcement of parental leanings. Thus, it is reasonable to conclude that early loyalties are a function of more explicit social bonding whether parental or peer (although often in opposing directions, noted as rebellion). It appears, then, that loyalty as observed at this phase is a bonding and social reinforcement process more so than anything innate to the young "consumer's" biogenetics.

This desire to emulate is not isolated to interests stemming from early educational experiences and activities. It is also known that occupations follow the same pattern found in religion and political views. This phenomenon is one of the oldest findings in sociology and has many explanations, including genetics and inherited intellectual patterns, aspirational and objective education, education-dependent job opportunities, income, and income-dependent occupational portals (for example, Blau and Duncan 1967; Durkheim 1933; Treiman 1977; Veblen 1919). For example, Beller and Hout (2006) and Laband and Lentz (1983) report intergenerational (fathers and sons) correlations of 0.30 to 0.40.

These data, however, do not fully address the central tenet proposed here, namely, that part of this high relationship is due to simple familial emulation in the same way and mechanism operating for religion and politics. The social canvas is rife with examples of families of military, law enforcement, medical, legal, artistic (especially in the acting profession), and countless other occupational threads. To cite a hackneyed phrase: "My daddy was a . . . ; his daddy was a . . . " and so on. The point relevant to this discussion is that this is not loyalty—it is an outgrowth of the early integration of a value set in a child at the critical stage of development where the social support mechanism ingrains a value system without the need for challenge. In fact, it goes beyond that—it provides a protective and combative environment that defends this value system. It is just too easy to refer to this phenomenon as loyalty. In fact, there is really no need to even ask the question: Why Y?

THE PREFRONTAL CORTEX

This section expands and proceeds to later developmental stages where adolescents develop cognitive preferences that they can explain (regardless of whether the explanations are accurate or whether others can relate to the explanation). This is the most intricate of all phases because it results from a confluence of biogenetic, psychological, and social forces (see Calvó-Armengol and Jackson 2009). It is this triangulation of sources that has the greatest and perhaps longest-lasting effect on what this author is now comfortable with entertaining as "true" loyalty. A foreboding is in order—lest the reader believe that a perpetual manifestation of loyalty emerges at this phase of life; this "true loyalty" conclusion will prove to be premature. Later, a stronger and less enduring environmental (physical, sociological, and so on) override may emerge, and is to be discussed.

Part of the reasoning informing this section derives from the now generally accepted sequence of cortical brain development. The fMRI field has largely determined where the lobe locations of the senses are processed (occipital, lateral, medial, frontal, and so on) and even where motor movement is contained (cerebellum, motor cortex). The last brain area to develop in humans is the prefrontal cortex (Stuss and Knight 2002), known not to mature until the early to mid twenties. This location controls reason and, more importantly, the opponent processes necessary to contain the harmful extremes of overstimulation. It is beyond the present scope to expand on this except to say that the age of "reason," maturation, and so on is now legally recognized to be 21 (although 18 is still operable in many locales and for many activities, such as driving, marriage, and legal responsibility).

The preceding is necessary to emphasize the point that much of "loyalty" displayed at this age range (that is, teens and early adulthood) will prove to be transient although, admittedly, many of these brain traces will endure or metamorphose as later maturity evolves (or is overlaid). Three consumption exemplars will be used to illustrate this phase; the first two will be seen to be more enduring than the third. Another way of saying this is that they will be less mutable because they are more rooted genetically and psychologically. The third is more socially oriented and, as one would expect, may be molded as the environment changes or is displaced, either through familial responsibilities or through ongoing maturation. Here, but to be discussed later, higher order values or goals will become prepotent and more causal $x \rightarrow y$ explanations will emerge. In order, these three topics are musical preferences, recreational and participative activity (primarily sports), and social memberships in the form of clubs and their related identity markers. Because of the enduring effects noted above, these interests will transition into discussion of more cognitive forms of loyalty as the age cohort progresses.

Music

It has long been known that music is partly inbred—genetic, if you will (Trehub 2003; see Levitin 2006 for overview). Normally it is thought to be contained and/or regulated in the right hemisphere of the brain (Bever and Chiarello 1974; Ivry and Robertson 1997; Zatorre 1998). For the present purpose, the nature of humankind to be "loyal" to musical preference is explored. I am not qualified to speak to the "natural instincts" that are thought to be inherent in vast numbers of individuals; the concern here is with loyalties to musical venues, variations, performers, and compositions.

Barring the debatable cultural preferences for harmony, loudness, tempo, and so on, music appears to be equally transliterate whether conveying semantic meaning or emotion (Balkwill and Thompson 1999; Juslin and Laukka 2003; Koelsch 2010). It appears that music is developmentally programmed in humans from age 2 and largely cortically myelinated in the late teens (for example, Holbrook and Schindler 1989; Levitin 2006, p. 232). Since it appears that musical tastes (that is, their nature such as classical, pop, gospel, rap, and so on) are more or less developmental, one is left to explain the preferences for performances and performers (musicians) net of the nature of their music and after the developmental influences have had their effect. As such, this same logic would appear to also explain preferences for other persona in the arts including drama, literature, architecture, and performing arts generally (dance, theater, other). It is at this point that "true" or "real" loyalty begins to emerge, either as a deeply held hybrid cognitive/affective preference or as a socially bonded activity. One can now see the meaning of the title to this chapter, that of a blending of genetic, psychological, and sociological forces.

The next section on sports activities will elaborate this triangulation more fully, but for now it is apparent that loyalty to all the manifestations of music begins with a need to express oneself harmonically, and to identify with persona that embed these rhythms within multisensory performances, usually with a compatible identity (performer or band), and within a social context that supports this preference. This social support does not have to be present; it can be imaginary or artificial, such as watching a digitized presentation. Because our social environment is, by definition, shared, one may question how some can find pleasure in listening alone, a very common experience. The answer is that individuals possess auditory imagery that invokes pleasure in its various manifestations (for example, Levitin 1994). Thus, loyalty exists nonetheless and is transferrable to other or subsequent purveyors of the same musical genre.

Activities (Sport)

This subtopic was chosen, not only because of its universal nature, but because it accesses most succinctly and distinctively the tripartite nature of loyalty. Physical activity is essential to human survival; some of which is obvious, from the need for an infant to feed via succulence to the need to ambulate for access to food, shelter, and sex, to the need to coordinate physical senses with other sensory cues in purposive fashion. Sport can be a singular activity (running), a multiparty activity (team sports generally), or a spectator activity in either a singular or group environment. The supposedly inactive nature of observing activity "from a distance" is assuredly lacking in exertion, but in fact involves mental, sensory, and minute mirroring of the activity even if it involves the physical accompaniments of emotion-responding (cheering, expressive anger).

It has other elements as well and here I reintroduce the $x \rightarrow y$ analogy. Sport presents the opportunity to engage one's goals in life. It answers the y question, if only momentarily. At the same time, it offers a solution to the craving for identity. Who am I? Why do I exist? What is my purpose? What should I do to fulfill this purpose? Sport is not the only answer to these questions—but it is an easy and easily obtainable or accessed answer.

It fulfills many current psychological needs, especially belongingness and/or affiliation.

Regardless of the higher-order needs sport provides, there are more immediate affective (that is, emotional) ties to games that add to its enduring nature. Sport is naturally emotive. It provides a required level of arousal to avoid languishing monotony. Initially, it may act as a target of curiosity either in terms of one's participation or as a spectator watching the Olympics (for example, Park et al. 2008, 2011). Later, sport provides a continual source of amusement. As no sporting outcome is "guaranteed," whether in terms of wins/losses, placing, beating the spread, or any other metric, sports have the inherent ability to excite, please, frustrate, or defeat one's emotional anticipations (Knobloch-Westerwick et al. 2009; Madrigal and Dalakas 2008). In short, intra-game or inter-game sport "jerks one's psychology around." Basketball, for example, has high intra-game jockeying of team position; hockey, in contrast, is a low-scoring game where final outcomes provide the "back and forth." Each has a different pulsing.

The developmental process of sport identification is well-researched among children (see James 2001); the biogenetic foundations have been discussed in the preceding. Not discussed are the apparent natural competitive genes possessed by humans. Excepting dominant displays, including combat, among animals for mating purposes, the origins of true competition beyond the attraction of the preferred mate is unclear. What is not unclear is the desire to be at the "top of one's game" in its many nuances, whether this is a personal best or Olympic medal or "Guinness records" best.

Goals are once again preeminent in humankind's quest. So we are back to the essential question of Why Y? One answer is provided by loyalty. The X in the equation is the explanation—understanding the goal; loyalty is one of the possible arrows, as in "I pursue an understanding of X by being loyal to Y." In the present context, "I am loyal to 'participating/spectating' in sport (team) Y because it yields physical benefits, psychological fulfillment, and social affiliation—each of which has ancillary benefits (health, serenity, social interdependencies)."

The development phases of sport loosely follow those of Piaget (1950), while the social influences are as described by Bandura (1969). Generally, children begin to identify with sports and teams in the "preoperational" era (age 2–7) and become more cognizant of their preferences in the preteen years (7–12). Parents', siblings', peers', and media influences are sequentially influential. Later, affiliation patterns are evident as educational and geographical involvement increases. Each of these "bondings" is related to a specific type of reward. Relating to parents' preference via conditioning yields nurturance, sibling-based attachments add to familial coherence and support, peer support provides the social envelope which will then be reinforced, augmented, or mutated throughout one's life experience. Even if one has no vested interest in "their" team, simple associations such as celebrating victory, wearing team apparel, being from (but not residing in) the same city as a winning team allow one to "bask in reflected glory," thereby providing both (false) pride and social acceptance by strangers (Cialdini et al. 1976).

The degree of fan identification appears to be a precursor to loyalty and at its extreme may approach unusually high loyalty displays. Sutton et al. (1997) have proposed three hierarchical attachment levels which may generalize to other "sport-like" activities such as gambling. Their levels of low (social), medium (focused), and high (vested) attachment correspond to the qualities of entertainment, performance, and emotional devotion respectively. Low-category fans find the focal sport entertaining to view whether either team wins/loses; medium-level fans are involved in the outcome as "fair weather friends," that is they are fans until the team is no longer a winner or, at least, a contender; while high-level fans are "do or die" supporters. The analogy to gambling is most apt. Some wagemakers just participate for the fun and excitement involved, regardless of the amount they lose; others participate if they wish to compete against others or the casino and hate to lose; while the third group is essentially addicted, which actually is a different state of mind (but, curiously, may still be a form of loyalty—to be discussed later).

Generally, these preferences will be sustained unless the pattern and/or intensity of reinforcement no longer becomes fulfilling. The staging of such "loyalty" follows the attitudinal-like framework suggested by Oliver (2010, ch. 15). Others (for example, Funk and James 2001; Iwasaki and Havitz 2004) follow different paths using attraction, involvement, commitment, and allegiance to achieve the same loyalty outcome. Unique to all "true" frameworks is that this loyalty must endure anti-loyalty resistance to a diminishing or changing of preference.

Is "sports loyalty" a true loyalty approaching an ultimate level? In some cases yes—although most are of a transitory nature—and in many, no. If one's support endures negative reinforcement (declining pleasure) or punishment (increasing displeasure), higher and higher levels of resolve must be present. The phrase "through thick and thin" sums this up (see Bristow and Sebastian 2001). The most loyal are those individuals that can resist continual disappointment (losses), teams moving to other locales, and forms of betrayal such as revelations of illegal activity (throwing games, as with the Chicago "Black"—actually White—Sox in the 1919 World Series).

Why then is sports loyalty so universal? It provides fulfillment of a goal—something to live for. And, as noted, it is easy and easily defended.

Personal sports, whether physically exerting or not (cards, fishing) are personally and socially involving; they give notice to others that one has consuming interests and therefore makes them interesting. (The social side of these activities is elaborated in the next section.) In fact, any consuming interest fulfills the goal of Why Y? The higher order of X—the because—does not have to be answered. How many parents have said that "it is good that (my child) has thus and so interest." No answer (to why it is good) is required. Everyone knows (or thinks they know) the answer. Of course sport is just one of many activities (hobbies are another) that fulfill the goal of being. It is as if to say that "I am here to (because I have been selected to) support Y. The X is answered.

CLUBS

This section is largely devoted to the sociological origins of loyalty. Having previously discussed genetic and psychological influences, it would seem that sociological factors may, in their own way, act in an overriding fashion as put forward previously. Indeed, many would argue that extreme cults do exactly that—they ask followers to give up all worldly possessions, their familial ties, and even their personal identity to become devotees. This author (Oliver 2010, pp. 448–9) has taken a variant of this position to make the point that social "contagion" can reach extremes whereby all other higher pursuits become subservient. Although I allude to more "normal" settings, such as hospices, one can easily recall historical precedents when even morality, as we know it, can be subjugated if not eliminated.

It has been widely noted that humans evolved as social creatures (for example, Christakis and Fowler 2009). While many examples in nature exist of species that are solitary (large cats—except in mating), others are notorious for their pack instincts (canines). Humans are on the "pack" side of the continuum. Whether for protection, mutual caregiving, or integration of separate but complementary skills, such as trade, solitary individuals have been found to have lesser survivability rates than dyads or groups.

This is not to say that the group preferences of individuals are purely a sociological phenomenon. Genetics play a role in a number of ways including the human mother–infant attachment required before weaning, the extended family heritage, and the debated necessity of human-to-human interaction such as play in normal development. This interacts, of course, with the psychological changes which also track development as observed in studies of individuals (and subspecies) raised in solitary versus group environments (Baumeister and Leary 1995). It is also the case that the brain requires observation of others for mimicry during maturation. More importantly, humans have a need for being part of "we" or "us" so that they can be unique from "them." This particular Y has always required an X.

This X is both a reason and an explanation for loyalty. In fact, social groups voicing their loyalties always have an X. We are loyal (Y) because we are of the same past (or background, such as ethnicity), present (residential communities), and future (professionals in training). Interestingly, age demographics share all of these similarities. Age cohorts were born together, exist in the present together, and will experience the future together with the same background as an anchor point. This, in part, explains the cultural specificity of some sports and why they never seem to successfully migrate across cultures (at least in the long run). Witness the resistance in the U.S. to cricket, lacrosse, rugby, jai-alai, pachinko, and despite its current popularity—soccer. And, to turn the tables, NFL football, NASCAR, and monster truck competitions are not popular outside the U.S.

And what of social isolates? Isolated individuals are frequently noted to search for others such as themselves so they can discover their roots, as either an intermediary X or as a final X. These may be persons with secular religious or interest views, those who collect unusual oddities, and those who feel there are others like themselves but who are widely dispersed (diasporadic) for political and other reasons. And what of those who think that "there must be others like me?" Fortunately, modern search engines allow for these persons to unite. Here, the Y is isolation—an inversion or limited case of loyalty (to oneself). It is this self-loyalty that results in a quest for the X, the explanation of Why am I? or Why is Y (singular loyalty)?

GENETIC, INDIVIDUAL, AND SOCIAL INTEGRATION: FULLY BONDED LOYALTY AND SOURCES OF ITS MUTATIONS

The components of loyalty have now been elaborated. It is clear that the strongest manifestation of loyalty is an amalgam of these three forces acting in concert. All human developmental phases beyond the formative years, the last being when the prefrontal cortex matures, are now subject to the ebb and flow of each of these components shifting positions of influence. Those subject to the greatest changes (that is, most malleable) are those having the greatest external influences, which is most probably the external social environment including those of a commercial or otherwise persuasive nature. Changes in loyalty preferences must come from "somewhere." Because the essential question of Why Y? never ceases including its extension (and existential meaning) and, therefore, begs an answer, individuals become search agents for the resolution to the apparent enigma: Why am I here? Not finding a ready answer, the easiest way to end the search is to explain it away via resignation to the "unknown made known" or to find "one's calling." The world provides numerous venues for both paths. These venues all fall within the rubric of loyalty.

The first section of this chapter began with an acknowledgment that the author's suspicion that the brain harbored a "loyalty structure" was incorrect. The brain only contains the basics of sensation processing and coordination. The limbic system is the source of our innermost feelings of pleasure or, to put it somewhat differently, feelings of the most pleasure one can achieve given life's circumstances. Loyalty is the modern-day outcome of this sense of seeking. At the same time that it gives answers, requiring little explanation beyond that of "just because," it also gives a motivation to pursue greater loyalty elsewhere, to shift loyalty in either degree or direction, or to shut it down completely and reset the search mode.

Individuals become loyal (or say they are) because of its temporary finality. This is me (with an unspoken "now"). The more ingrained the loyalty goal, the less thought given to the question of Why Y? For example, why does one eat and why does one prefer certain foods? Numerous answers are available because eating itself is necessary for survival. The body cares little where it gets nutrients as long as they are available. The consequences of nutrient deficiency have long been known; those of nutrient oversatiation are still being researched. Loyalty to food (generically) needs no explanation—it is biogenetic. Loyalty to foods—their specific nature—is both psychological and, to a greater extent, sociological. Loyalty to purveyors of food is a natural consequence of happenstance and availability, and is not of great consequence to the arguments here; in fact this loyalty is largely derivative.

In Oliver (2010, pp. 449–50), an attempt was made to account for a blend of personal identity with the cultural milieu surrounding the consumable. If one insists on an explanation of why loyalty to normal consumption activities is, in an extreme sense, more or less behaviorally trivial, one only need examine the current milieu of commerce which is rife with influences of the cultural and social environment, whether active, passive, or stationary, but enticing nonetheless. In the present, consumers are drawn to the consumable environment as opposed to the situation where the environment defines consumption for the consumers, although this obviously still does occur (as in captive environments such as cults). Consumers find greatest pleasure when discovering a natural match with both the consumable and its environment. Finding this combination is a temporary "fix," easily explained and defined as loyalty.

This is a particularly healthy situation for firms as their product or service is now inextricably embedded within the consumer psyche and lifestyle, and as part of consumers' self-identity and social identity. That is, consumers cannot conceive of themselves as being whole (fulfilled) without this integrated sense of loyalty. At the extreme, the subject of their loyalty is present intentionally and extensionally. Here, the consumer would say that this subject is "part of me" or an "extension of me" (Belk 1988). They live it.

Using fan clubs as an example, the personal identity of the fan advocate is typically not known to the team or artist. The allure of the larger consumption icon is sufficient to hold the consumer in the loyalty state. Many fans go to great lengths to support their icon: they travel extensively, wear special uniforms (for example, *Star Trek* devotees) and headgear (for example, sport caps with logos), and paint their bodies with team colors. Other forms of display insignia include badges, bumper stickers, affinity (credit) cards, and tattoos. One manifestation of this state is undying devotion, through good times and bad, such as existed when one example of the now famous prophecy "of the end of the world" failed to materialize (Festinger et al. 1956).

Clearly, individuals' willingness to remain faithful, renew, re-buy, or re-patronize cannot reach an ultimate extreme until they are willing to adore and commit unfailingly to (that is, to worship or love) an entity, institution, product, or service (Ahuvia 2005; Batra et al. 2012). Beyond this, the necessary additional adhesion stems from the social bonding of a "consumption" community and the synergy between community and consumers. In essence, consumers want to be loyal, the social organization or overseer wants them to be loyal, and, as a result, the two may become symbiotic. These are stringent criteria for the entity that wishes to have a loyal patronage base (Oliver 2010, p. 449).

What does it take to bring these requirements together? The answer is embedded in the central question: Why Y? If the search for this answer proves satisfactory, that is, the X makes "sense," one need look no further. Generally, apparently intuitive explanations are rarely questioned, as in the popular song "Born this way." Biogenetically, we are programmed with a brain structure that has evolved for eons; physiologically, we operate according to the numerous visceral and muscular-skeletal systems we inherit. Anthropological and medical science provides us with the Xs. These are the hard facts. The soft facts are provided by our psychological being. If we wish to answer the most obscure questions, as in the nature of our existence, there are philosophers, prophets, occultists, clairvoyants, mystics, and other purveyors of belief systems that will be acceptably satisfactory. Our minds have evolved to put the arrow between the X and the Y, however determined. This same evolution has enabled us to define not only the arrow's strength, but also its breadth.

The sociological system provides two mechanisms. First it attracts us to viable source structures. Curiosity and interest are two of many attractants. The explanations of the structure of the various systems are provided by writings (going back to cave drawings and scribes), verbal transfer—now known as word of mouth, and present-day media including the Web which encompass written, verbal, and electronic communicative forms. The second mechanism is that of support—expressed very loosely. Support can take the form of strict adherence enforced by reward and punishment such as in the military, cults, gangs, and structures based on invisible retribution including voodoo and Valhalla in Norse mythology. It is the province of these support systems to maintain loyalty, or the semblance of loyalty, once it threatens to dissipate. But, having said this, why is loyalty in certain domains less than durable?

TRANSIENT LOYALTY SYSTEMS

Much of what many believe to be loyalty may falter or fail at one or more of the durability criteria set forth here. These belief systems are labeled loyalty because science has no other semantic representation. The current quest among the fMRI community to find the human pleasure (and displeasure) structure centers have succeeded but have largely reached a technological plateau. Much as there is no single brain structure for satisfaction, excepting its emotional correlates of pleasure, high aroused pleasure (delight), and low (dis)pleasure, it is unlikely that satisfaction will be brain-mapped for the simple reason that it is a human-constructed hybrid cognitive-affective fulfillment response (Oliver 1997, p. 319; 2010, p. 342).

Loyalty differs in one significant manner. Its roots run more deeply in a biologic accounting. Whereas satisfaction requires a real or imagined need to be fulfilled, loyalty is more enduring; it can exist in the absence of fulfillment. In the description by this author, it can float away, becoming stable despite dissatisfaction (Oliver 2010, p. 452). This is particularly true for belief systems that are not disconfirmable. And, it has already been stated that disconfirmation in the example of sports, for example, does not necessarily result in a drop in loyalty. It can, but humans have developed an emotional response most commonly referred to as disappointment (Oliver 2010, p. 113) which maintains belief in the face of failure. But what about more vulnerable contexts?

Marketplace Loyalty (Is This Really Loyalty?)

Moving away from pure forms of social influence, we can enter the marketplace where social bonds and marketing appeals work in tandem or, oftentimes, at odds. Strangely, fashion artifacts (including automobilia, architecture, art, and so on) are dictated by the styles available, which are similar but different in their own subtle and not-so-subtle ways. Loyalties develop nonetheless to brands, styles, and concepts. And what of musical performances as previously discussed? Fans will go to great lengths to attend concerts in remote cities by their favorite groups. Restaurants are another example in this same context. In fact, all entertainment venues such as theaters, casinos, and movies of a particular theme (prequels and sequels) or containing favorite performers (too numerous to mention) are also prime candidates (Thomson 2006).

Product (Brand or Service) Loyalty

Product loyalty has no boundaries as it is commonly understood. As long as repeat purchasing is used as a proxy for loyalty, any rewards program, whether "locked in" or not (Johnson et al. 2003), will give the appearance of loyalty. In fact, these purchase frequency systems are generally referred to as "loyalty programs." Rarely, however, are patrons sampled as to their actual loyalty (assuming such measures are available and valid). Airlines were the first to use these strategies and just about every company, it seems, has some such program usually tied to a propriety (or affinity) credit card. Is this loyalty? No. It is transient loyalty at best. Marketplace loyalty is volatile and subject to the whims of the current preference and competitive environment. The marketplace is a fairly recent (in geologic time) phenomenon deriving from trade and stall-selling. We are not (yet) programmed to be "loyal" to things. We, in some sense, can be loyal to persons *if* they represent deities, saviors, lords or leaders, or parental images (see Yoon et al. 2006). But this crosses the boundary into more rooted and conditioned artifacts.

Multi-brand (Divided) Loyalty

In something of an anomaly, examples of multiple loyalties are common, particularly among everyday staples such as cereals. Proposed among the early writings on this topic was a model of multi-brand loyalty, which, as noted, would seem to be a contradiction in terms—but only if one views monogamy as the only permissible display of loyalty. These writings attempted to explain the concept in psychological terms, arguing that brands could be viewed as substitutes if they fell within a "latitude of acceptance" on the basis of quality (see Oliver 2010, pp. 431–2). Single-brand loyalty occurred when no competitive brand was in this region. Proponents of this view distinguished: "true" focal brand loyalty (loyalty to the particular brand of interest), multi-brand loyalty which includes the focal brand, "nonloyal" repeat purchasing of the focal brand, and happenstance purchasing of the focal brand by loyal or nonloyal buyers of another brand. Happenstance purchasing includes any repeat-purchase sequence due to factors other than "loyalty," such as unavailability of one's favorite brand, surrogate purchasing, and temporary constraints.

These examples show the folly of inferring any semblance of loyalty solely from repeat-purchase patterns subject to violation. Examples include withdrawal from the product category (for example, smoking cessation), and changes in need. This last phenomenon can occur in two different forms. In the first, the consumer "matures" whereby new needs supplant the old. For example, as a child grows, the toys and games played change to match the child's developmental phase, as with hobbies (to be discussed). A second form of need-based disloyalty is that alluded to previously whereby a competitive innovation appears that fulfills the consumer's needs, satisfying these needs more efficiently, or so it may seem. While it is also possible that the consumer's needs may have changed, so that a competitive offering is now the logical choice, competitors' messages frequently tout the ability of their product to fulfill needs at least as well (or better).

Addictive Loyalty

There are numerous activities that engender "loyalty" best referred to as addiction. Gambling is one such example. Some would argue that addictions should not be classified as loyalty behaviors; this author disagrees in principle. Any activities that individuals come to crave whether these are illegal (drugs), unhealthy (smoking), or legal (numerous products, services, or personal one-to-one behaviors) constitute relationships that occupy one's energies in an ongoing passionate manner not easily broken. Current thinking views these behaviors as related to activation or mimicry of our basic pleasure structures involving dopamine, norepinephrine, and the like (and hence biogenetic). Some have even referred to addiction as a rational behavior (Becker and Murphy 1988). Whether rational or not, addiction "loyalty" may be among the most difficult to break down, in terms of cessation or switching behavior. For many, it is much easier to exit social attachments than, for example, to quit smoking. And, in a more telling example, *The Wall Street Journal* (2012, p. D14) reports that 14 percent of college football fans would change their wedding date if it fell on a date for a big rival contest. Thus, addiction is loyalty; for others loyalty is the addiction; and for still others, loyalty and addiction are one and the same. In a sense, addictive loyalty flouts the boundary between the two.

Habits and Hobbies

These are interesting categories as they can be temporary to a particular age group (children's collectibles such as Beanie Babies, now passé) or, in some cases, last a lifetime (Barbie Dolls, where adult clubs have proliferated). Sports also fall in this category but many are age related and must be curtailed when the required stamina to participate cannot be maintained (for example, contact sports). This may not stop other forms of participating in the same category, such as coaching. Scouting is another fine example here as former scouts—an age-dependent activity—become scoutmasters so that they can continue to engage in this activity (and remain loyal to support its cause).

Collecting

Collecting is an excellent exemplar of this subset of loyalty. Like music, collecting has a developmental scheme beginning with children's toys and progressing to adult "investments" (Olmsted 1991). It can be a continual pursuit as in the aforementioned discussion of sport where the interest transitions from participation to spectatorship of teams or of one's children engaging in the sport. Collecting is also known to be bred in younger years and rekindled in adult lifestyles. For example, see Muensterberger (1994), a psychoanalyst, who traces it back to insecurities in childrearing. It can also be initiated in adult years as a new interest area that may develop for numerous reasons (for example, the study of genealogy). Communications technology is another current example, and still another, adventure travel, is common when time is freed up as in retirement. Muensterberger makes much of collecting's extreme manifestations and relates how collecting can become a passion, even an obsession, that can cause collectors to abandon family, friends, and job to obtain the rarest exemplar of "the collection."

Some of the world's financial crazes are cited as examples of the collecting tendency. Perhaps the greatest of these was the Dutch tulip mania of the seventeenth century. Art has followed similar "bubbles" in all of its forms including Chinese and Egyptian relics, old master paintings, and "new wave" representations in all varieties. The hackneyed phrase "boys and their toys" actually has a kernel of truth to it as it reflects exactly what is meant here. Loyalty to collecting or collections is one manifestation of those psychological longings.

Interpersonal Loyalty

This is a difficult category because it is so intertwined with friendships and avowed relations including marriages, partner unions, and numerous variations on friendships. One aspect of friendship worth noting is that no vows are made except those of a promissory nature, as in the previously noted BFF. These relations are easy to break, however, as only one partner need exit at any time. In group relationships (one with multiple others), this breakup may be hardly noticed, especially if the apparent bonding is not face-to-face (for example, on the Internet).

Marriage differs in one major aspect. Both parties agree under oath that "'til death do us part." Of interest is the fact that premarital and early married couples typically understate the probability of divorcing, frequently stating the possibility as "never" (Fowers et al. 1996). The actual U.S. statistics suggest that 40–50 percent will divorce. (This figure, although graphically accurate over the last few years, is immensely distorted because current marriages are compared to divorces stemming from unions over myriad intervals.) Nonetheless, there is a plethora of literature on marriages and their breakups and it would serve little purpose to rehearse that beyond what has been done (for example, Sternberg and Hojjat 1997).

Cults

It is important to delineate the popular meaning of a cult as an anti-this, anti-that group of individuals that intentionally does not conform to social norms as the prevailing culture knows them. Perhaps all remember the Hare Krishna members frequenting airports and other public places in their robes and shaved heads proselytizing to anyone who would listen. And, in a more frequently observed group, motorcyclists are still viewed by many as "outlaw bikers," stemming from the names of groups such as the Hells Angels [*sic*], who in their heyday largely rode Harley-Davidson motorcycles, thereby giving that brand a bad-boy image. One might ask how cults provide easy answers for Why Y? The answer is because they have all the answers. Particularly in the case of faith-based cults, parishioners have their sense of the world reprogrammed. The satisfactoriness of the answers exists in the lifestyle. Thought control is not a new phenomenon and no doubt dates back to unrecorded history when the first "immortal" issued rules for attaining eternal life via behavior change.

But, in fact, most sustainable cult communes appear normal in their demographic profile; they are upscale relative to their peers, stable, financially comfortable, and above average in intelligence and education (Atkin 2004). Atkin lists a number of popular brands that have achieved a semblance of cult status. This raises the inevitable question of consumer cults: are they bastions of loyalty?

Much like hobbies, I argue that these consumer collectives have a "shelf life." While in the appropriate life stage, the answer is yes—perhaps because of the sacrifices involved, particularly of advocacy and proselytizing. In faith-based circles, this frequently involves time (for example, voluntarism), money (for example, tithing), and the disposition of material possessions. And when does the shelf-life expire? There are two possible events. One is the aforementioned life phase; fashions (trends in particular) are especially susceptible. The other is changes in product meaning or signification. Currently (at the date of writing), tattoos are very popular as both statements and fashion trends. Already we are seeing surgeons performing more removals and tattoo shops doing more cover-ups, which may be a prelude to preference reversals.

LOYALTY "FOSSILIZATION"

It may be a truism, but age and long-term experience may result in apparent loyalty simply because of habit or resistance to change. These relationships may be loyal or not, but exist because of what many writers refer to as "inertia" (Huang and Yu 1999; Seetharaman and Chintagunta 1998). Some confuse inertia as loyalty but again, this cannot be ascertained until loyalty measures are available. Dissatisfaction-based lapsing has no common cause but it is easily identified when any of the performance referents (for example, expectations, equity) are negatively paired with observed performance. Of interest is the fact that individuals can tolerate or settle for dissatisfaction under at least two conditions. The first is compensatory satisfaction in any of the other comparative referent categories such as need fulfillment or value. The second is a lack of options; individuals "stuck" in unfortunate life situations display this phenomenon.

As stated, it is frequently observed that the elderly re-buy products and re-patronize services more often than the general population. In part this is due to limited access to outlets and/or limited mobility. It is also the case that habituation may have developed, and when queried, the consumer may say that he or she "always buys" this product or service. Is this a form of loyalty? It is repeat purchasing without question. The conundrum here is, again, no measures of true loyalty are administered, particularly to this population. Nonetheless, one can see that, on the basis of convenience alone, it is "easier" to re-buy a satisfactory (or even a dissatisfactory) product than to have to analyze each of a bundle of products, all fulfilling the same needs. This has been discussed in the literature as one of the disadvantages of technological innovation for the average consumer (Mick and Fournier 1998). The elderly would be even more adversely affected, thereby providing another reason for the observation that repeat purchasing is more common for older consumers.

ULTIMATE LOYALTY

This is not a widely accessed topic because it has not been researched to any extent. In fact, to this author's knowledge, there is no viable definition of "ultimate" loyalty. There are many examples of lifetime loyalty (for example, religion, marital couples who stay together throughout their lives) but is this ultimate loyalty or something of a long lasting nature that has not had sufficient time to expire? Oliver (2010, p. 432) adds the qualifier "against all odds and at all costs." Death is the only terminal expiration date as commonly accepted. Examples would include the military, where acts of heroism are frequently cited (and awarded) as demonstrating a high degree of loyalty to one's country, one's leaders, and one's comrades. Unfortunately, no test of the extent of loyalty is administered (or could be post facto). As this author states, "The consumption literature has not yet addressed this philosophically terminal loyalty form" (ibid., p. 452).

SUMMARY

In a phrase, loyalty, in whatever form, is goal-driven. It does not matter whether the goal is conscious, subconscious, or unconscious. In true behaviorist (but not behavior) fashion, individuals become attached to beliefs of their expressive capabilities because they have a "wherewithal." It is either an answer to the question of Why am I here? or to Why do I find the pursuit of X fulfilling? or to Why is X enjoyable? These various answers are provided by searching for and finding "discovery." This search can be introspective or it can be solely consummated by the words or the simple presence of others, or it can be a process initiated by introspection and then nurtured within the social envelope of groups, real or imagined.

The degree of loyalty—its permanence or transience—is determined by the depth of its emergence into one's being. Evolution can take this definition only so far. Once the requirements extend beyond those encased in our brain structures including the limbic system, conditioning and other learned responses become necessary. Drugs are known to be habit forming because they hijack our pleasure neurons, but loyalty to nonbarbiturate systems is captivating because rehearsal of their charms is conditioned to arouse these same pleasure responses. Developmental experience, environmental experience, and social experience all play roles in this process in the order that they impact the individual.

Indoctrination and more (or less) civil forms of mental programming have been known to operate since recorded history. More basic values, such as religion, political orientation, and close social ties, particularly familial, are among the most embedded and enduring. Mundane ties to marketplace artifacts are less secure. Such loyalties exist until they no longer "satisfy" (prove rewarding). Curiosity and novelty-seeking certainly play a role in this "switching" behavior, but this tendency is known to wane with age. Fashions, hobbies, sports, and even friendships are especially vulnerable. They maintain only when the social order is not disrupted or mutated. Another way of expressing this is to say that when the social support system depletes or is withdrawn, this aspect of the "three legged stool" collapses. Then one must rely on pure psychological resolve or find other compatible ways to stimulate the pleasure center of the brain. This is the "secret" to staving off disloyalty.

Already mentioned is the notion of "loyalty to disloyalty." This, too, is loyalty, but to a socio-estranged system. This is a judgment call, as many find disloyalty thrilling and some exercise it as a means of employment. All governments employ spies; companies use what is known as industrial espionage; con men, bilkers such as Ponzi and Madoff, Casanovas, and even the legitimate profession of magic also use this human vulnerability.

The conclusion one can draw is that loyalty is ubiquitous; it begins the moment we are born with its genetic predispositions. The brain has no "loyalty structure" or location. It only has pathways for motor neuron traces to give route to the impulses that manifest in what we have referred to, for lack of a better word, as loyalty. There is no value judgment intended. If it works for you, go for it. "Whatever" rings your bell, floats your boat, feeds you needs, and so on. A fitting end for this chapter is "To each their own."

REFERENCES

Ahuvia, Aaron C. (2005), "Beyond the extended self: loved objects and consumers' identity narratives," *Journal of Consumer Research*, **32** (1), 171–84.

Ambler, Tim, Sven Braeutigam, John Stins, Steven Rose and Stephen Swithenby (2004), "Salience and choice: neural correlates of shopping decisions," *Psychology & Marketing*, **21** (4), 247–61.

Atkin, Douglas (2004), *The Culting of Brands: When Customers Become True Believers*, New York: Penguin Group.

Balkwill, Laura-Lee and William Forde Thompson (1999), "A cross-cultural investigation of the perception of emotion in music: psychophysical and cultural cues," *Music Perception*, **17** (1), 43–64.

Bandura, Albert (1969), "Social learning of moral judgments," *Journal of Personality and Social Psychology*, **11**, 275–79.
Batra, Rajeev, Aaron Ahuvia and Richard P. Bagozzi (2012), "Brand love," *Journal of Marketing*, **76** (2), 1–16.
Baumeister, Roy F. and Mark R. Leary (1995), "The need to belong: desire for interpersonal attachments as a fundamental human motivation," *Psychological Bulletin*, **117** (3), 497–529.
Becker, Gary S. and Kevin M. Murphy (1988), "A theory of rational addiction," *Journal of Political Economy*, **976** (4), 675–700.
Belk, Russell W. (1988), "Possessions and the extended self," *Journal of Consumer Research*, **15** (2), 139–68.
Beller, Emily and Michael Hout (2006), "Intergenerational social mobility: the United States in comparative perspective," *The Future of Children Journal*, **16** (2), 19–36.
Berlyne, D.E. (1960), *Conflict, Arousal, and Curiosity*, New York: McGraw-Hill.
Berridge, Kent C. and Morten L. Kringelbach (2008), "Affective neuroscience of pleasure: reward in humans and animals," *Psychopharmacology*, **199** (3), 457–80.
Bever, Thomas G. and Robert J. Chiarello (1974), "Cerebral dominance in musicians and non-musicians," *Science*, **185** (4150), 537–9.
Blau, Peter M. and Otis Dudley Duncan (1967), *The American Occupational Structure*, New York: Wiley and Sons.
Bloom, Paul (2005), "Is God an accident?" *Atlantic Monthly*, **296** (3), 105–12.
Bloom, Paul (2007), "Religion is natural," *Developmental Science*, **10** (1), 147–51.
Bowlby, John (1982), *Attachment and Loss: Vol. 1: Attachment*, 2nd edn, New York: Basic Books.
Bristow, Dennis N. and Richard J. Sebastian (2001), "Holy cow! Wait 'til next year! A closer look at the brand loyalty of Chicago Cubs baseball fans," *Journal of Consumer Marketing*, **18** (3), 256–75.
Calvó-Armengol, Antoni and Matthew O. Jackson (2009), "Like father, like son: social network externalities and parent-child correlation in behavior," *American Economic Journal: Microeconomics*, **1** (1), 124–50.
Christakis, Nicholas A. and James H. Fowler (2009), *Connected: The Surprising Power of Our Social Networks and How They Shape Our Lives*, New York: Little, Brown.
Cialdini, Robert B., Richard J. Borden, Avril Thorne, Marcus Randall Walker, Stephen Freeman and Lloyd Reynolds Sloan (1976), "Basking in reflected glory: three (football) field studies," *Journal of Personality and Social Psychology*, **34** (3), 366–75.
Deppe, Michael, Wolfram Schwindt, Harald Kugel, Hilke Plaβmann and Peter Kenning (2005), "Nonlinear responses within the medial prefrontal cortex reveal when specific implicit information influences economic decision making," *Journal of Neuroimaging*, **15** (2), 171–82.
Dudley, Roger L. and Margaret G. Dudley (1986), "Transmission of religious values from parents to adolescents," *Review of Religious Research*, **28** (1), 3–15.
Durkheim, Émile (1933), *The Division of Labor in Society*, Glencoe, IL: Free Press.
Esch, Franz-Rudolf, Thorsten Möll, Bernd Schmitt, Christian E. Elger, Carolin Neuhaus and Bernd Weber (2012), "Brands on the brain: do consumers use declarative information or experienced emotions to evaluate brands?" *Journal of Consumer* Psychology, **22** (1), 75–85.
Festinger, Leon, Henry W. Riecken and Stanley Schachter (1956), *When Prophecy Fails: A Social and Psychological Study of a Modern Group that Predicted the Destruction of the World*, Minneapolis, MN: University of Minnesota Press.
Fowers, Blaine J., Kelly H. Montel and David H. Olson (1996), "Predicting marital success for premarital couple types based on PREPARE," *Journal of Marital & Family Therapy*, **22** (1), 103–19.
Funk, Daniel C. and Jeff James (2001), "The psychological continuum model: a conceptual framework for understanding an individual's psychological connection to sport," *Sport Management Review*, **4** (2), 119–50.

Holbrook, Morris B. and Robert M. Schindler (1989), "Some exploratory findings on the development of musical tastes," *Journal of Consumer Research*, **16** (June), 119–24.

Huang, Ming-Hui and Shihti Yu, (1999), "Are consumers inherently or situationally brand loyal? A set intercorrelation account for conscious brand loyalty and nonconscious inertia," *Psychology & Marketing*, **16** (6), 523–44.

Ivry, Richard B. and Lynn C. Robertson (1997), *The Two Sides of Perception*, Cambridge, MA: MIT Press.

Iwasaki, Yoshi and Mark E. Havitz (2004), "Examining relationships between leisure involvement, psychological commitment and loyalty to a recreation agency," *Journal of Leisure Research*, **36** (1), 45–72.

James, Jeffrey D. (2001), "The role of cognitive development and socialization in the initial development of team loyalty," *Leisure Sciences*, **23** (4), 233–61.

Jennings, M. Kent, Laura Stoker and Jake Bowers (2009), "Politics across generations: family transmission reexamined," *The Journal of Politics*, **71** (3), 782–99.

Johnson, Eric J., Steven Bellman and Gerald L. Lohse (2003), "Cognitive lock-in and the power law of practice," *Journal of Marketing*, **67** (2), 62–75.

Journal of Consumer Psychology (2012), Special issue: *Brand Insights from Psychological and Neurophysiological Perspectives*, **22** (1).

Juslin, Patrik N. and Petri Laukka (2003), "Communication of emotions in vocal expression and music performance: different channels, same code?" *Psychological Bulletin*, **129** (5), 770–814.

Keiningham, Timothy and Lerzan Aksoy (with Luke Williams) (2009), *Why Loyalty Matters*, Dallas, TX: Benbella Books.

Keleman, Deborah and Cara DiYanni (2005), "Intuitions about origins: purpose and intelligent design in children's reasoning about nature," *Journal of Cognition and Development*, **6** (1), 3–31.

Keller, Simon (2007), *The Limits of Loyalty*, Cambridge: Cambridge University Press.

Knobloch-Westerwick, Silvia, Prabu David, Matthew S. Eastin, Ron Tamborini and Dara Greenwood (2009), "Sports spectators' suspense: affect and uncertainty in sports entertainment," *Journal of Communication*, **59**, 750–67.

Koelsch, Stefan (2010), "Towards a neural basis of music-evoked emotions," *Trends in Cognitive Science*, **14** (3), 131–7.

Koski, Lilah Raynor and Phillip R. Shaver (1997), "Attachment and relationship satisfaction across the lifespan," in Robert J. Sternberg and Mahzad Hojjat (eds), *Satisfaction in Close Relationships*, New York: Guilford Press, pp. 26–55.

Laband, David N. and Bernard F. Lentz, "Like father, like son: toward an economic theory of occupational following," *Southern Economic Journal*, **50** (2), 474–93.

Levitin, Daniel J. (1994), "Absolute memory for musical pitch: evidence from the production of learned melodies," *Perception & Psychophysics*, **56** (4), 414–23.

Levitin, Daniel J. (2006), *This is Your Brain on Music: The Science of a Human Obsession*, New York: Plume (Penguin).

Litman, Jordan A. and Charles D. Spielberger (2003), "Measuring epistemic curiosity and its diversive and specific components," *Journal of Personality Assessment*, **80** (1), 75–86.

Madrigal, Robert and Vassilis Dalakas (2008), "Consumer psychology of sport: more than just a game," in Curtis P. Haugtvedt, Paul M. Herr and Frank R. Kardes (eds), *Handbook of Consumer Psychology*, New York: Psychology Press, pp. 857–76.

McClure, Samuel M., Jian Li, Damon Tomlin, Kim S. Cypert, Latané M. Montague and P. Read Montague (2004), "Neural correlates of behavioral preference for culturally familiar drinks," *Neuron*, **44** (October), 379–87.

Mick, David Glen and Susan Fournier (1998), "Paradoxes of technology: consumer cognizance, emotions, and coping strategies, *Journal of Consumer Research*, **25** (September), 123–43.

Mikulincer, Mario (1997), "Adult attachment style and information processing: individual differences in curiosity and cognitive closure," *Journal of Personality and Social Psychology*, **72** (5), 1217–30.

Muensterberger, Werner (1994), *Collecting, An Unruly Passion: Psychological Perspectives*, Princeton, NJ: Princeton University Press.
Oliver, Richard L. (1997), *Satisfaction: A Behavioral Perspective on the Consumer*, New York: Irwin/McGraw-Hill.
Oliver, Richard L. (1999), "Whence consumer loyalty?" *Journal of Marketing*, **63**, special issue, 33–44.
Oliver, Richard L. (2010), *Satisfaction: A Behavioral Perspective on the Consumer*, 2nd edn, Armonk, NY: M.E. Sharpe.
Olmsted, A.D. (1991), "Collecting: leisure, investment or obsession," in Floyd W. Rudmin (ed.), *To Have Possessions: A Handbook on Ownership and Property*, Conte Madera, CA: Select Press, pp. 287–306.
Park, Seong-Hee, Damon P.S. Andrew and Daniel F. Mahony (2008), "Exploring the relationship between trait curiosity and initial interest in sport spectatorship," *International Journal of Sport Management*, **9** (3), 1–17.
Park, Seong-Hee, Daniel Mahony, and Yu Kyoum Kim (2011), "The role of sport fan curiosity: a new conceptual approach to the understanding of sport fan behavior," *Journal of Sport Management*, **25**, 46–56.
Piaget, Jean (1950), *The Psychology of Intelligence*, London: Routledge.
Plassman, Hilke, Peter Kenning and Dieter Ahlert (2007), "Why companies should make their customers happy: the neural correlates of customer loyalty," *Advances in Consumer Research – North American Conference Proceedings*, **34**, 735–9.
Plassmann, Hilke, Thomas Zoëga Ramsøy and Milica Milosavljevic (2012), "Branding the brain: a critical review and outlook," *Journal of Consumer Psychology*, **22** (1), 18–36.
Pyysiäinen, Ilkka and Marc Hauser (2010), "The origins of religion: evolved adaptation or byproduct?" *Trends in Cognitive Science*, **14** (3), 104–109.
Schaefer, Michael, Harald Berens, Hans-Jochen Heinze and Michael Rotte (2006), "Neural correlates of culturally familiar brands of car manufacturers," *NeuroImage*, **31**, 861–5.
Scott, Gerald N. (1988), "Familial influence on religious involvement," in Darwin L. Thomas (ed.), *The Religion and Family Connection: Social Science Perspectives*, Provo, UT: Religious Studies Center, pp. 258–71.
Seetharaman, P.B. and Pradeep Chintagunta (1998), "A model of inertia and variety-seeking with marketing variables," *International Journal of Research in Marketing*, **15** (1), 1–17.
Sternberg, Robert J. and Mahzad Hojjat (eds) (1997), *Satisfaction in Close Relationships*, New York: Guilford Press.
Stuss, Donald T. and Robert T. Knight (eds) (2002), *Principles of Frontal Lobe Function*, New York: Oxford University Press.
Sutton, William A., Mark A. McDonald, George R. Milne and John Cimperman (1997), "Creating and fostering fan identification in professional sports," *Sport Marketing Quarterly*, **6** (1), 15–22.
The Wall Street Journal (2012), "The count," 7 September, D14.
Thomson, Matthew (2006), "Human brands: investigating antecedents to consumers' strong attachments to celebrities," *Journal of Marketing*, **70** (3), 104–19.
Trehub, Sandra E. (2003), "The developmental origins of musicality," *Nature Neuroscience*, **7** (6), 669–73.
Treiman, Donald J. (1977), *Occupational Prestige in Comparative Perspective*, New York: Academic Press.
Veblen, Thorstein (1915), *The Theory of the Leisure Class: An Economic Study of Institutions*, New York: Macmillan.
Yoon, Carolyn, Angela H. Gutchess, Fred Feinberg and Thad A. Polk (2006), "A functional magnetic resonance imaging study of neural dissociations between brand and person judgments," *Journal of Consumer Research*, **33** (June), 31–40.
Zatorre, Robert J. (1998), "Functional specialization of human auditory cortex for musical processing," *Brain*, **121** (10), 1817–18.

6 Customer engagement: a new frontier in customer value management

Sander F.M. Beckers, Hans Risselada and Peter C. Verhoef

INTRODUCTION

One of the most prominent developments in firms, and specifically within marketing, in the last decades has been the increasing amounts of customer data. This especially holds for service firms, such as banks, insurance companies, hotels, and so on. Service firms frequently interact directly with customers and have stored amounts of data of their customers. Moreover, through the use of loyalty programs, several service firms not interacting directly with customers, such as supermarkets, also have collected detailed knowledge about their customers (Dorotic et al. 2012). Firms have also heavily invested in customer relationship management (CRM) systems. According to Forrester, more than 72 percent of business-to-customer (B2C) firms regard retaining customers as one of their top priorities (Band 2010). Nowadays, firms have developed models to predict customer lifetime value and customer churn (Kumar and Shah 2009; Neslin et al. 2006). This has resulted in an increasing importance of customer value management as an important function within marketing and firms. Conceptually, customer value management (CVM) has its roots in relationship marketing. It entails maximizing the value of a company's customer base and analyzing individual data on prospects and customers. Firms use the resulting information to acquire and retain customers and to drive customer behavior with developed marketing strategies, in such a way that the value of all current and future customers is maximized. Companies can increase the value of their customer base by (1) attracting new customers, (2) increasing customer retention, (3) creating customer expansion, (4) winning back old customers, (5) supporting (active) relationship termination, and (6) effectively allocating resources among customers and marketing actions (that is, acquisition and retention) (Bolton et al. 2004; Verhoef et al. 2007).

Owing to the increasing interest in practice for CVM and the huge availability of customer data, researchers have extensively studied several topics in CVM, such as the implementation of CVM, customer lifetime value (CLV) models and multi-channel customer management (for example,

Neslin et al. 2006; Rust et al. 2004; Venkatesan and Kumar 2004). Verhoef and Lemon (2013) have discussed six major lessons that can be derived from this research. Although multiple steps have to be made, one can observe that CVM is moving to new frontiers. Specifically, Verhoef and Lemon (2013) argue that especially managing customer engagement and the customer networks in which engagement occurs are two important new emerging fields within CVM (see also Verhoef et al. 2010a). Kunz and Hogreve (2011) also consider customer engagement as an important new research field within service research. The increasing prevalence of new social media (for example, Twitter, Facebook, and YouTube) and the increasing acknowledgment of the importance of customer networks (for example, Van den Bulte and Wuyts 2007) are important facilitators of the increasing interest in customer engagement, since they have substantially increased the connectivity of customers (Libai et al. 2010), decreased the customer–firm interaction costs (Godes et al. 2005), and in some cases improved the quality of these interactions (for example, in terms of sensory content) (Libai et al. 2010; Ostrom et al. 2010). Customers communicate with other customers and/or companies more widely, faster, and with more qualitative detail than ever before. For instance, customers do so by tweeting about the latest movie they saw, by liking or commenting on a company's Facebook page, or by posting videos of themselves driving an expensive car. Hence, in a networked and information-rich environment, customer engagement becomes very relevant for companies. Within CVM this mainly implies that customers provide value to firms through transactions with firms (that is, being loyal, cross-buying), but also through non-transactional behavior. This is not a totally new idea. Already Hoekstra and Huizingh (1999) supported an extension of the CLV concept by arguing that it should also include the value of non-transactional behavior. The enormous adoption of the Net Promoter Score (Reichheld 2003) in practice also emphasizes that firms believe that non-transactional behavior (in this case, word-of-mouth) is an important value driver. Still, CVM research and specifically research on CLV has so far mainly focused on transactional behavior as an important value driver. Only recently have we started to acknowledge that CLV is a broader concept and should include customer engagement (Kumar et al. 2010a).

Given these noted developments, we focus in this chapter on customer engagement as a new frontier in CVM. Our main objective is to provide an overview of the emerging theory and research in this area and to come up with a list of future research topics on customer engagement. In doing so, we first provide a historic perspective on customer to firm orientations. Next, we briefly discuss CVM, as we consider this to be the starting point for the development of this new frontier (Verhoef et al. 2010a). Subsequently, we discuss customer engagement as a new frontier in CVM and explain how customer engagement can be seen as a next phase in customer–firm interactions in which customers become inside the domain of the company, hence the firm–customer relationship goes beyond a bilateral relationship (Prahalad 2004). To do so, we discuss the theory on customer engagement and emerging perspectives on its definition and scope. We discuss managing customer engagement in more depth subsequently and put special emphasis on the analysis of customer networks in which the engagement occurs.

DEVELOPMENT OF CUSTOMER TO FIRM ORIENTATIONS

Both academic and managerial interest in customer engagement are increasing and show no signs of flagging, even to such extent that the term 'customer engagement' can be considered a new buzzword in customer management (Verhoef et al. 2010a). 'Customer engagement' yields over 70 million hits on Google and has its own Wikipedia page. Also, many companies have adopted this important new term and many prestigious academic and managerial conferences include at least a section on the topic of customer engagement.

The next frontier of customer engagement within CVM can be best described from the historical perspective on customer-to-firm interactions (see Figure 6.1). Before the attention for relationship marketing and

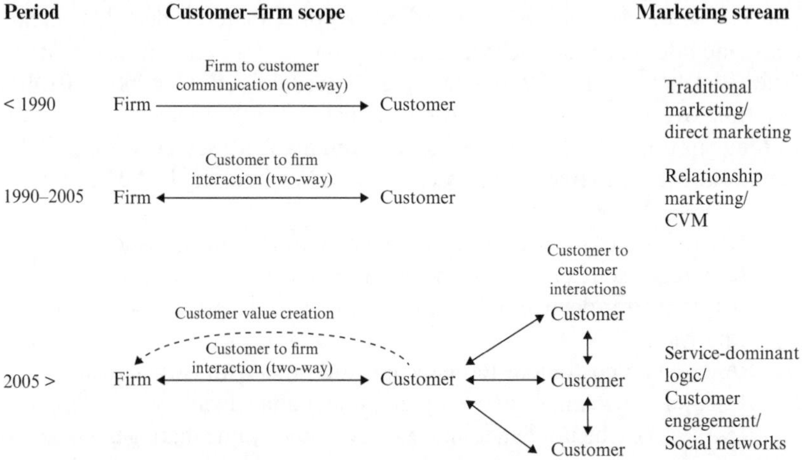

Figure 6.1 Scope of customer–firm interaction within marketing and service research

subsequently CVM (Dwyer et al. 1987; Morgan and Hunt 1994; Payne and Frow 2005), firms mainly focused on getting attention from customers by sending their messages to customers through mass media and sometimes more directed media, such as direct mailings. Within relationship marketing and customer management we observed a stronger focus on bi-directional relationships between customers and firms, in which customers and firms actively interact with each other. In these interactions both social value and economic value (that is, transactions) were exchanged (Fournier 1998). Still customers are not involved in the firm. In the era of customer engagement, we actually observe two developments. First, customers now can become actively involved in specific value-creating processes (Vargo and Lusch 2004). Second, customers also actively participate in customer networks, in which they also can create value for the firm through, for example, referrals. This has important consequences for value-creation.

CUSTOMER VALUE MANAGEMENT: EMERGING KNOWLEDGE

Since early 2000, we observe an increasing interest in research on customer management. Within this research stream the focus has been on customer-to-firm interactions. Interestingly, in these early days multiple impactful management books (for example, Blattberg et al. 2001; Rust et al. 2000) have been written on this topic, while research on this topic was still in its infancy. Top research on customer management really took off from 2003–04 onwards (Verhoef et al. 2010a). Approximately a decade later we can conclude that customer value management research is now a mature field (Blattberg et al. 2009; Kumar et al. 2006; Verhoef et al. 2007, 2010b). Multiple overview studies have been published that summarize the major findings in this field and in specific research areas. Research within CVM can broadly be centered on six research lines (Verhoef et al. 2007):[1]

1. Research on customer analysis: methods and technical issues
2. Research on customer acquisition methods
3. Research on determinants of customer retention and customer expansion
4. Research on customer lifetime value and links with firm value
5. Research on channels in customer value management
6. Research on the implementation of customer value management.

Research stream one focuses heavily on statistical methods to predict customer behavior. In the second research stream the focus is more on how firms can effectively acquire customers using several communication channels, such as direct mailings and email. Using econometric models, research stream three investigates the drivers of customer retention and/or customer expansion (Bolton et al. 2004). These models are also referred to as customer-based models. The fourth research stream builds on the research on retention and expansion, and focuses on the monetary value of customer relationships (Rust et al. 2004). Within this stream researchers have heavily emphasized customer lifetime value and customer equity as important customer and marketing metrics. Using models predicting customer purchase behavior (that is, churn, purchase frequency, cross-buying) and marketing costs, researchers have aimed to assess CLV (Donkers et al. 2007; Rust et al. 2011; Venkatesan and Kumar 2004). Researchers have also acknowledged the value consequences of other behaviors, such as product returns and credit-risk (Lhoest-Snoeck 2012; Petersen and Kumar 2009). Furthermore, research within this stream aimed to link this value with firm value and pledge for reporting this value in financial reports (Gupta et al. 2004; Kumar and Shah 2009; Wiesel et al. 2008). With these CLV models researchers also aim to efficiently allocate resources among customer value segments (Venkatesan and Kumar 2004) and/or general marketing investments (that is, increasing service quality vs. increasing brand awareness) (Rust et al. 2004). In this respect research in this area has also contributed to research on marketing and finance in which the Return on Investment of marketing investments has heavily been emphasized. The fifth research stream focuses on how channels can create value for customers and how customers use these channels (Neslin et al. 2006). Specifically, research has, for example, considered how the use of multiple channels is related to customer profitability (for example, Kumar and Venkatesan 2005) or which customer factors drive the adoption of new channels (Venkatesan et al. 2007). Finally, the last research stream considers how firms should implement CVM and whether CVM affects firm performance. Several studies have linked CVM implementation, specifically the use of customer analytics to exploit customer data resulting in customer insights, which can be used in managing customer interactions (for example, call center, website), and marketing decision making (for example, Reinartz et al. 2004; Jayachandran et al. 2006; Becker et al. 2009). Conceptually, Shah et al. (2006) have emphasized the importance of customer-centric organizations and how to move from a product-centric organization to a customer-centric focus of the firm. In that respect, Rust et al. (2010) have also emphasized the potential importance of chief customer officers within firms. While research has extensively focused on CVM implementations, empirical research on customer-centric organizations is, however, lacking.

Verhoef and Lemon (2013) have derived six general lessons that can be derived from this extensive research stream:

1. Use of CVM improves business performance.
2. CVM should be customer driven instead of IT driven.
3. Firms should adopt CLV as a core metric.
4. Firms should invest in strong customer intelligence capabilities.
5. Firms should understand the drivers of customer acquisition, retention and customer expansion.
6. Firms should manage their channels to create customer value.

For a more extensive discussion on these lessons, we refer to Verhoef and Lemon (2013). In sum, we conclude that research on CVM has become rather mature, which has provided some important implications for marketing theory and practice. One important challenge in the future within CVM is probably the emergence of big data (Davenport 2012; Rust and Huang 2012). Especially in an online environment, data becomes more massive, in which firms can potentially observe customers in their search and buying process online and through new devices, such as smart phones and tablets, providing huge opportunities for one-to-one marketing. Researchers have just started to develop models providing customers individual specific offers or real-time recommendations on their devices (for example, Chung et al. 2009). Future research will surely develop models that can effectively use the available data to enrich customer relationships and provide more value to the customers and the firm. Beyond this important development, one of the crucial trends in CVM is the increasing importance of customer engagement (Verhoef and Lemon 2013), which yields the next frontier in CVM. In the next section, we elaborate on this important trend. We start with highlighting emerging perspectives on the definition and scope of customer engagement, followed by a discussion on how customer engagement constitutes the next frontier in CVM.

DEFINITION OF CUSTOMER ENGAGEMENT

There remains debate about the meaning of customer engagement. As Bolton (2011, p.272) points out: "Although many organizations consider CE [customer engagement] important, this term has different meaning for different people." For instance, although various consultancy companies have started to develop measurement instruments for customer engagement (for example, www.allegiance.com), they attach different meanings to the construct. From an academic perspective, Van Doorn et al. (2010, p.253) were among the first to formally define customer engagement. They emphasize the behavioral focus of the term "engagement" and consequently define customer engagement behaviors as "the customer's behavioral manifestations toward a brand or firm, beyond purchase, resulting from motivational drivers," a definition that is consistent with that provided by the Marketing Science Institute (2010). Later, Brodie et al. (2011) started a debate surrounding this conceptualization. Precisely, they attempt to explore the theoretical foundations of the customer engagement construct and the term "engagement" and argue that besides a behavioral dimension, customer engagement also contains an emotional and cognitive dimension. Based on five fundamental propositions resulting from a synthesis of 'engagement' literature, Brodie et al. (2011, p. 260, emphases in original) define customer engagement as "a *psychological state* that occurs by virtue of *interactive, cocreative customer experiences* with a *focal agent/object* (for example, a brand) in focal service relationships." Reconciling both views on customer engagement, customer engagement can be seen as a latent state, which translates into observable customer engagement behaviors.

Beyond these two leading conceptual studies on customer engagement, So et al. (forthcoming) took up the challenge to develop a multifaceted customer engagement scale. To a large extent based on employee engagement literature, they view customer engagement as a second-order factor comprising five first-order factors; identification, enthusiasm, attention, absorption, and interaction. Their work presents managers a tool to measure customer engagement outcomes, without which managers tend to focus on other more accessible outcomes, such as increased sales.

To recap, in the emerging customer engagement literature there appears to be growing consensus that customer engagement is a multidimensional construct containing an attitudinal as well as a behavioral dimension. However, the exact dimensionality of the construct remains debatable. In addition, although there is merit for both an attitudinal dimension as well as a behavioral dimension of customer engagement, similar to the construct of customer loyalty (Van Doorn 2011), the latent dimension of customer engagement needs further refinement. Most importantly, it is unclear yet how the psychological dimension of customer engagement delineates (especially empirically) from alternative well-established constructs in customer management, such as commitment and involvement. Conceptually, So et al. (forthcoming, p. 10) argue for the overall customer engagement construct that "engagement requires more than the exercise of cognition" and that activity sets engagement apart from other constructs. Hence, for the overall customer engagement construct it is the behavioral aspect that distinguishes customer engagement from other constructs. How the psychological aspect of customer engagement delineates from other constructs in customer management (for example, flow, involvement, or commitment) is theoretically discussed on a fine-grained level by Patterson et al. (2006), Hollebeek (2011a, in particular table 3 on p. 793), and Hollebeek (2011b). Yet, these authors also underline that (the latent side of) customer engagement shares important overlaps with other constructs. While their theoretical studies address conceptual nuances between customer engagement and other, more well-established, customer management constructs, it is unsure (yet) whether the psychological and emotional aspects of customer engagement in fact can be empirically (and thus, managerial actionably) distinguished from other constructs, especially given the detailed and nuanced differences. Given this uncertainty, in marketing practice the psychological state belonging to customer engagement is acknowledged, "however, consistent with Van Doorn et al. (2010), managers tend to focus on measurable CE behaviors that extend beyond customer-firm purchase transactions" (Bolton 2011, p. 272).

Given the lack of clarity as to how the attitudinal dimension differentiates from other constructs in customer management (especially empirically), and, foremost, the managerial emphasis on dealing with observable customer engagement behaviors, throughout the remainder of this chapter we will limit our attention to the behavioral aspects of customer engagement.

CUSTOMER ENGAGEMENT: NEXT FRONTIER

The growing importance of customer engagement is not merely a new attention point or a new point on the radar for companies, but actually changes the rules of the game in customer–firm interactions. By undertaking customer engagement behaviors, customers become involved "in activities that were once reserved for the firm: promoting the brand, suggesting ideas for new products, choosing advertising copy, deciding on logos, and even reacting to competitive actions" (Libai 2011, p. 275). This development thus challenges the "classic" marketing productivity chain, in which customers are outside the domain of value creation (Lehmann 2004). By taking over (part of) company activities, customers move inside the domain of value creation, which makes them co-producers of value (Vargo and Lusch 2004). This new reality means that "firms no longer control marketing, but rather customers (via the Web, for example) define what a company is (and is not)" (Leeflang 2011, p.78). In other words, the boundary of the firm and the distinction between the firm and its customers are getting blurred (Sawhney and Prandelli 2000). In short, customer engagement behaviors are not a new light on the company's dashboard, but customers are actually put in the driving seat of the company and take over (part of) the steering wheel. We see this as a next step in the development of customer–firm interactions.

Types of Customer Engagement Behaviors

Under the behavioral dimension of customer engagement a wide range of specific behaviors are classified, such as customer-to-customer interactions, customer co-creation in new product development, and customer feedback (cf. Bijmolt et al. 2010; Verhoef et al. 2010a). Customer-to-customer interactions refer to communication between consumers about a company and/or brand (that is, word-of-mouth) (cf. Kumar et al. 2010a); for example, asking a friend for advice on mobile phone network providers. Another example is Jetstar, which set up a community where customers can share travel stories. Customer co-creation in new product development is "a collaborative new product development activity in which consumers actively contribute and select various elements of a new product offering" (Hoyer et al. 2010, p.283). Ample examples of customer co-creation can be found in multiple industries. For instance, in the airline industry, Air France invited customers to help design new tableware and Airbus held a contest in which customers could provide ideas for making aviation greener. Finally, customer feedback (that is, voice) is companies listening-in on their (potential) customers (Hirschman 1970). Informing a hotel about the quality of your stay is an illustration of an act of customer engagement that falls within customer feedback.

The distinctive forms of customer engagement behaviors are often studied in isolation. Exemplary are studies on the impact of word-of-mouth and customer recommendations (for example, Kumar et al. 2010b; Trusov et al. 2009), customer voice (for example, Van Oest and Knox 2011), and customer participation in new product development (for example, Burroughs et al. 2011; Hoffmann et al. 2010).

Managing Customer Engagement Behaviors

Despite customer engagement behaviors being often studied in isolation, our understanding of them can be enhanced by analyzing them from an integrated perspective. These separate behaviors belong to an overarching construct and share communality in that they change the way value is created within customer–firm interactions. Companies are now looking for ways to manage this new stage in customer-firm interactions. However, an investigation among Chief Marketing Officers shows that they struggle

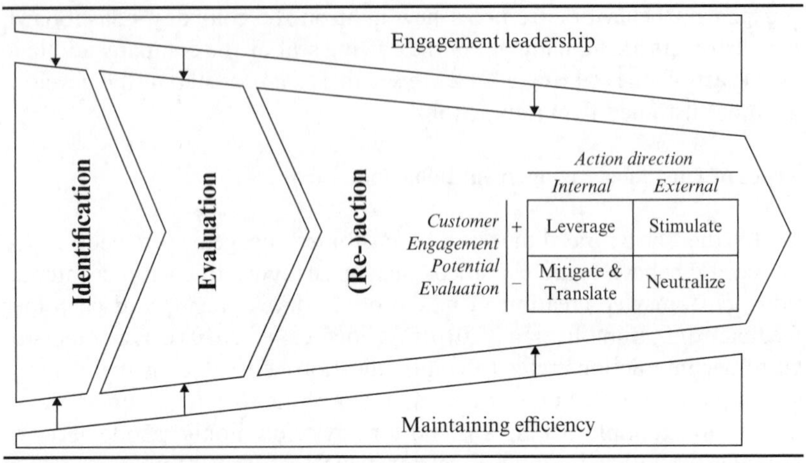

Source: Van Doorn et al. (2010).

Figure 6.2 Managing customer engagement

with how to deal with empowered customers (IBM 2011). Van Doorn et al. (2010) provide an overview of how to react to customer engagement behaviors (see Figure 6.2). They propose a three-step procedure in which, first, companies identify the occurring customer engagement behaviors (and the customers involved in them), then evaluate these behaviors, and finally take the right action for managing these behaviors. These actions range from leveraging, transmitting, and addressing both positive as well as negative customer engagement behaviors that are voiced internally to the company, to stimulating positive and preventing negative customer engagement behaviors that are voiced to external audiences. In addition, with respect to reacting to potential negative engagement behaviors, in marketing practice there is increasing attention for webcare activities. A study by Van Noort and Willemsen (2012) confirms that when dealing with online complaints, applying webcare can mitigate potential negative consequences. Also, reacting to such voiced complaints might provide a critical touch point in revitalizing the customer relationship, as indicated by the service recovery paradox (see for instance Smith et al. 1999). Within a service setting this effect is particularly pronounced for hotels and restaurants, assumedly because of high switching costs in these categories and thus the greater significance of an effective recovery (De Matos et al. 2007). Hence, managing customer engagement behaviors might be even more important for services with inherent high switching costs among service providers.

Proactive Management of Customer Engagement Behaviors

While there is clear merit in approaching the management of customer engagement behaviors by providing the right response, this is a rather reactive approach. Godes et al. (2005) indentify four approaches companies can take when dealing with social interactions, ranging from reactive to proactive. These approaches are observing the occurring interactions, moderating the interactions by fostering them, mediating the interactions by controlling the information flow to customers, and actively participating in and even creating these interactions themselves. In practice, it is observed that many companies try to take more control over customer engagement behaviors by opting for one of the more proactive approaches (that is, moderating, mediating, or participating). So, instead of reacting to occurring customer engagement behaviors, these companies start pursuing a more pro-active strategy to manage customer engagement behaviors (Verhoef et al. 2010a), for instance by stimulating word-of-mouth (Godes and Mayzlin 2009). Such strategies can be seen as a form of outsourcing company activities and value-creation to customers (Beckers et al. 2012). By giving customers a say in new product concepts, for instance through voting contests, some companies (partially) outsource the new product development function to customers. Other companies attempt to employ customers as salespersons for the company by setting up word-of-mouth campaigns; they thereby put advertising and acquisition activities in the hands of customers. Or companies set up online communities in which product support and other service activities are performed among customers.

However, although managers thus essentially outsource value-creation to customers by seeding customer engagement activities, the performance implications of these attempts are unclear. In fact, many managers fear "there is no room for error" when executing customer engagement strategies, and roughly half of these initiatives fail (Porter et al. 2011). Beckers et al. (2012) shed light on when (that is, under which circumstances) it can be beneficial for companies to proactively manage customer engagement behaviors. Using an event study, they find that half of companies' customer-engagement initiatives ultimately may erode company value, whereas the other half of these initiatives may actually increase company value. This result is similar to the findings reported by Porter et al. (2011). Based on the central premise that stimulating customer engagement behaviors represents a form of outsourcing, Beckers et al. (2012) use a transaction cost perspective to investigate variation in investors' evaluations towards various companies' customer engagement programs. Their results show that under the following circumstances proactively managing customer engagement behaviors can be a value-adding strategy: in initial stages (when customers' value-creating efforts are less likely to be redundant), when having a poor firm reputation (and therefore the risk of evoking negative customer engagement behaviors is less severe), and when facing low demand uncertainty (whereby the stability of customers' needs and wants in such environments makes them well suited for customer engagement initiatives).

CUSTOMER NETWORKS

Moving to the frontier of customer engagement, customer networks are becoming very important. After all, many customer engagement behaviors occur in networks (see Figure 6.1) and may affect the behaviors of others related to the engaged customers through customer-to-customer (C2C) interactions. There is ample evidence for so-called social contagion from aggregate level studies on, for example, innovation diffusion (for example, Bass 1969; Bell and Song 2007). The customer engagement concept acknowledges the effect of C2C interactions on the value of the customer to the firm (Libai et al. 2010; Verhoef et al. 2010a). From a customer value management perspective, however, it is not sufficient to know that positive effects of contagion and customer engagement exist. One needs to understand and measure the process on the individual level to be able to manage customer engagement. Furthermore, assessing the value of engagement behavior to increase accountability of social marketing efforts requires an individual approach. Insights from individual-level analyses help to answer questions such as: How do you value a customer that is not a regular buyer of your brand but regularly recommends it to his friends (influencer value; Kumar et al. 2010a)? What is the (negative) value of a complaint (Goldenberg et al. 2007)? And what should be the incentive for a referral or co-creation campaign (Kumar et al. 2010b)? In this section we discuss how individual customers may be affected by the behaviors of those in their networks and how marketers can analyze (the effects of) these C2C interactions. The fundamental premise is that understanding the network structure of individual consumers is an (almost) necessary requirement for the design of effective customer engagement behavior strategies (Katona et al. 2011).

Networks and Customer Behavior

The analysis of customer network data is a relatively new topic in the area of customer value management (Libai et al. 2010; Van Doorn et al. 2010).

The recent burst in the availability of network data has triggered the interest of marketers looking for ways to use C2C interactions for marketing purposes. This is illustrated by the huge social network advertising revenues that are expected to rise to US$7.72 billion in 2012 (eMarketer 2012) and by the exceptionally high valuations of social network sites (Baldwin 2011; Graig and Sorkin 2011). Despite a number of papers which provide evidence for the existence of the positive effects of C2C interactions on customer behavior, understanding of the phenomenon is still limited (Iyengar et al. 2011a).

Networks consist of actors and the ties between them. In the current setting, customers are the actors and the ties are formed by the interactions among them. Via these interactions customers potentially influence each other's behavior. In other words, the probability that a customer will engage in certain behavior is affected by the behavior of others he or she is related to. The majority of the studies investigate this phenomenon in the context of the adoption of new products or services (Bell and Song 2007; Choi et al. 2010). More recently these social influence effects have also been found in a customer retention context (Nitzan and Libai 2011). This illustrates the importance of understanding social influence on behavior in customer relationships and thus the importance of customer engagement for customer value management.

Network Data

The increasing importance of social networks is also fostered by technological developments and enormous growth in the popularity of the Internet. Consumers interact with others on various platforms, such as mobile telephony, email, online social networks, blogs, and review sites. A major difference between these C2C interactions and face-to-face contact is that these new types of interactions are digital and can thus be tracked. With these network data, models for behavior in customer relationships can be extended with a social influence component. This can be done in two ways. First, characteristics of the network and characteristics of the others in the network can be analyzed as drivers of customer behavior. This addresses the question of to what extent customers are influenced by others. Second, the influential power of customers can be measured by analyzing the behavior of multiple customers in their network. The identification of influential customers is important for setting up social marketing campaigns and managing customer engagement behaviors. In this way the consequences of customer engagement behaviors in the network of customers can be investigated (Libai et al. 2010; Van Doorn et al. 2010).

Data to Describe Networks

Customer-to-customer interactions form a network structure and thus researchers can use social network analysis techniques that have been developed in sociology (Van den Bulte 2010; Van den Bulte and Wuyts 2007). The way the network is defined is an important issue. Thus far, most studies have used either self-reported data or geographical data (zip codes) to build a network. Although the use of surveys is common (Wasserman and Faust 1994), they have several drawbacks, including dependence on respondents' memories, differences across respondents' interpretations, and self-report biases (Bertrand and Mullainathan 2001), all of which can lead to erroneous descriptions of the network. Geographical data are also commonly used because most customer and marketing databases contain zip code information (Bell and Song 2007; Nam et al. 2010). However, social interaction is not measured directly, and so the use of these data requires the assumption that people living close to each other influence each other (Choi et al. 2010; Iyengar et al. 2011a). It is unlikely to be an accurate description since social interaction is becoming less and less dependent on spatial proximity (Goldenberg et al. 2010; Haenlein 2011; Iyengar et al. 2011a).

As an alternative, online social networks are a potentially rich source of network data. The number of people in these networks is typically large and data are relatively easy to obtain (Godes and Mayzlin 2004; Lewis et al. 2008; Stephen and Galak 2010; Trusov et al. 2009). A disadvantage of this method is the difficulty in combining network information and behavioral and transactional data for the same person. Furthermore, people are typically connected in an online network to many others who are not relevant from a social influence perspective since it requires only very little effort to establish and maintain a 'friendship' tie (Ackland 2009; Trusov et al. 2010).

Another alternative specifically relevant in the telecom industry is the use of direct communication data from email or (mobile) telephony. In the latter case so-called call detail records (CDR) can be used to create networks. In CDR data, all phone calls and text messages are recorded individually. A person's mobile phone network is a good proxy for his or her social network (Eagle et al. 2009; Haythornthwaite 2005) and has been used to model retention (Nitzan and Libai 2011) and adoption (Hill et al. 2006).

Influential Customers

Social marketing campaigns, such as viral marketing and referral campaigns, solely rely on C2C interactions. A key issue in the design of such campaigns is the choice of the seeds. This is not only important from a social marketing campaigns perspective, but also from a mere service perspective. Customers who have a bad service experience may influence other customers, which might eventually lead to disloyalty for many customers, especially when customers are very influential (Nitzan and Libai 2011). The seeds are the first customers approached by the firm in the campaign. The most influential customers are obviously good candidates, because they will influence others and thereby spread the message (in case of a viral campaign, or a good or bad service experience) or persuade others to act (in case of a referral campaign). Determining which customers are most influential and why it is that some customers are more influential than others are two important research topics (Iyengar et al. 2011a, 2011b).

There are two well-established types of measures of influential power, objective measures based on network characteristics and subjective measures based on self-reports. Commonly used network characteristics are centrality measures, such as degree centrality, betweenness centrality, or closeness centrality (see Van den Bulte and Wuyts 2007 for a detailed discussion). The network characteristics are an important determinant of the influential power of a customer (Katona et al. 2011; Nitzan and Libai 2011). For example, Hinz et al. (2011) show that referral campaigns seeded on central customers outperform referral campaigns seeded on randomly selected customers. This is not obvious since a higher degree centrality has two opposing consequences. Customers with a higher degree centrality have a larger potential reach, because more people observe what these customers say or do. However, given that the time a customer can spend on influencing others is limited, the effect of a single interaction is likely to be lower in case of a higher degree centrality (Hinz et al. 2011; Leskovec et al. 2007). In the study by Hinz et al. (2011), the first effect apparently dominates the second effect, but it remains unclear whether this holds in general.

A popular self-reported measure for influence is opinion leadership (Childers 1986; King and Summers 1970). Self-reported opinion leaders are consumers that exert a disproportionate influence on those around them (King and Summers 1970). To measure opinion leadership, "most studies inquire about perceptions, discussions, or acts of influence in this topic area" (King and Summers 1970, p. 44). This illustrates that opinion leadership is quite a broad concept. It typically correlates with expertise (Childers 1986; Lyons and Henderson 2005; Van Eck et al. 2011), innovativeness (Lyons and Henderson 2005), and involvement or interest (Childers 1986; Darden and Reynolds 1971; Richins and Root-Shaffer 1988).

Network Value

An important aspect of customer value management is determining the value of the customer to the firm. It is clear from the foregoing discussion that customers affect each other's behaviors and thus that customer engagement behaviors generate value from the customer to the firm over and above their transactional value. Kumar et al. (2010a) label this value as influencer value, which captures the value-generating behavior of a customer driven by an intrinsic motivation to influence others. Determining the influencer value is an issue that is currently getting a lot of research attention. Libai et al. (forthcoming) argue that one should evaluate the changes in the value of the entire network of customer to determine the value of a customer's engagement behavior. This avoids multiple counting of customers that are affected by more than one contact.

A second way in which social influence and customer engagement translate into value of the customer to the firm is through referral campaigns. The so-called referral value (Kumar et al. 2010a) is different from influencer value in that referrals are typically not intrinsically motivated but driven by an incentive from the firm. Such incentives need to be aligned with the value that the referral generates (Kumar et al. 2010b). Schmitt et al. (2011) show that it is profitable for firms to acquire new customers by means of a referral campaign. Customers acquired through such a campaign are more loyal and have higher customer lifetime values than the average customer. They argue that this is because good (loyal and valuable) customers are more likely to participate in referral campaigns and are likely to bring in consumers like them. This illustrates that the characteristics of a customer's social network determine its value. The previously mentioned study by Hinz et al. (2011) on optimal seeding strategies is another example. Combining their findings on the best metric to select customers as seeds with the fact that customers acquired through referral campaigns are more valuable provides strong evidence for the value of customer networks to the firm.

SUMMARY AND CONCLUSION

To conclude, customer value management has developed to a mature and well-studied research field. Within customer value management, customer engagement presents the next frontier. In early stages (prior to 1990) the customer–firm interaction was a unidirectional relationship: from the firm to the customer (for example, mass media advertising). Later (roughly 1990–2005), this turned into a bidirectional relationship: from the firm to the customer and from the customer back to the firm (for example, customer feedback). Now (from 2005 onwards), the next step in customer–firm interactions is that the boundary between the firm and its customers is blurring. Customers, through their engagement, become part of the corporate domain and co-create value with companies. The exact conceptualization of customer engagement is an emerging construct, although there is consensus that engagement goes beyond purchase and contains a behavioral dimension, an emotional, and a cognitive dimension. This new stage in customer–firm interactions presents novel challenges in customer value management with a central role for the analysis of customer networks.

RESEARCH AVENUES

As a new frontier in customer management, research on customer engagement is in the beginning stages. In this young and intriguing research field there are ample opportunities for future research. Some of the most fundamental research questions, in particular with respect to the nomological network of customer engagement, and questions that are of particular interest for service firms are as follows:

- What are the drivers of customer engagement?
  - Intuitive drivers are for instance customer satisfaction, customer involvement, and customer loyalty, yet are there also additional drivers beyond these well-established constructs in customer management?
  - Are there unique drivers for engagement with service firms as compared to engagement with product firms? For instance, which roles do frontline employees play in shaping customer engagement? What is the impact of new service technologies?

- What are the outcomes of customer engagement for multiple stakeholders?
  - For employees: What is the interplay between customer engagement and employee engagement? How does customer engagement impact employees' job satisfaction, job performance, and job stressors?

    These outcomes for employees might be particularly relevant for service firms, due to the simultaneity of production and consumption in service settings, which makes engagement more likely to happen at the point of purchase.

- For companies: What impact does customer engagement have on brands, sales, revenues, and company value?
- For shareholders: What is the financial value of customer engagement?
- For customers: How does customer engagement impact customer satisfaction, customer loyalty, and customer purchasing behavior?
- For competition: How does engagement with firm X impact firm Y? For instance, Mayzlin and Yoganarasimhan (2012) investigate the much-observed phenomenon that blogs often link to other competing blogs.
- For society at large: Which social changes are induced by the blurring of the boundary between firms and customers due to customer engagement (behaviors)?

- How to measure these potential outcomes? For example, which data, which metrics, which methods to use?
  - How to measure the value to the firm of customer engagement in online social networks, such as likes, shares, re-tweets and so on?
  - How to assess potential cost reductions associated with value-generating activities of customer through their engagement behaviors? For example, by how much can firms reduce their advertising budget by using word-of-mouth campaigns?
  - How to determine reward incentives in customer networks?

- What are moderators of the effectiveness of customer engagement?
  - Is customer engagement suitable for every company? Are there differences in engagement outcomes for service firms compared to product firms? What is the role of the servicescape?
  - Which customers are likely to be engaged and the engagement of which customers is beneficial for service firms? For instance, what is the influence of a customer's interaction with employees, a customer's usage experience, and a customer's product knowledge?

- How does customer engagement evolve over time; that is, what are the dynamics of customer engagement?
  - Are online and off-line engagement complements or substitutes?
  - What is the lifecycle of customer engagement? For example, does complaint behavior typically start online and then turn into offline complaint behavior, or does it work the other way around?

Overall, we believe that the new frontier of customer engagement is very relevant for the development of customer management research in particular, while it also will impact service research and marketing research. We hope that this chapter will further stimulate research on this important topic.

NOTE

1. It is not our aim to provide an extensive overview of this research stream, as multiple overviews have been written on CVM, CLV, CRM, and multi-channel customer management. We refer to these reviews for an extensive overview of the field (for example, Blattberg et al. 2009; Kumar et al. 2006; Neslin and Shankar 2009; Verhoef and Lemon 2013).

REFERENCES

Ackland, Robert (2009), "Social network services as data sources and platforms for e-researching social networks", *Social Science Computer Review*, **27** (4), 481–92.

Baldwin, Clare (2011), "LinkedIn Ups IPO range, stokes social media frenzy," accessed 28 October 2011, at www.reuters.com/article/2011/05/17/us-linkedin-idUSTRE74G2GS20110517?feedType=RSS&feedName=internetNews.

Band, William (2010), "The Forrester Wave™: CRM suites for large organizations, Q2 2010," accessed 21 January 2013, at http://crmdynamics.blob.core.windows.net/xps-docs/06-16-10SuitesLarge.pdf.

Bass, Frank M. (1969), "New Product growth for model consumer durables," *Management Science*, **15** (5), 215–27.

Becker, Jan U., Goetz Greve and Sönke Albers (2009), "The impact of technological and organizational implementation of CRM on customer acquisition, maintenance, and retention," *International Journal of Research in Marketing*, **26** (3), 207–15.

Beckers, Sander F.M., Jenny van Doorn and Peter C. Verhoef (2012), "Outsourcing value creation to customers: when should companies stimulate customer engagement behaviors?," working paper, University of Groningen.

Bell, David R. and Sangyoung Song (2007), "Neighborhood effects and trial on the Internet: evidence from online grocery retailing," *Quantitative Marketing and Economics*, **5** (4), 361–400.

Bertrand, Marianne and Sendhil Mullainathan (2001), "Do people mean what they say? Implications for subjective survey data," *The American Economic Review*, **91** (2), 67–72.

Bijmolt, Tammo H.A., Peter S.H. Leeflang, Frank Block, Maik Eisenbeiss, Bruce G.S. Hardie, Aurélie Lemmens and Peter Staffert (2010), "Analytics for customer engagement," *Journal of Service Research*, **13** (3), 341–56.

Blattberg, Robert C., Gary Getz and Jacquelyn S. Thomas (2001), *Customer Equity: Building and Managing Relationships as Valuable Assets*, Boston, MA: Harvard Business School Press.

Blattberg, Robert C., Edward C. Malthouse and Scott A. Neslin (2009), "Customer lifetime value: empirical generalizations and some conceptual questions," *Journal of Interactive Marketing*, **23** (2), 157–68.

Bolton, Ruth N. (2011), "Customer engagement: opportunities and challenges for organizations," *Journal of Service Research*, **14** (3), 272–4.

Bolton, Ruth N., Katherine N. Lemon and Peter C. Verhoef (2004), "The theoretical underpinnings of customer asset management: a framework and propositions for future research," *Journal of the Academy of Marketing Science*, **32** (3), 271–92.

Brodie, Roderick J., Linda D. Hollebeek, Biljana Jurić and Ana Ilić (2011), "Customer engagement: conceptual domain, fundamental propositions, and implications for research," *Journal of Service Research*, **14** (3), 252–71.

Burroughs, James E., Darren W. Dahl, C. Page Moreau, Amitava Chattopadhyay and Gerald J. Gorn (2011), "Facilitating and rewarding creativity during new product development," *Journal of Marketing*, **75** (4), 53–67.

Childers, Terry L. (1986), "Assessment of the psychometric properties of an opinion leadership scale," *Journal of Marketing Research*, **23** (2), 184–8.

Choi, Jeonghye, Sam K. Hui and David R. Bell (2010), "Spatiotemporal analysis of imitation behavior across new buyers at an online grocery retailer," *Journal of Marketing Research*, **47** (1), 75–89.

Chung, Tuck Siong, Roland T. Rust and Michel Wedel (2009), "My mobile music: an adaptive personalization system for digital audio players," *Marketing Science*, **28** (1), 52–68.

Darden, William R. and Fred D. Reynolds (1971), "Shopping orientations and product usage rates," *Journal of Marketing Research*, **8** (4), 505–508.

Davenport, Thomas H. (2012), "Can you live without a data scientist?," *Harvard Business Review Blog Network*, at http://blogs.hbr.org/cs/2012/09/can_you_live_without_a_data_sc.html.

De Matos, Celso Augusto, Jorge Luiz Henrique and Carlos Alberto Vargas Rossi (2007), "Service recovery paradox: a meta-analysis," *Journal of Service Research*, **10** (1), 60–77.

Donkers, Bas, Peter C. Verhoef and Martijn G. de Jong (2007), "Modeling CLV: a test of competing models in the insurance industry," *Quantitative Marketing and Economics*, **5** (2), 163–90.

Dorotic, Matilda, Tammo H.A. Bijmolt and Peter C. Verhoef (2012), "Loyalty programmes: current knowledge and research directions," *International Journal of Management Reviews*, **14** (3), 217–37.

Dwyer, F. Robert, Paul H. Schurr and Sejo Oh (1987), "Developing buyer-seller relationships," *Journal of Marketing*, **51** (2), 11–27.

Eagle, Nathan, Alex S. Pentland and David Lazer (2009), "Inferring friendship network structure by using mobile phone data," *Proceedings of the National Academy of Sciences*, **106** (36), 15274–8.

eMarketer (2012), "Total worldwide social network ad revenues continue strong growth," accessed 7 July 2012, at www.emarketer.com/Articles/Print.aspx?R=1008862.

Fournier, Susan (1998), "Consumers and their brands: developing relationship theory in consumer research," *Journal of Consumer Research*, **24** (4), 343–53.

Godes, David and Dina Mayzlin (2004), "Using online conversations to study word-of-mouth communication," *Marketing Science*, **23** (4), 545–60.

Godes, David and Dina Mayzlin (2009), "Firm-created word-of-mouth communication: evidence from a field test," *Marketing Science*, **28** (4), 721–39.

Godes, David, Dina Mayzlin, Yubo Chen, Sanjiv Das, Chrysanthos Dellarocas, Bruce Pfeiffer, Barak Libai, Subrata Sen, Mengze Shi and Peeter Verlegh (2005), "The firm's management of social interactions," *Marketing Letters*, **16** (3), 415–28.

Goldenberg, Jacob, Sangman Han, Donald R. Lehmann, Janghyuk Lee and Kyung Young Ohk (2010), "Local neighborhoods as early predictors of innovation adoption," MSI working paper.

Goldenberg, Jacob, Barak Libai, Sarit Moldovan and Eithan Muller (2007), "The NPV of bad news," *International Journal of Research in Marketing*, **24** (3), 186–200.

Graig, Susanne and Andrew R. Sorkin (2011), "Goldman offering clients a chance to invest in Facebook," accessed 28 October 2011, at http://dealbook.nytimes.com/2011/01/02/goldman-invests-in-facebook-at-50-billion-valuation/.

Gupta, Sunil, Donald R. Lehmann and Jennifer Ames Stuart (2004), "Valuing customers," *Journal of Marketing Research*, **41** (1), 7–18.

Haenlein, Michael (2011), "A social network analysis of customer-level revenue distribution," *Marketing Letters*, **22** (1), 15–29.
Haythornthwaite, Caroline (2005), "Social networks and internet connectivity effects," *Information, Communication & Society*, **8** (2), 125–47.
Hill, Shawndra, Foster Provost and Chris Volinsky (2006), "Network-based marketing: identifying likely adopters via consumer networks," *Statistical Science*, **21** (2), 256–76.
Hinz, Oliver, Bernd Skiera, Christian Barrot and Jan U. Becker (2011), "Seeding strategies for viral marketing: an empirical comparison," *Journal of Marketing*, **75** (6), 55–71.
Hirschman, Albert O. (1970), *Exit, Voice, and Loyalty: Responses to Decline in Firms, Organizations, and States*, Cambridge, MA: Harvard University Press.
Hoekstra, Janny C. and Eelko K.R.E. Huizingh (1999), "The lifetime value concept in customer-based marketing," *Journal of Market-Focused Management*, **3** (3), 257–74.
Hoffman, Donna L., Praveen K. Kopalle and Thomas P. Novak (2010), "The right' consumers for better concepts: identifying and using consumers high in emergent nature to further develop new product concepts," *Journal of Marketing Research*, **47** (5), 854–65.
Hollebeek, Linda (2011a), "Demystifying customer brand engagement: exploring the loyalty nexus," *Journal of Marketing Management*, **27** (7–8), 785–807.
Hollebeek, Linda (2011b), "Exploring customer brand engagement: definition & themes," *Journal of Strategic Marketing*, **19** (7), 555–73.
Hoyer, Wayne D., Rajesh Chandy, Matilda Dorotic, Manfred Krafft and Siddarth S. Sing (2010), "Consumer co-creation in new product development," *Journal of Service Research*, **13** (3), 283–96.
IBM (2011), *From Stretched to Strengthened: Insights from the Global Chief Marketing Officer Study*, Somers, NY: IBM Global Business Services.
Iyengar, Raghuram, Christophe Van den Bulte and Jeonghye Choi (2011), "Distinguishing among multiple mechanisms of social contagion: social learning versus normative legitimation in new product adoption," working paper, The Wharton School, University of Pennsylvania.
Iyengar, Raghuram, Christophe Van den Bulte and Thomas W. Valente (2011), "Rejoinder--further reflections on studying social influence in new product diffusion," *Marketing Science*, **30** (2), 230–32.
Jayachandran, Satish and Rajan Varadarajan (2006), "Does success diminish competitive responsiveness? Reconciling conflicting perspectives," *Journal of the Academy of Marketing Science*, **34** (3), 284–94.
Katona, Zsolt, Peter P. Zubcsek and Miklos Sarvary (2011), "Network effects and personal influences: the diffusion of an online social network," *Journal of Marketing Research*, **48** (3), 425–43.
King, Charles W. and John O. Summers (1970), "Overlap of opinion leadership across consumer product categories," *Journal of Marketing Research*, **7** (1), 43–50.
Kumar, V., Lerzan Aksoy, Bas Donkers, Rajkumar Venkatesan, Thorsten Wiesel and Sebastian Tillmanns (2010), "Undervalued or overvalued customers: capturing total customer engagement value," *Journal of Service Research*, **13** (3), 297–310.
Kumar, V., Katherine N. Lemon and A. Parasuraman (2006), "Managing customers for value: an overview and research agenda," *Journal of Service Research*, **9** (2), 87–94.
Kumar, V., J.A. Petersen and Robert P. Leone (2010), "Driving profitability by encouraging customer referrals: who, when, and how," *Journal of Marketing*, **74** (5), 1–17.
Kumar, V. and Denish Shah (2009), "Expanding the role of marketing: from customer equity to market capitalization," *Journal of Marketing*, **73** (6), 119–36.
Kumar, V. and Rajkumar Venkatesan (2005), "Who are the multichannel shoppers and how do they perform? Correlates of Multichannel shopping behavior," *Journal of Interactive Marketing*, **19** (2), 44–62.
Kunz, Werner and Jens Hogreve (2011), "Toward a deeper understanding of services marketing: the past, the present, and the future," *International Journal of Research in Marketing*, **28** (3), 231–47.

Leeflang, Peter S.H. (2011), "Paving the way for 'distinguished marketing'," *International Journal of Research in Marketing*, **28** (2), 76–88.
Lehmann, Donald R. (2004), "Metrics for making marketing matter," *Journal of Marketing*, **68** (4), 73–5.
Leskovec, Jure, Lada A. Adamic and Bernardo A. Huberman (2007), "The dynamics of viral marketing," *ACM Transactions on the Web*, **1** (1), 228–37.
Lewis, Kevin, Jason Kaufman, Marco Gonzalez, Andreas Wimmer and Nicholas Christakis (2008), "Tastes, ties, and time: a new social network dataset using Facebook.com," *Social Networks*, **30** (4), 330–42.
Lhoest-Snoeck, Sietske M.J. (2012), "Customer value models in the energy market: understanding the role of acquisition and retention effects," doctoral dissertation, Department of Marketing, University of Groningen.
Libai, Barak (2011), "Comment: the perils of focusing on highly engaged customers," *Journal of Service Research*, **14** (3), 275–6.
Libai, Barak, Ruth N. Bolton, Marnix S. Bügel, Ko De Ruyter, Oliver Götz, Hans Risselada and Andrew T. Stephen (2010), "Customer to customer interactions: broadening the scope of word of mouth research," *Journal of Service Research*, **13** (3), 267–82.
Libai, Barak, Eitan Muller and Renana Peres (forthcoming), "Decomposing the value of word of mouth seeding programs: acceleration vs. expansion," *Journal of Marketing Research*.
Lyons, Barbara and Kenneth Henderson (2005), "Opinion leadership in a computer-mediated environment," *Journal of Consumer Behaviour*, **4** (5), 319–29.
Marketing Science Institute (2010), *2010–2012 Research Priorities*, Boston, MA: Marketing Science Institute.
Mayzlin, Dina and Hema Yoganarasimhan (2012), "Link to success: how blogs build an audience by promoting rivals," *Management Science*, **58** (9), 1651–68.
Morgan, Robert M. and Shelby D. Hunt (1994), "The commitment-trust theory of relationship marketing," *Journal of Marketing*, **58** (3), 20–38.
Nam, Sungjoon, Puneet Manchanda and Pradeep K. Chintagunta (2010), "The effect of signal quality and contiguous word of mouth on customer acquisition for a video-on-demand service," *Marketing Science*, **29** (4), 690–700.
Neslin, Scott A., Dhruv Grewal, Robert Leghorn, Venkatesh Shankar, Marije L. Teerling, Jacquelyn S. Thomas and Peter C. Verhoef (2006), "Challenges and opportunities in multichannel customer management," *Journal of Service Marketing*, **9** (2), 95–112.
Neslin, Scott A. and Venkatesh Shankar (2009), "Key issues in multichannel customer management: current knowledge and future directions," *Journal of Interactive Marketing*, **23** (1), 70–81.
Nitzan, Irit and Barak Libai (2011), "Social effects on customer retention," *Journal of Marketing*, **75** (6), 24–38.
Ostrom, Amy L., Mary Jo Bitner, Stephen W. Brown, Kevin A. Burkhard, Michael Goul, Vicki Smith-Daniels, Haluk Demirkan and Elliot Rabinovich (2010), "Moving forward and making a difference: research priorities for the science of service," *Journal of Service Research*, **13** (1), 4–36.
Patterson, Paul, Ting Yu and Ko De Ruyter (2006), "Understanding customer engagement in services," *Proceedings of ANZMAC 2006 Conference: Advancing Theory, Maintaining Relevance*, Brisbane, 4–6 December.
Payne, Adrian and Pennie Frow (2005), "A strategic framework for customer relationship management," *Journal of Marketing*, **69** (4), 167–76.
Petersen, J. Andrew and V. Kumar (2009), "Are product returns a necessary evil? Antecedents and consequences," *Journal of Marketing*, **73** (3), 35–51.
Porter, Constance Elise, Naveen Donthu, William H. MacElroy and Donna Wydra (2011), "How to foster and sustain engagement in virtual communities," *California Management Review*, **53** (4), 80–110.
Prahalad, C.K. (2004), "The cocreation of value," *Journal of Marketing*, **68** (1), 23.
Reichheld, Frederick F. (2003), "The one number you need to grow," *Harvard Business Review*, **81** (12), 46–55.

Reinartz, Werner, Manfred Krafft and Wayne D. Hoyer (2004), "The customer relationship management process: its measurement and impact on performance," *Journal of Marketing Research*, **41** (3), 293–305.
Richins, Marsha L. and Teri Root-Shaffer (1988), "The role of evolvement and opinion leadership in consumer word-of-mouth: an implicit model made explicit," *Advances in Consumer Research*, **15** (1), 32–6.
Rust, Roland T. and Ming-Hui Huang (2012), "Service marketing: insights and directions," *Fast Forward Series*, Boston, MA: Marketing Science Institute.
Rust, Roland T., V. Kumar and Rajkumar Venkatesan (2011), "Will the frog change into a prince? Predicting future customer profitability," *International Journal of Research in Marketing*, **28** (4), 281–94.
Rust, Roland T., Katherine N. Lemon and Valarie A. Zeithaml (2004), "Return on marketing: using customer equity to focus marketing strategy," *Journal of Marketing*, **68** (1), 109–27.
Rust, Roland T., Christine Moorman and Gaurav Bhalla (2010), "Rethinking marketing," *Harvard Business Review*, **88** (1–2), 94–101.
Rust, Roland T., Valarie A. Zeithaml and Katherine N. Lemon (2000), *Driving Customer Equity: How Customer Lifetime Value is Reshaping Corporate Strategy*, New York: The Free Press.
Sawhney, Mohanbir and Emanuela Prandelli (2000), "Communities of creation: managing distributed innovation in turbulent markets," *California Management Review*, **42** (4), 24–54.
Schmitt, Philipp, Bernd Skiera and Christophe Van den Bulte (2011), "Referral programs and customer value," *Journal of Marketing*, **75** (1), 46–59.
Shah, Denish, Roland T. Rust, A. Parasuraman, Richard Staelin and George S. Day (2006), "The path to customer centricity," *Journal of Service Research*, **9** (2), 113–24.
Smith, Amy K., Ruth N. Bolton and Janet Wagner (1999), "A model of customer satisfaction with service encounters involving failure and recovery," *Journal of Marketing Research*, **36** (3), 356–72.
So, Kevin Kam Fung, Ceridwyn King and Beverley Sparks (forthcoming), "Customer engagement with tourism brands: scale development and validation," *Journal of Hospitality and Tourism Research*.
Stephen, Andrew T. and Jeff Galak (2010), "The complementary roles of traditional and social media in driving marketing performance," working paper, INSEAD.
Trusov, Michael, Anand V. Bodapati and Randolph E. Bucklin (2010), "Determining influential users in Internet social networks," *Journal of Marketing Research*, 47 (4), 643–58.
Trusov, Michael, Randolph E. Bucklin and Koen H. Pauwels (2009), "Effects of word-of-mouth versus traditional marketing: findings from an Internet Social networking site," *Journal of Marketing*, **73** (5), 90–102.
Van den Bulte, Christophe (2010), "Opportunities and challenges in studying customer networks," in S. Wuyts, M.G. Dekimpe, E. Gijsbrechts and R. Pieters (eds), *The Connected Customer: The Changing Nature of Consumer and Business Markets*, London: Routledge, pp. 7–35.
Van den Bulte, Christophe and Stefan Wuyts (2007), *Social Networks and Marketing*, Cambridge, MA: Marketing Science Institute.
Van Doorn, Jenny (2011), "Comment: customer engagement: essence, dimensionality, and boundaries," *Journal of Service Research*, **14** (3), 280–82.
Van Doorn, Jenny, Katherine N. Lemon, Vikas Mittal, Stephan Nass, Doreén Pick, Peter Pirner and Peter C. Verhoef (2010), "Customer engagement behavior: theoretical foundations and research directions," *Journal of Service Research*, **13** (3), 253–66.
Van Eck, Peter S., Wander Jager and Peter S.H. Leeflang (2011), "Opinion leaders' role in innovation diffusion: a simulation study," *Journal of Product Innovation Management*, **28** (2), 187–203.
Van Noort, Guda and Lotte M. Willemsen (2012), "Online damage control: the effects of proactive versus reactive webcare interventions in consumer-generated and brand-generated platforms," *Journal of Interactive Marketing*, **26** (3), 131–40.

Van Oest, Rutger and George Knox (2011), "Extending the BG/NBD: a simple model of purchases and complaints," *International Journal of Research in Marketing*, **28** (1), 30–37.
Vargo, Stephen L. and Robert F. Lusch (2004), "Evolving to a new dominant logic for marketing," *Journal of Marketing*, **68** (1), 1–17.
Venkatesan, Rajkumar and V. Kumar (2004), "A customer lifetime value framework for customer selection and resource allocation strategy," *Journal of Marketing*, **68** (4), 106–25.
Venkatesan, Rajkumar, V. Kumar and Nalini Ravishanker (2007), "Multichannel shopping: causes and consequences," *Journal of Marketing*, **71** (2), 114–32.
Verhoef, Peter C. and Katherine N. Lemon (2013), "Successful customer value management: key lessons and emerging trends," *European Management Journal*, **31** (1), 1–15.
Verhoef, Peter C., Werner J. Reinartz and Manfred Krafft (2010), "Customer engagement as a new perspective in customer management," *Journal of Service Research*, **13** (3), 247–52.
Verhoef, Peter C., Jenny van Doorn and Matilda Dorotic (2007), "Customer value management: an overview and research agenda," *Marketing: Journal of Research and Management*, **3** (2), 105–20.
Verhoef, Peter C., Rajkumar Venkatesan, Leigh McAlister, Edward C. Malthouse, Manfred Krafft and Shankar Ganesan (2010), "CRM in data-rich multichannel retailing environments: a review and future research directions," *Journal of Interactive Marketing*, **24** (2), 121–37.
Wasserman, Stanley and Katherine Faust (1994), *Social Network Analysis: Methods and Applications*, Cambridge: Cambridge University Press.
Wiesel, Thorsten, Bernd Skiera and Julian Villanueva (2008), "Customer equity: an integral part of financial reporting," *Journal of Marketing*, **72** (2), 1–14.

PART III

CUSTOMER-CENTERED METRICS

7 Customer-based valuation: similarities and differences to traditional discounted cash flow models

Bernd Skiera and Christian Schulze

INTRODUCTION

Customer-based valuation uses information about the customer base (for example, number of customers, contribution margin per customer, retention rate) to determine the value of the firm. It thus relies on core metrics of marketing to determine a core metric of finance and accounting (equity value, also often referred to as market capitalization) and thus helps to bridge the current gap between accounting and finance on the one side and marketing on the other side.

The customer-based valuation approach has become very popular among researchers in marketing (Kumar and Shah 2009; Rust et al. 2004; Schulze et al. 2012; including the 2005 JMR Paul Green Award for the pioneering paper by Gupta et al. 2004) and the underlying idea of determining customer equity is used for reporting purposes as well (Kumar and George 2007; Skiera et al. 2011; Villanueva and Hanssens 2007; Wiesel et al. 2008). In finance and accounting, however, its popularity is much lower (Persson and Ryals 2010), which might stem from the fact that the differences between the traditional discounted cash flow approach and the customer-based valuation approach have not been examined in detail. Therefore, the aim of this chapter is to examine similarities and differences of both approaches in detail and to highlight under which circumstances the two approaches are likely to lead to substantial differences.

The remainder of the chapter is organized as follows. First, we describe the basic procedure of customer-based valuation in ten simple steps and then apply this approach in a simple numerical example. Second, we detail the key conceptual difference between customer-based valuation and the traditional discounted cash flow approach: the cohort-based view. Finally, we illustrate the advantages of the customer-based valuation approach over traditional discounted cash flow models in determining the value of high-growth firms with customer relationships that span several periods.

BASIC IDEA OF CUSTOMER-BASED VALUATION

Steps to Take in Customer-based Valuation

The essential idea of customer-based valuation is to take the following steps:

1. Estimate the average long-term value of one of the firm's current customers, that is estimate customer lifetime value (CLV) for the average current customer.
2. Multiply this value by the number of current customers to get "Customer Equity of current customers."
3. Estimate the average long-term value of one of the firm's future customers (that is, customers not yet acquired but expected for the future) including the costs for acquiring this future customer. The result is the customer lifetime value of a future customer.
4. Estimate the expected number of future customers.
5. Multiply the number of future customers by their average CLV and discount future cash flows appropriately to get "Customer Equity of future customers."
6. Add "Customer Equity of current customers" to "Customer Equity of future customers" to derive "Customer Equity before fixed cost."
7. Calculate the long-term value of fixed cost.
8. The difference between "Customer Equity before fixed cost" and the long-term value of fixed costs is "Customer Equity after fixed cost."
9. Add non-operating assets to "Customer Equity after fixed cost" to get firm value.
10. Subtract debt from firm value to calculate the equity value of the firm (also called shareholder value or market capitalization for publicly traded firms).

Setup of Illustrative Numerical Example

To illustrate the benefits of customer-based valuation, we use a simple numerical example. Assume the following situation: A firm with contractual customer relationships has carried over 50 existing customers from the previous year and will acquire 20 new customers in each of the following years. The acquisition of each new customer costs \$30, retaining each customer costs \$20 (also in the year of acquisition), revenue per customer and year is \$200 and the profit margin 50 percent. Consequently, the profit contribution per customer before retention cost is \$100. The average retention rate per customer is 80 percent, the firm's discount rate is 10 percent

Table 7.1 Setup of numerical example

Variable	Value
Number of current customers	50
Number of new customers per period	20
Revenues per customer and period	\$200
Profit margin	50%
Profit contribution per customer and period	\$100
Fixed cost	\$5,000
Retention rate	80%
Retention cost	\$20
Acquisition cost	\$30
Discount rate	10%
Nonoperating asset	\$0
Debt	\$10,000
Tax rate	0%

and all revenues and costs occur at the beginning of each year. Fixed costs are \$5,000 per year and the firm has debt of \$10,000. We neglect taxes for this illustrative example. We assume that all revenues and costs are cashed in immediately so that revenues equal cash inflows and costs equal cash outflows and summarize all values in Table 7.1. What is the value of this firm?

Results of Numerical Example

Following the ten steps presented above, we now calculate the value of the firm using the customer-based valuation approach. In our numerical example, the customer lifetime value before and after acquisition cost is easy to calculate as (see, for example, Schulze et al. 2012):

$$CLV_{current} = (m - c_{ret}) \cdot \frac{1 + d}{1 + d - r} = (\$100 - \$20) \cdot \frac{1 + 10\%}{1 + 10\% - 80\%}$$

$$= \$80 \cdot 3.67 = \$293 \qquad (7.1)$$

$$CLV_{future} = (m - c_{ret}) \cdot \frac{1 + d}{1 + d - r} - c_{acq} = \$293 - \$30 = \$263 \qquad (7.2)$$

where

c_{acq}: acquisition cost per customer,
c_{ret}: retention cost per customer and year,

Table 7.2 Results for the numerical example

Customer equity before fixed cost	\$72,600
Customer equity of current customers	\$14.667
Customer equity of future customers	\$57.933
– NPV of fixed cost in all periods	\$55,000
= Customer equity after fixed cost	\$17,600
– Debt	\$10,000
+ Nonoperating assets	\$0
= Shareholder value	\$7,600

$CLV_{current}$: customer lifetime value of current customers,
CLV_{future}: customer lifetime value of future customers, including their acquisition cost,
d: discount rate,
m: profit contribution per customer and year (before marketing costs),
r: retention rate.

Table 7.2 presents the results for the numerical example. It builds upon a well-known concept in finance called "terminal value," which is here the present value after year 2 of all future revenues and costs. In case of stable revenues and costs, the terminal value is easy to calculate as:

$$TV_{without\ current\ year} = N_{future} \cdot \frac{CLV_{future}}{d} \tag{7.3}$$

if it does not include the current year or as:

$$TV_{with\ current\ year} = N_{future} \cdot \frac{CLV_{future} \cdot (1 + d)}{d} \tag{7.4}$$

if it includes the current year.

The results displayed in Table 7.2 indicate that the net present value of the profit contribution realized in all periods with all customers, that is, customer equity before fixed cost, equals \$72,600. Customer equity of current customers is simply the product of the number of current customers times their customer lifetime value (50 · \$293.33 = \$14,667). Equation (7.4) can be used to calculate customer equity of all future customers (20 · \$263.33 · 1.1 / 0.1 = \$57,933). Similarly, the net present value of fixed cost in all periods is \$5,000 · 1.1 / 0.1 = \$55,000. The difference between customer equity before fixed cost and fixed cost is \$17,600. Subtracting debt yields the equity value of the firm, here called market capitalization of \$7,600. The ratio of customer equity of future customers to customer equity of current customers in this example is 1:4. According to our experience, this ratio is a typical one and rarely exceeds 1:2.5.

Figure 7.1 graphically summarizes the results and illustrates the importance of future profits. Future profits are reflected in the value of all future customers (that is, customer equity of future customers) and the future value of all current customers, that is, the difference between the customer equity of current customers and their current profit contribution). Thus, much of the future profit will be realized with customers that still need to be acquired.

DIFFERENCE TO TRADITIONAL DISCOUNTED CASH FLOW MODEL

All customer-based valuation models use the concept of calculating present values, a characteristic they share with discounted cash flow (DCF) models currently used for firm valuation in accounting and finance (for example, Brealey et al. 2008; Damodaran 2001). The main difference between a model of customer-based valuation and a traditional discounted cash flow model is the different source for the revenues and costs. In almost any traditional discounted cash flow model, the analyst estimates the free cash flow to the firm in each period. Thus, the period is the cash-generating source (see the horizontal arrow at the bottom of Figure 7.2). In contrast, in customer-based valuation customers are the source for all revenues and all costs except the fixed cost (see the vertical arrow on the right-hand side of Figure 7.2). The sum of these present values (labeled "Total present value" in Figure 7.2) is identical for both approaches.

Figure 7.3 displays the development of the present value of all profit contributions per cohort (that is, the profit contributions in different periods of one cohort). The value of the cohort of current customers is highest, which is not surprising as it summarizes all customers that were ever acquired and did not churn. The difference between the values of all other cohorts that all contain 20 new customers is then simply the difference in present value. The terminal value is high and captures 9.8 percent of the present value of total profit contribution. It reflects the importance of capturing the remaining value after the detailed planning horizon, here 22 periods.

Figure 7.4 presents the present value of all profit contributions per period (that is, the profit contributions of several cohorts that are all realized in one period). It indicates that the present value of profit contribution

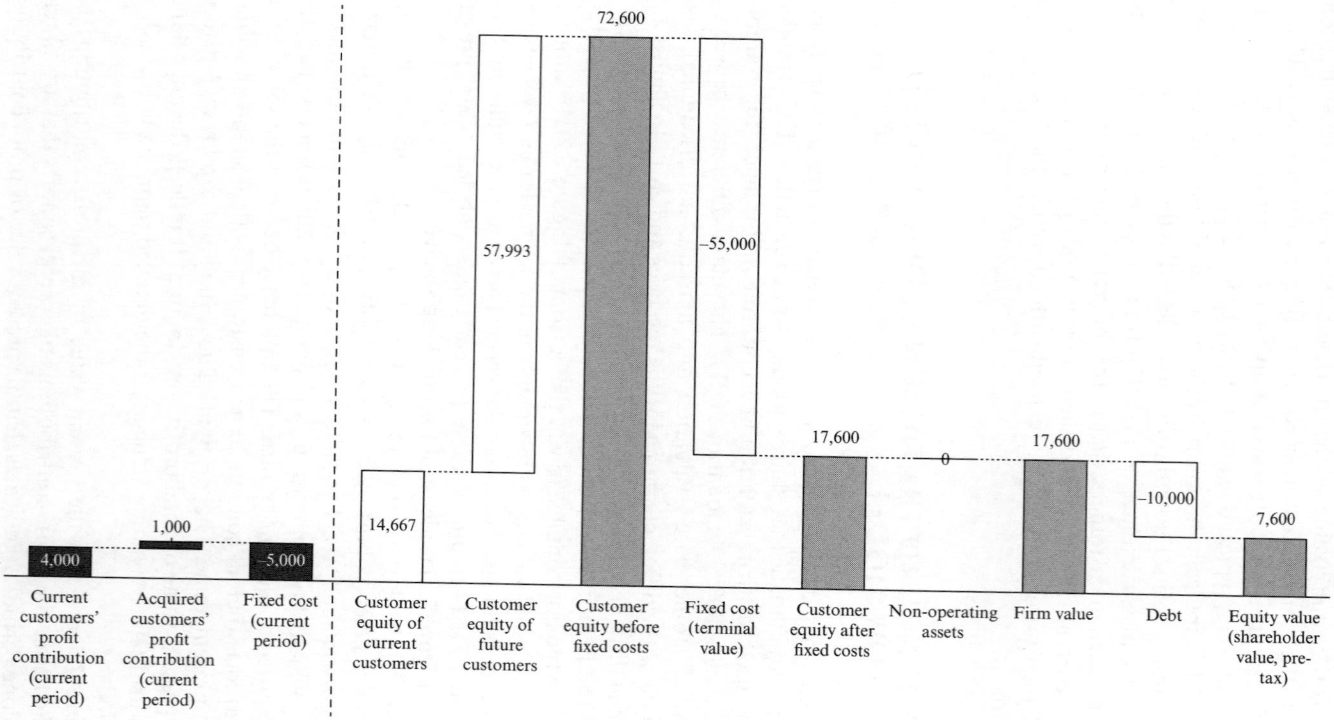

Figure 7.1 Distribution of value across components of shareholder value

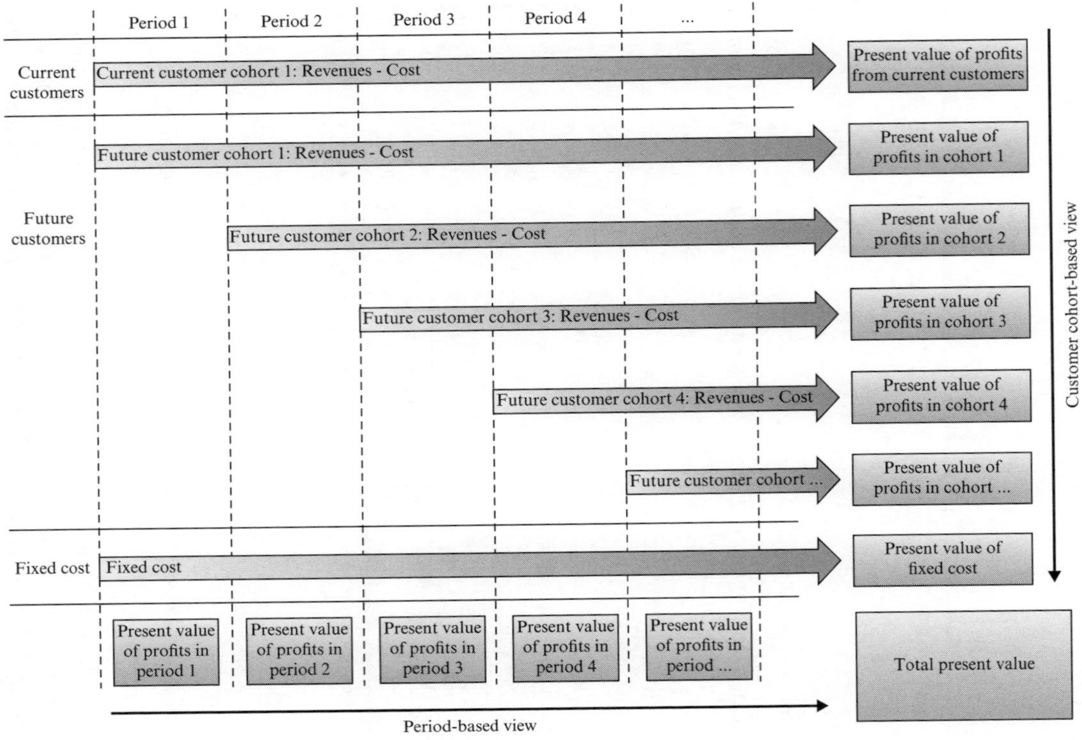

Figure 7.2 Difference between cohort-based and period-based valuation models

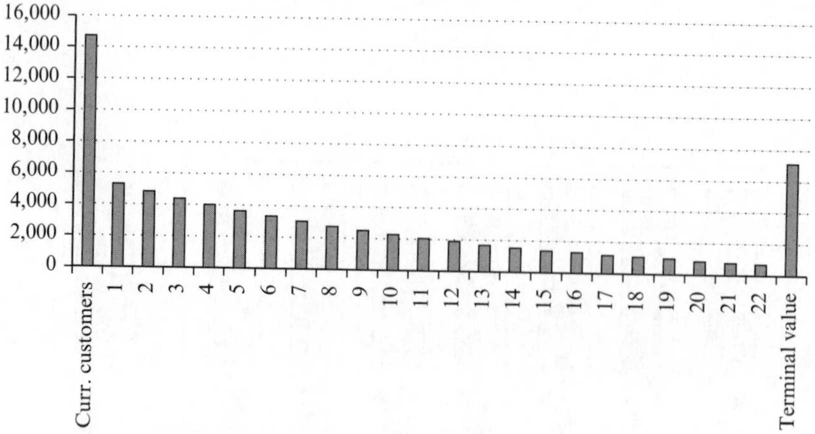

Figure 7.3 *Development of present value of profit contribution per cohort in numerical example*

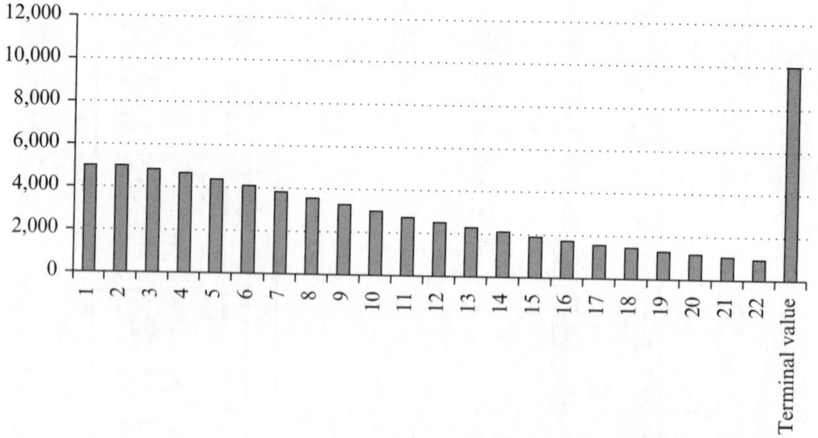

Figure 7.4 *Development of present value of profit per period over time in numerical example*

per period diminishes over time, which reflects the stronger discounting of future periods. The terminal value is twice as high as the present value of profit contribution in the first period and covers 13.8 percent of the present value of total profit contribution.

Figure 7.5 presents the (undiscounted) profit contributions per period. They are actually increasing, although at a decreasing rate that reflects that the maximum number of customers is 100 (= 20/(1 – 0.8)). Figure

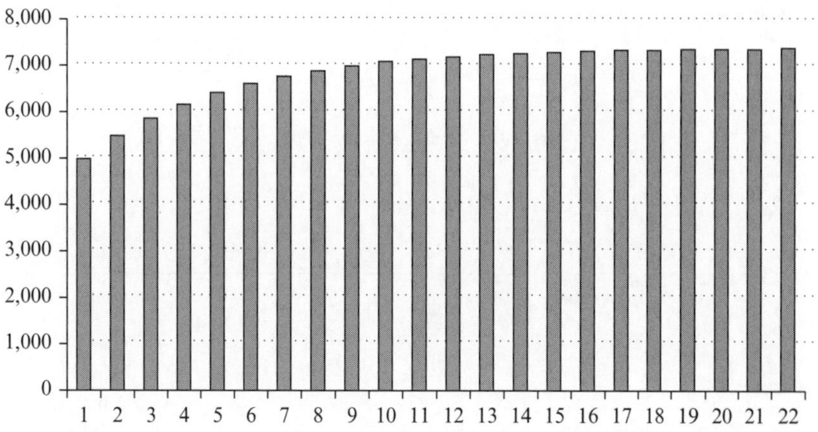

Figure 7.5 Development of profit per period over time in numerical example

7.5 also outlines that it is rather easy to project the profit contribution per period over time in our example, which might explain the popularity of this approach.

ADVANTAGES OF CUSTOMER-BASED VALUATION FOR VALUING HIGH-GROWTH FIRMS

The main difference between traditional discounted cash flow models and the customer-based valuation approach lies in the treatment of cohorts of customers instead of periods as the origin of cash flows. Both approaches need to yield the same value of the firm, and the numerical example showed that the prediction of profit contribution per period is relatively easy if the firm is in a fairly stable situation. For growth firms, however, the prediction of the development of profit contributions per period is much more difficult. Consider another numerical example of four start-up firms for which Figure 7.6 displays their increasingly negative *and* almost identical profits in their first five years. All four firms share a typical high-growth pattern for young firms and sport exactly the same number of customers in all years (following the diffusion curve of the technology substitution model with number of customers (t) = 100,000 / (1 + exp(5 – t)), see also Schulze et al. 2012) and debts and nonoperating assets are both zero. The crucial question is: Which of these four firms is most valuable despite their equality in profits and number of customers?

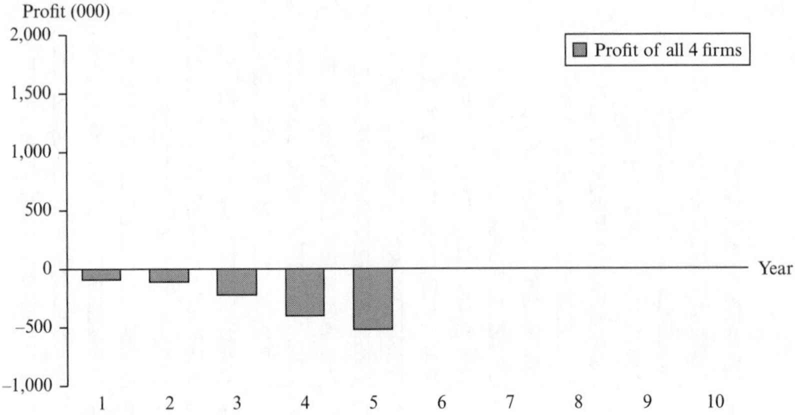

	Firm 1	Firm 2	Firm 3	Firm 4
Margin per customer	$60	$48	$43	$37
Acguisition cost per customer	$100	$80	$70	$60
Retention rate	56%	51%	47%	42%
Fixed cost	$17,500	$35,000	$47,500	$55,000
Discount rate	10%			
Number of customers	Number of customers(t) = 100,000 / (1+exp(5-t))			

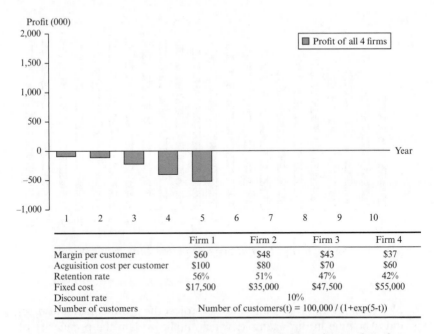

Figure 7.6 Identical profit from four high-growth firms during their first five years

A look at the firms' customer metrics in Figure 7.6 reveals that while bottom-line profits and customer development are identical, the firms differ in several important and easy to observe customer and financial metrics, namely, acquisition cost and yearly profit contributions per customer, retention rates, and yearly fixed cost. While those differences make it unlikely that the future development of all firms will be the same, the total effect of these differences is extremely difficult to eyeball.

The application of the customer-based valuation model of Schulze et al. 2012 to the four firms in Figure 7.6 shows that, despite their comparable profits and number of customers, the firms' customer equity before fixed cost differs substantially at the end of year five already (Figure 7.7). This gap widens even more when considering shareholder value.

Naturally, these large differences in customer equity are reflected in the firms' development in profits as shown in Figure 7.8. The application of customer-based valuation projects that, despite the increasingly negative profits until year 5, all firms will likely reverse this trend. The result is a so-called "hockey stick:" a prerequisite for positive firm values that is extremely difficult to predict with traditional discounted cash flow models. Additionally, the application of the customer-based valuation model

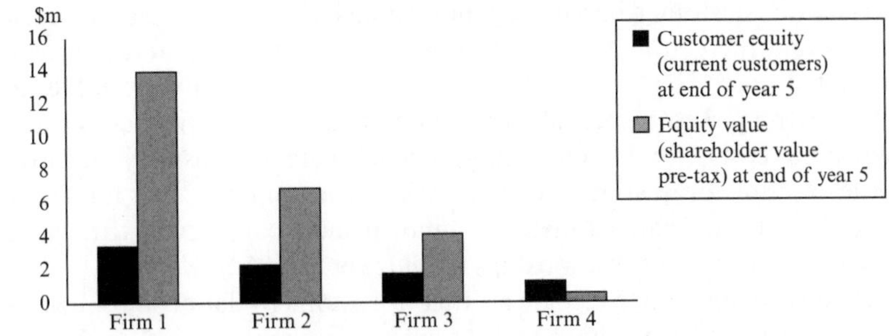

Figure 7.7 Customer equity and shareholder value for four high-growth firms

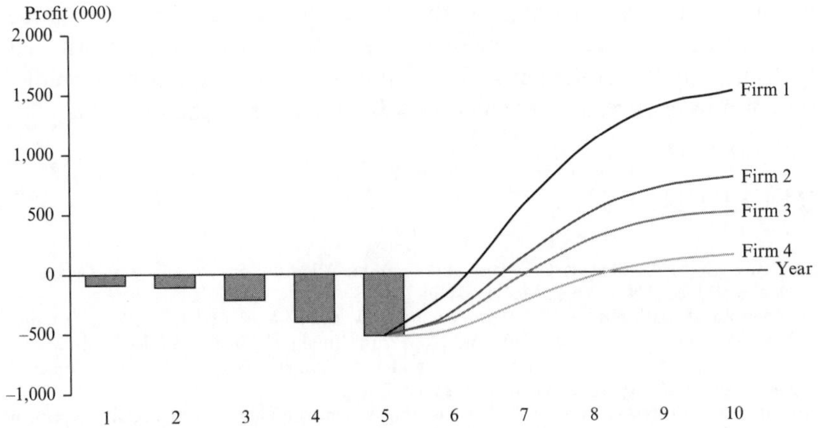

Figure 7.8 Profit development for four high-growth firms during first ten years

projects that, despite identical development until year 5, Firm A will generate more than $1.5 million in profits in year 10 while Firm D will barely run a profit in the same year.

Customer-based valuation models rely on the same basic principle of discounting future cash flows as traditional discounted cash flow models. However, through the additional use of customer metrics and a customer cohort-based view, they can better capture the connection between investments in one period and their returns at later points in time. This feature provides important insights about the value of current and future customers that cannot be inferred from periodic profits alone.

Moreover, customer-based valuation models lead to increased transparency and prediction accuracy in valuation scenarios where traditional discounted cash flow models have their shortcomings, for example, in high-growth markets (especially when combined with significant customer acquisition cost), for (often young) firms where increasingly negative profits require forecasting "hockey-stick" developments and for firms where short-term financial metrics cannot reliably capture the true value of long-term customer relationships (Schulze et al. 2012).

This distinction better recognizes that in customer relationships, investments in customer acquisition and the subsequent returns on the relationship rarely occur in the same time period. However, such investments and returns easily can be assigned to a customer cohort. Customer-based valuation also separately considers the impact of the number of acquired customers, the loyalty of these customers (via the retention rate), the investment required to acquire these customers (acquisition cost), the investments to retain these customers (retention cost) and the profit that each customer generates per period. This feature allows for an easy prediction of how changes in these metrics will influence shareholder value.

REFERENCES

Brealey, Richard A., Stewart C. Myers and Franklin Allen (2008), *Principles of Corporate Finance*, 9th edn, New York: McGraw-Hill.

Damodaran, Aswath (2001), *The Dark Side of Valuation. Valuing Old Tech, New Tech, and New Economy Companies*, London and New York: Financial Times, Prentice Hall.

Gupta, Sunil, Donald R. Lehmann and Jennifer A. Stuart (2004), "Valuing customers," *Journal of Marketing Research*, **41** (February), 7–18.

Kumar, V. and Morris George (2007), "Measuring and maximizing customer equity: a critical analysis," *Journal of the Academy of Marketing Science*, **35** (2), 157–71.

Kumar, V. and Denish Shah (2009), "Expanding the role of marketing: from customer equity to market capitalization," *Journal of Marketing*, **73** (November), 119–36.

Persson, Andreas and Lynette Ryals (2010), "Customer assets and customer equity: management and measurement issues," *Marketing Theory*, **10** (4), 417–36.

Rust, Roland T., Katherine N. Lemon and Valarie A. Zeithaml (2004), "Return on marketing: using customer equity to focus marketing strategy," *Journal of Marketing*, **68** (January), 109–27.

Schulze, Christian, Bernd Skiera and Thorsten Wiesel (2012), "Linking customer and financial metrics to shareholder value: the leverage effect in customer-based valuation," *Journal of Marketing*, **76** (March), 17–32.

Skiera, Bernd, Manuel Bermes and Lutz Horn (2011), "Customer equity sustainability ratio: a new metric for assessing a firm's future orientation," *Journal of Marketing*, **75** (3), 118–31.

Villanueva, Julian and Dominique M. Hanssens (2007), *Customer Equity: Measurement Management and Research Opportunities*, Foundations and Trends in Marketing series, vol. 1, Hanover, MA: Now Publishers

Wiesel, Thorsten, Bernd Skiera and Julian Villanueva (2008), "Customer equity – an integral part of financial reporting," *Journal of Marketing*, **72** (March), 1–14.

8 CRM metrics and strategies to enhance performance in service industries

V. Kumar, Nita Umashankar and Jee Won (Brianna) Choi

INTRODUCTION

The importance of the service sector is undeniable. In fact, services now dominate, making up about 70 percent of the aggregate production and employment in the Organisation for Economic Co-operation and Development (OECD) nations and contributing close to 75 percent of the gross domestic product (GDP) in the United States (Bartash 2012). In the past few decades, many leading firms have added services to their existing product offerings in an attempt to provide total customer solutions, and, thus, to improve their competitiveness and profitability (Lusch et al. 2007; Sawhney et al. 2006; Wise and Baumgartner 1999).

A service-centered view of marketing implies that marketing is a continuous series of social and economic processes that are largely focused on operant resources with which the firm is constantly striving to make a better value proposition than its competitors (Vargo and Lusch 2004a). Generally, the prototypical characteristics that have been identified as distinguishing services from goods include: intangibility, heterogeneity, inseparability, and perishability (IHIP). More recently, however, scholars have begun to question the validity and relevance of these four characteristics in distinguishing services from goods. For example, Vargo and Lusch (2004b) contend that the IHIP characteristics are remnants of the goods-based marketing model and lead to inappropriate normative strategies for service marketers. Lovelock and Gummesson (2004) also demonstrate that the IHIP paradigm fails to effectively and universally distinguish services from goods. We contribute to this debate by outlining challenges that service marketers face in an effort to characterize how services are unique and to motivate the need for customer relationship management (CRM) systems.

CHALLENGES IN SERVICES

Switching Costs

In noncontractual service settings, customers face lower switching costs. For example, when customers encounter service failures and poor service recovery efforts, they exhibit a high degree of switching behavior (Keaveney 1995). Still, customers face some level of switching costs, which service firms should be aware of. The first type of switching cost for service customers is procedural switching cost, which involves the time, effort, and hassle of finding and adapting to a new provider. The second type is social switching costs and relates to the potential loss of a personal bond or friendship with a service provider if the consumer switches. The third type, lost benefits costs, involves the potential loss of benefits such as special deals or concessions received from the service provider if the consumer switches (Burnham et al. 2003). All three types of cost need to be measured and managed. The use of procedural costs to encourage retention should be limited whereas developing social bonds to increase social switching costs and offering value-added benefits to encourage lost benefits switching costs should be encouraged (Burnham et al. 2003).

Quality/Productivity Trade-offs

Increasing service productivity often involves a trade-off, with better service typically requiring more labor intensity, lower productivity, and higher cost (Anderson et al. 1997; Marinova et al. 2008; Rust and Huang 2012). For example, for years, firms have outsourced their call centers overseas and decreased the use of more expensive domestic labor because of cost considerations, but now many firms, such as Dell and United Airlines, have reestablished their domestic call centers to achieve higher-quality service and increased customer satisfaction (Goolsby 2009; McCue 2004). Unlike for the goods sector, for the service sector, increasing customer satisfaction and increasing productivity often go hand in hand (Deming 1986). For example, more customer service representatives imply better service but lower productivity and higher cost. Rust and Huang (2012) find that large service firms tend to be too productive relative to the optimal level and, if so, should place less emphasis on cost reduction through automation and more emphasis on service quality.

Frequent Failures and Poor Recoveries

In spite of investing in service quality improvements, service firms are confronted with service failures, customer complaints, and dissatisfaction. For instance, despite a reduction in the number of flight delays, customer complaints have risen by 17 percent for airline firms (Martin 2011). Similarly, 27 percent of hotel customers experienced at least one service failure during their stay (Consumer Reports 2012) and 68 percent of customers who defected never returned due to ineffective recovery efforts (CustomerGauge News 2008). Experts in the airline industry strongly advocate the extreme importance of troubled airlines showing greater empathy to their customers in the face of delays to prevent the loss of their most frequent fliers (Koenig 2012).

Prior research suggests that highly effective recovery efforts can produce a "service recovery paradox" in which secondary satisfaction (that is, satisfaction after a failure and recovery effort) is higher than prefailure levels (McCollough et al. 2000; Smith and Bolton 1998). However, other studies offer contrary evidence, finding that post-recovery satisfaction levels are not restored despite effective recoveries (Bolton and Drew 1991; McCollough et al. 2000). Poor service recoveries have been shown to exacerbate already low customer evaluations following a failure, producing a "double deviation" effect (Bitner et al. 1990; Hart et al. 1990). Because many service relationships are ongoing, customers will likely experience multiple failures over the course of a relationship (Maxham and Netemeyer 2002). For example, despite effective recovery efforts, paradoxical increases diminish after more than one failure (Maxham and Netemeyer 2002).

Past research has assumed that all customers are alike in terms of their responses to service failures and firms' recovery efforts, overlooking why recovery efforts are effective for some customers and ineffective for others. In contrast, Ringberg et al. (2007) find that customers are guided by different cultural models in regards to their reactions to service failures and recoveries, validating the notion that customers are heterogeneous in how they gauge service encounters (Smith et al. 1999). For example, women want their views heard during service recovery attempts while men, in contrast, do not view this as important (McColl-Kennedy et al. 2003).

The Importance of Relationships

Relationships between customers and service employees and the firm are paramount in service settings. In some long-term relationships, a service provider may actually become part of the customer's social support network (Adelman et al. 1994). Such social support benefits are important to the customer's quality of life above and beyond the technical or core service offered (Zeithaml and Bitner 1996). Adopting a relational paradigm for services marketing offers obvious promises. For managers, strong and stable customer relationships deliver favorable word of mouth (Verhoef et al. 2002), justify price premiums (Bolton 1998), reduce employee training costs, and even lower staff turnover (Sheth and Parvatiyar 1995), all of which leads to higher firm profits. Yet, Fournier et al. (1998) challenge the effectiveness of customer relationship programs because loyalty in services remains elusive and unpredictable (Agustin and Singh 2005). Building customer loyalty remains a key priority but also a problem area for many service managers. At the same time, many firms underestimate the contribution of customer–staff interactions to customer loyalty. Although they recognize the salience of customer–staff relationships for favorable service experiences, many discourage staff from developing strong relationships with customers for fear that such relationships might divert customer loyalty to the staff rather than the firm (Bendapudi and Leone 2002; Palmatier et al. 2007). Yim et al. (2008) advocate for service firms to enhance customer–firm affection by adding excitement and intimacy to the service delivered, instead of following the satisfaction paradigm of monitoring satisfaction levels, reducing service failures, and promoting programs to "lock in" customers. Over the past few years, successful companies emphasize building a strong customer relationship. For example, airline Cathay Pacific has successfully launched a program that stresses "serving from our heart" to rejuvenate the firm's customer intimacy (Yim et al. 2008). Online retailer Zappos' generous return policy had a positive impact on customers' service experience such that Zappos learned its most profitable customers are those who return the most (Dugdale 2010).

The Interface of Services is Evolving

Internet technology offers the potential for creating new business models, radical new approaches to delivering information-based services, and new ways of relating to customers (Peterson et al. 1997; Reichheld and Schefter 2000; Rust and Kannan 2002). Existing service concepts are not readily applicable to Internet services. For example, Brown (2000, p. 62) argues that "the ability to obtain and consume services without interacting with a human provider challenges much of our existing knowledge." E-services, defined as "the provision of services over electronic networks like the Internet" (Rust and Kannan 2002), did not even exist when the field of services marketing first emerged. Much of the production task for these physically intangible services is turned over, typically at remote locations, to consumers who often provide not only their labor but also their own equipment as they access network systems (Boyer et al. 2002). Automation has played a significant role substituting for labor to increase service productivity. For example, consider telephone customer service. Originally, obtaining customer service over the telephone meant calling the company and talking to a customer service representative. Eventually, however, automated telephone systems became cost-effective and were implemented in many firms because they were cheaper to operate than a fully labor-based system, though such a transition has often frustrated customers (Rust and Huang 2012).

The Need for CRM

Overall, there is a need for service firms to periodically measure constructs of satisfaction, repurchase intentions, and positive word of mouth (WOM). By measuring constructs such as negative emotions and negative WOM, service firms and retailers will gain a more complete understanding of their customers because the damaging effect of negative emotions is high (Jones et al. 2007). Further, customers have varying motivations for engaging in relationships, and service providers should be aware of this. In a similar vein, it is suggested that service providers need to understand how customers perceive the relationship, in all of its aspects, to be able to develop it (Barnes 1994, 1995; Czepiel 1990; Fournier et al. 1998; Garbarino and Johnson 1999). Such information will shed light on customers' commitment to the firm, comfort with new channels and features of the firm, and satisfaction with the firm's service recovery efforts. In addition, the management of service productivity requires consideration of both efficiency (productivity) and effectiveness (service quality and customer satisfaction) (Rust and Huang 2012). However, the customer's behavior is often incomprehensible to the service provider due to the fact that the service provider is not able to fully or accurately interpret the customer relationship. Taken together, such issues facing service firms make it imperative that these firms invest in CRM systems to reduce uncertainty in their relationships with customers and address the challenges associated with services.

OVERVIEW OF CRM

Customer relationship management is the practice of collecting, storing, and analyzing customer-level information, and incorporating the results into the decision-making process of a firm (Aaker et al. 2012). Operationally, CRM can be described as the process for achieving a continuing dialogue with customers, across all available touch points, through differentially tailored treatment, based on the expected response from each customer to available marketing initiatives, such that the contribution from each customer to overall profitability of the company is maximized (Ramaseshan et al. 2006). As this definition reveals, CRM is an enterprise-wide process potentially affecting decisions as wide-ranging as marketing communications, pricing, customization of services, resource allocation across different customers or customer groups, and customer support services. In recent years, interest in CRM has been growing in both the academic literature and business press. For example, in 2004, McDonalds's launched a series of CRM efforts, such as touch-screen ordering system and improving the customer service hotline, to solve particular customer relationship problems. These efforts contributed in boosting sales and profits (Rigby and Ledigham 2004). In addition, the airline Emirates teamed up with Hewlett Packard to create an innovative in-flight communications and CRM system, which enhances customer experience and improves the level of customer service (HP website 2012).

Customer relationship management tools for the services industry can capture sales and service related interactions that the firm has with each individual customer. Such systems can track and detail customers' experiences with the firm and service employees, both offline and online. This includes workflow automation and a well-documented service history for customer support and the ability to add to a knowledge base that the firm will be able to tap into for future projects. With CRM initiatives, service firms can track customer-facing activities, identify trends, and provide personalized service with access to real-time actionable data.

Based on practitioner wisdom on CRM for service firms (for example, Vitberg 2011), we outline five common organizational problems and how CRM can solve these problems.

1. *Important prospect and customer data is scattered.* For service firms that do not have a CRM system, prospect and customer information can be found on business cards, notepads, Post-its, emails, documents, and spreadsheets. Important data is often only stored in people's minds, which results in costly inefficiencies and potential missed revenue opportunities. Customer relationship management consolidates disparate information and makes it accessible within a service organization.
2. *Management has limited visibility to sales pipeline information.* Without a CRM system, pipeline data can be a weekly information extraction and compilation exercise. Salespeople need to be repeatedly reminded to email a spreadsheet of potential deals and then an administrator

needs to manually consolidate the information for management. With a CRM system, a service firm has a centralized, Web-based system where salespeople can maintain their pipeline of sales opportunities.

3. *Customer service response is slower than it should be.* If a company does not have a structured and shared system for fielding customer service issues, additional service failures will ensue. A CRM system can provide customers with multiple options for issue submission where requests from all channels are funneled into a single shared repository.
4. *Marketing operates in isolation.* In many service firms, the marketing department does not receive any metrics as to which marketing efforts have been the most effective, which means that marketers operate with considerable uncertainty. With a CRM system, marketing functions are integrated into the sales department's operations. Since the progress of leads can be followed through the entire sales process, the marketing department can understand which campaigns are the most effective and better focus its future efforts.
5. *Internal collaboration consists of an overwhelming amount of email.* Within many service firms, internal communication and collaboration are accomplished by copying employees on several emails. Staff become overwhelmed with email and people often overlook critical information since they do not have time to process the huge flow of information. A CRM system can be a repository of quotation templates, customer email templates and presentation templates. There can be internal conversation threads that are similar to threads that can be found on social media sites.

COMPONENTS OF CRM SYSTEMS

CRM Database

Firms need to gather, store, and analyze data in order to make strategic marketing decisions. Such information is captured in transaction-related databases and customer databases. Transaction-related databases include information associated with customer transactions, such as type of product purchased, frequency of purchase, and transaction amount. A customer database includes information on the firm's customers, as opposed to the products owned by the customers. Examples of customer database information are demographic information (age, gender, marital status, education, number of people in the household, and income), basic contact information (name, address, zip code, and phone number), psychographic information (values, activities, interests, and preferences), and other relevant information (satisfaction, referrals, and loyalty). It is critical for managers to clearly understand their own customers not only to identify active and loyal customers but also to improve marketing strategies to effectively target inactive customers.

CRM Database for Service Firms

Databases allow key customer information to be shared throughout the organization and accessible to customer representatives. An accurate and current database of customer profiles, such as preferences, demographic information, and loyalty, allows marketing managers to create customized services based on customers' preferences. For example, an AT&T customer sales representative can access a customer's entire account history, allowing him or her to greet the caller by name, provide more detailed answers, and suggest customized service offerings. This improved database allows customers to get their questions answered and enhances their service experiences (Bitner et al. 2000).

CRM Technology

The rapid growth of technology has allowed for the strong development of CRM systems. In particular, three main components of CRM technologies have improved significantly: (1) customer touch point, (2) CRM application, and (3) data storage technology. Customer touch point allows the customer interaction to move away from traditional physical interaction to impersonal interactions such as Voice over Internet Protocol (VoIP), web-based (for example, email, website, Facebook, Twitter), phone-based (for example, telesales, automatic voice recognition systems) interactions, and location-based interactions (for example, Global Positioning System, location-based mobile applications). The widespread use of portable devices such as smartphones and tablets offers CRM applications in many forms, such as traditional enterprise resource planning (ERP) systems and mobile or web-based online portals. The growth of data storage technology has given rise to managing massive customer data. All of these technological developments allow CRM analysts to manage and analyze a tremendous amount of data to create a more complete profile of customers and subsequently target them more effectively.

CRM Technology for Service Firms

The increasing deployment of technology is altering the essence of service encounters formerly anchored in a "low-tech, high-touch" paradigm.

There is currently an emphasis on how service encounters can be improved through the effective use of technology. Technology is used to (1) customize service offerings, (2) recover from service failures, and (3) spontaneously delight customers (Bitner et al. 2000). To increase service productivity, many service firms utilize automation extensively to reduce the use of labor. However, greater use of automation does not always result in higher service quality, and the effectiveness of automation in providing service hinges on how advanced the technology level is. The benefit of automation and increased provision of services using technology includes the ability to collect data from automated and online service transactions. Such data can be used to augment both transaction and customer-based CRM databases.

CRM METRICS

Metrics help firms to track and access their performance and evaluate returns on their CRM initiatives. In the past, the academic literature has focused on developing metrics that measure the value of customers based on transactions between the customer and the firm. However, it is clear that the creation of value by customers for firms occurs through a more elaborate mechanism than through purchase alone (Kumar et al. 2010a). This includes behavioral manifestations (of customer engagement), in addition to purchases, which can be both positive (that is, posting a positive brand message on a blog) and/or negative (that is, organizing public actions against a firm; Van Doorn et al. 2010). Furthermore, it can be intrinsically or extrinsically motivated (Calder and Malthouse 2008; Deci and Ryan 1985). Customer value is, therefore, driven by the nature and intensity of "customer engagement" regarding the firm (and its product/service offerings; Kumar et al. 2010a).

Customer Engagement Value

High customer engagement is essential for future growth of the firm as low customer engagement prevents the firm from succeeding because of low sales and negative WOM. The rise in the Internet and social networks has broadened the scope of connection between customers through sharing reviews and preferences (Hennig-Thurau et al. 2010). Firms should understand and manage customer engagement both online and offline via WOM campaigns, referral reward programs, affiliate marketing, Internet-based viral marketing campaigns, and the new product development process (Kumar forthcoming). Customer engagement value (CEV) is composed of five core dimensions: customer life value (CLV), customer referral value (CRV), customer influence value (CIV), customer knowledge value (CKV), and customer brand value (CBV), where CBV is the foundation that drives the other four metrics.

Customer Lifetime Value

One of the most widely used and accepted measures of customer value is CLV (Blattberg et al. 2001; Gupta and Lehmann 2005; Kumar and Reinartz 2006; Rust et al. 2004a). Customer life value represents the sum of cumulated cash flows—discounted using the weighted average cost of capital (WACC)—of a customer over his/her lifetime with the firm. Customer life value is unique in that it incorporates elements of revenue, expense, and customer behavior to estimate profitability. By knowing the CLV of its customers, firms can decide which customers to provide preferential treatment to, which customers to interact with through inexpensive channels, when to contact a customer with an offer, which customer will make a profitable customer in the future, and what kind of marketing resources to allocate. The formula to compute CLV is:

$$CLV \text{ of customer } i = \sum_{t=1}^{T} P(Buy_{it}=1)) * \frac{AMGC_{it}}{(1+d)^t} - \sum_{t=1}^{T} M_{it} * \left(\frac{1}{(1+d)}\right)^t - A_i \tag{8.1}$$

where

CLV = customer lifetime value
$AMGC_{it}$ = average period gross contribution margin for customer i in period t
i = customer index
t = period for which net present value (NPV) is being estimated
T = future time period
d = discount rate
$P\ (Buy = 1)_{it}$ = probability that customer i will purchase in period t
M = marketing costs of the firm
A = acquisition costs of the firm.

Researchers have studied the drivers and consequences of increasing CLV to uncover optimal customer selection in marketing campaigns and measure marketing effectiveness, post-campaign. For example, Rust et al. (2004b) determine the drivers of customer choice and CLV by projecting the return on marketing expenditures for different types of campaigns and accounting for competitive information using a brand-switching matrix. Venkatesan and Kumar (2004) determine an optimal resource allocation strategy using genetic algorithms, resulting in a customer-level resource allocation strategy that maximizes each customer's lifetime value. In fact, Kumar (2008a) find that the CLV-based resource reallocation leads to an increase in revenue of about $20 million (a ten-fold increase) without any changes to marketing investments.

Customer Referral Value

Customer referral value measures the acquisition of new customers through firm initiated and incentivized formal referral programs. An important component of maximizing the value of a customer base is to determine how much of each customer's value stems from his or her referrals of new customers (CRV) as a result of a firm-initiated and incentivized referral program (Kumar et al. 2010a). Because referral programs reward existing customers and build the customer base, firms use them to encourage customers to make recommendations to others. Customer referral value is focused entirely on current customers converting prospects in their social network (both online and offline) into actual customers, for which they are rewarded. In many ways, these referring customers can be thought of as nonemployee salespeople earning a commission from the sale and can be an effective way of bringing in new customers.

For example, the social coupon service Groupon offers $10 Groupon Bucks for referring a friend and when that referral purchases a deal (Groupon Referral Program 2013). Similarly, Chase Bank's referral program rewards $25 to both referrer and referred customers whenever a referred customer opens a Chase checking account (Chase Referral Program 2012). As a result, the probability of conversion of prospects into newly acquired customers and the cost of this acquisition if successful for each type of referral needs to be included in the CEV equation and calculations. Kumar et al. (2010b) find that it is much more effective to target low CRV customers than random customers. Thus, service firms should heavily publicize their referral incentives to low CRV customers. Behavioral drivers of CRV include the average yearly profit from the customer, the average time between consecutive purchases from the customer (both related to CRV by an inverted U), the number of departments the customer purchased from, the number of channels the customer shopped from (both positively related), and whether the customer made referrals in the past (Kumar et al. 2010b). The CRV formula is expressed as (Kumar and Reinartz 2012):

$$CRV \text{ of customer } i = \sum_{t=1}^{T}\sum_{y=1}^{n1}\frac{(A_{ty} - a_{ty} - M_{ty} + ACQ1_{ty})}{(1+r)^t} + \sum_{t=1}^{T}\sum_{y=n1}^{n2}\frac{(ACQ2_{ty})}{(1+r)^t} \tag{8.2}$$

where

CRV = customer referral value
i = customer index
t = period for which NPV is being estimated
T = number of periods that will be predicted into the future (for example quarters, years)
A_{ty} = gross margin contributed by customer y who otherwise would not have bought the product
a_{ty} = gross cost of the referral for customer y
1 to $n1$ = number of customers who would not have joined without the referral
$n2 - n1$ = number of customers who would have joined anyway
M_{ty} = marketing costs needed to retain the referred customers
$ACQ1_{ty}$ = Savings in acquisition cost from customers who would not have joined without the referral
$ACQ2_{ty}$ = Savings in acquisition cost from customers who would have joined anyway
r = discount rate.

The CRV model considers four aspects of the referral process, which are (1) the timing of the referral to determine proper discounting periods, (2) the number of referrals made each year and the gross margin contributed by each referral, (3) the incentive a firm provides for referral behavior (that is, rewards) and the cost of that incentive associated with the incentive, and (4) acquisition costs saved from the referral process (Kumar et al. 2010b).

Prior research shows that customers who are more connected with prospects are better targets for referral programs, as these customers can interact and influence the prospects and increase CRV. Gupta and Mela (2008) have suggested that firms should invest in customers who are opinion leaders, even though they may not be profitable themselves. Furthermore, Kumar et al. (2010b) show that customers with high CLV are not necessarily those with high CRV. Thus, it is evidently necessary to consider both dimensions to calculate an effective CEV.

Customer Influence Value

Customer influence value measures customers' influence on other acquired customers as well as on prospects. For instance, WOM activity persuades and converts prospects to customers by minimizing buyer remorse to reduce defections, encouraging increased share of wallet of existing customers. With the growth of online social networks, influencing customer preferences and purchase decisions through these networks and WOM has become more important. Kumar and Mirchandani (2012) find that firms can improve the return on investment (ROI) of their social media campaigns by identifying the influencers and incentivizing them to spread a positive WOM about the service using social media (such as Facebook and Twitter). For example, Virgin Airline's latest digital marketing campaign encourages its most frequent flyers to share their flight experience on Twitter, Pinterest, and Facebook by posting comments and sharing its promotional interactive video, which provides a sense of flying with Virgin Airlines even for those who have never flown on the airline (Voight 2012). The CIV model combines the transactional value that each influencer brings to the firm—known as CLV—and the proportional CIV of each of his or her influences that is attributed to the individual's influence (Kumar et al. forthcoming). The formula to compute CLV is as follows:

$$CIV_\theta = \sum_i k_{\theta\to i} CLV_i + \sum_i k_{\theta\to i} \times CIV_i \tag{8.3}$$

where

CIV_θ = the CIV of a user θ
CLV = customer lifetime value
$\kappa_{\theta\to i}$ = Hubbell's influence of θ on *i*.

It is important to note that while the differences between CIV and CRV may seem subtle, they are in fact two separate constructs. Customer referral value focuses solely on turning prospects into customers through a formal incentivized referral program, while CIV focuses on both prospects as well as existing customers. It is important to note that CRV involves compensation for customers who make referrals (for example, \$100 for every successful referral), while CIV typically does not (for example, a blog post expressing satisfaction with a product). Another key difference lies in that once a prospect has been successfully acquired by a firm through a referral program, he or she can never "be referred again." In other words, a prospect can only contribute to an existing customer's CRV once. He or she can then be targeted by the firm with up-sell and cross-sell strategies.

However, this prospect can still be influenced by other individuals and contribute to their CIVs. Conversely, existing customers who want to increase their CRVs can only do so by successfully acquiring prospects for the firm, but they can increase their respective CIVs by influencing both other existing customers and prospects. In addition, while CIV can be positive, negative, or zero due to the spread of positive, negative, or no WOM, CRV can never be negative. This is because there are only two possible outcomes relevant to CRV; an individual makes a successful referral (CRV is positive) or not (CRV is zero). Furthermore, CIV stems from intrinsic motivations as opposed to CRV, which arises from extrinsic incentives. In addition, due to the complexity in tracking, CRV usually is calculated for only one generation of referrals while CIV focuses on the ripple effect and extends beyond the close social network of the customer to create a chain reaction with a wide group of customers (Hogan et al. 2004).

Customer Knowledge Value

Today, the meaning of value and the process of value creation are rapidly shifting to more personalized customer experiences, service provision, intangible resources, co-creation and relationships (Vargo and Lusch 2004a). Informed, networked, empowered, and active consumers are increasingly co-creating with the firm (Hoyer et al. 2010; Prahalad and Ramaswamy 2004). Customer participation and interaction with the firm and the people in both service creation and delivery directly influence service quality and behavioral outcomes (for example, service usage, repeat purchase behavior, and WOM)—as well as firm outcomes (efficiency, revenues, and profits; Bolton and Saxena-Iyer 2009). Customers can add value to the company by helping understand customer preferences and participating in the knowledge development process (Joshi and Sharma 2004). Since this is essential to the creation of successful new products that create value, contribution of customers to this value creation, that is, CKV, needs to be captured and included as part of CEV.

Customer knowledge value is also vital to quality/service improvement efforts. The recognition of the importance of customer feedback, complaint management, and service recovery has made the collection of customer satisfaction information a required element for firms wishing to attain or maintain their ISO 9001:2000 certification (Vavra 2002). This feedback has the potential to not only make the entire offering more attractive to existing and potential customers but also to improve process efficiencies (for example, reduced complaint management). For example, based on a recent survey by the Consumer Financial Protection Bureau, American Express has the fewest complaints among the five largest credit card companies in the United States. American Express has a very strong online community on Facebook and Twitter, where it allows its customers to easily provide feedback so it can improve its service to preemptively avoid service failures in the future (American Express Facebook Page 2013; Randal 2012).

Customer Brand Value

Social media plays a vital role in forming customer perception as consumers are constantly engaging and exchanging views with one another on social network platforms. The customer's perception of the brand is captured in the CEV framework under CRV. Customer brand value refers to the differential effect of a customer's brand knowledge, brand attitude, brand purchase intention, and brand behavior on his or her response to the marketing of a brand. Customer brand value impacts the aforementioned four metrics (CLV, CRV, CIV, and CKV) and indirectly contributes to the profitability of a firm.

The link between CLV and CBV is a dynamic process in which each component of CBV, such as brand knowledge, brand attitude, brand purchase intention, and brand behavior, contributes toward the CLV. The customer-level data is important to compute CLV and CBV. Customer life value is computed with customer transaction data. However, to compute CBV, firms need customer survey data that contains questions pertaining to each component of CBV. Once this information is available, firms need to estimate how these components affect each other. Conceptually, the CLV score is modeled as a function of the CBV components (Kumar 2008a).

CRM INITIATIVES

Key CRM initiatives include customer acquisition, retention, churn, and win-back, which are essential for establishing profitable CRM strategies. Service managers need to determine the correct approach in implementing the strategies to positively impact customers' decisions, thus resulting in higher profitability. Figure 8.1 illustrates specific strategies that can be used to address key CRM initiatives (Kumar and Peterson 2012).

CUSTOMER ACQUISITION

Firms use various marketing activities to acquire new customers, including mass media, price promotions and advertising, and personalized contacts.

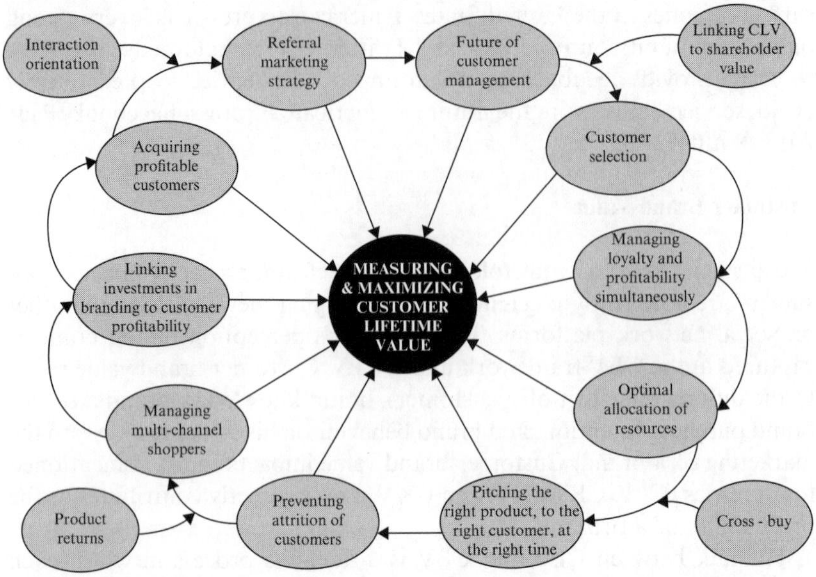

Source: Kumar (2008a).

Figure 8.1 The wheel of fortune strategies used for maximizing CLV

For many firms, marketing spending on acquiring customers represents an important expense, and it is widely known that the acquisition process has an important effect on future retention probability (Thomas 2001). Firms want to optimally allocate their limited acquisition budget to maximize customer equity and, therefore, shareholder value. Acquisition is the foundational step of the entire CRM process. Key components in the acquisition process include: identifying the right customers to acquire, predicting customers' response to promotional activities, understanding the long-term effects of marketing on customer acquisition, and using tested and proven metrics and models to maximize the efficiency of customer acquisition.

Customer acquisition strategies include (1) mass-level, (2) segment-level, and (3) one-to-one level strategies. Mass-level strategies involve any combination of mass marketing (radio, billboards, and so on) and direct marketing (telemarketing, mail, email, and so on) implemented to target 'eligible' customers rather than 'interested' ones. Although many of the same segmentation criteria from segment-level acquisition are present in one-to-one acquisition, they are taken to a new depth of detail for each customer. Where one-to-one acquisition has truly taken flight is in e-commerce and online interactions with customers. For example, Amazon.com successfully uses collaborative filtering to make customized music and book recommendations to users based on individual user preferences (Arora et al. 2008).

Acquisition metrics can be measured at both individual and aggregate level. Individual acquisition measures include the cost of acquiring a single customer using marketing resources, the revenues generated by the customer, and the profit generated by the customer, all of which contribute to a customer's lifetime value. Aggregate measures of acquisition include acquisition rate, aggregate acquisition cost, aggregate acquisition revenue, and aggregate acquisition profit. Acquisition rate refers to the percentage of people targeted by a marketing campaign who actually become customers. Managers use this metric because it is simple, easy to understand, easy to track, and can be tied to market share. A disadvantage of this metric is that there is no clarity as to whether one additional customer adds the same profit as the next customer. Aggregate acquisition cost, the average cost of acquiring a segment of customers, may be misleading because some customers might be very easy to acquire while others may not. By focusing on this metric, firms might overlook the variance in costs across customers and may target the easiest customers to acquire, for example, those with the lowest acquisition costs, as opposed to the most profitable customers. As Figure 8.2 illustrates, to understand return on acquisition, firms need to identify who is likely to be acquired, how long the customer will stay with the firm, and when the purchase activity is likely to occur (Reinartz et al. 2005).

Customer Acquisition for Services

Conventional acquisition strategies may be inappropriate for markets involving new services because they fail to account for the social effects (for example, WOM and imitation) that can influence future customer acquisition. Indirect social effects are integral to the service diffusion process in many markets because they help potential customers reduce the perceived risk of adoption. The contribution of these indirect social effects to the rate of category growth can be substantial (Rogers 1995). For example, in a study on the health and fitness service industry, Hurley (2004) finds that a majority of fitness centers listed WOM as their biggest source of member recruitment. Increased spending on retention can lead to incremental customer acquisition as satisfied customers share their experience with others.

With the growth of social coupon sites such as Groupon and LivingSocial, service firms, especially small local businesses, may be tempted to use social coupon deals in the hopes of attracting new customers. However, such a

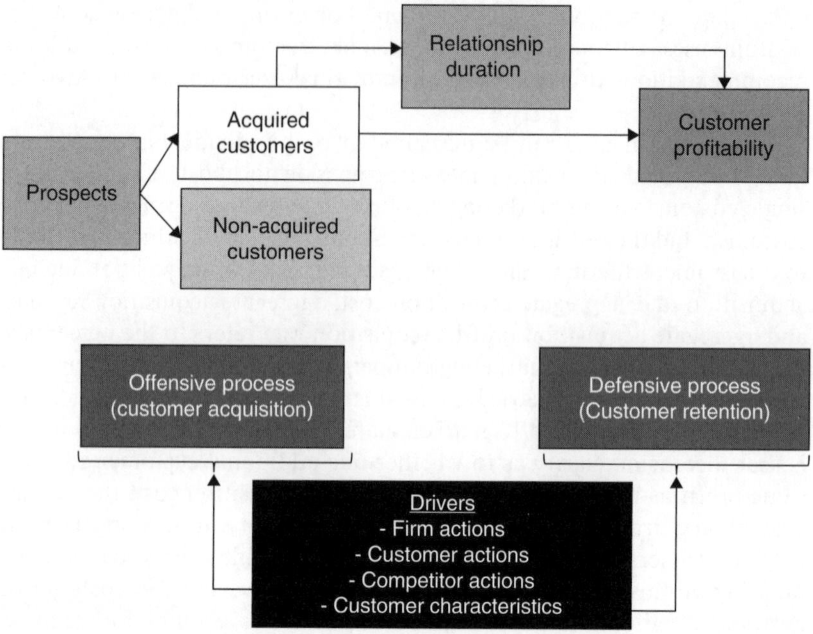

Figure 8.2 Acquisition and retention strategies

strategy may not always be profitable. Kumar and Rajan (2012) studied the impact of daily deal offers in multiple service industries and found that the current social coupon format does not ensure customer acquisition or yield profits. These price-conscious customers have less emotional attachment to the vendor and are less loyal. According to Rust et al. (1992), improving customer satisfaction helps service businesses because satisfied customers are less price sensitive, more likely to up-buy or cross-buy, and more loyal. Thus, to successfully acquire and retain customers with social coupon deals, service firms should focus on building customer satisfaction.

CUSTOMER RETENTION

Customer retention has been a dominant theme among scholars interested in CRM. Since the 1960s, firms have changed their focus from short term acquisition to long-term relationships and customer lifetime value. For example, for every 1 percent improvement in customer retention rate, a firm's value increases by 5 percent (Gupta et al. 2004). Affective commitment and loyalty programs that provide economic incentives positively affect both customer retention and customer share development (Verhoef 2003). For customer retention, a pertinent question that arises is: Who to retain? Data availability allows firms to measure an acquired customer's future profitability and thus helps determine whether that customer is worth the money and effort required to retain him or her. For example, in 2007 Sprint Nextel fired 1,000 customers who had become unprofitable. In order to minimize backlash for this abrupt cancellation, Sprint applied a credit to those customers' accounts that brought their credit to zero. Further, it is critical to decide when to engage in the retention process. Monitoring a customer's purchasing behavior is important in understanding when a firm should pursue the retention of that customer. Understanding attitudinal changes of a customer with regard to the firm's brand advises the firm on how and when to be aggressive in its retention strategies for that particular customer.

Retention metrics are divided into backward-looking and forward-looking metrics. For backward looking metrics at the aggregate level, firms measure the rate of retention, which refers to the percentage of people who are retained as customers at any given time. At the individual level, traditional metrics used for resource allocation are recency-frequency-monetary (RFM), share of wallet (SOW), and past customer value (PCV). Recency-frequency-monetary uses past customer information to evaluate customer value based on the time elapsed since the customer last placed an order with the company (recency), how often the customer orders from the company in a certain time period (frequency), and the amount that the customer spends on an average transaction (monetary). Share of wallet indicates the degree to which the customer meets his or her needs in a category with the firm. The SOW metric is widely used in retail businesses to identify whether customers are loyal to a specific store. Share of wallet is computed by dividing the value of sales of the focal firm to a customer in a category by the total amount spent by the customer in that category across all firms (Kumar and Rajan 2009). Past customer value is a metric based on the total contribution toward profit made by the customer in the past, adjusted for the time value of money. This metric assumes that past profitability of the customer indicates the level of future profitability. The value of a customer is determined based on the total contribution toward profit made by the customer in the past (Kumar and Rajan 2009).

In terms of forward looking retention metrics, at the individual level, firms compute CLV, which serves not only as a customer value metric but also as a retention metric. At the aggregate level, firms compute customer equity as a measure of retention. Refer to preceding sections for a more in-depth explanation of these metrics. Managers are encouraged to refrain from investing in customers with a low CLV and low SOW, as they add no value to the firm. Firms need to adopt a conversion strategy by upgrading and cross-selling products to high CLV and low SOW customers. Also, managers need to shift resources from low CLV and high SOW customers to high CLV and low SOW customers, with the goal of increasing their SOW. Heavy investments need to be made in high CLV and high SOW customers to maintain their loyalty. Firms can also calculate their customers' interpurchase times to impute potential competitive purchase behavior (Kumar 2008b).

Customer Retention for Service Firms

Retention strategies for service firms include increasing customer satisfaction, reducing service failures, and providing effective service recovery. The topic of customer satisfaction has been of great interest to marketing and consumer researchers for many years, driven in part by the notion that customer satisfaction can have long-term benefits, including customer loyalty and increased profitability. Prior research has recognized that both cognition and affect significantly predict satisfaction judgments. Satisfaction is a function of a comparison between expectations and performance (Oliver and DeSarbo 1988) and affect experienced during the consumption of a service (for example, joy, happiness, disgust). A large literature stream draws conceptual links between customer satisfaction and repurchase (Oliver 2009), and satisfaction has been linked empirically to a variety of customer repurchase behaviors (Bolton et al. 2006; Cooil et al. 2007). In practice, firms commonly emphasize satisfaction, assess their ability to deliver it, and believe it to be the best solution to ensure customer retention. Customer satisfaction ratings can be obtained from surveys, secondary data, or American Customer Satisfaction Index (ACSI) reports. The ACSI is an economic indicator that measures customer satisfaction; it is based on modeling customer evaluations of the quality of goods and services purchased in the United States from firms that have a substantial U.S. market share.

Researchers in the services area have extensively examined how customer satisfaction is impacted by service failures and service recovery efforts from the firm. For example, when a service failure occurs, the firm's response has the potential either to restore customer satisfaction and reinforce loyalty or to exacerbate the situation and drive the customer to a competing firm (Smith et al. 1999). The goal of service recovery is not merely to "survive" a bad customer experience by not losing the customer, but to take the opportunity to show customers just how important they are and how much you value their patronage (Patterson and Ward 2000). Well-executed service recoveries are important for enhancing customer satisfaction, building customer relationships, and preventing customer defections (Fornell and Wernerfelt 1987). Service recovery attributes affect customers' perceptions of distributive (perceived fairness of tangible outcomes of a dispute), procedural (perceived fairness of the policies by which the outcome is produced), and interactional (interpersonal treatment people experience during the conflict resolution) justice. Past research has found that compensation has the greatest effect on perceptions of distributive justice, an apology has the greatest effect on perceptions of interactional justice, and response speed is an important predictor of procedural justice (Blodgett et al. 1997; Clemmer and Schneider 1996; Smith et al. 1999; Tax et al. 1998). These results suggest that managers can view service recovery as a bundle of resources, in which each resource has a different proportional effect on the three dimensions of customers' justice evaluations.

CUSTOMER CHURN

Each year, firms spend vast amounts of money on promotional efforts, much of which are geared toward acquiring new customers. However, few executives appear to recognize the substantially higher cost of losing existing customers. Customer churn, also known as customer attrition or defection, is the loss of customers to the firm, and represents a growing problem for many firms and industries. In particular, customer churn has become a significant problem for firms in the publishing, financial services, insurance, electric utilities, healthcare, banking, Internet, telecommunications, and cable service industries. For example, in the cellular phone industry, annual churn rates range from 23.4 percent to 46 percent (Neslin et al. 2006). Customer churn can be difficult to identify and can be harmful to a firm's brand image and profitability, when it goes unnoticed. It is much easier and more cost-effective for firms to achieve higher profitability from reduced customer churn (Winer 2001). A study on this found that an estimated 4 percent of customers in the churn stage will actually voice their opinions, with the other 96 percent lost without voicing their discontent. And about 91 percent of the lost customers will never be won back (Thompson 2005).

Firms need to identify and address a customer early in the churn phase to prevent negative impact on the firm's profitability. Firms need to monitor customers' purchase behaviors, responses to marketing communication, duration between purchases, and utilize metrics to help identify customers who feel underappreciated. Questions to answer in order to take a holistic view of the churn process are: Which customers are likely to churn? Who are the customers who can be saved from the churn phase?

When are the customers likely to defect? Can we predict the time of churn for each customer and prevent customers from churning? How much do we spend on churn prevention? When should we intervene with respect to a particular customer?

Customer Churn for Service Firms

Service failures and failed recoveries are leading causes of customers' switching behavior in service organizations (Keaveney 1995). From a managerial standpoint, pertinent questions include: How can we get customers to complain to us rather than complain to their friends and/or switch service providers? Even if customers don't complain, can we identify when failures have occurred and respond to them? By studying the recovery practices of leading service firms, strategies to increase the percentage of service failures identified and reported can be observed. These strategies include (1) setting performance standards, (2) training customers on how to complain, and (3) using technological support offered through customer call centers and the Internet (Tax and Brown 1998).

Service firms have managed to construct useful and informative predictive models to help prevent churn. For example, communication service providers (CSPs) are forced to aggressively respond to competitive pressures, reduce customer churn, optimize product portfolios, and become more relevant and personalized. Communication service providers use business analytic solutions to predict business outcomes, spot trends as they emerge, improve customer service, drive customer value, and reduce churn by building a better understanding of the customer. As a result, some CSPs are able to improve their customer satisfaction with customized offers, reduce churn by 20 percent, and increase cross-sell outcomes by 5 percent to 10 percent over outbound campaigns.

CUSTOMER WIN-BACK

Win-back is the process of firms' revitalizing relationships with customers who have defected. The importance of winning back customers as a key element to a firm's CRM strategy cannot be underestimated. Research has shown that a firm has a 60 percent to 70 percent chance of successfully repeat-selling to an "active" customer, a 20 percent to 40 percent chance of successfully repeat-selling to a lost customer, and only a 5 percent to 20 percent chance of successfully closing the sale on a brand new customer (Griffin and Lowenstein 2001). Stauss and Friege (1999) find that the net return on investment from a new customer obtained from an external list is 23 percent compared with a 214 percent return on investment from the reinstatement of a customer who has defected. BellSouth lost around 21,000 small-business lines per month in 2001. In 2003, Bellsouth implemented a customer win-back strategy on package and price bundling offers, and managed to regain 26,000 customers per month (Caruso 2003).

Key components in the win-back process include (1) identifying the right customer to win back, (2) understanding what to offer customers in order to win them back, and (3) measuring the cost of win-back. At the individual level, firms should only try to win back customers with positive CLVs. For these customers, the question then becomes when to intervene and how much to spend on each customer. Firms need to decide which products to offer, including whether the intervention should entail additional features in the already adopted product or whether to offer new products. After deciding when to intervene, whether it is worth the cost, and what product to offer, the firm has to decide which contact channel to use to communicate the offer to the customer.

Customer Win-back for Service Firms

This entails an exchange in which the customer experiences a loss due to a service failure and the firm attempts to provide a gain, in the form of a service recovery effort, to make up for the customer's loss. In some cases, service firms engage in extensive efforts to reacquire lapsed customers or defectors. A common tactic to do so is lowering the price to reacquire a customer. For example, in the telecommunications industry, during the notorious long-distance telephone wars, a particular segment of customers frequently switched providers. These customers switched to benefit from an introductory offer of a competing provider, whereas others simply wanted to solicit a better offer from the original provider (Marple and Zimmerman 1999). Similarly, when AT&T's Internet service U-verse had a service outage due to software update failure, many of the affected customers vented their frustrations about the service failure and expressed their intention to cancel their subscriptions on AT&T online forums. To win back the dissatisfied customers, AT&T offered a sizable credit on the affected customers' service bills (Gross 2013).

To stimulate purchase activity, Amazon.com offers lapsed customers discounts on their next purchases. Similarly, Honey Baked Ham offers a $10 gift certificate to reactivate customers, and Self Care, a healthcare products marketer, offers discounts of up to 25 percent to customers who have not ordered from the company in 18 to 24 months. However, 100 percent retention or win-back is not always desirable or profitable, particularly when it requires setting a low retention price.

Summary of CRM Metrics

Overall, service managers should use appropriate metrics to quantify the various stages of their CRM initiatives. In doing so, managers can understand the success (or failure) of the CRM initiatives and can make the necessary changes to improve customer experience and profitability. Figure 8.3 outlines a dashboard of useful CRM metrics for service firms. Note that customers who are "won back" by the firm will then feed into acquisition-related metrics since they are reacquired by the firm.

CONCLUSION

Given that service markets have never been larger, competition in services has never been more intense, and employment growth within developed economies is almost exclusively derived from services, managing relationships with service customers is becoming increasingly critical. Further, service firms face unique challenges including low switching costs, quality/productivity trade-offs, frequent failures and poor recoveries, a unique reliance on relationships, and an evolving interface. Such challenges highlight the need for CRM systems in service firms. Service firms need to periodically measure constructs of satisfaction, repurchase intentions, and positive WOM to gain a more complete understanding of their customers because the damaging effect of negative emotions is considerable. Further, customers differ in their motivations for engaging in relationships, their comfort with new channels and features of the firm, and their satisfaction with the firm's service recovery efforts. Service providers should be aware of these differences. In addition, the management of service productivity requires consideration of both efficiency (productivity) and effectiveness (service quality and customer satisfaction). However, customers' behaviors are often incomprehensible to the service provider because the service provider is not able to fully or accurately interpret the customer relationship. Taken together, such issues facing service firms make it imperative that these firms invest in CRM systems to reduce uncertainty in their relationships with customers and address the challenges associated with services.

Data are increasingly available from multiple sources and data profiling is easier and more accurate than ever. Hence, this appears to be the appropriate time for implementing CRM initiatives in services firms. The goal of a successful service firm is to maximize CRM metrics, including customer engagement value, which comprises customer lifetime value, customer referral value, customer influence value, customer knowledge value, and customer brand value. To maximize these metrics, CRM strategies

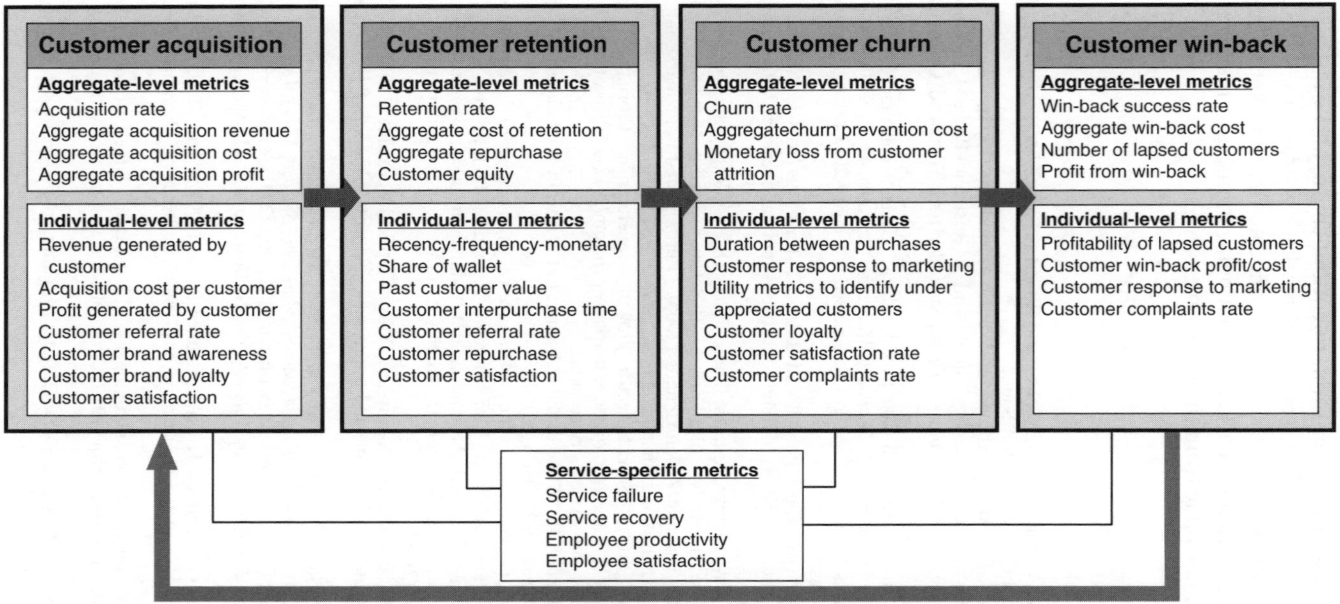
Customer acquisition
Aggregate-level metrics
Acquisition rate
Aggregate acquisition revenue
Aggregate acquisition cost
Aggregate acquisition profit
Individual-level metrics
Revenue generated by customer
Acquisition cost per customer
Profit generated by customer
Customer referral rate
Customer brand awareness
Customer brand loyalty
Customer satisfaction
Customer retention
Aggregate-level metrics
Retention rate
Aggregate cost of retention
Aggregate repurchase
Customer equity
Individual-level metrics
Recency-frequency-monetary
Share of wallet
Past customer value
Customer interpurchase time
Customer referral rate
Customer repurchase
Customer satisfaction
Customer churn
Aggregate-level metrics
Churn rate
Aggregatechurn prevention cost
Monetary loss from customer attrition
Individual-level metrics
Duration between purchases
Customer response to marketing
Utility metrics to identify under appreciated customers
Customer loyalty
Customer satisfaction rate
Customer complaints rate
Customer win-back
Aggregate-level metrics
Win-back success rate
Aggregate win-back cost
Number of lapsed customers
Profit from win-back
Individual-level metrics
Profitability of lapsed customers
Customer win-back profit/cost
Customer response to marketing
Customer complaints rate
Service-specific metrics
Service failure
Service recovery
Employee productivity
Employee satisfaction

Figure 8.3 Dashboard of metrics for service CRM

centered on customer acquisition, retention, churn, and win-back should be implemented. To adopt successful marketing strategies, service firms should use CRM systems to optimally allocate their marketing resources across services, pricing, marketing communications, and management to attain maximum value from their customers.

REFERENCES

Aaker, David A., V. Kumar, George S. Day and Robert P. Leone (2012), *Marketing Research*, 11th edn, Hoboken, NJ: Wiley & Sons.

Adelman, Mara B., Aaron Ahuvia and Cathy Goodwin (1994), "Beyond smiling: social support and service quality," in Roland T. Rust and Richard L. Oliver (eds), *Service Quality: New Directions in Theory and Practice*, Thousand Oaks, CA: Sage, pp. 139–73.

Agustin, Clara and Jagdip Singh (2005), "Curvilinear effects of consumer loyalty: determinants in relational exchanges," *Journal of Marketing Research*, **42** (1), 96–108.

American Express Facebook Page (2013), accessed 6 January 2013 at www.facebook.com/americanexpress.

Anderson, Eugene W., Claes Fornell and Roland T. Rust (1997), "Customer satisfaction, productivity, and profitability: differences between goods and services," *Marketing Science*, **16** (2), 129–45.

Arora, Neeraj, Xavier Dreze, Anindya Ghose, James D. Hess, Raghuram Iyengar, Bing Jing, Yogesh Joshi, V. Kumar, Nicholas Lurie, Scott Neslin, S. Sajeesh, Meng Su, Niladri Syam, Joacquelyn Thomas and Z. John Zhang (2008), "Putting one-to-one marketing to work: personalization, customization, and choice," *Marketing Letters*, **19** (3–4), 305–21.

Bartash, Jeffry (2012), "Service sector growth accelerates in February," accessed 5 November 2012 at http://articles.marketwatch.com/2012-03-05/economy/31123042_1_service-sector-ism-service-service-index.

Barnes, James G. (1994), "Close to the customer: but is it really a relationship?" *Journal of Marketing Management*, **10** (7), 561–70.

Barnes, James G. (1995), "Establishing relationships: getting closer to the customer may be more difficult than you think," *Irish Marketing Review*, **8** (May), 107–16.

Bendapudi, Neeli and Robert P. Leone (2002), "Managing business-to-business customer relationships following key contact employee turnover in a vendor firm," *Journal of Marketing*, **66** (2), 83–101.

Bitner, Mary Jo, Bernard H. Booms and Mary Stanfield Tetreault (1990), "The service encounter: diagnosing favorable and unfavorable incidents," *Journal of Marketing*, **54** (1), 71–84.

Bitner, Mary Jo, Stephen W. Brown and Matthew L. Meuter (2000), "Technology infusion in service encounters," *Journal of the Academic Marketing Science*, **28** (1), 138–49.

Blattberg, Robert C., Gary Getz and Jacquelyn S. Thomas (2001), *Customer Equity: Building and Managing Relationships as Valuable Assets*, Boston, MA: Harvard Business Review Press.

Blodgett, Jeffrey G., Donna J. Hill and Stephen S. Tax (1997), "The effects of distributive, procedural, and interactional justice on post-complaint behavior," *Journal of Retailing*, **73** (2), 185–210.

Bolton, Ruth N. (1998), "A dynamic model of the duration of the customer's relationship with a continuous service provider: the role of satisfaction," *Marketing Science*, **17** (1), 45–65.

Bolton, Ruth N. and James H. Drew (1992), "Mitigating the effect of service encounters," *Marketing Letters*, **3** (1), 57–70.

Bolton, Ruth N. and Shruti Saxena-Iyer (2009), "Interactive services: a framework, synthesis and research directions," *Journal of Interactive Marketing*, **23** (1), 91–104.
Bolton, Ruth N., Katherine N. Lemon and Matthew D. Bramlett (2006), "The effect of service experiences over time on a supplier's retention of business customers," *Management Science*, **52** (12), 1811–23.
Boyer, Kenneth K, Roger Hallowell and Aleda V. Roth (2002), "E-services: operating strategy—a case study and a method for analyzing operational benefits," *Journal of Operations Management*, **20** (2), 175–88.
Brown, Stephen W. (2000), "Pt. 4," in Raymond P. Fisk, Stephen J. Grove and Joby John (eds), *Services Marketing Self-Portraits: Introspections, Reflections, and Glimpses from the Experts*, Chicago, IL: American Marketing Association, pp. 53–69.
Burnham, Thomas A., Judy K. Frels and Vijay Mahajan (2003), "Consumer switching costs: a typology, antecedents, and consequences," *Journal of the Academy of Marketing Science*, **31** (2), 109–26.
Calder, Bobby J. and Edward C. Malthouse (2008), "Engagement and advertising effectiveness," in Bobby J. Calder (ed.), *Kellogg on Media and Advertising*, Hoboken, NJ: Wiley & Sons, pp. 1–36.
Caruso, Jeff (2003), "Carriers go bonkers over bundling," accessed 13 October 2003 at www.networkworld.com/columnists/2003/1013edit.html.
Chase Referral Program (2012), "Refer a friend," accessed 21 December 2012 at www.chase.com/ccp/index.jsp?pg_name=ccpmapp/shared/marketing/page/87531_raf&jp_aid=hpt_raf_ad&wt.ac=hpt_raf_ad&jp_avt=34731&WT.mc_id=q109_raf&jp_mep=hpt_raf&WT.pn_sku=raf&jp_cnv=https://resources.chase.com/secure/ReferAFriend/confirmationpage.aspx&jp_con=..ad_imageset_home.Tile.
Clemmer, Elizabeth C. and Benjamin Schneider (1996), "Fair service," in Teresa A. Swartz, David E. Bowen and Stephen W. Brown (eds), *Advances in Services Marketing and Management*, vol. 5, Greenwich, CT: JAI Press, pp. 109–26.
Consumer Reports (2012), "CR survey: Econo Lodge and Americas Best Value Inn are among lowest-rated hotels," accessed 10 December 2012 at http://pressroom.consumerreports.org/pressroom/2012/05/cr-survey-econo-lodge-and-americas-best-value-inn-are-among-lowest-rated-hotels.html.
Cooil, Bruce, Timothy L. Keiningham, Lerzan Aksoy and Michael Hsu (2007), "A longitudinal analysis of customer satisfaction and share of wallet: investigating the moderating effect of customer characteristics," *Journal of Marketing*, **71** (1), 67–83.
CustomerGauge News (2008), "The reasons customers defect," accessed 8 August 2012 at http://customergauge.com/2008/03/the-reasons-customers-defect/.
Czepiel, John A. (1990), "Service Encounters and Service Relationships: Implications for Research," *Journal of Business Research*, **20** (1), 13–21.
Deci, Edward L. and Richard M. Ryan (1985), *Intrinsic Motivation and Self-Determination in Human Behavior*, New York: Plenum.
Deming, W. Edwards (1986), *Out of the Crisis*, Cambridge, MA: MIT Press.
Dugdale, Addy (2010), "Zappos' best customers are also the ones who return the most orders," accessed 17 December 2012 at www.fastcompany.com/1614648/zappos-best-customers-are-also-ones-who-return-most-orders.
Fornell, Claes and Birger Wernerfelt (1987), "Defensive marketing strategy by customer complaint management: a theoretical analysis," *Journal of Marketing Research*, **24** (4), 337–46.
Fournier, Susan M., Susan Dobscha and David G. Mick (1998), "Preventing the premature death of relationship marketing," *Harvard Business Review*, **76** (January–February), 42–51.
Garbarino, Ellen and Mark S. Johnson (1999), "The different roles of satisfaction, trust, and commitment in customer relationships," *Journal of Marketing*, **63** (2), 70–87.
Goolsby, Kathleen (2009), "Enabling offshored call centers to move back on shore," accessed 16 May 2010 at www.outsourcingjournal.com/sep2009-callcenter.html.
Griffin, Jill and Michael W. Lowenstein (2001), *Customer Winback: How to Recapture Lost Customers—And Keep Them Loyal*, San Francisco, CA: Jossey-Bass.

Gross, Doug (2013), "U-verse back up after outage hit thousands," accessed 24 January 2013 at www.cnn.com/2013/01/24/tech/web/uverse-outage-att/index.html.
Groupon Referral Program (2013), "Refer a friend and earn $10 in Groupon Bucks!" accessed 5 January 2013 at www.groupon.com/visitor_referral.
Gupta, Sunil and Donald R. Lehmann (2005), *Managing Customers as Investments*, Philadelphia, PA: Wharton School Publishing.
Gupta, Sunil and Carl F. Mela (2008), "What is a free customer worth?" *Harvard Business Review*, **86** (November), 102–9.
Gupta, Sunil, Donald R. Lehmann and Jennifer Ames Stuart (2004), "Valuing customers," *Journal of Marketing Research*, **41** (January), 7–18.
Hart Christopher W.L., James L. Heskett and W. Earl Sasser Jr. (1990), "The profitable art of service recovery," *Harvard Business Review*, **68** (July/August), 148–56.
Hennig-Thurau, Thorsten, Ed Malthouse, Christian Friege, Sonja Gensler, Lara Lobschat, Arvina Rangaswamy and Bernd Skiera (2010), "The impact of new media on customer relationships: from bowling to pinball," *Journal of Service Research*, **13** (3), 311–30.
Hogan, John E., Katherine N. Lemon and Barak Libai (2003), "Quantifying the ripple: word-of-mouth and advertising effectiveness," *Journal of Advertising Research*, **44** (3), 271–80.
Hoyer, Wayne, Rajesh Chandy, Matilda Dorotic, Manfred Krafft and Siddharth Singh (2010), "Customer participation in value creation," *Journal of Service Research*, **13** (3), 283–96.
HP website (2012), "HP ElitePad takes flight with Emirates Airlines," accessed 10 December 2012 at www8.hp.com/us/en/hp-news/press-release.html?id=1333144#.URsL3KVg_g0.
Hurley, Teresa (2004), "Managing customer retention in the health and fitness industry: a case of neglect," *Irish Marketing Review*, **17** (1/2), 23–9.
Jones, Michael A., Kristy E. Reynolds, David L. Mothersbaugh and Sharon E. Beatty (2007), "The positive and negative effects of switching costs on relational outcomes," *Journal of Service Research*, **9** (4), 335–55.
Joshi, Ashwin W. and Sanjay Sharma (2004), "Customer knowledge development: antecedents and impact on new product performance," *Journal of Marketing*, **68** (4), 47–59.
Keaveney, Susan M. (1995), "Customer switching behavior in service industries: an exploratory study," *Journal of Marketing*, **59** (2), 71–82.
Koenig, David (2012), "American airlines stumbles on path to recovery," accessed 12 October 2012 at www.ajc.com/ap/ap/aerospace/american-airlines-stumbles-on-path-to-recovery/nSbBN/.
Kumar, V. and Werner Reinartz (2006), *Customer Relationship Management: A Databased Approach*. New York: Wiley& Sons.
Kumar, V. and Werner Reinartz (2012), *Customer Relationship Management: Concept, Strategy, and Tools. 2nd ed.*, Heidelberg: Springer Verlag.
Kumar, V. (2008a), *Managing customers for profit: Strategies to increase profits and build loyalty*, Upper Saddle River, NJ: Wharton School Publishing.
Kumar, V. (2008b), *Customer Lifetime Value: The Path to Profitability*, Delft: Now Publishers.
Kumar, V. (forthcoming), *Profitable Customer Engagement: Concepts, Metrics and Strategies*, London: Sage Publications.
Kumar, V. and Bharath Rajan (2009), "Profitable customer management: measuring and maximizing customer lifetime value," *Management Accoutning Quarterly*, **10** (3), 1–19.
Kumar, V. and Bharath Rajan (2012), "Social coupons as a marketing strategy: a multifaceted perspective," *Journal of the Academy of Marketing Science*, **40** (1), 120–36.
Kumar, V., Lerzan Aksoy, Bas Donkers, Rajkumar Venkatesan, Thorsten Wiesel and Sebastian Tillmanns (2010a), "Undervalued or overvalued customers: capturing total customer engagement value," *Journal of Service Research*, **13** (3), 297–310.
Kumar, V., Andrew J. Petersen and Robert P. Leone (2010b), "Driving profitability by encouraging referrals: who, when, and how," *Journal of Marketing*, **74** (5), 1–17.
Kumar, V. and Andrew J. Petersen (2012), *Statistical Methods in Customer Relationship Management*, Oxford: Wiley & Sons.

Kumar, V. and Rohan Mirchandani (2012), "Increasing the ROI of social media marketing," *MIT Sloan*, **54** (1), 55–61.

Kumar, V., Vikram Bhaskaran, Rohan Mirchandani and Milap Shah (forthcoming), "Creating a measurable social media marketing strategy: increasing the value and ROI of intangibles & tangibles for hokey pokey," *Marketing Science*.

Lovelock, Christopher H. and Evert Gummesson (2004), "Whither services marketing? In search of a new paradigm and fresh perspectives," *Journal of Service Research*, **7** (1), 20–41.

Lusch, Robert F., Stephen L. Vargo and Matthew O'Brien (2007), "Competing through service: insights from service-dominant logic," *Journal of Retailing*, **83** (1), 5–18.

Marinova, Detelina, Jun Ye and Jagdip Singh (2008), "Do frontline mechanisms matter? Impact of quality and productivity orientations on unit revenue, efficiency, and customer satisfaction," *Journal of Marketing*, **72** (March), 28–45.

Marple, Mark and Michael Zimmerman (1999), "A customer retention strategy," *Mortgage Banking*, **59** (11), 45–9.

Martin, Hugo (2011), "Complaints against airlines climb despite record on-time record," accessed 12 November 2012 at http://latimesblogs.latimes.com/money_co/2011/09/complaints-against-airlines-climb-despite-better-on-time-rates.html.

Maxham, James G. and Richard G. Netemeyer (2002), "Modeling customer perceptions of complaint handling over time: the effects of perceived justice on satisfaction and intent," *Journal of Retailing*, **78** (4), 239–52.

McColl-Kennedy, Janet R., Catherine S. Daus and Beverley A. Sparks (2003), "The role of gender in reactions to service failure and recovery," *Journal of Service Research*, **6** (1), 66–82.

McCollough, Michael A., Leonard L. Berry and Manjit S. Yadav (2000), "An empirical investigation of customer satisfaction after service failure and recovery," *Journal of Service Research*, **3** (2), 121–37.

McCue, Andy (2004), "For Dell, Indian call center failure a lesson," accessed 16 May 2010 at http://news.cnet.com/For-Dell,-Indian-call-centerfailure-a-lesson/2100-1001_3-5182611.html.

Neslin Scott A., Sunil Gupta, Wagner Kamakura, Junxiang Lu and Charlotte H. Mason (2006), "Defection detection: measuring and understanding the predictive accuracy of customer churn models," *Journal of Marketing Research*, **43** (2), 204–11.

Oliver, Richard L. (2009), *Satisfaction: A Behavioral Perspective on the Consumer*, New York: M.E. Sharpe.

Oliver, Richard L. and Wayne S. DeSarbo (1988), "Response determinants in satisfaction judgments," *Journal of Consumer Research*, **14** (4), 495–507.

Palmatier, Rob, Lisa K. Scheer and Jan-Benedict E.M. Steenkamp (2007), "Customer loyalty to whom? Managing the benefits and risks of salesperson-owned loyalty," *Journal of Marketing Research*, **44** (2), 185–99.

Patterson, Paul G. and Tony Ward (2000), "Relationship marketing and management", in T. Swartz and D. Iacobucci (eds), *Handbook of Services Marketing and Management*, Thousand Oaks, CA: Sage, pp. 317–42.

Peterson, Robert A., Sridhar Balasubramanian and Bart J. Bronnenberg (1997), "Exploring the implications of the Internet for consumer marketing," *Journal of the Academy of Marketing Science*, **25** (4), 329–46.

Prahalad, Coimbatore K. and Venkat Ramaswamy (2004), "Co-creation experiences: the next practice in value creation," *Journal of Interactive Marketing*, **18** (3), 5–14.

Ramaseshan, B., David Bejou, Subhash C. Jain, Charlotte Mason and Joseph Pancras (2006), "Issues and perspectives in global customer relationship management," *Journal of Service Research*, **9** (2), 195–207.

Randal, Maya Jackson (2012), "Capital One leads card complaints," accessed 22 December 2012 at http://online.wsj.com/article/SB10001424052702303379204577476971553430892.html.

Reichheld, Frederick F. and Phil Schefter (2000), "E-loyalty: your secret weapon on the Web," *Harvard Business Review*, **78** (July/August), 105–12.

Reinartz, Werner, Jacquelyn Thomas and V. Kumar (2005), "Balancing acquisition and retention resources to maximize profitability," *Journal of Marketing*, **69** (January), 63–79.
Rigby Darrell K. and Dianne Ledingham (2004), "CRM done right," *Harvard Business Review*, **84** (November), 1–13.
Ringberg, Torsten, Gaby Odekerken-Schröder and Glenn L. Christensen (2007), "A cultural models approach to service recovery," *Journal of Marketing*, **71** (3), 194–214.
Rogers, Everette M. (1995), *The Diffusion of Innovations*, New York: Free Press.
Rust, Roland T. and P.K. Kannan (eds) (2002), *e-Service: New Directions in Theory and Practice*, Armonk, NY: M.E. Sharpe.
Rust, Roland T. and Ming-Hui Huang (2012), "Optimizing service productivity," *Journal of Marketing*, **76** (2), 47–66.
Rust, Roland T., Tim Ambler, Gregory Carpenter, V. Kumar and Rajendra Srivastava (2004), "Measuring marketing productivity: current knowledge and future directions," *Journal of Marketing*, **68** (4), 76–89.
Rust, Roland T., Bala Subramanian and Mark Wells (1992), "Making complaints a management tool," *Marketing Management*, **1** (3), 40–45.
Rust, Roland T., Katherine Lemon and Valarie Zeithaml (2004), "Return on marketing: using customer equity to focus marketing strategy," *Journal of Marketing*, **68** (January), 109–26.
Sawhney, Mohanbir, Robert C. Wolcott and Arroniz Inigo (2006), "The 12 different ways for companies to innovate," *MIT Sloan Management Review*, **47** (3), 75–81.
Sheth, Jagdish N. and Atul Parvatiyar (1995), "The evolution of relationship marketing," *International Business Review*, **4** (4), 397–418.
Smith, Amy K. and Ruth N. Bolton (1998), "An experimental investigation of customer reactions to service failures: paradox or peril?" *Journal of Service Research*, **1** (1), 65–81.
Smith, Amy K., Ruth N. Bolton and Janet Wagner (1999), "A model of customer satisfaction with service encounters involving failure and recovery," *Journal of Marketing Research*, **36** (3), 356–72.
Stauss, Bernd and Christian Friege (1999), "Regaining service customers," *Journal of Service Research*, **1** (4), 347–61.
Tax, Stephen S. and Stephen W. Brown (1998), "Recovering and learning from service failure," *Sloan Management Review*, **40** (1), 75–88.
Tax, Stephen S., Stephen W. Brown, Murali Chandrashekaran (1998), "Customer evaluations of service complaint experiences: implications for relationship marketing," *Journal of Marketing*, **62** (2), 60–76.
Thomas, Jacquelyn (2001), "A methodology for linking customer acquisition to customer retention," *Journal of Marketing Research*, **38** (2), 262–8.
Thompson, Bob (2005), "The loyalty connection: secrets to customer retention and increased profits," accessed 24 April 2012 at www.rightnow.com/briefcase-files/PDFs/The_Loyalty_Connection_Secrets_to_Customer_Retention_and_Increased_Profits.pdf.
Van Doorn, Jenny, Katherine N. Lemon, Vikas Mittal, Stephan Nass, Doreen Pick, Peter Pirner and Peter C. Verhoef (2010), "Customer engagement behavior: theoretical foundations and research directions," *Journal of Service Research*, **13** (3), 253–66.
Vargo, Stephen L. and Robert F. Lusch (2004a), "Evolving to a new dominant logic for marketing," *Journal of Marketing*, **68** (1), 1–17.
Vargo, Stephen L. and Robert F. Lusch (2004b), "The four service marketing myths," *Journal of Service Research*, **6** (4), 324–35.
Vavra, Terry G. (2002), "ISO 9001: 2000 and customer satisfaction," *Quality Progress*, **35** (May), 69–75.
Venkatesan, Rajkumar and V. Kumar (2004), "A customer lifetime value framework for customer selection and resource allocation strategy," *Journal of Marketing*, **68**(4), 106–25.
Verhoef, Peter C., Philip H. Franses and Jenny C. Hoekstra (2002), "The effects of relationship constructs on customer referrals and number of services purchased from a multiservice provider: does age of relationship matter?" *Journal of the Academy of Marketing Science*, **30** (3), 202–26.

Verhoef, Peter C. (2003), "Understanding the effect of customer relationship management efforts on customer retention and customer share development," *Journal of Marketing*, **67** (4), 30–45.

Vitberg, Alan (2011), "Are professional services firms really ready for CRM?," accessed 20 November 2012 at www.vitbergllc.com/Professional-Services-Marketing-Digest/blog/bid/43892/Are-Professional-Services-Firms-Really-Ready-for-CRM.

Voight, Joan (2012), "Virgin America taps trendsetters for social video effort," accessed 21 December 2012 at www.clickz.com/clickz/news/2205496/virgin-america-taps-trendsetters-for-social-video-effort.

Winer, Russell S. (2001), "A framework for customer relationship management," *California Management Review*, **43** (Summer), 89–105.

Wise, Richard and Peter Baumgartner (1999), "Go downstream: the new profit imperative in manufacturing," *Harvard Business Review*, **77** (5), 133–41.

Yim, Chi Kin, David K. Tse and Kimmy Wa Chan (2008), "Strengthening customer loyalty through intimacy and passion: roles of customer–firm affection and customer–staff relationships in services," *Journal of Marketing* Research, **45** (6), 741–56.

Zeithaml, Valarie A. and Mary J. Bitner (1996), *Services Marketing*, New York: McGraw Hill.

9 It's not your score that matters: the importance of relative metrics

Timothy L. Keiningham, Lerzan Aksoy, Arne De Keyser, Bart Larivière, Alexander Buoye and Luke Williams

INTRODUCTION

> It's not just how many points you score that matters – you need to score more than your competitors.
>
> (Keiningham et al. 2011, p. 31)

In recent decades, customer loyalty has gained both academics' and practitioners' attention as being one of the most important determinants of company growth. Arguably the most important manifestation of this loyalty as it relates to firm growth is the share of category spending (that is, share of wallet) that customers allocate to the various brands that they use.

A great deal of research has examined the drivers of share of wallet (SOW). Most of this research has focused on the relationship between metrics like customer satisfaction, recommend intention, and repurchase intention on SOW. Yet while researchers agree that these variables are antecedents to SOW, research consistently finds weak relationships between satisfaction/intentions and SOW.

We argue that the primary cause for these weak relationships is not the metrics per se, but rather how these metrics are most typically analyzed. In particular, satisfaction and intentions are typically analyzed using absolute ratings. Instead, we propose that researchers and managers use relative metrics (that is, the focal brand in comparison with competitive alternatives) when linking to SOW.

This chapter explores the psychology of relative thinking, elaborates on previous academic research using a relative approach, and finally focuses on the implications and further research needed to advance the use of relative measures in research and practice.

THE GROWTH IMPERATIVE

Growth! It is arguably the most important gauge of a company's long-term success. As growth creates economic value for shareholders, it is the common goal of every public company chief executive officer (CEO) and one of the most important metrics by which the board of directors will assess his performance.

Despite every manager's desire to grow, however, research indicates that only one in ten companies is able to consistently deliver above average growth (Olson et al. 2008). Once company growth stalls, the odds of resurrecting even marginal growth rates are very low. Consequently, while there is no question that growth is imperative (both from a business and academic perspective), the dismal results for most companies prove that it's hard to know just how to make it happen.

Simplistically, there are two basic strategies for growing a business: (1) acquiring more customers, or (2) selling more to existing customers. It is clear that both activities are essential for a company's long-term health. It is generally accepted, however, that focusing on the existing customers tends to be more cost effective than acquiring new customers.

Research by McKinsey and Company (Coyles and Gokey 2002) and Ipsos Loyalty (McNerney and Keiningham 2011) appears to confirm this generally accepted truism (see Figure 9.1). Specifically, efforts to improve

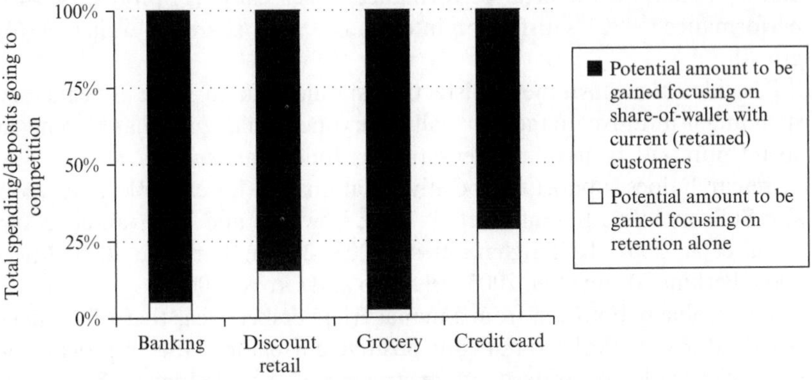

Note: An examination by Ipsos Loyalty found that the potential financial impact of improving the share of wallet of current customers far exceeded the potential from improving customer retention rates. Sample size for each category > 1,000.

Source: Ipsos Loyalty (2011).

Figure 9.1 The opportunity for growth through share of wallet

customers' share of spending (that is, share of wallet[1]) in combination with customer retention can add as much as ten-times greater value to a company than focusing on retention alone.

Despite the importance of SOW to firm financial performance, empirical evidence clearly demonstrates that in many categories, today's consumers divide their category spending among a greater number of brands than did previous generations. For example, Kraft foods—the largest food and beverage company in North America with products that regularly find their way into 99 percent of all households—has seen a tremendous decline in its customers' average share of category spending. Kraft defines a loyal customer as a person who bought 70 percent of the same brand within a category over the past three years. Three decades ago, the percentage of Kraft's customers believed to fit this description was approximately 40 percent. Today it is closer to 15 percent (Keiningham et al. 2005b).

THE CUSTOMER SATISFACTION–SHARE OF WALLET LINK

Researchers and practitioners generally accept that improving SOW is in large part driven by improving customers' perceptions of their experience. The underlying logic is a virtuous chain of effects that leads from positive customer perceptions of product/service performance to SOW and ultimately to financial performance, specifically: (1) product/service performance → (2) satisfaction/intentions → (3) share of wallet → (4) growth.

The idea that customer satisfaction should link to share of category spending is intuitive. In fact, virtually everyone would agree that we tend to spend more with firms that better satisfy us. Indeed, as expected, a large body of research does support this positive relationship (for example, Anderson and Sullivan 1993; Baumann et al. 2005; Bowman and Narayandas 2004; Cooil et al. 2007; Keiningham et al. 2003, 2005a; Larivière 2008; Mägi 2003; Perkins-Munn et al. 2005; Silvestro and Cross 2000).

The problem, however, from a managerial perspective is that while there is indeed a statistically significant positive correlation, the empirical evidence clearly demonstrates that the strength of the relationship between a customer's satisfaction level and his or her SOW is very weak (Hofmeyr et al. 2008; Mägi 2003) (see Figure 9.2). As a result, companies spend a great deal of time and money on efforts to improve customers' perceptions of the experience, but typically find that the impact on customers' share of spending shows very little improvement.

Researchers have proposed two possible reasons to explain this weak

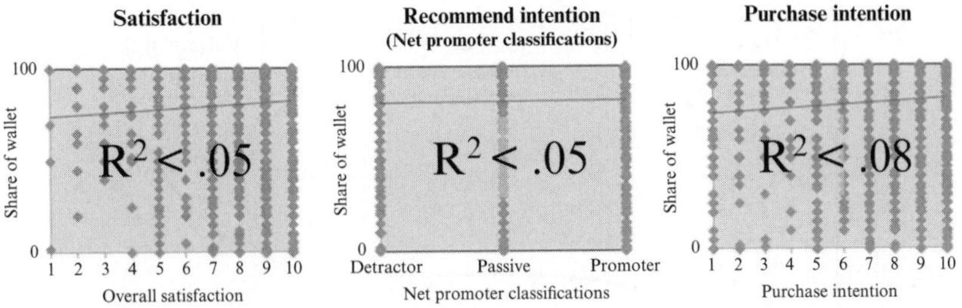

Note: Research shows that in most industries there is a very weak relationship between traditional satisfaction/loyalty metrics and the share of wallet that customers allocate to a firm.

Source: Keiningham et al. (2007).

Figure 9.2 The share of wallet breakdown V

relationship. First, customers appear to differ in their sensitivity to variations in satisfaction (Hofmeyr and Parton 2010). For example, demographic differences have been shown to impact the satisfaction–share of wallet relationship (for example, Cooil et al. 2007).

Second, researchers argue that satisfaction's impact on customer behavior (for example, retention, share of wallet, and so on) is nonlinear and asymmetric (for example, Anderson and Mittal 2000; Crotts et al. 2008; Keiningham and Vavra 2001). For example, Rust et al. (1994) propose three general zones of satisfaction in terms of satisfaction's impact on customer behavior: (1) Zone of Dissatisfaction (also, Zone of Pain), (2) Zone of Mere Satisfaction and (3) Zone of Delight (also, Zone of Complete Satisfaction) (see Figure 9.3).

Accounting for the asymmetric, non-linear pattern of satisfaction has significantly improved the satisfaction-loyalty model. Still, however, a large portion (around 70 percent) of a customers' wallet behavior remains unexplained (Hofmeyr and Parton 2010).

Hofmeyr and Parton (2010) argue that the overriding reason for the asymmetric, non-linear relationship between satisfaction and SOW is not satisfaction per se. Rather, it is because at some point higher levels of satisfaction correspond to a shift in a customer's preference ranking vis-à-vis competitive brands that the customer also uses. As a result, it is not the absolute satisfaction "score" that links to a customer's share of category spending—it is a customer's relative ranking of a brand that matters.

The idea that satisfaction is relative to competitive alternatives is not new. It is based upon fundamental psychological processes. But the application of relative measures, however, is not the norm.

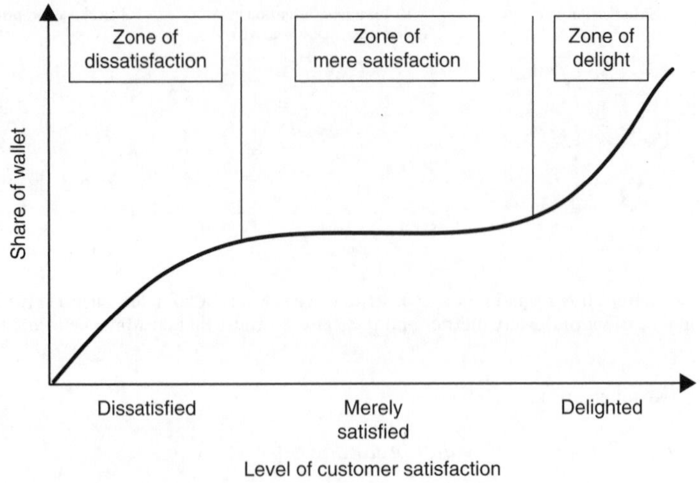

Source: Adapted from Rust et al. (1994, Fig. 3-1, p. 41).

Figure 9.3 The effect of satisfaction and delight

THE NEED FOR RELATIVE MEASURES

Despite their prevalence in business practice and academic research, the focus on absolute measures of customer satisfaction has the potential to mislead managers and researchers. Below are two of the most common problems.

The Illusion of Good and Bad Scores

The problem with looking solely at a firm's satisfaction score is that it is a poor indicator of the relative ranking that customers' assign to the brands they use. For example, imagine that a customer rated his satisfaction level a "9" on a ten-point scale. The most immediately relevant question to a manager is, "Is this a good or a bad score?" Most managers would argue that a "9" is a good satisfaction rating. But suppose the customer uses another brand in the category and for this brand he rates his satisfaction level a "10". In this case the competitor is the preferred brand. Similarly, imagine that another customer rated your brand an "8'. Most managers would not consider this to be a great score. But imagine the next highest score the customer assigns to a competitor brand is a "6". In this case, your brand is the customer's preferred brand.

As a result, given that satisfaction ratings are negatively skewed (that is, consumers tend to rate their satisfaction positively), most satisfaction ratings given by customers are not obviously good or bad relative to competitors customers also use. Clearly, extreme ratings at the lower end of the scale are bad, the highest rating point is good, but points in between are much less obvious. Without an understanding of how customers perceive a brand relative to competitors also used, there is great potential for managers to draw incorrect conclusions regarding customers' perceptions of their firm's performance.

The Illusion of Rating Equivalence

Managers typically treat customer satisfaction scores and other customer survey-based metrics as being equivalent across customers. For example, in the Net Promoter Score system, customers who rate their likelihood to recommend a 9 or 10 (on a 0 to 10 scale) are classified as "Promoters," a 7 or 8 as "Passives," and a 6 or lower as "Detractors." These groups are then treated as being homogeneous. For example, "Promoters generate 80 percent to 90 percent of referrals" (netpromotersystem.com 2012).

Unfortunately, such generalities are often very misleading. First, treating customers as homogeneous based upon their perceptions of the customer experience typically suffers from the ecological fallacy, that is, drawing false conclusions about individuals based upon population-level averages (Robinson 1950). In the case of this example, researchers Kumar et al. (2007) clearly demonstrate that only a small percentage of customers who state that they will refer the firm actually do so. Second, a host of demographic and cultural characteristics have been shown to impact how individuals respond to survey-based rating scales (for example, Iacobucci et al. 2003; van Herk et al. 2004). Without taking these factors into consideration, it is not possible to adequately assess the equivalence of consumers' ratings. Third, different respondents do not uniformly interpret scores or scale-labels, leading them to fill out satisfaction or other scales in a different manner. Research has shown customer characteristics to have a serious impact on survey responses, troubling the unambiguous relationship between customer satisfaction and SOW. A "9" doesn't have the same meaning for everyone. Some give it when they find you are performing well, whereas others score a "good" performance with a 7.

Working with relative scores can help to mitigate these three problems, thereby helping to improve the relationship between the customer experience variables (satisfaction, return intention, recommend intention) and SOW.

THE PSYCHOLOGY OF RELATIVE THINKING

There is a large body of research confirming the influence of competitive comparisons on both choice and post-purchase evaluations (Rust et al. 2000). For clarity and simplicity, we can think of these as falling into two distinct groups: pre-purchase and post-purchase influence.

Pre-purchase Influence

A typical representation of the consumer decision process in each basic consumer behavior course goes as follows: a consumer detects a certain problem/need and starts off by gathering relevant information on the different alternatives that can provide him/her with a solution. Next, a careful consideration of the alternatives in the consideration set is made, ultimately leading to a buying decision (Engel et al. 1995). Consumers, however, have finite limits to their information processing capacity (Malhotra 1982). To solve this inherent limitation of the human brain, decisions are often based on compensatory rules or heuristics.

Context and specific circumstances under which buying or other decisions are made seriously affect the use of the decision rules and the final outcome (for example, Payne 1982; Punj and Stewart 1983). These circumstances can be divided into individual difference variables (for example, age, sex, income), task variables, such the number of alternatives and time pressure, and context variables, such as the similarities/dissimilarities of the alternatives (Bettman et al. 1991).

The influence of alternatives, and thus the inherent need to employ relative thinking in loyalty research, becomes apparent. For example, the similarity/dissimilarity of alternatives clearly affects the probability of each alternative to be selected by consumers (for example, Huber 1983; Payne 1982). Consumers are likely to give little weight to features that are common across considered alternatives, but rather focus on differences. Additionally, the number of alternatives has a significant effect on the used decision rule (as described by Rust et al. 2000, p. 442). Research has shown that when the number of alternatives is relatively small, consumers tend to use compensatory rules, whereas, when the number of competing options is large, noncompensatory strategies, such as the elimination by aspects (EBA) rule, start to pop up (Bettman et al. 1991, Johnson and Meyer 1984).

Post-purchase Influence

Early research on post-purchase evaluations (that is, satisfaction/dissatisfaction) largely centered on focal brand expectations, leaving out any competitive notion. Woodruff et al. (1983), however, argued that norms based on consumer experiences with brands within a product category were a more natural comparison standard than focal brand expectations. Specifically Woodruff et al. (1983, p. 298) argue:

> The traditional view of confirmation/disconfirmation limits the comparison baseline to experiences with the focal brand, i.e., the one actually purchased and used. Clearly, focal brand expectations are likely to result from the decision to use the brand, but each consumer may have much broader experience within a product class. For example, a consumer's experiences may be with (1) a brand unit (e.g., a particular pair of Levi's jeans or a particular Wendy's restaurant), (2) other units of the same brand (e.g., several pairs of Levi's jeans or several Wendy's restaurants), (3) other similar brands (e.g., Wrangler's and Penney's jeans or McDonald's and Burger King restaurants), (4) a type of product consisting of a set of similar brands competing for the same use situation (e.g., work jeans or fast food restaurants), or even (5) a whole class of products comprising different product types competing for the same need or want (e.g., all slacks or all restaurants).

Follow-up research by Cadotte et al. (1987) confirmed this viewpoint. In their study, experience-based norms were shown to better explain variations in satisfaction than focal brand expectations. Additionally, Gardial et al. (1994) showed that in most cases consumers tend to rely on competitive comparisons/norms when evaluating their consumption experiences. This specifically means that competition serves as a benchmark to evaluate satisfaction with the focal firm, greatly impacting satisfaction scores and also calling for the need to have knowledge on the level of this reference point.

A parallel can be drawn with prospect theory (Kahneman and Tversky 1979). Three core propositions of the theory are (1) the reference point, (2) loss aversion, and (3) diminishing sensitivity.

1. *The reference point*. The evaluation of an alternative is relative to a reference point, which is called the adaptation level. This reference point can be the status quo (for example, staying at the same level), but can also refer to the outcome that is expected. Outcomes that are better than the reference point (for example, of a higher value) are considered "gains", going below this point is considered to be a "loss" (Kahneman 2011).
2. *Loss aversion*. Loss aversion is central to prospect theory. When compared, losses are always deemed larger than gains, even if the absolute/relative difference is the same. Kahneman and Tversky explain this by referring to the inherent human nature to treat threats as more urgent than opportunities.
3. *Diminishing sensitivity*. The marginal value of both gains and losses

decreases with their size (Hardie et al. 1993). For example, the first sip of a beer tastes best, after which the next gradually decrease in taste.

In accordance with the above description of post-purchase evaluations, it is clear that customers do not evaluate brands in isolation. Comparisons between different brands play a crucial role in consumer decision making. This reference point, which is formed by one's own expectations and the expectations of the performance of competing alternatives, is customer-specific as customers have differing expectations and may use different sets of providers.

RELATIVE MEASURES IN LITERATURE AND PRACTICE—AN OVERVIEW

Jacoby and Chesnut (1978) were among the first to discuss the relative nature of brand loyalty. Their work brought together different streams of brand loyalty research, and provided a comprehensive definition. They argue that to foster loyal customers, the product or brand information and the affect these customers have towards your brand have to be superior to other offerings. They note that, out of this evaluative process, a set of brands can be chosen, confirming the notion of multi-brand loyal customers:

> The sixth condition notes that brand loyalty is a function of decision-making, evaluative processes. It reflects a purchase decision in which the various brands have been psychologically (perhaps even physically) compared and evaluated on certain internalized criteria, the outcome of this evaluation being that one or more brands was (were) selected.
>
> (Jacoby and Chesnut 1978, p. 88)

A number of researchers have offered empirical and theoretical support for the use of relative measures. Below is a brief summary of the research to date in this area.

Hardie et al. (1993) demonstrated the superiority of relative choice models to nonreference models. Specifically, they developed a multinomial logit formulation of a reference-dependent choice model. While developing their choice and loyalty model, they based their assumptions on prospect theory by incorporating reference dependency, loss aversion, and diminishing sensitivity. Their findings include a superior fit and forecast capability for the reference-based model compared with a non-reference model, thereby confirming the value of competitive factors in loyalty models.

Dick and Basu (1994) developed a conceptual loyalty framework, mainly focusing on the relative nature of the construct. They defined relative attitude as the degree to which a customer's evaluation of one product or brand dominates that of other alternatives. These attitudes then relate to behavior, which is the ultimate outcome of customer loyalty.

> Attitudes have been related to behaviors, although it is important to note that one may hold a favourable attitude toward a brand but not purchase it over multiple occasions because of comparable or greater attitudinal extremity toward other brands. For purposes of predictive validity, it is hence advantageous to compare brands that are viewed by consumers to be relevant in a given consumption context. The nature of relative attitudes is likely to provide a stronger indication of repeat patronage than the attitude toward a brand determined in isolation. (Dick and Basu 1994, p. 101)

Van den Putte et al. (1996) compared different behavioral alternative models discussing the nature of multi-alternative situations. They found that using direct comparison scales (for example, a direct ranking scale on which respondents had to indicate their preference for a set of organizations by ranking the options from 1 to 9) increased explained variance of purchase intentions from 49 to 69 percent.

Bolton et al. (2000) developed a loyalty program membership model which accounted for competitive effects. Their findings suggested that customers make re-patronage decisions for a specific credit card company on the basis of their prior re-patronage intentions or behavior, which are updated by comparing their prior satisfaction level with the company versus that of the competitor(s) (Bolton et al. 2000). Furthermore, they partially confirmed prospect theory by demonstrating that in most cases losses weigh more heavily than gains.

Varki and Rust (1997) refined the use of analysis of variance (ANOVA) for comparing satisfaction ratings between firms. Their method allowed firms to identify, at an attribute level, which of its competitors performed better/worse. This had important implications for management, allowing them to take corrective steps where needed. Building on this work and the work of Hardie et al. (1993), Kumar (2002) developed a reference-dependent model of business customers' intent to repurchase from one of their existing supplier firms. His findings confirm that customers' repurchase intentions depend both on the satisfaction level with the supplier in question and the corresponding satisfaction level and costs of its referent competitor.

Olsen (2002) developed a relative chain-of-effects model. He reports a much stronger relationship between quality, satisfaction and loyalty when survey scales are presented in a relative way (that is, each question is posed for three alternatives in sequence) as opposed to an absolute presentation (that is, a battery of questions is asked for each alternative separately). This study, however, did not operationalize scores in a relative way.

Rust et al. (2004), in their return-on-marketing paper, posited customer lifetime value to depend on brand-switching patterns, amongst other things. The latter was estimated by means of a logit choice model incorporating customer ratings of customer equity (CE) drivers for several competing alternatives. This comparative approach allows comparing equity drivers' performance with those of competitors, providing management with a view on their overall competitive standing.

With regard to the relationship between satisfaction (and other perceptual or attitudinal metrics) and SOW, researchers have recognized that relative measures would be expected to perform better than absolute measures. For example, Mägi (2003, p.104) observes:

> A consumer who sees benefits in regularly using different stores would be more inclined to do so if several alternatives were equally satisfying, than if competing stores were seen as clearly inferior to the primary store. Thus it might be informative to use relative measures of satisfaction when predicting customer share.

Despite this recognition, academic research has overwhelmingly focused on absolute metrics. There are, however, some notable exceptions.

Wind (1970) linked two relative based attitude-measures to share of wallet in a business-to-business (B2B) context. He operationalized both a customer's attitude toward a given source relative to the ideal source (that is, the buyer's dissatisfaction gap) and his relative attitude to other sources (that is, the buyer's relative dissatisfaction gap with the second favorite source). The relative difference with the main competitor was found to be one of the most important predictors in the loyalty model.

Bowman and Narayandas (2004), again in a B2B context, included competitor performance in their model to predict SOW (operationalized as an indicator that satisfaction with the closest competition is equal to or exceeds satisfaction with the focal vendor). They found a negative effect, meaning that if the main competitor exceeded the focal vendor, SOW would drop. Furthermore, a significant interaction effect was found between comparative satisfaction and satisfaction with the focal vendor.

Ahearne et al. (2007) operationalized customer satisfaction and trust towards sales representatives in the pharmaceutical market as relative metrics. It is important to note, however, that their model estimates did not differ significantly to a model without competitive information.

Much of the call for the use of relative customer satisfaction (and other perceptual/attitudinal metrics) in the prediction of share has come from practitioners. For example, many managers adopted the customer value analysis (CVA) approach advocated by Bradley Gale (1994) in the book

Managing Customer Value. One of the primary points of differentiation of the CVA approach was the incorporation of relative brand position as key to linking customer perceptions to business outcomes (most notably market share). At one time this metric was widely used in industry, although it has fallen out of favor as many industries were unable to validate the claimed link to market share.

Hofmeyr et al. (2008) introduced a new brand attitudinal equity (AE) measure which was validated based upon its linkage to share of wallet. The AE measure was calculated by transforming satisfaction and other attitudinal metrics into relative ranks. For example, the highest satisfaction rating a customer gave to a brand in his/her consideration set would be assigned a "1," the second highest a "2," and so on. These ranks would then be transformed using the Zipf distribution. The parameters of the Zipf distribution were determined by fitting (in this case, back-solving) the relationship between the rank assigned by a customer to a brand and the corresponding SOW that the customer allocated to that brand. The results of this approach showed a large improvement model r-square. In particular, they found that the average r-square between satisfaction and SOW (at the customer level) using absolute measures was .24, while using the rank-based Zipf distribution transformation resulted in a .44 r-square.

Keiningham et al. (2011) introduced a power law for transforming satisfaction "rankings" into SOW predictions which they called the Wallet Allocation Rule (WAR). As with the Hofmeyr et al. (2008) approach, WAR calculations were based upon ranks. In the case of WAR, however, ranks were based upon the usage set (whereas Hofmeyr et al. (2008) used the consideration set). Keiningham and colleagues report that changes in customers' WAR scores and changes in their share of wallet over time showed a correlation of approximately .8, which translates into an r-square of approximately .6.

IMPLICATIONS AND FUTURE RESEARCH

Both theoretical and empirical research indicates that relative measures of perceptual and attitudinal data are superior to absolute measures in linking to customers' share of category spending. Yet despite widespread acceptance that perceptual measures like customer satisfaction are relative to competitive alternatives, the use of relative metrics in scientific research and in practice is rare.

Managers and researchers, however, would both tend to agree that the overriding goal of understanding customer perceptions and attitudes is to better understand customer behaviors resulting from them. Therefore, the use of relative measures needs to become the standard in both scientific research and management practice.

But exactly what relative measures should be the norm? Given the scarcity of research in the area, it is not clear what represents the best means of creating and using relative measures. Key questions to be answered include:

- Should relative measures be based upon difference scores, ranks, or some other method?
- What if any power law works best in linking these relative metrics to share of wallet, for example, Zipf distribution, WAR, and so on?
- Do some relative measures work better than others in linking to share of wallet?
- Are there demographic, industry, and country/culture factors that impact the relationship between relative metrics and share of wallet?

Additionally, managers will demand more than a linkage between relative perceptual/attitudinal measures and SOW. They will want to know what drives these relative measures so that they can identify the best opportunities for investment in improved SOW. Answering this important question will require research into the different approaches available for determining the drivers of relative performance.

Despite the need for additional research, however, methods have been proposed that managers and researchers can adopt now which should greatly improve the predictive power of their models (for example, Hofmeyr et al. 2008; Keiningham et al. 2011). Managers have long complained that satisfaction (and other perceptual/attitudinal metrics) do not link strongly enough to customers' actual buying behavior. The use of relative metrics removes that objection by providing a means for strongly linking to the share of category spending that customers allocate to the brands that they use.

NOTE

1. Share of wallet is defined as the percentage of money a customer allocates in a category that is assigned to a specific firm (Cooil et al. 2007).

REFERENCES

Ahearne, Michael, Ronald Jelinek and Eli Jones (2007), "Examining the effect of salesperson service behavior in a competitive context," *Journal of the Academy of Marketing Science*, **35** (4), 603–16.

Anderson, Eugene W. and Vikas Mittal (2000), "Strengthening the satisfaction-profit chain," *Journal of Service Research*, **3** (2), 107–20.

Anderson, Eugene W. and Mary W. Sullivan (1993), "The antecedents and consequences of customer satisfaction for firms," *Marketing Science*, **12** (2), 125–43.

Baumann, Chris, Suzan Burton and Greg Elliot (2005), "Determinants of customer loyalty and share of wallet in retail banking," *Journal of Financial Services Marketing*, **9** (3), 231–48.

Bettman, James R., Eric J. Johnson and John W. Payne (1991), "Consumer decision making," in Thomas S. Robertson and Harold H. Kassarjian (eds), *Handbook of Consumer Behavior*, Englewood Cliffs, NJ, Prentice-Hall, pp. 50–84.

Bolton, Ruth N., P.K. Kannan and Matthew D. Bramlett (2000), "Implications of loyalty program membership and service experiences for customer retention and value," *Journal of the Academy of Marketing Science*, **28** (1), 95–108.

Bowman, Douglas and Das Narayandas (2004), "Linking customer management effort to customer profitability in business markets," *Journal of Marketing Research*, **41** (4), 433–47.

Cadotte, Ernest R., Robert B. Woodruff and Roger L. Jenkins (1987), "Expectations and norms in models of consumer satisfaction," *Journal of Marketing Research*, **24** (3), 305–14.

Cooil, Bruce, Timothy L. Keiningham, Lerzan Aksoy and Michael Hsu (2007), "A longitudinal analysis of customer satisfaction and share of wallet: Investigating the moderating effect of customer characteristics," *Journal of Marketing*, **71** (1), 67–83.

Coyles, Stephanie and Timothy C. Gokey (2002), "Customer retention is not enough," *The McKinsey Quarterly*, (2), 81–9.

Crotts, John C., Bing Pan and Andrew E. Raschid (2008), "A survey method for identifying key drivers of guest delight," *International Journal of Contemporary Hospitality Management*, **20** (4), 462–70.

Dick, Alan S. and Kunal Basu (1994), "Customer loyalty: toward an integrated conceptual framework," *Journal of the Academy of Marketing Science*, **22** (2), 99–113.

Engel, James F., Roger D. Blackwell and Paul W. Miniard (1995), *Consumer Behavior*, 8th edn, Forth Worth, TX: Dryden Press.

Gale, Bradley T. (1994), *Managing Customer Value*, New York: Free Press.

Gardial, Sarah F., D. Scott Clemons, Robert B. Woodruff, David W. Schumann and Mary J. Burns (1994), "Comparing consumers recall of prepurchase and postpurchase product evaluation experiences," *Journal of Consumer Research*, **20** (4), 548–60.

Hardie, Bruce G.S., Eric J. Johnson and Peter S. Fader (1993), "Modeling loss aversion and reference dependence effects on brand choice," *Marketing Science*, **12** (4), 378–94.

Hofmeyr, Jan and Ged Parton (2010), "Rank matters," *Marketing Research*, **22** (3), 6–12.

Hofmeyr, Jan, Victoria Goodall, Martin Bongers and Paul Holtzman (2008), "A new measure of brand attitudinal equity based on the Zipf distribution," *International Journal of Market Research*, **50** (2), 181–202.

Huber, Joel (1983), "The effect of set composition on item choice – separating attraction, edge aversion, and substitution effects," *Advances in Consumer Research*, **10**, 298–304.

Iacobucci, Dawn, Doug Grisaffe, Adam Duhachek and Alberto Marcati (2003), "FAC-SEM: a methodology for modeling factorial structural equations models, applied to cross-cultural and cross-industry drivers of customer evaluations," *Journal of Service Research*, **6** (1), 3–23.

Jacoby, Jacob and Robert W. Chesnut (1978), *Brand Loyalty Measurement and Management*, New York: John Wiley.

Johnson, Eric J. and Robert J. Meyer (1984), "Compensatory choice models of noncompensatory processes – the effect of varying context," *Journal of Consumer Research*, **11** (1), 528–41.

Kahneman, Daniel (2011), *Thinking, Fast and Slow*, New York: Farrar, Straus & Giroux.

Kahneman, Daniel and Amos Tversky (1979), "Prospect theory: an analysis of decision under risk," *Econometrica*, **47** (2), 263–91.

Keiningham, Timothy L. and Terry G. Vavra (2001), *The Customer Delight Principle*, New York: McGraw-Hill.

Keiningham, Timothy L., Lerzan Aksoy, Alexander Buoye and Bruce Cooil (2011), "Customer loyalty isn't enough. grow your share of wallet," *Harvard Business Review*, **89** (10), 29–31.

Keiningham, Timothy L., Bruce Cooil, Lerzan Aksoy, Tor W. Andreassen and Jay Weiner (2007), "The value of different customer satisfaction and loyalty metrics in predicting customer retention, recommendation, and share-of-wallet," *Managing Service Quality*, **17** (4), 361–84.

Keiningham, Timothy L., Tiffany Perkins-Munn and Heather Evans (2003), "The impact of customer satisfaction on share-of-wallet in a business-to-business environment," *Journal of Service Research*, **6** (1), 37–50.

Keiningham, Timothy L., Tiffany Perkins-Munn, Lerzan Aksoy and Demitry Estrin (2005a), "Does customer satisfaction lead to profitability? The mediating role of share-of-wallet," *Managing Service Quality*, **15** (2),172–81

Keiningham, Timothy L., Terry G. Vavra, Lerzan Aksoy and Henri Wallard (2005b), *Loyalty Myths: Hyped Strategies That Will Put You Out of Business – and Proven Tactics That Really Work*. Hoboken, NJ: John Wiley & Sons.

Kumar, Piyush (2002), "The impact of performance, cost, and competitive considerations on the relationship between satisfaction and repurchase intent in business markets," *Journal of Service Research*, **5** (1), 55–68.

Kumar, V., J. Andrew Petersen and Robert P. Leone (2007), "How valuable is word of mouth?," *Harvard Business Review*, **85** (10), 139–46.

Larivière, Bart (2008), "Linking perceptual and behavioral customer metrics to multiperiod customer profitability – a comprehensive service-profit chain application," *Journal of Service Research*, **11** (1), 3–21.

Mägi, Anne W. (2003), "Share of wallet in retailing: the effects of customer satisfaction, loyalty cards and shopper characteristics," *Journal of Retailing*, **79** (2), 97–106.

Malhotra, Naresh K. (1982), "Information load and consumer decision-making," *Journal of Consumer Research*, **8** (4), 419–30.

McNerney, Matthew and Timothy Keiningham (2011), "The Wallet Allocation Rule: analyzing the relationship between brand perception and share of wallet," 3rd Annual LEAD Marketing Conference, Chicago, IL, Crowne Plaza Chicago O'Hare, 19–21 September, accessed 16 August 2013 at www.leadmarketingconference.com/Ipsos_at_LEAD_2011.pdf.

Netpromotersystem.com (2012), "Loyalty economics," accessed 4 August 2012 at www.netpromotersystem.com/system-processes/loyalty-economics.aspx.

Olsen, Svein O. (2002), "Comparative evaluation and the relationship between quality, satisfaction, and repurchase loyalty," *Journal of the Academy of Marketing Science*, **30** (3), 240–49.

Olson, Mathew S., Derek van Bever and Seth Verry (2008), "When growth stalls," *Harvard Business Review*, **86** (3), 50–61.

Payne, John W. (1982), "Contingent decision behavior," *Psychological Bulletin*, **92** (2), 382–402.

Perkins-Munn, Tiffany, Lerzan Aksoy, Timothy L. Keiningham and Demitry Estrin (2005), "Actual purchase as a proxy for share of wallet," *Journal of Service Research*, **7** (3), 245–56.

Punj, Girish N. and David W. Stewart (1983), "An interaction framework of consumer decision-making," *Journal of Consumer Research*, **10** (2), 181–96.

Robinson, William S. (1950), "Ecological correlations and the behavior of individuals," *American Sociological Review*, **15** (3), 351–7.

Rust, Roland T., Peter J. Danaher and Sajeev Varki (2000), "Using service quality data for competitive marketing decisions," *International Journal of Service Industry Management*, **11** (5), 438–69.

Rust, Roland T., Katherine N. Lemon and Valarie A. Zeithaml (2004), "Return on marketing: using customer equity to focus marketing strategy," *Journal of Marketing*, **68** (1), 109–27.
Rust, Roland T., Anthony J. Zahorik and Timothy L. Keiningham (1994), *Return on Quality: Measuring the Financial Impact of Your Company's Quest for Quality*. Burr Ridge, IL: Irwin Professional.
Silvestro, Rhian and Stuart Cross (2000), "Applying the service profit chain in a retail environment – challenging the 'satisfaction mirror'," *International Journal of Service Industry Management*, **11** (3), 244–68.
Van den Putte, Bas, Johan Hoogstraten and Roel Meertens (1996), "A comparison of behavioural alternative models in the context of the theory of reasoned action," *British Journal of Social Psychology*, **35** (2), 257–66.
Van Herk, Hester, Ype H. Poortinga and Theo M.M. Verhallen (2004), "Response styles in rating scales evidence of method bias in data from six EU countries," *Journal of Cross-Cultural Psychology*, **35** (3), 346–60.
Varki, Sajeev and Roland T. Rust (1997), "Satisfaction is relative," *Marketing Research*, **9** (2), 14–19.
Wind, Yoram (1970), "Industrial source loyalty," *Journal of Marketing Research*, **7** (4), 450–57.
Woodruff, Robert B., Ernest R. Cadotte and Roger L. Jenkins (1983), "Modeling consumer satisfaction processes using experience-based norms," *Journal of Marketing Research*, **20** (3), 296–304.

10 The satisfaction profit chain

Carly Frennea, Vikas Mittal and Robert A. Westbrook

Although marketing has historically been rooted in the production and exchange of goods and services, the emerging and dominant logic in marketing thought suggests the importance of firm investments in developing resources—tangible and intangible—to deliver customer value for fostering strong and positive customer perceptions, attitudes, and behaviors which drive firm performance (Rust and Oliver 1994; Vargo and Lusch 2004). Concurrently, therefore, a narrow focus on isolated marketing phenomena is giving way to a broader and more comprehensive consideration of the "big picture" through which firms can create value, deliver value, and receive value by interfacing with their customers (Rust and Chung 2006). Among the many frameworks, the service profit chain has emerged as a notable framework for studying these issues. In this chapter, we consider the service profit chain and its more general form, the satisfaction profit chain, to examine these issues. As explained later, though there are subtle differences between the service profit chain and the satisfaction profit chain, we use the term SPC to denote the more general framework. More specifically, we hope to accomplish three goals. First, we want to provide a conceptual, theoretical, and managerial overview of the SPC framework reviewing its empirical applications in published studies. Second, we hope to develop important research directions for scholarly work in this area. Third, we document a detailed illustration of the SPC framework to provide guidance for managers and practitioners who may wish to utilize the framework for improving organizational performance.

The satisfaction profit chain is a conceptual framework linking the delivery of customer experiences to their evaluation by customers, and thence to the market behavior of customers and the attendant financial impact. While the service profit chain has a similar scope, it concentrates on the service delivery process, and seeks to trace its effects on the firm's economic performance. In contrast, the satisfaction profit chain is more broadly focused on all major customer experiences and outcomes that affect the firm, regardless of whether they originate in service delivery or product consumption. In our view, the satisfaction profit chain is the more general conceptual framework, incorporating the service profit chain as a special case. To the extent that consumers today are faced with consumption systems—including both a product and service component—it is quite likely that applications of the SPC concept will extend the basic approach of the service profit chain to all customer experiences resulting from consumption of products as well as services. For instance, when consuming an automobile or a complex industrial good, the physical product as well as the associated service is a critical driver of customer perceptions and behaviors, which in turn drive firm financial performance. Thus, a more general satisfaction profit chain concept would be more relevant.

The SPC concept, in broad terms, seeks to describe how organizations transform inputs, or their operational choices and actions relative to market offerings, communications and ancillary services, into outputs, or measures of customer behaviors and firm performance, through customer perceptions, judgments, and attitudes. For firms, the SPC offers an integrative framework to answer such important questions as: Which operational factors are most important in determining customer perceptions of quality or performance on specific dimensions or attributes? How is the evaluation of specific aspects of service or product performance related to overall customer satisfaction, overall service quality, and their consequences such as customer loyalty, cross-buying, and share of wallet? How are these overall evaluations and customer behaviors associated with financial outcomes such as sales, profitability, and ultimately firm performance? How efficiently is the organization or its subunits transforming operational inputs into behavioral and financial outputs? The SPC provides both strategic and operational guidance to firms, incorporating both the design and management of firm business strategies. From a theoretical vantage point in the service literature, the satisfaction and service profit chains offer an integrated and comprehensive approach to quantifying the nature and magnitude of the links of the service delivery process.

THE SPC CONCEPT: ORIGINS AND DEVELOPMENT

Rust et al. (1994) were the first to conceptualize the SPC as a framework linking service quality to customer perceptions of service quality and financial outcomes with the objective of estimating return on quality. In this conceptualization, service investments improve customer perceptions of service (service quality), which in turn can drive sales, revenues and profits. Over time, the cost of investments and incremental financial performance can be used to estimate a return on quality at service firms. Heskett et al. (1994) adapted their framework to suggest that businesses have certain measurable relationships between profitability, customer loyalty, and employee productivity, loyalty, and satisfaction. Specifically, Heskett et al. (1994) articulated the following links: (1) profitability is driven primarily by customer loyalty, (2) customer loyalty is determined by customer satisfaction, (3) satisfaction is a function of the value of services provided to customers, (4) value, in turn, is the result of satisfied, loyal, and productive employees, and (5) employee efforts are driven by internal service quality, or the quality of the working environment. This framework focused attention—for managers and researchers—on quantifying the various linkages, so that the effects of all major service delivery elements might be traced ultimately to their impact on financial performance.

Today, the service profit chain has matured into a well-utilized framework in marketing. In the nearly two decades since its inception, numerous successful applications have been documented (see Table 10.2a for an overview). The maturation of the framework has occurred on many fronts. Perhaps the most notable aspect is the recognition that the framework actually extends beyond the context in which it was originally proposed, hence our use of the more encompassing term, the "satisfaction profit chain." First, in the satisfaction profit chain, customer satisfaction—and not just service quality—serves as a focal construct enabling the utility of the chain framework to be applied to the full range of market offerings, not only services. For example, it has been applied to services (Kamakura et al. 2002), consumer products companies (Pritchard and Silvestro 2005), and business-to-business (B2B) organizations (Bowman and Narayandas 2004). Over time, we think its applicability will also extend to technology settings, particularly self-service technologies (Meuter et al. 2000).

Second, in the initial conceptualization of the service profit chain, focus was limited to employee productivity as the primary antecedent to service quality. Since then, this narrow focus on employees has been replaced by a more encompassing recognition of the wide range of service and product factors that contribute to overall customer satisfaction and ultimately firm financial performance. Third, the initial concentration on business revenues and profits has given way to a broader focus on multiple dimensions of business performance, including market share, customer equity, and others. Fourth, while the original framework proposed simple linear linkages among the various elements of the service profit chain, increasingly research has identified moderators of the various linkages and documented the non-linear nature of many relationships. Finally, evidence across a number of studies now suggests the need to also directly link operational inputs and financial performance, as opposed to the earlier view that their effects were strictly mediated by intervening customer-based constructs such as attribute perceptions, overall customer satisfaction, and customer loyalty. The purpose of this direct and unmediated linkage is to account for the direct costs of the operational inputs, whose benefits may only be realized over time.

The theoretical relevance and managerial value of the SPC framework resides in its ability to depict and model the complex interrelationships among operational investments, customer perceptions, and the bottom line, as well as operational feedback on how efficiently the firm implements the strategic model. In this regard, the SPC is unique—and perhaps superior—compared to other managerial frameworks or marketing tools. For example, the customer lifetime value approach focuses on identifying the most profitable customers based on their discounted lifetime values. While useful for managing the customer base and high-level marketing strategies, this tool does not offer firms guidance on how specifically to manage internal resources and operations for said customer base. Another tool frequently used in marketing is conjoint analysis, which identifies the structure of customer preferences, given their evaluations of a set of alternatives composed of differing levels of product or service attributes (Green and Srinivasan 1990). Commonly used in product and product line design, it has also been applied to marketing mix strategy and competitive analysis, as well as less conventional areas such as litigation support and benefit package design (Green and Srinivasan 1990). Although it can be widely applied to derive valuable customer insights, conjoint analysis is not able to tell firms how they should allocate their operational resources to best affect consumer evaluations. Neither does it link customer evaluations to financial performance. Brand equity frameworks (Keller 1993) focus on the psychological processes that can enhance customer-based brand equity and may also focus on the impact of marketing-mix variables on brand equity; however, they do not take an integrative approach linking the antecedents of brand equity to financial performance.

Similar to the SPC framework is the customer equity framework (Rust et al. 2004) which models marketing investments to enhance customer equity, which in turn may affect financial performance. However, the focus of this framework is more at an overall marketing strategy level, while the SPC offers guidance on specific tactical choices as well. Finally, most closely related to the SPC framework is the return on quality (ROQ) framework (Rust et al. 1995). The ROQ tool explicitly models the impact of service quality improvements on profitability. Modern conceptualizations of the SPC have integrated the ROQ framework's emphasis on the cost of quality by incorporating a direct link between operational inputs and profits (Kamakura et al. 2002). In fact, the ROQ framework can be viewed as the first conceptual attempt to theoretically develop the underpinnings of the SPC framework.

ELEMENTS OF THE SATISFACTION PROFIT CHAIN

A systems perspective provides the theoretical basis for the SPC framework (Reidenbach and Oliva 1981). In a systems perspective "complex phenomena are conceptualized as a system that consists of various subsystems that work in tandem and evolve over time" (Mittal et al. 1999, p. 89). A system generally consists of a set of inputs, throughputs, and outputs with their interrelationships defining the system. Typically, these interrelationships can evolve over time and may vary across different systems and subsystems. In an organizational context (Morgan 1986), researchers have envisioned organizations as living systems that use inputs (for example, production factors), transform them (for example, through production), and produce outputs that satisfy customers' needs and wants (for example, utility). For marketing systems this approach is particularly useful and can be seen as the theoretical basis of the SPC framework (Kamakura et al. 2002). To fully understand the SPC it is therefore useful to understand the various inputs, throughputs and outputs, as well as their interrelationships. The framework generally implies inputs, as those decisions that are under the firm's control, throughputs as customer psychological processes (perceptions, judgments, attitudes, intentions), outputs as customer behaviors (for example, repurchase, cross-buying, word of mouth), and associated firm outcomes (for example, increased sales, profitability, market share). These are shown in Figure 10.1, and discussed next.

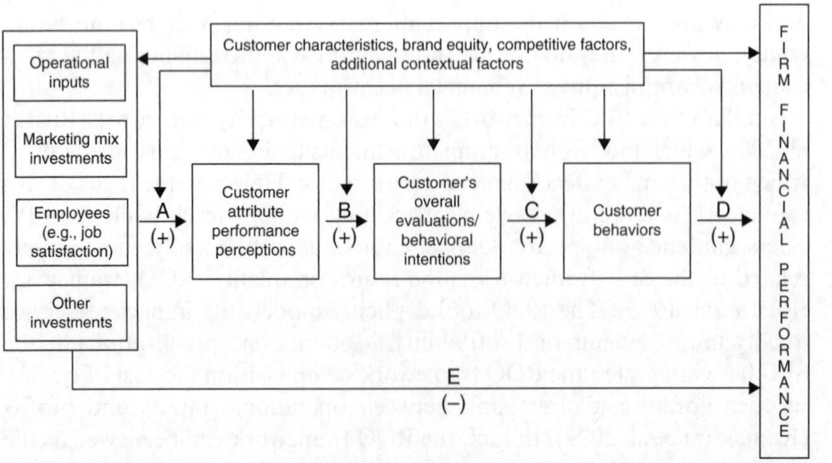

Figure 10.1 The satisfaction profit chain

Input: Operational Resource Investments

From a marketing perspective, the inputs to an SPC are the operational factors of the business, that is, those resources used by the firm to improve how customers perceive product and service attributes. They include production inputs such as employees, raw materials, technology, facilities, and infrastructure, but may also include inputs designed to directly affect customer perceptions (for example, brand equity and communication). The choice of production elements directly affects customers' perceptions of service or product attributes, such as waiting time at a bank, the timely departure of an airline flight, or the comfort of an automobile. Strategically, a firm should deploy resources to enhance inputs that impact those attributes most influential to customers' overall perceptions and judgments, and behaviors. In many cases inputs can be employee-focused constructs such as employee satisfaction, commitment, and performance (Gelade and Young 2005; Loveman 1998) because they presumably are associated with the level of effort that employees may input in improving service quality and satisfying customers.

Applications of the service profit chain have increasingly moved beyond the employee-centric logic traditionally specified as inputs, to include all types of firm-level inputs that influence customer perceptions and behavior. In part, the shift to a more general framework is a response to technological advances which have reduced the need for employees to interact with customers in industries previously characterized by extensive interaction. Self-service technologies are in effect technological interfaces that allow consumers to obtain a service without direct employee involvement (Meuter et al. 2000). In the banking industry, for example, automated teller machines (ATMs), online banking, and mobile banking have reduced the reliance on employees to deliver service, ultimately resulting in increased overall customer satisfaction. In addition, consumers can now perform a wide array of market behavior—purchasing groceries, mailing packages, and trading securities—without interacting with employees. In these situations, employee satisfaction may be less relevant to customer perceptions and behavior. This shift to reduced employee interaction has clear implications for other performance attributes that play a larger role in driving overall customer satisfaction. Thus, for instance, in high-technology firms the level of innovative product features may be an input, whereas for industrial/B2B firms, inputs may involve the level of on-site support provided by the firm to its customers in addition to the machinery supplied.

Throughput: Customer Assessments

The inputs or resource investments of firms result in market offerings, communications, and ancillary services that give rise to customer perceptions of differing levels of attribute performance. The throughput concept encompasses these mediating constructs—key customer perceptions at the attribute and overall level—through which the firm's operational inputs are transformed into outputs, its economic results. The literature amply demonstrates that attribute performance perceptions influence consumer evaluations of service and product quality (Bolton and Drew 1994), overall satisfaction (Anderson and Mittal 2000), and behavioral intentions (Rust et al. 2000). The theoretical basis for this link is the multi-attribute conceptualization of customer satisfaction and service quality (Anderson and Mittal 2000; Parasuraman et al. 1988), which argues that overall customer satisfaction—a global evaluation—is a function of attribute-level perceptions. Moreover, the conceptualization proposes that the extent to which a change in customers' attribute-performance perceptions leads to a change in the global customer evaluations indicates the importance of that attribute (Anderson and Mittal 2000). A firm's resource allocation to the various attributes seen by customers can then be based on their relative importance. Thus, the strategic purpose in quantitatively evaluating this link is to isolate the "key driver" attributes, those which have the highest impact on subsequent overall customer evaluations. The choice of which global evaluative construct to use—overall perceived service quality or overall satisfaction—is context dependent and will likely vary by firm. Methodologically, the importance of different attributes can be statistically determined using techniques such as regression analysis that assess the impact of a unit change in attribute performance on a corresponding change in overall satisfaction. Together, attribute performance perceptions and global evaluations constitute throughput.

Output: Customer Behaviors and Firm-performance Outcomes

While the preceding section describes the translation of firms' operational choices into customer perceptions, throughput also consists of the transformation of the latter into outputs, which includes both customer loyalty behaviors and financial outcomes. The theoretical basis for this link is the concept of attitude-intention-behavior consistency (Morwitz and Schmittlein 1992) in which overt customer behavior, on average, is determined by prior customer attitudes and behavioral intentions. Empirically it has been repeatedly demonstrated that overall satisfaction relates directly to both customer intentions and subsequent market behaviors (for example, Bolton 1998; Mittal and Kamakura 2001). The loyalty behaviors explored in any satisfaction or service profit chain application are of necessity specific to the firm and its market context. For instance, the most relevant loyalty behavior for telephone service providers is the duration of customer tenure (Bolton 1998). For durable goods, the actual repurchase of the same brand may be the behavior of interest, or in the case of automobiles, customer propensity to recommend the make and manufacturer to other customers. In the financial services industry, where a single customer can have multiple accounts with different providers, often firms find it useful to monitor "share of wallet," cross-sales, and duration of the customer's relationship with the firm (Kamakura et al. 2002; Loveman 1998). Similarly, in B2B contexts, where customers utilize multiple vendors, loyalty behaviors include share of wallet (Bowman and Narayandas 2004). In a retail grocery store application, loyalty behaviors consist of share of grocery budget, basket size, and word of mouth (Silvestro and Cross 2000).

Whatever customer behaviors are chosen for monitoring, they should be empirically related to firm revenues and/or profitability. In fact, there is a growing literature in marketing showing a positive association between several customer behaviors and firm-level outcomes. Thus, studies show that customer retention is associated with increased revenue (Loveman 1998), word of mouth is associated with firm stock performance (Luo 2009), and increased recommendations can increase sales performance (Chevalier and Mayzlin 2006).

Integrating Inputs, Throughputs, and Output: SPC Linkages

In the satisfaction profit chain, resource investments (operational inputs) have a positive and indirect impact on revenues and profit because they exert their effects through the mediating throughputs of customer attribute perceptions, overall customer satisfaction evaluations, and customer loyalty intentions. This should not mask the fact that resource investments initially have a direct negative effect on profits. Depending on the accounting framework being used, resource investments are typically a direct fixed or variable cost that must be paid for in the hopes that they will have a positive effect on throughputs and eventually outputs. The simultaneous positive and negative effect of operational investments—particularly on profits—was not modeled in the service profit chain framework until recently (Kamakura et al. 2002). As described earlier, this path was adapted from the ROQ framework (Rust et al. 1995), which explicitly considers the cost of service quality efforts. If managers ignore the negative feedback loop, they may overestimate the consequences of their resource investments and make suboptimal decisions. At the very least, failure to do so may result in the incorrect conclusion that higher customer satisfaction unconditionally increases firm profitability. Therefore, future applications of the service and satisfaction profit chain must take this negative direct effect into account to correctly understand and quantify the total effect of resource allocations on profits.

Although it has yet to be empirically modeled, researchers should also estimate reciprocal feedback effects in the service or satisfaction profit chain through the use of time series data. Feedback in general-systems theory refers to the process through which information concerning outputs is fed back into the system as an input and can cause change in throughput and/or output (Kast and Rosenzweig 1972). Conceptually, negative feedback may indicate a bank is falling short of performance targets and needs to make adjustments to its operational inputs to improve profits. The empirical implication is that a bank might have fewer resources with which to work and, as a result, in the next period may reduce certain inputs or allocate investments elsewhere (for example, reducing the number of full-time employees while adding an ATM to the lobby).

How do the three elements of the service or satisfaction profit chain comprise the system as a whole? A system is simply a set of interacting parts contained within a boundary. Systems are part of a larger hierarchy: composed of multiple interrelated subsystems at a lower level and part of a supra-system at the higher level. The system may be an entire organization (Kast and Rosenzweig 1972), a customer subgroup or segment (Danaher 1998), or a consumption process (Mittal et al. 1999). Subsystems may be functional areas in an organization or department, individual buyers within a customer segment, or product and service components of a consumption system. For example, a consumption system is comprised of product and service subsystems, which influence each other on top of their influence within their subsystem; that is, product satisfaction impacts behavioral intentions toward a service provider, and service satisfaction influences behavioral intentions toward a product manufacturer (Mittal et al. 1999). Behavioral intentions, in turn, determine customer behaviors manifested in the marketplace and the resulting financial returns to the business. Thus, two different inputs are managed in order to arrive at the same outcome.

Finally, an application of the SPC must address the context and/or external environment in which the chain of effects takes place. The external environment has various factors which may influence aspects of the service profit chain, such as the technical, the social-cultural, the competitive, the regulatory, and the political aspects (Reidenbach and Oliva 1981). For example, how do changes in employee protection laws and consumer protection laws affect the strategic and operational aspects of the service and satisfaction profit chains? Recent studies have incorporated factors such as the intensity of the competitive environment (Homburg et al. 2009) or competitor performance (Bowman and Narayandas 2004), implicitly recognizing that the SPC resides in an organization which is part of a larger supra-system. Expanding the context to larger systems such as the economic environment is especially important to address competitive dynamics among firms. For example, a firm which requires employees with specialized skills or a high level of customer proficiency in customer interactions is dependent on the quality of the labor market to deliver value to customers and returns to the business. They must also compete with competitors for the same pool of resources. From a theoretical perspective, both of these elements could be incorporated as moderating influences in the service or satisfaction profit chains. For instance, specialization may moderate the link between operational inputs and attribute performance. In addition, several firm-level factors such as the leverage of the firm, size of the firm, degree of specialization, the number of segments in which a firm competes, a firm's strategic emphasis (revenue growth or cost reduction) may all impact the magnitude of linkages in an SPC.

SATISFACTION PROFIT CHAIN: KEY ISSUES

Applying the Satisfaction Profit Chain: Strategic and Operational Model

A key advantage of the SPC framework is its ability to provide management with guidance at the strategic as well as the operational level. First discussed by Soteriou and Zenios (1999), the strategic model identifies the key links in the chain, while the operational model focuses on implementation, one link at a time, with the goal of enabling efficiency and achieving operational benchmarks. These benchmarks can be derived at the customer or subunit level (branches, stores part of a larger chain, general decision making units), depending on the data available to the firm. In the latter application, benchmarks evaluate and compare subunits based on their ability to implement elements of the strategic model. That is, operational analysis provides each subunit unique insight into its own position so that it can make adjustments to more efficiently implement the satisfaction or service profit chain. We emphasize that the operational model is not focused on output maximization alone but efficiency and profit maximization. Stated succinctly, "strategic benchmarking focuses on the things that really matter and efficiency benchmarks focus on how to do these things well" (Soteriou and Zenios 1999, p. 1222).

Table 10.1 Strategic and operational insight provided by the satisfaction profit chain

Strategic analysis (sets strategic direction for firm)	Operational analysis (benchmarking tool)
Which operational inputs have the largest impact on customer quality perceptions? How should the firm allocate its resource investments?	How well do subunits combine their resources? Which subunits most efficiently transform operational inputs into customer perceptions? How do subunits compare year to year?
What are the key value drivers for customers?	How do subunits compare in terms of which drivers of satisfaction are most important to customers? Which metrics should be used to measure employee and managerial performance?
How do customers demonstrate their loyalty? Which customer loyalty behaviors are most relevant to the firm?	Which subunits are able to most efficiently retain customers?
Which loyalty behaviors are related to financial performance?	Compared to the efficient benchmark, how well does the organization translate customer loyalty into profits?

Analysis at each level enables management to answer unique questions, and only by combining the two is it able to execute, implement, and monitor the satisfaction profit chain. To compare the strategic and operational uses of the chain framework, we present Table 10.1. Table 10.1 contains a list of representative questions the SPC can answer at each level, which we will explain in more detail subsequently. Throughout this discussion, we use the reoccurring example of a satisfaction or service profit chain at a bank (the setting of many empirical studies for the framework), but the approach is applicable in all other commercial, industrial, government, or nonprofit organizations. Although we consider strategic and operational applications one link at a time, it is important to recognize that the strategic model is first evaluated to identify key measures and linkages before modeling individual relationships at the operational level of analysis.

Firms can use the strategic model to determine which operational inputs have the largest impact on customer perceptions of attribute performance. For example, at a bank, performance perceptions of an attribute such as "waiting time in line" can be affected by operational inputs such as increasing the number of tellers, modifying the lobby layout, or increasing automation to provide faster service. Operational analysis can then be used to determine which subunits most efficiently transform operational inputs into customer perceptions. How many tellers do they have on the floor during a typical shift? How many ATMs are available in the lobby? What are their hours of operation? How many lanes do they have available for drive-up banking?

Moving forward along the chain, managers can then determine the key value drivers for the firm. That is, which attributes affect global consumer evaluations? Firms would then allocate investments to those inputs which most efficiently address the most important attributes in the amount and combination dictated by the operational model. Is waiting time more important than ease of online banking? What about proximity of ATM locations? Courtesy of employees? Type of accounts available? Again, the bank can compare branches in terms of which drivers of consumer evaluations (that is, satisfaction, service quality, or behavioral intentions) are more important to customers. Do they differ by subunit? If so, what are the characteristics of the branch serving customers who value the attribute "proximity of ATM locations" over the attribute "courtesy of employees"? Furthermore, this information can be used as a performance metric for branches as well as employees within a branch. If customers value waiting time, then reducing waiting time by x minutes per customer could be a performance target for the branch. Compensation for employees could also be partly based on achieving this target.

Next we turn to the link between global consumer evaluations and customer retention behaviors. How do customer evaluations of service quality and satisfaction translate into loyalty? At a bank, cross-selling and share of wallet are possible behaviors of interest. How well does each branch translate service quality into share of wallet? Which branches most efficiently retain customers? The final link in the service and satisfaction profit chain framework indicates, at the strategic level, which loyalty behaviors are related to financial performance, that is, profitability. It is important to monitor those behaviors related to profitability. Research has found several moderators of this relationship (discussed in the section titled "Empirical applications of the satisfaction profit chain"), thus firms need to not only evaluate the existence of this relationship, but also its magnitude and functional form.

Methodological Approaches to the Strategic and Operational Models

The strategic and operational levels of analysis in the service and satisfaction profit chain differ in the way they are statistically modeled. The strategic model is typically estimated using regression-based techniques.

Although early articles used regression equations to estimate each link individually (Bolton and Drew 1991; Bowman and Narayandas 2004; Loveman 1998), the entire system is better modeled using a simultaneous equation estimation technique. Structural equation modeling (SEM), hierarchical linear modeling (HLM) path models, and Bayesian network analysis all offer advantages over studying specific links in isolation. Unlike ordinary regression approaches, including advances such as two- or three-stage least squares regression, SEM can simultaneously estimate the interrelationships between numerous independent and dependent variables. In SEM, particular variables can be treated as independent for some links and dependent for other ones, which is especially relevant when chain constructs can be both antecedents for some purposes and consequences for others. Researchers have also found SEM to be a superior technique for modeling mediation (Iacobucci et al. 2007), which is a feature of many satisfaction profit chains. Hierarchical linear modeling path analysis situates a path model (a subset of SEM using only measured variables) in a hierarchical context, recognizing that service or satisfaction profit chain data is often gathered at different levels of aggregation (employee, customer, firm units, and time). Bayesian network analysis accommodates simultaneous cause and effect mapping, nonlinear relationships, and branching sequences common in survey data collection.

In contrast to the foregoing estimation methods for the strategic model, that for the operational model utilizes data envelopment analysis (DEA; Charnes et al. 1994). Data envelopment analysis is a nonparametric technique which measures the relative efficiency of multiple decision-making units (DMU) in transforming inputs into outputs. Efficiency is measured by comparing the inputs a DMU requires to those needed by a combination of the most efficient units operating under similar conditions in order to produce the same levels of outputs. In the bank example, a service quality DEA model, focused on the first link in the service profit chain, examines human and technological resources (for example, number of tellers, managers and employees, number of ATMs, number of accounts serviced) and how efficiently they are converted into service quality perceptions. Multiple DEA models can be estimated using different specifications for each link in the SPC. Rather than evaluating a DMU in relation to all other DMUs, DEA identifies a set of efficient units operating similarly to the unit under analysis. These efficient units (or branches) operating under similar conditions comprise one facet of the production efficiency frontier. Data envelopment analysis compares the inputs and outputs of all DMUs, identifies the most efficient set of DMUs to which a particular one will be compared, and creates a "virtual" production unit as a convex combination of the units in the efficiency frontier. This "virtual" production unit serves as a benchmark against which the relative efficiency of a unit can be determined. An advantage of DEA is that it accommodates economies as well as diseconomies of scale by only comparing units operating at similar levels, as well as the nonlinearities in the relationships between service perceptions, intentions and actual behavior (Anderson and Mittal 2000).

EMPIRICAL APPLICATIONS OF THE SATISFACTION PROFIT CHAIN

Table 10.2a presents a summary of our comprehensive review of the empirical literature on the satisfaction profit chain. We detail their components in Table 10.2b. In this section of the chapter, we make several generalizations about these studies, review limitations of the research to date, and, finally, highlight recent developments. We start by discussing the constructs representing inputs, throughput, and output. Interestingly, many empirical studies that deal with the service profit chain are situated in retail banking settings, though there is ample variation in the choice of inputs researchers have explored.

Early studies emphasized components of the employee experience, including satisfaction, loyalty, job climate, and productivity/effort, in keeping with Heskett et al.'s (1994) original conceptualization of the service profit chain. Consistent with our earlier discussion, there has been a decreasing emphasis—particularly in studies published in marketing journals—on employee-centric measures in the SPC over time. Most past studies have found a small or nonsignificant relationship between employee-related measures and throughput constructs such as attribute performance, service quality, and customer satisfaction (Homburg and Stock 2004; Loveman 1998; Silvestro and Cross 2000). Other studies outside the service profit chain stream of literature (for example, Schneider et al. 1998) have observed a reciprocal relationship between employee and customer perceptions. A recent meta-analysis (Brown and Lam 2008) found that employee satisfaction only explains between 4 and 6 percent of the variance in overall customer satisfaction. Although employee satisfaction can influence consumer satisfaction directly, there is strong evidence across past research that customer perceptions mediate this effect (Brown and Lam 2008). While partially driven by human factors, customer perceptions of attribute performance are a function of technological and physical factors as well. As such, making employee-related inputs the sole operational factor in service or satisfaction profit chain studies would be inadvisable.

A few recent applications have reflected this observation, and as a result,

Table 10.2a Summary of SPC studies

Study	Industry	Sample	Estimation method	Key results
Bolton and Drew (1991)	Telecomm	1,408 residential telephone subscribers	2LS regression	The authors developed a model of expectations, performance perceptions, service quality, and service value. Disconfirmation was found to be a major determinant of overall service quality, although perceived performance also had a direct effect. Assessments of service value were positively related to service quality evaluations, although the weighting of their drivers was different
Danaher and Rust (1996)	Telecomm	360 cellular phone customers	OLS regression	The authors investigated the indirect effects of service quality on customer behaviors. Service quality impacted usage rates and new customer attraction; the latter effect through word of mouth
Loveman (1998)	Banking	450 branches of regional bank	OLS regression	Testing individual links, the author found support for some, but not all, of the relationships in the SPC. Specifically, internal service quality was positively associated with employee satisfaction, and employee satisfaction was related to stated loyalty but not tenure. Tenure was correlated with customer satisfaction, but employee satisfaction was not. Customer satisfaction was positively correlated with customer loyalty while only some measures of loyalty were related to revenue
Carr (1999)	Banking	1,500 PNC bank customers	Not reported	The most satisfied customers had the highest account balances while those customers who were only satisfied had the same balance of those customers who were less than satisfied. Improving satisfaction also increased balances over time

Kimes (1999)	Hospitality	1,135 franchised Holiday Inn hotels	ANOVA	There was a positive relationship between product quality and operational performance. Hotels with at least one defect in the exterior, the guest rooms, and the guest bath had lower revenue per available room than hotels without such defects
Soteriou and Zenios (1999)	Banking	Customers of 144 branches of a Cyprus bank	DEA	The authors proposed a cascade of efficiency benchmarking models (operational efficiency, service quality efficiency, and profitability efficiency) and the links between them. Simultaneously examining operations (personnel and infrastructure), service quality, and profitability was superior to benchmarking dimensions separately
Silvestro and Cross (2000)	Grocery	6 UK grocery stores	Correlation	The authors found mixed support for the link between the input constructs and service value. There was a positive correlation between throughput constructs (service value and customer satisfaction), but only weak support for the positive relationship between customer satisfaction and customer loyalty. Customer loyalty positively correlated with financial performance
Garland (2002)	Banking	1,128 customers of a New Zealand bank	Descriptive statistics and OLS regression	Relationship length and share of wallet were major drivers of profitability

Table 10.2a (continued)

Study	Industry	Sample	Estimation method	Key results
Kamakura et al. (2002)	Banking	3,489 customers of 521 branches of a Brazilian bank	SEM and DEA	At the strategic level, the authors simultaneously investigated the links in the SPC and found operational resource investments impacted profits indirectly (positive relationship; via attribute performance perceptions, behavioral intentions, and customer behaviors) and directly (negative relationship). At the operational level, the authors demonstrated that firms must be efficient on both operations and customer retention to achieve high profitability
Kassinis and Soteriou (2003)	Hospitality	104 senior executives of high-end hotels in the EU	SEM	The authors explored the impact of environmental practices, a component of a firm's operations, on the external portion of the SPC. In essence, environmental management practices were conceived as an input in the SPC in lieu of traditional operational inputs. Environmental practices indirectly influenced financial performance through customer satisfaction and loyalty
Anderson et al. (2004)	Transportation	1,101 customers of a retail transport firm	Bayesian network analysis	In order to accommodate nonlinear relationships and branching sequences common in survey data collection, the authors proposed Bayesian network analysis as an alternative methodology for SPC studies. They demonstrated support for an SPC model where service inputs impacted attribute satisfaction, performance evaluations, and disconfirmation, which in turn drove retention and endorsement

Bowman and Narayandas (2004)	B2B	160 customers of processed metal suppliers	Regression (OLS, 2LS, 3LS, nonlinear, logit)	The authors adapted the SPC to a B2B context. Margin was positively impacted by share of wallet and negatively influenced by investments in customer management. Vendor attribute performance and customer satisfaction were mediating constructs between vendor effort and customer behaviors and profitability. Finally, the authors explored nonlinear relationships and differential responses as a result of customer specific factors such as competitive context and customer size
Homburg and Stock (2004)	7 industries	164 dyadic cases (164 salespeople and 328 B2B customers)	SEM	Using dyadic data, the authors systematically investigated the job satisfaction–customer satisfaction link of the SPC. Employee job satisfaction had both a positive direct effect on customer satisfaction as well as an indirect effect mediated by customer orientation. This effect was moderated by frequency of interaction, intensity of customer integration into value-creating process, and innovativeness of offerings. Customer satisfaction was also determined by quality of offerings and processes
Gelade and Young (2005)	Banking	1,407 branches of four retail banks	SEM	Employee climate evaluations and commitment were positively associated with customer satisfaction and sales. The authors found little support for the mediating role of customer satisfaction
Pritchard and Silvestro (2005)	Retail	75 stores of a UK home improvement chain	Correlation	The authors empirically tested a full model of Heskett et al.'s (1994) SPC and found support for only some of the linkages. Employee loyalty had a central role in their model as it was positively correlated with employee satisfaction, productivity, service value, customer satisfaction, and revenue growth. More importantly, although productivity and output quality

Table 10.2a (continued)

Study	Industry	Sample	Estimation method	Key results
				were positively correlated to profit growth, none of the customer measures (service value, satisfaction, or loyalty) related to financial performance
Larivière (2008)	Banking	522 customers of a Belgian bank	OLS regression	Different levels of share of wallet generated different levels of profitability as well as different profitability trajectories over time. The longitudinal relationship between share of wallet and profitability was nonlinear
Homburg et al. (2009)	Travel agency	258 employees and 597 customers of 109 travel agencies	HLM path model	The authors integrated a social identity-based path into the traditional satisfaction-based SPC model. The former included links between employee-company identification, customer-company identification, customer orientation, and employee-customer similarity. Higher customer-company identification increased willingness to pay, which in turn improves financial performance (sales/number of employees)
Evanschitzky et al. (2011)	Franchise services	50 outlets, 933 employees, and 20,742 customers	SEM and HLM	Employee satisfaction mediates the relationship between owner-franchisee satisfaction and customer satisfaction. No direct relationship was found. Improving employee satisfaction not only increased customer satisfaction scores, but also nearly doubled the impact of customer satisfaction on customer purchase intentions

incorporated nonhuman factors as operational inputs. The satisfaction profit chain model of Kamakura et al. (2002) included a construct related to customer perceptions of equipment as well as perceptions of employees, although the former was found to be a weaker antecedent of customer intentions to recommend the service than the latter. In a study focused on the relationship between job satisfaction and customer satisfaction, Homburg and Stock (2004) included quality of offerings as a control variable in their model and found it to be the most important predictor of customer satisfaction. Kassinis and Soteriou (2003) took a different approach to the satisfaction profit chain and examined a facet of the firm's operations, notably its environmental practices. Although they did not compare its explanatory power to that of employee factors, they did find an indirect effect on financial performance through overall customer satisfaction and loyalty.

While the link from employee satisfaction to customer satisfaction is far from straightforward, the pathways from customer satisfaction to customer loyalty behavior and financial outcome measures are consistently demonstrated in satisfaction profit chain applications and elsewhere. Reflecting this fact, every study of the satisfaction profit chain conducted in the last decade has included customer satisfaction as a throughput construct, in addition to perceived service quality. The increasing emphasis on customer satisfaction as a central mediating construct is likely due to evidence of its stronger effects on numerous measures of customer loyalty behaviors (Bolton et al. 2008; Keiningham et al. 2005) and firm financial performance (Anderson et al. 2004; Gruca and Rego 2005).

It is entirely possible that future research will include other focal constructs beyond service quality and customer satisfaction as overall evaluations. Homburg et al.'s (2009) inclusion of a social-identity-based path in the satisfaction profit chain is one such example. Researchers could also explore other customer metrics, such as brand equity (Keller 1993), customer-brand connection (Escalas and Bettman 2005), and commitment (Garbarino and Johnson 1999). The placement of these constructs in the satisfaction profit chain is not intuitively obvious; they may function as drivers of customer satisfaction or as moderators of a link in the chain of effects.

Despite its widespread application and evolution, empirical applications of the satisfaction profit chain may be further improved in several ways. First, as Table 10.2b shows, most empirical applications do not test a comprehensive and integrated SPC framework. Many studies do not test each link in the chain, and those that do frequently do so using independent equations or correlation analysis. For example, while Loveman (1998) provides the first comprehensive empirical study of the satisfaction profit

Table 10.2b Chain elements

Study	Input construct	Throughput constructs	Output constructs		Feedback loop
			Customer behavior	Financial metric	
Bolton and Drew (1991)	Attribute performance Expectations Disconfirmation	Service quality Service value			
Danaher and Rust (1996)	Service quality Advertising	Recommendation likelihood	Usage rate New customer market share		
Loveman (1998)	Internal service quality Employee satisfaction Employee loyalty	Customer satisfaction	Retention of checking accounts Number of services purchased per household Percentage of investable assets held with bank	Revenue	
Carr (1999)		Customer satisfaction	Account balance		
Kimes (1999)	Product quality (number of deficiencies per area)			Revenue per available room	

Soteriou and Zenios (1999)	Personnel (clerical and managerial Infrastructure/ equipment	Service quality		Branch profits	
Silvestro and Cross (2000)	Operating ratio Employee service capability Employee satisfaction Employee loyalty Productivity and output quality	Perceptions of service value Customer satisfaction	Share of grocery budget Basket size Customer referral	Profit margin	Employee satisfaction and operating ratio negatively correlated with profitability. Productivity positively correlated with profitability
Garland (2002)			Tenure with bank Share of wallet Presence of joint account	Dollar contribution	

Table 10.2b (continued)

Study	Input construct	Throughput constructs	Output constructs		Feedback loop
			Customer behavior	Financial metric	
Kassinis and Soteriou (2003)	Environmental management practices (use of energy saving, recycling, and water saving measures)	Customer satisfaction	Customer loyalty and retention	Market performance (growth in profits, revenue, and market share relative to industry)	
Anderson et al. (2004)	Service value (arrival time, delivery, employee courtesy, damage level)	Customer satisfaction (with timeliness, information, claim) Performance Disconfirmation	Retention Endorsement		
Bowman and Narayandas (2004)	Vendor effort (hours per month spent servicing a customer account)	Attribute level performance (sales rep. performance, product quality, product line breadth, responsiveness, and delivery) Customer satisfaction	Share of wallet	Profitability (margin)	Customer management effort negatively related to profitability

Homburg and Stock (2004)	Job satisfaction Quality of offerings Quality of customer-related business processes	Quality of customer interaction Customer satisfaction		
Gelade and Young (2005)	Climate (team, job enablers, and support) Employee commitment	Customer satisfaction		Sales achievement (branch sales as a percentage of target)
Pritchard and Silvestro (2005)	Service capability Internal service quality Employee satisfaction Employee loyalty Productivity	Output quality (stock availability) Service value Customer satisfaction	Recommendation likelihood Likelihood of revisit Average transaction size per store	Sales performance growth Net profit growth

Table 10.2b (continued)

Study	Input construct	Throughput constructs	Output constructs		Feedback loop
			Customer behavior	Financial metric	
Homburg et al. (2009)	Employee job satisfaction Employee-company identification	Customer orientation Customer satisfaction Customer-company identification	Customer loyalty (likelihood or booking with agency, recommendation, and returning to agency) Willingness to pay	Sales/number of employees	
Evanschitzky, et al. (2011)	Owner-franchisee satisfaction Employee satisfaction	Customer Satisfaction Customer purchase intentions			

chain (originally described as a service profit chain), he does so using regression equations in which each link in the model is estimated separately. Omission of links, especially at the beginning or end of the chain, do not allow for an integrated test of the framework. Of necessity, researchers must employ a simultaneous estimation approach involving path analysis or structural equations to be confident of correctly appraising the linkages in the model.

Second, studies have tended to focus on a single organization. Often this is unavoidable, because each application relies on measurements unique to the firm in question. Some researchers have addressed this issue (Homburg and Stock 2004), and future research should do likewise to ensure the generalizability of findings regarding the satisfaction profit chain. Third, the external validity of the relationships is hindered by limiting the context of study to the banking and hospitality industries. The SPC framework is no less useful to product firms, non-traditional service firms, as well as B2B firms (Bowman and Narayandas 2004). Researchers should continue to seek novel and varied settings for satisfaction profit chain studies.

Kamakura et al. (2002) make a strong case for including a direct relationship from operational inputs to financial outcomes. This link is consistent with the reasoning of the ROQ model (Rust et al. 1994). Only one other study using a multivariate methodological approach included this particular linkage. Bowman and Narayandas (2004), in their application of the satisfaction profit chain to business customers, demonstrate that customer management costs were negatively related to profitability. We believe that incorporating this link is critical to assess the profit implications of customer satisfaction and its inputs, and to move the ultimate criterion of the service profit chain away from a simplistic focus on firm revenue.

What are the most recent advances in the SPC framework? In a short time, researchers have evolved the satisfaction profit chain into new markets, added new paths, incorporated moderators, and used new methods (Anderson et al. 2004; Bowman and Narayandas 2004; Homburg et al. 2009). Bowman and Narayandas (2004) adapted the framework to address characteristics of business markets, including complexities of the decision-making unit, customers' use of multiple suppliers, and resource allocation at the individual customer level. The authors found support for all links in their chain (customer management effort → customer satisfaction → share of wallet → gross margin). Additionally, the authors included moderators to allow for the effects of customer characteristics (size), account characteristics (account management tenure), and competition. All three factors played a significant role in each linkage and resulted in asymmetrical relationships within the chain, which indicates that moderating influences cannot be overlooked in modeling the satisfaction profit chain. Homburg et al. (2009) included similar moderators in their social-identity satisfaction profit chain model, as well as the perceived similarity of employees and customers. Relationship tenure positively moderated the relationship between customer satisfaction and willingness to pay, customer satisfaction and customer loyalty, and customer-company identification and willingness to pay. Competitive intensity moderated the customer loyalty–financial performance link, such that loyalty increased financial performance only when competitive intensity was high. Employee-customer similarity did not have a significant moderating effect. Despite awareness that factors such as competitive intensity (Seiders et al. 2005), relationship age (Bolton 1998), and customer demographics (Mittal and Kamakura 2001) moderate individual links in the satisfaction profit chain, to our knowledge only two studies (Bowman and Narayandas 2004; Homburg et al. 2009) have explicitly included interactive effects. As stated earlier, incorporating interactive effects constitutes bringing aspects of the environmental supra-system into the satisfaction profit chain. For example, the competitive environment is explored by adding competitor satisfaction or industry concentration as moderators. In a similar fashion, including switching barriers could serve to incorporate the economic or regulatory environment into the satisfaction profit chain.

IMPLEMENTATING THE SPC: A DETAILED EXAMPLE

To illustrate the development and application of the satisfaction profit chain framework in an actual business setting, we consider the example of the ABC Corporation (identity disguised), a large and industry-leading commercial and industrial services company whose annual revenues exceeded $4 billion. Historically, ABC has relied on a growth strategy of acquiring smaller competitors who provided similar services, which had allowed it to generate strong and expanding earnings. At the time of the example, however, senior management had recognized that the extant growth strategy was unlikely to continue to generate the increases in profits that ABC required. Instead, management decided to focus on achieving organic growth of the company's revenues, while gradually improving its profit margin.

The company initially attempted to bring about growth in the customer base through enlarging and redirecting its field sales force. However, this effort produced little increase in revenues, while adding significant expense. At this juncture, senior management revisited the company's options for increasing its customer base, and decided that instead of new customer growth, it would emphasize retention by reducing customer losses to competitors. Many strategies to reduce customer losses were proposed by the executive team, including building the company's brand, centralizing customer call centers for improved customer service, instituting a loyalty rewards program, and advertising the company's recent achievements in sustainability to improve its reputation and appeal.

To help top management determine the most effective and efficient customer and margin growth strategies, ABC decided to develop a model of its satisfaction profit chain, which would provide both strategic and operational guidance. The company already had information on many of the necessary elements for constructing and analyzing the satisfaction profit chain within its business. Foremost among these were its measurement programs to monitor its service quality and to track its overall customer satisfaction. These programs had been implemented throughout the company's field operations to provide metrics for senior management as well as the management responsible for individual operating locations.

The service quality portion of the measurement program was intended to provide a comprehensive view of customers' ratings of ABC's service performance. It was comprised of eight broad areas of customer experience—service dependability, service personnel, on-site equipment, customer support, billing, sales personnel, value, and sustainability. From a management perspective, each of these areas of customer experience represented a potential point of emphasis for bringing about improvement in service quality.

The measurement of both service quality and overall customer satisfaction was accomplished in a common customer survey. Customers in each of the 200-plus geographic operating units were surveyed quarterly by telephone, for a total of approximately 5,000 interviews per year. Customers rated the company's performance on key specific service attributes within the eight areas of customer experience. In addition, the survey probed customers' overall satisfaction using a multi-item battery of rating scales. The same survey also gathered ratings of customers' intentions to renew service contracts and their willingness to recommend the company. For benchmarking purposes, competitors' customers were also surveyed using these same items, but in separate surveys.

To quantify the linkages in the model, the analysis began by creating reliable measures of service quality and overall customer satisfaction. Following exploratory and confirmatory factor analysis of the service attributes, measures of the quality of service were defined for each of the eight areas of customer experience with the company's services and operations, all of which possessed adequate internal consistency (alpha >.70). Then the structural linkages in the model were estimated statistically using both ordinary least squares (OLS) regression and maximum-likelihood

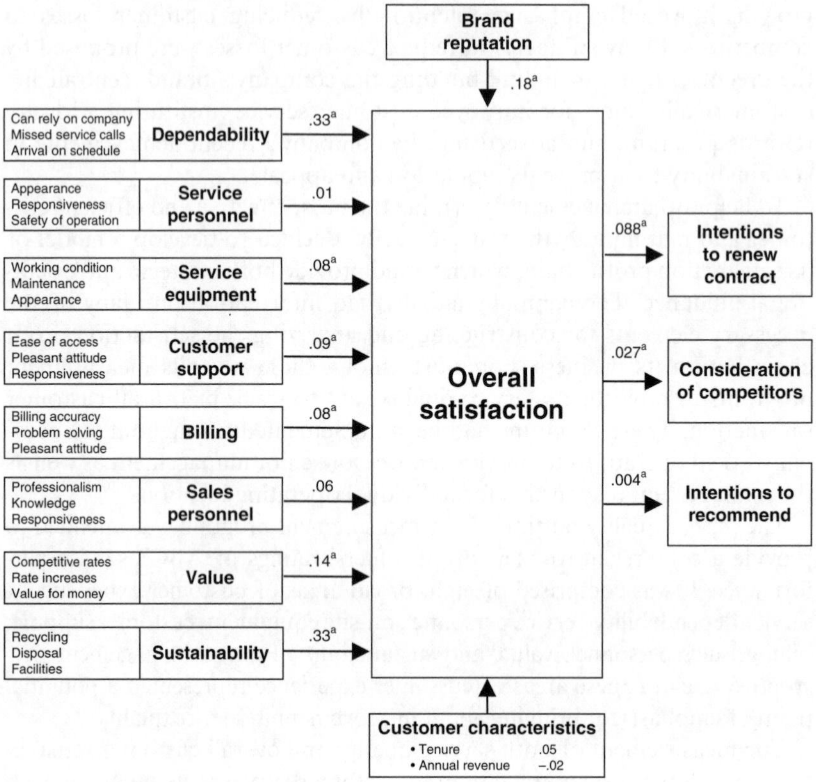

Note: [a] Statistically significant at p = .01 level.

Figure 10.2 Satisfaction profit chain for ABC Corporation

structural equations models. The OLS regression estimates of the company's satisfaction profit chain are shown in Figure 10.2. The measures of the eight areas of service experience accounted for over 70 percent of the variance in overall satisfaction, indicating that the service quality measures were reasonably complete as explanatory variables. The numeric values[1] above the arrows leading to overall customer satisfaction indicate the strength of the relationship between each of the eight areas of customer experience and overall customer satisfaction, controlling for each other. The structural equations model estimates were very comparable to those obtained from the regressions, but in the interests of space are not shown here. The regression estimates were used for presentation to the company's executives since there was greater familiarity with this analytical method than structural equations modeling.

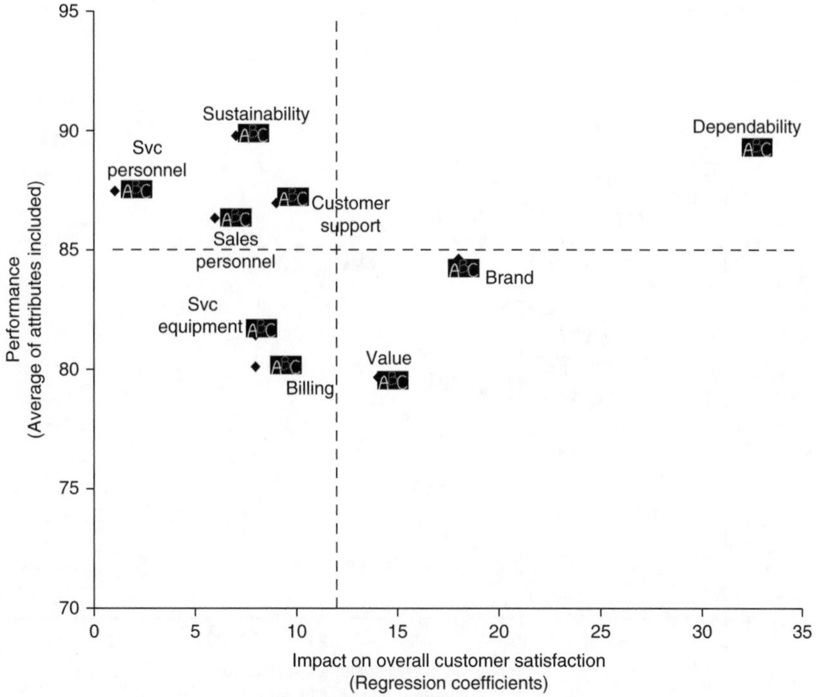

Figure 10.3 *Importance-performance map for ABC Corporation*

The top four areas of service experience relating to overall customer satisfaction were service dependability (.33), value (.14), brand reputation (.18), and customer support (.09). These results in and of themselves were very informative to the executives, some of whom were surprised that value was not the strongest contributing factor to overall satisfaction, while others were equally surprised that sustainability apparently had such limited impact. The importance of dependability came as a surprise to many senior executives, who had assumed it to be so commonplace within the company's delivery of service that it was not an issue to customers.

While the foregoing quantitative modeling of the satisfaction profit chain reveals the key drivers of overall customer satisfaction, to put these findings into proper perspective, the analysis also considered the performance of each of the eight areas of service experience. Figure 10.3 shows an importance-performance map to depict the level of performance (y-axis) along with the impact on overall satisfaction (x-axis). The logical focus for retaining ABC's customers was therefore value—it had one of the strongest associations with overall satisfaction and, at the same time, weakest

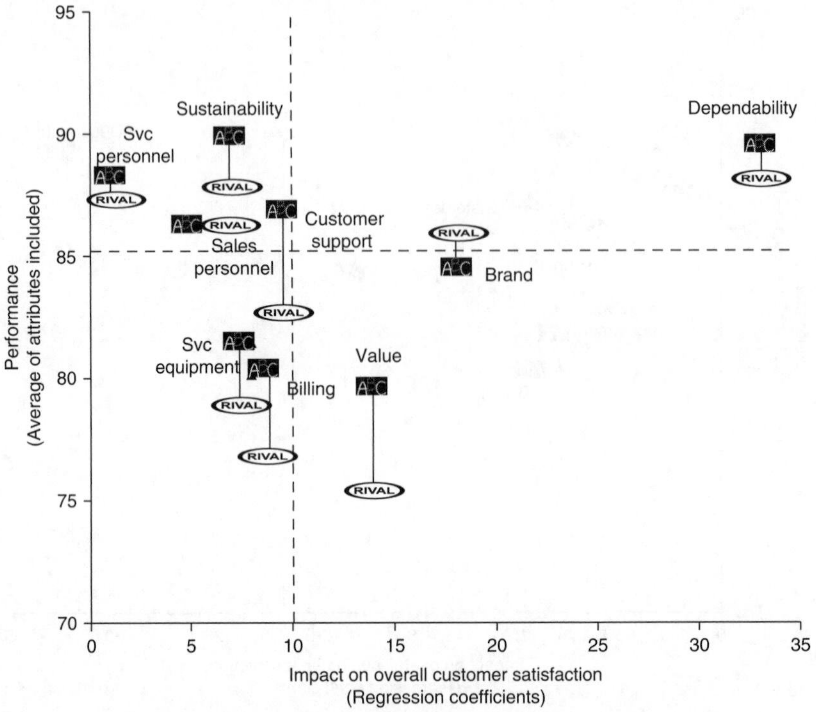

Figure 10.4 Benchmarked importance-performance map for ABC Corporation versus chief rival

performance. However, senior management was unwilling to consider reducing its prices and therefore margins as a means of improving customer satisfaction. Instead, they decided to focus on dependability, which had the strongest influence on customer satisfaction. Moreover, ABC had no meaningful performance advantage over its chief competitor in terms of dependability. This was clear from Figure 10.4, which also displays competitor performance. Figure 10.4 also showed ABC had a significant advantage over its chief rival in customer perceptions of value, customer support, billing, and on-site equipment.

As shown in Figure 10.2, the throughput portion of the satisfaction profit chain model found that overall customer satisfaction was linked to three types of customer intentions relevant to this firm: (1) customers' intentions to renew service contracts with the company, (2) customers' plans to consider alternative vendors to ABC, and (3) customers' willingness to recommend ABC to colleagues and associates.

The analysis traced the impact of these throughput variables by first

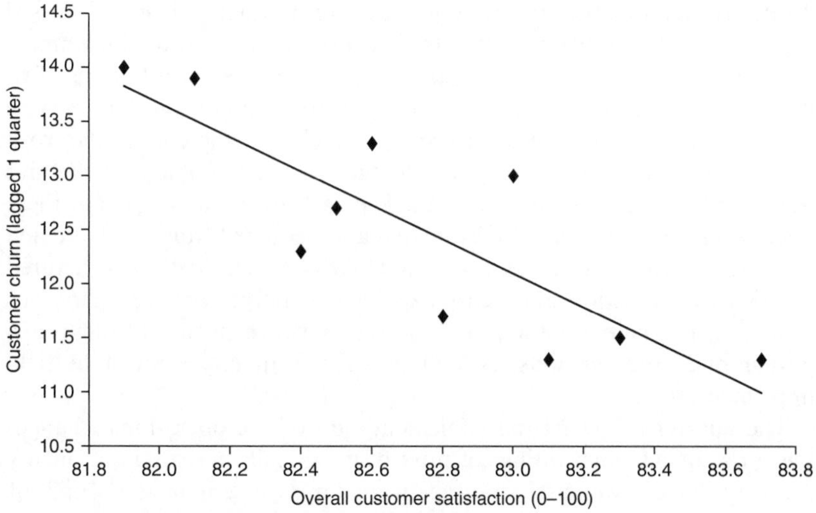

Figure 10.5 Relationship between customer satisfaction and churn

linking overall customer satisfaction to the company's customer churn statistics. This metric was derived from the ABC billing system, which indicated the number of customers who had terminated service. Churn was simply the proportion of all customers in the time period who ended their service. Figure 10.5 shows the relationship between overall customer satisfaction and customer churn. A 1 percent gain in overall satisfaction was estimated to reduce actual customer churn by 0.4 percent, which would yield an incremental gross margin of $40 million for ABC. From the earlier analysis of overall customer satisfaction, the latter would be improved most by increasing customers' perceptions of service dependability, rather than value, sustainability, billing, or service personnel. Even very modest improvements in customer perceptions of dependability had a notable impact on profitability. For every 1 percent improvement in dependability, overall satisfaction increased by 0.6 percent, which through its effect on lowering customer churn, would result in an estimated $22 million gain in gross margin.

To address the question of how to improve service dependability, the analysis identified that the key attribute driving perceptions of dependability was "No missed service calls" as opposed to "I can rely on ABC's service" or "My service is performed at the scheduled time." The implication of this finding was clear: Dependability would be most readily improved by specifically reducing the occurrence of missed service calls by ABC's field operations.

To determine how best to bring about lowering the incidence of missed service calls, the study team undertook a comprehensive root-cause analysis of the operational factors responsible for these service failures. Two key causes—out-of-date customer location information on daily service routes, and failure to check service personnel in at the end of the work day—were pinpointed by the team as the most actionable and effective ways of reducing missed service calls. The costs of pursuing each of these operational avenues were also estimated and deducted from the estimated incremental gross margin. In addition, ABC substantially restructured the field organization and centralized the corporate service operations function. This allowed for more coordinated investments through corporate budget allocations as well as greater quality control in field implementation.

The quarter following the implementation of the operational changes saw a rise in customer ratings of missed service calls in the service quality tracking, which was also reflected in an improvement in the scores of service dependability. During the next quarter, overall customer satisfaction scores also began to climb, reversing a four-year downward trend, as shown in Figure 10.6. Meanwhile, customer churn rates correspondingly

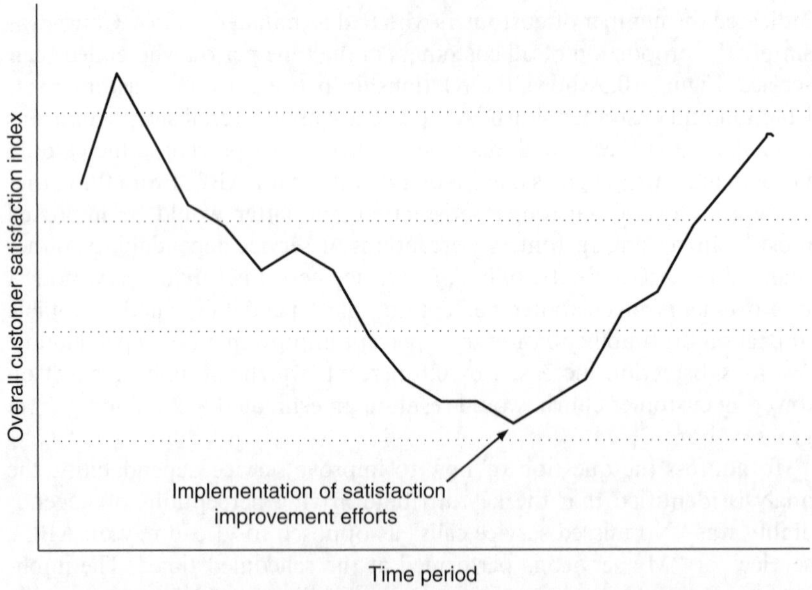

Figure 10.6 Results from use of satisfaction profit chain to guide ABC strategy and operations

began to decline, dropping from 13 percent to 10 percent. Financial statements confirmed the expected improvement in gross margin.

Thus, the satisfaction profit chain model constructed by ABC Corporation not only illuminated the path to achieving improved business growth and earnings during a difficult transition period, but also helped the executive team discover the importance of a customer-focused strategy.

CONCLUDING COMMENTS

Since its introduction by Rust et al. (1994), the SPC has become a strategically useful and theoretically challenging framework to understand marketing strategy from a customer-focused perspective. It can simultaneously provide guidance for strategy formulation and its tactical implementation. Its ability to incorporate a wide variety of firm inputs and efforts, link them to customer service perceptions and customer satisfaction, and then use customer-survey metrics to predict financial metrics provides a basis for making marketing strategy financially accountable. In addition to the dozen or so published studies in the academic literature, we are aware of several dozen cases where firms have applied the SPC framework to formulate, implement, and refine their strategy.

We have provided a review of the core concepts, as well as the empirical applications of the SPC framework. More importantly, we have identified useful research areas that can provide important research avenues. More generally, addressing the methodological and data-associated challenges, along with the incorporation of additional constructs (mediators and moderators) will be critical to conceptually refining the SPC concept. We hope that marketing scholars will continue researching this important area so that marketing concepts not only become financially accountable, but also more widely used by C-suite managers who seek higher returns to their marketing investments.

NOTE

1. Regression b coefficients.

REFERENCES

Anderson, Eugene W. and Vikas Mittal (2000), "Strengthening the satisfaction-profit chain," *Journal of Service Research*, **3** (2), 107–20.

Anderson, Eugene W., Claes Fornell and Sanal K. Mazvancheryl (2004), "Customer Satisfaction and Shareholder Value," *Journal of Marketing*, 68 (October), 172–85.

Anderson, Ronald, Robert D. Mackoy, Vincent B. Thompson and Gilbert Harrell (2004), "A Bayesian network estimation of the service-profit chain for transport service satisfaction," *Decision Sciences*, **35** (4), 665–89.

Bolton, Ruth N. (1998), "A dynamic model of the duration of the customer's relationship with a continuous service provider: the role of satisfaction," *Marketing Science*, **17** (1), 45–65.

Bolton, Ruth N. and James H. Drew (1991), "A multistage model of customers' assessments of service quality and value," *Journal of Consumer Research*, **17** (4), 375–84.

Bolton, Ruth N. and James H. Drew (1994), "Linking customer satisfaction to service operations and outcomes, in Roland T. Rust and Richard L. Oliver (eds), *Service Quality: New Directions in Theory and Practice*, Beverly Hills, CA: Sage Publications, pp. 173–200.

Bolton, Ruth N., Katherine N. Lemon and Peter C. Verhoef (2008), "Expanding business-to-business customer relationships: modeling the customer upgrade decision," *Journal of Marketing*, **12** (January), 46–64.

Bowman, Douglas and Das Narayandas (2004), "Linking customer management effort to customer profitability in business markets," *Journal of Marketing Research*, **39**, 433–47.

Brown, Steven P. and Son K. Lam (2008), "A meta-analysis of relationships linking employee satisfaction to customer responses," *Journal of Retailing*, **84** (September), 243–55.

Carr, Nicholas G. (1999), "Marketing: the economics of customer satisfaction," *Harvard Business Review*, **77** (March–April), 15–18.

Charnes, Abraham, William W. Cooper, Arie Y. Lewin and Lawrence Seiford (1994), *Data Envelopment Analysis: Theory, Methodology, and Application*, Norwell, MA: Kluwer Academic.

Chevalier, Judith A. and Dina Mayzlin (2006), "The effect of word of mouth on sales: online book reviews," *Journal of Marketing Research*, **36** (August), 345–49.

Danaher, Peter J. (1998), "Customer heterogeneity in service management," *Journal of Service Research*, **1** (2), 129–39.

Danaher, Peter J. and Roland T. Rust (1996), "Indirect financial benefits from service quality," *Quality Management Journal*, **2** (2), 63–85.

Escalas, Jennifer Edson and James R. Bettman (2005), "Self-construal, reference groups, and brand meaning," *Journal of Consumer Research*," **32** (December), 378–89.

Evanschitzky, Heiner, Christopher Groening, Vikas Mittal and Maren Wunderlich (2011), "How employer and employee satisfaction affect customer satisfaction: an application to franchise services," *Journal of Service Research*, **14** (2), 136–48.

Garbarino, Ellen and Mark S. Johnson (1999), "The different roles of satisfaction, trust, and commitment in customer relationships," *Journal of Marketing*, **63** (April), 70–87.

Garland, Ron (2002), "What influences customer profitability? Service-profit chain: non-financial drivers of customer profitability in personal retail banking," *Journal of Targeting, Measurement and Analysis for Marketing*, **10** (3), 233–48.

Gelade, Garry A. and Stephen Young (2005), "Test of a service profit chain model in the retail banking sector," *Journal of Occupational and Organizational Psychology*, **78** (1), 1–22.

Green, Paul E. and V. Srinivasan (1990), "Conjoint analysis in marketing: new developments with implications for research and practice," *Journal of Marketing*, **54** (October), 3–19.

Gruca, Thomas S. and Lopo L. Rego (2005), "Customer satisfaction, cash flow, and shareholder value," *Journal of Marketing*, **69** (July), 115–30.

Heskett, James L., Thomas O. Jones, Gary W. Loveman, W. Earl Sasser Jr. and Leonard A. Schlesinger (1994), "Putting the service profit chain to work," *Harvard Business Review*, **72** (2), 164–74.

Homburg, Christian and Ruth M. Stock (2004), "The link between salespeople's job satisfaction and customer satisfaction in a business-to-business context: a dyadic analysis," *Journal of the Academy of Marketing Science*, **32** (2), 144–58.

Homburg, Christian, Jan Wieseke and Wayne D. Hoyer (2009), "Social identity and the service-profit chain," *Journal of Marketing*, **73** (March), 38–54.

Iacobucci, Dawn, Neela Saldanha and Xiaoyan Deng (2007), "A meditation on mediation: evidence that structural equation models perform better than regressions," *Journal of Consumer Psychology*, **17** (2), 140–54.

Kamakura, Wagner A., Vikas Mittal, Fernando de Rosa and José Afonso Mazzon (2002), "Assessing the service-profit chain," *Marketing Science*, **21** (3), 294–317.

Kassinis, George I. and Andreas C. Soteriou (2003), "Greening the service profit chain: the impact of environmental management practices," *Production and Operations Management*, **12** (3), 386–403.

Kast, Fremont E. and James E. Rosenzweig (1972), "General systems theory: applications for organization and management," *Academy of Management Journal*, **15** (4), 447–65.

Keiningham, Timothy L., Tiffany Perkins-Munn, Lerzan Aksoy and Demitry Estrin (2005), "Does customer satisfaction lead to profitability," *Managing Service Quality*, **15** (2), 172–81.

Keller, Kevin Lane (1993), "Conceptualizing, measuring, and managing customer-based brand equity," *Journal of Marketing*, **57** (January), 1–22.

Kimes, Sheryl E. (1999), "The relationship between product quality and revenue per available room at Holiday Inn," *Journal of Service Research*, **2** (2), 138–44.

Larivière, Bart (2008), "Linking perceptual and behavioral customer metrics to multiperiod customer profitability: a comprehensive service-profit chain application," *Journal of Service Research*, **11** (3), 3–21.

Loveman, Gary W. (1998), "Employee satisfaction, customer loyalty, and financial performance: an empirical examination of the service profit chain in retail banking," *Journal of Service Research*, **1** (1), 18–31.

Luo, Xueming (2009), "Quantifying the long-term impact of negative word of mouth on cash flows and stock prices," *Marketing Science*, **28** (1), 148–65.

Meuter, Matthew L., Amy L. Ostrom, Robert I. Roundtree and Mary Jo Bitner (2000), "Self-service technologies: understanding customer satisfaction with technology-based service encounters," *Journal of Marketing*, **64** (July), 50–64.

Mittal, Vikas and Wagner A. Kamakura (2001), "Satisfaction, repurchase intent, and repurchase behavior: investigating the moderating effect of customer characteristics," *Journal of Marketing Research*, **38** (February), 131–42.

Mittal, Vikas, Pankaj Kumar and Michael Tsiros (1999), "Attribute-level performance, satisfaction, and behavioral intentions over time: a consumption-system approach," *Journal of Marketing*, **63** (April), 88–101.

Morgan, Gareth (1986), *Images of Organizations*, Beverly Hills, CA: Sage Publications.

Morwitz, Vicki G. and David Schmittlein (1992), "Using segmentation to improve sales forecasts based on purchase intent: which 'intenders' actually buy?" *Journal of Marketing Research*, **9** (November), 391–405.

Parasuraman, A., Valarie Zeithaml and Leonard L. Berry (1998), "SERVQUAL: a multiple-item scale for measuring consumer perceptions of service quality, *Journal of Retailing*, **64** (Spring), 12–40.

Pritchard, Michael and Rhian Silvestro (2005), "Applying the service profit chain to analyze retail performance: the case of the managerial strait-jacket?" *International Journal of Service Industry Management*, **16** (4), 337–56.

Reidenbach, R. Eric and Terence A. Oliva (1981), "General living systems theory and marketing: a framework for analysis," *Journal of Marketing*, **45** (Fall), 30–37.

Rust, Roland T. and Tuck Siong Chung (2006), "Marketing models of service and relationships," *Marketing Science*, **25** (6), 560–80.

Rust, Roland T. and Richard L. Oliver (1994), "Service quality: insights and managerial implications from the frontier" in Roland T. Rust and Richard L. Oliver (eds), *Service Quality: New Directions in Theory and Practice*, Beverly Hills, CA: Sage Publications, pp. 1–20.

Rust, Roland T., Katherine N. Lemon and Valarie A. Zeithaml (2004), "Return on marketing: using customer equity to focus marketing strategy," *Journal of Marketing*, **68** (January), 109–27.

Rust, Roland T., Anthony J. Zahorik and Timothy L. Keiningham (1994), "Return on quality (ROQ): making service quality financially accountable," Marketing Science Institute, report no. 94-106, April.

Rust, Roland T., Anthony J. Zahorik, and Timothy L. Keiningham (1995), "Return on quality (ROQ): making service quality financially accountable," *Journal of Marketing*, **59** (April), 58–70.

Rust, Roland T., Valarie Zeithaml, and Katherine Lemon (2000), *Driving Customer Equity: How Customer Lifetime Value is Reshaping Corporate Strategy*, New York: Free Press.

Schneider, Benjamin, Susan S. White, Michelle C. Paul (1998), "Linking service climate and customer perceptions of service quality: tests of a causal model," *Journal of Applied Psychology*, **83** (2), 150–63.

Seiders, Kathleen, Glenn B. Voss, Dhruv Grewal and Andrea L. Godfrey (2005), "Do satisfied customers buy more? Examining moderating influences in a retailing context," *Journal of Marketing*, **69** (October), 26–43.

Silvestro, Rhian and Stuart Cross (2000), "Applying the service profit chain in a retail environment: challenging the 'satisfaction mirror,'" *International Journal of Service Industry Management*, **11** (3), 244–68.

Soteriou, Andreas and Stavros A. Zenios (1999), "Operations, quality, and profitability in the provision of banking services," *Management Science*, **45** (9), 1221–38.

Vargo, Stephen L. and Robert F. Lusch (2004), "Evolving to a new dominant logic for marketing," *Journal of Marketing*, **68** (January), 1–17.

PART IV

MANAGING CUSTOMER CONTACTS

11 Service encounters in service marketing research

Mary Jo Bitner and Helen Si Wang

The service encounter or the "moment of truth" is one of the foundational constructs of service marketing. One of the earliest and most cited papers on this topic defined the service encounter as "the dyadic interaction between a customer and a service provider" (Surprenant and Solomon 1987, p. 87), meaning the moment in time when a customer interacts directly with a service provider. A broader view of the construct was also prevalent in a definition provided by Shostack (1985, p. 243) who described the service encounter as "a period of time during which a consumer directly interacts with a service." This broader definition suggests the term "service encounter" encompasses not only dyadic interactions with employees, but also customer interactions with technology, other customers, physical facilities, and other elements of the service. Later, Bitner and Hubbert (1994, p. 74) added an element to the definition which distinguishes it further from longer events or experiences in delineating a service encounter as "a discrete event occurring over a definable period of time." Over the years, the term "service encounter" has come to encompass technology-based encounters along with encounters that occur in person, over the telephone, or through the mail, and even within organizations (Zeithaml et al. 2013, ch. 4).

In tracing the term service encounter back to its origins, the earliest published papers on the topic include a paper by Solomon et al. (1985) appearing in the *Journal of Marketing* and a book entitled *The Service Encounter* (Czepiel et al. 1985). The book was the result of a conference that gathered researchers who led the early development of the service marketing field and research on service encounters (for example, David Bowen, Benjamin Schneider, Bernard Booms, Christopher Lovelock, Lynn Shostack, Michael Solomon, Mary Jo Bitner, Carol Surprenant, and others). These papers and books provided the impetus for long and deep lines of research on service encounters that have taken many different directions and spanned multiple disciplines.

Interestingly, prior to the mid-1980s no research in marketing had focused on service interactions between customers and providers and their impact on marketing outcomes. Since then, research has established the service encounter as a key determinant of customer satisfaction, perceptions of service quality, and ultimately customer loyalty (Gupta and Zeithaml 2006; Zeithaml et al. 1996). There has also been extensive research aimed at understanding the factors and dimensions of service encounters and underlying psychological drivers of service encounter satisfaction. As of today, tens of thousands of papers and books have been published using the term "service encounter." A search of Google Scholar on the search term "service encounter and marketing" revealed 194,000 results as of March 2013.

The service encounter construct is not only important to academic literature and theories of service marketing. It has also become an important focus for managers seeking to improve service quality and drive loyalty in their businesses. In the last several decades, managers in almost every industry have recognized the impact that their frontline employees and technologies have on customers in the "moment of truth", and many have built their marketing and loyalty strategies around effective customer–employee or customer–technology interactions. For example, at Zappos.com (owned by Amazon), the renowned online shoe retailer, every technology-based encounter is designed to build satisfaction and loyalty by providing easy access, well-researched information and photographs of shoe choices, along with an easy ordering and return process. Yet, the company also focuses on making every one of its phone encounters equally superior by allowing customer service representatives to spend whatever time is needed to help a customer who calls with questions or special requests. They know their success is built on consistent quality and excellence in these two very different types of encounters. The critical role of customer service in building relationships and even promoting and selling the firm's products and services has been recognized by many companies who invest heavily in customer service training and recruiting. For example, companies such as Harrah's Entertainment, Enterprise Rent-A-Car, Southwest Airlines, and Walgreens all spend substantial time and resources training their employees to excel at customer service in every encounter, and they reward them accordingly. Yet, just 30 years ago, few companies had strategies that recognized and measured the importance of these encounters or moments of truth.

In this chapter, we review the marketing discipline's research on service encounters, organizing our review around several themes that have been emphasized in the literature. Our discussion is based on three central themes: service encounter satisfaction, including its antecedents and consequences; service encounter dyads; and service encounters within experiences and networks. Within each theme, we also highlight current research directions and topics we believe represent the future of service encounter research in these domains. Owing to the large number of papers and book chapters published on service encounters, we will, for the most part, limit our discussion within each theme to highly cited papers and those published in prominent marketing and service journals or books. Our goal is to summarize influential research themes, highlight key research papers within each thematic area, and provide direction for future research, rather than to provide an exhaustive review of the literature.

SERVICE ENCOUNTER SATISFACTION

In this section we focus on research that explores the antecedents of service encounter satisfaction as well as its consequences and impact on downstream marketing outcomes. These have been two prominent themes of service encounter research, beginning very early in the service marketing discipline's history and continuing to the present.

Antecedents of Service Encounter Satisfaction

The foundation for most of the research on antecedents of service encounter satisfaction is the disconfirmation paradigm that contends that customer satisfaction with a service encounter depends on initial expectations for the encounter compared to actual perceptions of the encounter (Oliver 1980, 1997; Parasuraman et al. 1988). It is assumed that customers whose expectations are met or exceeded will be satisfied with the encounter. The same theoretical logic applies in research related to service quality perceptions. The fundamental disconfirmation paradigm has been widely used in service research with few challenges other than the debate over whether it is necessary to measure service expectations and how to measure them (Cronin and Taylor 1994; Parasuraman et al. 1994). For the most part, instead of debating and developing the underlying paradigm, research has focused on the predictors and outcomes of service encounter satisfaction. From a theory perspective, this has drawn researchers into areas such as customer–employee interactions, employee behaviors, customer-to-customer interactions, environmental psychology, the influence of servicescapes, and the effects of a broad range of psychological constructs such as mood, emotions, and attributions on service encounter satisfaction.

Critical Incident Research

Foundational work in service encounter satisfaction using the critical incident technique showed that the causes of dis/satisfaction in service encounters from the customer's perspective were linked to: employee responses to service delivery failures; employee responses to customer needs and requests; and unprompted and unsolicited actions on the part of employees (Bitner et al. 1990). These three broad categories were found to drive both satisfaction and dissatisfaction, depending on the particular actions of employees. For example, a service delivery failure might be remembered by the customer as satisfying or dissatisfying depending on how the failure was handled by the employee. Follow-up research that looked at critical service encounters from the employee's perspective found one additional cause, namely problematic customer behavior, as the source of customer dis/satisfaction (Bitner et al. 1994). The early critical incident studies served as the foundation for many studies in services and marketing using this technique to further explore encounter satisfaction in a variety of contexts (for example, Gremler 2004; Keaveney 1995).

Contextual Predictors of Service Encounter Satisfaction

While the early critical incident technique (CIT) research was very basic and largely descriptive in nature, it spawned considerable theoretical research examining specific behaviors such as employee effort (Mohr and Bitner 1995), employee rapport (Gremler and Gwinner 2000), employee adaptability (Gwinner et al. 2005), employee's service recovery behaviors (Tax et al. 1998), and employee coping behaviors and their effects on service encounter satisfaction. The early work on service recovery behaviors and complaint satisfaction formed the base of what has become a very deep and continuing stream of work on service recovery which we will not attempt to cover here (for reviews and recent papers see deMatos et al. 2007; Grégoire et al. 2009; Orsingher et al. 2010). What all of this research clearly established is that employees play a key role in service delivery outcomes and that the various types of behaviors and interactions can ultimately impact the level of customer satisfaction with the service and company. This research brought frontline service employees into the mainstream of marketing and service research. Prior to the research on service encounters, service employees were not viewed as a mainstream element of relevance to marketing theory or practice.

In addition to employee behaviors, research has shown other key predictors of service encounter satisfaction including the process of service delivery, technology interfaces, the customer him/herself, other customers, and the servicescape (Bitner 1992; Brady and Cronin 2001). Relying on a variety of theoretical foundations, research on these predictors has enriched our theoretical and managerial understanding of service encounters. Below we highlight some of the central topics, summarized in Figure 11.1.

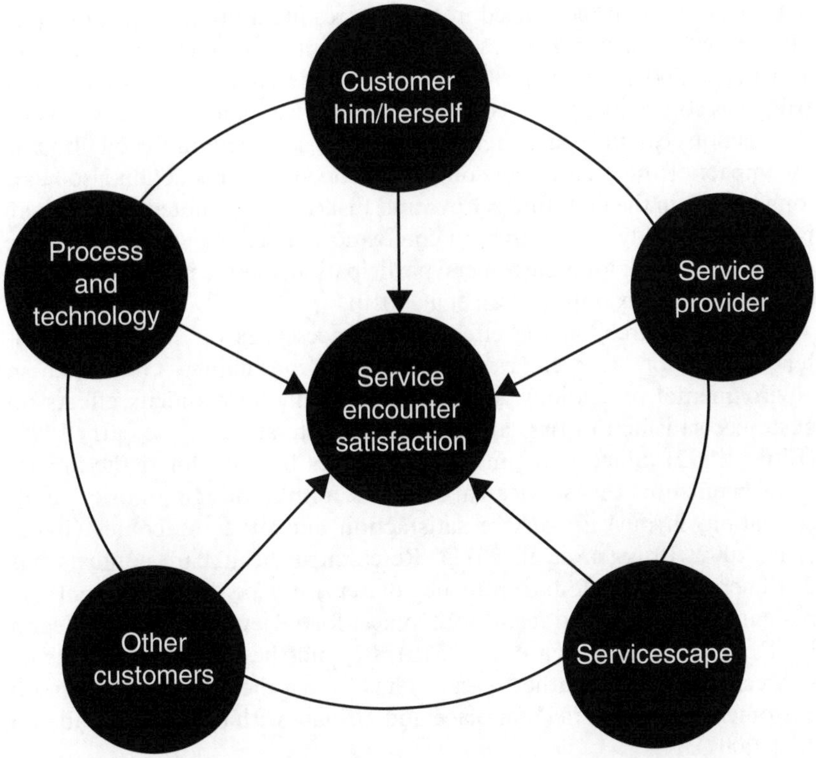

Figure 11.1 Contextual predictors of service encounter satisfaction

One particular service process element that has received significant research attention is waiting time. For services, waiting time is often a critical factor influencing customer satisfaction and many studies have examined aspects of its impact on satisfaction including length and type of delay (Taylor 1994, 1995), types of information shared during the wait (Hui and Tse 1996), stage in the service process where waiting occurs (Hui et al. 1998), and effects of the number of people in line (Zhou and Soman 2003). Other research has documented the increasing role played by technology in building service encounter satisfaction (Bitner et al. 2000; Meuter et al. 2000, 2005) as well as the nuances underlying satisfaction with technology-delivered service encounters (Dabholkar 1996; Holloway and Beatty 2008). As more and more services are delivered through self-service technology and "virtual servicescapes" are commonly experienced by customers, the opportunities for research on technology-based services remain open to further exploration and theory development.

It has long been recognized in the services literature that the customer him or herself also influences service encounter satisfaction (Bendapudi and Leone 2003; Bowen 1986). Through their behaviors, customers contribute as co-producers and co-creators of service value, and the quality of their actions can influence their own ultimate satisfaction. Recognition of the impact of other customers on service encounter satisfaction also has a long history in the literature (Grove and Fisk 1997). As noted earlier, there is a growing body of research on co-creation of service value and service outcomes that explores customers' participation and the impact on service evaluations (for example, Chan et al. 2010).

Finally, research on the effects of servicescapes on service encounter satisfaction is well established and continuing. Grounded in environmental psychology, servicescape terminology and its effects on customer satisfaction first appeared in the literature in the early 1990s (Bitner 1992). Since that time, many studies have explored the impact of elements of the servicescape (for example, design, music, modernization, layout) on service satisfaction and other outcomes (Baker et al. 2002; Bruggen et al. 2011). Research in healthcare contexts has documented the profound influence of servicescape design elements on patient satisfaction and health outcomes (for reviews see "Good Health By Design" 2011; Ulrich et al. 2010). Beyond the immediate effects of servicescape features, other research has shown the effects of design on customers' desire to stay in a place and affiliate with others (Rosenbaum et al. 2007).

Psychological Antecedents of Service Encounter Satisfaction

The previous section summarized central research themes related to contextual predictors of service encounter satisfaction and the factors that influence it from a service design and delivery perspective. In addition, there has been considerable research on the underlying psychological dimensions that influence service encounter satisfaction. Some of the primary theories that have been relied upon to understand customer satisfaction with service encounters are mood and emotion (Hennig-Thurau et al. 2006; Mattilla and Enz 2002), attribution theory (Bitner 1990; Folkes et al. 1987), role theory (Solomon et al. 1985), perceived control (Hui and Bateson 1991; Hui and Toffoli 2002; Noone et al. 2012), and equity theory (Olsen and Johnson 2003; Seiders and Berry 1998). Through this work we have gained a deeper appreciation for the psychology behind when and why customers are satisfied (or not) with particular service encounters.

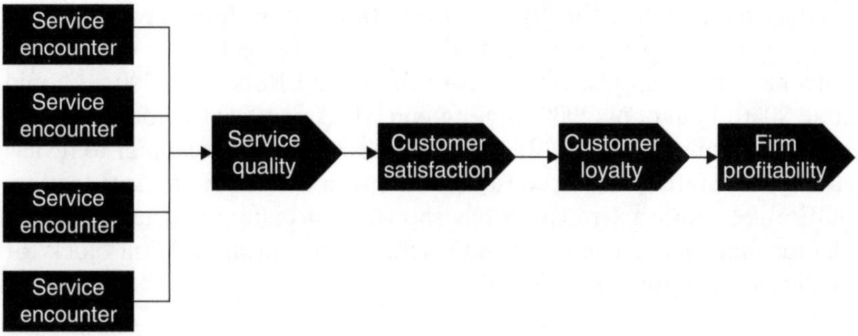

Source: Adapted from Zeithaml et al. (2013, p. 483).

Figure 11.2 Service encounters as drivers of service quality, customer satisfaction, customer loyalty and firm profitability

Consequences of Service Encounter Satisfaction

While research on the antecedents and predictors of service encounter satisfaction has dominated the published literature, the consequences of service encounter satisfaction and its impact on overall service quality, firm satisfaction, and other important downstream outcomes have also been the focus of research. In fact, service encounters have been referred to as the "building blocks of quality, value, and satisfaction" (Zeithaml et al. 2013, p. 93). What this means is that, while overall satisfaction and customer loyalty are critical to important firm outcomes such as customer loyalty and profitability, underlying those constructs are the day-to-day experiences of customers in service encounters. Figure 11.2 provides a visual representation of the connections between service encounters, quality, satisfaction, loyalty and firm profitability.

In their extensive review of several of the linkages shown in Figure 11.2, Gupta and Zeithaml (2006) suggest and provide evidence to support the following chain of relationships: customer perceptions or "what customers think" (for example, quality and satisfaction) are linked to customer behaviors or "what customers do" (for example, measurable behavioral outcomes like repeat purchase and loyalty), which predict firm outcomes or "what firms get" (for example, profits and other financial measures). Although they do not review the literature on it, their framework also suggests that marketing actions, including service encounters, will drive customer perceptions, setting off the downstream sequence of linkages in the framework. This seminal paper provides sound justification for considering service encounters as key drivers of customer perceptions and ultimately firm outcomes.

Other research has directly established the relationships between service encounter evaluations, service quality, and customer behaviors and firm outcomes (for example, Bitner 1990; Brady and Robertson 2001; Cronin et al. 2000; Paul et al. 2009; Spreng and Mackoy 1996; Taylor and Baker 1994; Zeithaml et al. 1996). It is beyond the scope of this chapter to review all of the literature on the consequences of service encounter satisfaction. Suffice it to say that research has shown, and many managers are convinced, that service encounter satisfaction is a critical building block for quality, satisfaction and loyalty.

Service Encounter Satisfaction—Future Research and Challenges

While research on the antecedents and consequences of service encounter satisfaction has a relatively long history, there are gaps in our knowledge and topics that remain to be explored. All of the influences shown in Figure 11.1 remain open to further research and deeper theoretical understanding. Further, as these areas evolve, they are taking on new directions and meanings, building from the foundations. For example, understanding of the customer's own role and other customers' roles as antecedents of service encounter satisfaction are being further developed in current research grounded in service-dominant logic, co-creation and service "value in use" (Grönroos 2011; Vargo and Lusch 2004). While the basic notion of service encounter satisfaction is still the foundation, current research is expanding the idea to focus on its co-creative and dynamic elements (for example, Chan et al. 2010; Wang et al. 2013). Research that cuts across service encounter satisfaction topics and weaves together current knowledge in innovative ways is also emerging. For example, researchers have combined theories of positive affect with theories of customer participation in examining the effect of positive affective state on a customer's level of participation, perceptions of quality, and satisfaction with healthcare encounters (Gallan et al. 2013).

From a managerial perspective, companies are beginning to realize that generic "good service" within a service encounter may not be enough to ensure superior outcomes, loyalty, or competitive advantage. Questions of "What precisely is good service in a given context?," "What do customers really expect?" and "How do expectations and perceptions evolve?" are important issues for companies, and thus compelling avenues for research. We have a strong and basic understanding of the answers to these questions; yet nuances, unexpected connections, and deeper theoretical understanding are still in needed. As one example, the notion of "branded customer service" is gaining momentum in practice. Branded customer service is more than good service; it is service that is carefully aligned with the company's brand position and where employees embody the brand position, personality, or meaning (Barlow and Stewart 2004). Some of the best examples of branded customer service are Southwest Airlines and Apple Computer. Empirically, branded customer service has been shown to impact brand satisfaction and customer-based brand equity, particularly for unfamiliar brands (Sirianni et al. 2013). This type of research takes us beyond the fundamentals of service encounter satisfaction and generic good service to begin to understand the nuances of branded service encounters and their impact on brand evaluations.

Finally, most of the published research on service encounter satisfaction is contextualized in consumer service settings. Yet, service encounters are clearly critical within business-to-business (B2B) relationships as well. While there are exceptions (Jayawardhena et al. 2007), our current understanding of the role of service encounters in B2B is limited.

SERVICE ENCOUNTER DYADS

Another core theme of service encounter research is the work on service encounter dyads. For many services, the dyadic interaction process between the customer and the service provider is the service, constituting an important part of service experience, and directly influencing service outcomes (for example, Bitner et al. 1990; Solomon et al. 1985). Central to service encounter dyads is the idea that the customer and the service provider mutually influence each other. Such a dyadic interaction not only causes a high interdependency between the service process and service outcomes (Chan et al. 2010; Ma and Dubé 2011), it also gives rise to a series of new cognitive, emotional, and behavioral phenomena in the service process and outcomes. In this section, we extend our exploration of service encounters from a single party's summary assessment, to a dyadic, moment-by-moment, and dynamic view. First, we review some of the important research on service encounter dyads. Then, in line with some of the most recent research, we explore conceptual and analytical potential for studying service encounter dyads.

A Dyadic Perspective

The conceptual focus on the dyadic view of service encounters has decades of history in the literature. Solomon et al. (1985) first developed a conceptual framework of dyadic service encounters based on role theory. They strongly argued that the service encounter is interactive and reciprocal, rather than something that can be looked at only from one party's perspective or at one point in time. Service outcomes rely on mutually satisfying factors and joint actions, rather than either party's perceptions and behaviors alone. In particular for low-involvement "mindless service encounters", Solomon et al. (1985) proposed using service scripts, a set of learned assumptions regarding each other's behaviors during the course of the interaction process, to understand the dyadic interaction process. Interdependency in the service process and service outcomes is conceptualized as the congruence or the positive or negative discrepancy in each other's scripted behaviors. Solomon et al.'s (1985) seminal conceptual focus on dyads inspired a series of studies focusing on the idea of interdependency. Some researchers re-examined important service outcome variables by acquiring measures from both the customer and service provider sides, such as service expectation–perception gap (Brown and Swartz 1989), Service Quality Index (SQI) (Farrell et al. 2001), and customer participation and value co-creation (Chan et al. 2010). Other research focused on the relational aspects unique to interaction dyads, such as commercial friendship (Price and Arnould 1999) and customer–employee rapport (Gremler and Gwinner 2000), and employee adaptive behavior (Gwinner et al. 2005).

Dyadic service encounters not only operate at the behavioral level, but also create emotional contagion, that is, the flow of emotions from one to another (Hatfield et al. 1994; Schoenewolf 1990). Extensive research has examined employee smiling behavior and authenticity of emotional labor display (Hennig-Thurau et al. 2006), dynamic impact of employees' multiple sequential emotional displays on customers' negative emotions (Du et al. 2011), employees' displayed emotions and their influences on customer affect and customer judgments of service quality (Pugh 2001), as well as customers' and employees' derived enjoyment from customer participation (Yim et al. 2012).

Researchers further find that the effects of interdependency are not universal. Gender, stereotype, and service brand can significantly moderate the dyadic interaction and related service outcomes. Mattila et al. (2003) found that men and women respond differently to positive and negative affective displays. Matta and Folkes (2005) argued that stereotypes have both positive and negative effects on consumers' perceptions of service providers, as well as of within-brand similarity and across-brand differentiation.

Dyads in Service Conversations

Decades of research developed rich theories on service encounter dyads by focusing on interdependency and adopting a dyadic lens. However, to conceptualize the customer–service provider interaction as a truly dyadic, moment-by-moment, and dynamic process calls for more in-depth analysis beyond summary measures acquired from both parties. New conceptual insights on 'how' the interdependency happens, rather than 'what' kind of interdependency, are yet to be explored. Traditional research methodology based on summary report and linear analytics, as important as they are, may hinder the further theoretical development of interdependency (Ma and Dubé 2011).

From this perspective, service conversational interaction provides us an ideal context to go into the micro-level of the dyadic interaction process. Service conversations are particularly important for professional services. In B2B services, such as information technology (IT) consulting and support services (for example IBM), management consulting or advertising agencies (for example, McKinsey or BBDO), clients convey their needs through conversations. Service providers develop better relationships with their clients and demonstrate their specific knowledge and skills in conversations. In B2C interpersonal professional services, such as healthcare, financial, or legal services, a few minutes of customer–service provider conversation may determine or significantly change an individual's health or everyday life. A service conversation identifies problems and co-creates solutions.

Most importantly, analyzing service conversations opens up new research methods to study the moment-by-moment dynamics of customer participation. To move the conversation along, both the customer and the service provider have to play their roles and co-create experiences for each other. Each of the customer's or the service provider's conversational speech patterns at any given moment demonstrate what sense they make out of the conversation—their mental representation of the service context (Duranti and Goodwin 1992). Thus, by analyzing the micro-level of sequences of service conversations, we are able to obtain more detailed and moment-by moment information about how the customer or the service provider interprets the context of conversational interactions they are engaged in. A service conversation allows us to go beyond the traditional method of retrospective summary self-report. Instead, it allows us to truly study service encounter dyads as dynamic processes.

Recent research has given increasing attention to conversation studies through videotapes, and third-party observations. Through analyzing customer-service provider conversational interactions, researchers have investigated customers' brand-code switching (Schau et al. 2007) and service provider–customer (anti)complementary interactions (that is, dominant–submissive or agreeable–quarrelsome) (Ma and Dubé 2011). Given these studies have focused on standardized, script-based, and relatively short service conversational encounters (that is, fast-food drive-through, dining services), we expect that conversations in professional services, characterized by highly dyadic involvement and richer content, will further extend our understanding of the dynamics of customer participation behaviors.

In a recent study we developed a conceptual framework to explain the coexistence of stable and dynamic customer conversational participation behavior in professional service settings (that is, financial services and health care services) (Wang et al. 2013). Empirically, we conducted a series of controlled experiments, simulating different dyadic service conversation patterns, as well as an observation study of online conversations. We adopt a phase-based sequence analysis approach and non-linear analytical models to examine the dynamics of interaction processes and link the characteristics of the temporal dynamics to service outcomes. The research demonstrates that time, as well as the customer's moment-by-moment perceived context complexity, determine the temporal dynamics of conversational interaction processes. Most importantly, what really influences service outcomes in terms of customer satisfaction, customer perceived service quality, and customer solution compliance, is not how long the service conversation goes, nor which party is taking control of the conversation. Rather, better service outcomes rely on how quickly the service conversation evolves to reduce customer perceived context complexity, changing their conversational participation from submissive to dominant patterns of information sharing.

Service Encounter Dyads—Future Research and Challenges

The dyadic service encounter is the service in many cases. For service managers, acknowledging process and outcome interdependency, and understanding both 'what' kind of interdependency and 'how' interdependency happens, are equally important. For simple and low-involvement services (for example, restaurant and retailing), managers can resort to rule-based service scripts to design more standardized service processes and manage the dyadic discrepancy to improve customer satisfaction. For more complex and high-involvement services (for example, healthcare and financial services), managers can utilize the temporal dynamics of interaction processes to influence customer behaviors, steering service processes and outcomes in more favorable directions.

The study of service encounter dyads calls for more dynamic and innovative conceptual and methodology development. With the rising of new technology, service encounters are extending from the traditional face-to-face interactions to human-to-human, human-to-machine interactions via telephone, online, social network, or even artificial intelligence. Interactions between dyadic parties can also be expanded to interactions among multiple parties such as the customer, the service provider, other customers, other service providers and social networks. These potentially new interactive phenomena call for more rigorous research methodology. Adopting tools of nonlinear dynamical systems (NDS) in psychology allows researchers to relax the assumption of scripted or planned dyadic behaviors. Rather, dyadic interaction can be modeled as a self-organizing system. Service outcomes or the unique characteristics of the service process emerge as a result of interaction itself, rather than aggregated individual efforts (Gorman et al. 2010)

SERVICE EXPERIENCES AND NETWORKS

Up to this point, we have discussed research on discrete service encounters, including research that focuses on customer satisfaction with a particular service encounter and research that focuses on the dyadic relationship between a customer and employee during a discrete encounter. Yet, it is clear that discrete service encounters most often occur within a sequence of encounters making up a total "event" or "experience" and even, at times, within a network of encounters with different, independent providers (Morgan et al. 2007; Tax et al. 2013).

Clarification of Encounter, Experience, and Network Terminology

Often the terms encounter, event, and experience are used interchangeably, resulting in a lack of clarity and at times confusion. We adhere to the older definitions of service encounter as noted earlier in the chapter (Bitner and Hubbert 1994; Shostack 1984; Surprenant and Solomon 1987). These definitions distinguish service encounters from related constructs and allow us to, in contrast, define a total, end-to-end customer experience as "service comprised of multiple encounters occurring over time, where the total time of the experience might be as short as minutes or hours, or as long as days, weeks, or years." For example, a cable company Internet repair experience could comprise encounters with a customer service representative, a scheduler/dispatcher, a repair person, and a phone follow-up satisfaction survey. All of these encounters would be part of the total repair experience and would involve interactions with different employees of the cable company. This experience would likely take several days. Shorter experiences are reflected in many restaurant, retail, and daily service events, where experiences take minutes or hours, but can still be made up of multiple discrete encounters. An example of a much longer end-to-end experience would be an undergraduate student pursuing a college degree over a several-year period where the number of distinct encounters with the university would be huge and diverse. Similar long experiences are prevalent in B2B consulting and solutions provision and industries such as healthcare. The point is that each discrete encounter can play a role in determining satisfaction and long-term relationship quality with a provider, but it is often part of an extended string of encounters.

Extending this idea even further, it is clear that not all encounters in an experience are necessarily with the same provider. Frequently customers string together encounters and experiences with a variety of different providers within a service network that comprise the final, total experience from their perspective. For example, in an experience such as home buying in the U.S., the customer strings together multiple encounters with independent providers (for example, a realtor, bank, employer, insurance company) to build a total home-buying experience. Each of these encounters and related experiences will ultimately influence the customer's total perception of the home-buying activity. Researchers have defined this type of context as a "service delivery network" (Morgan et al. 2007; Tax et al. 2013).

Research on Service Experiences and Networks

Conceptual work related to service experiences has referred to the stringing together of related services as the "customer activity chain" for a particular service domain (Sawhney et al. 2004) where the activity chain comprises all of the various activities and services required to accomplish a particular customer goal. Bettencourt (2010) refers to services within these types of customer activity chains as services that "solve customer problems" and help them get "jobs" done. Some of the most recent work in this area examines "service networks" as defined by customers. In this research, service networks are defined as "two or more organizations that, in the eyes of the customer, are responsible for the provision of a connected overall service experience" and are typically comprised of related, linked, or informal constellations of organizations that customers need to accomplish their goals (Tax et al. 2013). When organizations and researchers start to think of services in these ways, as complex chains of encounters and events, the enormous complexities and opportunities become apparent—both theoretically and managerially.

A service innovation and improvement technique that has long recognized the multiple encounters and sequential nature of service experiences is service blueprinting (Bitner et al. 2008; Patricio et al. 2011). Service blueprinting, as a technique, makes the role of individual encounters in these overall experiences very clear and explicit and is thus helpful in conceiving and studying complex service experiences. Most applications and publications on service blueprinting to date have focused on experiences with an individual service provider (Bitner et al. 2008; Shostack 1984, 1987). However, some of the more recent work is beginning to look at multi-level service blueprints and blueprints that cut across organizational boundaries and silos (Ostrom et al. 2010; Patricio et al. 2011).

To date, there has been relatively little empirical research examining customer evaluations of total experiences and service networks. The most cited paper is Arnould and Price (2003). In this paper the authors studied extraordinary experiences and extended service encounters, specifically in the context of river rafting. The research focused on evolving customer expectations, emotions that shape the experience and outcomes over time, and interactions among rafters and guides, all of which took place over days and weeks. Clearly, there were many, many service encounters taking place across the total rafting experience. Other research in hospitality and educational contexts has studied the changing nature of service expectations over time, and the role of individual service encounters that occur within the experience in shaping expectations (Boulding et al. 1993). In another paper, Verhoef et al. (2004) drew on strong theory in psychology and economics to examine relatively short customer service calls as a "sequence of events." In the research they looked at "peak performance events" and "final events" within a conversation to assess customer satisfaction with the call. The theoretical base in this study was very strong; however, the hypotheses could be tested in a more complex, longer-term service setting to get a better sense of the underlying relationships. Very recently, Saxena-Iyer et al. (2013) combined service theories of customer participation, quality, and goals to look at customer participation in service encounters over time and how customer participation in these encounters shapes perceptions of service quality, progress toward goals, and assessment of the provider in a career counseling context. Studying extended experiences in these ways is valuable in identifying the complexities and the changing nature of expectations, evolving human relationships, patterns of emotions, and ultimate outcomes. Yet, as each of these examples shows, this type of research is very challenging and requires unique data and access to customers over time.

Service Experiences and Networks—Future Research and Challenges

The domain of service experiences and service networks is wide open for research. Empirically we know very little about extended service experiences, whether they are physical face-to-face experiences, online or virtual experiences, or some combination. What is the role of discrete service encounters in these extended experiences? How are relationships built and what determines customer loyalty? What are the roles of other customers in these extended experiences? In a sense, all of the questions asked and answered about the antecedents and consequences of discrete service encounter satisfaction could be explored in the context of longer-term, extended service experiences.

Furthermore, many encounters and experiences today take place virtually through online delivery channels and social networks. What is the role of a service encounter in these contexts? What do customers expect and how do they evaluate individual encounters and end-to-end experiences in these virtual, extended service situations? What is the same and what is different from what we know about simple and discrete, face-to-face or technology-based encounters? What new theoretical paradigms might help us explain these types of service experiences where expectations may be nonexistent or easily and quickly changed?

Research on customer-defined service networks is just beginning (Tax et al. 2013). As companies work together formally and informally to assist customers in achieving their goals, many questions arise as to how to innovate, maintain quality, and govern these service networks where there may be contracts that define relationships among network members, or not. In many cases, the customer him or herself constructs the network and there are no formal ties among the organizations. Yet, from the customer's perspective the total experience is influenced by the performance of the various entities within the network whether or not they are formally related to each other (Morgan et al. 2007).

SERVICE ENCOUNTER RESEARCH: CONCLUSION AND LOOKING AHEAD

In this chapter, we have reviewed the three prominent themes in service encounter research within the service marketing field and provided some insights into future directions. Yet, we recognize and offer as a caveat that we have not covered the literature in an exhaustive way. We did not attempt to cover the literature on service encounters published in other disciplines (for example, management, service operations, human resources), nor did we cover closely related topics such as service recovery in detail. Other chapters in this book will likely cover some of these very important research topics and domains. We also recognize that service encounter research is by necessity interdisciplinary given that service encounter strategy and delivery touches elements of marketing, operations, human resources, and technology. Here we have focused on papers published in marketing and service journals almost exclusively; yet we know that every one of the prominent papers we have cited drew from multiple disciplines for its conceptual grounding and/or theoretical basis. We are strong proponents of an even greater cross-disciplinary focus in the future.

We started this chapter by stating that the service encounter is a foundational construct within service marketing research. Clearly it is a foundation; but just as clearly, it is still an active and even emerging research domain from various perspectives. It is amazing to realize just how quickly the research on service encounters has evolved—from the first mentions in the early 1980s, to the current day where the term is commonplace both in research and in practice. In the preceding sections we examined key themes in service encounter research to date including service encounter satisfaction (antecedents and consequences), service dyads, and service experiences and networks. Within each of these themes, there are research gaps and room for additional significant research, even in the service encounter satisfaction area—the oldest and most established of the three themes. Some specific gaps and research questions were identified within each theme, but there are certainly others that will be found or will emerge in the future.

Beyond the specific questions and topics mentioned already that form the core of current and emerging service encounter research, there are other service encounter topics of importance for research in the future. For example, most of the research on service encounters has been done in western cultures. While there is some research focused on global strategies and cross-cultural issues related to service encounters (for example, Liu et al. 2001; Mattila 1999; Patterson and Mattila 2008; Voss et al. 2004), this is an area ripe for further study given its importance to service managers and the theoretical complexities that underlie cross-cultural behaviors and strategies. Cultural differences invite service mangers to pay more attention when designing, managing, and evaluating service encounters and experiences as they expand globally. Cultural differences are also important in the context of service outsourcing and encounters via telephone and over the Internet that cross cultural boundaries (Mattila 1999). However, we also should also consider "how deep or pervasive these cultural differences are?" (Markus and Kitayama 1991), and when and whether they make a difference to marketing and service encounter strategy. Further, understanding encounters within total experiences and service networks across cultures would also be extremely challenging, but important.

Another broad domain of service encounter research that will certainly expand in the future is the domain of technology-delivered service where encounters are with machines and computers as well as with other customers and employees in technology-mediated contexts and through social networks and media. While there is a history of research on technology-delivered service (for example, Dabholkar 1996; Meuter et al. 2005), the world is changing so rapidly that new topics and issues are emerging in real time. For example, every "app" is a service. But, what is an ideal "app encounter" or "app experience" or "app network"? How might our established theories and understanding of more traditional service encounters help to predict and understand customers in these new contexts? What new theories are needed? Further, as people co-create services with companies and with each other online and through social media, how do these types of "service encounters" influence perceptions and loyalty? Is customer loyalty even relevant in these fast-changing, "free" and co-created service contexts?

Another important direction for service encounter research lies in the transformative service research (TSR) domain (Ostrom et al. 2010; Anderson et al. 2013). Transformative service research scholars urge us to begin looking at consumer well-being within service systems as a focus of research in order to better understand the service structures and institutions that shape outcomes for consumers and society at large. Shifting the dependent measure in service encounter research from satisfaction to well-being and/or quality of life is thus a promising avenue for future service encounter research that would tie it directly to TSR. Doing so would draw researchers into understanding different downstream outcomes as well as contextual predictors of service encounter well-being.

While service encounter publications represent some of the earliest and most widely acknowledged research in service marketing, it is clear that the topic is still a foundational element for current and emerging research. In addition to needing more work in service encounter satisfaction, service dyads, and service encounters within experiences and networks, research is also needed to better understand global/cross-cultural issues, technology-mediated service encounters, and the implications for well-being and transformative service research, as noted in the preceding paragraphs. The many limbs, branches, and sprouting leaves that we see in these research streams suggest that there are strong and deep roots in service encounter research, and much more to come. We look forward to seeing the directions the research takes in marketing as well as other disciplines.

REFERENCES

Anderson, Laurel, Amy L. Ostrom, Canan Corus, Raymond P. Fisk, Andrew S. Gallan, Mario Giraldo, Martin Mende, Mark Mulder, Steven W. Rayburn, Mark S. Rosenbaum, Kunio Shirahada and Jerome D. Williams (2013), "Transformative service research: an agenda for the future," *Journal of Business Research*, forthcoming.

Arnould, Eric J. and Linda L. Price (2003), "River magic: extraordinary experience and the extended service encounter," *Journal of Consumer Research*, **20** (June), 24–45.

Baker, Julie, A. Parasuraman, Dhruv Grewal and Glenn B. Voss (2002), "The influence of multiple store environment cues on perceived merchandise value and patronage intentions," *Journal of Marketing*, **66** (April), 120–41.

Barlow, Janelle and Paul Stewart (2004), *Branded Customer Service*, San Francisco, CA: Berret-Koehler.

Bendapudi, Neeli and Robert Leone (2003), "Psychological implications of customer participation in co-production," *Journal of Marketing*, **67** (January), 14–28.

Bettencourt, Lance (2010), *Service Innovation: How to Go from Customer Needs to Breakthrough Services*, New York: McGraw-Hill.

Bitner, Mary Jo (1990), "Evaluating service encounters: the effects of physical surrounding and employee responses," *Journal of Marketing*, **54** (2), 69–81.

Bitner, Mary Jo (1992), "Servicescapes: the impact of physical surroundings on customers and employees," *Journal of Marketing*, **56** (April), 57–71.

Bitner, Mary Jo and Amy R. Hubbert. (1994), "Encounter satisfaction versus overall satisfaction versus quality," in Roland T. Rust and Richard L. Oliver (eds), *Service Quality: New Directions in Theory and Practice*, New York: Sage Publications, pp. 72–84.

Bitner, Mary Jo, Bernard H. Booms and Mary Stanfield Tetreault (1990), "The service encounter: diagnosing favorable and unfavorable incidents," *Journal of Marketing*, **54** (January), 71–84.

Bitner, Mary Jo, Bernard H. Booms and Lois A. Mohr (1994), "Critical service encounters: the employee's view," *Journal of Marketing*, **58** (October), 95–106.

Bitner, Mary Jo, Stephen W. Brown and Matthew L. Meuter. (2000), "Technology infusion service encounters," *Journal of the Academy of Marketing Science*, **28** (1), 138–49.

Bitner, Mary Jo, Amy L. Ostrom and Felicia N. Morgan (2008), "Service blueprinting: a practical technique for service innovation," *California Management Review*, **50** (3), 66–94.

Boulding, William, Ajay Kalra, Richard Staelin and Valarie A. Zeithaml (1993), "A dynamic model of service quality: from expectations to behavioral intentions," *Journal of Marketing Research*, **30** (February), 7–27.

Bowen, David E. (1986), "Managing customers as human resources in service organizations," *Human Resource Management*, **25** (3), 371–83.

Brady, Michael K. and J. Joseph Cronin (2001), "Some new thoughts on conceptualizing perceived service quality: a hierarchical approach," *Journal of Marketing*, **65** (July), 34–49.

Brady, Michael K. and Christopher J Robertson (2001), "Searching for a consensus on the antecedent role of service quality and satisfaction: an exploratory cross-national Study," *Journal of Business Research*, **51** (1), 53–60.

Brown, Stephen W. and Teresa A. Swartz (1989), "Gap analysis of professional service quality," *Journal of Marketing*, **53** (April), 92–8.

Bruggen, Elisabeth C., Bram Foubert and Dwayne D. Gremler (2011), "Extreme makeover: short and long-term effects of a remodeled servicescape," *Journal of Marketing*, **75** (5), 71–87.

Chan, Kimmy Wa, Chi Kin Yim and Simon S.K. Lam (2010), "Is customer participation in value creation a double-edged sword? Evidence from professional financial services across cultures," *Journal of Marketing*, **74**, May, 48–64.

Cronin, J. Joseph, Jr. and Steven A. Taylor (1992), "Measuring service quality: a reexamination and extension," *Journal of Marketing*, **56** (3), 55–68.

Cronin, J. Joseph, Michael K. Brady and G. Tomas M. Hult (2000), "Assessing the effects of quality, value, and customer satisfaction on consumer behavioral intentions in service environments," *Journal of Retailing*, **76** (2), 193–218.

Czepiel, John, Michael R. Solomon and Carol F. Surprenant (1985), *The Service Encounter*, New York: Lexington Books.

Dabholkar, Pratibha A. (1996), "Consumer evaluations in new technology-based self-service options: an investigation of alternative models of service quality," *International Journal of Research in Marketing*, **13** (1), 29–51.

DeMatos, Celso Augusto, Jorge Luiz Henrique and Carlos Alberto Vargas Ross (2007), "Service recovery paradox: a meta-analysis," *Journal of Service Research*, **10** (August), 60–77.

Du, Jiangang, Xiucheng Fan and Tianjun Feng (2011), "Multiple emotional contagions in service encounters," *Journal of the Academy of Marketing Science*, **39** (3), 449–66.

Duranti, A. and Goodwin, C. (eds) (1992), *Rethinking Context*, Cambridge: Cambridge University Press.

Farrell, Andrew M., Anne L. Souchon and Geoffrey R. Durden (2001), "Service encounter conceptualization: employees' service behaviors and customers' service quality perceptions," *Journal of Marketing Management*, **17** (5/6), 577–93.

Folkes, Valerie S., Susan Koletsky and John Graham (1987), "A field study of causal inferences and consumer reaction: the view from the airport," *Journal of Consumer Research*, **13** (March), 534–9.

Gallan, Andrew S., Cheryl Burke Jarvis, Stephen W. Brown and Mary Jo Bitner (2013), "Customer positivity and participation in services: an empirical test in a health care context," *Journal of the Academy of Marketing Science*, **41** (3), 338–56.

"Good Health Care By Design" (2011), reprinted from *The Hastings Center Report*, **41** (1), 13–28.

Gorman, Jamie C., Polemnia G. Amazeen and Nancy J. Cooke (2010), "Team coordination dynamics," *Nonlinear Dynamics, Psychology, and Life Sciences*, **14** (3), 265–89.

Grégoire, Yany, Thomas M. Tripp and Renaud Legoux (2009), "When customer love turns into lasting hate: the effects of relationship strength and time on customer revenge and avoidance," *Journal of Marketing*, **73** (November), 18–32.

Gremler, Dwayne D. (2004), "The critical incident technique in service research," *Journal of Service Research*, **7** (1), 65–89.

Gremler, Dwayne D. and Kevin P. Gwinner (2000), "Customer–employee rapport in service relationships," *Journal of Service Research*, **3** (1), 82–104.

Grönroos, Christian (2011), "Value co-creation in service logic: a critical analysis," *Marketing Theory*, **11** (3), 279–301.

Grove, Stephen J. and Raymond P. Fisk (1997), "The impact of other customers on service experiences: a critical incident examination of 'getting along," *Journal of Retailing*, **73** (1), 63–85.

Gupta, Sunil and Valarie A. Zeithaml (2006), "Customer metrics and their impact on financial performance," *Marketing Science*, **25** (6), 718–39.

Gwinner, Kevin P., Mary Jo Bitner, Stephen W. Brown and Ajith Kumar (2005), "Service customization through employee adaptiveness," *Journal of Service Research*, **8** (2), 131–48.

Hatfield, Elaine, John T. Cacioppo and Richard L. Rapson (1994), *Emotional Contagion*, Paris: Cambridge University Press.

Hennig-Thurau, Thorsten, Markus Groth, Michael Paul and Dwayne D. Gremler (2006), "Are all smiles created equal?" *Journal of Marketing*, **70** (3), 58–73.

Holloway, Betsy Bugg and Sharon E. Beatty (2008), "Satisfiers and dissatisfiers in the online environment: a critical incident assessment," *Journal of Service Research*, **10**, 4, 347–64.

Hui, Michael, and John E. G. Bateson (1991), "Perceived control and the effects of crowding and consumer choice on the service experience," *Journal of Consumer Research*, **18** (September), 174–84.

Hui, Michael and Roy Toffoli (2002), "Perceived control and consumer attribution for the service encounter," *Journal of Applied Social Psychology*, **32** (9), 1825–44.

Hui, Michael and David K. Tse (1996), "What to tell consumers in waits of different lengths: an integrative model of service evaluation," *Journal of Marketing*, **60** (April), 81–90.
Hui, Michael, Mrugank V. Thakor and Ravi Gill (1998), 'The effect of delay type and service stage on consumers' reactions to waiting," *Journal of Consumer Research*, **24** (4), 469–79.
Keaveney, Susan M. (1995), "Customer switching behavior in service industries: an exploratory study," *Journal of Marketing*, **59** (April), 71–82.
Jayawardhena, Chanaka, Anne L. Souchon, Andrew M. Farrell and Kate Glanville (2007), "Outcomes of service encounter quality in a business-to-business context," *Industrial Marketing Management*, **36** (5), 575–88.
Liu, Ben Shaw-Ching, Olivier Furrer and D. Sudharshan (2001), "The relationships between culture and behavioral intentions toward services," *Journal of Service Research*, **4** (2), 118–29.
Ma, Zhenfeng and L. Dubé (2011), "Process and outcome interdependency in frontline service encounters," *Journal of Marketing*, **75** (3), 83–98.
Markus, Hazel R. and Shinobu Kitayama (1991), "Culture and the self: implications for cognition, emotion, and motivation," *Psychological Review*, **98** (2), 224–53.
Matta, Shashi and Valerie S. Folkes (2005), "Inferences about the brand from counterstereotypical service providers," *Journal of Consumer Research*, **32** (2), 196–206.
Mattila, Anna S. (1999), "The role of culture and purchase motivation in service encounter evaluations," *Journal of Services Marketing*, **13** (4/5), 376–89.
Mattila, Anna S. and Cathy A. Enz (2002), "The role of emotions in service encounters," *Journal of Services Research*, **4** (4), 268–77.
Mattila, Anna S., Alicia Grandey and Glenda Fisk (2003), "The interplay of gender and affective tone in service encounter satisfaction," *Journal of Service Research*, **6** (2), 136–46.
Meuter, Matthew L., Mary Jo Bitner, Amy L. Ostrom and Stephen W. Brown (2005), "Choosing among alternative service delivery modes: an investigation of customer trial of self-service technologies," *Journal of Marketing*, **69** (2), 61–83.
Meuter, Matthew L., Amy L. Ostrom, Robert I. Roundtree and Mary Jo Bitner (2000), "Self-service technologies: understanding customer satisfaction with technology-based service encounters," *Journal of Marketing*, **64** (July), 50–64.
Mohr, Lois A. and Mary Jo Bitner (1995), "The role of employee effort in satisfaction with service transactions," *Journal of Business Research*, **32** (3), 239–52.
Morgan, Felicia, Dawn Deeter-Schmelz and Christopher R. Moberg (2007), "Branding implications of partner firm-focal firm relationships in business-to-business service networks," *Journal of Business and Industrial Marketing*, **22** (6), 372–82.
Noone, Breffni M., Jochen Wirtz and Sheryl E. Kimes (2012), "The effect of perceived control on consumer responses to service encounter pace: a revenue management perspective," *Cornell Hospitality Quarterly*, **53** (4), 295–307.
Oliver, Richard L. (1980), "A cognitive model of the antecedents and consequences of satisfaction decisions," *Journal of Marketing Research*, **17** (November), 460–69.
Oliver, Richard L. (1997), *Satisfaction: A Behavioral Perspective on the Consumer*, New York: McGraw-Hill.
Olsen, Line Lervik and Michael D. Johnson (2003), "Service equity, satisfaction, and loyalty: from transaction-specific to cumulative evaluations," *Journal of Service Research*, **5** (3), 184–95.
Orsingher, Chiara, Sara Valentini and Matteo de Angelis (2010), "A meta-analysis of satisfaction with complaint handling in services," *Journal of the Academy of Marketing Science*, **38** (2), 169–86.
Ostrom, Amy L., Mary Jo Bitner, Stephen W. Brown, Kevin A. Burkhard, Michael Goul, Vicki Smith-Daniels, Haluk Demirkan and Elliot Rabinovich (2010), "Moving forward and making a difference: research priorities for the science of service," *Journal of Service Research*, **13** (1), 4–36.
Parasuraman, A., Valarie A. Zeithaml and Leonard L. Berry. (1988), "SERVQUAL: a multiple-item scale for measuring consumer perceptions of service quality," *Journal of Retailing*, **64** (Spring), 12–37.

Parasuraman, A., Valarie A. Zeithaml, and Leonard L. Berry (1994), "Reassessment of expectations as a comparison standard in measuring service quality: implications for future research," *Journal of Marketing*, **58** (February), 6–17.

Patrício, Lia, Raymond P. Fisk, João Falcão e Cunha and Larry Constantine (2011), "Multilevel service design: from customer value constellation to service experience blueprinting," *Journal of Service Research*, **14** (2), 180–200.

Patterson, Paul G. and Anna S. Mattila (2008), "An examination of the impact of cultural orientation and familiarity in service encounter evaluations," *International Journal of Service Industry Management*, **19** (5), 662–81.

Paul, Michael, Thorsten Hennig-Thurau, Dwayne D. Gremler, Kevin P. Gwinner and Caroline Wiertz (2009), "Toward a theory of repeat purchase drivers for consumer services," *Journal of the Academy of Marketing Science*, **37** (2), 215–37.

Price, Linda L. and Eric J. Arnould (1999), "Commercial friendships: service provider—client relationships in context," *Journal of Marketing*, **63** (4), 38–56.

Pugh, S. Douglas (2001), "Service with a smile: emotional contagion in the service encounter," *Academy of Management Journal*, **44** (5), 1018–27.

Rosenbaum, Mark S., James Ward, Beth A. Walker and Amy L. Ostrom (2007), "A cup of coffee with a dash of love: an investigation of commercial social support and third-place attachment," *Journal of Service Research*, **10** (August), 43–59.

Sawhney, Mohanbir, Sridhar Balasubramanian and Vish V. Krishnan (2004), "Creating growth with services," *Sloan Management Review*, **45** (2), 34–44.

Saxena-Iyer, Shruti, Ruth N. Bolton, Mary Jo Bitner and Michael M. Mokwa (2013), "Customer participation and service quality in extended consumption experiences," working paper, Arizona State University.

Schau, Hope, Stephanie Dellande and Mary C. Gilly (2007), "The impact of code switching on service encounters," *Journal of Retailing*, **83** (1), 65–78.

Schoenewolf, Gerald (1990), "Emotional contagion: behavioral induction in individuals and groups," *Modern Psychoanalysis*, **15** (1), 49–61.

Seiders, Kathleen and Leonard L. Berry (1998), "Service fairness: what it is and why it matters," *Academy of Management Executive*, **12** (May), 8–20.

Shostack, G. Lynn (1984), "Designing services that deliver," *Harvard Business Review*, **62** (January–February), 133–9.

Shostack, G. Lynn (1985), "Planning the service encounter," in John A. Czepiel, Michael R. Solomon and Carol F. Surprenant (eds), *The Service Encounter*, Lexington, MA: Lexington Books, pp. 243–54.

Shostack, G. Lynn (1987), "Service positioning through structural change," *Journal of Marketing*, **51** (January), 34–43.

Sirianni, Nancy J., Mary Jo Bitner, Stephen W. Brown and Naomi Mandel (2013), "Branded customer service: strategically aligning employee behavior with brand positioning," *Journal of Marketing*, forthcoming

Solomon, Michael R., Carol Surprenant, John A. Czepiel and Evelyn G. Gutman (1985), "A role theory perspective on dyadic interactions: the service encounter," *Journal of Marketing*, **49** (Winter), 99–111.

Spreng, Richard A. and Robert D. Mackoy (1996), "An empirical examination of a model of perceived service quality and satisfaction," *Journal of Retailing*, **72** (2), 201–14.

Surprenant, Carol F. and Michael R. Solomon (1987), "Predictability and personalization in the service encounter," *Journal of Marketing*, **51** (April), 73–80.

Tax, Stephen S., Stephen W. Brown and Murali Chandrashekaran (1998), "Customer evaluations of service complaint experiences: implications for relationship marketing," *Journal of Marketing*, **62** (April), 60–76.

Tax, Stephen S., David McCutcheon and Ian F. Wilkinson (2013), "The service delivery network (SDN): a consumer-centric perspective of the customer journey," *Journal of Service Research*, forthcoming.

Taylor, Shirley (1994), "Waiting for service: the relationship between delays and the evaluation of service," *Journal of Marketing*, **58** (April), 56–69.

Taylor, Shirley (1995), "The effects of filled waiting time and service provider control over the delay on evaluation of service," *Journal of the Academy of Marketing Science*, **23** (1), 38–48.
Taylor, Shirley and Thomas L. Baker (1994), "An assessment of the relationship between service quality and customer satisfaction in the formation of consumers' purchase intentions," *Journal of Retailing*, **70** (2), 163–78.
Ulrich, Roger S., Leonard L. Berry, Xiaobo Quan and Janet Turner Parish (2010), "A conceptual framework for the domain of evidence-based design," *Health Environments Research and Design Journal*, **4** (1), 95–114.
Vargo, Stephen L. and Robert F. Lusch (2004), "Evolving to a new dominant logic for marketing," *Journal of Marketing*, **68** (January), 1–17.
Verhoef, Peter C., Gerrit Antonides and Arnoud N. de Hoog (2004), "Service encounters as a sequence of events: the importance of peak experiences," *Journal of Service Research*, **7** (1), 53–64.
Voss, Christopher A., Aleda V. Roth, Eve D. Rosenzweig, Kate Blackmon and Richard B. Chase (2004), "A Tale of two countries' conservatism, service quality and feedback on customer satisfaction," *Journal of Service Research*, **6** (3), 212–30.
Wang, Helen Si, Mary Jo. Bitner, Amy L. Ostrom and G. Douglas Olsen (2013), "Customer participation in service conversations – an investigation of the dynamics of service context," working paper, Arizona State University.
Yim, Chi Kin, Kimmy Wa Chan and Simon SK Lam (2012), "Do customers and employees enjoy service participation? Synergistic effects of self- and other-efficacy," *Journal of Marketing*, **76** (6), 1–49.
Zeithaml, Valarie A., Leonard Berry and A. Parasuraman. (1996), "The behavioral consequences of service quality," *Journal of Marketing*, **60** (April), 31–46.
Zeithaml, Valarie A., Mary Jo. Bitner and Dwayne D Gremler (2013), *Services Marketing: Integrating Customer Focus Across the Firm*, 6th edn, New York: McGraw-Hill.
Zhou, Rongrong and Dilip Soman (2003), "Looking back: exploring the psychology of queuing and the effect of the number of people behind," *Journal of Consumer Research*, **29** (4), 517–30.

12 Frontline employees and performance: optimizing the frontline, maximizing the bottom line

Sandra Streukens and Tor W. Andreassen

INTRODUCTION

Starbucks and Nordstrom, a U.S. coffee chain and department store chain respectively, share a passion for service. While their service is complex in nature (that is, creating a positive customer experience), it can be decomposed into three parts. They offer a tangible component (for example, coffee and shoes) in a store, through the assistance of frontline employees who possess hard skills (that is, how to perform their job), and soft skills (that is, manage the human interaction in the moment of truth). While the tangible and store component separately and in combination are important, frontline employees' (FLE) performance in the moment of truth is critical to the customer experience and ultimately to sales performance. In fact, Starbucks reflect their appreciation of their FLEs in the often-cited slogan: "We are known for our coffee but our employees make us famous!" But what is the link between FLE behavior and sales performance and, related to this, how do you optimize FLE behavior in a way that maximizes profitability without losing focus on what actually drives FLE behavior?

In relation to the link between FLE behavior and (objective) sales performance, service researchers typically develop and test regression-based models that link data from employees to internal company data. Examples of these employee-revenue chains include the work of de Jong et al. (2004), Kamakura et al. (2002), and Loveman (1998). In its own right, research aimed at understanding these and other employee-revenue chains linking employee perceptions to objective performance contributes to an enhanced understanding of effective FLE management from both an academic and practical perspective. Nevertheless, decision-making models that take explicit advantage of this type of service management knowledge are scant in the existing literature. Aligned with this hiatus in service management research, many researchers (for example, Amundson 1998; Boudreau et al. 2003; Bretthauer 2004; Melnyk and Handfield 1998; Metters and Marucheck 2007) call for the development of decision-making models that unite mathematical rigor and behavioral services management premises. The practical need for such models is growing as a consequence of two trends in the Western service-based economies. First, increased competition forces service firms to be increasingly results oriented in order to survive. Second, customers have become a scarce resource pursued by an escalating number of aggressive suppliers.

The aim of our study is to develop and demonstrate a practical and versatile decision-making tool that assists managers in optimizing FLE management improvement initiatives in a way that maximizes profitability while at the same time being truly FLE oriented. In order to realize this, two elements are crucial. First, the employee-revenue chain that links soft employee perceptions to objective financial performance needs to be understood and quantified. The service literature frequently echoes that FLE self-efficacy is crucial (McKey et al. 2006; Schneider et al. 2005, 2009). However, there is surprisingly little empirical research on the antecedents of FLE self-efficacy and the nomological web connecting FLE self-efficacy to FLE objective financial performance. Therefore, the first part of our study proposes and assesses a model that provides insight into these relationships. Understanding what drives objective FLE performance is only part of the puzzle managers are faced with. In today's result-oriented business environment, questions regarding the optimal spending and allocation of resource to improve FLE performance and the associated expected returns and associated financial risk are taking center stage. Hence, the second key element of this study involves the development of a general mathematical model that provides an answer to these issues. In relation to the first element—the employee-revenue chain—the goal of this mathematical model is to take the insights stemming from the employee-revenue chain to the next level. This also implies that our optimization model to a very large extent is built on data that many companies collect already in the form of (periodic) employee surveys and sales data.

Before elaborating on the core issues of our work, we provide in the next section a more detailed discussion of our research objective and provide a graphical overview of the key elements.

BACKGROUND AND OVERVIEW

Figure 12.1 presents a macro-level overview of how typical marketing knowledge regarding employee-revenue chains can be used to make financially justified decisions pertaining to FLE investments. The model presented in Figure 12.1 is in line with principles underlying return on marketing (Rust et al. 1995, 2004).

As indicated in Figure 12.1, the employee-revenue chain takes a central

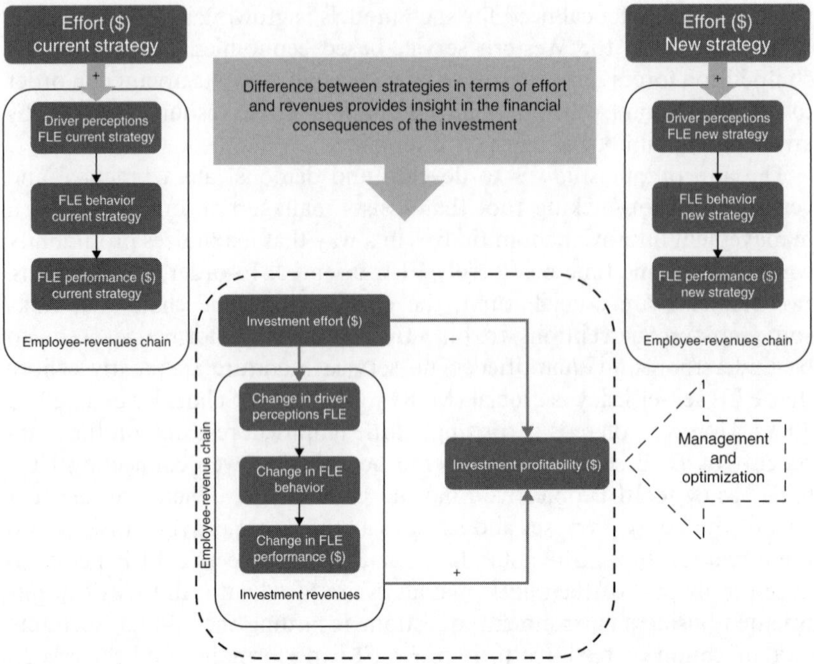

Figure 12.1 General model of investing in FLE management

position in effectively managing FLEs. It describes the revenue generating process that captures the notion that changes in FLE perceptions regarding the drivers have an impact on FLE behavior which subsequently results in enhanced financial performance. Following the model presented in Figure 12.1, FLE management investments are the difference between a current ("status quo") strategy and a new strategy. The current strategy is associated with the status quo levels of effort, driver perceptions, and financial performance. Following the logic of the employee-revenue chain, revenues can be increased by designing strategies that result in an increase of FLE perceptions regarding the drivers over and above the current strategy. The difference between the input and output of the status quo and new strategy provides insight into the financial consequences of the strategic investment. In order to arrive at investment strategies that are both FLE-focused as well as financially feasible, the remainder of our study is organized around two interrelated and complementary research objectives which we describe below.

Using an employee-revenues chain as the central element in decision-making models warrants the design of strategic improvement initiatives that are truly FLE focused. The notion that FLEs' behavior ultimately has a positive impact on financial performance has been documented in various academic studies (Bhattacharya et al. 2005; Koys, 2001; Loveman 1998). However, other research shows that this relationship is more complex. Homburg et al. (2011), for example, show that the relationship between employee behavior and financial performance is characterized by diminishing returns. In a similar vein, the empirical work of Franke and Park (2006) challenges the generally held belief that customer-oriented employee behavior is positive associated with financial performance. In particular, the latter authors fail to find a significant relationship between customer-oriented employee behavior and objective sales performance. Overall, this demonstrates the importance of studying the nomological web of relationships among key employee constructs and objective performance. Existing research (for example, Brown and Peterson 1994; Stajkovic and Luthans 1998) shows that self-efficacy is an important construct in explaining employee behavior and performance. Despite the ample amount of research underscoring the relevance of self-efficacy, little is known about the impact of self-efficacy on objective performance measures and the behaviors linking these two constructs. Likewise, the impact of the working environment on FLE self-efficacy remains under-explored so far. This leads to our first research objective:

Research objective 1 To empirically assess the relationships between FLE-environment fit, FLE self-efficacy, FLE behavior, and objective FLE performance

Without undermining the relevance of this first research objective, it is a necessary yet insufficient condition for financially justified FLE management. In line with the return on marketing movement initiated by Rust et al. (1995), an explicit trade-off between the costs and benefits associated with strategic initiatives is needed, making it possible to compare competing alternatives. Behavioral models like the employee-revenue chain central to our first research objective merely provide insight into the revenues associated with FLE management choices. Although Rust et al. (2004) show how knowledge from behavioral models can be used to make marketing decisions financially accountable, models that provide direction on how to optimize marketing decisions are still lacking. Similar to financial decision makers, marketing managers are struggling with questions such as how much to invest, how to optimally allocate the investments, and the associated rate of return and investment risk. Building on the empirical results obtained for our first research objective, our second research objective can be formulated as follows:

Research objective 2 [Building on the employee-revenues chain described in research objective 1] To develop and demonstrate a generally applicable mathematical model that allows for the optimization of FLE-management strategies that are both FLE-oriented and financially justified.

Building on the macro-level model presented in Figure 12.1, Figure 12.2 provides a more detailed overview of the structure and contents of our study.

The remainder of this chapter is organized as follows. In the next section we develop and assess the employee-revenue chain as put forward in our first research objective. In the fourth section we show how the empirical results associated with this employee-revenue chain can be used in building an FLE-management optimization model. In addition, we show how this model can be calibrated in practice and how it can answer key investment questions regarding the optimal spending level, the optimal allocation, and the associated return and risk. The final section summarizes the results, implications and limitations of our work.

UNDERSTANDING FLE OBJECTIVE FINANCIAL PERFORMANCE

This section focuses on the development and empirical assessment of an employee-revenues chain that explains FLE objective financial performance as a function of FLE behavior and perceptions. The structure of the employee-revenue chain and the accompanying hypotheses are presented in the lower left corner of Figure 12.2 (that is, research objective 1).

Model Development

FLE self-efficacy

Frontline employees' task-related self-efficacy, defined as the employee's beliefs in his or her abilities to perform job-related tasks (Bandura 1986), represents a core construct in explaining employee behavior and the resulting performance. Belief in one's capabilities, in turn, mobilizes the motivation, cognitive resources, and courses of action needed to meet given situational demands, making task-related or domain-specific self-efficacy one of the primary state-like motivational constructs that influence task performance (Chen et al. 2000). Moreover, Stajkovic and Luthans' (1998) meta-analysis demonstrates that self-efficacy is a critical driver of employee behaviors.

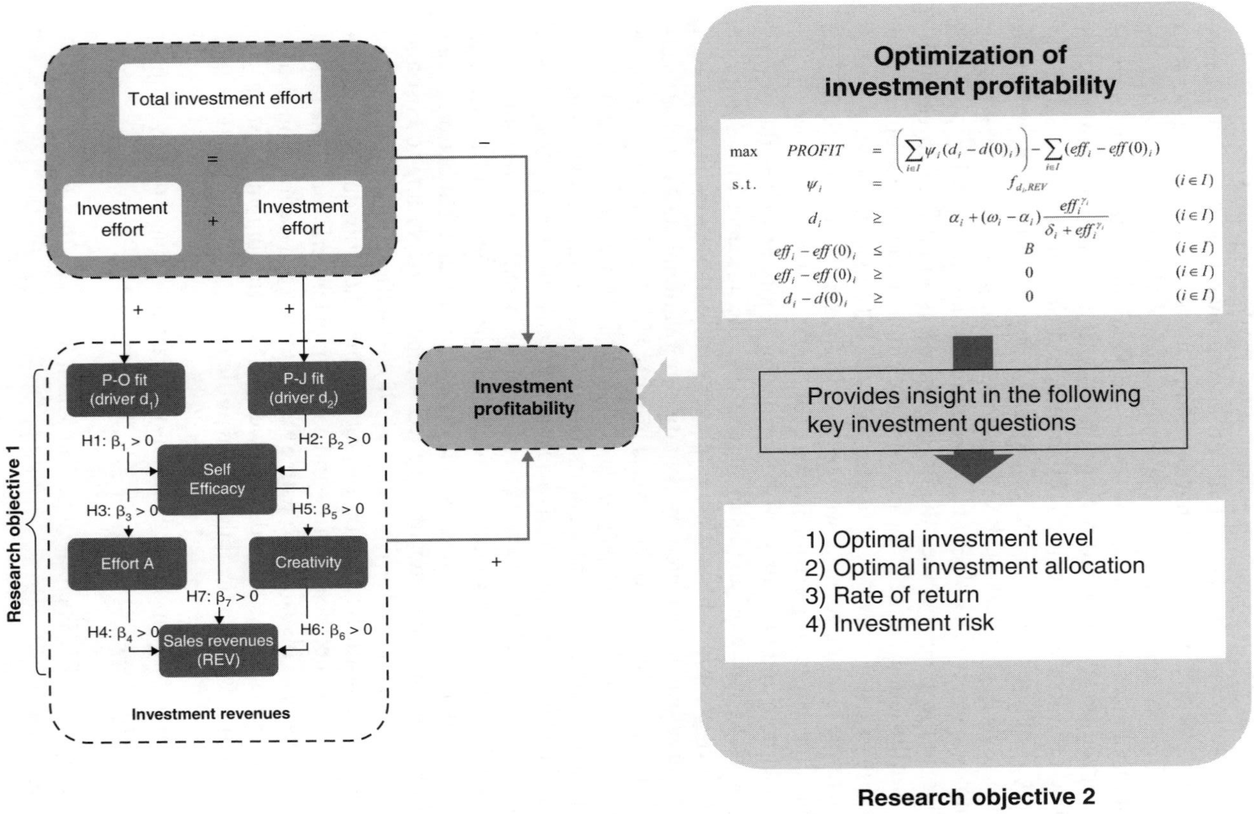

Figure 12.2 Overview of the current study

Person-environment fit as a source of FLE self-efficacy

In line with the tradition of interactional psychology, in which it is conceptually rooted, the central tenet of person-environment (P-E) fit theory is that positive employee behavior results from the congruence between attributes of the person and the environment. Although P-E fit can be conceptualized at a variety of levels, we focus in particular on person-organization (P-O) fit and person-job (P-J) fit as studies have shown that these are especially predictive of employee behaviors and are salient at many if not all stages of the employment process (Kristoff-Brown et al. 2005; Resick et al. 2007). P-O fit refers to the congruence between the employee's personal values and an organizational culture, whereas P-J fit refers to the match between the job requirements and the employee's abilities or the match between the needs of the employee and the supplies from the job (Kristof-Brown et al. 2005). As such, P-J fit should be judged relative to the tasks performed, whereas P-O fit focuses on the organization in which the job exists (Kristof-Brown et al. 2005).

Hackham and Oldham's (1976) job design theory as well as the empirical work of Parker et al. (2006) suggest that the influence on behavior of the work environment and an employee's fit to the environment is to a very large extent mediated by cognitive-motivational states such as self-efficacy. The literature offers several insights why P-E fit can be considered a source of FLE self-efficacy. In general, much information of employees' knowledge about their capabilities is generated from the social environment in which they work (Stajkovic and Luthans 1998). Fry (1990) argued that more control is experienced if abilities, needs, and resources are congruent with the demands. Conversely, Pervin (1968) and Pervin and Rubin (1967) state that when people experience a lack of fit between their abilities and the environment, they feel incapable. According to Gist and Mitchell (1992) as well as Chen et al. (1998), self-efficacy is the result of the examination of the self and the setting by which the individual assesses the availability of specific resources and constraints for performing the task at various levels. This is in line with Swann's (1990) self-verification theory which predicts that perceived fit provides self-confirming information.

Therefore, we state the following hypotheses:

Hypothesis 1 FLE perceived person-organization fit has a positive impact on FLE self-efficacy.

Hypothesis 2 FLE perceived person-job fit has a positive impact on FLE self-efficacy.

Connecting FLE self-efficacy and objective performance

According to Brown et al. (2005), FLE self-efficacy can be expected to have a positive impact on effort, as individuals who have positive self-efficacy beliefs focus their attention and motivation on the tasks necessary for achieving targeted performance levels and persevere in the face of difficulties. Following Krishnan et al. (2002), effort is defined as the amount of time and energy an FLE devotes to their customer contact tasks relative to their fellow FLEs. This implies that we view effort as being under "control" of the FLE. Empirical evidence on the relationship between FLE self-efficacy and effort is unanimous on the statistically significant positive nature of this relationship (see, for instance, Jaramillo and Mulki 2008; Krishnan et al. 2002). The same holds for the impact of effort on FLE performance (see, for instance, Brown and Peterson 1994; Rapp et al. 2008). Thus, we hypothesize:

Hypothesis 3 FLE self-efficacy has a positive impact on FLE effort.

Hypothesis 4 FLE effort has a positive impact on FLE objective sales performance.

Frontline employees' creative performance is conceptualized as the amount of new ideas generated and novel behavior exhibited by the salesperson in performing his job (Wang and Netemeyer 2004). In her model of creative action, Ford (1996) proposes that employee efficacy beliefs represent a necessary condition for creative behavior as creative behavior requires the employee must hold initial expectations that they can do so successfully. In line with the motivational nature of self-efficacy, efficacy levels are likely to influence the extent to which employees enjoy creativity-relevant activities, initiate creative action, and maintain actual creative levels in their work (Tierney and Farmer 2004). Moreover, Hartline and Ferrell (1996) suggest that increased levels of competence and confidence increase creative behavior as the FLE feels more able and therefore is more willing to adapt to customers' requests that require deviating from the standard routines. This leads to the following hypothesis:

Hypothesis 5 FLE self-efficacy has a positive impact on FLE creativity.

According to Wang and Netemeyer (2004), creativity is positively related to sales performance in the following ways. First, the effectiveness and efficiency in performing the relevant FLE service behaviors will increase. Second, creative identification of potential customers and their problems may lead to more successful development of customer relationships. Third, customized solutions are expected to delight customers and increase their satisfaction. Therefore, we hypothesize that:

Hypothesis 6 FLE creativity has a positive impact on FLE objective sales performance.

Inspection of the literature suggests that in order to understand the direct relationship between FLE self-efficacy and FLE performance, a distinction should be made between subjective and objective FLE performance. The relationship between FLE self-efficacy and subjective employee performance is generally found to be positive (for example, Krishnan, et al. 2002; Wang and Netemeyer, 2004). Building on the work of Brown et al. (2005), Fu et al. (2010), and Jaramillo and Mulki (2008), the relationship between FLE self-efficacy and objective employee performance is expected to be positive, yet less strong than its relationship with subjective performance. This leads to our final hypothesis stating that:

Hypothesis 7 FLE self-efficacy has a positive impact on FLE objective performance.

Empirical Assessment

Sampling

Data were collected from employees working for a Dutch retail chain selling consumer electronics. Given the relatively small population size (250 employees over 35 stores), we decided to conduct a census. All respondents were asked to fill out their unique personnel code enabling us to link employee perceptual and performance data. Ultimately, this resulted in an effective sample size of n = 107.

Surveying

All constructs in our model were measured using scientifically validated scales. The source of each particular measurement scale is presented in Table 12.1. All constructs were measured on a seven-point Likert scale. The salesperson's bonus—corrected for the number of working hours—was used as a proxy for economic performance. The bonus is a function of the number of specific products sold, and is used by company management as a measure of one's ability to sell in a customer-oriented and persuasive manner. Table 12.2 presents the inter-item correlation matrix.

Table 12.1 *Details measurement instruments and psychometric properties*

Construct	Item	Mean loading	Bootstrap Ci
P-O FIT	1	0.91	[0.85; 0.94]
Source: Cable and DeRue (2000)	2	0.85	[0.74; 0.92]
$\lambda_1 = 2.293$; $\lambda_2 = 0.385$; IC = 0.90; AVE = 0.76	3	0.86	[0.73; 0.92]
P-J FIT	1	0.81	[0.63; 0.90]
Source: Cable and DeRue (2000)	2	0.85	[0.71; 0.93]
$\lambda_1 = 2.869$; $\lambda_2 = 0.547$; IC = 0.90; AVE = 0.70	3	0.81	[0.69; 0.91]
	4	0.88	[0.74; 0.93]
SELF-EFFICACY	1	0.74	[0.61; 0.83]
Source: Krishnan et al. (2002)	2	0.82	[0.75; 0.88]
$\lambda_1 = 4.024$; $\lambda_2 = 0.687$; IC = 0.92; AVE = 0.67	3	0.84	[0.73; 0.90]
	4	0.83	[0.75; 0.89]
	5	0.87	[0.81; 0.91]
	6	0.80	[0.71; 0.87]
EFFORT	1	0.92	[0.87; 0.96]
Source: Krishnan et al. (2002)	2	0.89	[0.82; 0.94]
$\lambda_1 = 2.417$; $\lambda_2 = 0.342$; IC = 0.92; AVE = 0.80	3	0.87	[0.80; 0.93]
CREATIVITY	1	0.79	[0.70; 0.86]
Source: Wang and Netemeyer (2004)	2	0.72	[0.60; 0.81]
$\lambda_1 = 3.707$; $\lambda_2 = 0.842$; IC = 0.88; AVE = 0.52	3	0.77	[0.66; 0.85]
	4	0.69	[0.54; 0.81]
	5	0.58	[0.41; 0.72]
	6	0.70	[0.55; 0.80]
	7	0.78	[0.69; 0.85]

Analytical approach

Given our relatively small sample size and the exploratory nature of our study we opted for partial least squares (PLS) path modeling to estimate the various model parameters. To assess the significance of the estimates we constructed 95 percent percentile bootstrap confidence intervals based on 5000 bootstrap runs (Preacher and Hayes 2008).

Psychometric properties

For all reflective multiple measurement scales (that is, all constructs except performance) we empirically assessed the scale's unidimensionality (procedure Tenenhaus et al. (2005): unidimensional if $\lambda_1 > 1$; $\lambda_2 < 1$), internal

Table 12.2 *Correlation matrix*

	1	2	3	4	5	6	7	8	9	10	11	12	13	14	15	16	17	18	19	20	21	22	23	24
1 PO-fit01	1																							
2 PO-fit02	65	1																						
3 PO-fit03	67	62	1																					
4 PO-fit01	62	69	65	1																				
5 PJ-fit02	47	44	59	63	1																			
6 PJ-fit03	29	32	48	49	58	1																		
7 PJ-fit04	60	55	70	75	71	56	1																	
8 Self-efficacy01	35	35	27	20	26	27	20	1																
9 Self-efficacy02	36	30	25	23	18	24	25	54	1															
10 Self-efficacy03	26	16	21	13	14	24	10	72	62	1														
11 Self-efficacy04	39	34	30	22	14	20	21	56	66	63	1													
12 Self-efficacy05	40	32	36	24	26	36	29	53	61	63	71	1												
13 Self-efficacy06	30	19	26	15	24	22	28	41	59	59	54	72	1											
14 Effort-01	28	23	34	13	11	04	25	13	13	31	25	31	32	1										
15 Effort-02	19	25	23	11	08	05	23	20	20	31	26	30	29	76	1									
16 Effort-03	24	17	28	13	14	05	20	17	17	35	30	31	33	70	67	1								
17 Creativity-01	32	30	40	38	28	31	43	29	29	46	43	48	48	46	44	54	1							
18 Creativity-02	31	38	38	36	38	39	36	29	29	44	36	38	47	22	15	28	59	1						
19 Creativity-03	21	14	26	21	22	28	23	23	23	32	30	38	42	33	29	35	54	47	1					
20 Creativity-04	20	22	22	07	24	20	11	31	31	30	35	29	43	27	19	28	37	45	48	1				
21 Creativity-05	31	29	19	06	24	09	18	27	27	21	21	32	28	27	28	25	35	26	35	42	1			
22 Creativity-06	20	22	29	13	28	34	25	27	27	21	31	28	33	16	27	28	50	42	42	41	48	1		
23 Creativity-07	30	27	27	21	18	19	21	40	40	43	47	38	44	40	35	37	51	41	64	51	39	47	1	
24 Performance	21	11	15	10	05	06	20	31	31	36	38	35	45	33	30	25	23	08	17	09	05	12	10	1

	PO	PJ	SE	EF	CR	PE
PO	–	50	18	10	18	03
PJ	70	–	10	03	17	01
SE	42	32	–	15	38	20
EF	31	16	39	–	23	11
CR	43	41	62	48	–	03
PE	18	12	45	33	17	–

Note: The inset rectangle contains the latent construct correlations (lower triangle) as well as the squared latent construct correlations (upper triangle).

consistency reliability (procedure Jöreskog (1971): reliable if IC > 0.70), within-method convergent validity (procedures Hulland (1999): within-method convergent validity if loading > 0.50 and statistically significant, and Fornell and Larcker (1981): ave > 0.50) and discriminant validity (Fornell and Larcker (1981) criterion: ave(LV1) and ave(LV2) both larger than latent variable correlation between LV1 and LV2). As indicated by Tables 12.1 (unidimensionality, reliability, and within-method convergent validity) and 12.2 (discriminant validity), all scales possess favorable psychometric properties.

Hypothesis testing

Our structural model is well supported by the data given the statistically significant bootstrapped R^2-values for each endogenous construct (Self-efficacy: 0.19 CI_{95} = [0.12; 0.30]; Effort: 0.15 CI_{95} = [0.09; 0.22]; Creativity: 0.39 CI_{95} = [0.31; 0.47]; Performance: 0.31 CI_{95} = [0.21; 0.39]). Turning to the individual coefficients, we see that the majority of our hypotheses are supported. Self-efficacy is positively influence by person-organization fit (*H1* supported, b = 0.37 CI_{95} = [0.15; 0.62]), yet there is not relationship with the level of person-job fit (*H2* not supported). In turn, self-efficacy is an important determinant of employee creativity (*H5* supported, b = 0.63 CI_{95} = [0.51; 0.75]), employee effort (*H3* supported, b = 0.39 CI_{95} = [0.23; 0.56]), and objective employee performance (*H7* supported, b = 0.53 CI_{95} = [0.36; 0.69]). We find a significantly positive effect of employee effort on objective performance (*H4* supported, b = 0.26 CI_{95} = [0.09; 0.43]) as well as a significant negative relationship between employee creativity and objective performance (*H6* supported in opposite direction, b = −0.28 CI_{95} = [−0.49; −0.05]) (see Table 12.3).

Table 12.3 Hypothesis testing employee-revenue chain

Outcome (R^2)	Predictors	Coefficient	Bootstrap Ci	Result
Self-efficacy (0.178)	P-O fit	0.37	[0.15; 0.62]	*H1* supported
	P-J fit	0.07	[–0.16; 0.31]	*H2* not supported
Effort (0.153)	Self-efficacy	0.39	[0.23; 0.56]	*H3* supported
Creativity (0.384)	Self-efficacy	0.63	[0.51; 0.75]	*H5* supported
Performance (0.272)	Self-efficacy	0.53	[0.36; 0.69]	*H7* supported
	Effort	0.26	[0.09; 0.43]	*H4* supported
	Creativity	–0.28	[–0.49; –0.05]	Opposite effect

Summary

Although the results of our study further underscore the crucial role of FLE self-efficacy, it is evidenced that it also stimulates FLE behaviors (that is, FLE creativity) which have a negative effect on objective performance. Nevertheless, the total effect of FLE efficacy on objective performance appears to be positive.

Based on the entire chain of effects connecting FLE congruence perceptions to FLE objective performance, an evident conclusion is that companies should invest in strategic initiatives that lead to an increase in FLE congruence perceptions as this ultimately translates in enhanced performance. Yet, what remains unknown from our results is how much one should invest and how one should optimally allocate the investments, and what levels of return and risk are associated with the investment strategy. In the next section we describe how the results of employee studies like the one above can be used as input in a mathematical optimization model.

OPTIMIZING FLE MANAGEMENT INVESTMENTS

We start with the development of a generally applicable optimization model. Subsequently, we explain how to calibrate this model. In explaining the model calibration we return to the empirical results explained in the first section where applicable. The last part of this section shows how our model can be used to provide an answer to the key investment questions as mentioned previously and presented in Figure 12.2 (that is, research objective 2).

Model Development

To arrive at a decision-making model that allows for the optimization of investments in FLE behavior, both the revenues and costs of these investment schemes need to be taken into account (Rust et al. 2004; Zhu et al. 2004).

Investment revenues

Following the logic of employee-revenue chains, investment revenues are equal to the change in some FLE financial performance measures related to revenues (for example, sales) as a result of improving (some of) the drivers of employee behavior (that is, d_i, $i \in I$) relative to their current level (that is, $d(0)_i$, $i \in I$). Truly FLE-oriented investments require taking into account the entire nomological web of relationships connecting the drivers d_i to objective sales performance. According to the principles of network analysis, a set of recursive relationships connecting the drivers d_i to outcome variable *REV*, denoted by $f_{d_i,REV}$, can be captured in a single parameter ψ_i as shown in equation (12.1):

$$f_{d_i,REV} = \psi_i = \sum_{P:(d_i \rightarrow REV)} \left(\prod_{(d_i,REV) \in P} w_{ij} \right) \tag{12.1}$$

where w_{ij} equals the marginal effect of construct i on construct j.

Regardless of the exact nature of the nomological web in terms of constructs included and the functional form of the inter-construct relationships, the investment revenue *REV* as a function of driver improvement can be mathematically expressed as shown in equation (12.2):

$$REV = \left(\sum_{i \in I} \psi_i (d_i - d(0)_i) \right) \tag{12.2}$$

where

d_i = Level of driver i as a results of a targeted investment (that is, new strategy)
$d(0)_i$ = The status quo (that is, prior to investment) level of driver i
ψ_i = The impact of a unit-change in driver i on the relevant outcome variable.

Investment effort

In quantifying the relationship among investment effort (that is, cost) and investment profitability it is vital to take into account the dual nature of this relationship. First of all, there is a direct negative relationship between investment effort and investment profitability. Second, investment effort has an indirect positive impact on investment profitability. This latter effect can be explained as follows. Targeted investment efforts lead to an improvement in the associated drivers which subsequently ignites a chain of effects resulting in improved objective sales performance (see employee-performance chain).

Essential to capturing the positive indirect effect of investment effort on investment profitability is the calibration of a response function describing the relationship between investment effort and driver perceptions. Although our decision-making framework is not prescriptive regarding the type of response function, we use Little's (1970) ADBUDG function because of its flexibility and practical utility. This function is presented in equation (12.3):

$$d_i = \alpha_i + (\omega_i - \alpha_i) \frac{eff_i^{\gamma_i}}{\delta_i + eff_i^{\gamma_i}} \tag{12.3}$$

where d_i denotes the level of driver i as a result of an particular investment amount eff_i. Parameters α_i and ω_i restrict the response function to a meaningful range, whereas parameters γ_i and δ_i represent shape parameters.

Summing the investment expenditures aimed at improving the various drivers captures the total investment effort (that is, *TOT_EFF*) which has a direct negative impact on investment profitability. The function capturing the total level of investment effort is presented in equation (12.4).

$$TOT\_EFF = \sum_{i \in I} (eff_i - eff(0)_i) \tag{12.4}$$

where $eff(0)_i$ represents the spending level to maintain the current driver level $d(0)_i sd$ as implied by equation (12.3). Note that this is also in line with the situation presented in Figure 12.1 stating that the actual investment is the difference between the status quo strategy and the new strategy.

Investment profitability

Together, the investment revenue function and the total investment effort function form the investment profitability function as presented in equation (12.5):

$$PROFIT = \left(\sum_{i \in I} \psi_i (d_i - d(0)_i) \right) - \sum_{i \in I} (eff_i - eff(0)_i) \tag{12.5}$$

Designing an optimal investment strategy involves maximizing the profit function subject to the following four constraints. First, the relationship between investment effort and driver performance should follow the response function presented in equation (12.3). Second, the parameter ψ_i captures the nomological web $f_{d_i REV}$ as implied from underlying behavioral theory. Third, the total level of investment effort should not exceed a prespecified investment budget B. Fourth, two non-negativity constraints, implying that the performance of the drivers should at least be equal to their original level (that is, $d_i - d(0)_i \geq 0$) and the level of investment effort per driver should at least be equal to the status quo level (that is, $eff_i - eff(0)_i \geq 0$). Figure 12.3 summarizes the complete optimization framework.

Model Calibration

Investment revenues

As indicated in the previous section, quantifying the revenue generating process relies on standard analytical techniques such as multiple regression analysis or structural equation modeling using survey data and internal company data. In turn, network analysis allows capturing the effect of a change in driver performance in terms of financial perform-

$$
\begin{array}{llll}
\max & PROFIT & = & \left(\sum_{i \in I} \psi_i (d_i - d(0)_i)\right) - \sum_{i \in I} (eff_i - eff(0)_i) \\
\text{s.t.} & \psi_i & = & f_{d_i,REV} \quad (i \in I) \\
 & d_i & \geq & \alpha_i + (\omega_i - \alpha_i)\dfrac{eff_i^{\gamma_i}}{\delta_i + eff_i^{\gamma_i}} \quad (i \in I) \\
 & eff_i - eff(0)_i & \leq & B \quad (i \in I) \\
 & eff_i - eff(0)_i & \geq & 0 \quad (i \in I) \\
 & d_i - d(0)_i & \geq & 0 \quad (i \in I)
\end{array}
$$

Figure 12.3 Optimization framework

ance measure in a single figure (see also equation 12.1). Building on the employee-revenue chain addressed in this chapter the impact of a one-unit change in P-O fit would lead to a change of $\psi_1 = (\beta_1\,\beta_3\,\beta_4) + (\beta_1\,\beta_5\,\beta_6) + (\beta_1\,\beta_7)$ in sales performance, whereas a one-unit change in P-J fit would lead to a change of $\psi_2 = (\beta_2\,\beta_3\,\beta_4) + (\beta_2\,\beta_5\,\beta_6) + (\beta_2\,\beta_7)$ in sales performance. The different β coefficients represent the different marginal effects of the relevant independent variables on the relevant dependent variables in the set of structural relationships. Please note that the computation of the relevant marginal effects depends on the functional form of the equation. For the situation at hand, the β coefficients equal the unstandardized PLS structural model estimates. The current driver levels $d(0)_i$, which are also part of the revenues function, can be obtained by calculating the average scores of the relevant FLE perceptions. The driver levels as a result of the investments, d_i, are determined when running the optimization model. As for the current situation the results apply to the individual FLE level, a multiplication by the number of employees is needed to arrive at a revenue function that captures the investment revenues across all employees.

Investment effort

To calibrate Little's (1970) ADBUDG function, interviews with the decision-makers and/or the people at whom the efforts are directed (in our application FLEs) are needed. Typically, these interviews focus on the following four questions:

1. If effort eff_i is reduced to 0 what will then be the evaluation d_i?
This provides the value for parameter α_i. The value of α_i is typically the lowest value of the scale used to assess the perceptions regarding d_i. That is, parameter α_i represents the lower bound of the function.

2. If effort eff_i approaches infinity, when will then be the value of d_i?
   This answer provides the value for parameter ω_i. *The value of* ω_i *is typically the highest value of the scale used to assess the perceptions regarding* d_i. *That is, parameter* ω_i *represents the upper bound of the function.*
3. Regarding i, what is the current level of effort ($eff(0)_i$) and to what evaluation does that lead ($d(0)_i$)?
   Note that the current driver level is the average score of the driver and can be readily obtained from the data.
4. If, compared to the current situation, effort $eff(0)_i$ is doubled, to what level of d_i would that lead?
   Together with question 3, the answer to this question provides information on the values for the shape parameters γ_i *(S-shaped or concave function) and* δ_i *(elevation and steepness of function), which are chosen in such a manner that the curve matches the qualitative data obtained in the calibration phase as closely as possible.*

Calibration of the ADBUDG function for each driver d_i, will automatically provide an estimate of the total investment effort, which is also presented in equation (12.4).

Modeling Outcomes

This paragraph explains which analytical procedures underlie the assessment of the four key questions underlying each investment decision. As outlined previously (see also research objective 2 in Figure 12.2), these questions can be summarized as follows: (1) what is the overall optimal investment level? (2) What is the optimal allocation of the investment over the different drivers? (3) What is the rate of return associated with the investment? (4) What is the strategy's investment risk?

Optimal investment level

Investments remain feasible as long as the marginal revenues exceed the marginal costs. The optimum spending level is reached at the point where the marginal costs and revenues are equal. Mathematically, this means that the derivative of the profit function with respect to investment effort is equal to zero. Taking the profit function presented in equation (12.5) as our starting point and leaving out the parameters related to the status quo (that is, $d_i(0)$ and $eff(0)_i$) for the sake of clarity, this derivative is presented below (see equation (12.6)).

$$\max_{i \in I}(\psi_i d_i(eff_i) - eff_i)' = \max_{i \in I}\left\{\frac{\psi_i(\beta_i - \alpha_i)\psi_i\delta_i eff_i^{\gamma_i - 1}}{(\delta_i + eff_i^{\gamma_i})^2} - 1\right\} \quad (12.6)$$

Thus, in terms of equation (12.6), investing remains feasible as long as

$$\max_{i \in I} (\psi_i d_i(eff_i) - eff_i)' > 0,$$

whereas the optimal profitability level is obtained when

$$\max_{i \in I} (\psi_i d_i(eff_i) - eff_i)' = 0.$$

Optimal allocation

In order to optimize investment profitability, the optimal investment level should also be allocated optimally (Mantrala et al. 1992). Similar to deciding on the overall optimal investment level, the optimal allocation is directly related to the derivative of the profit function with respect to investment effort (see also equation (12.6)). Optimal allocation starts with assigning all investments to the driver with the highest partial derivative, say driver p. As these investments are characterized by diminishing returns, the associated partial derivative of driver p becomes smaller and at some point equals the partial derivative of the second most feasible driver, say driver q. Equation (12.7) summarizes this situation.

$$\frac{\psi_p(\beta_p - \alpha_p)\gamma_p \delta_p eff_p^{\gamma_p - 1}}{(\delta_p + eff_p^{\gamma_p})^2} = \frac{\psi_q(\beta_q - \alpha_q)\gamma_q \delta_q eff_q^{\gamma_q - 1}}{(\delta_q + eff_q^{\gamma_q})^2} \tag{12.7}$$

The equilibrium in equation (12.7) means that, economically seen, investing in drivers p and q is equally feasible. Optimal allocation is then warranted when investments are then divided over both drivers such that the partial derivatives remain equal. The allocation over the various processes or input variables remains economically feasible until for all drivers the partial derivative of the profit function with regard to y_i equals zero.

Although the previous paragraph describes the process underlying the determination of an optimal investment allocation from a mathematical perspective, it is important to point out that this process is not something that one needs to manage actively in practice. Rather, the mathematical framework provides a clear-cut solution in terms of the actual amounts or percentage of the overall optimal budget that should be spent on each individual driver. For example, for the optimal investment level B^*, 70 percent of the amount needs to be allocated to driver d_1 and 30 percent to driver d_2. The actual translation to actionable steps to be taken by management is made by turning to the data used to calibrate the response function linking effort and driver performance (that is, ADBUDG function).

Return on investment

As Rust et al. (2004) point out, it is important that marketing management investments should be placed on an even footing with other marketing-related investments (for example, investing in an advertising campaign) as well as other non-marketing investments (for example, increasing production capacity). Based on the output of our mathematical model, an estimate regarding the return on investment associated with a particular initiative can be readily obtained. In terms of the different elements of the optimization framework, the associated ROI can be expressed as shown in equation (12.8):

$$ROI = \frac{\sum_{i \in I} \psi_i (d_i - d(0)_i) - \sum_{i \in I} (eff_i - eff(0)_i)}{\sum_{i \in I} (eff_i - eff(0))_i} \tag{12.8}$$

Investment risk

Similar to all other investment decisions, the profitability projections associated with investment actions aimed at improving evaluative judgments are characterized by uncertainty or risk. In line with the notion that the variability in investment outcome reflects the amount of risk involved (Brealey and Myers, 2000), examining the robustness of the optimal solution to changes in the model's parameters provides an excellent way to assess the level of investment risk. A useful approach to assess the robustness of the investment profit projections is nominal range sensitivity analysis (Frey and Patil 2002; Morgan and Henrion 1990; von Winterfeldt and Edwards 1986). Nominal range sensitivity analysis evaluates the effects on a model's output due to changes exerted by varying individual model parameters across a range of plausible values while keeping the other parameter values at the nominal or base-case values. The robustness of the model is subsequently expressed as the positive or negative percentage change compared to the nominal solution.

Mathematically, the notion of nominal range sensitivity analysis is as follows. If the parameter value of a certain relation (k, l) is changed, say from w_{kl} to $w'_{kl} = w_{kl} + \phi$, and all other relations remain unchanged, that is, $w'_{ij} = w_{ij}((i, j) \neq (k, l))$, parameter $\psi_{p,q}$ describing the influence of driver z_p on outcome variable z_q to $\psi'_{p,q}$ is shown in equation (12.9):

$$\begin{aligned} \psi'_{p,q} &= \sum_{P:(z_p \to z_q)} \left(\prod_{(z_i, z_j) \in P} w'_{ij} \right) \\ &= \sum_{P:(z_p \to z_q):(k,l) \notin P} \left(\prod_{(z_i, z_j) \in P} w'_{ij} \right) + \sum_{P:(z_p \to z_q):(k,l) \in P} \left(\prod_{(z_i, z_j) \in P} w'_{ij} \right) \end{aligned} \tag{12.9}$$

$$= \sum_{P:(z_p \rightarrow z_q):(k,l) \notin P} \left(\prod_{(z_i,z_j) \in P} w_{ij} \right) + \sum_{P:(z_p \rightarrow z_q):(k,l) \in P} \left(\prod_{(z_i,z_j) \in P-(k,l)} w_{ij} \right) (w_{kl} + \varphi)$$

$$= \sum_{P:(z_p \rightarrow z_q):(k,l) \notin P} \left(\prod_{(z_i,z_j) \in P} w_{ij} \right) + \sum_{P:(z_p \rightarrow z_q):(k,l) \in P} \left(\prod_{(z_i,z_j) \in P} w_{ij} \right) + \sum_{P:(z_p \rightarrow z_q):(k,l) \in P} \left(\prod_{(z_i,z_j) \in P-(k,l)} w_{ij} \right) \varphi$$

The first two terms in the last row of equation (12.9) add up to $\psi_{p,q}$, whereas the last term (excluding parameter φ) in the last row of Equation (9) can be written as shown in equation (12.10):

$$\sum_{P:(z_p \rightarrow z_q):(k,l) \in P} \left(\prod_{(z_i,z_j) \in P-(k,l)} w_{ij} \right) = \sum_{P:(z_p \rightarrow z_q)} \left(\prod_{(z_i,z_j) \in P} w_{ij} \right) \cdot \sum_{P:(z_p \rightarrow z_q)} \left(\prod_{(z_i,z_j) \in P} w_{ij} \right)$$

$$= \psi_{p,k} \cdot \psi_{l,q} \tag{12.10}$$

Thus, substituting equation (12.10) for the corresponding term in equation (12.9) yields the following expression (see equation (12.11)) to calculate the influence of driver z_p on outcome variable z_q as a function of changes in the structural model parameters.

$$\psi'_{p,q} = \psi_{p,q} + \psi_{p,k}\psi_{l,q}\varphi \tag{12.11}$$

Using the optimal investment effort allocation scheme, compute the marketing investment profitability obtained with $\psi'_{p,q}$. Now, the robustness of the optimal solution is obtained by computing the relative difference in investment profitability obtained for parameters $\psi_{p,q}$ (original coefficients) and $\psi'_{p,q}$ (altered coefficients). The robustness of the optimal solution is then defined as shown in equation (12.12):

$$\left[\frac{|profit(\psi_{p,q}) - profit(\psi'_{p,q})|}{profit(\psi_{p,q})} \right] *100\% \tag{12.12}$$

Note that in assessing the robustness of the optimal solution, total profit is used rather than investment profit.

Evaluation Rather than Optimization

Although the focus of our model is on investment profit maximization, our model can also be used to evaluate (competing) investment strategies. This means that rather than running an optimization model, the revenues and costs associated with a particular investment are calculated using the formulae and associated parameter estimates as presented in the equations outlined above.

Optimization Software

Our decision-making model can be programmed and run in AIMMS. AIMMS is an advanced development environment for building optimization-based operation research applications and is used by leading companies throughout the world to support many different aspects of decision making. Besides the mathematical programming language that is originally used in AIMMS, an add-in for Microsoft Excel has been developed allowing the researcher to run optimization analyses like the ones described in this chapter in an Excel setting. This development makes the practical application of our marketing investment decision-making tool more accessible and attractive for prospective users.

DISCUSSION AND IMPLICATIONS

Driven by the practical and academic need for more research on effective management of FLE perceptions and behaviors (that is, the frontline) in terms of objective performance (that is, the bottom line), this chapter addressed the following two interrelated research objectives. First, to quantify the nomological web connecting key FLE constructs such as person-environment congruence, FLE self-efficacy, FLE behavior, and objective performance (that is, employee-revenues chain). Second, building on the insights from the previous objective, to develop a generally applicable optimization model that allows for the design of FLE management strategies that maximize financial performance while at the same time being truly FLE oriented.

Regarding the first objective, our study's three main findings can be summarized as follows. First, our research underscores the importance of FLE self-efficacy in understanding FLE objective performance. Second, the impact of self-efficacy on performance is characterized by an intricate pattern of relationships containing direct as well as positive and negative indirect effects via FLE behaviors. Third, P-O fit has a positive impact on self-efficacy and, ultimately, FLE objective performance.

Although the net overall impact of self-efficacy on objective sales performance is positive, it is important to note that the relationship between FLE creativity and objective sales performance is negative. Apparently, creativity in the moment of truth is not rewarded with enough sales to justify the efforts (see also Kumar et al. 2008). Based on this study's results, it is therefore argued that, in certain settings, sales performance benefits from keeping FLE creative performance within boundaries by stimulating the employees to perform more standardized behaviors that have been proven effective. An example could be for management to develop scripts that prescribe behavioral guidelines in different situations.

In light of the relationship between P-O fit and self-efficacy, and thus ultimately sales performance, paying attention to the fit between personal and organizational values in recruiting new employees is advisable. From an academic perspective, this finding is of interest given research by Arthur et al. (2006) which questions the use of P-O measures in employee selection and recruitment as they fail find support for a direct relationship between fit perceptions and employee performance measures. Apparently, to fully understand the performance consequences of P-O congruence it is necessary to take into account the constructs that mediate this relationship. Finally, for the service organization, the importance of P-O fit perceptions underscores the need to pinpoint the organizational values that are relevant to effective service delivery.

Building on study 1, study 2 developed a generally applicable optimization model that allows for the design of FLE-management strategies that are FLE-oriented and that maximize investment profitability. The model, which builds on the return on marketing logic, allows for an explicit assessment of the following four issues: (1) the determination of the optimal FLE investment level; (2) the optimal allocation of the FLE investment budget; (3) the return on FLE investment; and (4) the risk or robustness associated with an investment. In addition to optimization the model can be used to evaluate (competing) marketing investment alternatives. From a more practical perspective, an appealing characteristic of our model is that it builds on data (that is, employee survey data and sales performance data) and procedures (that is, regression analyses) that many service organizations are well acquainted with. Moreover, the data needed to calibrate model elements such as the ADBUDG response function are typically within close research of the service organization.

To further underscore the value of our model it should be noted that it can easily be extended to situations that are characterized by a different behavioral model. For example, rather than using an employee-revenues chain as proxy for the generation of investment revenues, one can also opt to include a customer-revenue chain or even a service profit chain (SPC)-like chain of effects (that is, employee-customer-revenues chain). In a similar fashion the model can be extended to accommodate a variety of dynamics such as customer acquisition, lag-effects, and the customers' ability to choose among alternative suppliers. Also, the type of response function describing the relationship between investment effort and driver perceptions (*in casu* the ADBUDG function) can be readily replaced by alternative functions.

Overall, our approach puts service managers in the position to assess the financial effects of FLE investments before making the actual decision. For service managers operating in countries with strong employee laws and protection making it difficult to reduce labor costs in the short-run, our model will prove to be very relevant.

LIMITATIONS

In study 1 we find a negative relationship between creativity and objective sales performance. Whether this relationship also holds in other settings needs to be further investigated. In professional service settings (that is, financial advice), employee creativity may be a prerequisite for arriving at a solution that is acceptable to the customer. Also, in situations where a long-term relationship exists between the service provider and the customer, employee creativity could be an element customers expect from the provider.

Limitations regarding the current specification of the behavioral part of our model (that is, employee-revenues chain) can be summarized as follows. First, relationships in the employee-revenues chain may be characterized by dynamic effects (for example, lagged effects and carry over effects). Second, in line with the logic of the service profit chain, customer perceptions are the connecting element between employee constructs and financial performance. Future work is needed to lay bare the nomological web of relationships that connect employee behaviors to objective sales performance. Likewise, it is important to make an explicit distinction between different sources of sales performance such as up-selling and cross-selling. By themselves, these are interesting areas for further academic research. It should be noted, however, that these types of relationships can be readily incorporated in our optimization model's revenue function (see also previous paragraph).

Finally, in our optimization model we did not take into account the degree of persistence characterizing different investments. An example of the level of persistence is the investment in a new information system that once it is in play remains of value for several time periods, in contrast to the effects of hiring additional FLEs to reduce customer waiting times that only last as long as the FLE is hired. To incorporate the level of persistence, the ADBUDG function can be extended with a persistence factor κ, which is high for investments that have a long-lasting effect, and low for investments that have a short-term effect only. Related to this, time series or panel data techniques can then be employed to capture these dynamic effects on FLE evaluative judgments, behaviors, and performance.

REFERENCES

Amundson, Susan D. (1998), "Relationships between theory-driven empirical research in operations management and other disciplines," *Journal of Operations Management*, **16**(4), 341–59.

Arthur, W., Jr., S.T. Bell, A.J. Villado and D. Doverspike (2006), "The use of person–organization fit in employment decision making: an assessment of its criterion-related validity," *Journal of Applied Psychology*, **91** (4), 786–801.

Bandura, Albert (1986), *Social Foundations of Thought and Action: A Social Cognitive Theory*, Englewood Cliffs: Prentice-Hall.

Bhattacharya, Mousumi, Donald Gibson and D. Harold Doty (2005), "The effects of flexibility in employee skills, employee behaviors, and HR practices on firm performance," *Journal of Management*, **31** (4), 622–40.

Boudreau, John, Wallace Hopp, John O. McClain and L. Joseph Thomas (2003), "On the interface between operations and human resource management," *Manufacturing & Service Operations Management*, **5** (3), 179–202.

Brealey, Richard A. and Stewart C. Myers (2000), *Principles of Corporate Finance*, New York: McGraw-Hill College.

Bretthauer, Kurt M. (2004), "Service management," *Decision Sciences*, **35** (3), 325–32.

Brown, Steven P. and Robert A. Peterson (1994), "The effect of effort on job satisfaction and sales performance," *Journal of Marketing*, **54** (April), 70–80.

Brown, Steven P., Eli Jones and Thomas W. Leigh (2005), "The attenuating effect of role overload on relationships linking self-efficacy and goal level to work performance," *Journal of Applied Psychology*, **90** (5), 972–9.

Cable, Daniel M. and D. Scott DeRue (2000), "The convergent and discriminant validity of subjective fit perceptions," *Journal of Applied Psychology*, **87** (5), 875–84.

Chen, Chao C., Patricia Gene Greene and Ann Crick (1998), "Does entrepreneurial self-efficacy distinguish entrepreneurs from managers?" *Journal of Business Venturing*, **13** (4), 295–316.

Chen, Gilad, Stanley M. Gully, Jon-Andrew Whiteman and Robert N. Kilcullen (2000), "Examination of relationships among trait-like individual differences, state-like individual differences, and learning performance," *Journal of Applied Psychology*, **85** (6), 835–47.

De Jong, Ad, Ko de Ruyter and Jos Lemmink (2004), "Antecedents and consequences of the service climate in boundary spanning self-managing teams," *Journal of Marketing*, **68** (2), 18–35.

Ford, Cameron M. (1996), "A theory of individual creative action in multiple social domains," *Academy of Management Review*, **21** (4), 1112–42.

Fornell, Claes and David F. Larcker (1981), "Evaluating structural equation models with unobservable variables and measurement error," *Journal of Marketing Research*, **28** (4), 39–50.

Franke, George R. and Jeong-Eun Park (2006), "Salesperson adaptive selling behavior and customer orientation," *Journal of Marketing Research*, **43** (November), 693–702.

Frey, H. Christopher, and Sumeet R. Patil (2002), "Identification and review of sensitivity analysis methods," *Risk Analysis: An International Journal*, **22** (3), 533–78.

Fry, P.S. (1990), "The person-environment congruence model: implications and applications for adjustment counselling with older adults," *International Journal for the Advancement of Counselling*, **13** (2), 87–106.

Fu, Frank Q., Keith A. Richards, Douglas E. Hughes and Eli Jones (2010), "Motivating

salespeople to sell new products: the relative influence of attitudes, subjective norms, and self-efficacy," *Journal of Marketing*, **74** (November), 61–76.
Gist, Marilyn E. and Terence R. Mitchell (1992), "Self-efficacy: a theoretical analysis of its determinants and malleability," *Academy of Management Review*, **17** (2), 183–211.
Hackman, J. Richard and Greg R. Oldham (1976), "Motivation through the design of work: test of a theory," *Organizational Behavior and Human Performance*, **16** (2), 250–79.
Hartline, Michael D. and O.C. Ferrell (1996), "The management of customer-contact service employees," *Journal of Marketing*, **60** (October), 52–70.
Homburg, Christian, Michael Müller and Martin Klarmann (2011), "When should the customer really be king? On the optimum level of salesperson customer orientation in sales encounters," *Journal of Marketing*, **75** (March), 55–74.
Hulland, John (1999), "Use of partial least squares (PLS) in strategic management research: a review of four recent studies," *Strategic Management Journal*, **20** (2), 195–204.
Jaramillo, Fernando and Jay Prakash Mulki (2008), "Sales effort: the intertwined roles of the leader, customer, and the salesperson," *Journal of Personal Selling & Sales Management*, **28** (1), 37–51.
Jöreskog, Karl G. (1971), "Statistical analysis of sets of congeneric tests," *Psychometrika*, **36** (2), 109–33.
Kamakura, Wagner A., Vikas Mittal, Fernando de Rosa and José A. Mazzon (2002), "Assessing the service profit chain," *Marketing Science*, **21** (3), 294–317.
Koys, D.J. (2001), "The effects of employee satisfaction, organizational citizenship behavior, and turnover on organizational effectiveness: a unit-level, longitudinal study," *Personnel Psychology*, **54** (1), 101–14.
Krishnan, Balaji C., Richard G. Netemeyer and James S. Boles (2002), "Self-efficacy, competitiveness, and effort as antecedents of salesperson performance," *Journal of Personal Selling & Sales Management*, **22** (4), 285–95.
Kristof-Brown, Amy L., Ryan D. Zimmerman and Eric C. Johnson (2005), "Consequences of individuals' fit at work: a meta-analysis of person-job, person-organization, person-group, and person-supervisor fit," *Personnel Psychology*, **58** (2), 281–342.
Kumar, J., Rajkumar Venkatesan and Werner Reinartz (2008), "Performance implications of adopting a customer-focused sales campaign," *Journal of Marketing*, **72** (September), 50–68.
Little, John D.C. (1970), "Models and managers: the concept of a decision calculus," *Management Science*, **16** (8), 466–85.
Loveman, Gary (1998), "Employee satisfaction, customer loyalty, and financial performance: an empirical examination of the service profit chain in retail banking," *Journal of Service Research*, **1** (1), 18–31.
Mantrala, Murali K., Prabhakant Sinha and Andris A. Zoltners (1992), "Impact of resource allocation rules on marketing investment-level decisions and profitability," *Journal of Marketing Research*, **29** (2), 162–75.
McKey, Daryl, Christina S. Simmers and Jane Licata (2006), "Customer self-efficacy and response to service," *Journal of Service Research*, **8** (3), 207–20.
Melnyk, Steven A. and Robert B. Handfield (1998), "May you live in interesting times . . . the emergence of theory-driven empirical research," *Journal of Operations Management*, **16** (4), 311–19.
Metters, Richard and Ann Marucheck (2007), "Service management – academic issues and scholarly reflections from operations management researchers," *Decision Sciences*, **38** (2), 195–214.
Morgan, Millett G. and Max Henrion (1990), *Uncertainty: A Guide to Dealing with Uncertainty in Quantitative Risk and Policy Analysis*, Cambridge: Cambridge University Press.
Parker, Sharon K., Helen M., Williams and Nick Turner (2006), "Modeling the antecedents of proactive behavior at work," *Journal of Applied Psychology*, **91** (3), 636–52.
Pervin, Lawrence A. (1968), "Performance and satisfaction as a function of individual-environment fit," *Psychological Bulletin*, **69** (1), 56–68.

Pervin, Lawrence A., and Donald B. Rubin (1967), "Student dissatisfaction with college and the college dropout: a transactional approach," *Journal of Social Psychology*, **72** (2), 285–95.
Preacher, Kristopher J. and Andrew F. Hayes (2008), "Asymptotic and resampling strategies for assessing and comparing indirect effects in multiple mediator models," *Behavior Research Methods*, **40** (3), 879–91.
Rapp, Adam, Raj Agnihotri and Lukas P. Forbes (2008), "The sales force technology–performance chain: the role of adaptive selling and effort," *Journal of Personal Selling and Sales Management*, **28** (4), 335–50.
Resick, Christian J., Boris B. Baltes and Cynthia W. Shantz (2007), "Person-organization fit and work-related attitudes and decisions: examining interactive effects with job fit and conscientiousness," *Journal of Applied Psychology*, **92** (5), 1446–55.
Rust, Roland T., Katherine N. Lemon and Valarie A. Zeithaml (2004), "Return on marketing: using customer equity to focus marketing strategy," *Journal of Marketing*, **68** (1), 109–27.
Rust, Roland T., Anthony J. Zahorik and Timothy L. Keiningham (1995), "Return on quality (ROQ): making service quality financially accountable," *Journal of Marketing*, **59** (2), 58–70.
Schneider, Benjamin, Mark G. Ehrhart, David M. Mayer, Jessica L. Saltz and Kathryn Niles-Jolly (2005), "Understanding organization-customer links in service settings," *Academy of Management Journal*, **48** (6), 1017–32.
Schneider, Benjamin, William H. Macey, Karen M. Barbera, and Nigel Martin (2009), "Driving customer satisfaction and financial success through employee engagement," *People & Strategy*, **32** (2), 22–7.
Stajkovic, Alexander D. and Fred Luthans (1998), "Self-efficacy and work-related performance: a meta-analysis," *Psychological Bulletin*, **124** (2), 240–61.
Swann, William B., Jr. (1990), "To be adored or to be known: the interplay of self-enhancement and self-verification," in Richard M. Sorrentino and Edward T. Higgins (eds), *Foundations of Social Behavior*, vol. 2, New York: Guilford, pp. 408–48.
Tenenhaus, Michel, Vincenzo Esposito Vinzi, Yves-Marie Chatelin and Carlo Lauro (2005), "PLS path modeling," *Computational Statistics and Data Analysis*, **48** (1), 159–205.
Tierney, Pamela and Steven M. Farmer (2002), "Creative self-efficacy: potential antecedents and relationship to creative performance," *Academy of Management Journal*, **45** (6), 1137–48.
Von Winterfelt, Detloff and Ward Edwards (1986), *Decision Analysis and Behavioral Research*, Cambridge: Cambridge University Press.
Wang, Guangping and Richard G. Netemeyer (2004), "Salesperson creative performance: conceptualization, measurement, and nomological validity," *Journal of Business Research*, **57** (3), 805–12.
Zhu, Zhen, K. Sivakumar and A. Parasuraman (2004), "A mathematical model of service failure and recovery strategy," *Decision Sciences*, **35** (3), 493–525.

13 Are you (appropriately) experienced? Service–sales ambidexterity

Ko de Ruyter, Paul Patterson and Ting Yu

Hey Joe, where you goin' with that gun in your hand . . . ?
("Hey Joe," recorded in 1967 by The Jimi Hendrix Experience)

In a classic recording, guitar hero Jimi Hendrix tells the story of Joe, going down to shoot his cheating old lady. But he never specifies in which hand Joe is holding his famous gun. Perhaps Joe's left hand would be quicker, but his right hand is stronger, and holding the gun with both hands could offer him a steadier shot. Hendrix himself was left handed but generally just restrung right-handed guitars and played them upside down; he also reportedly ate, drank, and held the telephone with his right hand. This "mixed-handedness" may even have been the foundation for his genius (Michaels 2010). That is, Hendrix tended to play intricate series of bends and slides with his right hand, while hitting strings and switching back and forth between pickups. Rather than using his hands independently, Hendrix's playing technique was based on close coordination between them, which reinforced the rich texture of his music. Moreover, "language and rhythm processing are lateralised to the left side of brain, while the processing of melody and harmony is lateralised to the right side" (Michaels 2010), so the ability to combine the use of both hands may have been part of what made Hendrix one of the most inventive guitar players of all time.

Boundary-spanning service employees often are expected to be nearly as inventive in pushing the boundaries of their work roles. Hendrix famously asked listeners if they were experienced; today, the question for service personnel is more often, can you gain sales experience? As productivity gains have become the mantra for service firms, frontline service environments increasingly move from cost to profit units, requiring employees to display "mixed-handedness," such that they seamlessly blend service provision with sales. The rationale for this simultaneous pursuit of both service and sales goals is simple: Rather than closing traditional, service-focused branches (that is, cost centers), organizations such as retail banks realize the advantages of converting them into revenue-generating centers (Pombriant 2005) to do more with less. As noted by Bitner et al. (1994), frontline personnel have extensive contact with customers, so they also become well aware of customers' needs and problems, and this information enables them to propose cross-selling proactively, a service that not only increases profits but also signals the firm's genuine interest in the customer. Thus, selling becomes a manifestation of good service. With the promise of increased revenues and higher customer retention rates, companies worldwide (for example, Starbucks, Formosa Hotels, Taiwan Post, Qantas Airlines, Singapore Airlines, Vietnam's HD Bank, Thailand's Kasikorn Bank, and Wells Fargo) have begun to ask their frontline employees to take on cross-selling responsibilities, as a means to achieve productivity increases.

Although a recent McKinsey & Co. report predicts an attractive return on the investments required to mix service with sales (Eichfeld et al. 2006), other consultants offer less optimistic projections (CSO Insights 2007; ICMI 2007b). Mounting anecdotal evidence suggests that service firms still struggle to ensure that their service representatives are responsive to customer problems and also sell new products and services. Service employees express their sense that selling is at odds with service provision, such that broadening their roles to include selling creates mental barriers and resistance. Even those service employees willing to engage in selling may lack the skills or ability to convert service encounters into sales talks (ICMI 2007b). Thus, we need more insights into which employees can or cannot simultaneously solve customer problems and generate new revenues—and why.

PURPLE HAZE AND OTHER SEATTLE EXPORTS

If we may extend our Hendrix references, service companies often appear to be operating in a purple haze, without any guidance for mapping the uncharted territory. Introducing service-to-sales conversions might appear to kill two birds with one stone, but the risk is that the stone also kills employee morale or creates customer discontent. Requiring frontline employees to pursue seemingly incompatible goals may result in lower service and sales levels and disappointing bottom-line results (Aksin and Harker 1999). In a recent study, Günes et al. (2010) demonstrate that adding sales to a list of key performance metrics can backfire, especially when cross-selling irritates customers and leads to negative critical incidents, managerial headaches, and reduced customer patronage. Dart (2009) reports that an emphasis on sales targets prompts increased customer complaints, and an ICMI (2007a) report concludes that, "eager to experience the potential benefits of a cross-selling strategy, many service and tech support centers leap without looking . . . the common result: lost customers, agents and revenues." Starbucks' initial failure in its efforts to combine service and sales provides a case in point.

The depressed share price and lack of U.S. growth of Starbucks, the seemingly untouchable coffee chain, has been attributed in part the demoralization of frontline baristas when management, in pursuit of productivity gains, imposed sales performance targets and competition to a setting that previously had been differentiated by the delivery of exceptional service and personal engagement with customers (Berfield 2009). Employee backlash was rapid; even long-time employees vented their angst on the StarbucksGossip.com blog. In response, Starbucks' chief executive officer (CEO) Howard Schultz proclaimed "We have lost our way" and "are in danger of our brand being commoditized," as a result of the diminished customer focus. Thus Starbucks quickly learned the importance of finding an approach that matches the firm's own capability to manage conflicting demands, namely, exploiting existing competencies and exploring new opportunities (Raisch and Birkinshaw 2008). The corporate about-face included a reduced focus on individual sales targets and increased emphasis on the core value of customer engagement.

As this vignette demonstrates, the infusion of service–sales blending is fundamentally changing the way firms market and manage services. Effectively aligning service provision and sales can create superior value and sustainable competitive advantage; ineffective approaches could be detrimental to firm survival. Hence, we need key theoretical tenets, to help researchers develop an in-depth understanding of this phenomenon and assist service managers in deploying it.

A few studies have started to explore the concept of ambidexterity as a theoretical lens for investigating effective service–sales conversion and examining how it can enable firms to leverage service strategies and operations (Jasmand et al. 2012; Yu et al. 2013a). The ambidexterity concept is well established in the domains of organizational strategy and behavior, as well as innovation and learning literature: It provides a means to understand how firms behave in mixed manners, which enable them to gain competitive advantages. Yet considerable gaps and dissentions continue to fuel debate about the exact nature of the concept, the factors that drive it, and their intricate relationships and impacts on service performance.

With this chapter, we seek to offer greater conceptual clarity regarding the notion of ambidexterity in a service and sales context, during a single encounter with customers. In so doing, we also hope to generate a robust basis for further service research that can help service companies develop and maintain their service and sales goal alignment. We thus begin with a discussion of ambidexterity and its operationalization as service–sales ambidexterity. After unpacking this focal construct, we review recent studies that identify its various drivers. We also assess empirical evidence regarding the impact of service–sales ambidexterity on key service firm performance characteristics. We conclude by discussing the lessons for managers and some avenues for research.

AMBIDEXTERITY

The word "ambidextrous" derives from the Latin root words *ambi*, meaning "both," and *dexter*, meaning both "right" (as opposed to "left") and "favorable." Thus, "ambidextrous" is literally "right on both sides." Jimi Hendrix was ambidextrous, though he might not have been aware of this skill. In management literature, "ambidexterity" provides a metaphor for describing an organization's ability to perform seemingly conflicting tasks or pursue disparate goals simultaneously (Gibson and Birkinshaw 2004; Lubatkin et al., 2006). This form of ambidexterity is necessary, because the task environment makes demands on an organization that may come in conflict (for example, short- versus long-term goals, service quality versus productivity, systematic versus experiential beliefs, short-term sales versus longer-term customer relationships). These trade-offs must be reconciled to support longer-term organizational performance (March 1991; O'Reilly and Tushman 2004; Tushman and O'Reilly 1996). As Michael Fraccaro, the head of learning, talent, resourcing and organization development at HSBC, Asia Pacific, asserts "True ambidexterity is about having the people within the organisation who have the mindset, skills and maturity to respond positively to different circumstances" (quoted in Knowledge at the Australian School of Business 2011). An impressive body of research on the notion of ambidexterity thus has emerged, though Raisch and Birkinshaw (2008, p. 376) point out that "ambidexterity is still in the process of developing into a new research paradigm . . . the research on organizational ambidexterity is strong in some areas while weak or virtually nonexistent in others." One of these "others" is service science literature, where ambidexterity demands delivering quality customer service while achieving sales targets.

Most uses of the concept of ambidexterity rely on a partition between exploration and exploitation. Exploitation seeks to refine and extend existing competencies and technologies to achieve positive, proximate, and predictable returns. Exploration instead focuses on experimentation with new alternatives (for example, new product development), which produces uncertain, distant, and often negative returns (March, 1991). Exploration and exploitation thus create unique organizational issues. For example, exploration demands a focus on long-term goals, risk taking, and innovation, whereas exploitation deals with short-term goals, efficiency, and production (Birkinshaw and Gibson, 2004; He and Wong, 2004). Yet both are crucial to organizational survival in the long term, such that every organization must find the right balance between them. High performance firms pursue both exploration and exploitation to manage their current market challenges but simultaneously adapt to changes in the business environment (Gibson and Birkinshaw 2004; Levinthal and March 1993). In these cases, empirical evidence supports the basic tenet that ambidexterity enhances performance (for example, Gibson and Birkinshaw 2004; He and Wong 2004; Lubatkin et al. 2006).

Service–Sales Ambidexterity

The remaining question is whether these positive outcomes can be generalized to all service firms that undertake the parallel pursuit of service and sales strategies. Service quality relates positively to customer loyalty (for example, Taylor and Baker 1994; Zeithaml et al. 1996) but also might compete with the execution of effective sales strategies. As ambidexterity orientations, exploration and exploitation thus may be non-substitutable and interdependent, which would imply the need for their multiplicative interaction, in which exploration and exploitation capacities combine to represent an organization's ambidextrous capacity (we discuss operational definitions subsequently) (Gibson and Birkinshaw, 2004; Jansen et al. 2005). Furthermore, service provision and selling are two distinct activities: Service represents a cost, whereas sales is usually regarded as a revenue-generating activity. Likewise, traditional service centers constitute cost centers, while sales departments are revenue-generating units. Yet the counterclaim to this traditional view notes that service firms need both. Furthermore, service and sales can be interdependent, such as when excellent customer service increases sales (Zeithaml, 2000) or when selling the right offering to the right customer at the right time and in right place enhances customers' perceptions of service, service quality, and satisfaction.

Highlighting these interdependencies, service firms ask more frontline service staff to provide quality service and engage in cross- and up-selling to generate revenues during encounters initially started in a service support context. Providing quality customer service involves actions aimed at supporting customers with problem-solving procedures and customized solutions. Because such acts often recur in response to similar requests, service workers tend to rely on well-practiced procedures and leverage their engrained knowledge and skills. By scripting encounters, service providers also can guarantee consistent quality and improved efficiency (Aksin et al. 2007)—the two key criteria for measuring service performance. If they must supplement these targets with selling objectives, service employees also must proactively identify customer needs that can be satisfied with additional products or service upgrades, which requires their solid knowledge of customer needs (Evans et al. 1999). Because sales activities largely depend on the timing of an appropriate offer (Günes et al. 2010), they require procedural flexibility. Such uncertainty and unpredictability contrasts with the reliability and efficiency focus of customer service. For example, when they blend service and sales efforts, frontline staff cannot use scripts, because a service-to-sales conversion results from a developing dialogue. A question about an energy bill might evolve into a discussion of the need for a new boiler or the installation of solar cells, but it does not move in that direction in every case. Therefore, to be ambidextrous, frontline service employees must be able to switch seamlessly across service and sales objectives and manage seemingly conflicting demands, as well as identify when or if to transform a service encounter into a sales call.

Some observers argue that the incompatibility in ambidexterity dimensions can best be resolved at the individual employee level (Gupta et al. 2006; March 1991), because employees can conduct such activities either simultaneously or sequentially (for example, Adler et al. 1999; Mom et al. 2009). From a strategic perspective, service and sales could enhance each other's effectiveness, such as when cross-/up-selling enhances service quality perceptions or customer service provision contributes to effective selling. At a more operational level, these efforts compete for scarce resources, such as the employee's time and attention, such that their simultaneous pursuit must involve trade-offs. They are not completely incompatible, but the required behaviors for customer service provision and selling exhibit contradictory, opposing behavioral and cognitive demands, as well as a shared set of capabilities, such as diagnostic behavior, empathy, and interpersonal adaptation (for example, Evans et al. 1999; Gwinner et al. 2005). Some employees thus multitask, relying on automatic processing while simultaneously carrying out nonroutine tasks (Wegner and Bargh 1998). If they conduct service tasks in a routine mode, they free up cognitive and attentional space for new and unfamiliar activities, such as cross- and up-selling (at the employee level, the term "exploitation" usually gets dropped, for its inappropriateness). Thus, frontline employees may be able to manage tasks that seemingly conflict but that share multiple common grounds, to simultaneously pursue service and sales objectives and thus display service–sales ambidexterity.

For this discussion, we also note that sometimes stating what a concept is *not* can clarify its quintessential attributes. The simultaneous pursuit of serving and selling cannot be captured by goal conflict, even if at first glance, ambidexterity and goal conflict seem similar. Goal conflict literature focuses on the conflict that arises from a trade-off across multiple goals (for example, due to time constraints); this conflict among goals reduces the performance devoted to each goal (for example, reduced goal commitment, shifts in goal prioritization) (for example, Cheng et al. 2007). Thus, goal conflict considers neither the characteristics of non-substitutability and interdependence nor the contradictory behavioral demands underlying the means to achieve goals. More generally, goal conflict literature addresses the "either/or," while ambidexterity considers complementariness and a "both/and" mindset. We therefore posit that goal conflict cannot capture the nature of the relationship between customer service provision and cross-/up-selling.

Structural Ambidexterity

Beyond the individual employee level, ambidexterity can be aggregated to departments, business units, and retail branches. At these higher levels, we need to distinguish between structural and contextual ambidexterity (Birkinshaw and Gibson 2004; Gupta et al. 2006). Structural ambidexterity implies that the firm achieves ambidexterity through its structural design, including loosely coupled and differentiated subunits, each of which specializes in either exploration or exploitation. Gibson and Birkinshaw (2004) describe structural ambidexterity as the result of a firm seeking structural solutions (subunit or temporal) to deal with internal tensions and conflict and still perform seemingly conflicting tasks or pursue disparate goals. If a firm needs to explore new opportunities while exploiting its existing capabilities (O'Reilly and Tushman 2004), it can apply structural ambidexterity and assign one business unit to focus on exploring the new business opportunities while another business unit continues to exploit its existing capabilities. Alternatively, the same business unit might explore business opportunities on some days but exploit existing capabilities on others. With a structural ambidexterity approach, employees' roles are clearly defined, and the employees need more specialized skills (Birkinshaw and Gibson 2004). Furthermore, with well-defined roles and task assignments (for example, for financial services, selling home loans or investment packages), employees also require more specialized skills (for example, persuasion) rather than general skills to pursue ambidexterity at the individual level.

Contextual Ambidexterity

Contextual mechanisms, such as the creation of appropriate organizational contexts (for example, servant leadership climate, intra- and inter-team support) or coordination mechanisms (for example, cross-functional interfaces), may be the most effective option for motivating people to work in a particular way in organizations (Gibson and Birkinshaw 2004; Mom et al. 2009). Senior managers shape their organizational context through the systems, incentives, and controls they put in place, as well as the behaviors they exhibit on a day-to-day basis. These contextual features then get reinforced by the actions and attitudes of people throughout the organization. An individual's ability to exhibit ambidextrous behavior thus can be facilitated (or constrained) by their organizational context. At the organizational level, contextual ambidexterity refers to the collective orientation of all employees toward the simultaneous pursuit of alignment and adaptability. Whereas alignment "refers to coherence among all the patterns of activities in the business unit; they are working together toward the same goals. Adaptability refers to the capacity to reconfigure activities in the business unit quickly to meet changing demands in the task environment" (Gibson and Birkinshaw 2004, p. 209). Thus successful ambidexterity demands not just formal structures (that is, structural ambidexterity) or vision and mission statements, but also a supportive context that empowers employees to make choices about how, when, and where to focus their efforts. So, basically, leadership gets displayed by everyone in the organization.

Recent research indicates that, at least in times of rapid change, organizations that embrace opposites emerge as the most innovative and flexible, and hence successful, firms (Knowledge at the Australian School of Business 2011). Within an organization (or unit), there may be one overarching organizational culture, but it also might accommodate multiple climates that may seem contradictory, such as control and flexibility, or short-term sales and long-term customer relationships, or meeting sales targets while providing excellent service. In this case, the focus shifts from trade-offs ("we can only excel at only one thing") to ambidexterity ("we can be good at both"). A recent study of several hundred global firms revealed that the business units that produced positive financial outcomes had multiple climates, such as control and flexibility or focusing inward and outward at the same time (MacCormick and Parker 2010). For Toyota, its long history of success may have stemmed from the routines and processes it built to emphasize multiple climates, such as "stable and paranoid," "systematic and experimental," and "formal and frank." In another illustration, Apple grew stronger because it encouraged the development of expertise in multiple areas, regardless of whether they appeared contradictory: sales and service, function and form, strategy and micro-management. Apple publicly called on employees across all functions, not just research and development (R&D) members, to innovate (MacCormick and Parker 2010). Its success argues strongly in favor of a contextual approach to ambidexterity.

FROM CONCEPT TO OPERATIONALIZATION

A common assumption is that an organization (or individual) performs either exploitation-like or exploration-like activities, but not both. The "opposite" of ambidexterity thus is the single pursuit of either activity, such as when a service employee only performs service provision. If the organization engages in neither type of activity, it stagnates and dies. If employees neither provide service nor sell, they would not be working—theoretically, they would be engaging in "non-dexterity." Thus, for an operational definition, the two ambidextrous dimensions are orthogonal and should be measured as separate sets of items. What remains unclear is how best to integrate the two sets of measures: through subtraction, addition, or multiplication. Subtracting appears least desirable, because it offers relatively low explanatory power. The additive model is superior in terms of its explanatory power (Jansen et al. 2009), though conceptually, it does not effectively reflect the non-substitutable, interdependent characteristics of the ambidexterity dimensions, particularly compared with the multiplicative approach (Gibson and Birkinshaw 2004). Therefore, most studies of service–sales ambidexterity adopt multiplicative functions, with the recognition that service provision and selling can be complementary and supportive. Because frontline employees can simultaneously engage in or quickly switch between the two activities, a multiplicative function also seems the most appropriate in an operational sense to capture the combined magnitude of service provision and selling activities. This operationalization further aligns with our argument regarding performance, in that the complementarity of service provision and selling boosts key performance parameters, such as customer satisfaction and sales performance. Other operationalizations could not be able to capture this connection (for an extensive discussion of operational definitions, see Cao et al. 2009).

Probing the Nature of Service–Sales Ambidexterity

In a qualitative study, Yu et al. (2013b) seek in-depth insights into the exact nature of service–sales ambidexterity by interviewing employees who experienced such a conversion in their organization. They focus on how employees of six branches of a large Australian retail bank experienced tension and complementarities in attaining both service and sales targets and what issues were involved in implementing service–sales ambidexterity at the business unit level. According to their findings, a trade-off exists between the two sets of activities, but its presence tends to be less prominent for servicing and selling tasks performed by individual staff. As one respondent argued:

> For someone to even make a comment on the fact sales is being compromised by service or vice versa, that's someone who doesn't comprehend that you know you can have everything . . . in some cases it might be sales are also service as well. You know providing sales are a service to a customer . . . we need to make sure that you sit them in front of you talk to them about what they want, let them tell you what it is they are here for, then garner the information that you need, and then develop a strategy for the customer. We are providing a service but we are also selling, but it's not selling for the sake of selling, it's selling to help the customer and assist them in their banking.
>
> (Yu et al. 2013b)

Thus, the employees recognized that cross- or up-selling had the potential to instill perceptions of good service, and adding sales objects could strengthen service provision. However, to serve effectively by selling well, the frontline employees needed to possess certain abilities and skills (for example, conversational) and that not every employee had:

> Some people are better at small areas of expertise and have little niches. Like at Broadmeadow there is a particular lady she is very good at making phone calls. She is just very comfortable and easy at talking to people. Whereas some of the girls are a bit 'what am I going to talk about?' They are nervous to ring up and make the call because they feel like they are not experts or trained at selling . . . They give you these lists of people to ring and they feel they are getting much out of it so it almost becomes a bit of 'what's the point?'
>
> (Yu et al. 2013b)

These findings thus highlight the importance of building employees' self-confidence by offering appropriate training focused on certain skill sets. They also needed help to find the delicate balance involved in combining service and sales activities. One respondent noted a fear of overselling, which could be perceived as poor service quality, for example: "Sometimes you may be compromised. In order to sell a product not necessarily to someone who actually wants it . . . You can have a conflict in that way. You might move the focus slightly, and try to get somebody to buy a product they won't use."

At this potential tipping point, sales attempts may hinder service to customers. In addition, some employees simply resisted implementing "yet another program" and would rather do what they have always done: "When I first started with [the bank], there wasn't such a big focus on pushing sales . . . It was all different back then . . . Personally, I would love to just be nice to my customers, go about doing what they want and not have to worry about the result of sales."

For organizations, these insights suggest the importance of recognizing that employees vary in their attitudes and willingness to take on sales as an extra activity. They need to ascertain whether each frontline employee is willing and able to be ambidextrous. Several recent studies address these issues, as we summarize in the remainder of this chapter.

Individual Drivers of Service–Sales Ambidexterity

Extant research has accumulated knowledge about the antecedents of ambidexterity at the organizational level. However, we know very little about what drives ambidexterity at the employee level, despite the acknowledged importance of individual ambidexterity (Mom et al. 2009; Raisch et al. 2009). Jasmand et al. (2012) propose that regulatory mode dimensions, such as locomotion and assessment, constitute individual antecedents of service–sales ambidexterity. Despite any compatibility of service and sales, the apparent operational conflict between them can evoke ambivalence. Regulatory mode theory aims to explain how people deal with such comparisons and changes in relation to their goal pursuits by describing people's motivational capacity to guide themselves, overcome obstacles, adapt to their environment, and resolve goal conflict (for example, Higgins et al. 2003). Locomotion refers to a preference for movement and change, including any activity that can be undertaken to avoid stasis. Locomotors like to get going and enjoy the realization of being in motion, regardless of whether they are moving in the right direction. They want to make things happen and derive intrinsic gratification from "getting on with it" (Kruglanski et al. 2010), as effectively summarized in Nike's well-known "Just do it" slogan (Kruglanski et al. 2000). In contrast, assessors prefer to evaluate a range of options before deciding to act; they are more inclined to think before they leap (Higgins et al. 2003). Colloquially, an assessment orientation seeks to "do things right."

These individual orientations seem particularly relevant when frontline service employees must include cross-/up-selling activities in a work environment that traditionally has focused on service provision. Service-to-sales conversion programs in frontline service units frequently feature relatively high uncertainty in terms of the appropriate performance indicators, not only for the new cross- and up-selling activities but also for activities to bridge the service provision and selling goals. Furthermore, management often unilaterally introduces sales objectives as performance indicators, leading employees to complain that they were hired to help customers, not sell to them. Locomotors might give it a go; assessors will evaluate how to combine the activities (or get their bearings) and accordingly perceive more obstacles down the road. People characterized by both regulatory modes combine the best of both words and thus move in the right direction. Thus, according to Jasmand et al. (2012), an employee's locomotion orientation enhances his or her service–sales ambidexterity, and the impact is amplified when the employee also is assessment oriented. And Jimi Hendrix used his right hand to manipulate the pick-ups of his Stratocaster in such a way that the melodic lines produced by his left hand made maximal impact.

Finally, contextually relevant factors may attenuate the impact of regulatory mode dimensions on ambidexterity at the individual level. When team identification is high, convergent thinking and consensus building are prominent, and the employee can diminish the regulatory impact of an assessment orientation. Jasmand et al. (2012) also note a detrimental effect of routine discretion, which lessens the cognitive effort inherent in an appraisal mode adopted by assessors. Because frontline service environment characteristics can hinder the valuable interplay of self-regulatory orientations, it becomes necessary to weight individual and contextual drivers at the same time. If an over strong team identification discourages divergent and critical thinking about service and sales alignment, workgroups should be urged to stop and question their existing views.

Adding Contextual Drivers to the Equation

To explore how organizational forces shape service–sales ambidexterity, Yu et al. (2013a) surveyed approximately 2,300 employees in 267 branches of a large retail bank and conducted in-depth interviews with selected frontline employees. Instead of focusing on their self-regulation, these authors accounted for the work context; that is, instead of placing the responsibility for blending service and sales on the individual employee, the study examined what happens when a retail outlet or branch takes ownership of both service and sales targets. For this service–sales ambidexterity at the unit level, employees must collectively decide how to divide their efforts and energy. Because the attainment of both types of objectives may be complementary at higher levels of aggregation, and even reinforce each other, a firm's work processes and systems might help facilitate and encourage boundary-spanning service employees to align their service and sales activities. Three contextual factors drive service–sales ambidexterity at the branch level. First, empowerment or perceived autonomy in service work allows frontline staff to decide when to engage (or not) in the different types of behaviors. For example, if work units have the discretion to decide that during peak service times, they will minimize up- and cross-selling attempts and not be ambidextrous, it can increase the overall effectiveness of a dual goal strategy. Second, team support in a collective work environment that recognizes the interdependence of members of a work unit exerts a positive influence on the degree of service–sales ambidexterity. In challenging work settings especially (for example, selling complex financial services), support from coworkers can help individual employees deal effectively with the complexities and align their seemingly conflicting objectives. Third, transformational leadership is key, because when supervisors display a helpful attitude, expressing involvement with the team, it enhances ambidexterity (Gibson and Birkinshaw 2004). Members of a work unit tend to develop shared beliefs about these drivers of service–sales ambidexterity, so Yu et al. (2013b) consider their impacts at both the employee and group (that is, consensus within each branch regarding the contextual drivers) levels.

The findings indicate strong support for the three drivers at the individual level, such that the organizational context determines the successful execution of a blended service–sales strategy. The authors also find support for the influence of empowerment and leadership at the branch level, but no significant impact of team support. Perhaps there is simply too much heterogeneity among team members for them to view the group as a resource for improving their ambidextrous capabilities.

In the in-depth interviews, several respondents went further, noting that autonomy in deciding what reward systems to implement led to the successful implementation of a service-to-sales conversion strategy: "We really felt strongly about being recognized and rewarded for both our serving and selling in trying to decide how to balance our time. Otherwise, it would be a no-brainer to just do what we were always doing, helping customers." The heterogeneity of the team also emerged as a clear issue; several respondents expressed a need to infuse the branch with fresh, unbiased colleagues: "Some of the old crowd around here don't even think. They come, do what they have always been doing, they go home. Can't really blame them, they have seen many programs come and go." At the same time, some respondents acknowledged the value of more experienced colleagues:

> Stephen downstairs has been with us longer than I can or even care to remember, and still outperforms the young crowd. He has developed this radar for customer needs and knows exactly when the time is right to sell a product as a service solution. It is amazing how quickly he has picked this thing up. He just does it, no questions asked.
>
> (Yu et al. 2013b)

In an earlier study, Yu et al. (2009) also assessed the impact of contextual drivers (performance management, social support) in an employee motivation and capability framework, to reflect on whether employees were willing (goal orientation) and able (self-efficacy) to be ambidextrous. Goal orientation as a motivational driver indicates a person's willingness to invest effort and energy in specific activities to achieve goals (Covington 2000), whereas self-efficacy pertains to the employee's confidence in his or her ability to carry out work-related tasks (for example, Crant 2000; Debowski et al. 2001). Goal orientation further comprises learning, performance-prove, and performance-avoid orientations (VandeWalle 1997). Employees who want to learn are less daunted by challenging tasks and more persistent in their attempts to master them by acquiring necessary skills and knowledge. Frontline staff with high learning orientations therefore should be better able to manage the dual demands of service and sales (Sujan et al. 1994). Both types of performance-oriented employees instead see challenging tasks as threats to their performance, such that they likely resist service–sales ambidexterity initiatives (Brett and VandeWalle 1999; VandeWalle et al. 1999).

Efficacy entails not just self-confidence but also proxy notions, such as "confidence in the skills and abilities of a third party or parties to function effectively on one's behalf" (Bray et al., 2001, p.426). In frontline work units, team leaders or supervisors often coach employees in how to undertake new activities and perform well, much like a personal trainer in the gym. Findings from physical exercise literature recognize that when people rely on external agents to help them perform tasks, it lowers their confidence in themselves. Accordingly, relying too closely on a supervisor when trying to master service–sales ambidexterity may keep an employee from developing personal competencies; Bandura (2001, p.13) suggests that "the price of proxy agency is a vulnerable security that rests on the competence, power, and favors of others."

Empirical evidence thus emphasizes contextual predictors of service–sales ambidexterity, such that a learning orientation promotes ambidextrous work unit behavior, whereas performance orientations have negative impacts. The confidence that workers develop in themselves increases their perceptions of their team's service–sales ambidexterity. Whereas proxy-efficacy as a moderator strengthens the impact of learning orientation on ambidexterity, it reduces the influence of self-efficacy. This two-sided effect suggests the need for more detailed explanations of the various ways leaders can influence workers' self-perceived motivation and ability, using various leadership styles, such as transactional, servant, or even spiritual leadership.

DOES AMBIDEXTERITY IMPLEMENTATION INFLUENCE ORGANIZATIONAL PERFORMANCE?

The case for adopting a service–sales ambidexterity strategy is compelling. But the litmus test for whether to pursue such a strategy must be the extent to which, if successfully implemented, it alters staff performance and results in improved productivity and financial performance at the branch and/or organizational levels. Research into this ambidexterity–performance linkage suggests two camps. Some studies employ soft or more subjective measures of performance, such as employee satisfaction, customer satisfaction, and employee (self-reported) or supervisor ratings of ambidexterity. A second camp uses hard, financial performance measures. In this section, we consider both types of evidence linking ambidexterity to performance.

A McKinsey & Co. report has indicated that firms can increase their revenues by 10 percent if they integrate cross- and up-selling functions in their traditional service centers (Eichfeld et al. 2006). Other observers predict a figure closer to 50 percent of total revenue (Murcott 2007). Ambidexterity also might parallel Rust et al.'s (2002) or Mittal et al.'s (2005) dual emphasis strategy, according to which capable firms adopt both cost and revenue emphases to manage their profitability through both efficiencies and customer satisfaction. Using managers' reports of firm performance and longitudinal secondary data of firm profitability and stock market returns, Rust et al. (2002) offer equivocal results; they find few performance differences between firms with a primarily sales focus and those that adopted both a sales and a cost reduction approach simultaneously. Mittal et al. (2005) in turn employ a longitudinal data set from 77 U.S. firms and conclude that achieving a dual emphasis (ambidexterity) is desirable for long-run financial success, but the process of achieving it is not necessarily financially rewarding in the short term. In other words, "Firms pursuing a dual emphasis need to consider both the short- and long-term consequences of their strategy" (Mittal et al. 2005, p. 544). Yu et al. (2013a), using cross-sectional data from a bank, examine the link between frontline employee service–sales ambidexterity and financial performance at the branch level. Controlling for branch size and location, they find a small but significant impact on branch profitability, such that ambidexterity explains 12.3 percent of its variance.

Among the studies using more subjective measures, Gibson and Birkenshaw (2004) find that business unit ambidexterity is positively associated with business unit performance, operationalized as employee satisfaction, customer satisfaction, and employees' realization of their full potential. Lubatkin et al. (2006) rely on self-reported measures of unit performance. These subjective, self-reported measures may suffer from common method and self-serving bias, so a more recent study, assessing the impact of ambidexterity performance across several service industries, uses supervisor ratings, rather than employee self-reports, of ambidexterity performance (Patterson et al. 2013). The combined evidence strongly indicates that successfully implementing a service–sales ambidexterity strategy makes a positive contribution to productivity and profitability at the branch (unit) and organizational levels. But as Mittal et al. (2005) note, this impact may unfold only over time.

CONCLUSION

This research review explores the possibility of combining service and sales in encounters with customers, as well as the extent to which service employees can be "reborn" as sales agents in a way that benefits customers. With this final section, we also aim to provide service researchers with some suggestions for further research that will explore the exciting opportunities for service–sales ambidexterity. Service firms may demand such studies as they seek to embrace service–sales ambidexterity as a viable strategy. As we have outlined, management literature offers mixed signals about this form of mixed-handedness, but to conclude this chapter we summarize the lessons learned.

Considering the avenues for further research, we need more work that clarifies the impact of ambidexterity on performance. Thus far, largely due to data availability, the focus has been on traditional, functionally driven performance measures, such as sales units, customer satisfaction, and service handling time. An appropriate assessment of service–sales ambidexterity performance may require new measures that take into account seemingly conflicting objectives but are based on underlying commonalities. For example, the successful alignment of service and sales might require employees to engage in diagnostic behavior and derive customers' latent needs. If these ambidextrous employees then develop an in-depth understanding of customer requirements, they could be of great value to new service development operations. The impact of such absorptive capacity on firms' service innovation strategy, and how to incorporate this impact into performance assessments, remains uncertain. It would be a worthwhile pursuit for additional research.

Moreover, we do not know the longer-term, relational consequences of a focus on service–sales alignment. Most existing studies are cross-sectional. Yet experiences and perceptions in frontline work environments are dynamic and need to be studied from a longitudinal perspective, using multiple measurements and reciprocal relationships across performance and service–sales ambidexterity. Considering the frequent reports of short-term efficiency losses, it seems imperative to assess the longitudinal impact of this type of ambidexterity.

In addition, the relatively few studies of service–sales ambidexterity seem focused exclusively on face-to-face service encounters or inbound telephone calls. Yet the past decade has witnessed a rapid increase in the number of customer contact points, with a special emphasis on social media. Contact points vary notably in their communication characteristics (for example, the presence of verbal versus nonverbal cues). Service delivery via email, for example, involves two-way communication but lacks a real-time quality. In this case, it may be more difficult for service representatives to drill down and discover what customer needs the firm could meet by offering up-selling opportunities. Further research should explore whether service–sales alignment differs across contact modes and if adjustments should be made at the individual, team, or branch level.

Finally, qualitative data suggest the presence of tipping points in service encounters, that is, moments at which further sales attempts may have negative effects or end the conversation. The existing body of research relies on surveys; it may be advisable to use recently developed text-mining techniques to achieve micro-level insights into conversational patterns and illocutionary acts and thereby determine where and when to introduce a sales opportunity into a dialogue, as well as identify which verbal cues signal that it is best to avoid selling at all.

Lessons Learned for Practitioners

In pursuit of productivity gains, service organizations increasingly ask their frontline employees to embark on the parallel pursuit of excellent service and extensive cross- and up-selling. But simply adding a sales function to employees' performance metrics may seriously backfire if done without due consideration of the many relevant issues and findings. For executives seeking to establish a service–sales ambidextrous organization (or units), we offer several key lessons:

- *Develop a climate for ambidexterity*. Research strongly indicates that, first and foremost, managers must systematically build a climate for ambidexterity. This lesson implies a shift of organizational and executive thinking, from trade-offs ("we can only excel at one thing or the other") to a more ambidextrous mindset ("we can excel at both") (MacCormick and Parker 2010). An individual employee's propensity to exhibit ambidextrous behavior is facilitated (or constrained) by the climate in which he or she works. Invisible stimuli and pressures can advance a "we can be good at both" mindset, which becomes employees' collective orientation toward the simultaneous pursuit of service and sales. Furthermore, such a climate establishes clear expectations, which also must be clearly communicated. Ultimately, by establishing systems, rewards, and controls and behaving appropriately, senior managers set the tone. As we noted, such climates already have been successfully implemented at firms such as Apple, Toyota, and HSBS.

- *Be both willing and able.* Although not entirely incompatible, the attitude and skill sets required for customer service provision and up-/cross-selling impose different cognitive and behavioral demands. Ambidexterity requires the presence of people whose skills, mindsets, and maturity levels allow them to respond effectively to various events and circumstances. Coupled with the empirical research findings to date, this requirement suggests that when recruiting, managers should look for candidates with strong self-efficacy and goal orientations (that is, ambition and drive to achieve personal goals). They also might seek out people with a locomotion orientation, who prefer movement and change in trying to achieve their goals. If possible, employees who also score high on assessment levels can better keep their desire to "get on with it" on track. Ideally, employees should be stimulated and trained to be both locomotors and assessors, who "just do the right thing every time." Achieving service excellence and sales outcomes also requires shared capabilities, including diagnostic behavior, empathy, and interpersonal adaptation. As a recruitment truism suggests though, managers should "recruit for attitude and train for skill." To implement a service–sales ambidextrous strategy, firms therefore might conduct personality tests to ensure job candidates have a disposition that is compatible with the varied task requirements they might face. Then the training modules can stimulate their self-regulation and reflection on personal motivation and give new employees guidelines for investing their energy effectively to meet their dual performance goals.
- *Recognize the importance of contextual drivers.* Three factors contribute to successful service–sales ambidexterity at the organizational unit (branch) level: empowerment, team support, and transformational leadership. When leaders "walk the walk" and set an example, they contribute to the service–sales climate and provide a supportive context that allows employees to make their own choices about when and how to focus their energies. This leadership then becomes a characteristic, exhibited by everyone in the unit, not

simply the formal unit manager, such that it moves both top-down and bottom-up (Birkinshaw and Gibson 2004). Frontline managers need to allow employees to trust their own judgments when it comes to balancing service and sales objectives. Ambidexterity can require trade-offs, and support from direct colleagues can help employees make them. Therefore, the firm should implement processes and systems to facilitate knowledge sharing and social support, such as through role-playing and team-building exercises based on realistic challenges. The reward systems also should recognize all the elements involved in aligning service and sales. That is, employees need to be recognized when they take an opportunity to up-sell, even if it increases their customer handling time.

Because many boundary-spanning employees today are required to develop a willingness and ability to serve well by selling well, we confront a new generation of salespeople. Turning them into "rock legends" will take time, patience, and a deliberate strategic choice by service firms that provide an environment that gives frontline employees sufficient confidence to grow into their new roles, set new objectives, and discover their inner Hendrix. Service–sales ambidexterity may be a balancing act, but as research shows, the act can ultimately be rewarding to employees, companies, and their customer audiences.

REFERENCES

Adler, Paul S., Barbara Goldoftas and David I. Levine (1999), "Flexibility versus efficiency? A case study of model changeovers in the Toyota production system," *Organization Science*, **10** (1), 43–68.

Aksin, O. Zeynep and Patrick T. Harker (1999), "To sell or not to sell: determining the trade-offs between service and sales in retail banking phone centers," *Journal of Service Research*, **2** (1), 19–33.

Aksin, O. Zeynep, Mor Armony and Vijay Mehrotra (2007), "The modern call center: a multi-disciplinary perspective on operations management research," *Production and Operations Management*, **16** (6), 665–88.

Bandura, Albert (2001), "Social cognitive theory: an agentic perspective," *Annual Review of Psychology*, **52** (1), 1–26.

Berfield, Susan (2009), "Baristas, patrons steaming over Starbucks Via: aggressive rollout of new instant coffee product brewing discontent," *Bloomberg Businessweek*, accessed 1 March 2011 at http://today.msnbc.msn.com/id/33890453/ns/business-local_business/.

Birkinshaw, Julian and Cristina Gibson, 2004, "Building ambidexterity into an organization," *Sloan Management Review*, **45** (4), 47–55.

Bitner, Mary J., Booms, Bernard H., and Mohr, Lois A. (1994), "Critical service encounters: the employee's viewpoint," *Journal of Marketing*, **58** (4), 95–106.

Bray, Steven R., Nancy C. Gyurcsik, S. Nicole Culos-Reed, Kimberley A. Dawson and Kathleen A. Martin (2001), "An exploratory investigation of the relationship between

proxy efficacy, self-efficacy and exercise attendance," *Journal of Health Psychology*, **6** (4), 425–34.
Brett, Joan F. and Don Vandewalle (1999), "Goal orientation and goal content as predictors of performance in a training program," *Journal of Applied Psychology*, **84** (6), 863–73.
Cao, Qing, Eric Gedajlovic and Hongping Zhang (2009), "Unpacking organizational ambidexterity: dimensions, contingencies, and synergistic effects," *Organization Science*, **20** (4), 781–96.
Cheng, Mandy M., Peter F. Luckett and Habib Mahama (2007), "Effect of perceived conflict among multiple performance goals and goal difficulty on task performance," *Accounting and Finance*, **47** (2), 221–42.
Covington, Martin V. (2000), "Goal theory, motivation, and school achievement: an integrative review," *Annual Review of Psychology*, **51** (1), 171–200.
Crant, Michael J. (2000), "Proactive behavior in organizations," *Journal of Management*, **26** (3), 435–62.
CSO Insights (2007), *Sales Performance Report 2007: Call Center Marketing & Sales Optimization Study*, Jim Dicky and Berry Trailer (eds), Boulder, CO: CSO Insights.
Dart, Jonathan (2009), "Bank workers forced to push loans to public," *Sydney Morning Herald*, 1 February.
Debowski, Shelda, Robert E. Wood and Alber Bandara (2001), "Impact of guided exploration and enactive exploration on self-regulatory mechanisms and information acquisition through electronic search," *Journal of Applied Psychology*, **86** (6), 1129–41.
Eichfeld, Andy, Timothy D. Morse and Katherine W. Scott (2006), "Using call centers to boost revenue," *McKinsey Quarterly*, May.
Evans, Kenneth R., Todd J. Arnold and John A. Grant (1999), "Combining service and sales at the point of customer contact a retail banking example," *Journal of Service Research*, **2** (1), 34–49.
Gibson, Cristina B. and Julian Birkinshaw (2004), "The antecedents, consequences, and mediating role of organizational ambidexterity," *Academy of Management Journal*, **47** (2), 209–26.
Güneş, Evrim D., O. Zeynep Akşin, E. Lerzan Örmeci, and S. Hazal Özden (2010), "Modeling customer reactions to sales attempts: if cross-selling backfires," *Journal of Service Research*, **13** (2), 168–83.
Gupta, Anil K., Ken G. Smith and Christina E. Shalley (2006), "The interplay between exploration and exploitation," *Academy of Management Journal*, **49** (4), 693–706.
Gwinner, Kevin P, Mary Jo Bitner, Stephen W Brown and Ajith Kumar (2005), "Service customization through employee adaptiveness," *Journal of Service Research*, **8** (2), 131–48.
He, Zi-Lin and Poh-Kam Wong (2004), "Exploration vs. exploitation: an empirical test of the ambidexterity hypothesis," *Organization Science*, **15** (4), 481–94.
Higgins, E. Tory, Arie W. Kruglanski and Antonio Pierro (2003), "Regulatory mode: locomotion and assessment as distinct orientations," in M.P. Zanna (ed.), *Advances in Experimental Social Psychology*, New York: Academic Press, pp. 293–344.
ICMI (2007a), "2007 survey on cross-selling summary, operations management", International Customer Management Institute, CMP Media, LLC.
ICMI (2007b), "Call center management review: 2007 call center cross-selling survey report," International Customer Management Institute, CMP Media, LLC.
Jansen, Justin J.P., Frans A.J. Van den Bosch and Henk W. Volberda (2005), "Exploratory innovation, exploitative innovation, and ambidexterity: the impact of environmental and organizational antecedents," *Schmalenbach Business Review*, **57** (4), 351–63.
Jansen, Justin J. P., Michiel P. Tempelaar, Frans A.J. van den Bosch and Henk W. Volberda (2009), "Structural differentiation and ambidexterity: the mediating role of integration mechanisms," *Organization Science*, **20** (4), 797–811.
Jasmand, Claudia, Vera Blazevic and Ko de Ruyter (2012), "Generating sales while providing service: a study of customer service representatives' ambidextrous behavior," *Journal of Marketing*, **76** (1), 20–37.
Knowledge at the Australian School of Business (2011), "Beyond specialisation: how

businesses benefit when opposites attract," 23 November, accessed 12 February 2013 at http://knowledge.asb.unsw.edu.au/articlepdf/1522.pdf?CFID=34694651&CFTOKEN=33145743&jsessionid=d0303dd98998e994798c33193d237d3e6d2d.

Kruglanski, Arie W., Erik P. Thompson, Tory E. Higgins, M. Nadir Atash, Antonio Pierro, James Y. Shah, and Scott Spiegel (2000), "To 'Do the right thing' or to 'Just do it': locomotion and assessment as distinct self-regulatory imperatives," *Journal of Personality and Social Psychology*, **79** (5), 793–815.

Kruglanski, Arie W., Edward Orehek, Tory E. Higgins, Antonio Pierro and Idit Shalev (2010), "Modes of self-regulation: assessment and locomotion as independent determinants in goal pursuit," in R.H. Hoyle (ed.), *Handbook of Personality and Self-Regulation*, Malden, MA: Blackwell-Wiley, pp. 375–402.

Levinthal, Daniel A. and James G. March (1993), "The myopia of learning," *Strategic Management Journal*, **14** (Winter), special issue, pp. 95–112.

Lubatkin, Michael H., Zeki Simsek, Yan Ling and John F. Veiga (2006), "Ambidexterity and performance in small- to medium-sized firms: the pivotal role of top management team behavioral integration," *Journal of Management*, **32** (5), 646–72.

MacCormick, Judith and Sharon K. Parker (2010), "A multiple climate approach to understanding business unit effectiveness", *Human Relations*, **63** (11), 1771–806.

March, James G. (1991), "Exploration and exploitation in organizational learning," *Organization Science*, **2** (1), 71–87.

Michaels, Sean (2010), "Was Jimi Hendrix's ambidexterity the key to his virtuosity? Guitar hero's 'mixed-handedness' was secret to his genius, argues American psychologist," *Guardian*, 25 February, accessed 12 February 2013 at www.guardian.co.uk/music/2010/feb/25/jimi-hendrix-ambidexterity-virtuosity.

Mittal, Vikas, Eugene W. Anderson, Akin Sayrak and Pandu Tadikamalla (2005), "Dual emphasis and the long-term financial impact of customer satisfaction," *Marketing Science*, **24** (4), 544–55.

Mom, Tom J.M., Frans A.J. van den Bosch and Henk W. Volberda (2009), "Understanding variation in managers' ambidexterity: investigating direct and interaction effects of formal structural and personal coordination mechanisms," *Organization Science*, **20** (4), 812–28.

Murcott, Mary (2007), *Service to Sales—A Global (and Candid) Perspective*, Colorado Springs, CO: ICMI Press.

O'Reilly III, Charles A. and Michael L. Tushman (2004), "The ambidextrous organization," *Harvard Business Review*, **82** (4), 74–81.

Patterson, Patterson G., Ting Yu and Narumon Kimpakorn (2013), "Killing two birds with one stone: cross-selling during service delivery," proceedings from the 2013 Naples Forum on Service, Naples, June (in press).

Pombriant, Denis (2005), "Adding sales to the call center agenda," Executive White Paper – Beagle Research Group, May.

Raisch, Sebastian and Julian Birkinshaw (2008), "Organizational ambidexterity: antecedents, outcomes, and moderators," *Journal of Management*, **34** (3), 375–409.

Raisch, Sebastian, Julian Birkinshaw, Gilbert Probst and Michael L. Tushman (2009), "Organizational ambidexterity: balancing exploitation and exploration for sustained performance," *Organization Science*, **20** (4), 685–95.

Rust, Roland T., Christine Moorman and Peter R. Dickson (2002), "Getting return on quality: revenue expansion, cost reduction, or both?" *Journal of Marketing*, **66** (4), 7–24.

Sujan, Harish, Barton A. Weitz and Nirmalya Kumar (1994), "Learning orientation, working smart, and effective selling," *Journal of Marketing*, **58** (3), 39–52.

Taylor, Steven A. and Thomas L. Baker (1994), "An assessment of the relationship between service quality and customer satisfaction in the formation of consumer purchase intention," *Journal of Retailing*, **70** (2), 163–78.

Tushman, Micheal L. and Charles A. O'Reilly III (1996), "Ambidextrous organizations: managing evolutionary and revolutionary change," *California Management Review*, **38** (4), 8–30.

VandeWalle, Don (1997), "Development and validation of a work domain goal orientation instrument," *Educational and Psychological Measurement*, **57** (6), 995–1015.

VandeWalle, Don, Steven P. Brown, William L. Cron and John W. Slocum Jr. (1999), "The influence of goal orientation and self-regulation tactics on sales performance: a longitudinal field test," *Journal of Applied Psychology*, **84** (2), 249–58.

Wegner, Daniel M. and John A. Bargh (1998), "Control and automaticity in social life," in D.T. Gilbert, S.T. Fiske and L. Gardner (eds), *The Handbook of Social Psychology*, New York: McGraw-Hill, pp. 446–96.

Yu, Ting, Paul Patterson and Ko de Ruyter (2009), "Achieving ambidexterity in retail banking: the role of branch context," International Conference on Service Science and Innovation. Conference proceedings, 11–12 August, Taipei.

Yu, Ting, Paul G. Patterson and Ko de Ruyter (2013a), "Achieving service–sales ambidexterity," *Journal of Service Research*, **16** (1), 52–66.

Yu, Ting, Paul G. Patterson and Ko de Ruyter (2013b), "A qualitative analysis of service–sales ambidexterity," unpublished manuscript.

Zeithaml, Valarie A. (2000), "Service quality, profitability, and the economic worth of customers: what we know and what we need to learn," *Journal of the Academy of Marketing Science*, **28** (1), 67–85.

Zeithaml, Valarie A., Leonard L. Berry and A. Parasuraman (1996), "The behavioral consequences of service quality," *Journal of Marketing*, **60** (2), 31–46.

PART V

PRODUCT AND PRICING

14 The pricing of services

Steven M. Shugan

INTRODUCTION

This chapter considers the pricing of services. Given the vast nature of the pricing literature, this chapter focuses on three pricing topics that are particularly relevant for service industries.

The first topic is advance pricing of services. Advance pricing is a pricing strategy for time-sensitive services where the service provider sells the service at different prices for different future times. For example, an airline offers a product line where the line consists of flights leaving on different days at different times. In this situation, the service provider can link the price to the duration of time between the time of the future consumption of the service and the purchase (or the commitment to purchase) the service. The specified time for future consumption may be very specific. For example, many entertainment services sell tickets for specific future dates and times. Other examples of specific future times include conferences, tours, cruises, professional courses, and so on. The time of consumption might also be a well-defined interval. For example, homecare services such as lawn services and exterminating might sell their service for a specific future week or future month. Finally, the future time of consumption might be a complex condition often related to industry seasons. For example, an amusement park ticket might specify admission during future off-peak days (for example, Monday through Thursday) or future off-peak months (September through November). As the current time approaches the time of consumption, the price of the service usually increases to the highest level. This situation differs from, for example, the sale of manufactured fashion goods where the price steadily declines as the fashion season progresses. This situation also differs from manufactured goods that can be consumed at any point in time and the service provider exercises no control over when the manufactured good is consumed. For example, after a consumer purchases a soft drink or a motion-picture DVD, the seller has little control over when the soft drink is consumed or the motion-picture DVD is viewed.

The second pricing topic in this chapter is the pricing of capacity-constrained services where either future demand is uncertain or future available capacity is uncertain. In this situation, the capacity-based price is linked to the remaining capacity. Although the time until consumption is usually related to remaining capacity because remaining capacity often decreases over time, linking the current price to remaining capacity differs because it makes future prices less predictable. For example, transportation services such as airlines and railroads often link their fares for particular flights or trains to the number of unsold or available seats. Lodging services such as hotels often link prices to the number of remaining available rooms. Generally, prices increase as remaining capacity diminishes. However, as the time of consumption approaches, the remaining capacity is sometimes sold at lower prices. Although capacity can be an issue for manufacturers with limited quantities of their manufactured product, these sellers are often able to use inventory control and just-in-time logistics as their primary methods for managing demand uncertainty.

The third pricing topic is seasonal pricing. Seasonal pricing involves pricing for the predictable demand peaks or, at least, the predictable part of the demand peak. Seasons can consist of hours, days, weeks, months, holidays, and so on. For example, restaurants expect increases in demand during weekend evenings and off-peak demand during late weekday afternoons. Movie theaters expect peak demand during school holidays such as Thanksgiving and Independence Day. Retailers expect peak demand during the Christmas holiday season. Although manufactured goods can also be seasonal, building inventory for the peak season is the primary method for managing predictable seasonality.

Note that the pricing of a particular service might involve all three of these pricing issues (that is, advance pricing, capacity-constrained pricing, and seasonal pricing). For example, an airline might link the initial price of a flight to the number of unsold seats but, as the time approaches departure, the airline might link the final prices to the time to departure. Moreover, the airline might also consider seasonality when setting the initial price so that the base price (given a nearly empty flight) might depend on the hour, day and month of departure and the expected demand conditions existing at that point in time. However, the theories and implementations underlying advance pricing, capacity-based pricing and seasonal pricing are very different. Advance pricing attempts to exploit consumer uncertainty regarding future consumption states. Capacity-based pricing attempts to continuously update the expected future demand based on current and recent sales. Finally, seasonal pricing attempts to predict future demand based on demand patterns observed in past seasons.

ADVANCE PRICING

Many (or most) service providers exercise some control over the time of consumption. This control is often absent from firms in other sectors of the economy. For example, restaurants, physicians, management consultants, plumbers and many others make appointments or reservations for specific times. In fact, many of these service providers can determine the exact time at which the service is delivered. A restaurant, for example, can deny service at 7.30 p.m. but allow service at 8.30 p.m. A restaurant can also sell promotional discount cards (for example, $15 for $20 worth of food) in December for use on weekdays in January. Contrast this situation with manufactured products such as motion-picture DVDs or food products such as apples. Unlike the theatrical exhibition at the local theater, a consumer can view the motion-picture DVD at any desired time and place. Unlike the apple consumed at the local restaurant, a consumer can eat a purchased apple at any desired time and place. For this reason, service providers have a marketing mix variable that other sellers often lack. Service providers can forward sell at an advance price by getting purchase commitments before the period of consumption. Service providers can then sell at a spot price at the time of consumption.

There are three critical questions regarding the management of advance selling or pricing at a time in advance of consumption. The first question is whether advance pricing is profitable. The second question is, in theory, how to set the advance price. The third question is how to implement advance pricing.

Let us start by considering why advance pricing is profitable. Forward selling at an advance price is usually only profitable if either the advance price has a higher profit margin or the advance price generates additional demand for the service. Parenthetically, there are two other dubious arguments regarding why advance pricing can be profitable but neither argument is very compelling. First, it is possible, but unlikely, that advance pricing reduces the seller's risk. For example, the seller of a concert could advance sell to hedge against bad weather or some other event that might diminish spot demand for the concert. Doing so transfers the risk from the seller to the buyer where the buyer now assumes the risk for bad weather or some other event that makes the concert less desirable. However, finance theory suggests that service providers should be risk neutral or, at least, far less averse to risk than ordinary consumers. Moreover, a simpler solution is to transfer risk to insurance companies and financial markets that are often eager to assume risk at a smaller monetary premium than most consumers. Consequently, it is more profitable and plausible to reduce risk by buying insurance rather than expecting consumers to assume those risks.

A second, also less compelling, argument for advance pricing is that advance pricing provides information about future demand. For example, a hotel could advance sell rooms or an airline could advance sell seats on a flight in order to estimate the demand for those rooms or that flight. However, service providers would need to give consumers some significant benefit for making advance purchase commitments. Supplying that benefit would incur a substantial cost for the service provider. A less expensive alternative would be to allow consumers to make reservations that do not involve a firm purchase commitment. For example, the reservation could be free, involve a small monetary charge, or could be cancelled without charge for a specified period. These reservations would provide the service provider with information about future demand without the need to entice consumers into making advance purchase commitments. Reservations systems, in some cases, might still need to provide the consumer (precisely, the marginal customer) with some incentive for making the reservation but that incentive would be far less costly than the incentive that would be required to induce the consumer into making a rigid advance purchase commitment.

Hence, it seems that forward selling at an advance price that differs from the spot price is only a viable strategy when the advance price either increases the profit margin or increases demand. For a higher profit margin, the advance price would usually need to be higher than the future spot price (that is, the price at the time of consumption), unless selling in advance reduces costs in some significant way (for example, the service provider can more efficiently deliver services given advance purchase commitments). However, potential buyers would know that the advance price is possibly higher than the future spot price. Consequently, for the service provider to enjoy a higher advance price, the potential buyer must have some reason to buy in advance because buying in advance (where the advance price is higher than the spot price) implies both paying a higher price and parting with money sooner rather than later.

There are some reasons why a buyer might be willing to pay more in advance but these reasons only apply in some very specific situations. First, the buyer might believe that limited capacity (discussed in the next section) might impede a later purchase. In that case, if future capacity becomes unavailable, the spot price becomes, de facto, infinite. Of course, a profit-maximizing service provider should probably raise the price as the service provider's capacity becomes exhausted. Hence, this situation should be rare unless the service provider fails to retain full pricing authority.

A second reason that a potential buyer might pay a higher price in advance is that the buyer prefers to accomplish the purchasing task sooner rather than later. For example, the traveler might want to purchase an airline ticket before booking hotels, making restaurant reservations and purchasing tours. It might be of some comfort to the traveler to know that flights are booked and it is unnecessary to book those flights in the future. The consumer might also pay in advance as a means for self-imposed budgeting. These motivations are psychological rather than economic because, for example, when future airline flights are always available at a lower cost, there is no economic reason to purchase the airline ticket sooner. Hence, these situations for paying a higher advance price are also probably rare.

A third reason that a potential buyer might pay a higher price in advance is some idiosyncratic feature of the transaction. For example, an immediate transaction might be tax deductible in the current year while a future payment may not be. An immediate transaction might allow the use of funds in an expiring expense account. An immediate transaction might be required for another purchase (for example, purchasing insurance before shopping for an automobile). An immediate transaction might be made in exchange for other concessions offered by the service provider. For example, the service provider might give the buyer some ancillary benefits (for example, the best table in the restaurant, a free drink with the ticket purchase, a package deal).

Given that high advance purchase prices are rare, we must conclude that the most common motivation for a potential buyer to make an early commitment to purchase in advance is that the advance price is lower than the spot price. Consequently, the buyer gets a discount for making an early or advance purchase. Service providers are essentially paying buyers to make advance purchase commitments and purchase at lower advance prices than the higher spot prices.

That raises the question regarding why the service provider should be willing to discount the advance price when the discount lowers the profit margin. If the service provider sells at the higher spot price, the service provider enjoys a higher profit margin. So, the only remaining logical way a lower advance price could be more profitable is that the lower advance substantially increases the demand for the service.

However, merely increasing demand is not sufficient to justify an advance price discount. Any discount will usually increase demand whether that discount is in the advance or the spot period. Consequently, even when a discount in the spot price will increase demand, the service provider could still offer that discount in the spot period and there would be no reason for the consumer to advance purchase. For example, suppose the spot price is \$100 and the discounted advance price is \$90. If the service provider enjoys more profits at an advance price of \$90 rather than an advance price of \$100, maybe the service provider would enjoy more profits at a spot price of \$90 rather than a spot price of \$100. In other words, a spot price of

$100 is not optimal if a discounted spot price of $90 provides the same or greater profits (that is, there is a sufficient increase in demand to offset the decrease of $10 in the unit profit margin) than a spot price of $100. We must conclude that advance selling is only profitable when a discount in the advance period increases demand more than a discount in the future spot period.

There are at least two situations when a discount in the advance period yields a larger increase in demand than a discount in the spot period. The first situation is when there are different buyers or market segments in each period and these different segments have a different sensitivity to price. Buyers in one period are willing to pay a higher price than buyers in the other period. However, that situation alone is insufficient to justify an advance price that differs from the spot price. For example, suppose that buyers in the future spot period are more sensitive to price than buyers in the advance period who are willing to pay more. In that case, the service provider would want to charge a lower spot price and a higher advance price. However, given a higher advance price, all buyers would wait and buy in the spot period generating no advance sales at the higher advance price. So consider the opposite situation, when buyers in the spot period are willing to pay more than buyers in the advance period. Now the service provider can charge a low price in the advance period for making an early purchase. However, all buyers would now purchase in the advance period unless buyers in the spot period are unable to advance purchase.

Hence, there are at least two additional conditions required before advance purchase discounts are both feasible and potentially more profitable than spot selling alone (that is, in the case where there are different segments in each period). First, the buyers in the spot period must be willing to pay more than buyers in the advance period, and second, buyers in the spot period must be unable to buy in the advance period. Although these conditions are restrictive, there are a few service providers that face this situation. This situation can occur in the travel industry where hotels, airlines and car rental agencies, for example, face leisure and business travelers. Leisure travelers plan trips in advance and are more sensitive to price. Business travelers must often travel with little advance planning for a last minute meeting or meetings that run longer than expected. Business travelers are not potential buyers in the advance period and are often willing to pay more in the spot period than leisure travelers.

We do observe advance purchase discounts in the travel industry and these discounts represent a simple form of price discrimination (that is, third-degree price discrimination) where business travelers often pay more than leisure travelers. However, high spot prices also deter purchases by last-minute leisure travelers who sometimes also plan last-minute leisure trips. Hence, other forms of price discrimination (beyond advance purchase discounts) are sometimes more profitable than advance pricing at a discounted advance price. For example, a price or fare discount requiring a Saturday night stay-over might be unimportant to leisure travelers while being unattractive to business travelers. A price or fare discount requiring a weekend or midday departure might again be unimportant to leisure travelers while being unattractive to business travelers. This type of price discrimination has been extensively studied in the economics literature.

Beyond the different segment situation, there is still another more general situation when advance pricing is profitable. This situation occurs when buyers have a different willingness to pay in different consumption states and future consumption states are unknown. A consumption state is simply the circumstances that influence the utility that a consumer gets from a service. For example, a diner values a restaurant meal more when he or she is hungry. A student values an evening movie ticket more when a difficult course assignment is not due the next morning. A passenger values an ocean cruise more when he or she has available vacation time. Business travelers tend to value taxi cab rides more when they are rushed. Consumers value dry-cleaning services more when a garment is stained shortly before the garment is required. Consumers are willing to pay more for bottled soft drinks when they are thirsty.

The bottled soft drink example differs from all the other examples. Consumers have control over the consumption of the bottled soft drink because consumers can inventory the soft drink until the preferred time of consumption. In the other examples, the service provider has some or complete control over the time of consumption. For example, consider a soft drink sold at a motion-picture theater rather than a supermarket. In the theater, consumers are in either a thirsty state or not. Theater owners expect that only consumers in a thirsty state will buy and, consequently, adopt a higher price, in part, because consumers in a thirsty state are willing to pay more. The supermarket, in contrast, expects that nearly all of the consumers who are buying soft drinks are not in a thirsty state and are buying soft drinks with an expectation of inventorying the soft drink for later consumption. Consequently, the supermarket must adopt a lower price than the motion-picture theater, in part, because consumers in the supermarket can postpone their purchase and buy elsewhere, given that consumption will occur at a later time regardless of where the soft drink is purchased. Perhaps, consumers who buy refrigerated soft drinks at the supermarket reveal that they are in a thirsty state and, consequently, are willing to pay more than consumers buying unrefrigerated soft drinks. Hence, the supermarket knows that it can cover the cost of refrigeration because consumers in a thirsty state will pay for the benefit of refrigeration. Of course, few consumers in the supermarket are in a thirsty state and so the supermarket sells few refrigerated soft drinks compared to the unrefrigerated soft drinks.

Note that consumers who make advance purchases of a soft drink at the supermarket expect only to drink the soft drink in a future thirsty state and, consequently, they know their current and future utility for the soft drink. However, suppose consumers made advance purchases of the soft drink at the motion-picture theater. For example, a theater offers consumers a voucher for a soft drink to be consumed at the theater the following weekend. Consumers who purchase this voucher do not know their future consumption state. They can only value the voucher based on its expected utility. Hence, in the supermarket example, the soft drink represents a manufactured product which is sold, inventoried and, at the consumer's discretion, consumed. In the movie-theater example, the soft drink represents a service and the service provider offers the service at a specified time interval and the utility of the service depends on the consumer's state during that time interval.

Conceptually, the expected value of the voucher is the weighted average of the utilities of the product or service in each possible consumption state. Although there are many states, the number of states does not have a material impact on the final conclusion, so for simplicity consider the soft drink example with only two states. The two states are "thirsty" and "not thirsty." When consumers are thirsty they will pay more for the soft drink service than when they are not thirsty. Hence, the value of the voucher is less than the value of the soft drink service in the "thirsty state" because it is possible the consumer will not be in the "thirsty state." However, the value of the voucher is more than the value of the soft drink service in the "not thirsty state" because it is possible the consumer will be in the "thirsty state."

To be precise, suppose consumers will pay \$5 for a soft drink in the "thirsty state" but only \$1 for a soft drink in a "not thirsty state." If there is a 10 percent chance of being in a thirsty state, conceptually, the consumer would be willing pay .1(\$5) +.9(\$1) or \$1.40 for the voucher. Of course, the consumer might consider the risk of not buying the voucher, being in a future "thirsty state" and paying \$5 for the soft drink. The consumer might also consider the risk of buying the voucher and not being in a future "thirsty state." However, assume the consumer will pay \$1.40 for the voucher and the movie theater charges \$1.40 for the voucher. To differentiate this example from the previous price discrimination example where the airline exploited the difference between business and leisure travelers, consider the case when all consumers are the same. Of course, if consumers are not the same, advance selling might exploit both consumer consumption state uncertainty as well as price discrimination.

If the motion picture theater charged $1.40 for the voucher, all consumers would advance purchase the voucher. The theater would enjoy revenue of $1.40N where N is the number of consumers who advance purchase at the advance price of $1.40. Now suppose the theater only spot sold the soft drink at the time of consumption (no vouchers). Then, the motion picture theater would charge $5 to exploit consumers in a "thirsty state." However, only 10 percent of the consumers would be in a "thirsty state." Consequently, theater revenue would be (.1)($5)N or $.5N. The revenue would be far less than the revenue from the voucher. In fact, for this example, advance selling revenues are 1.4/.5 or 280 percent of spot revenues. Other numbers yield different numerical results but, qualitatively, advance selling at an advance price nearly always yields revenues that are many times greater than the maximum possible spot revenues.

The preceding example does not consider the cost of the soft drink. The additional revenue in the advance period comes from additional demand rather than price discrimination. Additional demand implies supplying an additional quantity of the service and, consequently, additional cost. In this example, more soft drink is sold in the advance period. It is likely that the theater's increased soft drink costs are small compared to the increased revenue. However, it is possible that very costly services with slim profit margins will find it unprofitable to sell to consumers who are in consumption states corresponding to a low willingness to pay. In that case, advance selling is no more profitable than spot selling at a high price that covers the high cost. Moreover, price discrimination is also no more profitable than spot selling at a single high price for the same reason. As is usually the case for all marketing strategies, advance selling usually provides greater profits when service providers have sufficient profit margins to allow some flexibility in their pricing decisions.

Although mathematical proofs are beyond the scope of this chapter, it is possible to prove that advance selling is no less profitable than only spot selling. Also, advance selling is often many times more profitable than spot selling alone. The reason is that advance selling is an excellent way to profit from consumption uncertainty. In the advance period, neither the service provider nor the consumer knows the consumer's future consumption state. There is a type of symmetry in information (or lack of information) between the consumer and the service provider. In fact, the service provider might have more information about future consumption states because the service providers have had experience with many consumers over many past periods.

In contrast, the spot period brings an asymmetry which is disadvantageous to the service provider. Consumers know their own consumption state but the service provider does not. Moreover, unlike the case of price discrimination between business and leisure travelers, there is no easy way to identify which consumers are in favorable consumption states and charge those consumers more than consumers who are only willing to pay less. In fact, consumers could be identical in every other respect beyond the consumption state. Consequently, the service provider gains from negotiating with the consumer in the advance period and those gains become the advantage of advance selling.

In the previous example, advance selling at the optimal price causes all consumers to advance buy because consumers are homogenous with respect to their willingness to pay. However, if consumers do differ on their willingness to pay or responsiveness to different levels of service, and those differences are likely, then exercising price discrimination can be profitable. Price discrimination policies could include spot selling at a high spot price, advance selling at different prices in different periods and offering different prices to different market segments. Hence, advance selling is not necessarily an exclusive strategy but can be combined with other pricing strategies and often is part of a more comprehensive pricing strategy.

However, there is one issue that arises when incorporating an advance selling strategy within a more comprehensive pricing strategy. It is necessary for the consumer to believe that the advance price is discounted. The consumer must believe that the future spot price will be higher than the current advance price. The best way to create that belief is to ensure that spot prices are always higher than all preceding advance prices. Prices for service delivery at any specified time should always be increasing as that time approaches. Otherwise, consumers will wait and advance selling becomes less effective.

There are several ways to ensure that the spot price is higher than the advance price. One method is to increase the quality of the service until the cost is sufficiently high so that the best spot price is a high spot price. For example, suppose that consumers in a favorable (high willingness-to-pay) state will pay a \$5 spot price and other consumers are only willing to pay \$3. If half the consumers are in each state and the marginal cost of service delivery is zero, then the profit from spot selling at \$5 is (1/2)(\$5) N = \$2.50N and the profit from spot selling at \$3 is (\$3)N. Hence, it is more profitable to spot sell to everyone at \$3 rather than to only half the consumers at \$5. Advance selling will not work because advance pricing at (1/2)(\$3) + (1/2)(\$5) = \$4 causes consumers to not advance buy but wait for the \$3 spot price.

However, suppose the service provider increases the quality of the service so that there is a marginal cost of \$1.2 for delivering the service. In that case, the profit from spot selling at \$5 is (1/2)(\$5 – \$1.2)N = \$1.9N and the profit from spot selling at \$3 is (\$3 – \$1.2)N = \$1.8N, where the number of consumers N is probably larger given the increased quality. Hence, it is now more profitable to spot sell at $5 rather than $3. Advance selling is now both feasible and more profitable than only spot selling. Hence, one method for making advance selling profitable is to increase the quality of the service to create a credible and optimal high spot price.

Other methods for convincing the consumer that the spot price will be higher than the advance price include selling sufficient capacity so that very little capacity remains for spot-period sales. Another method is to establish a reputation of never lowering the spot price even when it appears that doing so would increase spot profits. Another method to ensure a high spot price would be to offer a price guarantee to the consumer. The guarantee would allow the consumer to get a refund of any overpayment caused by the advance price being higher than the spot price. A guarantee of that type would convince consumers that buying in the advance period would be no more costly than buying in the spot period.

In sum, advance selling can either be an implementation of price discrimination where consumers with different responsiveness to price pay different prices. Advance selling can also be a method for exploiting consumer uncertainty about future consumption states and selling to the consumer when there is symmetry in information between the consumer and the service provider. In either case, advance selling can be very profitable compared to spot selling alone.

CAPACITY-CONSTRAINED PRICING

This section considers ways that capacity constraints impact the pricing strategies of service providers. This section differs from seasonal pricing in, at least, one important respect. Seasons are, to a large extent, predictable. In fact, seasonality could be defined as predictable variation in demand that tends to be periodic. In contrast, capacity-constrained pricing involves demand peaks which are unpredictable. Moreover, even though prices are usually easier to quickly change than other strategic variables, it is often difficult to adjust prices for unpredictable demand peaks. For example, a restaurant is unable to raise prices when several large parties of diners unexpectedly and simultaneously arrive. A copying service is unable to raise prices when several customers unexpectedly and simultaneously place large orders.

Before considering the pricing strategy for capacity-constrained services, remember that there is also a capacity strategy. Capacity could be increased until the capacity is sufficiently large so that there is seldom a need to deny service or delay service delivery. However, it is rarely (if ever) optimal to increase capacity to that extent or even nearly to that extent. The reason is that maintaining capacity incurs a cost. There are the costs of keeping employees who may be unwilling to only work sporadically. There are costs associated with maintaining facilities. There are costs associated with lease payments on equipment and the opportunity costs associated with maintaining investments in higher levels of capacity compared to lower levels of capacity. Consequently, it is usually unprofitable to maintain capacity levels that completely avoid denial of service or service delays.

Remember also that the objective of optimizing capacity utilization is usually not consistent with the objective of profit maximization. Although it is certainly valuable to monitor capacity utilization to determine how much surplus capacity exists during different periods, that information is often more valuable for capacity decisions than pricing decisions. Prices should be set to maximize profits. If the optimal price generates demand that is insufficient to employ all or even most of available capacity, that is not a reason to decrease the price to fill additional capacity. No factory, for example, sets prices to sell the maximum number of manufactured products that the factory can produce. Similarly, no service provider should attempt to sell all available capacity. Of course, when capacity is strictly binding and the service provider can sell no additional units, then a price increase should be considered. This section explores optimal pricing strategy when demand is unpredictable, capacity is limited, and the objective is profit maximization (not capacity utilization).

The most frequently used remedy for unpredictable demand peaks that exceed available capacity is to inventory customers until sufficient capacity becomes available. For example, there are frequently queues of customers at amusement parks, banks, restaurants, and so on. The queues occur with sufficient frequency that customers often come to expect them. Beyond literal queues, demand peaks also create congestion that diminishes the consumer's utility for the service. For example, a boat ride or tour might be less enjoyable when operating at capacity and the maximum number of customers is trying to simultaneously receive the service. Airports and many other service facilities become unpleasant and sometimes dysfunctional as they reach capacity. Although the service provider is usually unable to adjust the nominal rate or nominal price during times of peak demand, the service provider can effectively change the price by either compensating customers during times of peak demand or charging consumers for decreasing their wait time. Although these strategies can sometimes work in very opposite directions, both strategies can increase profits under different situations.

When deciding how to compensate or charge consumers for waits, it is important to consider the immediate profit implications, the long-term profit implications and the incentives created by the compensation strategy. Researchers, for example, have argued that compensating consumers during times of peak demand only exacerbates the problem because compensation both decreases the effective price of the service and decreases the incentive to avoid congestion. Consequently, compensation causes more consumers to arrive at the service and the service becomes still more congested. Compensation must increase again to deter congestion and further increases in compensation continue to further increase congestion.

The outcome for the service provider is often unclear. There are negative factors for the service provider. First, there is the cost of the compensation. Second, the increased congestion often decreases the customer's willingness-to-pay for the service. Third, the increased congestion could deter some customers from arriving and those deterred customers might have a higher willingness-to-pay than the less congestion-sensitive customers who do arrive.

In contrast, there are also positive benefits for the service provider that offers compensation during times of congestion. First, compensation can cause more customers to wait for available capacity and a persistent customer inventory can allow better capacity utilization (that is, more customers are served). Second, compensation can cause some customers to arrive at the service who might not otherwise arrive because they had expected congestion even though there is no congestion. Third, compensation (particularly non-monetary compensation) can increase the utility of the entire service delivery system and increase the willingness-to-pay, at least for some consumers. Finally, non-monetary compensation can achieve other marketing objectives such as the promotion of ancillary goods and services (for example, free samples at restaurant queues).

Monetary compensation for congestion, long waits or simply denial of service can include vouchers, discounts off the purchase price and coupons for future purchases. Nonmonetary compensation can include alternative services at another facility, coupons for future purchases, higher priority on future service delivery, complementary ancillary services, upgraded future services, and various gifts. For example, hotels can offer alternative accommodations at alternative but superior facilities. Airlines can offer upgrades on alternative future flights. Restaurants can offer complementary drinks, appetizers and desserts. Amusement parks can offer additional free attractions such as parades and fireworks. The basic strategy should be to devise non-monetary compensation that costs the service provider very little (for example, priority in a queue, an upgrade to an otherwise empty premium seat) but has great value to the consumer (precisely, the marginal customer). Of course, there is often still an opportunity cost associated with non-monetary compensation.

Beyond compensation during the peak, potential capacity constraints also influence the off-peak price. Remember that, unlike predictable seasonal peaks where the regular price varies across seasons and reflects expected demand during each season, it is difficult to temporarily raise the price during an unexpected peak. A restaurant, for example, cannot suddenly decide that demand is unusually high and issue new menus with higher prices. Consequently, menu prices and the prices of any service must reflect the service provider's expectations regarding the probability of both high and low demand periods. Prices that are too low might miss the opportunity for higher profit margins during times of unexpectedly high demand. Prices that are too high might further depress demand during periods of already low demand.

In the past, there has been no easy solution to this problem. It does little good to lower prices after consumers have already arrived at the service facility because those lower prices will be unable to attract a sufficient number of new consumers in time to remedy the temporary lull in demand. It also does little good to advertise lower prices during lulls in demand because it is unclear how long the lull in demand will last. By the time that new potential consumers become aware of a temporary price reduction during an unexpected off-peak period, the demand situation at the service provider's location might change.

However, emerging technology can change this situation. Global positioning systems can locate consumers by their current location. During periods of slack demand, service providers can send offers or mobile coupons to consumers in the immediate vicinity. Third party facilitators can provide this capability (for example, MobSav.com), navigational devices can provide this capability (for example, Garmin), and cellular phones can provide this capability (for example, Yowza, MobiQpons, and Cellfire). In fact, it is unnecessary to send a physical or electronic coupon. The service provider can simply temporarily lower the price during the off-peak period, and use all of the new emerging technologies to announce that temporary low price and the time when that low price expires.

Still another strategy for coping with temporary lulls in demand is to encourage customers who are currently at the service provider's facility to consume more. For example, ancillary services might be temporarily discounted. Restaurants with a surplus of seating might temporarily offer discounted desserts or discounted after-dinner drinks because lingering patrons are no longer occupying valuable table space (that is, constrained capacity). Airlines with surplus seating might temporarily allow passengers to relocate on the plane to more spacious or better seats. At minimum, the service provider should use temporary lulls in demand to increase service quality. With a surplus of personnel and a surplus of physical capacity, the service provider can easily provide the existing customers with a better service experience at very little additional cost.

Finally, it is important to note that the capacity-constrained pricing strategy is part of a more general service strategy that includes setting the optimal level of service quality. Too often, marketing theory treats pricing as if it were an independent decision unrelated to millions of other marketing decisions. One rationale for this independence is that service providers can easily and quickly change price compared with other decisions (for example, capacity, quality, advertising, promotions, bundling, and so on) that take more time to design and implement. However, that rationale neglects the fact that marketing strategy should simultaneously consider all decision variables regardless of whether future changes in those variables are difficult or not. Moreover, even when it is difficult to change some non-pricing decision, most non-pricing decisions still interact with the pricing decision. For example, a service provider can decide to avoid congestion and minimize any deterioration in service quality during times of unexpected peak demand by maintaining a higher capacity level (for example, more personnel, larger facilities, more equipment). The resulting higher level of capacity justifies charging a higher price. Some segment of consumers is often willing to pay that higher price, even during periods of slack demand, because the higher level of capacity provides insurance against the risk of arriving during an unexpected period of excessive demand. The marketing decision is whether to target that segment of consumers or target a different segment that is not averse to waiting.

Moreover, advertising and positioning strategies will also interact with the pricing decision in the same way. Advertising and positioning strategies will either tend to emphasize higher capacity (for example, delivery services with next day delivery, retailers with guaranteed maximum checkout times and a pleasant environment during required waits) at a higher regular price, or alternatively, a very low regular price with minimum capacity and no guarantees.

SEASONAL PRICING

The Prevalence of Seasonality

Seasonality in the service sector is ubiquitous. Seasonality implies predictable demand peaks during specific time intervals which might be defined in terms of hours, days, weeks or years. There are strong seasonal patterns in almost every aspect of service delivery including the demand for the service, the availability of seasonal component products, the ability to launch new products, the availability of labor, advertising costs, and, often, which consumer segment is currently buying the service. Virtually every service industry in every country is seasonal. Seasonality transcends services such as snow removal, landscaping and transportation services. Seasonality dictates business strategy in highly seasonal services such as accounting, advertising, construction, amusement parks, beauty salons, restaurants, car rentals, tourism, cinemas, communications, construction materials, education, public utilities, employment agencies, financial services, and lodging. Moreover, seasonality in one industry (for example, retailing) can create seasonality in other industries (for example, trucking) when one industry supplies the other. Many service providers experience regular seasonal patterns related to other periodic exogenous factors that are usually beyond the control of a single firm's control including holidays (for example, Martin Luther King day), government actions (for example, tax deadlines), the school year, industry traditions (for example, sports seasons, trade shows, new auto releases), the weather (for example, summer, winter), social traditions (for example, mealtime hours, business hours) and historic events cause seasonal demand peak. Seasonality also impacts customization strategies and word-of-mouth diffusion. Even political terms of office can inspire a type of seasonality.

Types of Seasonality

Although seasonality is often considered as a generic peak in demand, close examination reveals that there are different types of seasonality. These types are not mutually exclusive and a service provider can experience one or more types of seasonality. However, it is important to distinguish between the different types of seasonality because these different types of seasonality imply different pricing strategies.

For example, airlines, coffee shops and movie exhibitors often have more customers during seasonal peaks. However, these additional customers usually consume the same quantity of the service. For example, movie goers still see only one movie on Friday night and consumers of coffee still buy a single cup. In contrast, electrical utilities, snow-removal services and landscaping services often face increased consumption by current customers during seasonal peaks. Each user of electricity consumes more electricity and each user of a landscaping service requires more effort during the peak growing season. Some services face both types of peaks. For example, restaurants might have more customers during lunch and dinner hours, but have greater consumption per diner during dinner hours. This section considers several types of seasonal peaks.

The Consumption Peak

Consumption peaks occur when each consumer consumes more of the service during the peak and those peaks are, in some part, predictable. There may be more consumers that demand service during the peak but the main feature of the consumption peak is the increased consumption (higher volume) by existing customers. For example, grocery stores may experience increased purchases on weekends by consumers doing weekly purchases in contrast to small replenishment purchases during weekdays. Hotels might observe longer stays during summer months (vacation months) than during winter months. In addition, hotels might observe longer stays during weekends than weekdays even though, in this case, total demand for hotel rooms might actually decrease during these periods of increased consumption (for example, on weekends).

The optimal pricing strategy for a pure consumption peak, given no increase in the number of customers, is often a price decrease (that is, compared with off-peak prices). The primary reason for a price decrease is that high-volume customers are more valuable than low-volume customers. It is therefore optimal to offer high-volume customers a lower price than low-volume customers to attract more of those customers. High-volume customers, who consume more of the service, are more valuable to the service provider because those customers usually represent a larger profit margin than customers who purchase smaller quantities of the service. For example, a gambler who stays at a casino for several days is likely to generate more revenue for the casino than a gambler who stays for only the afternoon. Another reason is that high-volume customers usually create less congestion and consume fewer resources than low-volume customers who consume smaller quantities of the service. For example, a diner who orders only pie and coffee consumes nearly as much table space and restaurant resources as a diner who orders an expensive dinner with expensive wine. High-volume consumers who create less congestion are more valuable because they do not deter additional customers. A third reason why price decreases are usually optimal is that the per-unit marginal cost of serving a high-volume customer is usually lower than the per-unit marginal cost of serving a low-volume customer. A pizza delivery service might incur very little addition cost for delivery of ten pizzas compared to delivery of one pizza. A university might incur roughly the same administrative costs for a part-time student who takes one course per semester as a full-time student who takes four courses per semester.

Although it is beyond the scope of this chapter, it is also usually optimal to offer a higher quality service during consumption peaks than during the off-peak period. The reason is that, like lower prices, higher quality also attracts more high volume customers and, given that high-volume customers often provide higher margins (given that they purchase more units), it is worthwhile trying to attract more of these high-volume customers by offering higher quality.

The Cost Peak

A cost peak occurs during periods when the service provider incurs greater costs during particular periods. For example, service providers using part time labor and shipping incur higher costs during holidays. For example, service providers with energy intensive services observe seasonal increases in the cost of energy and gasoline. Service providers using seasonal fruits and vegetables incur higher costs during off-seasons (often winter months). In most cases, unlike unpredictable fluctuations in demand, seasonality is often sufficiently predictable to allow the development of seasonal strategies involving planned changes in prices and service quality.

The optimal seasonal pricing strategy for a cost season depends on whether service providers in a particular industry have the ability to temporarily change their cost structure (that is, lower costs) during the cost peak by lowering quality. For example, when a service provider requires particular foods or components that are out of season and costly to obtain, these service providers can offer lower-quality frozen versions of those foods or components. When natural snow is in short supply, ski resorts might employ artificial snowmaking but stop short of producing the same snow depths.

Before considering the simultaneous pricing and quality strategy, consider the situation when it is costly or otherwise difficult to change the service delivery quality during cost peaks. In that case, the optimal strategy is usually to pass some of the increased cost on to consumers in the form of a higher service price. Although the service price increases, the extent to which the service price can be increased depends on several factors. One of those factors is obviously the consumer's sensitivity to price. When the consumer (precisely, the marginal customer) is more price-sensitive, larger price increases become less profitable. Consequently, less of the cost increase is passed on to consumers or end-users.

Another often misunderstood factor is the nature of competition. When competition is more severe, price increases are usually larger and a greater proportion of the costs are passed on to customers. When competition is weak and the service provider is a monopolist, the price increases tend to be much smaller. Despite some popular wisdom or myth in the popular press, it not in the monopolist's best interest to pass on large increases in costs because the monopolist bears the entire brunt of the decrease in demand caused by the higher price. In contrast, the service provider in a highly competitive market has a very slim profit margin. In fact, in perfect competition, the service provider's profit margin is so small that the profit margin only allows the service provider to earn a minimal return on investment to remain an ongoing business. Consequently, all service providers in highly competitive industries have no choice but to pass on cost increases to their customers or go out of business. When some service provider does go out of business, the remaining service provider must still pass on nearly all of their increased costs.

The situation changes when the service provider can lower service quality to decrease costs. In fact, the situation dramatically changes. It is generally much more profitable to reduce quality when costs increase rather than to pass on all of the additional cost. The reason is that at the previous optimum (before the cost increase), the optimal quality was set at the point when the consumer (precisely, the marginal consumer) was unwilling to pay more (at least, more than the cost) for additional quality. Now that the cost has increased, consumers are willing to forgo some quality for lower prices. After the service quality is decreased, the situation changes and it can be optimal to lower the service price. Remember that the same price now represents an effective price increase because the consumer receives less service or a lower quality service for that same price. Moreover, a slight decrease in price can justify the decrease in quality. Whether a price decrease is optimal depends on the precise shape of the demand function and the market's willingness to pay for quality but most common demand functions suggest it is optimal to lower price while decreasing the service quality.

The Arrival Peak

Arrival peaks occur when more consumers arrive during the seasonal peak and those arrival peaks are, in some part, predictable. Price increases are always optimal when more buyers arrive during the peak. Moreover, quality increases are also often optimal.

There are four reasons why price increases are optimal for arrival peaks. First, the arrival of more consumers during the arrival peak increases congestion and congestion decreases consumer willingness to pay for the service. Raising the price helps alleviate congestion by discouraging less price-sensitive buyers. Second, raising the service price increases the profit margin and, given that more consumers are arriving, raising the profit margin does not significantly decrease total demand. Third, raising the price retains less price-sensitive customers who may be more averse to congestion than more price-sensitive customers. Finally, raising the price allows increases in quality. Increases in quality can slightly increase congestion but those increases help attract additional customers with a higher willingness to pay. Consequently, although the service-pricing decision and service-quality decision during an arrival peak must be coordinated, it is optimal to increase both the service price and service quality.

The Cross-selling Peak

A cross-selling peak occurs when consumers during the season often simultaneously purchase more than one service. For example, before the summer vacation season, consumers may simultaneously purchase a variety of automotive services including oil changes, new tires, tune-ups and other maintenance services. During morning breakfast hours, consumers who purchase coffee from a coffee vendor are more likely to purchase muffins, bagels and other bakery goods. Cross-selling peaks cause lower optimal prices. That fact has been known for some time. However, cross-selling peaks also encourage higher service quality during the peak. The reason is that when arriving consumers buy more than one service at a time, they provide a greater per customer profit margin which makes those customers more valuable. Hence, the service provider should expend a greater effort to attract consumers who buy ancillary services. A lower price and a higher service quality provide a coordinated strategy for attracting those buyers.

Framing Peak Seasonal Prices

Psychological theory tells us that presentation or framing is important. Customers may like a concept when presented in one way but not another. Considerable research suggests that price is no exception.

It is often useful to present peak seasonal prices as regular prices rather than premium prices. In that way, off-peak prices become prices discounted from the regular price. For example, the matinee price for a movie is considered to be a discount off the regular price. Weekend and night telephone rates are discounts from the daytime rate. In each case, the consumer who uses the service during the peak pays a regular price, but the regular price is higher than the off-peak price. Other examples include family nights at sporting events, two-for-one drink specials, free off-peak upgrades on car rentals or hotel rooms, coupons good only during off-peak hours, early-bird dinner specials, special off-peak admission to amusement parks, and so on.

Whether to Announce Seasonal Peak Prices

In most cases, the service provider announces both the off-peak and peak seasonal prices. Telephone companies, amusement parks, landscaping services, and accounting services, for example, announce higher rates during their peak seasons. Here, the user knows, in advance, the price during the peak season. Announcing a high peak price signals consumers that, despite increased peak congestion, raising the price will help mitigate that increased congestion and mitigate longer waiting times. The high peak price suggests that price rationing will minimize the probability that demand will exceed available capacity.

Although announcing peak-prices has advantages, there are also disadvantages. Rather than announcing peak prices, the service provider can vary the peak price as additional information about peak demand becomes available. Rates can begin to change as capacity fills. In this situation, neither the service provider nor the consumer knows tomorrow's rate. Consider, for example, a hotel booking space for a date in the future. On that date, the hotel plans to offer the first 20 percent of its rooms at a discount rate, the next 50 percent of its rooms at a regular rate, the next 20 percent at a high rate and the last 10 percent at a very high premium rate. As the date approaches, the hotel implements the plan and the rate rises as the hotel fills. At some point, the hotel may no longer have a binding capacity constraint. However, as noted earlier, decreasing spot price inhibits advance selling at an advance price.

Still another reason for not announcing peak prices is the opportunity to auction limited remaining capacity. Demand that exceeds capacity generates no revenue. Auctioning the last available capacity does extract the maximum revenue. Despite the theoretical attractiveness of auctions, they are rare. Airlines do auction overbooked seats by offering greater and greater payments to flyers willing to surrender their current seats for seats on the next flight. Ushers may extract higher and higher tips for the best of the remaining seats. Tickets for sporting events may increase as the stadium fills. However, social pressures and transaction costs sometimes make auctions infeasible.

Different Objectives for Private and Public Sectors

When managing public services, the objective may not be optimal seasonal pricing to maximize profits. The objective may only be to reduce peak season demand. Within a larger context, it may be socially desirable to encourage citizens to consume less during times of peak seasonal demand. The benefits may be associated with the conservation of scare resources, the general public welfare, or political objectives. For example, it might be desirable to avoid high prices that would preclude service to all but high income individuals. This situation can occur for many public services including the national parks, electrical utilities, the public highway system and public transportation systems.

When seasons are predictable (for example, rush hour), public services might want to shift demand to off-peak periods. This type of demand shifting is usually unprofitable for private sector services because price rationing is usually more profitable. It can only be profitable when the demand peak is unpredictable, so that a price increase is not possible. For example, although a restaurant may use a reservation system to shift patrons to another time slot when there is an unexpected peak in demand, when the peak is predictable, the restaurant would usually choose to charge higher prices during the peak and offer patrons lower prices off-peak (for example, offer early dinner specials). Public services, in contrast, may be unwilling to raise prices during periods of peak demand for social welfare reasons. Of course, the same laws of supply and demand apply to public services as private services. The consequence is a shortage of the service, rationing, congestion, undue burden on scarce public resources, and long queues. Although these consequences might be sufficiently negative to shift some demand to the off-peak, raising the peak price would increase revenues which could be used to increase peak capacity.

SUMMARY

This chapter considered advance pricing, capacity-constrained pricing and seasonal pricing. Advance pricing gives the consumer a discount for purchasing in an advance period before the consumption or spot period. It can be profitable for three reasons. First, it exploits consumers who are willing to pay more by charging them more than other consumers (that is, price discrimination). Second, it exploits consumer uncertainty about future consumption states. Third, it exploits uncertainty about future consumption states. Capacity constrained pricing occurs when (1) there are unpredictable peaks in demand, (2) capacity constraints prevent serving all customers, and (3) there is an inability to temporarily increase the service price during the peak period, in part, because the peak is unpredictable. The optimal strategy is to encourage additional consumption off-peak and provide non-monetary compensation during the peak. Finally, seasonal pricing occurs when there are predictable demand peak. The optimal strategy depends on the type of peak. Consumption peaks (where consumers consume more) yield lower optimal prices. Cost peaks (where costs increase) yield higher optimal prices when quality changes do not occur. Arrival peaks (where more consumers arrive) yield higher optimal prices. Finally, cross-selling peaks (where consumers buy more ancillary services) yield lower optimal prices.

BIBLIOGRAPHY

Avlonitis, George J. and Kostis A. Indounas (2007), "Service pricing: an empirical investigation," *Journal of Retailing and Consumer Services*, **14** (1), 83–94.

Chao, Hung-Po and Robert Wilson (1987), "Priority service: pricing, investment, and market organization," *The American Economic Review*, **77** (5), 899–916.

Chen, Rachel R., Eitan Gerstner and Yinghui (Catherine) Yang (2009), "Research note—should captive sardines be compensated? Serving customers in a confined zone," *Marketing Science*, **28** (3), 599–608.

Desiraju, Ramarao and Steven M. Shugan (1999), "Strategic service pricing and yield management," *Journal of Marketing*, **63** (1), 44–56.

Rabinovich, Elliot and Joseph P Bailey (2004), "Physical distribution service quality in internet retailing: service pricing, transaction attributes, and firm attributes," *Journal of Operations Management*, **21** (6), 651–72.

Radas, Sonja and Steven M. Shugan (1998), "Seasonal marketing and timing new product introductions," *Journal of Marketing Research*, **35** (3), 296–315.

Rust, Roland T. and Tuck Siong Chung (2006), "Marketing models of service and relationships," *Marketing Science*, **25** (6), 560–80.

Shugan, Steven M. (2000), "Services and seasonal demand in handbook of services marketing and management," in Teresa A. Swartz and Dawn Iacobucci (eds), *Handbook of Services Marketing and Management*, Thousand Oaks, CA: Sage Publications, pp. 147–70.

Shugan, Steven M. (2002), "Service marketing and management: capacity as a strategic marketing variable," in Barton A. Weitz and Robin Wensley (eds), *The Handbook of Marketing*, Thousand Oaks, CA: Sage Publications, pp. 484–512.

Shugan, Steven M. and Aydın Alptekinoğlu (2011), "Seasonal prices, capacity and congestion," working paper, University of Florida.

Shugan, Steven M. and Jinhong Xie (2000), "Advance pricing of services and other implications of separating purchase and consumption," *Journal of Service Research*, **2** (3), 227–39.

Shugan, Steven M. and Jinhong Xie (2004), "Advance selling for services," *California Management Review*, **46** (3), 37–54.

Shugan, Steven M. and Jinhong Xie (2005), "Advance selling as a competitive marketing tool," *International Journal of Research in Marketing*, **22** (3), 351–73.

Tung, Wei, Louis M. Capella and Peter K. Tat, (1997), "Service pricing: a multi-step synthetic approach," *Journal of Services Marketing*, **11** (1), 53–65.

Xie, Jinhong and Steven M. Shugan (2001), "Electronic tickets, smart cards, and online prepayments: when and how to advance sell," *Marketing Science*, **20** (3), 219–43.

15 Marketing innovation: probabilistic goods and probabilistic selling

Jinhong Xie and Scott Fay

OVERVIEW

"Probabilistic goods" and "probabilistic selling" are two terms defined recently in the marketing literature (Fay and Xie 2008) to refer to a newly observed marketing innovation. The term "probabilistic goods" (also called opaque products) represents a new product concept that is not a concrete product, but rather an offer involving the probability of obtaining any one of a set of multiple distinct products/services. "Probabilistic selling" is an emerging marketing strategy whereby a seller creates probabilistic goods using existing (component) products/services and adds probabilistic goods to its product line.

Priceline.com is an early example of a seller offering probabilistic goods in the travel industry (for example, airlines, hotels, car rentals). Using this website, consumers can purchase travel services for which some specific attributes of the service (for example, the itinerary of the flight, the location of the hotel, or the identity of the car rental company) are not revealed until after payment. However, Priceline offers probabilistic goods via a unique pricing model: Rather than facing posted prices, buyers bid for prices (known as "Name Your Own Price" or NYOP). If the bid is accepted, the buyer's credit card is charged. Early research on opaque products was stimulated by Priceline's specific business model, but most studies focused on the NYOP pricing policy (for example, Fay 2004; Hann and Terwiesch 2003; Spann et al. 2004).

Fay and Xie (2008) explore whether or not probabilistic selling can potentially benefit many firms in a wide range of industries. They demonstrate that the profit advantage of probabilistic selling is far more general than previously realized, and is neither dependent upon the special characteristics of the travel industry nor limited to Priceline's specific NYOP model. The concepts of probabilistic goods and probabilistic selling can be applied to any market setting with multiple products/services. For instance, a retailer can offer a consumer the choice of paying full price to obtain her preferred color of sweater (for example, red or blue), or paying a lower price to take a 50-50 chance of receiving either a red or a blue sweater. A cruise line can provide a vacationer with two options: Book the cruise trip of her choice (for example, a Western Caribbean cruise) or save money by taking a trip chosen by the cruise line from among several alternatives, including that particular cruise. A health club offering three group fitness classes a day can charge higher prices to those who want to select their own class time but give discounts to those who are willing to attend a class assigned by the club.

Fay and Xie (2008) develop a general theory of probabilistic selling, which reveals that the essence of the profit advantage of probabilistic selling comes from consumer heterogeneity in their product preference strength, which is an underexplored buyer characteristic in marketing theory and practice. Probabilistic selling introduces uncertainty as a new product attribute. On the supply side, it creates a new mechanism for market segmentation based on the strength of buyers' product preferences. On the demand side, it implies a new choice for consumers, one that is not possible under traditional selling: choosing between information and price. Taken together, this new segmentation tool available to the seller and the new tradeoffs available to the buyer create a profit advantage of probabilistic selling in several important dimensions, among which are market expansion, price discrimination, demand uncertainty management, capacity utilization, and flexible and efficient product line extension.

Recent market observations also provide growing evidence to support the general applicability of probabilistic selling. Until recently, it was difficult to find firms that offered probabilistic goods to consumers, with the exception of the two online travel intermediaries, priceline.com and hotwire.com. In today's online markets, however, one can easily find various probabilistic goods offered by service providers, manufacturers, and retailers. Yet, probabilistic goods and probabilistic selling are still new concepts unfamiliar to many marketers. Even among those that do offer probabilistic goods, some only use the strategy to dispose of overstocks and thus may not benefit fully from this innovative strategy.

In this chapter, we present a theory of probabilistic goods and probabilistic selling based on recent research (Fay 2008; Fay and Xie 2008, 2010). Specifically, we will illustrate how probabilistic goods fundamentally differ from traditional goods, why and when a firm can benefit from introducing them, how to design probabilistic goods and set prices, and how to use probabilistic selling to address the challenge of demand uncertainty and enhance capacity utilization. We will also discuss technology and market factors that facilitate and hinder the implementation of probabilistic selling. We hope this discussion will enhance understanding of the probabilistic selling strategy and stimulate more interest in this emerging marketing innovation from academics, marketing managers, business educators, and consultants. To make the chapter readable to a more general audience, we demonstrate the theory of probabilistic selling via some illustrative examples.[1]

1 PROBABILISTIC SELLING IN THE MARKETPLACE

Although probabilistic goods and probabilistic selling are still relatively new concepts to many marketers and consumers, in the past several years there have been an increasing number of market applications, especially in two major industries: travel and retailing.

1.1 Applications in the Travel Industry

Many online travel service providers are offering discounted probabilistic services to travelers (see Table 15.1 for some examples). As shown in Table 15.1, these probabilistic travel services are offered under some unusual names that convey the uncertainty and opaqueness involved, such as "Hidden Hotels," "Secret Sale," "Secret Carrier," "Blind Booking," "Mystery Hotel," and "Undercover Hotels."

The specific formulation of a probabilistic service can differ across providers. Using the category of probabilistic airline tickets, Table 15.2 offers some examples as to how opacity varies across different travel websites, that is, which specific variables are unknown to buyers until after the completion of the transaction. As shown in Table 15.2, in most cases, travelers buying probabilistic tickets cannot specify the name of the airline or the travel itinerary. Interestingly, in some cases, travelers may not even select when to travel (Freedom Air) or where to go (Germanwings).[2] Recently, a new variable, Airline Alliance, has been used in the design of probabilistic tickets at fly.com, where those interested in opaque tickets can select a specific airline partnership (for example, SkyTeam, Oneworld and Star Alliance) even though they cannot specify the name of the airline. According to fly.com, they use this arrangement "so those who have a preference can easily choose flights available on their alliance of choice."[3]

1.2 Applications in the Retailing Industry

Initially, probabilistic goods were only observed in the travel industry. However, recent research suggested that they could be advantageous to firms in many other market settings (Fay 2008; Fay and Xie 2008, 2010).

Table 15.1 Examples of probabilistic travel services

Website offering probabilistic travel services	The name of the probabilistic travel services offer
Priceline.com	"Name your own price" (http://www.priceline.com/)
Hotwire	"Hidden Hotels" (http://www.hotwire.com/)
Travelocity.com	"Top Secret Hotels" (http://leisure.travelocity.com/Promo. . .s_main,00.html)
Expedia.com	"Unpublished Rate hotels" (http://www.expedia.com/daily/hotels/. . .es/default.asp)
Wotif.com	"Wot Hotel" (http://www.wotif.com/search/TextSearch?searchTerms=%22Wot+Hotel?%22)
Germanwings.com	"Blind Booking" (https://www.germanwings.com/skysales/BlindBooking.aspx?culture=en-GB)
HotelDirect.co.uk	"Hidden Gem' Hotels" (http://www.hoteldirect.co.uk/webapp/. . .ms&city=London)
Kayak.com	"Secret Carrier" (http://www.kayak.com/)
Quickbook.com	"Secret Sale" (http://www.quikbook.com/secret-sale)
Booklt.com	"Mystery Hotel" (http://bookit.com/us/louisiana/new-orleans/hotels/4-star-french-quarter-mystery-hotel/)
LastMinuteTravel.com	"Top Secret ® Hotels" (http://www.lastminute.com/site/trave. . .op-secret.html)
Superbreak.com	"Mystery Hotels" (http://www.superbreak.com/marketing/mystery-hotels)
DHR.com	"Undercover Hotels" (http://www.dhr.com/deals/hotels/undercover-hotels/)
Asiawebdirect.com	"Mystery Hotels" (Asia) (http://www.asiawebdirect.com/mysteryhotels/)
Easytobook.com	"NH Mystery 4 star Hotel Amsterdam" (Netherland) (http://www.easytobook.com/en/netherlands/north-holland/amsterdam/nh-mystery-hotel/)
Otel.com	"Mystery Hotels" (http://www.otel.com/mystery-hotels.php)

Indeed, various probabilistic goods are offered by online retailers today. For example, swimoutlet.com, lane4swim.com, 1worldsarongs.com, tmall.com, bustedtees.com, agonswim.com, store.americanapparel.net, noisebot.com, buloso.com, and many other online retailers offer discounted probabilistic apparel and shoes (framed as "grab bag," "mystery bag," "random color," "surprise print," "random t-shirt," or "let us choose the style"), where color, patterns, and styles are not known to the consumer prior to purchase.

Table 15.2 Attributes known to buyers at the time of booking

Website	Departure city	Departure (return) date	Destination	Airline	Itinerary	Airline alliance
PriceLine	Yes	Yes	Yes	No	No	No
Hotwire	Yes	Yes	Yes	No	No	No
Kayak	Yes	Yes	Yes	No	No*	No
Germanwings	Yes	Yes	No	No	No	No
Freedom Air	Yes	No	Yes	No	No	No
Fly.com	Yes	Yes	Yes	No	No	Yes
Vayama.com	Yes	Yes	Yes	No	No*	No

Note: * While the specific itinerary is not revealed, the website shows the approximate departure and arrival time (for example, depart from MCO between 8 and 9a.m. and arrive Beijing between 4 and 5 p.m.).

Retailers offer probabilistic goods via a variety of formats. For example, swimoutlet.com offers 63 percent savings for a Nike women's swimsuit if consumers are willing to give up their demand for a specific print. As stated in the website,[4] "The Nike® Swim Cut-Out Tank Grab Bag is an affordable and fun way to get a high-quality suit at a very affordable price. You pick the suit, and we pick the print." Bustedtees.com, an Internet t-shirt company, offers probabilistic bundles of t-shirts: "Get 4 random BustedTees for only $30, a savings of over 60%. You pick the size, we'll pick the shirts."[5] Buloso.com (Taiwan) implements its probabilistic selling strategy by framing traditional goods and probabilistic goods as "store pick-up price" and "online price" (for example, "store pick up price ¥39: at your choice of color," "online price ¥20: without choosing color" for toothbrush holders).[6]

Recently, some major online retailers, such as Amazon,[7] Nextag,[8] and Bizrate,[9] have also started to offer various discounted probabilistic goods, such as sportswear, women's clothing, men's ties, and children's toys. Like other websites that offer probabilistic goods, when buying probabilistic apparel from Amazon, buyers can only select size, but not the style/color/design. Also, consumers are informed: "No Return on this style. Exchanges are for size only."[10]

1.3 Technologies that Facilitate Probabilistic Selling

In brick-and-mortar retailing, it is very difficult and inefficient to display and sell probabilistic goods. For instance, it would be cumbersome for consumers to bring multiple items of apparel to the cash register in order for a random draw (for example, a coin flip) to determine which item the consumer receives (and then have the retailer re-stock the remaining items). However, advances in technology are making it easier to implement the probabilistic selling strategy, and the Internet allows probabilistic goods to be offered more efficiently. For example, an online seller can easily create a webpage that illustrates the two possible component goods using existing product descriptors. Integrated software and data communication networks can help the retailer automate the assignment decision and transmit this outcome to buyers. As more e-commerce occurs and as more technologies become available to make it easier to manage probabilistic goods, the probabilistic selling strategy will become increasingly feasible for a wider array of industries. Hence, developing a deeper understanding of this marketing innovation is particularly timely and important. In the rest of this chapter, we will provide answers to some theoretical and practical questions related to probabilistic selling.

2 AN IMPORTANT MARKETING INNOVATION

Probabilistic selling is an exciting marketing innovation that advances the product concept by introducing "uncertainty" as a new dimension to product attributes. In this section, we will discuss why this extension to the product concept is novel and significant from both a supply- and a demand-side perspective.

2.1 A New Mechanism for Market Segmentation

From a seller's perspective, introducing uncertainty as a product attribute creates a new mechanism for market segmentation, based on consumer heterogeneity in product preference strength.

Consumer heterogeneity exists in all markets and consumers differ in their product preferences. For example, some favor traditional but others desire contemporary furniture; some are more interested in a short three-day cruise, but others prefer a long 12-day trip; some like complicated and intense video games, but others enjoy simple, relaxing games. Firms undertake great effort to tailor their products toward the needs of different consumer segments. By offering products that differ in various attributes (for example, style, color, speed, location, time, and warranty policy), firms increase total sales and improve profit. Although less emphasized by researchers and marketers, is it evident that consumers also differ in the strength of their product preferences. Some would be willing to pay considerably more for their preferred option than for a less-preferred option (for example, a Friday versus a Saturday concert; a 100 percent cotton versus a 60 percent cotton shirt), but others may be willing to pay only a slightly higher price for their preferred option. Buyer heterogeneity in product preference strength is an underexplored consumer characteristic in marketing theory and practice. Probabilistic selling creates an opportunity for firms to improve profit by exploiting this unique buyer property.

Under traditional selling, products do not differ in the level of uncertainty involved; the seller offers only components goods for sale and discloses all available attribute information. Under probabilistic selling, however, uncertainty is used as a product attribute in the product line design. The seller offers both component goods, for which a buyer knows exactly what product/service he or she is purchasing, and probabilistic goods, for which a buyer is uncertain about the item she will receive after payment. It is reasonable to believe that uncertainty reduces consumers' product valuations. However, the magnitude of such an uncertainty-caused disutility differs across consumers depending on the relative strength/weakness of their product preferences. For example, it is extremely important for a traveler who needs to go to Paris for her best friend's wedding to fly to the specific destination at the specific time. The same can be said for a business traveler who has a meeting in Berlin. For such consumers, the uncertainty about where and when to fly (for example, when using "blind booking" by Germanwings) would lead to an enormous level of disutility. However, for a college student planning her first visit to Europe without strong preferences about a specific arrival city and travel time, the uncertainty involved in "blind booking" may create a low level of disutility (or even generate a positive utility if she loves "surprises"). Similarly, a "random color" offered by an online store selling children's hats would significantly reduce the purchase utility for a mother who has already bought several hats for her daughter, but now needs a new pink hat to match her daughter's new pink coat. However, it would not be so critical for a mother who simply needs to buy a hat (any hat) to keep her daughter warm in winter.

The discussion above suggests that consumers with strong preferences would prefer component over probabilistic goods because the uncertainty involved in the latter significantly reduces their product valuations (and may even lead to a negative utility). Consumers with weak product preferences would be interested in probabilistic goods since they are not negatively impacted by the uncertainty involved and enjoy the accompanying lower price (especially for those who cannot afford the higher prices of the component goods). As a result, by introducing uncertainty as a new product attribute, probabilistic selling enables the seller to segment markets based on buyer product preference strength. In section 3, we demonstrate in more detail how this new market segmentation mechanism can improve the seller's profit.

2.2 A New Choice for Consumers

At first glance, from the consumer's perspective, probabilistic selling seems to restrict their product choice. However, this marketing innovation actually offers consumers a choice that is impossible under traditional selling, that of choosing between information and price. Under traditional selling, consumers are required to specify the product they buy. For example, before paying for an airline ticket, a consumer must specify a specific itinerary, that is, the carrier, the departure airport and time, the destination, the number of stops, when and where to stop, and the length of each stop. Before paying for a swimsuit, a consumer must confirm the brand, print, style, material, and size. Thus, all consumers pay for full information regardless of whether the information is important to them or not. Under probabilistic selling, however, products differ in the level of uncertainty involved, and consumers can make tradeoffs between information and price. Those with strong preferences value information highly and thus buy component goods at a higher price. However, those with weak preferences are tolerant of uncertainty and, thus, are willing to purchase a probabilistic good in order to receive a discount.

A striking implication of offering buyers the choice between information and price is that this additional purchase option helps the seller both address demand uncertainty and increase capacity utilization. We demonstrate these results in sections 3.4 and 3.5.

3 PROFIT ADVANTAGES OF PROBABILISTIC SELLING

In this section, we discuss several major profit advantages of probabilistic selling. Five numerical cases are presented in Tables 15.3 and 15.4. We use these cases to illustrate intuitively the profit advantage of probabilistic selling and to discuss the economic forces driving these advantages.

3.1 Enlarging Market Size

One fundamental advantage of probabilistic selling is that it can allow the seller to increase market coverage. We illustrate this advantage in case 1, where a seller offers two products (j = 1, 2) and faces four potential segments of customers (A, B, C, D), each of equal size (normalized to be

Table 15.3 Profit advantage of probabilistic selling: market expansion and price discrimination

In the following three cases, two products are available in a market with four consumer segments: A, B, C, D, which can differ in which product they prefer and how much they will be willing to pay for their preferred and less-preferred product.

Case 1: Probabilistic selling enables market expansion (The market is not fully covered under TS)

- Buyer valuation for products 1 and 2: A{10,0}, B{6, 4}, C{4, 6}, D{0,10},
- Product cost: $c_1 = c_2 = \$3$.

Traditional selling (TS)			Probabilistic selling (PS) ($\varphi = 50\%$)			
p_1	p_2	Total sales	p_1	p_2	p_0	Total sales
10	10	2	10	10	5	4
$\pi^*_{TS} = (\$10 - \$3) \times 2 = \$14$			$\pi^*_{PS} = (\$10 - \$3) \times 2 + (\$5 - \$3) \times 2 = \$18$			

$$\Delta\pi\% = \frac{(\pi^*_{PS} - \pi^*_{TS})}{\pi^*_{TS}} = \frac{(18 - 14)}{14} = 29\%$$

Case 2: Probabilistic selling facilitates price discrimination (The market is fully covered under TS)

- Buyer valuation for products 1 and 2: A{10,0}, B{6, 4}, C{4, 6}, D{0,10},
- Product cost: $c_1 = c_2 = \$0$.

Traditional selling (TS)			Probabilistic selling (PS) ($\varphi = 50\%$)			
p_1	p_2	Sales	p_1	p_2	p_0	Sales
6	6	4	10	10	5	4
$\pi^*_{TS} = \$6 \times 4 = \$24$			$\pi^*_{PS} = \$10 \times 2 + \$5 \times 2 = \$30$			

$$\Delta\pi\% = \frac{(\pi^*_{PS} - \pi^*_{TS})}{\pi^*_{TS}} = \frac{(30 - 24)}{24} = 25\%$$

Case 3: Probabilistic selling in vertically-differentiated markets (All consumers value product 1 more than product 2)

- Valuation for products 1 and 2: A{10,0}, B{6, 4}, C{6, 4}, D{10,0},
- The seller knows which product is more popular (i.e., there is no demand uncertainty),
- Marginal cost of the product: $c_1 = c_2 = \$0$.

Table 15.3 (continued)

Traditional selling (TS)			Probabilistic selling (PS) ($\varphi = 50\%$)			
p_1	p_2	Sales	p_1	p_2	p_0	Sales
10	4	4	10	10	5	4
$\pi^*_{TS} = \$10 \times 2 + \$4 \times 2 = \$28$			$\pi^*_{PS} = \$10 \times 2 + \$5 \times 2 = \$30$			
$\Delta\pi\% = \frac{(\pi^*_{PS} - \pi^*_{TS})}{\pi^*_{TS}} = \frac{(30 - 28)}{28} = 7\%$						

one). Each consumer will purchase at most one product, and a consumer's valuations for the two products are V_1 and V_2, respectively. Specifically, the four consumers' valuations for products 1 and 2 are: A{10,0}, B{6, 4}, C{4, 6}, D{0,10}. These valuations imply that consumers differ both in their preferred product (that is, A and B prefer product 1, and C and D prefer product 2) and in the strength of their product preference (that is, A and D have strong preferences, and B and C have weak preferences). The two products have the same costs, $c_1 = c_2 = 3$. Table 15.3 shows the optimal prices and profits under both traditional selling (TS) and probabilistic selling (PS).

As shown in Table 15.3, under TS, the optimal price is \$10. Only two consumers (A and D) will buy at this price and the seller earns a maximum profit of $\pi^*_{TS} = (\$10 - \$3) \times 2 = \$14$. Under PS, the seller sets three prices, \$10 for product 1, \$10 for product 2, and \$5 for a probabilistic good (which can be either product 1 or product 2 with an equal probability). Consumers A and D will pay \$10 to receive their preferred product. Consumers B and C will not buy component goods since they are only willing to pay \$6 for their preferred product. Rather, they choose to pay \$5 to take the chance of receiving either product 1 or product 2, because their valuation for the probabilistic good is \$(4+6) × 0.5 = \$5. As a result, the total demand under PS is four and the seller earns a profit of $\pi^*_{PS} = (\$10 - \$3) \times 2 + (\$5 - \$3) \times 2 = \$18$. In this case, by offering a probabilistic good, the seller doubles the demand and increases profit by $\frac{(\pi^*_{PS} - \pi^*_{TS})}{\pi^*_{TS}} = 29\%$.

Probabilistic selling can increase the total market size because, when uncertainty is used as an additional product attribute, the seller is able to offer a longer product line with the same number of component products. As shown in case 1, with two component products, the seller can offer buyers three choices under PS but only two under TS. Since the probabilistic good is priced less than the component goods (\$5 versus \$10), PS

Table 15.4 Profit advantage of probabilistic selling: managing demand uncertainty and enhancing capacity utilization

In the following two cases
1. Consumers' valuations for their *preferred* and *less-preferred* product are: A{10,0}, B{6, 4}, C{6, 4}, D{10,0}.
2. Marginal cost of the product is: $c_1 = c_2 = \$0$

Case 4: Probabilistic selling helps to manage demand uncertainty (The seller: uncertain about which product is more popular, no capacity constraints)

Traditional selling (TS)			Probabilistic selling (PS) ($\varphi = 50\%$)			
p_1	p_2	Sales	p_1	p_2	p_0	Sales
6	6	4	10	10	5	4
$\pi^*_{TS} = \$6 \times 4 = \$24$			$\pi^*_{PS} = \$10 \times 2 + \$5 \times 2 = \$30$			

$$\Delta\pi\% = \frac{(\pi^*_{PS} - \pi^*_{TS})}{\pi^*_{TS}} = \frac{(30 - 24)}{24} = 25\%$$

Case 5: Probabilistic selling enhances capacity utilization (The seller: uncertain about which product is more popular, with capacity constraints)

Traditional selling (TS)			Probabilistic selling (PS) ($\varphi = 50\%$)			
p_1	p_2	Sales	p_1	p_2	p_0	Sales
10	10	2	10	10	5	4
$\pi^*_{TS} = \$10 \times 2 = \$20$			$\pi^*_{PS} = \$10 \times 2 + \$5 \times 2 = \$30$			

$$\Delta\pi\% = \frac{(\pi^*_{PS} - \pi^*_{TS})}{\pi^*_{TS}} = \frac{(30 - 20)}{20} = 50\%$$

expands the market to include those consumers who would be priced out of the market under TS (B and C in case 1).

Fay and Xie (2008) derive conditions under which market expansion via probabilistic selling is profitable. First, the product cost cannot be too high, that is, market expansion is advantageous only if the cost to serve the newly acquired consumers is lower than their product valuations. This condition holds in many markets with high fixed costs but low variable costs, such as airlines, hotels, software, information goods, and fashion products. Second, introducing probabilistic goods can create a cannibalization effect, that is, some consumers who would have purchased component goods at a high price under traditional selling will buy probabilistic goods at the discounted price under probabilistic selling. Hence, market expansion via probabilistic selling would be advantageous in markets only if this cannibalization effect is not too large. Specifically, consumer uncertainty sensitivity and price sensitivity must not be strongly correlated. We suspect that this condition holds in many markets. For example, business travelers are typically not sensitive to price but are very sensitive to uncertainty. Professional photographers are much more sensitive to camera specifications than are amateurs, and the former are also willing to pay a higher price for their photographic equipment.

3.2 Facilitating Price Discrimination

Can probabilistic selling improve profits in markets where market expansion is not possible (for example, the seller already serves all potential consumers under traditional selling)? We now illustrate another profit advantage of probabilistic selling: facilitating price discrimination. We consider case 2, in which the market is fully covered under TS.

Demand under case 2 is the same as in case 1. The only difference between the two cases is that the cost is lower in case 2, $c_1 = c_2 = 0$. Given the low product cost, under TS, it is optimal to charge a low price, $P_{TS} = \$6$, and sell to all four consumers. The seller earns a profit of $\pi^*_{TS} = \$6 \times 4 = \$24$. For PS, the optimal prices in case 2 are the same as in case 1. The seller's profit is: $\pi^*_{PS} = \$10 \times 2 + \$5 \times 2 = \$30$. Hence, for case 2, compared to TS, introducing a probabilistic good improves profit by $\frac{(\pi^*_{PS} - \pi^*_{TS})}{\pi^*_{TS}} = \frac{(30 - 24)}{24} = 25\%$.

Case 2 shows that PS can improve profit even without the benefit of market expansion, because the strategy allows the seller to segment the market based on buyer product preference strength, and thus implement price discrimination. As shown in case 2, under TS, all buyers pay the same price (\$6) but, under PS, buyers with strong preferences pay a higher price (\$10) and buyers with weak preferences pay a lower price (\$5). Since buyers differ in their strength of product preference in almost all markets, probabilistic selling can potentially enhance many sellers' ability to price discriminate.

Fay (2008) shows that probabilistic selling can facilitate price discrimination and induce market expansion even when a firm faces competition. In this chapter, we assume a monopolist produces both product 1 and product 2. However, Fay (2008) finds that, if products 1 and 2 are produced by competing firms and the probabilistic good is offered by an intermediary, then the probabilistic good will still attract the consumers with weak preferences. Thus, offering probabilistic goods may enable firms to sell to consumers that they would not otherwise have targeted. Furthermore, knowing that the intermediary will focus on weak-preferenced consumers, a firm has an incentive to target its product to consumers who strongly prefer this product over that of its competitor. As a result, probabilistic selling relaxes price competition and allows price discrimination to remain viable in a competitive setting.

3.3 Vertically Differentiated Markets

Both cases 1 and 2 are horizontally differentiated markets where consumers differ in their preferred products. Can probabilistic selling still be advantageous in vertically differentiated markets where all consumers prefer the same product? We illustrate the profit advantage of probabilistic selling in such markets in case 3.

In case 3, all consumers prefer product 1 to product 2. Specifically, the four consumer product valuations are A{10,0}, B{6, 4}, C{6, 4}, and D{10,0}. We assume that the seller is aware that product 1 is more popular than product 2 (we will consider the case with demand uncertainty in cases 4 and 5). The product cost is $c_1 = c_2 = 0$. Under TS, it is optimal to charge a high price for product 1 ($10) and a low price ($4) for product 2. At these prices, A and D will buy the popular good and B and C will buy the less popular good. The seller earns a profit of $\pi^*_{TS} = \$10 \times 2 + \$4 \times 2 = \$28$. As shown in Table 15.3, even if *all* consumers prefer the same product, PS can still increase profit by $\Delta\pi^*_{PS} = \frac{(30 - 28)}{28} = 7\%$.

Case 3 illustrates that offering a probabilistic good can improve profit not only in horizontally differentiated markets but also in markets that are vertically differentiated. Note that, in case 3, the seller can price discriminate under both TS and PS. However, the seller can induce purchase from the low-valuation consumers (B and C) at a higher price under PS ($5) than under TS ($4), because consumers who pay the discounted price will certainly receive their less-preferred product under TS, but will have a 50 percent chance of receiving their preferred product under PS. As a result, although the seller can implement price discrimination under both TS and PS, the latter earns the seller a higher profit.

Furthermore, in case 3, the price of the less-popular product is much lower than that of the popular product under TS, but they are the same under PS. Based on a formal analytical model that allows some consumers to strictly prefer the less popular good, Fay and Xie (2008) show that, in general, introducing a probabilistic good reduces price differentiation between component goods. In order to segment the market under TS (and thus attract consumers who do not have very high values for either product), the seller must charge different prices for the two component products, that is, a low price for the unpopular product. However, under PS, the seller can reach the lower-valuation consumers who only have weak preferences for the more popular item by offering a discounted probabilistic good. This strategy enables the seller to maintain high prices even for the less popular good, and thus earn high margins on sales to consumers who strongly prefer the less popular product.

Finally, in general, the potential advantage of probabilistic selling is higher in horizontally differentiated markets than in those that are vertically differentiated (for example, 25 percent in case 2 versus 7 percent in case 3) because it is easier to implement price discrimination under TS in vertically differentiated than in horizontally differentiated markets. Another issue that may hinder the potential benefit of probabilistic selling in vertically differentiated markets is seller credibility. When some products are more popular or are perceived to have higher quality than others, consumers may question whether the seller would ever assign the more popular or the higher-quality product to buyers of the probabilistic good. We will discuss this seller credibility issue in more detail in section 5.

3.4 Managing Demand Uncertainty

Demand uncertainty occurs in many markets. For example, it is hard for a shoe manufacturer to predict which specific style of its newly designed line of boots will be "hot" for the coming winter. A city tour company may not be able to accurately predict which of tomorrow's sightseeing tours will be more popular than the others. Demand uncertainty can negatively affect profit because the seller is unable to set product prices based on their relative popularity. We illustrate in case 4 (see Table 15.4) that probabilistic selling can weaken the negative impact of demand uncertainty on profit.

Consumers' willingness-to-pay and product costs are the same under case 4 as in case 3; the only difference between the two is that, in case 4, the seller faces demand uncertainty, that is, the seller is unaware of which product is the more popular one. Under TS, without knowing the relative popularity of the two products, the seller charges the same price for both and thus cannot price discriminate. As shown in Table 15.4, the optimal price is \$6 for each product. Each of the four consumers buys a unit of the popular good and the seller earns a profit of \$24. In this case, PS increases profit by $\frac{(\pi^*_{PS} - \pi^*_{TS})}{\pi^*_{TS}} = \frac{(30 - 24)}{24} = 25\%$.

Comparing case 4 with case 3, we see that sellers facing demand uncertainty benefit more from probabilistic selling than sellers without such uncertainty (25 percent versus 7 percent). Fay and Xie (2008) prove that this is a general finding. Probabilistic selling acts as a buffer against demand uncertainty. In the absence of demand uncertainty (case 3), under TS, the seller charges a premium for the more popular product (that is, $P_2^{TS} < P_1^{TS}$). However, in the presence of demand uncertainty (case 4), the seller is unable to base prices on the (unknown) demand for each product. This information disadvantage lowers the profit under traditional selling. However, introducing a probabilistic good removes this information disadvantage. Under PS, the price of the probabilistic good does not change under demand uncertainty (case 3 versus case 4), because the expected value of the probabilistic good is unaffected, and the price of the probabilistic good is set at this expected value. In our example (see Table 15.3), prices of the component goods are likewise unaffected by demand uncertainty. Fay and Xie (2008) show that, when some consumers strictly prefer the less popular good, demand uncertainty can affect component prices. However, even in this more general setting, demand uncertainty changes the component prices more when a firm is using traditional selling than when engaging in probabilistic selling.

3.5 Enhancing Capacity Utilization

In many markets, sellers not only face demand uncertainty but also capacity constraints. For example, retailers often must place inventory orders months prior to the selling season and are unable to replenish inventory if the demand for a product exceeds this pre-season order. In many service industries (for example, airlines, hotels, vacation resorts, theaters, hospitals, auto repairs, and education classes), the service providers are subject to a fixed service capacity (seats, rooms, and time). Can probabilistic selling help sellers in such markets? We demonstrate the impact of capacity constraints on the profit advantages of probabilistic selling in case 5.

The only difference between case 4 and case 5 is that the seller faces capacity constraints in the latter. Specifically, for each product, the seller has only three units for sale. As in case 4, without knowing which good will be more popular, the seller in case 5 cannot tailor prices to the (unknown) demand for each product under TS. Unlike case 4, however, the seller in case 5 does not have enough capacity to serve all four consumers. Hence, it is optimal to charge a higher price, \$10, and sell only to consumers with high valuations (A and D). The maximum profit under TS is $\pi_{TS}^* = \$10 \times 2 = \$20$. In this case, probabilistic selling increases profit by $\frac{(\pi_{PS}^* - \pi_{TS}^*)}{\pi_{TS}^*} = \frac{(30 - 20)}{20} = 50$, which is twice as much as that in case 4.

The fact that the profit advantage of probabilistic selling is larger when capacity is limited than when it is unlimited (50 percent versus 25 percent in case 4) is somewhat surprising. Given that market expansion is one potential benefit of the probabilistic selling strategy, one would question whether introducing probabilistic goods would ever benefit sellers with limited capacity (since increasing the total demand does not seem to be particularly beneficial given the capacity constraints).

What are the economic intuitions behind this surprising result? The coexistence of demand uncertainty and capacity constraints creates a difficult challenge for the seller: mismatch between demand and capacity (that is, some products have excess demand but others have excess capacity). Under traditional selling, this problem is very hard to resolve because, without knowing which product will be perceived more favorably by consumers, the seller is unable to use prices to optimally shift demand towards the product with underutilized capacity. However, under probabilistic selling, consumers with weak product preferences are motivated to buy the discounted probabilistic goods. As a result, many weak-preferenced consumers will end up consuming the less popular product (even though a majority, or even all, of them prefer the more popular product). This not only increases sales for the less popular product, but also effectively "saves" the limited capacity of the popular product for those with strong product preferences (for example, consumers who will not buy the less popular product regardless of its price). Compared with traditional selling, probabilistic selling increases capacity utilization (less unsold inventory of the unpopular product and less lost demand for the popular product), and thus increases profit.

Fay and Xie (2008) derive conditions under which capacity constraints make probabilistic selling more advantageous. Specifically, they show that capacity constraints increase the profit advantage of probabilistic selling when capacity is in a mid-range and demand uncertainty is sufficiently high. This is because, when demand uncertainty is very low or capacity is sufficiently large, the mismatch is not a major problem for the seller. When capacity is sufficiently low, the seller would allocate few (if any) units of its scarce capacity to the lower-margin probabilistic good, which weakens the benefit of probabilistic selling.

3.6 Efficient and Flexible Product Line Extension

A probabilistic good is not a concrete product but a "virtual" product or service (that is, a chance to receive any one of a set of multiple distinct products/services). A seller currently carrying any number of component products or services can extend its product line, that is, add probabilistic goods, without incurring the cost of developing new products or services. As we show in section 4, sellers can use uncertainty-based product design to create a large number of probabilistic goods with its existing products.

Using probabilistic goods for product line extensions would be particularly valuable if it were very costly or difficult to add new concrete products or services. For instance, although a theater that is already open every night of the week may not be able to introduce an additional performance, it could add probabilistic tickets to its product offerings (for example, a "Surprise Week-Night" ticket, which could turn out to be a ticket for a Monday, Tuesday, Wednesday or Thursday night performance). The "virtual" nature also allows the length of the product line to fluctuate according to market factors (for example, a cruise line could offer a four-day "Eastern or Western Bahamas" cruise in the peak season, but not in the off-peak season).

4 DESIGNING PROBABILISTIC GOODS

In this section, we discuss issues related to the design of probabilistic goods.

4.1 Uncertainty-based Design

As noted at the end of the previous section, introducing uncertainty as a new product attribute allows the seller to greatly extend its product line without adding new products.

First, the seller can use its existing products to create multiple probabilistic goods that differ in the level of uncertainty involved. For example, a seller that currently carries three different styles of a handbag can offer a three-style probabilistic handbag that contains component goods with all three different styles, and some two-style probabilistic handbags that only contain two component goods. Since a three-style probabilistic handbag involves a higher level of uncertainty than a two-style probabilistic handbag, the seller can offer a deeper discount to the former, that is, set prices based on the level of uncertainty involved.

Second, the seller can create multiple probabilistic goods that differ in the type of uncertainty involved. For example, an airline can offer different probabilistic tickets that vary in the type of information that is unknown to buyers before payment, for example, some with unknown carriers, some with unknown departure/arrival times, and some with unknown destinations. A health club can offer different probabilistic classes that differ in the variables that the buyer is willing to let the club decide, such as class locations, time, exercise styles, and instructors. Buyers who are sensitive to one type of uncertainty (for example, location) may not be sensitive to another type of uncertainty (for example, time). Offering multiple probabilistic goods that involve different types of uncertainty further segments consumers based on the type of uncertainty to which they are least sensitive, thereby allowing the seller to charge a higher price for probabilistic goods and further improve the profit advantage of probabilistic selling.

Finally, the seller can also allow consumers to design their own probabilistic goods. Advances in information technology and e-commerce offer various user-friendly tools that allow buyers to specify how many and which specific component products they would like to include in the probabilistic goods set. The seller can charge a higher price for buyer-designed than for seller-designed probabilistic goods since the former are generally less risky to buyers than the latter.

In sum, probabilistic selling creates new opportunities for the seller to apply uncertainty-based product design and pricing, which can help the seller to effectively segment markets, increase total sales, and improve profit.

4.2 Selecting the Component Products

While it is apparent that a wide spectrum of probabilistic products that could be offered by sellers exists, it would be useful to have general guidance as to which sets of component goods are likely to maximize the benefits of probabilistic selling. Fay and Xie (2008) find that the profit advantage of probabilistic selling is highest when the horizontal differentiation of the component products in the set is at an intermediate level. Introducing probabilistic goods can generate a cannibalization effect, that is, some consumers who would have paid full price under traditional selling will buy probabilistic goods at a discounted price under probabilistic selling. Low horizontal differentiation of the component products implies a strong cannibalization effect, that is, reduced sales of the component goods. For example, consider a personal computer (PC) manufacturer who currently sells a laptop computer with three different colors, black, silver, and pink, and is interested in creating a probabilistic good using a black and a silver laptop. At first glance, this seems to be a logical design since black and silver are common colors for laptops and are considered acceptable by most consumers. However, such a design implies that most consumers, including those who would have paid a higher price for a black laptop (or a silver laptop) otherwise, would be interested in the discounted probabilistic laptop. As a result, introducing such a probabilistic laptop can significantly hurt the sales of component goods and reduce overall profit. Alternatively, the seller can consider creating a probabilistic good using two more-differentiated colors of the laptop (for example, black/pink, or silver/pink). Such a design implies that some consumers will dislike but others will like the probabilistic laptop. For example, most business consumers would not want to take the chance of being assigned a pink laptop, but many high school girls would be happy to pay a lower price and receive either a black or a pink laptop.

On the other hand, if the component products are extremely differentiated, the profitability of probabilistic selling is also undermined, since such a design implies a high risk to buyers of the probabilistic good and large reductions in their willingness-to-pay. For example, consider a seller who offers a probabilistic floor lamp that can turn out to be one of two lamps with very different styles (for example, contemporary versus traditional) or different functions (for example, reading versus decoration). Since the components are highly differentiated, most consumers would be sensitive to the uncertainty involved. A deep discount is necessary to induce consumers to buy such a high-risk probabilistic good, which can significantly weaken the profit advantage of probabilistic selling.

4.3 Determining the Probability Associated with Each Component Good

Another important issue regarding the design of a probabilistic good is how to set the probability that the buyer will be assigned a specific component product. Consider a seller who currently offers two colors of sweaters, red and blue, and is interested in introducing a probabilistic sweater with a probability of φ to be a red sweater and a probability of $1 - \varphi$ to be a blue sweater. How should the seller determine the value of φ? Fay and Xie (2008) formally model the seller's decision about the probability selection and find that introducing a probabilistic good can be advantageous for any arrangement in which each component good has a positive probability of being assigned as the probabilistic good (that is, $0 < \varphi < 1$). However, the seller can gain the most from probabilistic selling by assigning an equal probability to each component product as the probabilistic good. In our example of a two-color probabilistic sweater, it is optimal to offer the buyer of the probabilistic sweater an equal probability of receiving a red or a blue sweater (that is, $\varphi^* = ½$).

To understand why an equal probability is optimal, consider what happens if the seller assigns the probability of receiving a red sweater at some level higher than ½ (rather than equal to ½). First, increasing the probability of receiving a red sweater makes the probabilistic sweater more attractive to consumers who prefer the color red. This creates a cannibalization effect: some consumers who would have purchased the red sweater at a higher price under $\varphi = ½$ now buy the discounted probabilistic sweater under $\varphi = ½$. Second, a higher φ means a lower probability of receiving a blue sweater, which makes the probabilistic sweater less attractive to consumers who prefer the color blue. This creates a demand reduction effect: some consumers who would have purchased the probabilistic product under $\varphi = \frac{1}{2}$ now do not buy anything under $\varphi > \frac{1}{2}$. Moreover, the seller is unable to reduce the two negative effects on profit by adjusting the price of the probabilistic good, because increasing the price of the latter intensifies the demand reduction effect and decreasing its price intensifies the cannibalization effect.

5 IMPLEMENTATION OF PROBABILISTIC SELLING

The preceding sections have identified a number of potential profit advantages of probabilistic selling. This section discusses several obstacles to implementation that sellers must address in order to implement the probabilistic selling strategy effectively. In particular, sellers must (1) be able to credibly commit to the uncertainty involved in probabilistic goods, (2) effectively limit opportunistic buyer behaviors, and (3) effectively communicate to consumers so that buyers fully understand their options and tradeoffs when purchasing probabilistic goods.

5.1 Seller Credibility

For probabilistic selling to be advantageous, consumers have to believe that the outcome of buying a probabilistic good is uncertain. In other words, the seller must be able to commit credibly to the uncertainty involved in probabilistic goods. This commitment not only requires the seller to introduce uncertainty truthfully, but also to convey such uncertainty to consumers effectively, that is, consumers' expectations are of critical importance. Failing to do so, the probabilistic good would cannibalize full-price sales and market expansion would be lessened. To illustrate this scenario, consider what the impact on case 1 (from Table 15.3) would be if consumers expected that a buyer of the probabilistic good would certainly receive product 1 (rather than with a probability of 50 percent, as we assumed earlier). Buyer A would now purchase the probabilistic good (rather than product 1) since it is less expensive (and the buyer expects the probabilistic good to turn out to be product 1 anyway). Furthermore, buyer C would choose not to purchase anything (that is, she is willing to purchase the probabilistic good if she anticipates a 50 percent chance of receiving her preferred item, but not if she thinks she is certain to receive her less-preferred product). In sum, the firm makes one full-priced sale (of product 2 to buyer D) and two probabilistic good sales (to buyers A and B). The resulting profit is (\$10 − \$3)*1 + (\$5−\$3) * 2 = \$11, which is strictly less than the profit under traditional selling.

This example highlights the importance of ensuring that consumers are uncertain about their product assignments in order for probabilistic selling to segment consumers effectively and profitably. One situation in which it may be difficult to convey such uncertainty credibly is when the component products have asymmetric costs. While the seller may want consumers to believe they are equally likely to receive either product, the seller may have the financial incentive *ex post* to assign the low-cost product since, once the sale is made, the buyer's order can be fulfilled at a lower cost by assigning the product that is less expensive to produce. If consumers observe production costs, they may have a natural inclination to expect the probabilistic good to be the low-cost one. The consequence of lacking credibility is that the advantage of introducing a probabilistic product is completely eliminated. For example, if, due to asymmetric costs, consumers expect that the probabilistic good will be the low-cost product, then no one will be willing to pay full price for the low-cost good regardless of how strongly they prefer this product. As a result, probabilistic selling fails to segment on the basis of the strength of consumer preference.

Although it may be challenging for a seller to credibly commit to uncertain product assignments, several options are available to sellers to obtain credibility under probabilistic selling: (1) remove the allocation decision from their control so that they no longer have the discretion to make assignments on the basis of factors such as costs and remaining inventory levels; (2) build a reputation for non-deterministic allocations by varying assignments across transactions and ensuring that consumers have access to credible information about previous assignments of the probabilistic good.

First, consider the approach of removing the allocation decision from the seller's control. The source of the difficulty of establishing uncertainty credibility is that consumers know that the seller has the incentive to assign products in a nonrandom way. If the seller could somehow tie its hands and thus prevent itself from making nonrandom assignments, then uncertainty credibility could be established. One way to achieve this would be to have assignments based on some random event that is entirely outside the seller's control and is publicly observed. For instance, a seller could offer a probabilistic good in which the buyer receives product 1 if the last digit of the Dow Jones Industrial Average at the close of the day's trading session is even, and receives product 2 if this last digit is odd. Another means would be to transfer the allocation decision to a third party, such as by offering the probabilistic good through an intermediary. An intermediary, who exclusively or predominantly sells probabilistic goods, would have an incentive to ensure that assignments are made randomly since its business model is entirely predicated on assuring this uncertainty. Indeed, assuring uncertainty credibility could be the reason we observe that many hotels offer regular hotel rooms on their own websites but use online travel agents, such as priceline.com, hotwire.com, hoteldirect.co.uk, and hotel.de, to sell their rooms as "mystery rooms."

Second, consider the approach of establishing a reputation of uncertainty credibility via transparent observation of previous assignments. The seller can establish such a reputation if consumers are able to observe prior assignments in order to verify that the assignments of probabilistic products vary across transactions. The Internet has facilitated the spread of word of mouth, thus enabling users to learn more easily about past allocations of the probabilistic good. For instance, several websites (for example, betterbidding.com and biddingfortravel.com) provide forums whereby consumers report the flight itineraries and hotels they have received from Priceline. By viewing these listings, potential buyers of a probabilistic good on Priceline can estimate the probability that they will be assigned to a particular property. The extent of information on such forums can be enormous. For example, biddingfortravel.com contains over 300,000 postings. As probabilistic products become available in non-travel markets, additional forums are likely to arise. Sellers could accelerate this process by financially backing the development and promotion of such sites. Furthermore, there may be opportunities to make the sites easier to use and more informative. For example, existing forums rely on self-reports, that is, users manually report the product or service they received. Lack of verifiability and the fact that only certain consumers (either very pleased or very unhappy) are generally willing to exert the required reporting effort can lead to biased or inaccurate reports. However, a seller could introduce an automated reporting system in which the allocation is automatically posted whenever a probabilistic good is purchased. Such an automated procedure would increase both the amount and the accuracy of information that is available to potential buyers.

Another possibility is that third parties may seize the opportunity to present assignment information in a more manageable and a more comprehensive manner. For example, *Consumer Reports WebWatch* recently spent approximately $38,000 booking airline seats, hotel rooms, and rental cars in order to report differences between opaque travel websites and non-opaque sites. The existence of such independent information helps to establish probabilistic sellers' credibility. In sum, if consumers can obtain reliable information about past assignments (either from fellow consumers, an intermediary, or directly from the seller), it is possible for sellers to establish a credible reputation for making non-deterministic product assignments.

5.2 Opportunistic Buyer Behavior

When offering probabilistic products, sellers must be aware of (and limit) two potential buyer opportunistic behaviors: (1) opportunistic product returns, and (2) arbitrage.

First, under probabilistic selling, a buyer could purchase the discounted probabilistic good, keep it if it turns out to be her preferred good, but return it if she or he is allocated his or her less-preferred product. The implication of such opportunistic behavior (if there are no transaction costs to consumers) is that all consumers, with either strong or weak preferences, would be interested in probabilistic goods and would not be willing to pay full price for the component goods. For the probabilistic product to attract only consumers with weak preferences, the latter must truly commit to being flexible as to which product they will consume. To induce such commitment, sellers offering probabilistic goods should maintain a strong return policy for purchases of the probabilistic good, such as "No Return on this style. Exchanges are for size only" (amazon.com[11]), and "All sales are final" (swimoutlet.com[12]).

Second, under probabilistic selling, a buyer can purchase the discounted probabilistic good and then resell the received item at a higher price. Notice that the resold item is no longer opaque. The reseller could undercut the component good prices, thus eliminating the seller's ability to charge a premium for the component products. Preventing arbitrage is critical to the success of many other marketing strategies involving discounted prices (such as quantity discounts, advance selling, and bundling).

Fortunately, new technologies may help sellers enforce no-return and no-resale policies. For instance, smart cards, radio-frequency identification (RFID) chips, biometric palm readers, and electronic tickets enable the seller to ensure that a particular product or service can only be consumed by the original buyer (Shugan and Xie 2005; Xie and Shugan 2001). Even without such advanced technologies, arbitrage is easily avoided for services that are delivered at the time of purchase.

Furthermore, buyer opportunistic behaviors are less of a concern if there are substantial frictional costs associated with refunds or reselling. For instance, if the buyer must pay for shipping, it will not be worthwhile to return the product if it is relatively inexpensive. Thus, it may be particularly easy to implement probabilistic selling for products that are inexpensive or costly to ship. Resale through secondary markets, such as eBay, would also be less of a threat if shipping costs were high relative to the product's value. In addition, arbitrage through resale is less likely if the product is perishable or is a fashion good (that is, rapidly declines in value over time).

Finally, it is important to note the restrictions on refunds and reselling are simply meant to prevent arbitrage and thus ensure that the buyers of probabilistic goods truly incur the risk associated with uncertain product assignments. Policies can still be instituted to provide consumers with quality assurance. For instance, a seller of probabilistic good could offer a replacement policy in which buyers are guaranteed that the product will arrive free of defects, whereby a replacement of the exact same size/pattern/style would be offered in the event that the product arrives in a damaged condition.

5.3 Communication with Consumers

Communication with consumers is critical to the success of probabilistic selling. It is very important for sellers to clearly communicate what the product offering entails and what specific terms apply to probabilistic products (for example, nonrefundable and nontransferable). This is especially important because consumers may have had very little, if any, past experience with probabilistic goods and the sales policies associated with them may significantly differ from policies that apply to other products sold by the retailer.

In such communication, the focus should be on providing an accurate depiction of the risk that a buyer of a probabilistic good will incur. Persuasive advertising that seeks to downplay the risk is likely to undermine profit. Recall that probabilistic selling relies on segmentation, that is, getting strong-preferenced consumers to pay a premium while offering targeted discounts to consumers with weak preferences. If a strong-preferenced consumer were to purchase the probabilistic good, the seller not only loses the potential sale of a full-priced item, but also faces a potentially unhappy buyer (if he or she receives his or her less-preferred item). Effective communication with consumers is a tool for encouraging consumers to appropriately self-segment. For example, some sellers directly alert buyers about the risk involved: "Keep in mind, though, that you never know what team you will receive."[13] "These suits could be pretty, ugly, or in between."[14] Other sellers inform consumers about the uncertainty in a less direct (and more positive) approach: "If you like surprises, then this grab bag is perfect for you."[15]

The seller should also make every possible effort to facilitate word-of-mouth communication. In today's markets, most consumers will search online consumer reviews before making their purchase. The seller can effectively inform consumers about how probabilistic selling works by encouraging experienced buyers of probabilistic goods to share their information. For example, consider the comments made by an unsatisfied buyer at swimoutlet.com: "I am so disappointed when I received the 2 swimsuits from the grab bag. I would never thought they would be the same!" [*sic*]. Such comments, though negative, would benefit the seller, since it effectively alerts potential buyers about the risk of receiving the exact same items when ordering multiple probabilistic goods. Such comments will discourage consumers with strong preferences (that is, those who really want to obtain different items) from buying probabilistic goods, but would not bother consumers with weak preferences. In online consumer reviews, some consumers reveal their own type and offer advice to their fellow consumers: "I am a person who likes surprises and I find this way of shopping very exciting. But if you are too picky about color and style, this is NOT your store." Informative word-of-mouth communication is particularly important to the success of probabilistic selling since this novel selling strategy can be advantageous only if some consumers (that is, those with weak preferences) like, but others (that is, those with strong preferences) dislike probabilistic goods.

In sum, the objective of sellers' communication efforts should be to shape consumers' expectations so that they can accurately assess the risk involved in purchasing a probabilistic product. Underestimating this risk will cannibalize component good sales; overestimating it will undermine probabilistic good sales. Thus, misunderstandings of risk in either direction undermine the profitability of probabilistic selling.

6 CONCLUSION

As a marketing innovation, probabilistic selling creates new profit opportunities for firms and offers options to consumers that were previously unavailable. This emerging marketing strategy can potentially lead to a win-win situation, both improving profit and increasing social welfare (Fay and Xie 2012).To further explore the potential of this marketing innovation and integrate it with firms' existing strategic decisions, some recent studies have extended the research on probabilistic selling in several new dimensions.

6.1 Inventory Decisions

Fay and Xie (2012) integrate the demand-side decision (pricing) and supply-side decision (inventory) in the probabilistic selling business model. They illustrate that, when introducing probabilistic goods, the seller should order less inventory (relative to the scenario of traditional selling) if costs are very low, but more inventory otherwise. They also demonstrate that probabilistic selling can be used as an effective inventory-management tool, reducing the units to salvage, and thus improving inventory efficiency.

6.2 Time of Commitment

Fay and Xie (2012) derive the optimal time a firm should commit to a buyer of a probabilistic good (that is, by assigning her a specific item). They discover that, in the presence of demand uncertainty, the firm may actually earn a higher profit by committing to consumers early, that is, before the firm has the opportunity to acquire more demand information. This profit advantage occurs because early commitment limits a firm's ability to assign the buyer a less popular good, thereby increasing buyers' willingness to pay for probabilistic goods. Specifically, early commitment is more profitable when the product cost is low, but otherwise later commitment is more advantageous.

6.3 Last-minute Selling via Opaque Intermediaries

Jerath et al. (2010) compare the benefits of last-minute sales to consumers directly versus through an opaque intermediary in the travel industry. They find that the direct channel dominates when consumer valuations for travel are high and/or little service differentiation exists between competing service providers; otherwise, the opaque intermediary channel dominates. As the probability of high demand increases, the profit advantage of opaque selling increases.

6.4 Probabilistic Selling versus Markdowns

Rice et al. (2013) compare probabilistic selling with markdown selling (that is, price reduction over time). They show that both strategies implement price discrimination by adding a "damaged" good to a firm's product line (an uncertain product under probabilistic selling and delayed consumption of a product under markdown selling). However, the former is based on buyer heterogeneity in preference strength, whereas the latter is based on buyer heterogeneity in patience. Probabilistic selling is most advantageous when low-valuation consumers are relatively less "picky" than they are "impatient," and high-valuation consumers are relatively more "picky" than they are "impatient."

Over the past several years, the marketing innovation of probabilistic selling has received increasing attention from practitioners. Its market adoptions have spread beyond the travel industry and are growing rapidly (for example, some major online retailers such as Amazon are starting to offer probabilistic goods). As advances in technology continue to make it easier and more efficient to implement the probabilistic-selling strategy, more firms in a wide range of industries will have the opportunity to benefit from this important innovation.

NOTES

1. Readers who are interested in more rigorous mathematical derivations can find detailed analytical analysis in Fay and Xie (2008, 2010).
2. In the examples of probabilistic goods given in the text and Tables 15.1 and 15.2, buyers of the probabilistic good are assigned a component product immediately after purchase. Even more opacity is created if the assignments are delayed. Gallego and Phillips (2004) use the term "flexible product" to refer to the situation when the seller assigns one of the alternatives to each purchaser at a substantially later date. Mang et al. (2012) study an Australasian low-cost airline that offers flexible tickets. Gallego and Phillips (2004) provide additional examples of flexible products being offered outside of the travel industry: Internet service providers, such as Yahoo, MSN, and Lycos, selling advertising space on a "run-of-network basis," carriers of air cargo offering "time-definite products" in which the carrier does not specify which flight will carry the shipment, and several European tour operators giving discounts to customers who allow the tour operator to choose the property of their stay.
3. milepoint.com/forums/threads/one-on-one-with-warren-chang-vice-president-and-general-manager-fly-com.13164/.
4. www.swimoutlet.com/product_p/33164.htm, on which, buyers can choose size but not color/style/fabric.
5. www.bustedtees.com/grabbag.
6. www.buloso.com/Shop/itemDetail.aspx?mNo1=150255.
7. For example, www.amazon.com/dp/B004UMQOQS?tag=wpmumu8945839-20
8. For example, www.nextag.com/Speedo--2700202/the-incredibles/brand-html.
9. Foe example, www.bizrate.com/mens-swimwear/1525144281.html.
10. www.amazon.com/dp/B004UMQOQS?tag=wpmumu8945839-20.
11. www.amazon.com/dp/B004UMQOQS?tag=wpmumu8945839-20.
12. www.swimoutlet.com/product_p/2046.htm.
13. www.agonswim.com/nonCustom/grabBag/grabBag.cfm.
14. www.grabbagswimwear.com/index.php?main_page=product_info&products_id=2.
15. www.amazon.com/Womens-Luck-Grab-Sarongs-World/dp/B001AOO4X4.

REFERENCES

Fay, Scott (2004), "Partial-repeat-bidding in the name-your-own-price channel," *Marketing Science*, **23** (3), 407–18.

Fay, Scott (2008), "Selling an opaque product through an intermediary: the case of disguising one's product," *Journal of Retailing*, **84** (1), 59–75.

Fay, Scott and Jinhong Xie (2008), "Probabilistic goods: a creative way of selling products and services," *Marketing Science*, **27** (4), 674–90.

Fay, Scott and Jinhong Xie (2010), "The economics of buyer uncertainty: advance selling vs. probabilistic selling," *Marketing Science*, **29** (6), 1040–57.

Fay, Scott and Jinhong Xie (2012), "Timing of commitment as a strategic variable: using probabilistic selling to enhance inventory management," 6 December, accessed

12 September 2013 at http://ssrn.com/abstract=1757856 or http://dx.doi.org/10.2139/ssrn.1757856.

Gallego, Guillermo and Robert Phillips (2004), "Revenue management of flexible products," *Manufacturing & Service Operations Management*, **6** (4), 321–37.

Hann, Il-Horn and Christian Terwiesch (2003), "Measuring the frictional costs of online transactions: the case of a name-your-own-price channel," *Management Science*, **49** (11), 1563–79.

Jerath, Kinshuk, Serguei Netessine and Senthil K. Veeraraghavan (2010), "Revenue management with strategic customers: last-minute selling and opaque selling," *Management Science*, **56** (3), 430–48.

Mang, Stefan, David Post and Martin Spann (2012), "Pricing of flexible product," *Review of Managerial Science*, **6** (4), 361–74.

Rice, Dan, Scott Fay and Jinhong Xie (2013), "Probabilistic selling vs. markdown selling: price discrimination and management of demand uncertainty in retailing," *International Journal of Research in Marketing*, forthcoming.

Spann, Martin, Bernd Skiera and Bjorn Schafers (2004), "Measuring individual frictional costs and willingness-to-pay via name-your-own-price mechanisms," *Journal of Interactive Marketing*, **18** (4), 22–36.

Shugan, Steve and Jinhong Xie (2005), "Advance-selling as a competitive marketing tool," *International Journal of Research in Marketing*, **22** (3), 351–73.

Spann, Martin, Bernd Skiera and Bjorn Schafers (2004), "Measuring individual frictional costs and willingness-to-pay via name-your-own-price mechanisms," *Journal of Interactive Marketing*, **18** (4), 22–36.

Xie, Jinhong and S. Shugan (2001), "Electronic tickets, smart cards, and online prepayments: when and how to advance sell," *Marketing Science*, **20** (3), 219–43.

16 New service development from the perspective of value co-creation in a service system

Bo Edvardsson, Anders Gustafsson, Per Kristensson, Bard Tronvoll and Lars Witell

INTRODUCTION

New service development (NSD) is the engine of renewal to create a profitable business. Companies try to increase their competitiveness through innovative activities and interactions that create value for the involved actors, such as existing customers, potential new customers and other shareholders (for example, Edvardsson et al. 2000; Gustafsson and Johnson 2003). New service development often stems from an improved way to use existing resources to co-create value. New resources or new technologies are also sometimes used and integrated within systems that are capable of creating value. These value-creating systems or service systems constitute the basic context and enabler of value co-creation and thus the foundation for NSD. A service system is an appropriate frame for studying new service development, because it moves away from traditional perspectives "rooted in technological product inventions" (Michel et al. 2008, p. 54).

Value is always co-created with the customer through the activation of sets of resources (Vargo and Lusch 2004). Service companies accordingly need to design resource integration mechanisms within the service system that support customers and other value co-creation actors to enhance NSD and innovation. Customers also co-develop value as one mode of co-creation in which they and other actors can be actively involved in fostering NSD. Customers interact and develop relationships within the system in order to exploit and enhance their own resources and to gain the benefit of those of others. Denoting the customer as the key actor and resource integrator implies a new and radically changed status for customers. Customers are an important source in the NSD process. Consequently, to understand and enhance these processes, we must understand the service; the service system in which new service development takes place; and the customer's ability to acquire, integrate, and use the available resources in a specific context.

New service development processes in a business context are understood as various phases from idea generation to market launch with a sustainable acceptance in the market. We argue for a systemic perspective on NSD where actors, and in particular customers, are the focus. The key actor is always the customer because companies can only offer value proposition (Lusch et al. 2007), that is, they can align their resources in the service system and aim to facilitate the customer's value co-creation process. It is the customer's knowledge and skills (operant resources) that are the driving force behind value creation and NSD. As a consequence, customer involvement becomes central to the development process. We want to highlight the role that customers play in NSD and why, when, how, and through what methods to involve the customer. A high degree of customer involvement means a change from NSD *for* the customer to NSD *with*, or even *by*, the customer.

By co-development, we mean being proactive and interacting and communicating in order to co-create new service with the customer. It gives significant business potential in using the customer's knowledge, skills and motivation throughout the NSD process. The customer as a co-developer is of relevance not only for private and public service companies, but also for manufacturing companies in the transition from product orientation to service orientation.

This chapter focuses on NSD and is based on a series of research studies performed by researchers at CTF – Service Research Center, Karlstad University. The aim is to show why, when, how, and through what methods to involve the customer in different stages of the NSD process. We use service systems as the base for NSD since new services are most often based on a reconfiguration of existing resources within the system. Different models and tools have been developed in service research which is presented, including a discussion of the managerial NSD implications.

SERVICE SYSTEM

Vargo and Lusch (2011, p. 3) argue that "A system orientation is important to both academics and practitioners because it has different implications for understanding and applying principles of value co-creation, as is particularly essential in an increasingly interconnected, and thus increasingly dynamic, world." Edvardsson and Tronvoll (2013) continue this line of argument by stating that understanding value co-creation in service systems is essential to analyze and manage NSD and innovation. Furthermore, they argue that value is created collaboratively in interactive configurations of resources and guided by norms and rules in the system. That is, companies do not develop and offer services; rather, they design and communicate new value propositions, develop and manage service systems capable of realizing the new value propositions, and ensure that value co-creation results in favorable, memorable customer experiences.

Value-creating systems have often been described as constellations of resources (Normann 2001), a configuration of resources (Spohrer et al. 2007), value networks (Lusch et al. 2010), or service ecosystems (Vargo and Lusch 2011). To co-create value, customers and other actors, for example employees and partners, need a support system in order to integrate and operate on resources during their co-creation of value. As resource integration and value co-creation take place within a service system, all beneficiaries, including the customer, the employees, the company, and other actors, become resource integrators and value co-creators in a complex joint endeavor. Spohrer et al. (2007, p. 72) describe service systems as "value co-creation configurations of people, technology, value propositions connecting internal and external service systems, and shared information (language, laws, measures, and methods)." Maglio and Spohrer (2008, p. 18) built on this definition when describing a service system as an open system capable of: (1) improving the state of another system through sharing or applying its resources, with the understanding that the second system agrees that interaction constitutes value; and (2) improving its own state by acquiring external resources, with the understanding that the first system perceives value when interacting with other systems.

Vargo and colleagues (Lusch, et al. 2010; Vargo and Lusch 2011) have emphasized the dynamic aspect of value-creating systems by introducing the notion of a "service ecosystem." They argue that: "networks are not just networks (aggregations of relationships); they are dynamic systems" (Vargo and Lusch 2011, p. 185), described as relatively self-contained and self-adjusting systems of resource-integrating actors connected by shared institutional structures. Earlier, Merz et al. (2009, p. 38) elaborated on the idea of networks as "resource integrators that collectively function as an interdependent ecosystem to mutually create value, as perceived phenomenologically (that is, in context)". Lusch et al. (2010, p. 31) argue that, when networks successfully institutionalize resources, they become joined together as a service ecosystem or "a spontaneously sensing and responding spatial and temporal structure of largely loosely coupled value proposing social and economic actors' interactions through institutions and technology, to (1) co-produce service offerings; (2) exchange service offerings; and (3) co-create value."

WHY COLLABORATE WITH CUSTOMERS IN NSD?

According to Prahalad and Ramaswamy (2000, p. 80), "customers are fundamentally changing the dynamics of the marketplace". In essence, what they meant is that the role of the customers is changing from viewing them as passive recipients to active co-creators. To illustrate with a real world example, consider Lego, the success of which is largely due to the company's close collaboration with key customers, using their specific competencies to develop market offerings that they and other customers also desire.

However, the idea that customers are active agents is not new. Customers have always participated in creating value, for example, when they are selecting, transporting, assembling, repairing, and using goods and services they have purchased. What is new is the situation that encourages customers to become co-inventors of tomorrow's offerings. According to Bendapudi and Leone (2003), what we are seeing are customers who create conditions for a customized consumption experience for themselves. This shift in the perspective of companies to viewing customers as active co-inventors rather than as passive recipients of something produced far away from them is captured in the move from the traditional sales replica "What can we do for you?" to "What can we do together?"

At the same time as Prahalad and Ramaswamy (2000) argue the changing role of customers, researchers at the CTF – Service Research Center at Karlstad University (Sweden) undertook the question of the value of customer contributions at the front end of NSD projects. To be more specific, the question is about the merit of customers' ideas in comparison to ideas that came from developers working in-house. Is it really possible that customers' ideas can outperform well-educated developers with many years of working life experience?

Customer Co-creation during NSD

Getting new and valuable ideas is an important activity for companies that expect to succeed in developing new services (Kristensson et al. 2004). A unique idea for a new offering may represent a new way of responding to yet unfulfilled customer needs in a way that is profitable for the company and turns out to be value-creating for the customer, a true win-win scenario that is fundamental to business today. Due to this situation, business self-help management books, business gurus, as well as scholarly research, have proposed that customers should be viewed as a potentially great source of finding new innovative ideas that can build business.

Unfortunately, especially at the time of the millennium, not many companies seemed convinced that this strategy would work for them. The most extreme action of being customer oriented in the development process appeared to be by conducting large-scale surveys or maybe creating a focus group. Inviting customers to become collaborators and to suggest ideas for future offerings seemed like an ideal scenario. As traditional market research techniques only manage to skim the surface of customer needs and desires, such actions do not seem to do enough. As many product and service offerings become more and more technologically complex, it will be even more difficult to acquire knowledge about customer needs using such techniques. Background research on the value of customer input in service development seems to be an important research gap to fill.

Real-life Experiment at the Largest Telecommunication Operator in Scandinavia

In 2000, Telia, the largest telecommunication (telecom) operator in Northern Europe, was interested in innovating new non-voice mobile phone services but faced the usual problem of not knowing what the typical customer wanted. Therefore, getting into the minds of potential and existing customers was crucial. One excellent way of doing so is, of course, to let customers initiate what the company should develop in the future. Indeed, having several actual and potential customers carving out ideas, in the immediate area of use for the customer, sounds like a potential way of providing the company with opportunities for new offerings.

Because mobile phones and their associated services are technical in nature, market research techniques, as described above, did not provide much useful information. Customers simply stated that they were satisfied with the product as it was or they came up with solutions that the product developers were already aware of. So, a new project was set up where customers were asked to be the creative source for new mobile phone service ideas.

An experimental design was used where Telia's customers were given the task to create ideas for new value-adding services (Kristensson et al. 2004 contains a more thorough description of the experiment). The outcome, that is, the ideas about new mobile phone services, was to be compared with service ideas generated by a group of in-house developers at Telia. In this way it would be possible to compare and assess the true merit of ideas generated by customers. The question of why companies should involve customers in NSD would get an empirical answer (instead of arm-chaired hunches and a management guru's gut feeling).

The research project contained four phases. In the first phase, all customers listened to a brief lecture about telecom and its technology to provide a sense of understanding of the possibilities (and limitations) that today and tomorrow's mobile technology will enable. All users were also equipped with mobile phones and a free subscription so that they could use the cell phone whenever they needed.

In the second phase, all participants (that is, customers) were to create ideas for new services that they themselves would appreciate in their own everyday life. It should be noted that since the participants were instructed to create services that would provide benefits for themselves, they were told not to sit at home and simply engage in an individual brainstorming process. Rather, they were to function as usual, and whenever a problematic situation occurred, or they experienced some kind of emotion or experience, they were instructed to consider if they thought the mobile phone could play a value-adding role for them. If so, they recorded their idea. This means that all types of situations that customers experienced in their daily life, at work or privately, functioned as stimuli to coming up with ideas for a mobile phone service. Interviews carried out after the project was over showed that this process worked rather automatically for the users. Since they had learned about the possibilities regarding mobile phone opportunities in the future, whenever a small problem or situation of some kind occurred they came to think about how a mobile phone service could solve these situations in a smoother way.

In the third phase, all the participants were asked to transcribe their ideas into a more detailed service description. In the service description, the participants were asked to write a brief description of the service idea and state how the service would create value for them.

In the final and fourth phase, all ideas were taken to screening. All ideas were ranked on a scale from 1 (low) to 10 (high). Three dimensions—originality, value, and ease of implementation—were used. A score of 1 represented the least original, least valuable, and most difficult to produce. Similarly, a score of 10 corresponded to the most original, most valuable, and easiest to produce. There were four panels, consisting of three people in each panel, judging the ideas against the three criterions. All ideas were made unidentifiable so that the judges in the panels did not know whether the idea was invented by a customer or by a professional research and development (R&D) member.

From a research point of view, it was of interest to investigate what a group of users would be able to identify in terms of ideas compared to a group of in-house developers. Our question was whether ideas generated by professional service developers were more original, valuable, and realizable than ideas generated by users. From Telia's point of view, it was of interest to discover new ideas for new mobile phone services.

As shown in Table 16.1, the results from co-creation during NSD projects at Telia, it is clear that users can be a valuable source for innovative

Table 16.1 Means (all panels aggregated) for four dimensions of creative output for professional in-house developers and customers

	Originality	Value	Ease of implementation	Number of ideas
Professional in-house developers	4.00	4.38	6.82**	4.58
Customers	4.48**	4.85*	6.01	6.47*

Note: **<.001 and *<.05.

ideas. Users are, simply put, capable of being creative if they are allowed to collaborate during circumstances that differentiate from traditional market research. These results are impressive, and it is important to remember that customers outnumber members of R&D departments and thus represent a much more diverse group of people (for example, regarding education, age, home setting, interests, and so forth). Therefore, customer ideas are also likely to not only be of more value, but also be more heterogeneous, diverse, and varying than the ideas from the R&D department.

WHEN SHOULD WE LISTEN TO CUSTOMERS?

Despite the general consensus that co-creation with customers is beneficial, there is a lack of agreement regarding how and why this is (Witell et al. 2011). Also, is it always beneficial to listen to what customers have to say? An Apple designer states, "At Apple we don't waste our time asking users, we build our brand through creating great products we believe people will love" (Skibstedt and Bech Hansen, 2011). The essence of this message is that the demand for something fundamentally new is completely unpredictable. Even users themselves have no idea whether they will like an entirely new product before they start using it (and perhaps then only after years of use). In contrast, Prahalad and Ramaswamy (2004) describe and argue at a very general level that companies that use co-creation are extremely successful in their efforts, and that more companies should adopt this strategy. We do not believe that it is always beneficial to listen to customers in the same manner but, depending on what a company wants to accomplish, they may want to adapt their strategy.

We argued that the co-creation process in NSD is generally a communication process. Furthermore, the process of communication and socially rich interactions with customers is one of the determinants for new service success. Research has thus far focused predominantly on when to listen to customers (Gruner and Homburg, 2000), rather than how companies should communicate with customers. Gruner and Homburg (2000, p. 4) concluded that intensive communication with customers is generally considered to be a determinant of product success and that previous studies had provided a "limited insight into the interaction with customers". Consequently, one of the more interesting aspects of co-development is the communication process between a company and its customers and how this process can improve product and market success.

Value in Context

Previous research is clear regarding the difficulty of understanding value-creation processes. Von Hippel (1994) explained that customer value is "sticky information," which means it is costly to transfer from one place to another because it is tacit. Therefore, companies find it difficult to identify, understand, and adopt knowledge about the value-creation processes that customers experience. The value-creation processes are inherently subjective and must be understood in relation to each specific time, place and service system in which they occur. Accordingly, as already noted, companies have started to treat their customers as active collaborators when developing various offerings. This contrasts with the traditional view of customers as passive informants from whom information can be extracted by means of surveys or focus groups.

It has been suggested that companies that apply a proactive market orientation work more closely with their customers. Proactive market orientation can be achieved by working closely with lead users or by conducting market experiments to discover future needs that are typically difficult to foresee or articulate. Witell et al. (2011) suggested that it is necessary to distinguish co-creation for use from co-creation for others: customers perform co-creation for use for their own benefit, while co-creation for others is oriented towards other customers. Therefore, co-creation in the development process mainly concerns co-creation for others. Furthermore, given that it can be difficult to identify or express certain customer needs, it is assumed that co-creation for others typically depends on opportunities for interaction and communication. Essentially, customer co-creation concerns different ways of communicating and interacting with customers in their context and, for the company, the intended service system context.

Companies often know more about their solution to a certain problem than they do about the customer's needs regarding the same problem. Companies should communicate with customers in the development process in order to understand how the solution can be applied to satisfy the customer's needs. In research this is referred to as "absorptive capacity" (the company's capacity to assimilate customer needs) and is a major challenge for companies developing new offerings. Cooperation with all parts of a network (including customers) is essential in order to create an attractive offering.

Customer Co-creation as Communication and Interaction with Customers

Bonner (2010) showed that the communication literature offers a novel and valuable opportunity to examine the quality of communication in development processes, particularly with regard to need-related information that can be difficult to transfer from a customer to a company. Based on the organizational communication literature, Mohr and Nevin (1990) and Bonner (2010) analyzed the frequency, direction, modality, and content of marketing channel communication. In this chapter, marketing channel communication is used as a way of learning from and with customers to better understand how they integrate resources during a value co-creation process, which results in a deeper understanding of customers' needs and how to support them. The underlying idea is in line with the common notion that intense co-creation leads to higher product success (Kristensson et al. 2004).

The four dimensions result in an interactive communication climate that is conducive to the learning, sharing, and understanding of customer needs. Frequent, bidirectional, face-to-face, and active communication is likely to enable bilateral trust and high-quality information exchange about customers' needs. Active communication enables customers and companies to meet and exchange information regarding needs that might otherwise be difficult to express or transfer. In line with this we define customer co-creation as a communication and resource integration process that is used when attempting creative problem solving. Consequently, passive co-creation is considered less beneficial for the outcome of the innovation and involves less frequent, unidirectional, electronic, and anonymous communication in which there is an uneven distribution of initiative and creativity. Therefore, it is less beneficial for a development process.

The first dimension, frequency, refers to the amount of time that the involved parties use for communication. In the context of customer co-creation, frequency refers to such aspects as the amount of ongoing feedback between a company and its customers. It may also concern the number of mutual experiments or the amount of iteration that takes place with customers during the development of a specific version of the offering within a development project. Frequency can also refer to the extent to which a learning process about customers' needs occurs and leads to the generation of new ideas in a development project.

The second dimension of the communication process that characterizes co-creation regards direction. Direction refers to the democratic aspect of communication; namely, the extent to which one party exerts power over the other(s). This could apply to issues such as whether both parties take equal initiative to interact and assume approximately the same workload. With regard to customer co-creation, direction is believed to be important when it is difficult to estimate future customer usability. In other words, when it is difficult to foresee or imagine value co-creation, there must be an even distribution of communication between parties in order to envision or understand future customer needs. Furthermore, when there is an even distribution of communication and interaction, both parties can be expected to contribute to the end result, which should lead to more novel ideas.

The third dimension, modality, refers to how information is transmitted. For example, it could apply to aspects of the communication process, such as whether the dialogue takes place face to face or whether it is possible to provide immediate feedback. It may also apply to the degree to which communication is focused on a specific recipient. With regard to customer co-creation, modality refers to the extent to which communication takes place face to face or in other ways (such as electronically) and the extent to which a customer is given the opportunity to deal directly with critical aspects in a development project. This assumes that electronic communication typically addresses many recipients. Research confirms that group decision making is hampered when it is done through electronic communication as compared to face-to-face communication. Also, when customers are excluded from any part of a development project, it is most likely to be the critical parts, for which customer input might have the greatest impact.

The final dimension that characterizes customer co-development regards content, or what is transmitted during communication. In the context of co-creation between a company and its customers, content can relate to whether the focus is on customer needs and difficulties related to value-creation. On the other hand, customers may sometimes be invited to companies with the purpose of strengthening the relationship rather than improving the outcome of the development processes. This chapter focuses on whether companies enable customers to share their inventiveness at the locations where their needs are most likely to be present in the future (without trying to determine them in a superficial laboratory, for example). The reason for this is related to the frequently documented difficulty of expressing needs. It is assumed that latent needs are more easily detected if a search is conducted at the same time as the user experiences them.

One issue is whether all dimensions of customer co-development have an effect on new service success in all kinds of development projects, or whether the effect depends on the degree of innovativeness of a development project (incremental versus radical). Based on the literature on customer co-creation for others, it is difficult to identify any research suggesting that active participation of customers in a development project would have any negative influence on product success, which is why this question is especially interesting.

A Cross-sectional Survey

A more thorough description of the method can be found in Gustafsson et al. (2012). Data was collected through a paper-based survey sent to service or product development managers selected from an externally purchased database. The procedure yielded 334 company responses which is a response rate of 20.0 percent. Complete data was obtained for manufacturing and service companies in industries such as the machine industry, pulp and paper, fabricated metal goods, machinery and equipment, renting and real estate, construction services, consumer services, and business services. All questions in the survey, including those regarding activities and performance, were asked at the project level. The respondents categorized all projects as improvements, incremental innovations, or radical innovations. We used this categorization to further focus the differences between incremental (207 companies) and radical innovations (77 companies).

The survey instrument was developed on the basis of previous research and existing research instruments (Bonner 2010; Mohr and Nevin 1990; Song and Perry 1997a, 1997b). Twenty items were used to operationalize the six latent constructs that covered customer co-creation, product success, and market success. Each item was scored on a ten-point scale that ranged from "completely disagree" to "completely agree." The proposed model was estimated using partial least-squares (PLS) across companies. Partial least-squares is an estimation procedure that integrates aspects of principal-components analysis with multiple regressions (Wold 1982). The model for incremental innovations worked well, while for radical innovations we had to redo the analysis with fewer indicators in order to make it fit into the criteria of what constitutes a good model.

All constructs were modeled using reflective indicators; that is, indicators were created based on the assumption that they all reflect the same underlying phenomenon (Chin 1998). Jackknife estimates were generated in order to evaluate the significance of the paths in the model (Chin 1998). Jackknifing generally involves deleting every *n*th case or observation, estimating the model parameters, and then repeating this sample–resample

Table 16.2 *An overview of how the different dimensions of customer co-development influences project success for incremental and radical innovation*

	Frequency	Direction	Modality	Content
Incremental innovation	0.15*	0.17*	*NS*	0.21*
Radical innovation	0.34*	NS	NS	−0.25*

Note: *<.05 and NS = non-significant.

procedure in order to generate a set of standard errors for the model parameters. Following Tukey's guidelines, 5 percent of the sample was removed during the re-sampling procedure, which resulted in 20 sub-samples per model. Simple *t*-statistics were then computed in order to determine whether the parameters are different from zero.

Customer Communication for Incremental and Radical Innovation

Table 16.2 depicts the results from the study. When working with incremental NSD, more is more; a company cannot do too much in order to understand the customer perspective and allow customers to co-develop as much as possible. This is no surprise considering what previous research has prescribed both regarding what is lacking in NSD (customer interaction) and what is successful (listening to customers).

What is more surprising and interesting is what happens when dealing with radical new services. The communication model does not work well at all; communication for radical innovations is quite different. Essentially, radical innovations are difficult for customers to imagine; they are unthinkable in advance and, in fact, if companies listen to customer solutions, may actually be harmful (as indicated by the negative sign). Thus spending time with customers and trying to understand their context is beneficial for market success when working with radical new services. The logic is not that difficult to understand; when customers make concrete suggestions they do this based on their previous experiences of a solution that already exists. If companies listen to this they may lose some of the desired market newness. We may also revisit the examples in Prahalad and Ramaswamy (2004) and scrutinize the purpose in each described case. Our interpretation is that in all these cases customers helped the companies to make incremental developments and essentially make the new service ready for the market.

HOW SHOULD WE LISTEN TO THE CUSTOMER?

There is a trend to suggest that traditional market research techniques such as interviews and focus groups are reactive and do not provide the right information. In previous sections we suggested that a company should involve customers to co-create with them when developing new offerings. Involvement of customers in service development co-creates much better knowledge than do traditional market research techniques But what facts and empirical evidence do we actually have to support this claim? Based on the research at the largest telecom operator in Scandinavia, we know that customers can provide ideas that are more original and of higher value than professional in-house developers. But, there is no knowledge on how we should listen to customers and how the method used influences what the customer can contribute.

Reactive and Proactive Market Research

A company can use responsive or proactive market research techniques to identify customer needs or ideas (Johnson 1998; Narver et al. 2004). Responsive market research concerns a firm's attempts to discover, understand and satisfy the expressed needs of its customers. Proactive market research, on the other hand, has been described as a process in which the firm must discover, understand and satisfy the latent needs of its customers (Witell et al. 2011).

Some of the more common market research techniques that companies use to generate customer information include surveys, in-depth interviews, and focus groups (Verma et al. 2008). These techniques, which concentrate on capturing customers' previous experiences with an offering, have been designed so that the customers respond to an existing product or service from the company. Accordingly, these market research techniques have been categorized as reactive or backward looking (Johnson, 1998). Companies that use reactive market research techniques decide what type of questions should be asked or they limit the responses from customers by asking about a customer's previous experience with a product or service. This limits the possibility of the customer providing new insights and thoughts that lie outside the questionnaire or interview guide. In such cases, customers are likely to describe their future needs based on their experiences with previous usage (Trott 2001).

While reactive market research techniques capture customers' spoken needs, proactive market research techniques seek to capture latent customer needs. Proactive market research techniques assist in the development of innovative new offerings that build on gaining greater access to customers' underlying values and behaviors (Johnson 1998).

Real-life Experiment at a Microwave Oven Manufacturer

In 2006, we worked with Whirlpool, a large manufacturer of microwave ovens. In the microwave oven market, manufacturers sell their different products under a variety of different brands, ranging from low-priced ovens with few functions to high-end ovens with many functions. Both the technology and the market are mature and manufacturers are interested in identifying new ways of providing customer value. The strategy of Whirlpool is to make the best appliances through constant innovation throughout their product range, which covers laundry, kitchen and other solutions for the home.

The development process often includes a phase of idea generation. At Whirlpool, idea generation consists of four main activities: generation, screening, identification, and evaluation. In order to build on previous research that claims customers provide more innovative ideas than product developers (Kristensson et al. 2004), customers were invited to participate in idea-generation activities. The first activity, that is, idea generation by customers, was intended to provide innovative ideas. In the second activity, that is, company screening of ideas, engineers and marketers made a preliminary screening to identify the ideas with the most innovative potential.

In the research project, each customer was assigned randomly to provide new ideas through reactive or proactive market research techniques, ranging from interviews and focus groups to customer involvement (further description can be found in Witell et al. 2011). Participation was voluntary and all customers were informed of their task two weeks before the actual experiment. Customers were told that they were going to participate in a study regarding microwave ovens and that their ideas were of interest for the future development of products and services.

A professional interviewer and moderator conducted in-depth interviews and focus groups, and instructed the group participating through customer involvement. The in-depth interviews were one to two hours in duration. The interviewer started all interviews by asking the customers about their microwave oven use, and, as the interview proceeded, more questions were directed towards their needs and wishes for the future. Each focus group session had five or six customers and lasted for two hours. The moderator began by asking about present microwave use and then moved the discussion towards needs and wishes for the future. Questions and discussion topics included a hypothetical situation in which a person's kitchen burned down and they had to rebuild it again. In addition, triggers were introduced during all market research techniques in order to encourage creativity. Examples of triggers were online microwave cookbooks, baking cakes in the microwave, watching microwave oven chefs on YouTube, and making and eating microwave popcorn.

Customers in the experiment on customer involvement included ordinary customers. The procedure for the experiment was similar to the one previously described. Customers participated in the experiment for seven days, during which time they received training in how to use a microwave and were asked to focus on the problems and difficulties they experienced when using their microwaves at home. All participants were provided with a camera with which they could photograph occasions when they encountered specific problems or thought of opportunities while using their microwaves. All ideas and perceived problems were noted in an idea book, which was submitted at the end of the seven days.

Ideas provided through the three market research techniques were ranked by two panels regarding originality (the newness of an idea) and value (the value from a customer's point of view). Each of the panels comprised four judges, all of whom were employed by the microwave oven manufacturer. The panel members each had at least five years of experience in their line of business and decided which development projects the company should initiate. Each judge was instructed to rate the ideas on a scale from one (lowest) to ten (highest).

From a research point of view, it was of interest to investigate if the different market research techniques provided different kinds of ideas. Our question was whether ideas generated by proactive market research techniques were more original and valuable than ideas from reactive market research techniques. From Whirlpool's point of view, it was of interest to discover new ideas for their range of offerings.

The results of the experiment suggest that proactive market research techniques provide ideas that are more original than those from the interviews and focus groups, but there is no difference regarding the customer value of the ideas (see Table 16.3).

The experiment suggests that using proactive market research techniques

Table 16.3 Means of panel evaluation for originality and value for interviews, focus groups and customer involvement

	Originality	Value	Number of ideas[x]
Interviews	3.69	6.64	4.64
Focus groups	3.33	6.40	4.86
Customer involvement	4.55*	6.36	5.64

Note: *<.05 and [x]=no statistical test done.

in the development process provides ideas that are significantly more innovative than those generated through traditional market research techniques. Customer involvement appears to derive customer ideas from an experience that has triggered their understanding of how value-in-context is created. In contrast, customers participating in traditional market research methods, such as focus groups and in-depth interviews, have had to rely on their memories of previous experiences in order to provide ideas. Traditional market research techniques seem restricted by the fact that users have difficulty imagining or remembering scenarios in which they have experienced certain needs. Because cognition is often limited to the situations in which people find themselves at that point in time, focus group participants are likely to be limited to making suggestions connected to that particular moment, or to standard situations that are typically shared by most people.

METHODS FOR LISTENING TO AND INVOLVING CUSTOMERS IN NSD

How can companies capture the most essential and at the same time actionable information? "You can't just ask customers what they want and try to give that to them . . . Everything at Apple starts and ends with the customer experience" (Steve Jobs, in Isaascon 2011, p. 231). Thus, it is important to understand how to develop a competitive advantage through favorable customer experiences.

This section provides an overview of methods for obtaining information from customers in their own habitat, business or life context to facilitate the NSD process, and how to integrate a new service in an existing service system. This overview is grounded in a literature review and based on an article in *Technovation* (Edvardsson et al. 2012). This section also presents a framework that suggests four modes of customer integration and categories of customer information in which data is classified either as in situ (data captured in a customer's use situation) or ex situ (data captured outside the use situation) and as either in context or ex context. Context is defined as a constellation of resources and the involved actors in a service system (Edvardsson 1997). Accordingly, in context refers to methods in which the customer is in the actual use context and has access to various resources, while ex context refers to a situation in which the customer is outside the use context and, therefore, has no direct access to the resources.

Customers' knowledge and experiences can be gained in different forms; for example, (1) problems and complaints, (2) ideas and suggestions, (3) behaviors and emotions that are important or sought after, and (4) visualizations, simulations or prototypes. All of these forms of information are

Resource context (resource constellations available to the customer)	Use situation (activities and interactions in a specific situation): **In situ**	Use situation (activities and interactions in a specific situation): **Ex situ**
In context	***The correspondent***, reporting live from the situation	***The reflective practitioner***, reporting from the armchair
Ex context	***The tester***, reporting from the virtual heaven	***The dreamer***, the creative who generates wild and imaginative ideas

Source: Edvardsson et al. (2012).

Figure 16.1 Framework for relating use information to methods for NSD

tightly linked to use knowledge, for which customers have a clear advantage over a company in terms of identifying and communicating them to another party. Figure 16.1 shows potential customer information in the form of four modes from the categorization of the situational and contextual variables. The methods for each mode are described in the following section.

- *The correspondent*. A customer who experiences a real service context and who is in or just about to enter a real-life value-creating situation. Information made possible by the position is resource anchored from the actual service context and from a use situation when value is created.
- *The reflective practitioner*. A customer who is in or has experience in a service context and who is not connected to a real-life value-creating situation. Information made possible by the position is resource-anchored from the actual service context and is decoupled from a real-life value-creating situation.
- *The tester*. A customer who has learned about the service context from outside and who simulates or tests a real-life value-creating situation. Information made possible by the position is decoupled from the actual service context experience and comes instead from a simulated or imagined use situation.

- *The dreamer*. A customer who has learned about a service context from outside and who is not connected to a real-life value-creating situation. Information made possible by the position is decoupled both from the actual service context experience and from a real-life value-creating situation.

Mode 1—The Correspondent

This mode is characterized by customers who are in a use situation with the intention to co-create value. This position has the potential to generate use-related information on the most important resources, resource integration activities and experience drivers.

Empathic design (Leonard 1995) is based on observation of customer behavior during the co-creation of value, including resource integration (for example, watching someone trying to use a photocopier), how use different resources available in a specific context, and how customers interact with other actors. This set of techniques investigates customers' use in order to find a suitable solution to service or product issues (Leonard and Rayport 1997).

The lead user method (Urban and von Hippel 1988; von Hippel 1986) focuses on pursuing trends from customers at the forefront in specific areas and use situations. They are lead users and have developed and adopted ways of co-creating value that most customers will experience at a later stage. The lead user method captures ideas, ways of co-creating value and customer experiences in its natural context. The aim is to develop novel ideas and processes that enable new service and more attractive customer experience.

Mode 2—The Reflective Practitioner

Much of the information used in service innovation originates from customers who are not in the service situation or do not really have an expressed need for service, but instead have experience from the service's resource context. The mode is characterized by users who are in, or have experience in, the actual service context but are ex situ; in other words, they are not in a real-life service situation that creates or intends to create value. They possess in-depth experience from specific use contexts and thus are capable of expressing what they would like to be changed and developed to arrive at a more favorable customer experience.

Participatory design (Ellis and Kurniawan 2000) is a method based on collaboration with and involvement of targeted customers throughout or in parts of the NSD process, such as in idea generation and evaluation or during concept testing. Consequently, developers can derive customers' reactions to and experiences of, as well as intentions to buy, various service concepts before the final development and market launch.

Living labs (Bergvall-Kåreborn et al. 2009; Schaffers et al. 2007) is a 'family of methods' that contains many different tools where simulation and visualization techniques are used. It usually involves a virtual spatial and servicescape context, either with physical material or with computer software. In living labs, customers act alone in the co-creation of value, in interaction with other customers as well as with employees and other stakeholders.

Mode 3—The Tester

Tester has no real-life experience regarding the service system and resource context, and will only have limited knowledge about what forms the basis for value co-creation and attractive customer experiences in context. However, these customers might be less restrictive in their thinking and provide more novel suggestions and "thinking out of the box". Conversely, the customers are in situ, which means that they have a real need and they want a service solution to a real-life problem. Therefore, the customers are in a position where they know what service will fulfill their needs, but they do not know the constellation of resources that could realize a new and attractive service.

Researchers using the information acceleration method (Urban et al. 1996) construct a virtual buying environment that simulates the information that is available to consumers when they make a purchase decision. The customer can actively use a modeled service in a specific context, making it possible for NSD developers to observe how value is co-created and whether there are any problematic aspects that need to be addressed before a market launch.

Mode 4—The Dreamer

The most common way to capture customer-centric information from this position is through methods in which the customer and the NSD developers asking for the information do not face each other, such as a survey or similar approach. Prospective users are encouraged to indicate their values, priorities, preferences, and other attributes related to use situations in the future by comparing them with the conditions and services available today.

The TRIZ method is based on the assumption that universal principles of invention exist that form the basis for creative innovation (Chai et al. 2005). TRIZ is highly versatile and can be used for ideation, customization, and problem-solving. TRIZ can also help to better understand resource integration and how customers use products and services, what value customers expect, and what value-drivers are critical as well as unimportant for an attractive experience. The final output is a list of possible innovative conceptual resource configurations to facilitate the NSD process and the service design.

In the free elicitation method (Bech-Larsen and Nielsen 1999), users are asked to express their feelings and preferences in relation to probes or cues by verbalizing the first thing that comes to mind. This is a method to capture what is on the top of the customer's mind and the most important customer experience-driver to create a basis for the NSD process, especially in the early phases.

Li et al. (2009) argued that service quality function development (SQFD) is a useful and rather common approach in NSD. The model is based on the notion that there are different gaps in the service development process. In the initial stage, companies collect information about customers through interviews or questionnaires to define their expectations, and analyze customer complaints to define what is most important for the customer in order to create an attractive new service.

SUMMARY AND CONCLUSIONS

In this chapter we have focused on the customer as the key actor when new service development is co-developed. This is enabled through the service system and the framework of why, when, how, and method used to involve the customer in developing new service. Our main question is, why is it worthwhile to involve customers in co-creating future offerings? The main reason, and the major explanation to the results, is likely to have to do with the difficulty in understanding customer needs. Von Hippel (2001) argues that use-environments are characterized by "sticky" or difficult-to-transfer information. Many times the reason why information is difficult to transfer has to do with the situation that customer needs are so deeply embedded in complex service systems and use-environments. Consequently, when customers are co-developers in an NSD project, it is important that they are in contact with, and act within, the service system where the new service is meant to create value-in-use. Ideas generated by a customer in the customer's own environment are more likely to contain those unique resources that companies seek but which are difficult to detect. Needs and requirements are likely to be, more or less consciously and deliberately from the customer's point of view, automatically built into the ideas generated. Ideas that a customer comes up with are likely to be about situations that often are embedded deeply in the users' own environments, and these are difficult to reach for companies and may also be hard to verbally explain in other types of market research (Kristensson et al. 2004).

Feelings and needs and the circumstances surrounding a certain offering may be the same as when you actually are experiencing the need. Before or after or in another service system the need is likely to take a different form and is therefore difficult to discover. An example of this would be when you have forgotten to bring a towel in your sport bag, intended for the shower after working out at the gym. When are you most likely to discover that you have neglected to pack this necessary value proposition? Will it be at work, in the car going to the gym, doing exercises in the gym, or when you are just about to take a shower? The answer seems obvious; you will discover your need when the need is present. In any other situation, you are much less likely to become cognitively aware of your need. Using this assumption, the empirical research presented here suggests that a company should invite customers to co-create with them when they develop a new service offering.

In essence, customer co-creation is a matter of communication. Companies cannot uncritically let customers co-create in all NSD projects; at least, not without some thought. Companies need to be aware that there are nuances and a number of challenges for the involved beneficiaries when it comes to designing service systems to enable value co-creation, and thus companies need to carefully consider why they want to involve the customers as co-developers in different phases on the NSD process. When companies want to achieve incremental innovations it is straightforward and more is more; customer input does help firms to be more successful in developing new offerings. For radical innovations, how companies co-develop with their customers is more complex. Spending time with customers and trying to understand their context is always beneficial, while being too constrained may hamper the radical capabilities. However, communication is essential here and, given the right way of communicating, the result may be different. The essential message is that companies need to adopt a mode of communication suited to purpose, that is, how radical the new service should be.

One piece of evidence that suggests that companies do not always think about how to involve customers is that interviews and focus groups are used in too many NSD projects. Managers often use interviews and focus groups because they know how to use them, know which consultant to use, and know how to interpret the results. The overuse of these market research techniques suggests that they are used in unsuitable situations and then provide bad information for certain decisions in the development process. Interviews and focus groups are suitable for capturing customers' spoken needs, which is useful for incremental innovations. These market research techniques should only be used in incremental innovation NSD projects.

Other market research techniques can be more useful for capturing latent needs and achieving radical innovations. Our research shows that methods of customer involvement provide more original ideas than traditional market research techniques. Through the involvement of customers, service developers obtain useful knowledge about customers' value-in-use contexts. Even though customer involvement is an interesting technique, there are other alternatives market research techniques that could provide similar results; examples are the lead user method and ethnographic methods such as contextual inquiry.

REFERENCES

Bech-Larsen, T. and N.A. Nielsen (1999), "A comparison of five elicitation techniques for elicitation of attributes of low involvement products", *Journal of Economic Psychology*, **20** (3), 315–41.

Bendapudi, N. and R.P. Leoni (2003), "Psychological implication of customer participation in co-production," *Journal of Marketing*, **67** (1), 14–28.

Bergvall-Kåreborn, B., C. Ihlström Eriksson, A. Ståhlbröst and J. Svensson (2009), "A milieu for innovation: defining living labs," ISPIM Innovation Symposium, New York City, p. 12.

Bonner, J.M. (2010), "Customer interactivity and new product performance: moderating effects of product newness and product embeddedness," *Industrial Marketing Management*, **39** (3), 485–92.

Chai, K., J. Zhang and K. Tan (2005), "A TRIZ-based method for new service design," *Journal of Service Research*, **8** (1), 48–66.

Chin, W.W. (1998), "The partial least squares approach to structural equation modeling", in G.A. Marcoulides (ed.), *Modern Methods for Business Research*, Mahwah, NJ: LEA.

Edvardsson, B. (1997), "Quality in new service development: key concepts and a frame of reference," *International Journal of Production Economics*, **52**, 31–46.

Edvardsson, B. and Olsson, J., (1996), "Key concepts in new service development", Service Industries Journal, Vol. 16 No. 2, pp. 140–64.

Edvardsson, B. and B. Tronvoll (2013), "A new conceptualization of service innovation grounded in S-D logic and service systems," *International Journal of Quality & Service Sciences*, in press.

Edvardsson, B., A. Gustafsson, M.D. Johnson and B. Sandén (2000), *New Service Development and Innovation in the New Economy*", Lund: Studentlitteratur.

Edvardsson, B., A. Gustafsson, P. Kristensson, P., Magnusson and J. Matthing (2006), *Involving Customers in New Service Development*, London: Imperial College Press.

Edvardsson, B., P. Kristensson, P, Magnusson E. and Sundström (2012), "Customer integration in service development and innovation – methods and a new framework," *Technovation*, **32** (7–8), 419–29.

Ellis, R.D. and S.H. Kurniawan (2000), "Increasing the usability of online information for older users: a case study in participatory design", *International Journal of Human-Computer Interaction*, **12**, 263–76.

Gruner, K.E. and C. Homburg (2000), "Does customer interaction enhance new product success?," *Journal of Business Research*, **49** (1), 1–14.

Gustafsson, A. and M.D. Johnson (2003), *Competing in a Service Economy: How to Create a Competitive Advantage through Service Development and Innovation*, San Francisco, CA: Jossey-Bass.

Gustafsson, A., P. Kristensson and L. Witell (2012), "Customer co-creation in service innovation – a matter of communication?," *Journal of Service Management*, **23** (3), 311–27.

Isaascson, W. (2011), *Steve Jobs*, New York: Simon and Schuster.

Johnson, M.D. (1998), *Customer Orientation and Market Action*, Upper Saddle River, NJ: Prentice Hall.

Kristensson, P., A. Gustafsson T. Archer (2004), "Harnessing the creative potential among users," *Journal of Product Innovation Management*, **21** (1), 4–14.

Leonard, D. (1995), *Wellsprings of Knowledge: Building and Sustaining the Sources of Innovation*, Boston, MA: Harvard Business School Press.

Leonard, D. and J.F. Rayport (1997), 'Spart innovation through empathic design," *Harvard Business Review*, **75** (6), 102–13.

Li, J.-H., L. Xu and X.-L. Wu (2009), "New service development using GAP-based QFD: a mobile telecommunication case," *International Journal of Services Technology and Management*, **12**, special issue, 146–74.

Lusch, R.F., S.L. Vargo and M. O'Brien (2007), "Competing through service: insights from service-dominant logic", *Journal of Retailing*, **83** (1), 5–18.

Lusch, R.F., S.L. Vargo and M. Tanniru (2010), "Service, value networks and learning", *Journal of the Academy of Marketing Science*, **38** (1), 19–31.

Maglio, P.P. and J. Spohrer (2008), "Fundamentals of service science", *Journal of the Academy of Marketing Science*, **36** (1), 18–20.

Merz, M.A., Y. He and S.L. Vargo (2009), "The evolving brand logic: a service-dominant logic perspective", *Journal of the Academy of Marketing Science*, **37** (3), 328–44.

Michel, S., S.W. Brown and A.S. Gallan (2008), "An expanded and strategic view of discontinuous innovations: deploying a service-dominant logic", *Journal of the Academy of Marketing Science*, **36** (1), 54–66.

Mohr, J. and J. Nevin (1990), "Communication strategies in marketing channels: a theoretical perspective", *Journal of Marketing*, **50** (1), 36–51.

Narver, J.C., S.F. Slater and D.L. MacLachlan (2004), "Responsive and proactive market orientation and new product success", *Journal of Product Innovation Management*, **21** (5), 334–47.

Normann, R. (2001), *Reframing Business: When the Map Changes the Landscape*, Chichester: Wiley.

Prahalad, C.K. and V. Ramaswamy (2000), "Co-opting customer competence", *Harvard Business Review*, **78** (1), 79–87.

Prahalad, C.K. and V. Ramaswamy (2004), *The Future of Competition: Co-Creating Unique Value with Customers*, Boston, MA: Harvard Business School Press.

Schaffers, H., M. Cordoba, P. Hongisto, T. Kallai, C. Merz and J. Rensburg (2007), "Exploring business models for open innovation in rural living labs," 13th International Conference on Concurrent Enterprising, Sophia-Antipolis, France, p. 13.

Skibstedt, J. and R. Bech Hansen (2011), "User-led innovation can't create breakthroughs; just ask Apple and IKEA", accessed 7 September 2011 at www.fastcodesign.com/1663220/user-led-innovation-cant-create-breakthroughs-just-ask-apple-and-ikea.

Song, X.M. and M.E. Parry (1997a), "A cross-national comparative study of new product development processes: Japan and the United States," *Journal of Marketing*, **61** (2), 1–19.

Song, X.M. and M.E. Parry (1997b), "The determinants of Japanese new product successes," *Journal of Marketing Research*, **34** (1), 64–76.

Spohrer, J., P.P. Maglio, J. Bailey and D. Gruhl (2007), "Steps toward a science of service systems," *Computer*, **40** (1), 71–7.

Trott, P. (2001), "The role of market research in the development of discontinuous new products," *European Journal of Innovation Management*, **4** (3), 117–25.

Urban, G.L. and E.von Hippel (1988), "Lead user analyses for the development of new industrial products," *Management Science*, **32** (2), 791–805.

Urban, G.L., J.R. Hauser, W.J. Qualls, B.D. Weinberg, J.D. Bohlmann and R.A Chicos

(1996), "Information acceleration: validation and lessons from the field," *Journal of Marketing Research*, **34** (1), 143–53.
Vargo, S.L. and R.F. Lusch (2004), "Evolving to a new dominant logic for marketing", *Journal of Marketing*, **68** (1), 1–17.
Vargo, S.L. and R.F. Lusch (2011), "It's all B2B . . . and beyond: toward a systems perspective of the market," *Industrial Marketing Management*, **40** (2), 181–7.
Verma, R., C. Anderson, M. Dixon, C. Enz, G. Thompson and L. Victorino (2008), "Key elements in service innovation: insights for the hospitality industry," *Cornell Center for Hospitality Research Managerial Reports*, **8** (18).
Von Hippel, E. (1986), "Lead users: a source of novel product concepts," *Management Science*, **32** (7), 791–805.
Von Hippel, E. (1994), "'Sticky information' and the locus of problem solving: implications for innovation", *Management Science*, **40** (4), 429–39.
Von Hippel, E. (2001), "Perspective: user toolkits for innovation," *Journal of Product Innovation Management*, **18** (4), 247–57.
Witell, L., P. Kristensson, A. Gustafsson and M. Löfgren (2011), "Idea generation: customer co-creation versus traditional market research techniques," *Journal of Service Management*, **22** (2), 140–59.
Wold, H. (1982), "Systems under indirect observation using PLS", in C. Fornell (ed.), *Second Generation of Multivariate Analysis Methods*, New York: Praeger, pp. 325–47.

17 Hybrid offerings: research avenues for implementing service growth strategies

Werner Reinartz and Wolfgang Ulaga

A business absolutely devoted to service will have only one worry about profits. They will be embarrassingly large.

(Henry Ford)

In the business-to-business (B2B) domain, the march towards a more significant share of turnover generated from the provision of services seems, at least in the coming years, unstoppable (for example, Antioco et al. 2008; Davies et al. 2006; Neu and Brown 2008). There are a number of explanations why product-centered companies are pursuing service strategies. Among these, three drivers of growth in B2B services are of particular interest:

1. *Outsourcing trends*. Over the past years, asset optimization has become an issue of growing concern to many business customers. With increasing expectations for a higher return on assets, more flexible production units, and further technological advances, customers increasingly focus on their core businesses and are more willing to outsource nonstrategic processes. As a consequence, vendors in many business markets have witnessed an increased demand for services.
2. *Saturation of installed base*. Many companies have discovered that it has become increasingly difficult to continue the growth of their installed base. Indeed, in many product markets, a firm's installed base outnumbers new equipment sales by far. As an example, with global revenues of \$1.8 billion in 2009, Electro-Motive Diesel (EMD) has the largest installed base of diesel-electric locomotives in the world and sold approximately 300 new locomotives worldwide while servicing an installed base of more than 70,000 engines throughout the world. Similarly, Fenwick, a leading European manufacturer of forklifts and part of the LINDE Material Handling Group, sold approximately 15,000 forklift trucks in France while also serving an installed base of 130,000. Since the mid-1990s, Fenwick developed multiple services based upon its traditional products. Currently, half of the company's sales are derived from a broad variety of services ranging from rentals and fleet management to smart services such as condition monitor-

ing, security management and even a training school for forklift truck drivers.

3. *Commoditization in product markets*. An increasing number of business customers rely on purchasing as a strategic weapon to improve their bottom line. Yet, as customers develop global sourcing strategies and scrutinize even long-established relationships, suppliers increasingly feel the pressure on equipment sales. Ongoing price erosions are fueled even further by a growing trend toward commoditization of products. Indeed, in many industries, it has become increasingly difficult for manufacturers to differentiate solely on the physical features of the product. Most suppliers, even from emerging economies, are able to satisfy the required product standards. Thus product parity, or the similarity of objective product performance, is propelling many product manufacturers into a hypercompetitive position.

From a scholarly perspective, we possess significant knowledge about the processes, antecedents, and consequences of designing and delivering successful service offerings (Parasuraman et al. 1988; Rust and Oliver 1994; Zeithaml et al. 1990). Yet extant literature predominantly refers to pure services in consumer marketing settings, some of which include the airline industry, financial services, hospitality, or retailing. The focus on pure services ignores a domain, which may be critical, known as hybrid offerings. Hybrid offerings are combinations of "one or more goods and one or more services which create more customer benefits than if the good and service were available separately" (Shankar et al. 2007, p. 2). This focus corresponds with the increasing research interest in the successful deployment of goods–service combinations (Antioco et al. 2008; Davies et al. 2006; Ostrom et al. 2010; Wise and Baumgartner 1999). In a recent paper (Ulaga and Reinartz 2011), we examined the key success factors for designing and delivering hybrid offerings in business markets. Employing case studies and in-depth interviews with senior executives in the manufacturing company setting, we created a resource–capability framework as a basis for research and practice.

Despite the general agreement among both executives and scholars about why goods-centric firms strive for growth through innovative hybrid offerings, we require an improved understanding of how they successfully implement such service-growth strategies. Extant literature in this domain, thus far, has not sufficiently addressed the critical challenges faced in the implementation process. Hence, to clarify this critical next step and to identify avenues for future research, the objectives of this book chapter are twofold:

- to outline the key characteristics of our original framework (Ulaga and Reinartz 2011), and
- to extend the framework by discussing implications in two critical areas which are immediately concerned with implementation challenges, that is, the required sales transformation process and the impact of leveraging smart technologies for service growth.

HYBRID-OFFERING FRAMEWORK

Ulaga and Reinartz (2011) implement a qualitative approach to investigate both the required resources and capabilities for a successful hybrid-offering approach. A pilot study, as well as 22 in-depth interviews with senior managers from large B2B manufacturing firms, constitute the data basis for the study. The core issues to be addressed include the identification of key resources and capabilities that goods-focused manufacturers will find essential when developing and generating successful hybrid offerings and also generating a typology of specific roll-out approaches for hybrid offerings which will then lead to specific recommendations.

The initial step will involve the identification of the unique resources that manufacturing firms either possess or can build more easily in comparison with pure service firms and that may be extremely critical and useful for developing hybrid offerings (Table 17.1). Generally speaking, a firm's resources are the stocks of available factors owned or controlled by the firm (Amit and Schoemaker 1993).

In contrast to resources, capabilities refer to a firm's capacity to deploy its resources (Amit and Schoemaker 1993). We derive a set of capabilities that are of particular use for the successful launch of hybrid offerings, appear to be more likely developed by goods-dominant firms with their unique resources, and are new to services and marketing literature (Table 17.2).

Finally, we emphasize two outcome variables that are of importance; specifically, cost reduction achieved through hybrid offerings and/or additional revenue generation. While these positional outcome variables are generic, albeit central, to the resource-based view literature, it must still be recognized that other outcome variables should not be disregarded. For example, the impact of hybrid offerings on customer satisfaction, on customer retention, or on the offering firm's image might also be taken into consideration. In combination, the conceptual framework outlines the key capabilities that are grounded in specific resources and are leading to a positional advantage for a successful hybrid-offering deployment (Figure 17.1).

The second essential aspect of our framework involves the development of a typology of hybrid offerings that permits an elaboration on the

Table 17.1 Definitions of resources

Resources	Definition
1. Installed base product usage and process data	The stock of product usage and customer process data collected through a firm's installed base of goods and/or used in customers' operations
2. Product development and manufacturing assets (PDMA)	The stock of resources invested in a firm's research and development (R&D) and manufacturing infrastructure. PDMA are of tangible and intangible nature
3. Product sales force and distribution network	The stock of resources tied in a firm's direct sales organization and channel intermediaries to cover its sales territory
4. Field service organization	The stock of resources allocated to a network of specialized technicians aimed at deploying and servicing the firm's installed base

Table 17.2 Definitions of capabilities

Capabilities	Definition
A. Service-related data processing and interpretation capability	The manufacturer's capacity to analyze and interpret installed base product usage and process data to help customers achieve productivity gains and/or cost reductions
B. Execution risk assessment and mitigation capability	The manufacturer's capacity to evaluate the uncertainty whether contractually agreed-upon outcomes will be realized and to design and implement safeguarding mechanisms to meet performance commitments while maintaining internal profit targets
C. Design-to-service capability	The manufacturer's capacity to integrate tangible and intangible offering elements synergistically to tap its potential for new revenue generation and/or cost reduction
D. Hybrid-offering sales capability	The manufacturer's capacity to reach key decision makers in the customer organization, coordinate key contacts in the customer and vendor firms, sell value based on specific documentation and communication tools, and align its sales force with the field organization and channel partners to grow revenues
E. Hybrid-offering deployment capability	The manufacturer's capacity to rely on flexible platforms that allow for standardizing production and delivery processes while safeguarding its ability to adapt to individual customers' needs

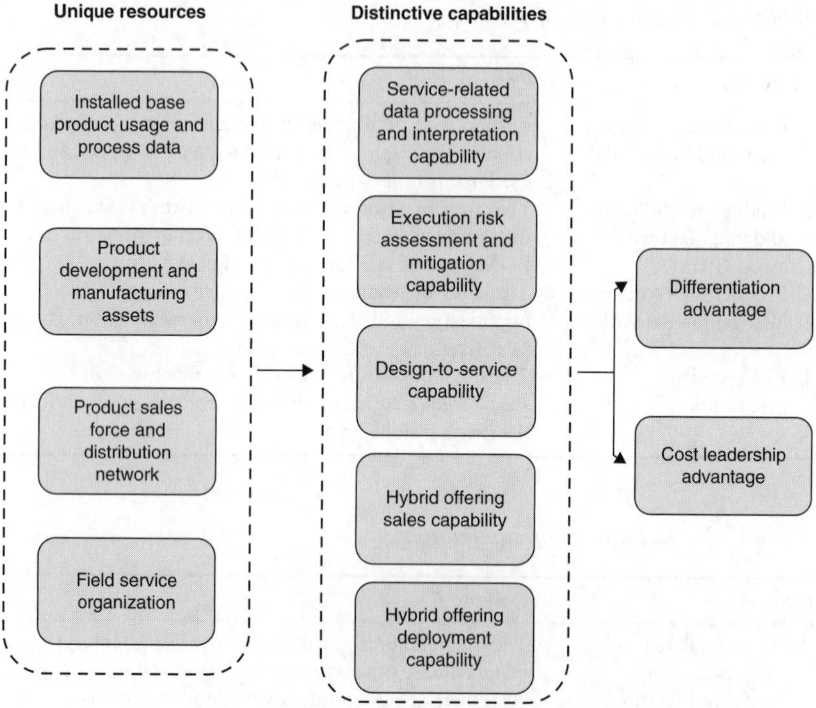

Figure 17.1 Manufacturer-specific resources and capabilities for successful hybrid offerings

granular discussion of the effects of resources and the capabilities on positional advantage. The key aspect to recognize in this instance is that services materialize in very heterogeneous good–service combinations. Therefore, it is essential that the framework addresses such heterogeneity. Even though an aggregate of classifications does exist in the literature (Boyt and Harvey 1997; Frambach et al. 1997; Lovelock 1983; Mathieu 2001; Samli et al. 1992), none of these classifications are particularly useful in the context of hybrid offerings. The newly proposed classification is constructed on two underlying dimensions and thus identifies four good–service combinations. The first dimension refers to whether the service is directed toward the supplier's good or geared toward the customer's process. The second dimension involves whether the supplier's value proposition is grounded in the promise to perform a deed (input based) or achieve performance (output based). The combination of these two dimensions elicits four categories that vary fundamentally in the key resources and capabilities required to deploy hybrid offerings in business markets (see Table 17.3).

Table 17.3 Classification scheme of industrial services for hybrid offerings

		Service recipient	
		Service oriented toward the supplier's good	Service oriented toward the customer's process
Nature of the value proposition	Supplier's promise to perform a deed (input based)	1. *Product lifecycle services (PLS)* Definition: Services to facilitate the customer's access to the supplier's good and ensure its proper functioning during all stages of the lifecycle Examples: Delivery of industrial cables Inspection of an ATM machine Re-grooving of an industrial tire Recycling of a power transformer	3. *Process support services (PSS)* Definition: Services to assist customers in improving their own business processes Examples: Energy efficiency audit for a commercial building Logistics consulting for material-handling processes in a warehouse
	Supplier's promise to achieve performance (output based)	2. *Asset efficiency services (AES)* Definition: Services to achieve productivity gains from assets invested by customers Examples: Remote monitoring of a jet engine Welding robot software customization	4. *Process delegation services (PDS)* Definition: Services to perform processes on behalf of the customers Examples: Tire fleet management on behalf of a trucking company Gas and chemicals supply management for a semi-conductor manufacturer

Product lifecycle services (PLS) refer to the range of services that facilitate the customer's access to the manufacturer's good and ensure its proper functioning during all stages of its lifecycle whether before, during, or after its sale. These services are directly in correlation with the supplier's good, therefore, the value proposition is derived from the most generic definition of service: a promise to perform a deed on behalf of the customer. While, in many cases, PLS are a 'must have' and, therefore, difficult to employ as a basis for differentiation, they may play an important role in establishing the vendor's reputation as a competent service provider.

In seeking that differentiation, certain firms move toward asset efficiency services (AES) to actively differentiate through new and distinctive value-added services that encompass their goods. Asset efficiency services target achieving productivity gains from assets invested by customers. Similar to PLS, asset efficiency services are directed toward the supplier's own product. More importantly, unlike PLS, AES are typically not considered as "must haves" among customers who displayed a higher willingness to pay for value-added AES.

While the two previous categories focus on services attached to a supplier's good, process support services (PSS) and process delegation services (PDS) place direct emphasis on their customers' processes. Process support services are the range of services provided by a manufacturer to assist customers in improving their own business processes. Thus, the value proposition focuses on leveraging the supplier's specialized competences to assist customers in optimizing processes or specific process elements within their operations. In other words, manufacturers commit to performing specific, process-oriented tasks that will assist customers in those things they must complete. However, vendors do not take responsibility for customer processes, nor do they manage processes on their behalf.

Process delegation services are the range of services a manufacturer provides when it performs processes on behalf of customers. Process delegation services are directed at the customer process, but contradictory to input-based PSS whereby customers retain control, suppliers go one step further in the PDS process and focus their value proposition on the promise to achieve process performance (that is, they are output-based offerings). The notion of "process delegation services" is deliberately favored over the frequently utilized and still ill-defined term of "customer solutions" in order to better capture the essence of such complex performance-based offerings. In our research, we identify six key characteristics of PDS: (1) integration of tangible and intangible elements into complex hybrid offerings; (2) customization of good–service combinations to account for individual customer needs; (3) co-creation and joint implementation of contractual arrangements; (4) alignment of interests of all parties involved;

(5) risk transfer from the customer to the vendor; and (6) gain-sharing of the value created in such complex agreements.

The benefit of the proposed framework is that it explicitly defines the capabilities that are valuable to manufacturers for venturing into hybrid offerings. Naturally, the relative importance of the various capabilities differs for each of the four types in Table 17.3. Generally speaking, as firms begin with PLS and eventually progress up to PDS, more and higher levels will be required of the various capabilities. Likewise, the mix of hybrid offerings tends to evolve over time, indicating that firms increase to higher levels only after consolidating their position in lower categories.

More importantly, the set of capabilities leads to the next, natural questions of how to build and how to manage those respective capabilities. Building on the existing framework, two important dimensions must be expounded upon. The first dimension—sales transformation process—relates to hybrid-offering sales capability. The second dimension—impact of smart technologies—provides further granularity on service-related data processing and interpretation capability.

SALES TRANSFORMATION PROCESS

Anecdotal evidence suggests that a manufacturer's sales force constitutes a major hurdle in the path toward a service-centric business model. For example, in our study (Reinartz and Ulaga 2008, pp. 94–5), we discovered evidence for powerful resistance to change from within sales organizations, such that even following extensive training, firms experience high levels of disturbance, faced with "little choice but to fire and hire; a few . . . replaced 80% of their existing sales forces." Similarly, we (Ulaga and Reinartz 2011) ascertained that only one-third of industrial salespeople transition smoothly to sales of hybrid offerings, and the majority of sales representatives require massive training in order to master the challenges, or prefer to be reassigned to sales of just goods-centric offerings. These disconcerting anecdotes emphasize the pivotal role of sales in the shift from a goods-centric to a service-centric business model. If "product salespeople are from Mars, while service salespeople are from Venus" (Ulaga and Reinartz 2011, p. 13), to what extent does the shift in corporate strategy toward a service-centric business model affect a company's industrial sales force? Are there fundamental differences between selling goods and hybrid offerings in industrial markets and, if so, how do these differences affect the nature of the selling process? Which distinctive sales capabilities are required to sell hybrid offerings in B2B markets? Finally, which personality traits resonate most with high-performing hybrid-offering salespeople as opposed to outstanding goods-centric sales representatives? To the best of our knowledge, academic research must still explore many of the critical aspects related to steering industrial sales organizations away from a product-centric toward a service-centric focus in order to increase revenues from hybrid offerings.

Extant Research on Product versus Services Sales in Industrial Markets

More than 30 years ago, Dubinsky and Rudelius (1980–81, p. 65) questioned: "Do you sell industrial services the same way as industrial products? Answers are vague or nonexistent." In their survey of 154 sales representatives, they discovered that salespeople emphasize various selling techniques for industrial goods and services such that "because of the intangibility of service, the same selling techniques used to sell a product are not always applicable when used to sell a service" (Dubinsky and Rudelius, 1980–81, p. 74). Despite continued research within the sales management domain, it appears that the answer to their key question remains far from obvious. Clarifying whether such differences exist and understanding how they affect the sales process, required sales skills, and distinctive salesperson attributes represent key prerequisites for mastering the transformation from a traditional goods-centric to a service-knowledgeable industrial sales force.

This transition has not gone unacknowledged. For example, Rackham and DeVincentis (1999) emphasize the requirement for different types of sales forces with opposing characteristics, and Cron and Decarlo (2010) note that executives believe that implementing their solution-selling model is one of the top three challenges for sales organizations. Thus growing consensus suggests that sales approaches and models cannot sufficiently nor currently account for the changes in complex B2B markets (Plouffe et al. 2008; Wang and Netemeyer 2004; Williams and Plouffe 2007), especially in relation to service transition strategies. Plouffe et al. (2008, p. 87) contend that "sales researchers have . . . ignored one of the most important trends in contemporary business—the shift away from a traditional goods-based economy toward service-based offerings." Hence, Tuli et al. (2007) ask for additional studies on solution sales cycles, and Bonney and Williams (2009) argue that, because solution sales require new sales capabilities, salesperson opportunity recognition should provide an innovative cognitive-based construct to explain solutions for salespersons' success. Storbacka et al. (2011) develop a framework for managing solution sales that identifies 28 pertinent management practices.

Ulaga and Loveland (2012) specifically examine key challenges that goods-dominant sales organizations are confronted with when transitioning toward hybrid-offering sales. Relying on focus groups and in-depth interviews with 38 sales executives at industrial corporations, these authors confirm the pivotal role of the industrial sales force in successfully mastering service transitioning strategies in business markets. The authors discovered that the firms in their sample underestimated the magnitude of change required at the level of their industrial sales organization. In-depth interviews and focus groups revealed that minor changes did not suffice in increasing revenues and profits through hybrid offerings that went beyond the manufacturers' traditional goods-centric sales core. As sales executives in their study explained, even firms with a dominant market position and a successful sales force often stumble when they venture into selling good–service combinations. The extensive human resource problems noted by our participants, including a powerful resistance to change and excessive agitation, offer a clear illustration of the issues at stake in the transformation.

Second, Ulaga and Loveland (2012) find four distinctive characteristics of the hybrid-offering sales process which are in contrast with traditional goods-centric sales. These specificities refer to (1) a sales model firmly grounded in a co-creation perspective as opposed to a traditional persuasion model in goods-centric sales; (2) the emphasis on specifying hybrid-offering requirements in cooperation with the customer rather than matching customer-initiated specifications with a vendor's preexisting (goods-based) offering; (3) the involvement of a broader and deeper network of stakeholders in both the customer's and vendor's organizations, rather than the narrower set of relationships with key actors in purchasing or operations; and (4) a focus on increasing the customer share throughout the vendor's installed base and not just acquiring new accounts and closing deals.

According to the authors, these distinctive characteristics impart important ramifications for the development of sales capabilities that are relevant to hybrid-offering sales. Ulaga and Loveland (2012) identify four key capabilities specifically resonating with hybrid-offering sales: (1) to gain a deep understanding of a customer's business model and operations and to leverage this intimate knowledge to identify selling opportunities; (2) to reach beyond a comfort zone of established contacts and manage a complex network of relationships in customer and vendor organizations; (3) to proactively manage customer expectations to ensure profitability not only for the initial sale but, over time, for contracts attached to hybrid-offering sales; and (4) to practice value selling in the context of hybrid offerings, such as by assisting customers in understanding the value of the intangible service elements as a component of industrial good–service combinations.

Finally, they identify 12 potentially relevant personality traits for a hybrid-offering sales context and discuss how the seven most frequently cited traits relate to performance. Specifically, they emphasize the roles of learning orientation, customer-service orientation, intrinsic motivation, general intelligence, emotional stability, teamwork orientation, and introversion (low extraversion). The authors additionally recognize that certain traits traditionally identified as relevant for goods-dominant sales appear irrelevant (or even detrimental) in a hybrid-offering sales context. Selected traits that emerge as particularly beneficial for the sale of industrial goods–service combinations similarly appear insignificant or even problematic in a goods sales context. In summary, these qualitative findings suggest that the profiles of a high-performing goods salesperson and a stellar performer in hybrid-offering sales likely diverge on several key personality traits. Thus, Ulaga and Loveland (2012) appear to confirm anecdotal evidence presented by Reinartz and Ulaga (2008) and Ulaga and Reinartz (2011) suggesting that goods salespeople are from Mars while, on the contrary, hybrid-offering salespeople appear to hail from Venus.

Future Research Agenda on the Sales Transformation Process

In combination, the emerging literature that is focused on the sales-force transition from a goods-centric sales force to a sales organization capable of growing revenues based on hybrid offerings emphasizes a number of important implications. First, hybrid-offering sales do not appear as being simply an extension of goods sales. Companies may be able to increase their sales of standard product lifecycle services such as extended warranties attached to equipment by employing their existing industrial sales force, but it would be inappropriate to expect competent, experienced, goods-centric salespeople to perform "business as usual" to sell complex combinations of goods and services in industrial markets. In particular, there appears to be a serious disparity between the demands placed on existing industrial sales forces and their capability to effectively sell hybrid offerings, as evidenced by the high rates of turnover among (otherwise efficient and effective) sales representatives.

Second, given the magnitude of transformation involved, the literature suggests that top management must become more deeply involved in managing the transformation. A company's industrial sales force plays a pivotal role in ensuring a successful service transition strategy. Steering the industrial sales organization from a goods-centric to a service-centric sales model requires full attention from C-level management. Such attention affects the manner in which salespersons are recruited, allocated, and trained. Consequently, industrial firms would be well advised to take an unbiased look at how they design their sales organization, develop coordination mechanisms for specialized sales forces, and redesign incentive structures to align the sales organizations with their overall corporate strategies.

Research on implementing service transitioning strategies on the sales organization's level remains in its infancy. Many questions to debate offering fruitful avenues for research on hybrid-offering sales are still unanswered. First, the initial findings presented by Ulaga and Loveland (2012) might explain some of the discrepancies in extant sales literature related to the links between job performance and the personality traits of industrial salespeople. Prior research has tended to view sales of industrial goods, services, and combinations thereof, as essentially identical. However, their results suggest the need to consider the specific sales context when determining the necessary traits for any particular sales job. Continued research is required to empirically validate the qualitative findings of prior studies in this domain. For example, combining survey data regarding personality traits with archival performance data related to goods versus hybrid-offering sales would provide an increased fine-grained understanding of the meaning and importance of the personality traits of high-performing goods and hybrid-offering salespeople.

Second, additional research might investigate how the sales process, required capabilities, and personality traits vary across the various categories of hybrid offerings. To accomplish this, scholars could rely on the taxonomy developed by us (Ulaga and Reinartz 2011) and presented in this chapter. Because hybrid offerings build more on customer processes and increasingly focus on outcomes, the traits identified in our study are likely to become ever more central to successful job performance.

Third, scholars could investigate a broader set of behaviors and traits. For example, researchers have suggested the value of an "intraorganizational navigation" construct (Plouffe and Gregoire 2011), or the ability of salespeople to work proactively across the internal environment of their firms. Other studies argue a competitive advantage of salespeople who can mobilize internal assets and build a strong understanding of their customers through robust networks (Hutt and Walker 2006). Understanding how to build and leverage such networks appears as a promising topic for future research.

Fourth, firms are not paying enough attention to how hybrid-offering sales are evaluated or rewarded. The sales and delivery processes are more complex, take longer to complete, and their outcomes are more difficult to measure, which creates a problem for customers as well who must wait to determine how efficiently and effectively the hybrid offerings deliver the desired results. Thus, periods of evaluation and incentives must be lagged as well. Therefore, investigating incentive systems and evaluation methods for hybrid-offerings sales—and determining how to measure the performance outcomes of hybrid offerings and the salespeople who sell them—represents an important theoretical and managerial concern when moving forward.

IMPACT OF SMART TECHNOLOGIES

While it is apparent that a service offering, in general, is very much the norm rather than the exception, currently, a company's service offerings must be differentiated from traditional services (for example, PLS); customers must perceive them as possessing entirely new value. One increasingly important way to do this is to make new service offerings "smart"—they must be preemptive and proactive rather than reactive—meaning that, in order to head off an undesirable event or to enable new opportunities, the action is based upon some form of automated field intelligence. Thus, if a vendor wants to advance beyond PLS, chances are that smart technologies will play a significant role.

Smart services are a fast-growing segment within the services domain extending to many business-to-business as well as business-to-consumer (B2C) settings, for example, mechanical engineering, healthcare, information and communication technology (ICT), automotive, and household appliances (Fano and Gershman 2002). In industries that rely on advanced ICTs, for example, medical devices, the percentage of smart service-enabled devices among companies' serviceable assets had dramatically increased from 11.7 percent in 2007 to 27.9 percent in 2009 (Dutta 2009; Wünderlich et al. 2013). This statistic implies that smart services are moving away from niche markets and penetrating the mainstream marketplace. Based on our research and interviews, enabling services and hybrid offerings to transform to 'smart' is one of the more prominent vectors of growth and differentiation in the service space.

In order to accomplish this, we first define what constitutes a "smart" service and, based on these defining characteristics, conceptualize smart services. Second, we illustrate the opportunities and challenges of two very differing smart services types, specifically, machine-to-machine (M2M) services and smart interactive services. We conclude with potential avenues for further research.

Definition and Conceptualization of Smart Services

Smart services can be defined by their cutting-edge use of ICT. Information and communication technology based functionalities are increasingly interjected into physical goods. The defining characteristic of smart services is the delivery to or through intelligent products featuring connectivity. These services wirelessly capture and analyze real-time product performance data that enables preemptive services based on actual evidence above and beyond proactive and reactive service provisioning (Allmendinger and Lombreglia 2005). Smart services are technology-mediated services, whereas classical services represent typically face-to-face services. However, it is important to note that a smart service encapsulates more than just mere technology. It also refers to a customer-centric view and strategy transforming that technology into a value-added service from the customer's point of view (knowwpc 2008). Hence, in order to deliver a service that is smart, a customer–provider interaction becomes essential. This heterogeneous group of services can exhibit various levels of customer and provider activity within the interaction that is involved in the service delivery process. Therefore, the type and the degree of interaction are both appropriate dimensions to differentiate smart services (Wünderlich et al. 2013). The type of interaction distinguishes between the provider's and the customer's activity level, and the degree of interaction refers to the intensity of this activity level. The activity levels of both the customers and the providers can range from low to high. A low customer activity level includes, for example, the mere deployment of smart objects, whereas a high customer activity level encompasses several conscious actions in sequence. A low provider activity level refers to the mere provision of connectivity between objects or the activation of procedures to be performed individually by the customer; a high activity level of the provider includes additional actions and increased intensity.

In the following discussion, we focus mainly on those two types of smart services that entail the most diverging characteristics regarding the customer–provider interaction continuum, specifically M2M and interactive services. Machine-to-machine services refer to smart services that are a component of both a low provider's and a low customer's activity level (Wünderlich et al. 2013). These types of smart services involve machines utilizing network resources to communicate with remote application infrastructures without any, or only a very low level, of human intervention to monitor and control either the machine itself or the surrounding environment. This indicates that M2M services do not just create a passive data collection point but also an intelligent inter-machine coordination ecosystem. To capture a so-called event, temperature or inventory level, for example, M2M services employ a device (for example, sensor or meter) which relays via a network to an application—the software program—translating the captured event into certain meaningful information, such as items requiring restocking (Krishnan and Sanyal 2010). Machine-to-machine services are smart services that can be highly automated and standardized and in which the degree of customer–provider interaction is rather low with systems as the counterpart on the provider side. Hence, no user collaboration and coproduction with the service provider is possible. In contrast, interactive services refer to smart services that possess both a high level of the provider's and the customer's activity. On the one hand, this type of smart service describes an embedded technology within the product that communicates object to object. On the other hand, it also includes a high level of personal interaction between the service-provider employee and the customer as a component of the service delivery process. It requires user collaboration with the service provider and leads to potentially high levels of service coproduction (Wünderlich et al. 2013). Examples in this category include industrial remote interactive repair and troubleshooting, information technology (IT) remote deployment, and infrastructure management. Unlike M2M services, interactive services cannot be automated and standardized but are highly customized, with people instead of systems as a counterpart on the provider side (Schumann et al. 2012).

The promise for smart services is great. For example, companies employing a smart service can, on average, support asset uptimes that are 12 percent higher than those companies that do not utilize smart services. In this case, the difference of a 12 percent asset uptime can equate to about €23 million in annual revenues for a €192 million company (nPhase 2007). In terms of revenue, M2M services are predicted to dramatically increase from €91 billion in 2010 to €714 billion in 2020, a compound annual growth rate (CAGR) of 22.9 percent (Machina Research 2011). However, the necessity of high coordination capabilities and investments in hardware, for example, leads the provider to confront several risks associated with smart services. Thus, it should be pointed out that the process of the shift from (simple) PLS to smart services may not be only advantageous for the provider but may also contain challenges, as discussed in the following section.

Opportunities and Challenges in the Shift from Classical to Smart Services

Opportunities and challenges of M2M services

Machine-to-machine services enable an enhancement in the level of automation and standardization and, hence, optimize asset performance and utilization. Owing to the preemptive control ascertained with M2M services, further manifold efficiency gains such as minimization of failures, prevention of problems, and shortening response and downtimes may be realized. This efficiency and control of resources can, sequentially, lead to a decrease in cost level but an increase in productivity level. Obtaining data from remote diagnostics and real-time statistics advances the provider's capability of smarter and better informed decision making which can then, subsequently, advance the service offering's quality, leading to financial opportunities such as increasing revenues. The possibility of monitoring and controlling business processes anytime and anywhere, providing that Internet access is available, permits a high degree of flexibility, convenience, and availability for customers. Typically, these service-based offerings represent AES-type offerings which are likely to provide new sources of ongoing revenues throughout the product lifecycle. Accordingly, we conclude that the opportunities of M2M services mainly refer to internal opportunities, such as operational and capability as well as financial aspects, for a provider.

However, the shift from classical to M2M services may also pose certain challenges. Owing to the fact that, with M2M services, a greater amount of data is available for more participants, business processes will transform and providers must improve the training of their employees (Lawton 2004) to improve their abilities in manipulating these data numbers in order to create viable information. To deploy a suitable M2M solution, a high-technology readiness is required with a diversity of hardware and software components that must be integrated to lead to a high degree of complexity (Lawton 2004). It becomes essential for the provider to acquire internal resources, capabilities, and competencies from a variety of internal stakeholders in order to develop suitable M2M services. This confusing realm can result in failure for a provider when developing effective M2M services, as the provider is not able to optimally allocate required resources over the different domains. Hence, the provider faces certain capability challenges shifting from classical to M2M services. Investments in these components may be very expensive, and the provider's intense efforts to gather resources and capabilities and the high level of complexity may make it difficult to increase margins for these types of smart services, leading to financial challenges for the providers. In addition to these internal challenges, external challenges such as market challenges, that is, the possibility that the customer does not adopt the M2M service, are a key concern.[1] One explanation for this nonadoption may perhaps be due to a security concern of the customer fearing hackers breaking into the M2M applications designed to control, for example, building security or environmental-control systems (Lawton 2004). Another explanation why customers do not wish to adopt M2M services could be the absence of transparency of service provision processes in smart service settings (Wünderlich et al. 2013). Hence, the provider must create transparency in the service provision processes and their quality for the customers, as it is difficult for the customer to evaluate the time, effort, and quality of the service work when they are not able to ascertain if the provider is actually involved in the project. A further aspect that is important to mention is the relationship challenge in the M2M

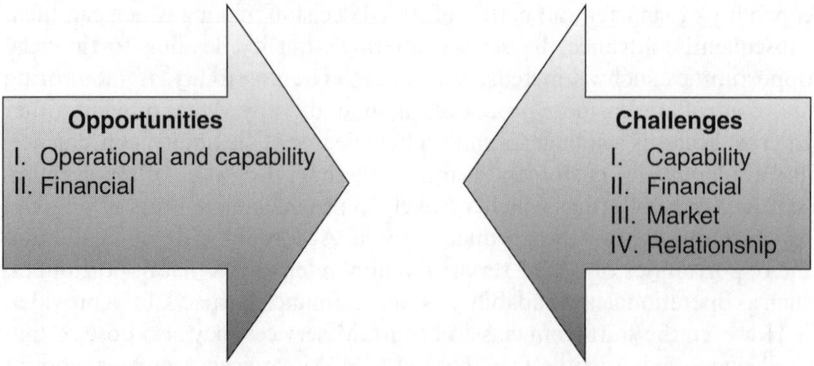

Figure 17.2 Opportunities and challenges in the shift from classical to M2M services

service setting that combines the internal and external provider's perspective and refers to the loss of personal interaction and social exchange. In M2M services, the provider and the customer interact solely on an object-to-object basis, which means a lack of personal contact and, hence, reduces possibilities of exchanging and developing friendliness and empathy—important determinants for developing trust, value, and customer loyalty. Furthermore, this lack of personal contact can also reduce the potential for cross-selling and up-selling for the provider, owing to limited information on its customer needs (Schumann et al. 2012). Figure 17.2 summarizes these opportunities and challenges of shifting from classical to M2M services.

Opportunities and challenges of interactive services

In contrast to the opportunities of M2M services, the opportunities of interactive services focus mainly on the possibility to build close, long-lasting and collaborative relationships between the service provider and its customers. Here, similar to PDS, highly customized services are offered, instead of automated and standardized ones. The stronger interactivity in terms of communication and information exchanges between the provider and customer that is required in interactive service selling (compared to classical, face-to-face and M2M service selling) should produce strong, collaborative relationships with high levels of trust and cooperation (see also Fang et al. 2008; Kumar and Reinartz 2012). The required user collaboration with the service provider can result in high levels of service coproduction—one of the main drivers of service usage, service effectiveness, customer satisfaction, value perception, quality, and recovery (Wünderlich et al. 2013). Owing to the technology mediation in smart service selling, these services are more intangible to the customer and, therefore, are more difficult to evaluate, leading to a decrease in market transparency but an increase in the customer's perceived purchase risk (Fang et al. 2008). Owing to the fact that the service provider has developed an individually tailored, highly customized and integrated smart interactive service to solve a customer's particular problem, the provider becomes increasingly important to the customer and, likewise, the customer becomes dependent or locked into the relationship. Ensuring that the customer's needs and requirements are fulfilled, and effective interactive services are developed, respectively, the customer participates in interactive service selling and adopts this new type of smart service. Hence, long-term and loyal relationships can be established by selling smart interactive services, accelerating customer lifetime value (see also Kumar and Reinartz 2012).

Based on the opportunities of interactive services as outlined above, it becomes clear that one of the main challenges from the provider's point of view is the market challenge; the risk that the customer does not participate in interactive service selling or does not adopt this new type of customized smart service, which will then lead to failure of establishing loyal relationships. Since interactive services require that providers as well as customers have both tacit (experiential) and codified knowledge (Chesbrough 2004), information sharing is a critical component of participation in interactive services (Bolton and Saxena-Iyer 2009). Hence, one market challenge for the provider is to guarantee information-sharing behavior to the customer in order to develop suitable and customized interactive services. Only if the provider has knowledge about the customer's specific problems and needs can an effective smart interactive service be developed, implemented and fulfill the customer's requirements and needs. Regarding the participation in, and adoption of, smart interactive services, the perception of control and transparency of the customer through technology-mediated interaction plays an additional major role.[2] Control over and transparency in the service process itself and the provider's actions are very important for the customers. Whereas in a classical, face-to-face service setting, the customer has the ability to directly monitor and take corrective actions, this is not possible within a smart (interactive) service setting. Hence, customers believe these smart (interactive) services to be risky and, therefore, search for tangible and transparent cues about this interactive collaboration process. Thus, the provider faces certain capability challenges for building these cues. In this context, the creation of trustworthiness—comprising goodwill, reliability, and expertise of the service provider—through technology-mediated interaction becomes essential because the provider's actions are not directly visible to the customer.[3] This perception of the provider's trustworthiness may positively influence a customer's attitudinal and behavioral responses

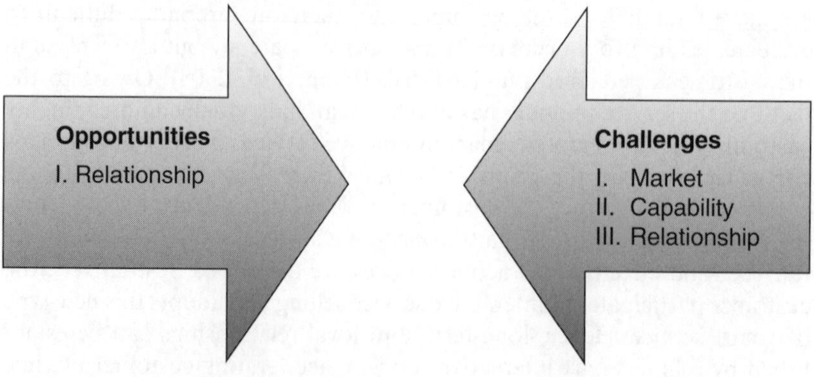

Figure 17.3 Opportunities and challenges in the shift from classical to interactive services

to smart (interactive) services. One aspect that can assist in positively influencing trustworthiness and control perceptions is the discernment of social presence of a service employee, reflecting another capability challenge for the service provider. The perception of social presence of a service employee describes the extent to which an interactive smart service allows the customers to experience the human interaction partner as being virtually present. Owing to the fact that interactive services are intensively coproduced by both the provider and the customer, the customer's attitude toward this collaboration as reflected in willingness to collaborate, perceptions of role clarity, guidance, and self-efficacy, presents a relationship challenge for the provider in the shift to interactive smart services. This customer's collaboration belief can be seen as an important driver of attitudes and behaviors toward the interactive service. Figure 17.3 summarizes these opportunities and challenges of shifting from classical to interactive services.

In summary, concerning the opportunities and challenges of M2M and interactive services, we emphasize that these are (a) mainly technology and complexity related for M2M services, and (b) mainly relationship and collaboration related for interactive services. Based on the apparent opportunities and challenges of M2M and interactive services, a future research agenda for these smart services is formulated.

Future Research Agenda for Smart Services

Research directions for M2M services

With respect to avoiding capability risks, it is necessary, from the provider's point of view, to understand how business processes must be changed and how employees are to be trained to enable them to manipulate significant amounts of data. Furthermore, it is important to analyze how internal decision-making processes should be optimally coordinated among various internal stakeholder groups. Finally, which resources, capabilities, and competencies are necessary at different stages of the M2M service development and implementation process? Focusing the market challenges of M2M services, one fruitful avenue for further research is to investigate customers' adoption and usage drivers of M2M services. Examples include the manner in which the provider can create more transparency for the consumer in the service provision processes in order to facilitate the evaluation of time, effort, and quality of the service. Additionally, the knowledge of customer needs in an object-to-object communication setting as a determinant to effectively design smart service offerings is essential. Effective smart service offerings can lead to a high degree of customer satisfaction and, hence, it is important to analyze under which conditions M2M services lead to an increase in customer satisfaction. This increase in customer satisfaction can, in turn, offer certain relationship opportunities for the provider. In this context, it is especially relevant to investigate how the loss of personal interaction and societal exchange is perceived by the customer and how the reduced possibilities of exchanging and developing friendliness, empathy, and sympathy can be compensated in this object-to-object communication setting.

Research directions for interactive services

During interactive services experiences, it would probably be valuable to empirically investigate what service design features and provider actions encourage customers to share different types of information with the provider (Bolton and Saxena-Iyer 2009), allowing the provider an opportunity to develop effective interactive service offerings and eliminate the market challenges, respectively. Furthermore, it might be interesting to analyze whether and how customer perceptions of control and transparency, trustworthiness, social presence, and collaboration influence the acceptance of interactive services, and whether some factors are more or less important depending on the acceptance stage (the following aspects refer to Wünderlich et al. 2013). Focusing on control and transparency as capability challenges, a provider should know what kind of tangible and intangible features (for example, buttons, control panels, mechanisms, and processes) increase or decrease customer control beliefs. Additionally, which factors influence the perceived transparency of a smart service process, and can an increase in transparency reduce customer risk perceptions? Regarding a provider's trustworthiness, it might be fruitful to analyze how a customer judges this trustworthiness and to investigate possible dimensions and drivers of that trustworthiness. To overcome further capability challenges, a provider should know what affects trustworthiness before, during, and after the smart interactive service interaction. Enforcing trust building and offering control mechanisms describes a trade-off; hence, it should also be questioned where the ideal trade-off is in order to raise customer perceptions and whether this trade-off changes in the event that the customer experiences a service failure. Does the provision of control mechanisms automatically lead to a higher perception of trustworthiness? Regarding the social presence in the smart interactive service setting, it is essential to realize how social presence can be established and with which media it can best be established, respectively. Furthermore, a provider should know to what extent this social presence can, in turn, increase trustworthiness and decrease risk perceptions in this context. Owing to the fact that collaboration between the customer and the provider is essential in a smart interactive service context, the main future research questions concern the relationship challenge. In this context, it might be interesting to analyze how to increase the customer's motivation to collaborate, for example, whether descriptions of roles should be formally fixed or freely negotiated and whether customer collaboration is always beneficial for the provider. If this is not always the case, it must be examined under which circumstances this collaboration is beneficial. Cumulatively, there is a need for a better understanding of how characteristics of interactive services (servicescape, design, people, processes, and technology) influence customers' perceptions (for example, of service quality), preferences and behavior (for example, usage) concerning interactive services (Bolton and Saxena-Iyer 2009).

NOTES

1. The classification into capability, financial, and market challenges refers to a classification used by Sawhney et al. (2004) to classify the risks occurring in the process of service migration. For the argumentation concerning the capability, financial, and market challenges, see also Kumar and Reinartz (2012) who examine the disadvantages of the shift to hybrid offerings. Their argumentation also holds for the context of smart services.
2. The following issues refer to aspects mentioned in the context of smart interactive services by Wünderlich et al. (2013).
3. It becomes clear that, for example, control, transparency, and trustworthiness are challenging aspects for providers in both smart service settings—M2M and interactive services. The opportunities and challenges mentioned for M2M and interactive services are thus not to be seen as mutually exclusive but rather describe the most prevalent aspects occurring in the two different smart service settings. Because control, transparency, and trustworthiness are aspects mentioned in the context of smart interactive services by Wünderlich et al. (2013), we also refer to those aspects as challenges mainly occurring in the interactive service context and not in the M2M service context.

REFERENCES

Allmendinger, Glen and Ralph Lombreglia (2005), "Four strategies for the age of smart services," *Harvard Business Review*, **83** (10), 131–45.
Amit, Raphael and Paul J.H. Schoemaker (1993), "Strategic assets and organizational rent," *Strategic Management Journal*, **14** (1), 33–46.
Antioco, Michael, Rudy K. Moenaert, Adam Lindgreen and Martin Wetzels (2008), "Organizational antecedents and consequences of service business orientations in manufacturing companies," *Journal of the Academy of Marketing Science*, **36** (3), 337–58.
Bolton, Ruth and Shruti Saxena-Iyer (2009), "Interactive services: a framework, synthesis and research directions," *Journal of Interactive Marketing*, **23** (1), 91–104.
Bonney, F.L. and B.C. Williams (2009), "From products to solutions: the role of salesperson opportunity recognition," *European Journal of Marketing*, **43** (7–8), 1032–52.
Boyt, Tom and Michael Harvey (1997), "Classification of industrial services: a model with strategic implications," *Industrial Marketing Management*, **26** (4), 291–300.
Chesbrough, Henry (2004), "A failing grade for the innovation academy," *Financial Times*, 25 September.
Cron, W.L. and T.E. Decarlo (2010), *Sales Management: Concepts and Cases*, 10th edn, Hoboken, NJ: John Wiley & Sons.
Davies, Andrew, Tim Brady and Michael Hobday (2006), "Charting a path toward integrated solutions," *MIT Sloan Management Review*, **47** (3), 39–48.
Dubinsky, Alan J. and William Rudelius (1980–81), "Selling techniques for industrial products and services: are they different?" *Journal of Personal Selling and Sales Management*, **1** (1), 65–75.
Dutta, Sumair (2009), *The Evolution of Remote Product Service and the Emergence of Smart Services*, Boston, MA: Aberdeen.
Fang, Eric, Robert W. Palmatier and Jan-Benedict Steenkamp (2008), "Effect of service transition strategies on firm value," *Journal of Marketing*, **72** (September), 1–14.
Fano, Andrew and Anatole Gershman (2002), "The future of business services in the age of ubiquitous computing," *Communications of the ACM*, **45** (12), 83–7.
Frambach, Ruud T., Inge Wels-Lips and Arjan Guendlach (1997), "Proactive product service strategies: an application in the European health market," *Industrial Marketing Management*, **26** (4), 341–52.
Hutt, M.D. and B.A. Walker (2006), "A network perspective of account manager performance," *Journal of Business & Industrial Marketing*, **21** (7), 466–73.
knowwpc (2008), "Smart services: customer focus turns technology into solutions," accessed 23 September 2012 at http://knowwpcarey.com/article.cfm?cid=25&aid=399.
Krishnan, V. and Bhaswar Sanyal (2010), "M2M Technology: Challenges and Opportunities," Tech Mahindra, White Paper, 2010.30.
Kumar, V. and Werner Reinartz (2012), *Customer Relationship Management – Concept, Strategy, and Tools*, Berlin/Heidelberg: Springer.
Lawton, George (2004), "Machine-to-machine technology gears up for growth," *Computer*, **37** (9), 12–15.
Lovelock, Christopher H. (1983), "Classifying services to gain strategic marketing insights," *Journal of Marketing*, **47** (3), 9–20.
Machina Research (2011), "M2M global forecast & analysis 2010–20," accessed 23 September 2012 at www.machinaresearch.com/sitebuildercontent/sitebuilderfiles/machina_research_press_release_m2m_global_forecast_analysis_2010_20.pdf.
Mathieu, Valérie (2001), "Product services: from a service supporting the product to a service supporting the client," *Journal of Business & Industrial Marketing*, **36** (1), 39–58.
Neu, Wayne and Stephen W. Brown (2008), "Manufacturers forming successful complex business services," *International Journal of Service Industry Management*, **19** (2), 232–51.
nPhase (2007), "The Art of Smart Services – Volume 1: Building the Business Case," QUALCOMM White Paper, May.
Ostrom, Amy L., Mary Jo Bitner, Stephen W. Brown, Kevin Burkhard, Michael Goul,

Vicki Smith-Daniels, Haluk Demirkan and Elliot Rabinovich (2010), "Moving forward and making a difference: research priorities for the science of service," *Journal of Service Research*, **13** (1), 4–36.
Parasuraman, A., Valarie A. Zeithaml and Leonard L. Berry (1988), "SERVQUAL: a multiple-item scale for measuring consumer perceptions of service quality," *Journal of Retailing*, **64** (1), 12–40.
Plouffe, C.R. and Y. Gregoire (2011), "Intraorganizational employee navigation and socially derived outcomes: conceptualization, validation, and effects on overall performance," *Personnel Psychology*, **64** (3), 693–738.
Plouffe, C.R., B.C. Williams and T. Wachner (2008), "Navigating difficult waters: publishing trends and scholarship in sales research," *Journal of Personal Selling & Sales Management*, **28** (1), 79–92.
Rackham, N. and J.R. DeVincentis (1999), *Rethinking the Sales Force: Redefining Selling to Create and Capture Customer Value*, New York: McGraw-Hill.
Reinartz, Werner and Wolfgang Ulaga (2008), "How to sell services profitably," *Harvard Business Review*, **86** (5), 90–98.
Rust, Roland T. and Richard Oliver (1994), "Service quality: insights and managerial implications from the frontier," in R.T. Rust and R.L. Oliver (eds), *Service Quality: New Directions in Theory and Practice*, Thousand Oaks, CA: Sage Publications.
Samli, A. Coskun, Laurence W. Jacobs and James Wills (1992), "What presale and postsale services do you need to be competitive?" *Industrial Marketing Management*, **21** (February), 33–41.
Sawhney, Mohanbir, Sridhar Balasubramanian and Vish V. Krishnan (2004), "Creating growth with services," *MIT Sloan Management Review*, **45** (2), 34–43.
Schumann, Jan H., Nancy V. Wünderlich and Florian v. Wangenheim (2012), "Technology mediation in service delivery: a new typology and an agenda for managers and academics," *Technovation*, **32** (2), 133–43.
Shankar, Venkatesh, Leonard L. Berry and Thomas Dotzel (2007), "Creating and managing hybrid innovations," AMA Winter Educators' Conference, San Diego, CA, February.
Storbacka, K., P. Polsa and M. Sääksjärvi (2011), "Management practices in solution sales – a multilevel and cross-functional framework," *Journal of Personal Selling and Sales Management*, **31** (1), 35–54.
Tuli, Kapil R., Ajay K. Kohli and Sundar G. Bharadwaj (2007), "Rethinking business solutions: from product bundles to relational processes," *Journal of Marketing*, **71** (3), 1–17.
Ulaga, W. and J. Loveland (2012), "Implementing service growth strategies in industrial markets: the role of the sales force," *Proceedings AMA Summer Marketing Educators' Conference*, Chicago, 16–19 August.
Ulaga, Wolfgang and Werner Reinartz (2011), "Hybrid offerings: how manufacturing firms combine goods and services successfully", *Journal of Marketing*, **75** (6), 5–23.
Wang, G. and R.G. Netemeyer (2004), "Salesperson creative performance: conceptualization, measurement and nomological validity," *Journal of Business Research*, **57** (8), 805–12.
Williams, B.C. and C.R. Plouffe (2007), "Assessing the evolution of sales knowledge: a 20-content analysis," *Industrial Marketing Management*, **36** (4), 408–19.
Wise, Richard and Peter Baumgartner (1999), "Go downstream: the new profit imperative in manufacturing," *Harvard Business Review*, **77** (5), 133–41.
Wünderlich, Nancy V., Florian v. Wangenheim and Mary Jo Bitner (2013), "High tech and high touch: a framework for understanding user attitudes and behaviors related to smart interactive services," *Journal of Service Research*, **16** (1), 3–20.
Zeithaml, Valarie A., A. Parasuraman and Leonard L. Berry (1990), *Delivering Quality Service: Balancing Customer Perceptions and Expectations*, New York: Free Press.

PART VI

DIGITAL SERVICE MARKETING

18 Adaptive personalization of mobile information services

Tuck Siong Chung and Michel Wedel

1 INTRODUCTION

In the past decade, the development and use of information services have been expanding exponentially. Innovations in communication technology have reduced fixed and variable cost, and have increased the demand for these services. At the same time, due to increased market opportunities and low barriers to entry, competitive pressures have risen and service providers have tried to command higher margins by innovating and by differentiating their offerings (Rust and Chung 2006). Technology innovations have thus made personalization profitable in mass production (Varki and Rust 1998). As a consequence, consumer choice options continue to increase rapidly, especially in categories such as music, news, travel, entertainment, and games. As a result of the very large number of available alternatives, consumers of these services increasingly rely on product reviews. Almost three-quarters of consumers in the U.S. reported having done so.[1] Over half of consumers consider user reviews to be the most trustworthy source of product information. However, online user reviews have limitations. These reviews rely on proactive user input, which many consumers are unwilling or unable to give. Furthermore, users differ in the way they use "star" rating scales or binary "like" items. Finally, online product and service ratings are subject to shilling attacks (see Chung et al. 2009 and Rust et al. 2010 for reviews).

In most information service categories, personalization has not only become feasible, but has evolved as an important competitive strategy as well. It makes the meeting of individual customer needs better and makes competitive retaliation more difficult (Sun 2006; Syam and Kumar 2006). Personalization is predicated based on sufficiently detailed customer data and analytical tools that help in recognizing differences in behavior between consumers and in identifying marketing opportunities. With continuing advancements in technology, marketers have had access to ever more detailed customer data to help personalize services, and to increasing means to reach individual customers. Targeting customers at a more detailed level leads to greater revenue as a result of customers' willingness to pay for products and services that better meet their individual needs. However, personalization often comes at an increased cost. Costs of personalized service development, distribution, advertising, pricing and promotion can be substantial. Companies therefore need to make strategic choices separately for each marketing mix variable between targeting their customers at the mass, segment, or individual levels, using profitability as a guide. For example, fast-moving consumer products companies such as PepsiCo develop and sustain global brands, advertise to segments in the market, and deliver sales promotions online at the individual level and through social media. Especially for products for which substantial economies of scale exist in development, distribution, advertising, pricing or promotion, mass- or segment-level marketing will lead to higher profitability. Economies of scale can potentially be realized for each element of the marketing mix, but particularly in product development and distribution of traditional product categories such as fast-moving consumer goods, cars, durables and electronics.

However, if economies of scale are small or negligible and production, distribution and communication processes are flexible, it is profitable to target customers individually. Such negligible economies of scale typically occur for information service categories, such as music, news, gaming, e-books, and movie-streaming. Personalized marketing for these categories is particularly effective in the online environment (Zhang and Wedel 2009), which is increasingly the primary channel through which such services are delivered and marketed. Online companies in particular may exploit high levels of detail for each of their marketing control instruments. Production, logistics, pricing, advertising, promotion, and after sales service are all viable candidates for personalization. New media continue to drive down the costs of personalization and continue to contribute to its success and profitability. Moreover, personalization can only be fully implemented with sufficiently detailed individual-level customer behavior data. Advancements in interactive media have facilitated the collection of such data and have reduced its cost.

Recently two converging trends, the increasing penetration of mobile devices and the increasing penetration of social networks, are producing significant opportunities for further growth of service personalization. This is true especially when mobile devices like iPhone and Android devices have been introduced into the market and become exceedingly versatile. They possess capabilities like global positioning, web surfing, social networking, e-book reading, gaming, and music and video playing, just to name a few. Currently, there are over 5 billion mobile devices being used across the world (BBC News 2010). The dividing line between cell phones and personal computers is increasingly harder to define, with the advent of devices that fall in between the two categories like tablet computers and e-readers with web-browsing functionality. Moreover, facilitated by impressive computing and storage capabilities, a wide range of domain-specific information services has been developed. Over 1.5 billion apps were downloaded from the App-store within the first year of its operation in categories such as games, news, sports, health, reference, and travel. Mobile devices are now the primary source not only for telecommunication, but also for music, information, shopping, entertainment, and news. Just a few examples of the information services developed are Pandora, which offers a personalized radio station on mobile phones, and its competitors Spotify and Last.fm, and Flipbook, which is a news aggregator that displays news headlines and pictures in a magazine style, and its competitors Zite and Google Currents, which have similar functionality.

However, providing information services over mobile devices also comes with its challenges. In particular, because of the size of the display and users' shorter attention spans on these devices, it is more difficult for users to browse the many available alternatives to find personally relevant information services. Providing consumers with more limited, but more relevant, choice options is thus critical and personalization of information based on the user's demographic profile, preference, and current location and task is becoming increasingly popular.

In addition, more and more services on the Internet facilitate social networking, where individuals link to a network of other individuals. Some of the most successful Internet companies of recent years have developed and taken advantage of this capability, including Facebook, LinkedIn and Twitter. Facebook had over 500 million users in 2011 (www.Bloomberg.com). Mobile social networking is on the rise. The audience for mobile social networking in the European Union (EU) region grew by over 40 percent in 2011, with over 55 million mobile users in the five largest EU countries alone.[2] These users access social networking sites via their mobile devices, more than half on a daily basis. The advent of mobile social networking apps is to a large extent responsible for this growth. Myspace, Facebook and MSN are worldwide leaders in mobile social networking. Facebook alone has over 400 million mobile users worldwide; its mobile usage grew over 50 percent in 2011. The number of mobile social networking services is also continuing to expand. For example, Brightkite and Fon11 allow people to keep track of the location of their friends in their network, and of these friends' status, at any moment. With these services, users send updates via Global Positioning System (GPS), text or email messages, to update their location, pictures, and profile. Strands started out as a mobile social networking service for music discovery. It now features a mobile Web portal and a personalized radio station. Strands' mobile social networking service enables its users to find music and network with their friends via their mobile phones. The music streaming service Spotify, with more than 10 million users, has partnered with Facebook to give people access to their friends' favorite music and playlists, and allow for active music sharing as well. Itsmy, with more than 1 million registered mobile users, has launched 100,000 personal mobile television channels, one for every ten of its users.

From these trends we can see that closed-loop marketing (CLM) is emerging as a major strategic option. There has been an increase in the popularity of this approach in online and mobile applications in several industries. In CLM research and development (R&D), marketing research and marketing are not seen as separate stages located in functionally and physically distinct departments of the company. Instead, CLM comprises a cycle in which customer information is continuously collected and updated, and advanced analytics are used to forecast customer behavior and to redesign and personalize products, services and marketing effort in short cycles (see Figure 18.1). Closed-loop monitoring has already realized some of its potential in the financial, hospitality, retailing, and pharmaceutical industries, among others (Capgemini 2008). Yet, it is likely to have even greater potential for online and mobile personalization of information services. Whereas many of the current approaches require the manual execution of the different CLM stages, information technology enables fully automated CLM systems in online and mobile environments. Some

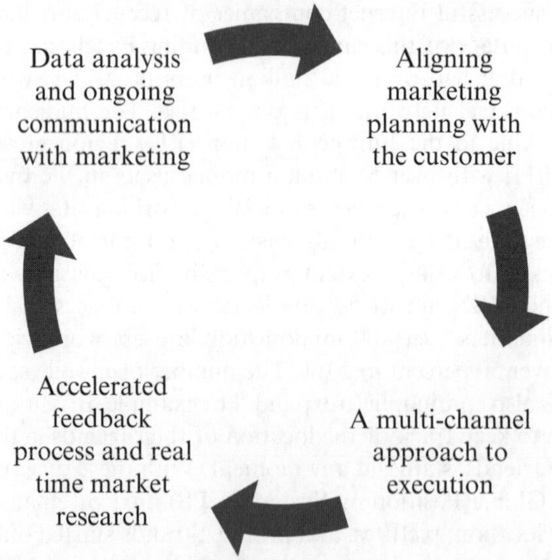

Figure 18.1 Closed loop marketing

mobile information service applications already have implemented such automated and continuous CLM systems. Examples are Pandora, which automates the delivery of mobile music in a closed-loop cycle, and Google Currents, which does the same for news. In addition, several mobile services now utilize the information in the user's social network to personalize information services. These trends set the stage for adaptive personalization systems. A simple early example of an adaptive system is Microsoft Office, which reorders menu options depending on how often they are used, with the purpose of assisting ease of use of the system. It seems that a final stage in the evolution from recommendation—to personalization—to adaptive personalization systems has begun to materialize.

2 RECOMMENDATION SYSTEMS

Recommendation systems have proved to be powerful personalization tools, with eye-catching applications for books, movies and music by Amazon.com, Netflix.com and Apple's Genius. For televisions, TiVo pioneered the personalized recording of television programs based on users' rating of programs through its TiVo Suggestions service. Recommendation systems generally fall into two categories: content filtering and collaborative filtering systems. There are, however, hybrid recommendation systems that combine features of content and collaborative filtering systems. Content-filtering systems involve digital agents that produce recommendations based on the target customer's past preferences for products/services, and the similarity between those products/services. Academic research has shown that these agents may indeed affect customer preferences (Cosley et al. 2003; Häubl and Murray 2003), result in lower prices paid for services (Diehl et al. 2003), and improve the quality of consumer choices (Ariely et al. 2004; Häubl and Trifts 2000). However, their effectiveness depends critically on the extent to which they learn the individual consumer's decision rules (Aksoy et al. 2006), and recommendations for unfamiliar items may be evaluated less positively by users, depending on the recommendation context (Cooke et al. 2002). Collaborative filtering, on the other hand, predicts a customer's preferences using those of other, similar customers. While so-called memory-based systems use measures of similarity between customers' preferences or behaviors, model-based systems use mathematical and statistical techniques to predict preferences for recommended items.

Memory-based systems have been popular in practice because they are simple to implement, easily scalable, and robust. The Nearest Neighbor Algorithm is widely used in commercial systems. Van Roy and Yan (2010) show that asymptotically linear collaborative filtering algorithms, such as a modified Naïve Bayes and Kernel Density Estimation algorithm, greatly outperform Nearest Neighbor algorithms when the data is distorted, for example through manipulation by vendors. They show that there is much room for improving existing commercial personalization algorithms. This is supported by anecdotal evidence of earlier failures of recommendations delivered by popular systems such as Amazon, TiVo, and Netflix. The marketing literature has therefore largely focused on the development of potentially more powerful model-based recommendation systems (Ansari et al. 2000; Bodapati 2008; Ying et al. 2005). Indeed, research has almost invariably shown that model-based systems outperform simpler recommendation engines, but at the cost of a substantially larger computational burden. Content and collaborative filtering based recommendation systems have been shown to learn at different rates (Ariely et al. 2004).

Many recommendation systems are based on user reviews and ratings of users' satisfaction with specific services (songs, books, movies, restaurants). As many as 70 percent of shoppers claim to check online product reviews before making a purchase, and a high rating increases the likelihood of purchase for over half of consumers. Online reviews are trusted more than television, magazine and newspaper advertising.[3] Sixty percent of retailers now facilitate online reviews of their products and services. Although quite popular in practice, there are several problems associated with explicitly asking individuals to evaluate specific services they have used. It turns out that because many consumers are unwilling to actively provide this input, most of the information in the recommendation systems in question is missing (Ying et al. 2006). In addition, when asked to provide an evaluation on the most often used 5-star rating scale, individuals respond idiosyncratically (Rossi et al. 2001). Some may use only one or both of the extreme ends of the scale while others tend to score in the middle, depending on their personality, culture or geographic location. Even tendencies to respond to a simple binary "like" request may differ between individuals. Furthermore, recommendation systems based on user input are vulnerable to shilling attacks. Here, crafted ratings are submitted by companies in order to influence the system to make commercially desired recommendations (Lam and Riedl 2004). Such shilling attacks may seriously undermine the effectiveness of recommendation systems that are based on user input in practice. As a consequence, more and more companies have moved towards the use of unobtrusively obtained measures as input for recommendation systems, including click-stream, purchase, and usage data. Amazon is an example that combines both information on visited pages as well as products purchased by the target and similar consumers.

Another drawback is that most recommendation systems produce recommendations for consumers based on their predicted likes, preferences, or choices, but not necessarily based on their predicted responsiveness to the recommendations themselves (Bodapati 2008). Taking receptivity to recommendations into account in making recommendations can change the nature of recommendations and greatly increase their effectiveness. Furthermore, these and other recommendation systems suffer from the 'cold-start' problem: for new products or services, no ratings are available yet and recommendations cannot be made. Finally, scalability presents an important challenge for many recommendation systems regardless of whether they use ratings input or not (Bodapati 2008; Montgomery et al. 2004). The databases used to generate recommendations are massive in terms of the number of individuals, choice alternatives and their attributes. Massive datasets are an issue when the algorithm is computationally intensive (Ansari et al. 2000; Ying et al. 2006). The recent Netflix recommendation tournament has brought that issue to the fore. In practice, therefore, recommendations are often computed statically, at fixed time intervals, rather than in continuous time based on all of the most recent information.

There is a trend to utilize social networks for delivering product/service recommendations. For example on Facebook, users can "like" products, which are then recommended to friends in their network. Over half of the users of Twitter recommend companies or services. These tweets are effective, because 90 percent of people trust recommendations from people they know: about one-quarter of consumers now turn to social networks for advice on services they like to purchase.[4] Thus, recommendations delivered through social networks can be more effective than online recommendations in general. In addition, they improve the scalability of the recommendation engines in question, being based on a smaller subset of similar customers for each target user. Strands, for example, exploits the social network by allowing users to discover new music through friends in their network. Most news websites, including those of the *New York Times* and the *Wall Street Journal*, offer users the option to "like" or "share" a news article on the website with friends in their network. These systems, however, again require proactive effort on behalf of the user. In addition, sharing news or music through a social network flags the user as the source, which in some cases may not be desirable to the user and might hamper the spread of content through the network. Yet, social networking is continuing to increase the effectiveness of recommendations.

3 PERSONALIZATION

Whereas recommendation systems involve presenting the user with a selection out of a large existing set of service offerings, personalization adapts the service offering to the individual user's needs. The recognition of consumer heterogeneity has been fundamental to the academic study of marketing, and to the effectiveness of marketing practice. In developed countries, the rapid rise of the information economy and more connected, mobile, affluent, and demanding consumers have caused consumer markets to fragment and consumer heterogeneity to increase, forcing firms to offer products and services that better meet the needs of individual customers. Advancements in technology have enabled customizing and personalizing services to the needs of the individual (Khan et al. 2009; Varki and Rust 1998). Customization and personalization capitalize on consumer heterogeneity and involve tailoring of one or more aspects of the marketing mix to the individual customer (Arora et al. 2008). Arora et al. (2008) make the following distinction between customization and personalization. Customization involves the firm facilitating the customer, tailoring products and services to his or her preferences. An example is Dell.com, which allows customers to customize their computer they buy in terms of pre-specified product features. To enable customization, consumer input is required: a primary approach to customization requires customer input in the form of checking boxes that indicate interests in categories of products/services. My.Yahoo, for example, offers these options for news and enables users to customize web-content in categories such as sports, technology, finance, news, and shopping. The mobile news aggregator Flipbook allows users to customize the sources of the news they receive (*New York Times*, NBC, ABC, NPR, and so on). Although initial customization is fast and refinements can be made, problems with this approach are that the categories are often too coarse to limit the time users have to spend on initial customization, that they are identical for all users because it is difficult to anticipate all relevant options for each particular user, and that they only allow services to be filtered but not prioritized.[5]

Personalization, on the other hand, involves the firm itself tailoring the marketing mix to the customer, based on available customer information (Arora et al. 2008). An example is Pandora, which tailors the delivery of music to users based on their initial music selections and the similarities between songs based on song attributes extracted from the Music Genome database (Castelluccio, 2006). Personalization offers the advantage of greater customer satisfaction (Arora et al. 2008). Conceptually, personalization consists of three stages (Murthi and Sarkar 2003): learning consumer preferences, matching service alternatives to consumers, and evaluation of the effectiveness of learning and matching stages. In online and mobile CLM systems, these three stages can be fully automated in a continuous cycle of personalization. There are three main ways in which services can be personalized (Adomavicius and Tuzhilin 2005). Passive Personalization displays personalized service information in response to related customer activities. For example, Catalina Marketing Services is an industry leader of personalized coupons delivered at the checkout counter of brick-and-mortar retail stores, based on shoppers' purchase histories. Pull Personalization provides a personalized service when a customer explicitly requests it. A personalized fashion website such as Shoedazzle.com uses this approach. When signing up, users fill out a short survey about style and brand preferences. Then, they get to see a boutique with products, designed and produced by Shoedazzle, which they are most likely to enjoy based on the survey results. Push Personalization sends information about a personalized service or the service itself directly to new customers without their explicit request. Pandora, already referred to above and recently integrated with TiVo, does that by creating online or mobile personalized radio stations.

4 ADAPTIVE PERSONALIZATION

The problems with ratings-based recommendation systems have prompted companies to use data unobtrusively obtained from customers as input for recommendation engines and personalization of services. The main advantage of using that type of data is that proactive user input is not required, and recommendations are based on revealed, rather than stated, preferences. A downside is that there is less control over the services and service attributes that are "evaluated" by customers, and thus over the input of the system. Consumers can only choose from the set of alternatives that was personalized to them, which constrains the set of choices that can be observed over time. The downside is thus that these systems may zoom in on a too narrow set of preferences for the consumer (Chung et al. 2009). Yet, the advantages often outweigh the disadvantages and more and more companies use click-stream, download, purchase and usage data as input for recommendation and personalization engines (Bodapati 2008). In many cases, however, the systems in question are static, or at most update information and personalize services at regular time-intervals.

Adaptive personalization systems (APS) have emerged that take full advantage of unobtrusively obtained customer information to provide personalized services in real time (Chung et al. 2009; Rust and Chung 2006). Groupon.com is a popular service that, on its website or by email, presents daily deals for products and services from local or national retailers. If a certain number of people sign up for the deal, then it becomes available to all, if not then no one gets it that day. Importantly, Groupon Now is a service that personalizes the deals delivered by email or on mobile devices. Subscribers need to enter their preferences in their profile. The service gets smarter over time: as it gets to know the individual subscriber better, the deals will be personalized better.

These and other APS require minimal proactive user input and are mostly based on observed purchase or usage data. Most importantly, they learn consumer tastes adaptively over time from small amounts of information, and are able to track consumers' changing preferences. In order to prevent the systems from zooming in on too narrow a subset of consumer preferences, they need to build in an element of surprise. That is, service items for which user preferences are not necessarily predicted to be high may be recommended anyway, if that item is popular in the population, popular in the user's social network, or simply by chance. Such personalization may allow not only the system, but also the user him or herself to learn about preferences for new alternatives (Chung et al. 2009). The adaptive personalization approach provides implicit feedback on the effectiveness of recommendations. This is the case because the system keeps track of the extent to which previous recommendations are being used and can thus target users based on their responsiveness to recommendations for personalized services (Bodapati 2008). From a user's viewpoint, these systems are easier to use. The user only needs to use the service and usage data is automatically recorded: proactive user input is not required, or is not required as much. Figure 18.2 provides a stylized flow diagram of an adaptive personalization system that includes social networking features. Adaptive personalization systems implement CLM strategies by collecting and analyzing data, predicting user behavior, personalizing services, and evaluating the effectiveness of the recommendations, in a continuous and automated cycle.

5 ADAPTIVE PERSONALIZATION IN THE MARKETING LITERATURE

The nascent marketing literature on adaptive personalization is summarized in Table 18.1. One of the first articles that developed an adaptive personalization approach is that of Zhang and Krishnamurthi (2004). The purpose of these authors was to personalize online promotional price discounts, in line with services such as Catalina. To do this, they used an integrated purchase incidence, quantity and timing model that forecasts consumers' response to promotional effort over time. Heterogeneity was modeled with a mixture model formulation. The authors employed a numerical profit-maximization procedure to adaptively determine the timing and depth of promotions, tailored to individual consumer segments. Their approach adapts to variety-seeking/inertia tendencies of consumers differently. A comparison shows that the approach yields substantially

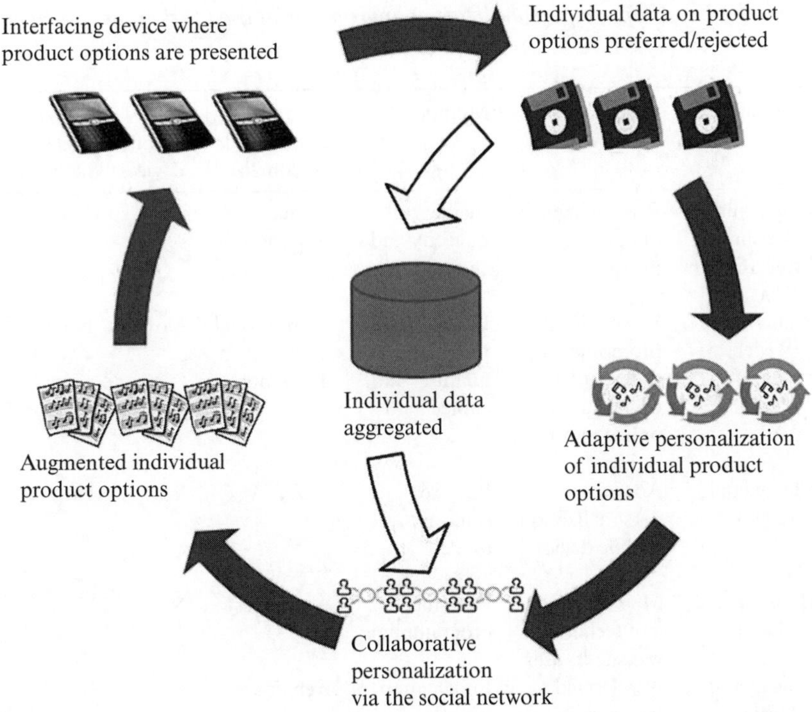

Figure 18.2 Adaptive personalization system

higher profits than extant industry practices of online price discounting. In an application and extension of this model-based approach, Zhang and Wedel (2009) investigated the profit implications of adaptive personalization online and offline, comparing three levels of granularity: mass, segment, and individual. The results show that individual-level adaptive personalization is profitable, but mostly in the online channel. Especially offline, differences in profitability of personalization at the three different levels of individuality are small. In the context of mobile information services, the former result is of relevance since such services can be, and are ideally, offered online and/or through mobile devices, as is currently the case with Groupon. Comparisons with current practices similar to those of Catalina are favorable to the approach proposed by Zhang and Wedel (2009), in particular in online settings, where they can yield increases in profitability between 20 and 60 percent.

In the first mobile personalization approach in the marketing literature, Chung et al (2009) design and evaluate an adaptive personalization

Table 18.1 Adaptive personalization approaches in the marketing literature

Journal paper	Research focus	Method	Product customized/ personalized	Use of mobile devices	Use of social networks
Zhang and Krishnamurthi (2004)	Personalizing online promotions	Incidence, quantity and choice model	Online promotions	No	No
Zhang and Wedel (2009)	Personalized promotions at different levels of granularity, online and offline	Latent class Incidence, quantity and choice model	Promotional price discounts	No	No
Chung et al. (2009)	Adaptive personalization mobile devices	Particle filtering, model averaging	Music	Yes	No
Hauser et al. (2009)	Matching look and feel of website to user	Dynamic programming	Web pages	No	No
Atahan and Sarkar (2011)	Accelerated learning of user profiles	Information theory heuristics	Web links	No	No
Chung et al. (2012)	Adaptive personalization mobile devices	Naïve Bayes, social network filtering	News	Yes	Yes

approach for mobile devices. Their approach deals with personalization of music, in line with commercial services such as Pandora. As input, the system uses whether or not a person has listened to a song and for how long. Further, attributes of the songs are used as predictor variables for that behavior. To deal with the issue of scalable real time personalization a particle filtering algorithm was developed. The particle filtering algorithm is a dynamic Markov Chain Monte Carlo method often used in artificial intelligence. Importantly, it can handle the constraints of personalization via mobile devices. The algorithm is particularly effective in a situation where the music preferences of users change in real time. In addition, Chung et al. (2009) used a hybrid personalization model that combined the benefits of both a model-based and a collaborative approach. Collaborative personalization was carried out via a Bayesian model averaging approach. Furthermore, the approach involves a variable selection step that captures the changes in weights users placed on the different product attributes and removes nonessential variables from the estimation. Finally, an element of surprise is brought in through random recommendations, which avoids the system zooming in on a too narrow set of user tastes too early on. The model is unobtrusive to the users and requires no user input other than the user listening (or not) to the songs automatically downloaded in the device. It learns and adapts to users' changes in preferences dynamically. A field test of the approach shows that it adapts better to user tastes than an approach that is similar to the Pandora algorithm, and results in a 20 percent higher percentage of songs that users listen to completely.

Hauser et al. (2009) develop a system for adaptive personalization of website design. They call the approach "website-morphing," and it involves matching the content, look and feel of the website to a fixed number of cognitive styles. They infer four style dimensions based on 13 items: analytic/holistic, impulsive/deliberate, visual/verbal and leader/follower. These lead to $2^4 = 16$ cognitive style segments. The probability of each cognitive style segment is estimated for website visitors, based on initialization data that, next to the observed segments, involves the respondents' click-stream and paired comparison judgments of alternative web-page morphs. In a second loop, the optimal morph assignment, a multi-arm bandit problem, is computed using dynamic programming. The website morphs are defined on three dimensions—graphical/verbal, small/large information load, and focused/general content—which leads to eight possible morphs to be assigned to one of the 16 segments. The dynamic program maximizes the sum of the expected immediate profit and the discounted future profit obtained from the user making a purchase on the website. It balances the trade-off between exploitation, which is presenting product options that best suit users' predicted preferences, and exploration, which is introducing surprise to help improve estimation. The solution of the morph assignment is computationally feasible, because it is that arm in the multi-arm bandit problem that has the largest Gittins index. Hauser et al. (2009) show that morphing may substantially improve the expected profitability of the website compared to a standard website design, by about 20 percent if ten or more clicks are observed to classify visitors into cognitive style segments.

Another challenge of an adaptive personalization system has to do with the provision of reasonable personalization only after receiving a small amount of data. When this is not possible, users may drop out from the personalization system as they fail to see the benefit offered by the system. Atahan and Sarkar (2011) deal with this issue by providing a technique that accelerates the learning of user profiles. Using information theoretic heuristics, the technique involves providing service offerings to the users that maximizes expected information gain at every instance of personalization.

Chung et al. (2012) developed an approach to personalization of news articles on mobile devices. The basic idea is that Really Simple Syndication (RSS) news-feeds are downloaded into a user's mobile device, where the headlines of the articles are presented in a news scroll. The user can bring up an article by tapping the corresponding headline in the scroll. The action is logged by the system, which also records the time the user spends reading the article. Similar to some of the other more successful adaptive personalization approaches, this system relies on automated analysis of the service content, in this case a text-analysis of the news articles. The approach sorts keywords in terms of their odds-ratio between articles that were read and those that were not. Based on the top discriminating keywords it then employs a modified Naïve Bayes classifier, which accounts for key-word dependence, to compute the probability that new news-feeds will be read by the user. This involves only closed form calculations that can be executed in real time. Being the first approach in the literature to use the social networks for recommendations, Chung et al. (2012) also include a news-feed in the scroll if there is substantial uncertainty whether or not the user will read it (that is, the classification odds are close to one), and if at least one friend in the users' social network has read the article. This utilizes the social network in a way that promotes shared knowledge among friends and colleagues, but also includes serendipity that is needed for the system to continue to learn new user preferences for news. A social-influence parameter allows the impact of the social network to be tuned. In an experimental implementation of the system on mobile devices, Chung et al. (2012) show that using articles through the social network improves the quality of personalization, leading to more readership of the news articles and more time spent on the articles. Increasing the social influence by tuning the social influence parameter improves performance, up to a point, and the performance of the system improves substantially over time. A comparison with current practices employed by, for example, Yahoo! news, which involve users indicating whether or not they like categories of news (sports, politics and so on), results in up to triple the percentage of articles read (33 percent), and triple the time spent reading them (150 seconds per article).

6 DISCUSSION AND FUTURE OUTLOOK

The future for APS looks bright and many avenues for further development are open. We believe that APS are only in their initial stages and that their performance will continue to improve and their scope will continue to expand. Many of the features of an APS make it more acceptable to the end user than a traditional recommendation system. We have cited several examples of companies that already successfully employ such systems, including Groupon, Pandora, and Google. For those and other companies in the information services industry, this presents an effective way of implementing fully automated CLM systems which already have demonstrated their efficacy in several offline industries. The nascent marketing literature summarized in Table 18.1 gives a sense of the exciting developments in this field and the gains that can be expected by continuing development and improvement of APS, in particular at the intersection of mobile and social networking applications. The use of scalable and closed form computations, and the potential use of cloud computing to bypass the computational limitations of mobile devices, makes expansion of the scale and scope of adaptive personalization highly probable in the near future (Chung et al. 2009, 2012).

The technology acceptance model (Davis 1989) cites two determinants for a new technology to be accepted by users, namely, perceived usefulness and perceived ease of use. The perceived usefulness of an adaptive personalization system is demonstrated to users through its improved performance over time and the delivery of information services that match the user's taste better and better. In addition, the accelerated learning of user profiles makes the system more personally relevant to the user, thereby encouraging its acceptance (Atahan and Sarkar 2011). Another feature that makes adaptive personalization systems more personally relevant is that they often mimic how the user makes decisions in real life, for example, by utilizing models based on utility maximization (Murthi and Sarkar 2003). Next to improving personalization, this also provides greater validity of the system to the user. For example, Zhang and Krishnamurthi (2004) incorporate the variety-seeking/inertia tendencies in a utility-maximizing model of individual decision making, and Chung et al.'s (2009) procedure reflects that individuals do not consider all service attributes in their decision making and their use of non-compensatory decision rules.

Adaptive personalization systems reduce the number of choice options available to users. While some researchers consider this to be a limitation because they assume that users generally like more choice options, too many choices can be overwhelming. Iyengar and Lepper (2000) show that shoppers are more likely to purchase a service when they are given a small rather than large number of options. In addition, shoppers are also more satisfied with their choices from a more limited selection. This aspect of narrowing overwhelming choice options to a more manageable set is a key feature of most of the APS in practice, and of those proposed in the academic literature (Chung et al. 2009, 2012). The key, of course, is that the limited set of options that is available matches consumers' tastes better. In addition, the systems in question are easy to use, not only because of the reduction in options, but also because of their simple user interfaces. The systems provided by Chung et al. (2009) and Chung et al. (2012) are examples, but this holds even more for the approach proposed by Hauser et al. (2009) that changes the online interface to suit the usage style of users. Such improved and adaptive interfaces are particularly important for mobile devices, where consumers' attention spans are shorter and the space for presenting information is limited. In the future it is likely that not only the content of information services (Chung et al. 2009), but also their price and promotions (Zhang and Krishnamurthi 2004) and matching user interfaces (Hauser et al. 2009) are simultaneously personalized.

But, APS also allow users to explore their own preferences through the exposure to options they may not initially have chosen and may even have been unaware of. This is a crucial aspect of recommendation and adaptive personalization systems, and prevents the latter from zooming in on user preferences too much too early on. This aspect is reflected in several of the approaches proposed in the academic literature (Table 18.1). Specifically, Hauser et al. (2009) morph websites to simultaneously optimize current rewards and discounted future rewards from "exploration". Chung et al. (2009) explicitly include random recommendations of music and recommendations of music that is popular in the population as a whole, which allow the system to keep on learning new user preferences. Chung et al. (2012) do this via the user's social network. Serendipity built into the system allows not only the system, but also the user him or herself to learn about his or her preference for new service options.

One of the most promising features of the APS is perhaps the incorporation of social network filtering. Rather than using a simple collaborative filtering approach to improve on personalization, unobtrusive filtering of content through the users' social network captures the influence of the preferences and behaviors of the user's friends on the user, and creates a shared service experience among them (Chung et al. 2012). We call this "collaborative personalization," which is particularly important for experiential categories with strong social influences, such as movies, books, news and music. Future personalization approaches could extend these approaches by incorporating the frequency and nature of social interactions, users' certainty of their preferences, the size of the social network, and the geographic location of the user and of her friends in the social network using GPS capability (Narayan et al. 2011). The potential applications of systems that incorporate social network filtering are enormous. Effectively, such systems may capture dynamics of service choices not only for a single individual, but also capture group dynamics, and provide a wealth of unobtrusively collected customer data that companies can leverage. It may help to predict adoption, diffusion, and lifecycle of information services, help firms to proactively and strategically seed new product launches in social networks, and may better help identify trends and opportunities for service innovation.

NOTE

1. www.bazaarvoice.com/resources/stats (accessed 21 December 2011).
2. www.bazaarvoice.com/resources/stats (accessed 21 December 2011).
3. www.bazaarvoice.com/resources/stats (accessed 21 December 2011).
4. www.bazaarvoice.com/resources/stats (accessed 21 December 2011).
5. www9.org/w2-mobileweb/PazzaniMobileWeb.html (accessed12 October 2011).

REFERENCES

Adomavicius, Gediminas and Alexander Tuzhilin (2005), "Towards the next generation of recommender systems: a survey of the state-of-the-art and possible extensions," *IEEE Transactions on Knowledge and Data Engineering*, **17** (6), 734–49.

Aksoy, Lerzan, Paul N. Bloom, Nicholas H. Lurie and Bruce Cooil (2006), "Should recommendation agents think like people?" *Journal of Service Research*, **8** (4), 297–315.

Ansari, Asim, Skander Essegaier and Rajeev Kohli (2000), "Internet recommendation systems," *Journal of Marketing Research*, **37** (3), 363–75.

Ariely, Dan, John G. Lynch. Jr. and Manuel Aparicio IV (2004), "Learning by collaborative and individual-based recommendation agents," *Journal of Consumer Psychology*, **14** (1 and 2), 81–95.

Arora, Neeraj, Xavier Dreze, Anindya Ghose, James D. Hess, Raghuram Iyengar, Bing Jing, Yogesh Joshi, V. Kumar, Nicholas Lurie, Scott Neslin, S. Sajeesh, Meng Su, Niladri Syam, Jacquelyn Thomas and Z. John Zhang (2008), "Putting one-to-one marketing to work: personalization, customization, and choice," *Marketing Letters*, **19** (3–4), 305–21.

Atahan, Pelin and Sumit Sarkar (2011), "Accelerated learning of user profiles", *Management Science*, **57** (2), 215–39.

BBC News (2010), "BBC measuring the Information Society 2010", *BBC News*, 9 July.

Bodapati, Anand (2008), "Recommender systems with purchase data," *Journal of Marketing Research*, 45 (February), 77–93.

Capgemini (2008), "Closed loop marketing: unlocking the benefits of customer centricity," accessed 18 August 2011 at www.us.capgemini.com/lifesciences/.

Castelluccio, Michael (2006), "The Music Genome Project," *Strategic Finance*, **88** (6), 57–8.

Chung, Tuck Siong, Michel Wedel and Roland T. Rust (2012), "Adaptive mobile personalization using social networks," working paper, Nanyang Business School, Nanyang Technical University.

Chung, Tuck Siong, Roland T. Rust and Michel Wedel (2009), "My mobile music: an adaptive personalization system for digital audio players," *Marketing Science*, **28** (1), 52–68.

Cooke, Alan D.J., Harish Sujan, Mita Sujan and Barton A. Weitz (2002), "Marketing the unfamiliar: the role of context and item- specific information in electronic agent recommendations," *Journal of Marketing Research*, **39** (4), 488–97.

Cosley, Dan, Shyong K. Lam, Istvan Albert, Joseph A. Konstan and John Riedl (2003),

"Is seeing believing? How recommender interfaces affect users' opinions," *Recommender Systems and Social Computing*, **5** (1), 585–92.
Davis, Fred D. (1989), "Perceived usefulness, perceived ease of use, and user acceptance of information technology," *MIS Quarterly*, **13** (3), 319–40.
Diehl, Kristin R., Laura Kornish and John G. Lynch Jr. (2003), "Smart agents: when lower search costs for quality information increase price sensitivity," *Journal of Consumer Research*, **30** (1), 56–71.
Häubl, Gerald and Valerie Trifts (2000), "Consumer decision making in online shopping environments: the effects of interactive decision aids," *Marketing Science*, **19** (1), 4–21.
Häubl, Gerald and Kyle B. Murray (2003), "Preference construction and persistence in digital marketplaces: the role of electronic recommendation agents," *Journal of Consumer Psychology*, **13** (1–2), 75–91.
Hauser, John R., Glen L. Urban, Guiherme Liberali and Michael Braun (2009), "Website morphing," *Marketing Science*, **28** (March), 202–23.
Iyengar, Sheena S. and Mark R. Lepper (2000), "When choice is demotivating: can one desire too much of a good thing?" *Journal of Personality and Social Psychology*, **79** (6), 995–1006.
Khan, Romana, Michael Lewis and Vishal Singh (2009), "Dynamic customer management and the value of one-to-one marketing," *Marketing Science*, **28** (6), 1063–79.
Lam, Shyong K. and John Riedl (2004), "Shilling recommender systems for fun and profit," in *WWW '04: Proceedings of the 13th International Conference on World Wide Web*, New York: ACM Press, pp. 393–402.
Montgomery, Alan L., Kartik Hosanagar, Ramayya Krishnan and Karen B. Clay (2004), "Designing a better shopbot," *Management Science*, **50** (2), 189–206.
Murthi, B.P.S. and Sumit Sarkar (2003), "The role of the management sciences in research on personalization," *Management Science*, **49** (10), 1344–62.
Narayan, Vishal, Vithala R. Rao and Carolyne Saunders (2011), "How peer influence affects attribute preferences: a Bayesian updating mechanism," *Marketing Science*, **30** (2), 368–84.
Rossi, Peter E., Zvi Gilula and Greg M. Allenby (2001), "Overcoming scale usage heterogeneity: a Bayesian hierarchical approach," *Journal of the American Statistical Association*, **96** (453), 20–31.
Rust, Roland T. and Tuck Siong Chung (2006), "Marketing models of service and relationships," *Marketing Science*, **25** (6), 560–80.
Rust, Roland T., Christine Moorman and Gaurav Bhalla (2010), "Rethinking marketing," *Harvard Business Review*, **88** (1), 94–101.
Sun, Baohong (2006), "Technology innovation and implications for customer relationship management," *Marketing Science*, **25** (6), 594–7.
Syam, Niladri B. and Nanda Kumar (2006), "On customized goods, standard goods, and competition," *Marketing Science*, **25** (5), 525–37.
Van Roy, Benjamin and Xiang Yan (2010), "Manipulation robustness of collaborative filtering," *Management Science*, **56** (11), 1911–29.
Varki, Sajeev and Roland T. Rust (1998), "Technology and optimal segment size," *Marketing Letters*, **9** (2), 147–67.
Ying, Yuan Ping, Fred Feinberg and Michel Wedel (2006), "Leveraging missing ratings to improve online recommendation systems," *Journal of Marketing Research*, **43** (3), 355–65.
Zhang, Jie and Lakshman Krishnamurthi (2004), "Customizing promotions in online stores," *Marketing Science*, **23** (4), 561–78.
Zhang, Jie and Michel Wedel (2009), "The effectiveness of customized promotions in online and offline stores," *Journal of Marketing Research*, **46** (April), 190–206.

19 It's the social, stupid! Leveraging the 4C markers of social in online service delivery

Ko de Ruyter and Tom van Laer

In an attempt to capitalize on the benefits of social media, Royal Dutch Airlines (KLM) launched Club China, a social network aimed at business travelers and entrepreneurs who do business in the emerging economy. For the airline, it represents a way to develop extended connections with high margin service segments. For customers, the community goes far beyond traditional travelers' loyalty programs that rely on selective incentives (that is, frequent flyer points). Its primary proposition is based on "linking value," that is, the added value of social bonds (Cova 1997) that provide relevant information and relationships with peers. Immaterial value also stems from being part of an exclusive club, which in turn reflects the customers' entrepreneurial identity. Club China's online forum allows customers to maintain valuable contacts, share experiences through personal stories, pose questions, and propose new service concepts. Experts offer insights into matters related not just to business operations and investments but also to social issues, such as how to improve life in China's factory towns and the use of renewable energy in rural industrial centers. Members also can choose their seatmates for a flight by using a "meet and seat" functionality based on Facebook and LinkedIn profiles. Dedicated phone support services are available of course, and offline events take place in both China and the Netherlands. A myriad of services aimed at professional development and relationships through social media thus enhance the airline's core service, namely, transporting people from A(msterdam) to B(eijing).

As this little vignette shows, social media have evolved from small talk with family and socializing with friends or colleagues to big opportunities for businesses. They challenge existing conceptions of market relationships and customer roles. For service firms in particular, they are transforming existing business models and core service delivery processes, because service delivery is all about interactions. In a social media reality, these interactions become much more transparent and increasingly beyond the control of the service provider; firms simply are not in a position to dictate the terms of engagement. Rather, companies increasingly seem like the "uninvited crashers of the Web 2.0 party," a role that some firms have trouble accepting (Fournier and Avery 2011, p. 193). Keeping track of and adjusting to these developments is proving difficult even for technology-knowledgeable practitioners—as well as for services researchers, whose studies at the intersection between services and social media are only beginning to emerge. As our understanding of a profoundly networked marketplace grows, it becomes more apparent that we must come to terms with the basic forces that drive change. Media and technology platforms are essential parts of the equation, but we also need to recognize that various tools and applications will come and go, and their "solutions" will generate new problems.

If social media are fundamentally changing the way firms market and manage services, then we must identify the key tenets that drive this transformation into social service delivery. Social media essentially enable relationships among people and between customers and companies. Service marketers need to learn how to nurture these relationships through their strategically active participation. A fan base on Facebook, a follower relationship on Twitter, or a connection on LinkedIn represent human communications that go beyond the mere exchange of information.

Services research offers little guidance. As Kozinets et al. (2011, p. 207) observe, few authors seek to offer frameworks for "connecting the reality and potential of social media with transformative concerns." To develop a deeper, more fundamental understanding of the transformative impact of social media on service firms and their customers, we direct attention to their social components and examine in detail how doing so may leverage firms' service strategies and operations.

THE MARKERS OF "SOCIAL"

The term "social" inherently refers to association, originating from the Latin word *socius* (Dolwick 2009). Its connotation refers to both individualistic and communal elements of how people associate (Lorenzo-Molo and Udani 2012). In their associations, people create, recreate, and disseminate information. Through user-generated content, customers share their experiences with products and services; online reviews, recommendations, and testimonials thus have replaced traditional marketing information channels as the most trusted source for informing purchasing or strategic alliance decisions (Godes and Mayzlin 2004). Because online experience and opinion sharing has reached such prominence, new evaluative criteria are needed to assess the effectiveness of the process by which customers serve customers by sharing their experiences (Liu et al. 2011).

Content is widely available and accessible, so customers will react to it, and service firms are drawn into participatory conversations, in which it is less acceptable to rely on professional spokespersons. Instead, cross-sections of employees, fellow customers, and even competitors join the conversation, with a reach that has taken a lot of companies by surprise. It took three years to reach the 1 billion Tweet limit; today, 1 billion Tweets are sent every three days (www.twitter.com). Companies such as Best Buy and Dell have established listening centers and allow large cross-sections of their employees to talk back via Facebook or offer Twitter-based, real-time customer support. As people share more stories, narrative becomes the primary format of online conversations and the currency of persuasion. Adopting a "conversational human voice" thus may be an essential element of building and maintaining relationships in a networked marketplace (Kelleher 2008).

In addition to rational motives, such as information sharing, emotional motives, such as the need for social connection and self-expression, also govern customers. That is, people present aspects of their selves to others in their social networks, and in these environments, their visibility gets filtered through features such as wall posts, symbols, likes, and number of connections. In KLM's Club China, some members send subtle signals of their expertise. Social media present ample opportunities for value creation through self-knowledge and self-enhancement (Banaji and Prentice 1994; Hollenbeck and Kaikati 2012). In addition to identity construction, they feature serious issues related to control over personal information and social privacy.

Finally, many companies organize and facilitate online conversations in collectives and integrate communities at various stages of their value chains. Crowdsourcing platforms and after-sales support communities "constitute an online social structure woven from continuous interactions among individuals focused around shared interests and common practices" (Dahlander and Frederiksen 2012, p. 989). In this sense, they add informational and social value to core service propositions, as KLM's Club China example makes clear. Communities such as these provide social support (Ballantine and Stephenson 2011) and fulfill needs for connection, interaction, and belongingness (Zaglia 2013). These platforms represent a relational perspective on innovation, because they gather wisdom and creativity from the collective. Thus, in line with recent theorizing about the nature of social media, we advance four markers of "social" with the potential to extract additional value in service delivery: (1) conversation, (2) content, (3) construction of identity, and (4) community.

CONVERSATION

Recent years have experienced unparalleled growth in the volume and importance of online conversations. Customers use this form of discourse to scrutinize, discuss, and evaluate products and services. Because markets are a form of conversation, firms face the challenge of entering a conversation in this social media environment, analyzing what is being said, and determining how to talk back. Facebook's size is often discussed relative to the size of countries, because millions of users comment directly on products and service experiences (NM Incite 2011). A substantial percentage of tweets also focus on brand, product, and service experiences (Jansen et al. 2009). Online retailers, such as Amazon.com and Bertelsmann.com receive hundreds of customer reviews on a daily basis. These developments have been referred to as the "big data" challenge: The sheer volume and lack of structure of the qualitative information available in online, text-based conversations presents a formidable challenge (Cao et al. 2011; Singh et al. 2011). Most online businesses claim their performance is hampered by their inability to efficiently decipher or reliably analyze conversations among their online customers (Bonnet and Nandan 2011).

The rise of online conversations even has surpassed traditional, one-directional, firm-to-customer messages, forcing companies to reinvent their business models to remain competitive. For example, enabling any customer to write product and service reviews has been key to Amazon's exponential growth. A 2005 Deloitte market study shows that 69 percent of those who read customer reviews share them with people in their social circle, thus magnifying their impact (Kambil et al. 2005). An even more recent Nielsen (2010) survey shows that 41 percent of customers are willing to share negative product experiences online through Twitter or by writing a review. Online conversations can thus add as well as subtract value.

The unstructured, text-based nature of online customer conversations renders traditional methods for detecting customer perceptions (for example, preference data, satisfaction surveys) virtually obsolete. Even widely used quantifiable rating scales (for example, star ratings) fail to capture the sentiment and impact of text-based conversations. For example, despite mildly positive quality ratings (for example, 6.2 out of 10 on imbd.com, 67 percent freshness score on the Rotten Tomatoes movie review site), the motion picture *Bruno* fell $20 million short of box office expectations. After the fact, this performance emerged as in accordance with information-rich narrative reviews that expressed audience members' disappointment (Corliss 2009).

The nature of online conversations may demand more attention devoted to computer-aided text analysis (Lee and Bradlow 2011). Text mining commonly proceeds in three steps: (1) structuring any form of written texts into a database, (2) extracting word usage patterns from these textual accounts, and (3) using quantitative analysis to make inferences from the texts to the context in an objective and systematic manner (Pollach 2012). The central premise of text mining reflects the assumption that the frequency with which particular words and concepts occur in a text is a measure of their relative importance, attention, or emphasis (Krippendorff 2004), such that it conveys psychologically relevant information, over and above the words' literal meaning (Pennebaker et al. 2003).

Forrester (2009) in turn predicts that the value of text analytics will increase from $499 million in 2011 to $978 million in 2014. This set of tools enables marketers to deal with social media conversations by analyzing vast amounts of unstructured data and quantifying information that is mostly qualitative in nature. There is emerging evidence of the usefulness of text mining tools, demonstrated across diverse forms of online content, such as blogs (Cohn et al. 2004), web forums (Dino et al. 2009), instant messaging (Slatcher and Pennebaker 2006), and online group negotiations (Huffaker et al. 2011). How people put their words together to create a message (that is, communication style) is the question underlying text analytics. Whereas the average native English speaker has an impressive vocabulary of well over 100,000 words, fewer than 400 are so-called function words (Pennebaker et al. 2007). This deceptively trivial percentage (less than 0.04 percent) accounts for more than half of the words people use in their daily conversations (Rochon et al. 2000).

Function words not only have powerful impacts on the reader but also reflect a great deal about the writer. Tausczik and Pennebaker (2010, p. 29) posit that "intertwined through these content words are style words, often referred to as function words. Style or function words are made up of pronouns, prepositions, articles, conjunctions, auxiliary verbs, and a few other esoteric categories." These categories identify not only what people convey (that is, sentential meaning) but also how they write (sentential style), so both have diagnostic value that affects decisions (Bird et al. 2002). In contrast with non-functional words (for example, nouns, verbs, adjectives), which convey content, function words set the tone for social interactions and are key to understanding the relationships among speakers, objects, and other people (Chung and Pennebaker 2007).

Building on communication accommodation theory, researchers have argued that symbolic actions, inherent to communication styles, form the basis for linguistic style adaptations. The central premise is that conversation partners align their communication style to become "more like their fellow interactants in a bid to decrease social distance, seek or signal approval, and thereby accommodate" (Giles et al. 2007, p. 142). People consciously or subconsciously accommodate their conversation partners to develop closer relationships and signal empathy, credibility, and a common social identity. Within the context of social media conversations, the words used in text-based posts are the sole symbols available to form an impression about people (Ma and Agarwal 2007). Conversations in social media communicate specific linguistic styles that reveal aspects of the authors' personality. Research has revealed that alignment in conversational style, or linguistic style match (LSM), irrespective of content, increases rapport, credibility, and shared perceptions between conversants (Ireland and Pennebaker 2010). For example, for couples on a first date, LSMs predict subsequent relationship viability; Huffaker et al. (2011) show that in online negotiations, greater matches in function word usage increase interpersonal rapport and agreement between potential coalition partners. Therefore, in relation to textual conversations in social media, LSM may be a sensitive, unobtrusive symbol of conversant affinity, diagnostic of behavioral outcomes, regardless of the interaction environment, perceived quality, length, or objective.

Ludwig et al. (2013a) analyzed the linguistic content and style properties of verbatim customer reviews on Amazon.com and assessed their impact on online retail sites' conversion rates. This online retailer adds customer reviews as an important information service to its website to assist its customers in making purchase decisions. For 17 consecutive weeks, information about a total of 591 books and 18,682 customer reviews was recorded and used to determine whether the tone of voice expressed in these reviews drove sales conversion. As predictors, changes in affective content and linguistic style properties of the book reviews were taken into account too. The authors also posited that in online reviews, authors likely read other reviews about their product of interest (for example, science fiction books) and write reviews for an audience that shares this interest (Forman et al. 2008). Therefore, within product interest groups or genres, reviews likely reflect a certain linguistic style associated with that interest group, and reviewers nonconsciously mimic it in their own writing. In line with communication accommodation theory, reviewers' adjustments to a genre-specific linguistic style should elicit perceptions of shared identity and rapport among the reading collective (Giles 2009). Such perceived rapport sends important signals to readers of the review that likely influence customers' judgments and behaviors if they process the information heuristically, as is common in online information searches (Jones et al. 2004). When new reviews align with the genre's way of conversing, it should lead to a closer match with the interest group's linguistic style and thus a positive change in conversion rates. A dynamic panel data model reveals that the influence of positive affective content (for example, conveying emotions such as happiness, sadness, or anger) on conversion rates is asymmetrical, such that greater increases in positive affective content in customer reviews exert a smaller effect on subsequent increases in conversion rate; no such tapering-off effect occurs for negative content. Beyond the semantic content, the authors demonstrate that the linguistic style in which such reviews are written also has direct implications for conversion rates. Taken together, positive changes in affective content and increasing congruence with the product interest group's typical linguistic style jointly increase conversion rates. These findings suggest that firms should not only pay attention to what customers are saying but also how they express themselves, emphasizing the importance of LSM as a social media metric.

Ludwig et al. (2013b) also examine whether style matching has predictive value in real-time conversations in social media by investigating its impact in crowdsourcing platforms. In these settings, companies solicit customers to submit ideas, suggest service improvements, and discuss experiences. Popular examples include Dell's IdeaStorm ("where your ideas reign") and Audi's Virtual Lab, where brand enthusiasts develop concepts for infotainment services. Their study used text mining to monitor the conversations of more than 74,000 members across 37 crowdsourcing platforms. In addition, a pre-study comparing the results of a short survey (N = 622) and participants' LSM scores served to corroborate whether LSM could be equated with participants' social identification levels. Members' linguistic style matches with the common style of conversing on a particular platform signaled social identification with the channel and affected participation quantity and quality. Quality was operationalized by the level of cognitive effort that participants exerted to post in discussions, focusing on the use of causal words (for example, because, cause, and effect) and other words suggestive of cognitive processing (for example, realize, and understand). Because these authors monitored the conversations for 10 weeks, it was possible to identify trends and reversals (that is, instability) and determine their impacts on the quantity and quality of posts as well. Whereas a stronger alignment trend led to greater participation quantity and quality, frequent reversals in members' LSM developments suggested lower participation quantity. Finally, at the platform level, greater synchronicity in the linguistic style across all participants helped stimulate participation behavior. Collaboration in social media platforms thus offers a unique opportunity to tap a reserve of expertise and creativity and involve customers as co-creators of new service concepts. To effectively exploit this opportunity, text analysis provides valuable insights into how crowdsourcing can be leveraged to enhance service delivery.

CONTENT

The earliest conceptions of social media made clear that they entail people's regular sharing of (written) stories on weblogs (blogs), supplemented by photos and videos, about themselves and their experiences, with interested friends and relatives. For most social media users today, the focus is on updating their status on Facebook, Twitter, or other social media sites. These extended stories explain who the posters are and what they have been doing (Kozinets et al. 2010). For these purposes, a "story" is any account of an event or sequence of events, leading to a transition from an initial state to a later or end state, which a storyteller conveys to a recipient (Bennett and Royle 2004). Telling stories is a valuable exercise for both storytellers and recipients. Stories constitute a powerful device to frame a service or product experience (Gergen and Gergen 1988; Shankar et al. 2001; Thompson 1997) and can therefore influence the storyteller's likelihood of repeating the narrated experience and/or to advise others about that experience (Moore 2012).

For the story recipient, stories associated with advertising, branding, communication, other consumers, and service research all provide benefits, for both potential consumers and the companies. Zappos generates so much positive electronic word of mouth with its fantastic service experience that the company can afford to spend significantly less on traditional marketing than its rivals. These stories recount the origin of the business, how the company has solved problems, and the role the business plays in the wider landscape of the market. Stories show the human side of the business, bringing the brand to life, such as the dramatic origins of Facebook or the ups and downs of Apple. Despite anecdotal evidence of the persuasive power of stories though, service professionals and researchers still know little about how to leverage storytelling in social media.

A growing number of companies places high value on the stories that customers and employees tell as important assets. When companies realize that storytelling can enhance service delivery, they start looking for stories everywhere, updating their websites with "tell us your story" pages (for example, Dell, Starbucks) and asking customers to post testimonials on YouTube (for example, cosmetic surgery clinics). These efforts can yield hundreds of captivating stories, shedding light on unique and authentic customer experiences. On some websites, the experiences get stored in so-called storybanks, central digital repositories that can be used to instruct, entertain, and inform employees (Goodman 2009). KLM's Club China is a particularly good example of the power of storybanking. The social network challenged the first major wave of members who went to do business in or with China to share their stories and to post this content to the

Club China website, as well as on Facebook and Twitter. Club China thus introduced the traditional passion for storytelling into its social media environment. Stories also can be shared from anywhere in the world by anyone with an Internet connection. Currently, Club China has almost 100 members who actively write and post stories to the site: "Club China members share their business experiences with you! How did they get their start? What were their key learnings in setting up their business in China?" (www.flyingblueclubchina.com). The goal is clear and timely: By using social media to capture and share customer stories, Club China not only highlights the power of customer connections but also builds momentum and visibility for the KLM brand. To reach this goal, it needs to curate its growing collection of stories to ensure that only those stories that engross customers get posted.

Stories in social media also engross and persuade through narrative transportation (Escales 2004, 2007; Green and Brock 2000, 2002; Slater and Rouner 2002). Gerrig (1993) uses the term "transportation" to describe the feeling of entering the world evoked by a story. Narrative transportation is the extent to which (1) a customer empathizes with the story characters and (2) her or his imagination is activated by the story events, which leads her or him to experience suspended reality during the story reception. As a result of being transported, readers are no longer aware of their beliefs, attitudes, and intentions prior to reading, because they are engrossed in the story events.

In contrast, when confronted with an analytical, factual claim that counters their attitudes and intentions, customers are inclined to rationalize and draw on their prior beliefs to generate negative cognitive responses (Petty et al. 1983). Negative cognitive responses offer counterarguments, and the persuasive attempt will probably fail, because facts are not perceived as an attempt to start a dialogue. However, narrative transportation inhibits such negative cognitive responses (Green and Brock 2000). Consequently, it "may lead to at least temporary acceptance of values and beliefs that represent a shift from the individual's existing beliefs" (Slater and Rouner 2002, p. 177). In other words, whereas readers tend to argue against analytical persuasive messages that are inconsistent with their prior attitudes and intentions, they do not do so when confronted with a story-based claim, even when it runs counter to their attitudes and intentions (Slater and Rouner 1996). Instead, transported readers empathize with the main story character (Green and Brock 2002). Whereas once customers had to read professional, analytical reviews for opinions on restaurants and travel, today the customer reviews on websites such as Urbanspoon.com and Tripadvisor.com enable them to identify and empathize with fellow customers, transporting them into their service delivery experiences.

In social media settings, people also tend to share negative service delivery experiences. Voicing discontent online forms a threat to consumers' confidence in companies (Ward and Ostrom 2006). Even unconfirmed messages can develop rapidly into stories with serious destructive potential (Elsner et al. 2010), because peers who read about these experiences tend to empathize with the protagonist. Well-known companies have experienced massive reputation damage based on posts in social media. Consider the example of United Airlines and Dave Carroll. United Airlines's careless handling of Carroll's $3,500 guitar in March 2008 led the Canadian artist to record a song—and YouTube music video—called "United Breaks Guitars," which by August 2010 had been seen more than 9 million times and exerted a negative impact on the company's bottom line. For such companies, a strategy of reticence, or hoping that the storm of negative word of mouth will just blow over, is not effective. Rather, the highly reactive social media environment demands a quick and appropriate response to avoid the further erosion of customer trust and subsequent loss of market share (Li et al. 2004).

An online experiment has shown which service recovery responses in social media works best in which conditions (van Laer and de Ruyter 2010). For example, the narrative content of a response contributes to an effective restoration of trust. These authors distinguish apologetic versus denying responses, such that users reading a narrative apology in response to a trust violation came to empathize with the accused party and were consequently transported. The feeling of empathy had a positive influence on how the users felt about the expression of regret in the apology. Conversely, such an effect did not occur when they processed a denial. These results demonstrate that companies can restore most of their trust and retain customers by posting the right response in the wake of negative stories in social media: apologizing in the form of a narrative that triggers customers' affective reactions.

Commonly, a company's spokesperson or public relations (PR) professional formulates the reply to a trust violation, presumably to exploit his or her greater credibility (in comparison with the accused person). However, in social media, source credibility may be largely irrelevant. In this context, statements from official spokespeople appear to be "cheap talk," whereas customers relate more with workers in the lower ranks (Gaines-Ross 2010). After the explosion of BP's Deepwater Horizon drilling platform, for example, more people chose to follow a Twitter account holder posing as an employee (Leroy Stick [an alias]) than the actual BP corporate response Twitter feed. Van Laer and de Ruyter (2010) also examine the narrative content of responses to social media messages about service failures specifically in relation to the perspective of the specific narrator, arguing that telling a story from the point of view of the person directly involved enhances the probability that social media users empathize with this person and his or her world view. In their experiment, a personal response by the employee directly responsible for the service failure was more effective in restoring trust than a response issued by the company's spokesperson. The implication is that successful trust restoration depends on who communicates for the company. If a firm chooses to respond to a trust violation in social media with a narrative apology, consumers' opportunity to feel for the involved party becomes crucial and, in effect, determines whether they will trust the firm again. A study by Kearney (2011) reveals that the majority of companies still do not respond to customer comments on Facebook pages. Emerging research shows that they must think more carefully about their social service recovery strategy; it has become clear that an appropriately humanized response strategy can protect and enhance a company's reputation. In such a strategy, the art of storytelling takes center stage.

CONSTRUCTION OF IDENTITY

The rapidly growing use of social media also influences the way customers present themselves. In virtual meetings and marketplaces, it becomes possible to maintain multiple forms of identity that contribute to personal branding (Chung and Lee 2010). Work on self-presentation and self-disclosure in computer-mediated environments thus emphasizes that social media are services that motivate people to construct their online identity (boyd and Ellison 2007; Schau and Gilly 2003). This research highlights two main components of any constructed identity: personal and social (Skitka 2003). Personal identity is "the person's construction and maintenance of an autobiography—a life story that is built, told to (and by) others in various contexts, and from time to time revised to fit changing experiences or preferences" (Hewitt 2003, p. 111). Personal identity refers to pursuits that set a person apart from referent others. For example, users can manage a profile page and wall of posts that bear detailed witness to their personal experiences, brand preferences, and significant (or less significant) events. In contrast, social identity refers to pursuits that associate a person with referent others. This component of identity derives from membership in popular interest groups (Tajfel and Turner 2004), including brand fan pages such as Coca-Cola's (54 million members).

Yet some carefully constructed identities reportedly are violated when social media users are exposed to ridicule and insults or sometimes even bodily harm (Parker 2012; *The Economist* 2011). Cases of so-called cyber harassment have caused members to exit social networking sites, a trend that has affected Facebook and Twitter, as well as the weblog communities run by Procter & Gamble, Porsche, Sony, and Walmart (Avery 2010; Edelman 2010; Martin and Smith 2008; Moore 2009). In response, some companies attempt to intervene in peer-to-peer (P2P) conversations to counteract cyber harassment, such as by altering the privacy controls on user accounts to regulate access to personal information (Krasnova et al. 2010; Sledgianowski and Kulviwat 2009). Paradoxically though, tightening the rules of engagement limits the freedom of self-expression and identity building undertaken by benevolent customers (Kleinrock 2004). Thus Facebook was criticized recently for failing to tell members it was disabling a feature that shares user addresses and telephone numbers with external applications and websites (Bowen 2011; Purdy 2011). Social media communities often regard sudden, unexplained decisions by network providers to intervene in their conversations as violations of their painstakingly crafted personal and social identities (Raphael 2009; Walters 2009)—an issue that provokes strong feelings and complaints about any restrictions on people's freedom of expression (Urban et al. 2009). Therefore, it is important to determine how to address cyber harassment in a way that members regard as necessary, appropriate, and in their best interests, instead of as unjust.

The tension between perceptions of intervention as an immoral identity violation versus a morally defensible anti-harassment tool provides a foundation for emerging research focused principally on social media provider interventions and communications about the decision to intervene. Mayer et al. (2009) find that when a service provider's decision to intervene in a conversation violates personal or social identity, it has a negative influence on acceptance of the decision. They further note that the two components differ with respect to the influence they exert on people's reactions to decisions: People are more prone to accept decisions to intervene when the decision (slightly) violates social identity. For social identity violation, it seems "sorrow shared is sorrow halved," so decisions may be endured more easily when shared with others.

Decisions by social network providers also may be framed to dampen violating perceptions. For example, van Laer (2011) shows that framing decisions to restrict expression by a list of factual arguments explaining the rationale for the decision were viewed as greater violations of personal identity than of social identity. When the basis for the decision to intervene was provided using an anecdote about a particular cyber harassment episode (that is, an experiential account, narrating the rationale for the changed policy), people perceived no difference in the violations of either identity and deemed the measures equally acceptable. Van Laer (2011) thus asserts that decisions based on experiential evidence or customer stories increase the acceptability of the measure, because customers can more easily imagine that they could be the victims of cyber harassment too one day. This phenomenon—experiencing the event from one's own perspective—is called self-referencing (Escalas 2007; Burnkrant and Unnava 1989), which can be prompted by expressions such as "Imagine yourself . . ." (Escalas 2004). A self-referencing strategy encourages people to use their personal identity, thoughts, feelings, likes, and dislikes to process the information. If they do so, but the decision to intervene is presented as a list of factual arguments, people take a more critical look at the information. Not surprisingly, the use of this strategy appears to decrease the possibility that people accept a decision (Burnkrant and Unnava 1989, 1995; Meyers-Levy and Peracchio 1996). Instead, a self-referencing strategy combined with an anecdote about a cyber harassment episode helps users imagine themselves as victims and increases the chances that they will accept the decision to intervene. That is, the best way to get users to accept decisions to intervene in their identity construction seems to be through an experiential account of cyber harassment in which users imagine themselves as victims and are stimulated to invent different outcomes for the cyber harassment experience (that is, social media provider intervention). Customers' acceptance of the boundaries of identity construction thus can be framed as a customer experience with which they identify more easily. Social networks should review their privacy policies and service strategy, instead of blindly extending or limiting freedom of expression in social media.

COMMUNITY

Two decades ago, Rheingold (1994, pp. 57–8) recognized that community is an important element of online environments and thus defined online communities as "social aggregations of a critical mass of people on the Internet who engage in public discussions, interactions in chat rooms, and information exchanges with sufficient human feeling on matters of common interest." Today, such platforms have become important marketing tools. Virtual communities serve brand building, customer relationship management, and idea generation purposes (for example, Algesheimer et al. 2005), and increasingly service delivery and after-sales support goals too (for example, Mathwick et al. 2008). Socially embedded service delivery augments informational elements with value accrued through peer connections. These social networks enable members to "build and maintain a network of friends for social and professional interaction" (Trusov et al. 2009, p. 92). Online forums therefore have been ranked among the top 25 management tools in use today, and they form an important part of many firms' social media marketing strategy (Rigby 2011).

Scholars identify social capital as a key metric for assessing the viability of peer-to-peer problem-solving (P3) communities. This intangible resource is part of and accumulated within the community's social structure, governed by relational norms of voluntarism, reciprocity, and social trust (Mathwick et al. 2008). In contrast with the accumulation of financial capital, social capital accrues through shared, mutual benefits that arise from social investments. In an online social network, these benefits may be instrumental in nature, such as enhanced stocks of knowledge and information resources gained through the support of and guidance from other members (Adler and Kwon 2002). That is, virtual P3 communities have both informational and social value propositions. After-sales service support in this setting commonly entails minimal employee involvement (employees participate on a rotation basis to guarantee the quality of responses and correct undesirable behavior), creating a very low-cost channel. Customers post questions, issues, or problems about product use, and often incredibly quickly, fellow customers suggest high-quality solutions and provide answers. These peers thus participate by serving other customers as partial employees, activities traditionally designated to frontline service staff. Mathwick et al. (2008) show that social capital, as determined by the normative influences of voluntarism, reciprocity, and social trust, is an important impetus for a community's informational and social value proposition and thus of member commitment toward the community. These authors also provide evidence of the emergence of different factions within collectives, demarcating "newbies" from established "wikis." The newcomers appear to join virtual P3 communities to gain access to the problem-solving and information exchange; they regard social support and solidarity as a notable but relatively unimportant result of the community's social capital. Among more established members, the opportunity to receive social support is a key driver of continued active membership though. Longer-term members come to regard one another as "family," and the camaraderie they experience fuels their continued commitment to the community.

In many companies, the business case for the use of virtual networks relies on cost reductions. But others have begun to explore online social networks as revenue-generating service channels, such as when basic services are available for free, but upgraded or premium services can be accessed according to a subscription-based model. Yet we lack much insight into the viability of such an approach, and several authors argue that these revenue models are perhaps overly complicated, because so many online services are free of charge that a critical mass is needed before any of them can reap the financial benefits. Service researchers have begun to investigate how value creation through community can be capitalized upon.

Extending social capital to community value creation, Vock et al. (2013) argue that viewing the community as an entity may provide additional insights into the formation of community value propositions and ultimately the willingness to pay a subscription fee. These authors introduce the concept of entitativity, which refers to "the degree to which a collection of persons are perceived as being bonded together in a coherent unit" (Lickel et al. 2000, p. 224), or simply the "groupness" of a group (Hamilton et al. 2002, p. 140). Entitativity denotes whether members of an online community or social network view themselves as members of a single and meaningful entity. Campbell (1958) proposed several elements that determine whether people experience entitativity, including similarity and proximity, boundedness, sharing a common fate (for example, collective goals), and collective movement. Lickel et al. (2000) argue that the degree of interaction among members of a collective is also an important factor that leads to perceptions of entitativity.

A focus on this construct helps us understand how community, as a marker of social, introduces value-added elements that change the nature of service delivery. Online communities and networks vary considerably in their demographics, such as size and membership profile, and their purpose; in turn, they vary with respect to whether they are tight-knit entities or loose aggregates of anonymous members. Research in social psychology demonstrates that when members perceive they are a part of an entitative group, they feel more committed and are willing to invest in the collective (Hamilton et al. 2002). Social networks perceived as high in entitativity likely display high degrees of interaction, collective goal orientation, and a focus on communal outcomes, and as a result, a higher social value proposition. In addition, entativity influences the perceived economic value of online collectives, perhaps because the members of the in-group are positively biased about the community's potential to realize positive achievements and material goals.

Vock et al. (2013) confirm the impact of entativity on community value propositions and willingness to pay across two social networks that differ in outlook: (1) a community whose primary purpose is to help members find and interact with former classmates and (2) a professional network that enables members to find jobs, people, and business opportunities or recommend others. Differences emerge between these communities. In the former, entativity exerts a direct impact on members' willingness to pay a premium; in the professional network, the impact is more indirect and moves through the social, economic, and functional value that members derive from their interactions with other network members.

Whether direct or indirect, the results demonstrate that it may be viable for community facilitators to pursue a strategy aimed at realizing financial returns. Because of their feeling of "we-ness," members are willing to pay a premium for the services the community offers. Online social networks, such as LinkedIn, encourage the formation of special interest groups that are accessible only to specific members. These groups are more specifically defined and often founded with a specific communal focus. KLM's Club China also has a specific focus on forging relationships within a narrowly defined network. In this way, perceptions of entitativity increase, and profitable value propositions can be offered to these communities.

As firms seek to explore the knowledge and creativity of their customers, it is also becoming rapidly clear that online networks are socially complex phenomena with a myriad of challenges. Most research has focused on the infusion of value-laden propositions, depicting online communities as virtual spaces characterized by altruism, mutuality, and reciprocity, such that individuals serve the interest of the collective and co-create services (for example, Mathwick et al. 2008). The coexistence of regular and premium members, and newbies and wikis, suggests that different factions appear within online networks, so there may be a need for a regulatory mechanism to forge relationships between loosely aligned members with differing commitment, self-interest, knowledge, and ability. Without contractual obligations or formal authority, an important issue is finding ways to govern the behavior of members to ensure quality content and enhance service delivery.

Social collectives commonly develop behavioral governance "from the bottom up," that is, mainly through social norms. Research on online communities has demonstrated that the norm of reciprocity (that is, an implicit obligation to return any favors received) strongly governs behavior (Wasko and Faraj 2005). In addition, online collectives have introduced various incentive structures that seek to exploit the impact of status recognition. Companies as diverse as Apple, Amazon, Hewlett-Packard, Sears, and Yelp all have implemented recognition schemes to motivate customers to contribute. Moreover, public displays of accumulated symbolic capital can serve as a proxy for members who search for expert content.

At the heart of these recognition systems is a mechanism that allows peers to award points, depending on the perceived quality of the contributions or answers to questions posed. Such points serve as selective incentives that allow members to improve their status ranks on the basis of their individual merit. Public recognition systems are critical to many online collectives. Yet they also prompt some undesirable results. An explicit focus on status motivates people to manipulate the system to achieve higher status more quickly. Because not all members have equal opportunities to advance, factions of "haves" and "have nots" also come into existence. Wiertz et al. (2010) show that the presence of a meritocratic governance system thus interacts with a system of normative governance, such that a sense of reciprocity develops in relation to the point system. In response to the tensions between ranked and unranked factions in a service support community, members increasingly adhere to a norm that requires them to reciprocate points for the answers and solutions they receive. Thus the system is sabotaged, which ultimately threatens the continuity of the community. That is, a public recognition system offers a way to judge the quality of the community's knowledge resource, but it also emphasizes the differences between ranked and unranked, such that it profoundly affects the community's social strata. This research corroborates evidence on dysfunctional social interactions in online collaboration systems that undermine the quality and usability of public resources as diverse as Wikipedia and Google Maps.

In summary, services in social media are a complex issue, encompassing both bright and dark sides, such as the voluntary nature of conversations through storytelling and identity building, to peer-to-peer collaborative efforts. Further research may be able to chart those aspects and assess what needs to be done to come to terms with their negative sides.

CONCLUDING REMARKS

Social media hold the promise of transforming service delivery from a faceless voice or fingers on the other end of the line or email, into a social process in which customers engage service providers and other customers in real time, in real language, and through a real voice. Yet many industry reports show that the majority of firms remain socially shy, and delivering on social media's promised value propositions involves many challenges. To meet these challenges, service firms are looking to academic research for guidance. Therefore, this chapter offers several suggestions for ways in which social media could add significant value, according to the 4C markers of social: (1) conversation, (2) content, (3) construction of identity, and (4) community. Service firms should rely on these insights as they embrace social media in their service delivery strategy and operations. In this final section, we therefore provide service researchers with some directions for research, in relation to how each of the 4C markers of social may transform the nature of service delivery.

We argue that it is important to analyze customers using text analyses of the words used in a conversation. The analysis of large volumes of unstructured, verbatim data may yield valuable consumer insights, as demonstrated in relation to the predictive capability of customer reviews in relation to conversion rates and the quality and quantity of idea generation in crowdsourcing environments. Matching linguistic styles also offers a way to dynamically monitor real-time conversations in social media. Possible research extensions could assess conversation styles across different personas (for example, popular archetypical customer profiles, widely adopted in business practice to replace market segments) and—through dynamic website adaptations—present profiles with information in a style congruent with their own. Furthermore, the development of intelligent virtual agent technology has made it easier for online customers to engage in real-time conversations with companies, as Kohler et al. (2011) show. Further research on linguistic style matching may provide important inputs into how virtual service employees can effectively converse with customers and turn service encounters into transporting experiences.

In relation to the second marker of social, content, we have argued that in social media, customers share experiences by telling stories. Such a vivid narrative format has the ability to transport readers, so different rules of persuasion come into play. Social media content already is moving beyond the use of words to compose stories, as audio-visual components become more important, such as photo albums on Facebook or videos on YouTube, posted by customers who wish to tell a story about what they experienced. Researchers therefore should explore the role of increased media richness in the degree of transportation of readers or viewers of such narratives. We have not yet explored the various impacts of these developments. On the one hand, the less a message triggers the senses, the more imaginative effort may be required, resulting ultimately in higher engagement levels and engrossment. On the other hand, as Polichak and Gerrig (2002) suggest, audio-visual content generates a richer participatory response by triggering the sense of hearing too. Ongoing research needs to resolve these issues.

In relation to the construction of identity, we note that successful online identity management depends on the different identities consumers use to engage with social media. We can distinguish personal and social identities already, but there may be more. A coherent service strategy also should incorporate consumers' online personal branding. Additional research could investigate whether profiles might become internalized offline over time, in which case social media usage may be an interesting boundary condition: When people log on more frequently, do they experience less strain associated with a perceived discrepancy between their offline and online identities? Furthermore, service researchers should assess ways to monitor and recognize which peer-to-peer conversations are prone to result in identity violations. Further research can examine ways to present privacy regulations in a way that makes them stand out from the background chatter and ensure user satisfaction and loyalty.

Finally, with regard to community, this chapter reveals that online forums constitute multiple value propositions; the notion of social capital transforms a functional service delivery experience into a sense of belonging and an opportunity for self-actualization. Furthermore, emerging research demonstrates that informational, social, and functional value propositions are independent predictors of community performance metrics, such as participatory behavior, continuing commitment, and willingness to pay or upgrade. However, not much is known about what these value propositions mean for different stakeholders. For example, health professionals evaluate the value of health communities primarily from a medical perspective, in which doctors act as custodians of content, largely oblivious of the social value that these platforms offer to patients. It would be worthwhile to explore what happens when formalized medical information contrasts with patient experience and thus provide guidance for resolving such discrepancies in complex service delivery situations. Community represents an arena for the development of informational value, enriched with the social value of layperson interactions. That is, service encounters can be redefined by incorporating social value attributes.

By paying careful attention to the 4C markers of social, service researchers and practitioners can continue to develop our understanding of how service delivery is, more than ever before, a collaborative venture between consumers and producers that stimulates innovation, mutual learning, and, ultimately, customer loyalty.

REFERENCES

Adler, Paul.S. and Seok-Woo Kwon (2002), "Social capital: prospects for a new concept," *Academy of Management Review*, **27** (1), 17–40.

Algesheimer, René, Utpal M. Dholakia and Andreas Herrmann (2005), "The social influence of brand community: evidence from European car clubs," *Journal of Marketing*, **69** (3), 19–34.

Avery, Jill (2010), "Gender bender brand hijacks and consumer revolt: the Porsche Cayenne story," in Jill Avery, Sharon Beatty, Morris B. Holbrook, Robert V. Kozinets and Banwari Mittal (eds), *Consumer Behavior: Human Pursuit of Happiness in the World Of Goods*, Cincinnati, OH: Open Mentis, pp. 645–9.

Ballantine, P.W. and R.J. Stephenson (2011), "Help me, I'm fat! Social support in online weight loss networks," *Journal of Consumer Behaviour*, **10** (6), 332–7.

Banaji, M.R. and D.A. Prentice (1994), "The self in social contexts," *Annual Review of Psychology*, **45** (1), 297–332.

Bennett, Andrew and Nicholas Royle (2004), *Introduction to Literature, Criticism and Theory*, 3rd edn, Harlow: Pearson.

Bird, Helen, Sue Franklin and David Howard (2002), "'Little words' – not really: function and content words in normal and aphasic speech," *Journal of Neurolinguistics*, **15** (3–5), 209–37.
Bonnet, Didier and Priyank Nandan (2011), "Transform to the power of digital – digital transformation as a driver of corporate performance," report, Capgemini Consulting.
Bowen, Jeff (2011), "Platform updates: New user object fields, edge.remove event and more," Facebook, 15 January, accessed 11–12 December 2012 at http://developers.facebook.com/blog/post/446.
boyd, danah m. and Nicole B. Ellison. 2007. "Social network sites: definition, history, and scholarship," *Journal of Computer-Mediated Communication*, **13** (1), 210–30.
Burnkrant, Robert E. and H. Rao Unnava (1989), "Self-referencing: a strategy for increasing processing of message content," *Personality and Social Psychology Bulletin* **15** (4), 628–38. doi: 10.1177/0146167289154015.
Burnkrant, Robert E. and H. Rao Unnava (1995), "Effects of self-referencing on persuasion," *Journal of Consumer Research*, **22** (1), 17–26.
Campbell, Donald T. (1958), "Common Fate, Similarity, and Other Indices of the Status of Aggregates of Persons as Social Entities," *Behavioral Science*, 3(1), 14–25.
Cao, Qing, Wenjing Duan and Qiwei Gan (2011), "Exploring determinants of voting for the "helpfulness" of online user reviews: a text mining approach," *Decision Support Systems*, **50** (2), 511–21.
Chung, Christy and Matthew Lee (2010), "A theoretical model of intentional social action in online social networks," *Decision Support Systems*, **49** (1), 24–30.
Chung, Christy and James.W. Pennebaker (2007), "The psychological function of function words," in K. Fiedler (ed.), *Social Communication: Frontiers of Social Psychology*, New York: Psychology Press, pp. 343–59.
Cohn, Michael A., Matthias R. Mehl and James W. Pennebaker (2004), "Linguistic indicators of psychological change after September 11, 2001," *Psychological Science*, **15** (10), 687–93.
Corliss, R. (2009), "Box-office weekend: Brüno a one-day wonder?," accessed 5 June 2011 at www.time.com/time/arts/article/0,8599,1910059,00.html.
Cova, Bernard (1997), "Community and consumption: towards a definition of the 'linking value' of product or services," *European Journal of Marketing*, **31** (3/4), 297–316.
Dahlander, Linus and Lars Frederiksen (2012), "The core and cosmopolitans: a relational view of innovation in user communities," *Organization Science*, **23** (4), 988–1007.
Dino, Amanda, Stephen Reysen and Nyla R. Branscombe (2009), "Online interactions between group members who differ in status," *Journal of Language and Social Psychology*, **28** (1), 85–93.
Dolwick, J.S. (2009), "'The Social' and beyond: introducing actor-network theory," *Journal of Maritime Archaeology*, **4** (1), 21–49.
Edelman, David C. (2010), "Branding in the digital age," *Harvard Business Review*, **88** (12), 62–9.
Elsner, Mark K., Oliver P. Heil and Atanu R. Sinha (2010), *How Social Networks Influence the Popularity of User-Generated Content*, Cambridge, MA: Marketing Science Institute.
Escalas, Jennifer Edson (2004), "Imagine yourself in the product: mental simulation, narrative transportation, and persuasion," *Journal of Advertising*, **33** (2), 37–48.
Escalas, Jennifer Edson (2007), "Self-referencing and persuasion: narrative transportation versus analytical elaboration," *Journal of Consumer Research*, **33** (4), 421–9.
Forman, Chris, Anindya Ghose and Batia Wiesenfeld (2008), "Examining the relationship between reviews and sales: the role of reviewer identity disclosure in electronic markets," *Information Systems Research*, **19** (3), 291–313.
Forrester (2009), "Text analytics takes business insight to new depths," Forrester Report, Cambridge, MA.
Fournier, Susan and Jill Avery (2011), "The uninvited brand," *Business Horizons*, **54** (3), 193–207.
Gaines-Ross, Leslie (2010), "Reputation warfare," *Harvard Business Review*, **88** (12), 70–76.
Gergen, Kenneth J. and Mary M. Gergen. 1988. "Narrative and the self as relationship,"

in Leonard Berkowitz (ed.), *Advances in Experimental Social Psychology*, New York: Academic Press, pp. 17–56.

Gerrig, Richard J. (1993), *Experiencing Narrative Worlds: On the Psychological Activities of Reading*, New Haven, CT: Yale.

Giles, H. (2009), "The process of communication accommodation," in N. Coupland and A. Jaworski (eds), *The New Reader in Sociolinguistics*, Basingstoke: Macmillan.

Giles, H., M. Willemyns, C. Gallois and M.C. Anderson (2007), "Accommodating a new frontier: the context of law enforcement," in K. Fiedler (ed.), *Social Communication*, Hove: Psychology Press, pp. 129–62.

Godes, David and Dina Mayzlin (2004), "Using online conversations to study word-of-mouth communication," *Marketing Science*, **23** (4), 545–60.

Goodman, Andy (2009), "A bank that always builds interest," *free-range thinking* (April), accessed 14 December 2012 at www.agoodmanonline.com/pdf/free_range_2009_04.pdf.

Green, Melanie C. and Timothy C. Brock (2000), "The role of transportation in the persuasiveness of public narratives," *Journal of Personality and Social Psychology*, **79** (5), 701–21.

Green, Melanie C. and Timothy C. Brock (2002), "In the mind's eye: transportation-imagery model of narrative persuasion," in Melanie C. Green, Jeffrey J. Strange and Timothy C. Brock (eds), *Narrative Impact: Social and Cognitive Foundations*, Mahwah, NJ: Lawrence Erlbaum, pp. 315–41.

Hamilton, David L., Steven J. Sherman and Luigi Castelli (2002), "A group by any other name – the role of entitativity in group perception," *European Review of Social Psychology*, **12** (1), 139–66.

Hewitt, John P. 2003. *Self and Society: A Symbolic Interactionist Social Psychology*, 9th edn. Boston, MA: Allyn and Bacon.

Hollenbeck, C.R. and A.M. Kaikati (2012), "Consumers' use of brands to reflect their actual and ideal selves on facebook," *International Journal of Research in Marketing*, **29** (4), 395–405.

Huffaker, D.A., R. Swaab and D. Diermeier (2011), "The language of coalition formation in online multiparty negotiations," *Journal of Language and Social Psychology*, **30** (1), 66–81.

Ireland, M.E. and J.W. Pennebaker (2010), "Language style matching in writing: synchrony in essays, correspondence and poetry," *Journal of Personality and Social Psychology*, **99** (3), 549–71.

Jansen, Bernard J., Mimi Zhang, Kate Sobel and Abdur Chowdury (2009), "Twitter power: tweets as electronic word of mouth," *Journal of the American Society for Information Science & Technology*, **60** (11), 2169–88.

Jones, Quentin, Gilad Ravid and Sheizaf Rafaeli (2004), "Information overload and the message dynamics of online interaction spaces: a theoretical model and empirical exploration," *Information Systems research*, **15** (2), 194–210.

Kambil, Ajit, Patrick Conroy and Ryan Alvanos (2005), "A view from the glass house: how to compete in the transparent marketplace," in Deloitte Review, Deloitte.

Kearney, A.T. (2011), "Social media study, an investigation into the social media practices of Interbrand's top 50 brands for 2011," accessed 11–12 December 2012 at www.marketwire.com/press-release/2nd-annual-at-kearney-social-media-study-finds-most-top-consumer-brands-still-not-getting-1610947.htm.

Kelleher, T. (2008), "Organizational contingencies, organizational blogs and public relations practitioner stance toward publics," *Public Relations Review*, **34** (3), 300–302.

Kleinrock, Leonard (2004), "The Internet rules of engagement: then and now," *Technology in Society*, **26** (2–3), 193–207.

Kohler, T., J. Fueller, K. Matzler and D. Stieger (2011), "Co-creation in Virtual worlds: the design of the user experience," *MIS Quarterly*, **35** (3), 773–88.

Kozinets, R.V., F.M. Belz and P. McDonagh (2011), "Social media for social change," in D.G. Mick, S. Pettigrew, C.C. Pechmann and J.L. Ozanne (eds), *Transformative Consumer Research for Personal and Collective Well-Being*, New York: Routledge Academic, pp. 205–23.

Kozinets, Robert V., Kristine de Valck, Andrea C. Wojnicki and Sarah J.S. Wilner (2010),

"Networked narratives: understanding word-of-mouth marketing in online communities," *Journal of Marketing*, **74** (2), 71–89.

Krasnova, Hanna, Sarah Spiekermann, Ksenia Koroleva and Thomas Hildebrand (2010), "Online social networks: why we disclose," *Journal of Information Technology*, **25** (2), 109–25.

Krippendorff, Klaus (2004), *Content Analysis: An Introduction to its Methodology*, Thousand Oaks, CA: Sage Publications.

Lee, Thomas Y. and Eric T. Bradlow (2011), "Automated marketing research using online customer reviews," *Journal of Marketing Research*, **48** (5), 881–94.

Li, Charlene, Josh Bernoff and Tenley McHarg (2004), *Best Practices | Blogging: Bubble or Big Deal? When and How Businesses Should Use Blogs*, Cambridge, MA: Forrester Research.

Lickel, Brian, David L. Hamilton, Grazyna Wieczorkowska, Amy Lewis, Steven J. Sherman and A. Neville Uhles (2000), "Varieties of groups and the perception of group entitativity," *Journal of Personality and Social Psychology*, **78** (2), 223–46.

Liu, Ben, Elena Karahanna and Richard Watson (2011), "Unveiling user-generated content: Designing websites to best present customer reviews," *Business Horizons*, **54** (3), 231–40.

Lorenzo-Molo, C.F. and Z.A.S. Udani (2012), "Bringing back the essence of the 'S' and 'R'to CSR: understanding the limitations of the merchant trade and the white man's burden," *Journal of Business Ethics*, October, 1–14, doi 10.1007/s10551-012-1513-1.

Ludwig, Stephan. Ko de Ruyter, Mike Friedman, Elisabeth C. Brüggen, Martin Wetzels and Gerard Pfann (2013a), "More than words: the influence of affective content and linguistic style matches in online reviews on conversion rates," *Journal of Marketing*, **77** (1), 87–103.

Ludwig, S., J.C. de Ruyter, M. Wetzels, D. Mahr and E. Bruggen, (2013b), "Take their word for it, the symbolic role of linguistic style matches in user-innovation communities," *Management Information Systems Quarterly*, forthcoming.

Ma, M. and R. Agarwal (2007), "Through a glass darkly: information technology design, identity verification, and knowledge contribution in online communities," *Information Systems Research*, **18** (1), 42–67.

Martin, Kelly D. and N. Craig Smith (2008), "Commercializing social interaction: the ethics of stealth marketing," *Journal of Public Policy & Marketing*, **27** (1), 45–56.

Mathwick, Charla, Caroline Wiertz and Ko de Ruyter (2008), "Social capital production in a virtual P3 community," *Journal of Consumer Research*, **34** (6), 832–49.

Mayer, David M., Rebecca L. Greenbaum, Maribeth Kuenzi and Garriy Shteynberg (2009), "When do fair procedures not matter? A test of the identity violation effect," *Journal of Applied Psychology*, **94** (1), 142–61.

Meyers-Levy, Joan and Laura A. Peracchio (1996), "Moderators of the impact of self-reference on persuasion," *Journal of Consumer Research*, **22** (4), 408–23.

Moore, Sarah G. (2012), "Some things are better left unsaid: how word of mouth influences the storyteller," *Journal of Consumer Research*, **38** (6), 1140–54.

Moore, Victoria (2009), "The fake world of Facebook and Bebo: how suicide and cyber bullying lurk behind the facade of 'harmless fun', " *Daily Mail* (Femail), 4 August, accessed 16 December 2012 at www.dailymail.co.uk/femail/article-1204062/The-fake-world-Facebook-Bebo-How-suicide-cyber-bullying-lurk-facade-harmless-fun.html.

Nielsen (2010), "Global trends in online shopping," in *Nielsen Global Consumer Report*, New York: Nielsen.

NM Incite (2011), "How social media impacts brand marketing," NM Incite.

Parker, Ian (2012), "The story of a suicide: a gay freshman and the online world," *The New Yorker*, 6 February.

Pennebaker, James W., Matthias R. Mehl and Kate G. Niederhoffer (2003), "Psychological aspects of natural language use: our words, our selves," *Annual Review of Psychology*, **54** (1), 547.

Pennebaker, James W., Cindy K. Chung, Molly Ireland, Amy Gonzales and Roger J. Booth (2007), "The development and psychometric properties of LIWC2007," Austin, TX: LIWC.net.

Petty, Richard E., John T. Cacioppo and David Schumann (1983), "Central and peripheral routes to advertising effectiveness: the moderating role of involvement," *Journal of Consumer Research*, **10** (2), 135–46.

Polichak, James W. and Richard J. Gerrig (2002), "'Get up and win!' Participatory responses to narrative," in Timothy C. Brock, Melanie C. Green and Jeffrey J. Strange (eds), *Narrative impact: Social and Cognitive Foundations*, Mahwah, NJ: Lawrence Erlbaum.

Pollach, Irene (2012), "Taming textual data: the contribution of corpus linguistics to computer-aided text analysis," *Organizational Research Methods*, **15** (2), 263–87.

Purdy, Douglas (2011), "Improvements to permissions for address and mobile number," Facebook, 18 January, accessed 16 December 2012 at http://developers.facebook.com/blog/post/447.

Raphael, J.R. (2009), "Facebook privacy change sparks federal complaint," *PCWorld*, 14 January, accessed 16 December 2012 at www.pcworld.com/article/159703/facebook_privacy_change_sparks_federal_complaint.html?tk=rel_news.

Rheingold, Howard (1994), *The Virtual Community: Finding Connection in a Computerised World*, London: Secker and Warburg.

Rigby, Darrell K. (2011), "Management tools 2011: an executive's guide," Bain & Company Report, accessed 9 March 2011 at www.bain.com/bainweb/PDFs/cms/Public/Bain_Management_Tools_2011.pdf.

Rochon, Elizabeth, Eleanor M. Saffran, Rita S. Berndt and Myrna F. Schwartz (2000), "Quantitative analysis of aphasic sentence production: further development and new data," *Brain and Language*, **72** (3), 193–218.

Schau, Hope Jensen and Mary C Gilly. 2003. "We are what we post? Self-presentation in personal web space," *Journal of Consumer Research*, **30** (3), 385–404.

Shankar, Avi, Richard Elliott and Christina Goulding (2001), "Understanding consumption: contributions from a narrative perspective," *Journal of Marketing Management*, **17** (3/4), 429–53.

Singh, Surendra N., Steve Hillmer and Wang Ze (2011), "Efficient methods for sampling responses from large-scale qualitative data," *Marketing Science*, **30** (3), 532–49.

Skitka, Linda J. (2003), "Of different minds: an accessible identity model of justice reasoning," *Personality & Social Psychology Review*, **7** (4), 286–97.

Slatcher, Richard B. and James W. Pennebaker (2006), "How do I love thee? Let me count the words," *Psychological Science*, **17** (8), 660.

Slater, Michael D. and Donna Rouner (1996), "Value-affirmative and value-protective processing of alcohol education messages that include statistical evidence or anecdotes," *Communication Research*, **23** (2), 210–35.

Slater, Michael D. and Donna Rouner (2002), "Entertainment-education and elaboration likelihood: understanding the processing of narrative persuasion," *Communication Theory*, **12** (2), 117–244.

Sledgianowski, Deb and Songpol Kulviwat (2009), "Using social network sites: the effects of playfulness, critical mass and trust in a hedonic context," *Journal of Computer Information Systems*, **49** (4), 74–83.

Tajfel, Henri and John Turner (2004), "An integrative theory of intergroup conflict," in Mary Jo Hatch and Majken Schultz (eds), *Organizational identity: A Reader*, Oxford: Oxford University, pp. 56–65.

Tausczik, Yla R. and James W. Pennebaker (2010), "The psychological meaning of words: LIWC and computerized text analysis methods," *Journal of Language and Social Psychology*, **29** (1), 24–54.

The Economist (2011), "Creepy crawlies," *The Economist*, 23 April, pp. 63–4.

Thompson, Craig J. (1997), "Interpreting consumers: a hermeneutical framework for deriving marketing insights from the texts of consumers' consumption stories," *Journal of Marketing Research*, **34** (4), 438–55.

Trusov, Michael, Randolph Bucklin and Koen Pauwels (2009), "Estimating the dynamic effects of online word/of/mouth on member groth of a social network site," *Journal of Marketing*, **73** (5), 90–102.

Urban, Glen L., Cinda Amyx and Antonio Lorenzon (2009), "Online trust: state of the art, new frontiers, and research potential," *Journal of Interactive Marketing*, **23** (2), 179–90.

Van Laer, Tom (2011), "Return of the narrative: studies on transportation in social media," doctoral dissertation, Maastricht University, Maastricht.

Van Laer, Tom and Ko de Ruyter (2010), "In stories we trust: how narrative apologies provide cover for competitive vulnerability after integrity-violating blog posts," *International Journal of Research in Marketing*, **27** (2), 164–74.

Vock, Marlene, Willemijn van Dolen and Ko de Ruyter (2013), "Understanding willingness to pay for social network sites," *Journal of Service Research*, **16** (August), 311–25.

Walters, Chris (2009), "Facebook's new terms of service: 'We can do anything we want with your content. Forever.' (Your rights)," Consumer Media LLC, 15 February, accessed 16 December 2012 at http://consumerist.com/2009/02/facebooks-new-terms-of-service-we-can-do-anything-we-want-with-your-content-forever.html.

Ward, James C. and Amy L. Ostrom (2006), "Complaining to the masses: the role of protest framing in customer-created complaint web sites," *Journal of Consumer Research*, **33** (2), 220–30.

Wasko, Molly and Samer Faraj (2005), "Why should I share? Examining social capital and knowledge contribution in electronic networks of practice," *MIS Quarterly*, **29** (1), 35–58.

Wiertz C., C. Mathwick, K. de Ruyter and B. Dellaert (2010), 'A balancing act: exploring governance in a virtual P3 community' (extended abstract), *Advances in Consumer Research*, **37** (peer reviewed).

Zaglia, M.E. (2013), "Brand communities embedded in social networks," *Journal of Business Research*, **66** (2), 216–23.

20 A meta-analytic investigation of the antecedents of digital piracy

Steven A. Taylor, Chiharu Ishida and Horace Melton

INTRODUCTION

Digital piracy (hereafter referred to as DP) remains a problem for marketers of digital products such as software, music, and movies (Bocij 2006; Cockrill and Goode 2012; Higgins and Marcum 2011; Hinduja 2006; Taylor 2012a, 2012b; Taylor et al. 2009). The vast majority of DP occurs over the Internet (Higgins and Marcum 2011), making attenuation of DP difficult to monitor and enact. A few theoretical frameworks have been applied to explain DP-related behaviors, but only a few theories exist trying to generally explain illegal behaviors, and little research has sought to test the generalizability of explanatory theories specific to DP. Consequently, a problem with the literature on DP is that, typical with areas of inquiry in their infancy, it includes a number of areas of emphasis that have largely evolved independent of one another. This can make difficult the ability to test the merits of competing more general underlying theoretical explanations of DP intentions and behaviors. Consequently, we argue that the body of knowledge related to DP will benefit from a systematic review of the literature with an eye toward integrating existing theoretical explanations.

In this chapter we address this void by conducting a series of meta-analyses related to underlying influences on the formation of DP intention/behaviors. Aquinis et al. (2011) assert that meta-analysis is the dominant approach to research synthesis. Pratt et al. (2010) concur, with the primary advantages of helping to mitigate (1) potential investigator bias, (2) failures to specify the criteria used to review studies leading to poor replicability, (3) challenges associated with handling large volumes of data, and (4) the inability to furnish more precise point estimates attenuating efforts to compare theoretical variables within and across explanatory paradigms (also see Rosenthal and DiMatteo 2001).

The remainder of this chapter is divided into several sections. First, we discuss the known theoretical underpinnings of DP intentions and behaviors. Knowledge of existing theoretical and empirical evidence related to DP is necessary to guide coding practices for meta-analyses. Second, we discuss the methods and results related to the meta-analyses of DP intention/behavior formation conducted here. Finally, we discuss the implications of the reported findings.

IDENTIFYING THE KEY CONSTRUCTS AND THEIR INTERRELATIONSHIPS

Digital piracy is defined as the illegal act of copying digital goods, software, digital documents, digital audio (including music and voice), and digital video for any reason other than to create a backup without explicit permission and compensation to the copyright holder (Gopal et al. 2004). This definition appears to enjoy a measure of commensurability (Hennig-Thurau et al. 2007, Higgins and Marcum 2011, Higgins et al. 2008, Taylor et al. 2009). What is less clear is the best representation of the theoretical framework underlying antecedent influences on DP intentions and behaviors. The current meta-analysis attempts to help fill this gap in the literature by providing structure for inquiries.

The current research capitalizes on Higgins and Marcum's (2011) theoretical model explaining the formation of DP-related behaviors. Higgins and Marcum (2011) review the predominant theories that have been used to understand DP in the business, information technology, and business ethics literatures, and they propose an additive model wherein influences related to self-control theory (Gottfredson and Hirschi 1990) and social learning theory (Akers 1998; Bandura 1986) are hypothesized to be the primary antecedent influences on DP intentions. Their model also suggests that variables that are associated with these two theories mediate the influence of demographics on the formation of DP intentions. The argument is that multiple risk factors and theoretical assumptions may be used to understand DP as there does not appear to be an underlying single cause or correlate. Higgins and Marcum (2011) ultimately argue that various theories should be taken together as influences on DP intentions, thereby allowing reconciliation of the identified theories in their proposed integrated model. We endeavor to contribute to this cause by conducting a test of an expanded version of their proposed theoretical model based upon a series of meta-analyses. Figure 20.1 presents the model assessed here. Similar to Geyskens et al. (1999), we categorize effect sizes (that is, correlations) based on the operationalization of constructs.

Consistent with Higgins and Marcum's (2011) conceptual model, we propose that DP-related behavioral intentions mediate the influences of self-control and social learning on DP-related behaviors.[1] In fact, much

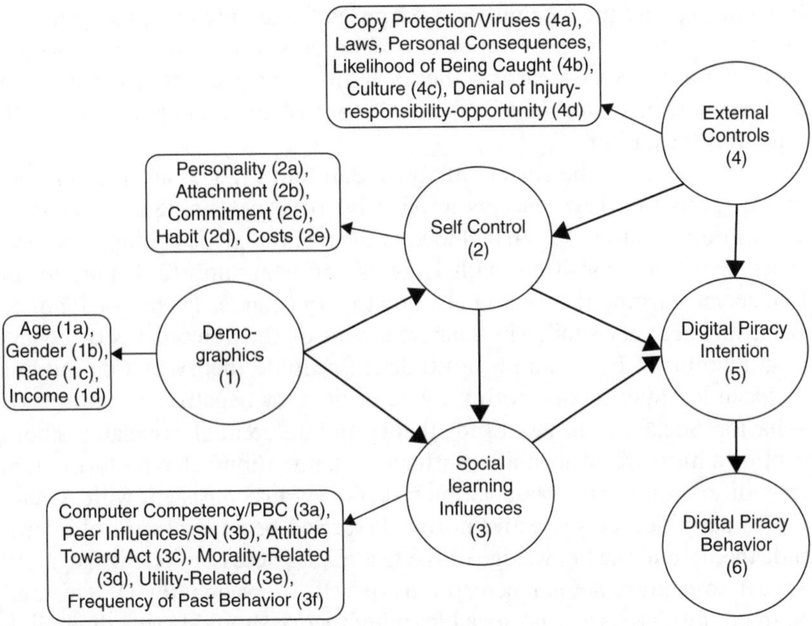

Figure 20.1 The research model and meta-analytic codes

of the reported research measures DP-related behavioral intentions as opposed to DP-related behaviors given the challenges associated with observing the illegal behavior.

Social Learning Theory

Pratt et al. (2010) describe the central principle of social learning theory as the proposition that crime is learned through social interaction. In short, the argument is that people vary in their exposure to behavioral and normative patterns through their association with others (that is, differential association) which then are subject to differential reinforcement, defined as the balance of anticipated and actual rewards/punishments resulting from behavior. Bandura (2001) characterizes social learning theory as agentic. That is, people are agents of experience rather than simply undergoers of experience. In this view, Bandura asserts that human agency is characterized by a number of core features that operate through phenomenal and functional consciousness, including (1) temporal extension of agency through intentionality and forethought, (2) self-regulation by self-reactive influence, and (3) self-reflectiveness about one's capabilities, quality of functioning, and the meaning and purpose of one's life pursuits. Thus, the argument is that the most important reinforcers of criminal behaviors are social in nature. Social learning theory, in this view, has both a direct effect and partially mediates the effects of self-control and demographics on DP intention formation.

For purposes of the current analysis, Bandura's (2001) agentic perspective suggests that key concepts implicit in social psychological models of self and/or intentionality be included in the meta-analytic coding. This perspective appears consistent with Higgins and Marcum's (2011) argument that social learning theory and attitude theory (that is, Theory of Planned Behavior) are very similar in their treatment of the antecedents of behavioral intentions. For example, attitudes in attitude theory and definitions in social learning theory both provide positive or negative evaluations of behavior. Social norms in attitude theory and differential associations both capture a measure of normative influences in intention/behavior formation. In addition, differential association (Akers 1998) is consistent with Ajzen's (1988) definition of subjective norms. Perceived behavioral control in attitude theory and the knowledge of the techniques necessary to engage in DP appear to capture similar perceptions of self. Consequently, Higgins and Marcum (2011) assert that social learning theory should have a direct link to DP intentions (and intentions → behaviors) because the main components of attitude theory are consonant with those of social learning theory.

In summary, Higgins and Marcum (2011) suggest that the influences associated with social learning theory (1) represent a latent concept, (2) are antecedent to DP-related intentions/behaviors, and (3) mediate the influences of both self-control and demographics on DP-related behavioral intentions/behaviors. Figure 20.1 presents the categories we identified as related to social-learning which influence DP-related intentions/behaviors, including computer competency/perceived behavioral control, peer influences/social norms, attitudes toward the act of DP, individualistic morality-related considerations,[2] utility-related concepts (consistent with the expectancy-value model of attitudes), and measures of frequency of past behavior.[3]

Self-control

Higgins and Marcum (2011) continue by arguing that self-control, in the context of DP, refers to the inability to resist temptation when an opportunity presents itself because the individual is unable to foresee the long-term consequences of his or her behavior. Bouffard and Rice (2011) advocate Hirschi's (2004) redefinition of self-control as the tendency to consider the full range of potential costs relevant to the criminal act, suggesting that such costs vary in number and salience based upon one's level of self-control. In addition, Hirschi (2004) suggested that low self-control is influenced by an individual's level of social bonding. Bouffard and Rice (2011) empirically validate this assertion. However, Higgins et al. (2009) reformulated the theory of self-control and DP to reconcile with advances in general control theory. Specifically, they endorsed a social-bonding perspective that focuses on self-control generally, not just low self-control.

Readers may question why "self-control" is modeled as a unique exogenous influence from "perceived behavioral control" common to attitude models such as the Theory of Planned Behavior. From an attitudinal perspective Ajzen (2002) concedes that there are conceptual and methodological ambiguities associated with the concept of perceived behavioral control. He concludes that perceived behavioral control is best interpreted as a unitary latent concept comprised of separable components reflecting beliefs about self-efficacy and controllability. This perspective subsumes all versions of control, and it is based upon the definition that it denotes the subjective degree of control over performance of a behavior itself. Thus, in the view of Ajzen (2002), self-control as a separate unique construct independent of other social learning influences in models of DP-related behaviors appears unnecessary.

However, Higgins and Marcum (2011) assert that self-control is an independent and unique antecedent influence on DP-related behavioral intentions/behaviors from social learning components, and it mediates the influence of demographics on DP-related behavioral intentions/behaviors. Within their framework they provide three primary reasons why self-control should be included in the proposed theoretical model explaining DP behaviors: (1) self-control appears to be a stable human characteristic, indicating dynamic measures appear appropriate to develop proper policy to attenuate the practice; (2) self-control is developed early in life, and it likely underlies more adult influences such as computer literacy, attitudes, peer associations, and/or morality (that is, the factors of social learning theory); and (3) self-control helps shape individuals' definition of and attitudes toward crime, and peer association provides the mechanism that can explain how definitions and techniques toward criminal activity are formed.

Thus, Higgins and Marcum (2011) envision self-control as a latent concept comprised of three primary factors of personality, attachment to social ties, and commitment. Commitment is "the rational component in conformity" (Hirschi 1969, 2004) and it refers to the fear of law-breaking behavior in this context. Through an individual's commitment to social bonds s/he decides to acquire digital goods by conventional means as they perceive they have more to lose by violating laws. Wolfe and Higgins

(2008) specifically consider the influences of self-control versus perceived behavioral control within the context of college student drinking. These authors present empirical evidence that (1) self-control and perceived behavioral control are unique concepts, and (2) that an additive (not interactive) relationship exists between the concepts in the prediction of alcohol use. Tavousi et al. (2009) present further empirical evidence that perceived behavioral control and self-efficacy are unique constructs vis-à-vis substance abuse. Thus, there currently appears to exist no agreement as to whether perceived behavioral control as a social learning influence should be separated from other forms of control germane to DP. It appears clear that Higgins and Marcum (2011) do not envision their view of control as exactly the same thing as perceived behavioral control as found in traditional attitude models. Consequently, the current research follows the conceptualization advocated by Higgins and Marcum (2011) as depicted in Figure 20.1.

Operationally, there are a number of influences to be considered within the domain of self-control as presented here. Turner and Piquero (2002) assert that both behavioral and attitudinal measures of self-control are indicative of an individual's true level of self-control (although behavioral measures consistently explain more variance). Higgins et al. (2008) compare three different perspectives on self-control vis-à-vis DP behavior, including personality characteristics, social bonding measures, and the self-generated view of inhibitions. Results support the conclusion that all three measures of self-control have an important role in understanding the likelihood to perform DP. Higgins et al. (2009) call for general measures of self-control, not just traditional measures of low self-control. In coding results for purposes of meta-analyses, studies were scrutinized to ascertain whether the author(s)' intention was to measure perceived behavioral control or another form of self-perceived control. Measures observed within the following meta-analysis relate to direct predictors of the general concept of self-control, behavioral and attitudinal measures of self-control, and concepts such as habit of engaging in DP, public self-consciousness, general perceptions of costs/price of engaging in DP, ego involvement, and deficient self-regulation (see Figure 20.1). LaRose et al. (2003) assert that self-deficient regulation in this context is generally based on social-cognitive theory (Bandura 1989), and specifically related to self-regulatory mechanisms (Bandura 1991). Thus, self-deficient regulation describes the process of self-control through the sub-functions of self-monitoring, judgmental processes, and self-reaction. Consequently, in this view, deficient self-regulation is defined as a state in which conscious self-control is relatively diminished.

External Controls

The current analysis further extends Higgins and Marcum's (2011) model in an arguably important way based on the issue of control. "Control" as viewed by Higgins and Marcum (2011) appears to relate to a mix of individuals' more stable characteristics and choices, whereas social learning influences more generally appear largely related to individuals' choices. Readers will note measures of social learning theory and self-control both share linkages to intrinsic forms of motivation. Reeve (2005, p. 134) defines intrinsic motivation as, "the innate propensity to engage one's interests and to exercise one's capabilities and, in doing so, to seek to out and master optimal challenges" (Deci and Ryan 1985). From a self-determination perspective, this is considered a higher form of motivation (Ryan and Deci 2000). An emphasis on self-control and social learning influences appears consistent with Taylor et al.'s (2009) argument advocating persuasive marketing communication-based approaches to combating DP (that is, internally motivate people to resist engaging in DP) as opposed to emphasizing external control measures such as legal threats or copy-protection schemes.

However, marketers of easily replicable digital products have also often relied heavily on external (external to the individual) forms of controls (for example, physical constraints such as copy protection, or the presence or absence of existing laws versus an individual's specific response to the presence of specific laws). From a self-determination perspective, this is considered a lower form of motivation based upon rewards and punishments (Reeve 2005, Ryan and Deci 2000). How these more external constraints should be coded in the current study is not obvious in Higgins and Marcum's (2011) conceptual model. Yet some DP-related studies have included variables with regards to anti-piracy measures taken by digital product owners/publishers (for example, Andrés 2006; LaRose et al. 2006). Furthermore, we note that such protections may directly influence perceived consequences should the individuals be caught, in terms of perceived prosecution risk and knowledge of laws (for example, Fetscherin 2009; Goles et al. 2008; Jacobs et al. 2012; Liao and Liu 2010; Peace et al. 2003).

Therefore, for the purpose of meta-analysis, we added a coding category titled "External Controls" capturing empirical evidence related to physical copy protection, the risk of downloading a virus, the likelihood of being caught and penalized, cultural influences, and denial of injury/responsibility arguments (see Figure 20.1). We hypothesize that these measures will have both a direct influence on DP-related intentions, as well as an indirect effect through an individual's self-control. This hypothesis is based on the self-determination continuum of types of motivation (Ryan and Deci 2000).

Demographics

The final major exogenous construct in Figure 20.1 involves demographic characteristics (Blackwell and Piquero 2005). Demographics are considered in Higgins and Marcum's (2011) proposed model to serve as exogenous influences on both self-control and the influences of social learning theory. The crux of their argument is that the influence of gender and race on DP-related intentions will be mediated by self-control and social learning and that the remaining variation of gender on DP-related behaviors will be accounted for by the motivation process, although they concede that the specific role of demographic influences remains to be better understood.

Summary

Higgins and Marcum (2011) propose an untested theoretical model explaining the formation of DP-related behaviors. This model serves as a basis for organizing a series of meta-analyses, consistent with the calls of those authors for empirical validation of their model. The current research extends their proposed model by considering various conceptualizations and measures of "control." The next section presents the methods underlying this analysis.

METHODS

Our meta-analyses began by planning and preparing the literature review. There are a number of issues that merit consideration. First, Card (2012) argues that since individual studies are the unit of analysis for meta-analyses, the goal of the literature review is to obtain a complete, representative, unbiased collection of studies from which inferences can be made about a larger population of studies. However, one cannot know with certainty whether or not they have identified every possible published and unpublished study. For example, the "file drawer" problem refers to instances involving only the examination of published work, and in meta-analyses it is well recognized by social scientists (Aquinis et al. 2011, Borenstein et al. 2009, Cumming 2012). Aquinis et al. (2011) assert that while researchers typically use the failsafe N method (computing the number of missing studies needed to make a significant effect insignificant) to address the potential bias, these authors instead recommend examining a combination of funnel plots and the "trim and fill" method of publication bias analysis (see Duval 2005). The current research acknowledges and implements this recommendation. The trim-and-fill method uses "an iterative procedure to remove the most extreme small studies from the positive side of the funnel plot, re-computing the effect size at each iteration until the funnel plot is symmetric about the (new) effect size" (Borenstein et al. 2009, p. 286).

Second, Card (2012) identifies a potential apples and oranges problem with meta-analyses (that is, combining diverse methods and populations of interest in the sample of studies). Our review of the DP-related literature identifies very diverse methods and measures attempting to explain the formation of DP-related intentions and behaviors. Thus, the current research takes a general approach to the processes underlying DP. Card (2012) argues that it is appropriate to combine a diverse range of studies when the goal of the meta-analysis is to consider a broad population of studies. This is the approach adopted here.

The third issue involves articulating a sampling frame, together with inclusion and exclusion criteria. The desired sampling frame for the current research (those included in the sample) involves all identified published articles, unpublished (rejected) articles, and dissertations related to explanations of DP-related intentions or behaviors. Excluded studies include purely theoretical explanations, qualitative inquiries, and quantitative studies that either do not include any of the identified relationships in Figure 20.1 with either DP-related intentions or behaviors, or do not provide sufficient information to code for meta-analyses (after sending requests for the information to study authors).

The fourth issue involves planning the search strategy to identify potential sources of studies. Significant improvements have occurred in recent years in online libraries and article databases, many of which now include published dissertations. To capture published works individual searches were conducted of the ABI-Inform, Article First, Psych Info, Academic Search, Elsevier, and Emerald Full-Text online article databases using the keywords "digital piracy," "piracy," "software and crime," and "music and crime," among others. To capture unpublished works, a call for unpublished work was made using ELMAR, a popular listserv for business-related social scientists. We also conducted Google and Google Scholar searches, as well as a physical university library search (to identify books or book chapters in print meeting our sample criterion). We also further contacted the Editor for a forthcoming special issue on DP in an academic business journal. Two graduate students and three PhD-trained scholars independently searched the literature to identify potential articles to include in the meta-analysis.

Fifth, the scholars associated with this article independently reviewed identified studies for appropriateness and containing the necessary correlation matrices. Studies deemed appropriate for the meta-analysis, but not containing a correlation matrix, merited a personal email to the lead author or study contact asking for the correlation matrices. Finally, we had several PhD-trained subject matter experts review our list of studies, and included forward and backward searches as the process progressed.

Having articulated our search strategy to identify studies to populate our meta-analysis, we next turned to the coding of identified correlation matrices. The effect size is Pearson's product moment correlation, *r*. In spite of the popularity of using correlations as effect size estimates for meta-analyses, some researchers advocate the use of alternative effect size variables such as regression beta (β) coefficients instead of correlation coefficients (for example, Pratt et al. 2010). However, the established view appears to be that a beta coefficient is not a surrogate for effect size in meta-analyses. As Peterson and Brown (2005, p. 175) note, "Logic dictates that unless an effect-size metric reflects a simple bivariate or zero-order relationship between two variables, effect sizes cannot be meaningfully combined and aggregated across studies." This is because a beta coefficient reflects the influence of all predictor variables in a multiple regression model.

We then categorize correlations based on the operationalization of constructs. Coding was first conducted independently by three PhD-trained scholars, and then reconciled (see the section below about interjudge reliability). Figure 20.1 presents the previously discussed coding used here to assign studies from the literature to appropriate relationships within the assessed theoretical model. Readers will note that we employed the practice of including multiple effect sizes from individual studies when appropriate. Pratt et al. (2010) justify this practice for two reasons: (1) selecting only one effect size estimate per study limits the ability of meta-analyses to examine how methodological variations across studies potentially influence effect size estimates; and (2) it is difficult to select a single methodologically defensible decision rule for selecting among effect size estimates within a study, and ignoring other effect size estimates from the same study. The obtained correlations were input into the Comprehensive Meta-Analysis 2.0 software package (www.meta-analysis.com/). The random effects (as opposed to fixed effects) model was employed for calculations of effect sizes since it is unlikely that all studies are functionally equivalent (Borenstein et al. 2009; Cummings 2012). Readers will note that the bibliography does not contain the citations for all the studies in the following meta-analyses because of concerns about article length. A complete list of the articles included in the following meta-analyses is available upon request from the corresponding author.

Interjudge Reliability of Coding

Based on the procedures developed by Perreault and Leigh (1989) and recommended by Kirca et al. (2005) in their market orientation meta-analysis, we calculated an interjudge reliability index for the three-judge coding of the observations. Perreault and Leigh (1989) developed a reliability index that overcomes the limitations of Cohen's Kappa by computing a sample-based estimate of reliability, and accounts for frequency of agreement among judges and the number of categories from which a judge can choose in classifying an observation. Interjudge reliability is determined by the formula

$$I_r = \{[(F_o/N) - (1/k)] * [k/(k-1)]\}^{.5}$$

where F_o = frequency of judgments on which judges agree, N = number of judgments, and k = number of categories from which a judge can choose in classifying an observation. We calculated an interjudge reliability index of .92 indicating the reliability of our coding process is high (Perreault and Leigh 1989, p. 147). Initial differences in coding were resolved through discussion among research team members.

RESULTS

Table 20.1 presents the results of the meta-analyses conducted here. Forty-two studies met all the criteria for inclusion in the study, representing 912 unique correlations associated with the research model presented as Figure 20.1, and a combined sample size of 764,032 unique observations. However, prior to discussing the findings of the meta-analysis conducted here, the issue of potential publication bias merits further discussion. To address concerns about potential publication bias, the trim-and-fill method represents a sort of sensitivity analysis that estimates how a summary effect size would change by adding potentially missing values. In short, the method assumes that funnel plots should be symmetric if a meta-analysis has captured all relevant studies. Asymmetric funnel plots generally suggest studies may be missing from the analysis, although small studies with large effect sizes can cause this as well. Thus, these adjusted effect size estimates represent conservative estimates. Table 20.1 summarizes these results, as well as presenting the results of the current research's trim-and-fill corrected effect sizes, which can be considered more conservative estimates of obtained effect sizes.

The first ten rows of results reported in Table 20.1 (the first block of

Table 20.1 Meta-analytic results

Path	Characteristics			Effect size and 95% interval			Test of null (2 tail)		Heterogeneity				Tau²			
	No. studies	No. of correlations	Sample size	Point estimate random	Lower limit	Upper limit	Z-value	p-value	Q-value	Df (Q)	p-value	I^2	Tau^2	Std error	Variance	Tau
Demographics ↔ Self-control	8	43	97,312	−0.013	−0.039	0.012	−1.040	0.298	579.609	42	**0.000**	92.754	0.006	0.002	0.000	0.076
	Trim and fill (7R)			0.012	−0.013	0.037			668.425							
Demographics ↔ Social learning	11	120	134,857	0.007	−0.012	0.025	0.695	0.487	1317.168	119	**0.000**	90.965	0.009	0.002	0.000	0.095
	Trim and fill (9L)			−0.010	−0.030	0.010			1853.520							
Demographics ↔ External controls	8	56	54,990	0.012	−0.018	0.042	0.771	0.441	639.489	55	**0.000**	91.399	0.011	0.003	0.000	0.105
	Trim and fill (14L)			−0.045	−0.078	−0.012			1169.933							
Demographics ↔ DP intentions	5	19	6,732	−0.046	−0.102	0.011	−1.570	0.116	101.044	18	**0.000**	82.186	0.013	0.005	0.000	0.115
	Trim and fill (4L)			−0.085	−0.144	−0.026			163.915							
Demographics ↔ DP behaviors	10	32	94,037	−0.013	−0.054	0.027	−0.637	0.524	1120.218	31	**0.000**	97.223	0.012	0.004	0.000	0.111
	Trim and fill (0)			–	–	–			–							
Self-control ↔ Social learning	17	154	111,845	**0.075**	0.052	0.099	6.275	**0.000**	2375.529	153	**0.000**	93.559	0.020	0.003	0.000	0.142
	Trim and fill (16R)			**0.116**	0.088	0.143			3935.697							
Self-control ↔ External controls	7	15	6,620	**0.087**	0.019	0.154	2.492	**0.013**	100.419	14	**0.000**	86.058	0.015	0.008	0.000	0.123
	Trim and fill (0)			–	–	–			–							
Self-control ↔ DP intentions	14	20	8,116	**0.212**	0.046	0.367	2.494	**0.013**	1105.099	19	**0.000**	98.281	0.146	0.057	0.003	0.382
	Trim and fill (0)			–	–	–			–							
Self-control ↔ DP behaviors	10	19	28,663	0.052	−0.054	0.158	0.962	0.336	141.429	18	**0.000**	98.725	0.055	0.026	0.001	0.234
	Trim and fill (0)			–	–	–			–							

Social learning ↔ External controls	16	128	75,408	**0.116**	0.077	0.155	5.752	**0.000**	3802.125	127	**0.000**	96.660	0.050	0.009	0.000	0.223
	Trim and fill (28L)			0.027	−0.017	0.071			6854.181							
Social learning ↔ DP intentions	27	192	59,265	**0.281**	0.234	0.327	11.157	**0.000**	7371.913	191	**0.000**	97.741	0.123	0.016	0.000	0.351
	Trim and fill (33L)			**0.190**	0.138	0.240			10722.175							
Social learning ↔ DP behaviors	15	56	54,160	**0.204**	0.156	0.251	8.114	**0.000**	1846.404	55	**0.000**	97.021	0.034	0.008	0.000	0.185
	Trim and fill (15L)			**0.124**	0.072	0.176			3331.8982							
External controls ↔ DP intentions	10	22	6,832	0.081	−0.046	0.206	1.257	0.209	592.574	21	**0.000**	96.456	0.089	0.030	0.001	0.298
	Trim and fill (3L)			−0.004	−0.148	0.140			1007.9030							
External controls ↔ DP behaviors	12	28	21,071	−0.011	−0.075	0.053	−0.342	0.733	523.036	27	**0.000**	94.838	0.025	0.010	0.000	0.159
	Trim and fill (5L)			−0.087	−0.166	−0.006			189.0984							
DP intentions ↔ DP behaviors	7	8	4,124	**0.269**	0.116	0.410	3.393	**0.001**	169.346	7	**0.000**	95.866	0.050	0.034	0.001	0.223
	Trim and fill (0)			–	–	–			–							
Sum	177	912	764,032													

Note: Significant point estimates are bolded. The term "Trim and Fill" refers to Duval and Tweedie's trim-and-fill (2000a, 2000b) method. The associated number in parentheses represents the number of studies trimmed to adjust the observed random effects, with "R" and "L" representing right or left of the mean respectively.

rows) present tests of the average mean effect sizes of the meta-analytic correlations between demographics and the other model variables (see the column titled "Point estimate random" in Table 20.1). The significance level of the Z-value is used to reject (or not) the null hypothesis that the mean effect is not different from zero and there is no association between identified variables. In the case of the current research, the evidence does not support rejecting the null hypothesis of no association between demographic influences and other model variables. The next eight rows of evidence (the second block) suggest that measures of self-control are statistically (positively) associated with social learning, external controls, and DP intentions. However, we observe no direct association between measures of self-control and DP behaviors. Of the identified statistically significant associations, the relationship between self-control and DP intentions appears the strongest observed association. Thus, there exist direct associations between self-control and social learning, external controls, and DP intentions.

The next six associations in Table 20.1 (the third block of rows) concern social learning theory influences, with evidence suggesting statistically significant (positive) associations between social learning and external controls, DP intentions, and DP behaviors. Thus, social learning concepts appear importantly related to many model concepts, including those in self-control, external control, and both DP intentions and behaviors. The next four rows of evidence presented in Table 20.1 (the fourth block of rows) concern the influence of external controls. We have previously established identified relationships between external controls and both self-control and social learning influences. However, here we accept the null hypothesis that external control has no effect vis-à-vis DP intentions and behaviors. Thus, external control concepts appear related most directly to individuals' perceptions of self-control and social learning influences. The final block of rows in Table 20.1 validates the statistically significant (positive) relationship and relatively strong association between DP intentions and DP behaviors across the studies considered here. Table 20.2 summarizes these findings as a correlation matrix of observed effect sizes and 95 percent confidence intervals.

Table 20.1 also presents a consideration of heterogeneity within the observed associations. Cumming (2012) states that a set of studies is homogenous if sampling variability can reasonably account for the variation between studies. Heterogeneity is apparent when variation between studies is larger than this. Cummings (2012) identifies the Q statistic as a measure of the extent of heterogeneity. The Q statistic and its p-value serve as a test of significance (Borenstein et al. 2009). A statistically significant Q-value suggests that the included studies do not share a common effect

Table 20.2 *Summary of observed effect sizes and confidence intervals**

	Demographics	Self-control	Social learning influences	External controls	Digital piracy intention	Digital piracy behavior
Demographics	1					
Self-control	0.012 (−.013–.037)	1				
Social learning influences	−.010 (−.030–.010)	**.116** (.088–.143)	1			
External controls	−.045 (−.078– −.012)	**.087** (.019–.154)	.027 (−.017–.071)	1		
Digital piracy intention	−.085 (−.144– −.026)	**.212** (.046–.367)	**.190** (.138–.240)	−.004 (−.148–.140)	1	
Digital piracy behavior	−.013 (−.054–.027)	.052 (−.054–.158)	**.124** (.072–.176)	−.087 (−.166– −.006)	**.269** (.116–.410)	1

Note: *Reported correlations and associated 95% confidence intervals are adjusted by Dual and Tweedie's (2000a, 2000b) trim-and-fill method. Bolded values are statistically significant at $p \leq .05$.

size and further supports a reliance on the random effects model versus the fixed effects model in meta-analysis (consistent with the method adopted here). Such was the case here with literally every identified association possessing a statistically significant P-value associated with the Q-statistics in Table 20.1. Another measure of potential heterogeneity involves the I^2 statistic, which measures the extra amount of between-studies variability beyond that expected under the fixed effects model (that is, the percentage of the observed variance that comes from real differences between studies—Borenstein et al. 2009; Card 2012; Cummings 2012). The results reported here identify consistent substantial percentages of observed variances in effect sizes between studies attributable to "real" differences between studies, further suggesting a strong reliance on random-method models in this area of inquiry. The final statistic that can be viewed to consider heterogeneity in meta-analytic results concerns τ (tau). Tau represents the standard deviation of the true population effect size across studies, with T representing the sample estimate of the parameter. The current research employs the method of moments (or DerSimonian and Laird method) as this method does not make any assumptions about the distribution of random effects. Borenstein et al. (2009) assert that τ^2 serves as the between-studies variance in the analysis and our estimate of τ serves as the standard deviation of the true effects. These metrics are particularly useful in that they are sensitive to the metric of the effect size, and they are not sensitive to the number of studies (Borenstein et al. 2009). The τ^2 scores in Table 20.1 appear to support the conclusions associated with observed between-study variability above. The tau scores in Table 20.1 range from 0.076 to 0.382, also suggesting some variance between true effect sizes associated with the current research. Taken together, all three measures of heterogeneity suggest heterogeneity exists among the true underlying effect sizes of the relationships observed here. Together, these results support the use of the random effects model in this meta-analytic study of DP instead of the fixed-effect model. At a minimum, service researchers should compute both random and fixed estimates of DP-related effect size scores and assess observed heterogeneity in their own meta-analyses.

Card (2012) asserts that when meta-analyses contain substantial heterogeneity in effect sizes across studies (as is observed here), it is usually informative to investigate the sources of the heterogeneity through moderator analyses. Cumming (2012) states that moderator analyses in this context seek to identify an association between a moderator and the main effect size. Two potential moderators were identified for consideration here based upon a review of the studies included in the meta-analyses. The first is the context of the inquiry (that is, DP related to music, software, video, or other). The second involves the nature of the sample (student versus non-student). The null hypothesis for this analysis is that context as a moderator is not statistically related to effect size.

We investigate the sources of heterogeneity for the results reported in Table 20.1 using meta-regression (random effects, method of moments model[4]). Borenstein et al. (2009) state that the random-effects model will (1) lead to more moderate weights assigned to each study than the fixed-effects model, (2) assign more weight to small studies and less weight to large studies, (3) increase the confidence interval and slope for each coefficient, and (4) reduce the likelihood for observed statistical significance for each coefficient as well as the model as a whole. Readers will note in Tables 20.3 and 20.4 that there is a Q-statistic associated with moderator analyses that differs from that reported in Table 20.1. Card (2012) states that the logic in testing categorical moderators in meta-analyses is based on the ability to separate total heterogeneity (Q_{Total}) into between-group heterogeneity ($Q_{Between} = Q_{Model}$) and within-group heterogeneity ($Q_{Residual} = Q_{Within}$). Card (2012) continues by suggesting that the key question when evaluating categorical moderators is whether or not there exists greater than expected $Q_{Between}$. If so, this implies that the groups based on the categorical study characteristic (context and nature of the sample in the case of the current study) differ and therefore the moderator is reliably related to the observed effect sizes. Tables 20.3 and 20.4 present the results of these analyses.

Table 20.3 first presents the results of mixed-effect (method of moments) regression results related to the context of studies as a moderator. The first column of numbers provides a point estimate for the slope of the relationship between two variables. The p-value associated with each represents whether or not the slope is statistically significant in that potential group differences are identified by a statistically significant slope. Assessing the column titled p-value in Table 20.3, it is apparent that only two of the possible 15 associations assessed in Table 20.3 suggest that the slope is likely not zero (that is, demographics ↔ DP behaviors, self-control ↔ external controls). This suggests that the context for studying DP may not prove to be particularly problematic in future studies related to DP. Table 20.4 presents the same analyses vis-à-vis student versus non-student samples. These results suggest a bit more potential moderation in that four of the 15 relationships studied here present evidence of a positive slope in analyses (demographics ↔ DP behaviors and self-control ↔ social learning influences, plus external controls ↔ DP intentions and external controls ↔ DP behaviors). These results suggest that service researchers consider assessing DP-related intentions and behaviors across both student and non-student samples whenever possible.

Tables 20.3 and 20.4 present additional information of researcher

Table 20.3 Mixed-effects (method of moments) regression results for context

Path		Point estimate	Std error	Lower limit	Upper limit	Z-value	p-value		Q-value	Df (Q)	p-value	Tau^2
Demographics ↔ Self-control	Slope	−0.01168	0.02340	−0.05753	0.03418	−0.49912	0.61770	Model	0.24912	1	0.61770	0.00581
	Intercept	0.00042	0.03070	−0.05975	0.06060	0.01382	0.98898	Residual	59.39820	41	**0.03144**	
								Total	59.64732	42	**0.03772**	
Demographics ↔ Social learning	Slope	0.00460	0.00995	−0.01490	0.02411	0.46278	0.64352	Model	0.21417	1	0.64352	0.00906
	Intercept	−0.00031	0.01754	0.03468	0.03406	−0.01778	0.98581	Residual	148.4357	118	**0.03039**	
								Total	148.6498	119	**0.03404**	
Demographics ↔ External controls	Slope	0.00851	0.01666	−0.02414	0.04116	0.51064	0.60960	Model	0.26076	1	0.60960	0.01106
	Intercept	0.00031	0.02748	−0.05355	0.05417	0.01134	0.99095	Residual	134.6893	54	**0.00000**	
								Total	134.9500	55	**0.00000**	
Demographics ↔ DP intentions	Slope	−0.01312	0.02515	−0.06242	0.03617	−0.52188	0.60176	Model	0.27236	1	0.60176	0.01370
	Intercept	−0.01928	0.05840	−0.13375	0.09519	−0.33014	0.74130	Residual	16.66289	17	0.47742	
								Total	16.93525	18	0.52756	
Demographics ↔ DP behaviors	Slope	−0.11749	0.04818	−0.21191	−0.02307	−2.43875	**0.01474**	Model	5.94749	1	**0.01474**	0.01200
	Intercept	0.11863	0.05769	0.00557	0.23169	2.05649	0.03974	Residual	125.6533	30	**0.00000**	
								Total	131.6008	31	**0.00000**	
Self-control ↔ Social learning	Slope	−0.00529	0.01293	−0.03063	0.02005	−0.40889	0.68262	Model	0.16719	1	0.68262	0.02041
	Intercept	0.08802	0.03250	0.02432	0.15173	2.70817	0.00677	Residual	264.3860	152	**0.00000**	
								Total	264.5532	153	**0.00000**	
Self-control ↔ External controls	Slope	0.09816	0.03454	0.03047	0.16586	2.84218	**0.00448**	Model	8.07801	1	**0.00448**	0.00864
	Intercept	−0.06408	0.060298	−0.18822	0.05408	−1.06291	0.28782	Residual	16.42369	13	0.22701	
								Total	24.50170	14	**0.03982**	
Self-control ↔ DP intentions	Slope	0.07373	0.09055	−0.10374	0.25121	0.81427	0.41549	Model	0.66304	1	0.41549	0.15922
	Intercept	0.08609	0.18262	−0.27185	0.44402	0.47139	0.63736	Residual	19.62788	18	0.35415	
								Total	20.29091	19	0.37727	

Self-control ↔	Slope	0.06325	0.04667	−0.02823	0.15473	1.35521	0.17535	Model	1.83660	1	0.17535	0.04277
DP behaviors	Intercept	−0.09483	0.11840	−0.32690	−0.13723	−0.80094	0.42317	Residual	21.51739	17	0.20400	
								Total	23.35400	18	0.17735	
Social learning ↔	Slope	0.01279	0.02679	−0.03971	0.06529	0.47755	0.63297	Model	0.22805	1	0.63297	0.04997
External controls	Intercept	0.09977	0.04056	0.02028	0.17926	2.46012	0.01389	Residual	146.2080	126	0.10521	
								Total	146.4361	127	0.11430	
Social learning ↔	Slope	−0.00818	0.02767	−0.06242	0.04605	−0.29571	0.76745	Model	0.08745	1	0.76745	0.12490
DP intentions	Intercept	0.30144	0.05019	0.20308	0.39980	6.00662	0.00000	Residual	203.5618	190	0.23762	
								Total	203.6492	191	0.25222	
Social learning ↔	Slope	0.00004	0.02403	−0.04706	0.04715	0.00173	0.99862	Model	0.0000	1	0.99862	0.03500
DP behaviors	Intercept	0.20673	0.05029	0.10817	0.30529	4.11099	0.00004	Residual	63.0727	54	0.18626	
								Total	63.0727	55	0.21248	
External	Slope	0.13184	0.06830	−0.00203	0.26572	1.93019	0.05358	Model	3.72565	1	0.05358	0.07793
Controls ↔ DP	Intercept	−0.10449	0.11410	−0.32812	0.11913	−0.91583	0.35976	Residual	24.91033	20	0.20488	
intentions								Total	28.63598	21	0.12302	
External	Slope	−0.04978	0.03494	−0.11825	0.01870	−2.42467	0.15425	Model	2.02970	1	0.15425	0.02514
controls ↔ DP	Intercept	0.05925	0.05898	−0.05635	0.17486	2.00455	0.31511	Residual	84.61519	26	0.00000	
behaviors								Total	86.64488	27	0.00000	
DP intentions ↔	Slope	−0.08306	0.09415	−0.26759	0.10147	−0.88219	0.37767	Model	0.77827	1	0.37767	0.05950
DP behaviors	Intercept	0.43104	0.19799	0.04298	0.81910	2.17702	0.02948	Residual	7.964246	6	0.24074	
								Total	8.74246	7	0.27168	

Table 20.4 Mixed-effects (method of moments) regression results for sample

Path		Point estimate	Std error	Lower limit	Upper limit	Z-value	p-value		Q-value	Df (Q)	p-value	Tau²
Demographics ↔	Slope	No separate groups with the sample-related potential moderator.						Model	Not applicable.			
Self-control	Intercept							Residual				
								Total				
Demographics ↔	Slope	0.03889	0.03724	−0.0411	0.11189	1.04415	0.29642	Model	1.09025	1	0.29642	0.00904
Social learning	Intercept	−0.03503	0.04090	−0.11519	0.04514	−0.85633	0.39182	Residual	147.8525	118	**0.03270**	
								Total	148.9428	119	**0.03282**	
Demographics ↔	Slope	0.00493	0.03084	−0.05551	0.06537	0.15998	0.87290	Model	0.02559	1	0.87290	0.01104
External controls	Intercept	0.00599	0.04006	−0.07253	0.08452	0.14959	0.88109	Residual	135.0185	54	**0.00000**	
								Total	135.0441	55	**0.00000**	
Demographics ↔	Slope	−0.13126	0.07423	−0.27676	0.01423	−1.76821	0.07703	Model	3.12658	1	0.07703	0.01128
DP intentions	Intercept	0.10684	0.09042	−0.07037	0.28405	1.18163	0.23735	Residual	16.71395	17	0.47390	
								Total	19.84052	18	0.34187	
Demographics ↔	Slope	−0.28689	0.04817	−0.38131	−0.19248	−5.95557	**0.00000**	Model	35.46880	1	**0.00000**	0.01157
DP behaviors	Intercept	0.30478	0.05693	0.19320	0.41637	5.35350	0.00000	Residual	99.01404	30	**0.00000**	
								Total	134.4829	31	**0.00000**	
Self-control ↔	Slope	−0.04863	0.02417	−0.09599	−0.00126	−2.01211	**0.04421**	Model	4.04858	1	**0.04421**	0.02017
Social learning	Intercept	0.14695	0.03744	0.07357	0.22032	3.92526	0.00009	Residual	263.2337	152	**0.00000**	
								Total	267.2822	153	**0.00000**	
Self-control ↔	Slope	0.14360	0.08058	−0.01433	0.30154	1.78209	0.07474	Model	3.17583	1	0.07474	0.01265
External controls	Intercept	−0.08548	0.10212	−0.28564	0.11468	−0.83706	0.40256	Residual	15.29285	13	0.28943	
								Total	18.46868	14	0.18626	

Self-control ↔ DP intentions	Slope	0.39034	0.39589	−0.38558	1.16627	0.98599	0.32414	Model	0.97217	1	0.32414	0.14626
	Intercept	−0.19470	0.42469	−1.02708	0.63768	−0.45845	0.64663	Residual	21.06398	18	0.27620	
								Total	22.03615	19	0.28246	
Self-control ↔ DP behaviors	Slope	0.03084	0.11139	−0.18747	0.24916	0.27691	0.78185	Model	0.07668	1	0.78185	0.05592
	Intercept	0.00861	0.16771	−0.32010	−0.33732	0.05134	0.95905	Residual	17.96830	17	0.39084	
								Total	18.04498	18	0.45269	
Social learning ↔ External controls	Slope	0.05175	0.05739	−0.06074	0.16424	0.90169	0.36722	Model	0.81304	1	0.36722	0.04977
	Intercept	0.05723	0.06882	−0.07766	0.19212	0.83162	0.40563	Residual	146.1762	126	0.10554	
								Total	146.9892	127	0.10833	
Social learning ↔ DP intentions	Slope	0.05570	0.06470	−0.07112	0.18252	0.86087	0.38931	Model	0.74110	1	0.38931	0.12383
	Intercept	0.22542	0.07800	0.07253	0.37830	2.88983	0.00385	Residual	204.5988	190	0.22223	
								Total	205.3398	191	0.22658	
Social learning ↔ DP behaviors	Slope	0.01706	0.06442	−0.10920	0.14331	0.26477	0.79118	Model	0.07010	1	0.79118	0.03493
	Intercept	0.18634	0.08147	0.02667	0.34601	2.28735	0.02218	Residual	63.11898	54	0.18518	
								Total	63.18908	55	0.20955	
External controls ↔ DP intentions	Slope	0.30976	0.15405	0.00782	0.61169	2.01071	**0.04436**	Model	4.04296	1	**0.04436**	0.07389
	Intercept	−0.28425	0.19148	−0.65955	0.09104	−1.48450	0.13768	Residual	26.06964	20	0.16352	
								Total	30.11260	21	0.08975	
External controls ↔ DP behaviors	Slope	−0.13736	0.04312	−0.22188	−0.05285	−3.18553	**0.00144**	Model	10.14760	1	**0.00144**	0.02406
	Intercept	0.16739	0.06421	0.04154	0.29324	2.60682	0.00914	Residual	79.04605	26	**0.00000**	
								Total	89.19365	27	**0.00000**	
DP intentions ↔ DP behaviors	Slope	No separate groups with the sample-related potential moderator.						Model	Not applicable			
	Intercept							Residual				
								Total				

interest. Q_{Model} can be considered a between-group subgroup analysis in this context. $Q_{Residual}$ is analogous to Q_{Within} in terms of subgroup analysis. Thus, the final columns in Tables 20.3 and 20.4 reflect that there exist cases wherein part of the observed effect sizes can be attributable to either between-groups variance (demographics ↔ DP behaviors; self-control ↔ social learning influences; self-control ↔ external controls; external controls ↔ DP intentions; external controls ↔ DP behaviors), within-group variance (demographics ↔ self-control; demographics ↔ social learning influences; demographics ↔ external controls; demographics ↔ DP behaviors; self-control ↔ social learning influences; and external controls ↔ DP behaviors), or both (demographics ↔ DP behaviors; self-control ↔ social learning influences; and external controls ↔ DP behaviors). Readers will note a measure of consistency associated with which specific relationships express issues related to potential heterogeneity.

Discussion of Results

We consider these results to represent broad strokes in our canvas of understanding of the formation of DP-related intentions and behaviors. First, the results appear to support the conclusions that social learning and self-control theories appear promising avenues of investigation in marketing efforts to attenuate DP-related practices. Second, the evidence to date appears to support a strong relationship between DP-related intentions and behaviors, preserving the likely efficacy of survey-based research methods. Third, the role of demographics is not clarified by the reported meta-analyses. We find little evidence that demographics are related to any of the other key concepts in the model assessed here. Finally, a similar conclusion can be made concerning external control measures, which are not found to be directly associated with either DP-related intentions or behaviors. If external measures such as legal threats and copy protection are ineffective in changing behavior, then one begins to question the utility of their use from a marketing perspective. This finding also appears to support the arguments of Taylor et al. (2009) for a marketing-communications-based approach to combating DP as opposed to more direct legal threat strategies.

However, care must be taken to not over-interpret the results reported here. The observed measures of heterogeneity in Table 20.1 support this conclusion given the consistent observations (1) that the studies included in this meta-analysis do not appear to share a common effect size based upon the observed p-values associated with Q-values (that is, the true effect size in the population varies); and (2) very high observed variances emitting from real differences between studies (I^2). Thus, DP-related meta-analytic studies involving these antecedent variables should use the random effects model whenever possible. Cumming (2012) argues the random effects model assumes that there is a distribution of population parameters (not a single true effect), and that different studies estimate different values from that distribution. In addition, there is evidence of potential moderating influences among DP studies related to sample type and focus of inquiry. Future research in DP should strongly consider the use of invariance studies to better understand the reported results (see Vandenberg and Lance 2000).

STUDY LIMITATIONS

All studies possess limitations, and this study is no exception. First, our assessment of the conceptual model of Higgins and Marcum (2011) assesses associations (bivariate correlations) and not causation. Second, and related to the first point, while mediating influences are theorized in the conceptual model presented as Figure 20.1, we provide no true tests of mediation/moderation. The relative strength and nature of predictive relationships is yet undetermined and within the purview of future research. Third, some may disagree with our coding decisions vis-à-vis a general approach. It is clear that finer levels of discrimination are available to future meta-analyses, potentially reducing some of the observed heterogeneity observed here. Finally, while we sought correlation matrices for every identified study in our literature review, there were a few instances when we received no responses back for our requests. This occurrence reinforces our strategy of reporting effect sizes corrected for potential "file drawer" problems.

MANAGERIAL AND FUTURE RESEARCH IMPLICATIONS

The meta-analytic results reported here generally support Higgins and Marcum's (2011) conceptual model of the antecedents of DP-related intentions/behaviors. This implies a number of managerial implications for service marketers of easily replicable digital products. First, the importance of self-control and social learning influences in the model are validated by the weight of the evidence to date. However, the effect size and confidence interval associated with external control measures demonstrates no evidence that such strategies influence DP-related behaviors or behavioral intentions. Rather, it is the measures of self-control and social learning influences that seem to dominate the model. This suggests an emphasis on fostering intrinsic motivation within potential digital pirates as opposed to an emphasis on extrinsic forms of motivation. This conclusion appears consistent with the recommendations of Taylor et al. (2009) concerning marketers' strategies to try to attenuate the practice of DP. It is the intrinsically-motivating concepts of self-control and social learning that appear to offer the clearest associations with underlying DP intentions/behaviors.

Also, a variety of interesting future research issues emerge from the analyses presented here. One of the most interesting observations from this study concerns the appropriate conceptualization and operationalization of the perceived control construct. The current research finds that psychologically-based measures such as perceived behavioral control and self-control theory appear related to DP-related behaviors and intentions. External measures of control are more suspect. Also, it is unclear whether marketing communication strategies can be better directed toward self-control rather than social learning influences. If in fact self-control is more closely associated with a stable human characteristic, this may suggest an emphasis on efforts to use social learning influences to attenuate DP. Future research should consider providing greater insight into how best to view control within the context of DP.

Ferguson and Brannick (2012) present evidence that publication bias may not be as much of an issue as viewed in the literature. Their study suggests that publication bias was worrisome in about 25 percent of the meta-analyses that they analyzed, and that meta-analyses that included unpublished studies were more likely to show bias than those that did not (probably due to selection bias in unpublished literature searches). Nonetheless, in the current research we included unpublished studies whenever possible and provide both raw and corrected effect sizes based on the current state of practice. Future research remains to validate whether or not the file drawer problem is truly problematic.

The results reported in Table 20.1 validate the importance of adjustments by the trim-and-fill method (Duval and Tweedie 2000a, 2000b). We recommend that service marketers who use meta-analytic methods in the future report both obtained and adjusted (for potential file drawer bias) effect sizes such as done here in Table 20.1. Readers can then make informed interpretations of results. We further suggest that random instead of fixed methods are generally preferred in this area of inquiry, as discussed throughout this chapter.

Finally, some readers may inquire, "Why not use the correlation matrix constructed in Table 20.2 as input into multivariate analyses?" We chose not to do this based on the arguments of Card (2012), who asserts that one issue involves the potential for different correlations from very different sets of studies to yield a correlation matrix that is non-positive definite. Another issue concerns assumed heterogeneity among studies comprised in the meta-analyses. Card (2012) suggests that observed heterogeneity does not allow for setting the kinds of equality constraints necessary to use structural equation modeling (SEM)-based methods of prediction such as proposed by Cheung and Chan (2005). Readers are also invited to consider Cheung's (2008) more recent model for integrating meta-analyses into SEM. We leave to future research efforts to assess the predictive characteristics of DP-related data.

NOTES

1. This conceptualization of intention mediating the relationship between antecedents of DP and actual DP behavior is further bolstered by the wealth of literature related to the intention-behavior relationship. For example, theoretically, behavioral intentions are a key component of attitude theory (Bagozzi et al. 2001, Eagly and Chaiken 1993), goal theories (Webb and Sheeran 2006), as well as the folk Theory of the Mind (Malle et al. 2001). Webb and Sheeran (2006) present evidence that medium-to-large changes in behavioral intentions ($d = 0.66$) are associated with small-to-medium changes in behavior ($d = 0.36$).
2. A word about moral behaviors appears warranted as an element of social learning influences in this context. Higgins and Marcum (2011) observe that moral considerations tend to demonstrate a negative link to DP. However, the other concepts coded as social learning influences represent largely positively valenced linkages. Thus, we anticipate that any observed effect sizes based upon moral influences vis-à-vis DP-related behaviors intentions will serve to attenuate the overall observed effect size between social learning influences and DP-related intentions/behaviors in our reported results. That said, we chose to code all of these influences together in our analyses as the goal of the research reported here is to sift out the strength of the relative influences of social learning versus various forms of control on DP-related intentions and behaviors.
3. The reason that frequency of past behavior (FPB) was coded as a measure of social learning instead of self-control (for example, habit-related) is based on the prominence of FPB in emerging attitudinal models that explain the formation of behavioral intentions (Taylor 2007, 2012a).
4. Borenstein et al. (2009) note that considering that the studies considered here derive from different studies in the literature it is plausible that the impacts of the covariates assessed here capture some, but not all, of the true variation among effects. This suggests the use of the random-effects model. Under the random-effects model the effect size is the mean of the true effect sizes for all studies with a given value of the covariates. This is important because different error terms are used to compute tests of significance and confidence intervals from the fixed-model method.

REFERENCES

Ajzen, Icek (1988), *Attitudes, Personality, and Behavior*, Milton Keynes: Open University Press.

Ajzen, Icek (2002), 'Perceived behavioral control, self-efficacy, locus of control, and the theory of planned behavior," *Journal of Applied Social Psychology*, **32** (4), 665–83.

Akers, Ronald L. (1998), *Social Learning and Social Structure: A General Theory of Crime and Deviance*, Boston, MA: Northeastern University Press.

Andrés, Antonio Rodríguez (2006), "The relationship between copyright software protection and piracy: evidence from Europe," *European Journal of Law and Economics*, **21** (1), 29–51.

Aquinis, Herman, Dan R. Dalton, Frank A. Bosco, Charles A. Pierce and Catherine M. Dalton (2011), "Meta-analytic choices and judgment calls: implications for theory building and testing, obtained effect sizes, and scholarly impact," *Journal of Management*, **37** (1), 5–38.

Bagozzi, Richard P., Zeynep Gurhan-Canli and Joseph R. Priester (2001), *The Social Psychology of Consumer Behavior*, Buckingham: Open University Press.

Bandura, A. (1986), *Social Foundations of Thought and Action: A Social Cognitive Theory*, Englewood Cliffs, NJ: Prentice Hall.

Bandura, A. (1989), "Human agency in social cognitive theory," *American Psychologist*, **44** (9), 1175–84.

Bandura, A. (1991), "Social cognitive theory of self-regulation," *Organizational Behavior and Human Decision Processes*, **50** (2), 248–87.

Bandura, A. (2001), "Social cognitive theory: an agentic perspective," *Annual Review of Psychology*, **52** (1), 1–26.

Blackwell, Brenda Sims and Alex R. Piquero (2005), "On the relationship between gender, power control, self-control, and crime," *Journal of Criminal Justice*, **33** (1), 1–17.

Bocij, Paul (2006), *The Dark Side of the Internet*, London: Praeger.

Borenstein, Michael, Larry V. Hedges, Julian P. T. Higgins and Hannah R. Rothstein (2009), *Introduction to Meta-Analysis*, Chichester: John Wiley & Sons.

Bouffard, Jeffrey A. and Stephen K. Rice (2011), "The influence of the social bond on self-control at the moment of decision: testing Hirschi's redefinition of self-control," *American Journal of Criminal Justice*, **36** (2), 138–57.

Card, Noel A. (2012), *Applied Meta-Analysis for Social Science Research*, New York: Guilford Press.

Cheung, M.W.L. (2008), "A model for integrating fixed-, random-, and mixed effects meta-analyses into structural equation modeling," *Psychological Methods*, **13** (3), 182–202.

Cheung, M.W.L. and W. Chan (2005), "Meta-analytic structural equation modeling: a two-stage approach," *Psychological Methods*, **10** (1), 40–64.

Cockrill, Antje and Mark M.H. Goode (2012), "DVD pirating intentions: angels, devils, chancers, and receivers," *Journal of Consumer Behavior*, **11** (1), 1–10.

Cumming, Geoff (2012), *Understanding the New Statistics: Effect Sizes, Confidence Intervals, and Meta-Analysis*, New York: Routledge, Taylor & Francis Group.

Deci, E.L. and R.M. Ryan (1985), *Intrinsic Motivation and Self-Determination in Human Behavior*, New York: Plenum.

Duval, S. (2005), "The trim-and-fill method," in H.R. Rothstein, A.J. Sutton and M. Borenstein (eds), *Publication Bias in Meta-Analysis: Prevention, Assessment and Adjustment*, Chichester: John Wiley.

Duval, S. and R. Tweedie (2000a), "A nonparametric 'trim and fill' method of accounting for publication bias in meta-analysis," *Journal of the American Statistical Association*, **95** (449), 89–98.

Duval, S. and R. Tweedie (2000b), "Trim and fill: a simple funnel-plot-based method of testing and adjusting for publication bias in meta-analysis," *Biometrics*, **56** (2), 455–63.

Eagly, Alice H. and Shelly Chaiken (1993), *The Psychology of Attitudes*, Fort Worth, TX: Harcourt Brace Jovanovich.

Ferguson, Christopher J. and Michael T. Brannick (2012), "Publication bias in psychological science: prevalence, methods for identifying and controlling, and implications for the use of meta-analyses," *Psychological Methods*, **17** (1), 120–28.

Fetscherin, Marc (2009), "Importance of cultural and risk aspects in music piracy: a cross-national comparison among university students," *Journal of Electronic Commerce Research*, **10** (1), 42–55.

Geyskens, I., J.-B. E.M. Steenkamp and N. Kumar (1999), "Meta-analysis of satisfaction in marketing channel relationships," *Journal of Marketing Research*, **36** (2), 223–38.

Goles, Tim, Bandula Jayatilaka, Beena George, Linda Parsons, Valrie Chambers, David Taylor and Rebecca Brune (2008), "Softlifting: exploring determinants of attitude," *Journal of Business Ethics*, **77** (4), 481–99.

Gopal, R., G. Sanders, S. Bhattacharjee, M. Agrawal and S. Wagner (2004), "A behavioral model of digital music piracy," *Journal of Organizational Computing and Electronic Commerce*, **14** (2), 89–105.

Gottfredson, M. and T. Hirschi (1990), *A General Theory of Crime*, Stanford, CA: Stanford University Press.

Hennig-Thurau, Thorsten, Victor Henning and Henrik Sattler (2007), "Consumer file sharing of motion pictures," *Journal of Marketing*, **71** (4), 1–18.

Higgins, George E. and Catherine D. Marcum (2011), *Digital Piracy: An Integrated Theoretical Approach*, Durham, NC: Carolina Academic Press.

Higgins, George, E., Scott E. Wolfe and Catherine D. Marcum (2008), "Digital piracy: an examination of three measurements of self-control," *Deviant Behavior*, **29** (5), 440–60.

Higgins, George E., S. E. Wolfe and C. D. Marcum (2009), "Digital piracy and neutralization: a trajectory analysis from short-term longitudinal data," *International Journal of Cyber Criminology*, **2** (2), 324–36.

Hinduja, Sameer (2006), *Music Piracy and Crime Theory*, New York: LFB Scholarly Publishing LLC.

Hirschi, Travis (1969), *Causes of Delinquency*, Berkeley, CA: University of California Press.

Hirschi, Travis (2004), "Self-control and crime," in R.F. Baumeister and K.D. Vohs (eds), *Handbook of Self-Regulation: Research, Theory, and Applications*, New York: Guilford.

Jacobs, Ruud S., Ard Heuverlman, Maurice Tan and Oscar Peters (2012), "Digital movie piracy: a perspective on downloading behavior through social cognitive theory," *Computers in Human Behavior*, **28** (3), 958–67.

Kirca, Ahmet H., Satish Jayachandran and William O. Bearden (2005), "Market orientation: a meta-analytic review and assessment of its antecedents and impact on performance," *Journal of Marketing*, **69** (April), 24–41.

LaRose, Robert, Ying Ju Lai, Ryan Lange, Bradley Love and Yuehua Wu (2006), "Sharing or piracy? An exploration of downloading behavior," *Journal of Computer-Mediated Communication*, **11** (1), 1–21.

LaRose, Robert, Carolyn A. Lin and Matthew S. Eastin (2003), "Unregulated Internet usage: addiction, habit, or deficient self-regulation?" *Media Psychology*, **5** (3), 225–53.

Liao, Yu Qing and Quan Liu (2010), "Applying dual digital watermarking technology in digital rights management," *Information Sciences and Interaction Sciences (ICIS) 3rd International Conference Proceeding*, 23–25 June, pp. 616–19.

Malle, Bertram, Louis J. Moses and Dare A. Baldwin (2001), *Intentions and Intentionality: Foundations of Social Cognition*, Cambridge, MA: MIT Press.

Peace, A. Graham, Dennis F. Galletta and James Y.L. Thong (2003), "Software piracy in the workplace: a model and empirical test," *Journal of Management Information Systems*, **20** (1), 153–77.

Perreault, William D. and Laurence E. Leigh (1989), "Reliability of nominal data based on qualitative judgments," *Journal of Marketing Research*, **26** (May), 135–48.

Peterson, Robert A. and Steven P. Brown (2005), "On the use of beta coefficients in meta-analysis," *Journal of Applied Psychology*, **90** (1), 175–81.

Pratt, Travis C., Francis T. Cullen, Christine S. Sellers, L. Thomas Winfree, Jr., Tamara D. Madensen, Leah E. Daigle, Noelle E. Fearn and Jacinta M. Gau (2010), "The empirical status of social learning theory: a meta-analysis," *Justice Quarterly*, **27** (6), 765–802.

Reeve, John Marshall (2005), *Understanding Motivation and Emotion*, 4th edn, Hoboken, NJ: John Wiley & Sons.

Rosenthal, R. and M.R. DiMatteo (2001), "Meta-analysis: recent developments in quantitative methods for literature reviews," *Annual Review of Psychology*, **52** (1), 59–82.
Ryan, R.M. and E.L. Deci (2000), "Self-determination theory and the facilitation of intrinsic motivation, social development, and well-being," *American Psychologist*, **55** (1), 68–78.
Tavousi, M., A.R. Hidarnia, A. Montazeri, E. Hajizadeh, F. Taremain and F. Ghofranipour (2009), "Are perceived behavioral control and self-efficacy distinct constructs?," *European Journal of Scientific Research*, **30** (1), 146–52.
Taylor, Steven A. (2007), "Broadening and deepening attitude-based models of goal-directed behaviors," *British Journal of Social Psychology*, **46**, 739–68.
Taylor, Steven A. (2012a), "Evaluating digital piracy intentions on behaviors," *Journal of Service Marketing*, **26** (7), 472–83.
Taylor, Steven A. (2012b), "Implicit attitudes and digital piracy," *Journal of Research in Interactive Marketing*, **6** (4), 281–97.
Taylor, Steven A., Chiharu Ishida and David W. Wallace (2009), "Intention to engage in digital piracy: a conceptual model and empirical test," *Journal of Service Research*, **11** (3), 246–62.
Turner, Michael G. and Alex R. Piquero (2002), "The stability of self-control," *Journal of Criminal Justice*, **30** (6), 457–71.
Vandenberg, Robert J. and Charles E. Lance (2000), "A review and synthesis of the measurement invariance literature: suggestions, practices, and recommendations for organizational research," *Organizational Research Methods*, **3** (1), 4–70.
Webb, Thomas L. and Paschal Sheeran (2006), "Does changing behavioral intentions engender behavior change? A meta-analysis of the experimental evidence," *Psychological Bulletin*, **132** (2), 249–68.
Wolfe, Scott E. and George E. Higgins (2008), "Self-control and perceived behavioral control: an examination of college student drinking," *Applied Psychology in Criminal Justice*, **4** (1), 108–34.

PART VII

RETHINKING THE MARKET FUNCTION

21 Rethinking the roles of marketing and operations: a service-ecosystems view

Stephen L. Vargo, Robert F. Lusch and Melissa Archpru Akaka

INTRODUCTION

The study of service(s) has gained increasing attention in recent years, as researchers and managers struggle to understand dynamic and intangible aspects of markets that are not well explained by traditional, manufacturing models of value creation (Chase and Haynes 2000; Vargo and Lusch 2004b). One of the major issues with conventional production-based models is that they distinguish the role of firms as "producers," or creators, of value and the role of customers as "consumers," or destroyers, of the value created by the firm (Normann 2001). In fact, the study of service(s) has been partly driven by an effort to improve the understanding of value creation when "production" and "consumption" processes converge, and "relationships" between firms and customers (Gronroos 1995; Gummesson 1987) are seen as central aspects of exchange and value creation (for example, Lovelock 2000; Zeithaml et al. 1985). This redirection of service-related research—toward an interactive and customer-inclusive view (Chase 1978)—has blurred the lines between historically divided firm functions in academia and practice (Lovelock 2000), and implies a need for cross-fertilization across disciplines.

A look back at the evolution of service(s) research indicates that a variety of service-related disciplines, particularly marketing and operations, have contributed toward an effort to address the issue of "inseparability" as well as other issues regarding seemingly "unique" characteristics of services (Vargo and Lusch 2004b)—for example, intangibility, heterogeneity, and perishability (Zeithaml et al. 1985). One emerging research stream—"service-dominant (S-D) logic"—suggests that all of these characteristics, which were once identified as unique to services, are in fact descriptive of all of social and economic exchange, especially when viewed in terms of value and its creation (Vargo and Lusch 2004a, 2004b, 2008). Thus, service(s) research can, and has already begun to, impact mainstream marketing research and practice.

However, as Vargo and Lusch (2004a) point out, like traditional business and economic disciplines, service(s) research is generally grounded in a very goods- and production-centered logic—that is, goods-dominant (G-D) logic. Because of this, many of the models developed for studying and understanding service(s) focus on customers as occasional contributors to the production of service (for example, self-service). This inclusion of the customer in firm-centered production processes has drawn attention toward customers as value creators, but also has made it increasingly difficult to distinguish the roles of different functions of the firm and its respective disciplines, such as marketing, operations and information technology. For example, with regard to the role of marketing, Lovelock (2000, p. 424) raised the question, "How should marketing relate to operations and human resources in those service environments where production and consumption take place simultaneously?"

Efforts to combine "production" and "consumption" processes into "lean solutions" (Womack and Jones 2005) extend the view of value creation beyond firms' production activities. Furthermore, an increasing emphasis on "customer competence" (Prahalad and Ramaswamy 2000) and the consideration of value networks (Lusch et al. 2010; Normann 2001) highlight the roles of multiple stakeholders and their contributions to value creation. These recent attempts to better understand varying roles in value creation suggest that a broader, more inclusive view is needed to inform the dynamic changes that are taking place across various, not just "service", industries (Vargo and Akaka 2009; Vargo and Lusch 2004a).

In this chapter, we argue that S-D logic (Vargo and Lusch 2004a, 2008) and its view on service—the application of competences for the benefit of another—as the basis of exchange, provides a robust and interactive framework for rethinking the purpose of the firm and its role(s) in value creation, specifically those related to marketing and operations. In particular, we articulate a service-ecosystems view of value co-creation, which is based on an "actor-to-actor" (A2A) framework (Vargo and Lusch 2011a) that emphasizes the dynamics of market interactions as well as the social forces (that is, institutions) that drive value creation (Vargo and Lusch 2011a, 2011b). This framework interconnects the value-creation processes of firms with various stakeholders by suggesting that all social and economic actors are resource integrators, as well as service providers and beneficiaries, that enact practices to create value for themselves and for others, or co-create value.

Importantly, this view removes the distinction between "producers" and "consumers" (Vargo et al. 2008) as separate actors and focuses on all actors as service providers and beneficiaries. This shift toward an A2A perspective (Vargo and Lusch 2011a) extends the view of marketing and operations beyond internal firm functions, by pointing toward marketing as the central role of a firm (Drucker 2003), and expanding the roles of operations and marketing beyond firms, to include practices and processes of various stakeholders, including customers.

We begin this chapter with an overview of an S-D logic, service-ecosystems view to provide an alternative approach for thinking about the roles of firms in value creation. To develop a fuller understanding of the roles of marketing and operations, we draw on a dynamic view of roles as resources in service ecosystems (Akaka and Chandler 2011; Baker and Faulkner 1991). Rather than focusing on roles as fixed to specific positions, such as firms as producers and customers as consumers, we argue that roles (for example, marketing and operations) can be considered as sets of practices (Akaka and Chandler 2011). In this view, roles connect one actor to other actors and can be integrated and recombined depending on the context of value creation. This reconceptualization of the nature of roles provides a framework for studying the unbundling and rebundling (Normann 2001) of value-creating practices across markets. It underscores the importance of multiple stakeholders in the co-production of compelling value propositions, as well as co-creators of value. We conclude with an example of the roles of marketing and operations in value co-creation, from a dynamic service-ecosystems view.

SERVICE ECOSYSTEMS

Service-dominant logic has been discussed as a potential underlying framework for weaving together traditionally diverse disciplines in the study of service (Spohrer et al. 2007). We argue here that this emerging and evolving logic can help to better integrate service(s) research, including that related to marketing and operations, and provide a more encompassing theoretical foundation for the study of service. This is because, alternative to traditional services (plural) research, which center on the study of intangible units of output, S-D logic views service (singular)—the application of competences for the benefit of another—as the basis of all exchange. Importantly, S-D logic's conceptualization of service broadens the scope of service research to include all exchange-related practices and processes (Vargo and Akaka 2012) and provides insight to rethinking the traditional roles of marketing and operations in value creation.

Service-dominant logic is grounded in ten foundational premises (FPs) that center on (1) service as the basis of exchange (FP1), (2) value co-creation (FP6), (3) resource integration (FP9), and (4) contextual value (FP10) (Vargo and Lusch 2004a; 2008). Recent extensions of S-D logic promote a stakeholder co-creation perspective (Lusch and Webster 2011), argue for an actor-to-actor approach (Vargo and Lusch 2011a) and emphasize the role of networks (Akaka et al. 2012; Lusch et al. 2010) and systems dynamics (Vargo and Akaka 2012) in service-for-service exchange. This service-centered, systems-oriented view has led to the introduction and elaboration of the concept of a service ecosystem (Akaka et al. 2012; Chandler and Vargo 2011; Lusch 2011; Vargo and Akaka 2012; Vargo and Lusch 2011a).

Grounded in S-D logic, service ecosystems are defined as "relatively self-contained self-adjusting systems of resource integrating actors connected by shared institutional logics and mutual value creation through service exchange" (Vargo and Lusch 2011b). This dynamic view emphasizes the systemic nature of value co-creation and the influence of social factors in service-for-service exchange. Recent elaborations on service ecosystems point toward the importance of *networks* of relationships and resources (Akaka et al. 2012) and *institutions* (Vargo and Lusch 2011a, 2011b) that constitute the context through which value is co-created, as well as the practices (routine actions) that guide the reproduction of both (Giddens 1984; Vargo and Akaka 2012). The following sections review S-D logic's central concepts and elaborate the nature of service ecosystems and how value is co-created within and among them.

Service

As mentioned, S-D logic is based on the central tenet that service is the basis of exchange (Vargo and Lusch 2004a; 2008). That is, all exchange is based on service, and all economies are service economies. This inclusive definition of service broadens the scope and reach of service-related research. Rather than treating services as inferior products, as is done within G-D logic, S-D logic underscores the centrality of applying knowledge and skills for the benefit of others in all social and economic exchange.

Although material and symbolic resources maintain an important role within S-D logic— as intermediaries, or vehicles, for the provision of service—goods (tangible products) are not the primary resources in value creation. This is because these "operand" resources—those that require action taken upon them to be valuable—only become valuable through human evaluation or value determination. Because views on value differ from person to person, and are influenced by service beneficiaries as well as service providers, this service-centered perspective emphasizes the application of competences of all parties engaged in exchange as a requisite for value creation. Thus, perhaps the second most important concept of S-D logic is value co-creation.

Value Co-creation

One of the central premises of S-D logic is that value is always *co-created* by the customer (Vargo and Lusch 2004a, 2008), and, thus, all actors engaged in exchange are always (not only in special cases) active participants in value creation. In this view, value is ultimately derived and determined by a service beneficiary (for example, customer), through the use of, or experience with, a market offering, in a particular context. Thus, service beneficiaries are not only part of value creation, but they are central to it. The role of service providers (e.g. firms), then, is to assist service beneficiaries in creating value for themselves, and for others, in the context of their own lives. For firms, this is accomplished through the development of value propositions (Lusch et al. 2007), which a potential customer can accept, reject, ignore, or modify for integration with various other resources to solve a variety of problems. It is important to note that S-D logic's A2A view broadens a customer-centric view on value creation to include the roles of other stakeholders (for example, suppliers, associations, and government agencies) in value co-creation.

In addition to a "stakeholder" view of value co-creation, S-D logic's conceptualization of value co-creation extends beyond inviting customers to participate in the production of "services" (Ordanini and Pasini 2008). Vargo and Lusch (2006) distinguish between "co-production" and value co-creation by suggesting that co-production can be considered as a particular value co-creation process, which involves the collaboration of multiple stakeholders (for example, firms, customers, and suppliers) in the development and design stages of generating a market offering or value proposition. Although co-production is considered a sub-process of value co-creation, it is a critical consideration for managers attempting to increase their firms' contributions to value creation because many of the changing market roles are currently tied to co-production (Akaka and Chandler 2011).

On the other hand, within an S-D logic, service-ecosystems view, value is always co-created among multiple actors. Thus, the co-creation of value relies on the competences of firms, customers and other stakeholders. This draws attention toward the primacy of *operant* resources—those that are capable of acting on other resources (for example, knowledge and skills)—over *operand* resources (for example, goods and money) in value creation (Constantin and Lusch 1994; Vargo and Lusch 2004a). In the co-creation of value, it is important to reiterate that before value can be realized by the beneficiary (for example, customer), the firm's offering or value proposition, must be integrated with other resources, some of which are also obtained through the market and some of which are privately (for example, personal, friends, and family) or publicly (for example, government resources) accessed. Thus, value creation is always a collaborative and interactive process, driven by the application and integration of operant (and sometimes operand) resources.

Resource Integration

The process of value co-creation appears increasingly complex, as more social and economic actors, service providers and beneficiaries, are included in the process. What is fundamentally an exchange of service-for-service has become increasingly complicated through the development of networks, large organizations, indirect and monetized exchange, and rapid advances in information technology. Importantly, a service-ecosystems view moves away from a focus on dyadic exchange, to various forms of interaction and resource integration. This broader view of interaction in markets emphasizes the strength of "largely loosely coupled" relationships or "weak ties" (Granovetter 1973) in value co-creation (Vargo and Lusch 2011a).

Although complexities of the market may appear to be increasing, an S-D logic, service-ecosystems view emphasizes that organizations, money and goods are only vehicles for exchange, and that service remains the basis for all exchange. Furthermore, this service-centered perspective offers a balanced approach to exchange, which considers all social and economic actors as resource integrators, and points toward an A2A view on market interaction and value creation (Vargo and Lusch 2011a).

This A2A view of market interaction and emphasis on all actors as resource integrators draws attention toward the micro-level actions and interactions that contribute to the co-creation of both value and markets (Chandler and Vargo 2011). In particular, Korkman et al. (2010) draw on S-D logic and argue that value is co-created and resources are integrated through the enactment of practices. The study of practices in market interactions and value creation has gained attention in recent years (Kjellberg and Helgesson 2006; Schau et al. 2009), and has been most extensively discussed in the literature regarding "markets as practices" (Kjellberg and Helgesson 2006) In particular, Kjellberg and Helgesson (2006) identify three market practices—exchange, normalizing and representation—that contribute to the ongoing reproduction of markets.

Vargo and Akaka (2012) draw on the literature regarding market practices (Kjellberg and Helgesson 2006) and suggest that resource integration should be considered as a central practice for value co-creation in service ecosystems. They argue that, as individual actors (for example, firms, customers, and countries) enact practices to create value for themselves and for others, they integrate a variety of market- and nonmarket-facing resources. In other words, as actors enact particular resource-integration practices, they interact with other actors and contribute to value co-creation processes. These processes intersect with other value co-creation processes and form networks of relationships (Akaka et al. 2012). However, the enactment of practices not only contributes to the development of relationships, but also reproduces the social structures that compose service ecosystems as well (Edvardsson et al. 2011; see also Giddens 1984). In other words, the enactment of resource-integration practices both draws on and contributes to the context (including networks and institutions) through which value is derived (Vargo and Akaka 2012).

Value-in-context

Service-dominant logic's concepts of service, value co-creation and resource integration underscore the contextual factors and social forces that influence, and are influenced by, actions and interactions among actors. Thus, in this view, value co-creation is always a collaborative process, driven by the application of operant resources, which takes place in the context of a unique set of exchange relationships (systems) and is guided by intersecting institutions (that is, social structures) (Giddens 1984). Importantly, S-D logic redirects attention away from traditional notions of normative economic value, value-in-exchange, toward a focus on real value, or value-in-use (Smith 1776 [2000]). More specifically, an S-D logic ecosystems view emphasizes a phenomenological and experiential view of value, which has most recently been discussed as "value-in-context" (Vargo et al. 2008).

In complex market environments, there is often a tendency to view organizations, as well as their functional departments, "as entities in and of themselves" without accounting for the employed individuals who generate and transfer knowledge internally and externally. Chandler and Vargo (2011) elaborate the complex interactions in service ecosystems by identifying micro, meso, and macro levels of interaction in value co-creation, as well as a meta layer that provides a dynamic systems view of how the levels relate and evolve. In this multi-level view, department- and firm-level systems emerge through repeated interaction (for example, exchange) among individuals.

Although marketing and management typically have been studied within the structure of the firm, the construction of a firm actually involves a complex system of routine actions (that is, practices), as well as networks of relationships and resources (Akaka et al. 2012), social norms (that is, institutions) and collective meanings (Vargo and Lusch 2011a). Furthermore, firms are nested within broader ecosystems, composed of

Table 21.1 Alternative views on value and value creation

	G-D logic	S-D logic
Nature of value	Value-in-exchange	Value-in-context
Process of value creation	Added value	Value co-creation
Role of firm	Producer	Resource integrator
Role of customer	Consumer	Resource integrator
Context of interaction	Dyad	Ecosystem

multiple practices, networks, and institutions. Thus, social context is composed of micro, meso and macro levels of interactions and relationships, as well as intersecting and overlapping social structures, such as institutions. Table 21.1 compares an S-D logic ecosystems view with traditional, G-D logic views on value and value creation.

The shift toward service-centered thinking for the roles of the firm requires refocusing the creation of value from the production of units of output to the process of service provision (Vargo and Lusch 2004a). Service-dominant logic provides a framework for this shift in thought as it "superordinates service (the *process* of providing benefit) to products (*units of output* that are sometimes used in the process)" (Lusch et al. 2007, p. 6, emphasis in original). This focus on process integrates the traditional firm roles of "production" and "distribution"—that is, operations and marketing—into a broader process of value creation and emphasizes the competencies and collaboration required for creating value in complex systems of exchange. The S-D logic, service-ecosystems view provides a framework for rethinking the roles of marketing and operations (and other disciplines) as discussed in the section that follows.

RETHINKING THE ROLES OF MARKETING AND OPERATIONS

The integration of the roles of marketing and operations in both academia and practice has already begun (for example, Balasubramanian and Bhardwaj 2004; Karmarkar 1996; Malhotra and Sharma 2002). Karmarkar (1996, p. 125) argues, "the operations function was traditionally managed as a cost center, but it is now apparent (and in retrospect, obvious) that production and operations decisions also affect such market related variables as time, quality (conformance and performance), and customer support." Along a slightly different vein, Malhotra and Sharma (2002) discuss the conflicts that arise between marketing and operations because of separate department goals, for example, marketing's goal to increase product diversity versus manufacturing's goal of reducing costs through longer production of a narrower product line. However, the authors also establish broad areas of mutual interest and integration between the two functional areas that lead to the overarching goal for both marketing and operations of maximizing organization performance, and call for further research aligning the objectives between disciplines.

Extending the integration of roles in value creation beyond firm-centered efforts, Womack and Jones (2005) emphasize the need for lean solutions, which brings together both "production" and "consumption" processes and streamlines the value-creation processes for both firms and customers. This emphasis on the customer's role in value creation has also been recognized in Prahalad and Ramaswamy's (2000) work on "customer competences" and Christensen et al.'s (2007) discussion on identifying the "jobs" that products take on when they are used by customers. In addition, service-related research has also drawn attention toward the role of customers, particularly in service encounters or direct interaction with firms (Orsini and Karagozoglu 1988; Paul 1994).

To articulate the roles of the firm in service provision, several service researchers have applied a dramaturgical perspective (for example, Bitner 2000; Grove et al. 2000; Soloman et al. 1995). For example, Grove et al. (2000) suggest that the two main roles of a firm involve "front stage" and "back stage" activities. In this view, customers are considered as "audience" members who are an important, but not central, part of the processes by which value is created. Although this view considers multiple roles in value creation, it emphasizes a distinction between goals of those who deal directly with customers and those who do not. Lovelock (2000) identifies one of the problems is that operations may want less time spent with customers to increase efficiency and marketing want more time with customers. In this view, the problems arise when the "front" and "back" stage actors do not have the same goals and are not both directed toward understanding the perspectives and practices of customers.

The inclusion of the customer within this framework has begun to blur the lines between operations and marketing activities. However, further investigation into the roles of marketing and operations is needed to address the disconnection between roles related to the front stage, the back stage and the audience, and provide a unifying framework for clarifying the roles of firms (and others) in value creation. Furthermore, the consideration of customers as the "audience" makes it difficult to understand the participation of the customer in value creation, and the level of involvement required. We argue that the S-D logic, service-ecosystems view discussed above provides a framework for rethinking the roles of marketing and operations. This is based on (1) the integration of roles as resources in service ecosystems, (2) the centrality of marketing in value co-creation, and (3) the ubiquity of operations and marketing, as well as resource integration, in service ecosystems. These ideas are elaborated below.

Integrating Roles as Resources in Service Ecosystems

As mentioned, an S-D logic ecosystems approach emphasizes the idea that customers always contribute to value co-creation. However, it is the re-integration of roles related to co-production—a subset of value co-creation processes (Lusch and Vargo 2006)—that is changing the dynamics of markets and requires more attention, especially for those aimed at developing more compelling value propositions (Akaka and Chandler 2011). The recognition of customer enactment of what have been conventionally known as firm-related practices has been especially prevalent in recent years with the introduction of new forms of information technology that enable customers to access more information, learn new practices, and interact with different (and more) actors. Concepts such as self-service (Meuter et al. 2000), mass customization (Gilmore and Pine 1997), and user innovation (von Hippel 2009) reflect the movement from thinking about customers as passive "consumers" to, at least part-time, "producers."

Akaka and Chandler (2011) provide insight to the shifting roles of customers, by arguing that roles can be integrated (combined and recombined) as resources (Baker and Faulkner 1992) depending on the context of value creation. This view provides an alternative perspective of roles than is applied in prior service-related literature, which presumes that actors are assigned particular positions (for example, front stage or back stage) and will enact or "act out" their roles in order to meet or conform to expectations associated with a particular position (for example, Grove et al. 2000; Solomon et al. 1985). Recent research on market-related actions centers on the concept of *practices* (Kjellberg and Helgesson 2006), and explicates the way in which the routine actions of multiple actors contribute not only to the creation of value, but also can shape and reshape markets as well. Drawing on a practice approach to better understand the changing roles of customers and firms, Akaka and Chandler (2011, p. 251) argue for a reconceptualization of roles as "a set of practices (repeated activities) that connect one actor to one or more actors." This conceptualization of roles draws on a dynamic service-ecosystems view, and centers on the idea that roles of actors are not fixed, and can move from person to person, and change over time.

Redefining roles as sets of practices that connect one actor to other actors underscores the way in which roles can be integrated as resources

Figure 21.1 Roles as enacted positions

in value creation. The traditional treatment of roles in prior service literature suggests that roles are adopted, learned and/or fulfilled based on the expectations associated with a particular social position (for example, Solomon et al. 1985). In this case, roles are treated as operand resources, those that must be acted upon or acted out (fulfilled) to provide support or benefit. Figure 21.1 depicts a traditional view of the roles of the firm, in which the roles of marketing and operations (and other firm functions) are enacted from the positions or departments.

Alternatively, the consideration of roles as sets of practices suggests that integrating unique combinations of practices—combining and recombining roles—can lead to changes in social positions, and thus networks. In particular, Baker and Faulkner (1991, p. 281) argue, "Roles are used to create positions and their relationships (that is, social structures). Social structures are created by concretizing (abstract) roles into real positions." In this case, roles can be conceptualized as resources (Baker and Faulkner 1991) because they guide the actions and interactions among actors, but also support the development of relationships and social networks (for example, markets). This approach highlights the operant nature of roles because, as they (sets of practices) are enacted, they can act on other resources and create change (Akaka and Chandler 2011). Figure 21.2 illustrates the integration of sets of practices by different actors and illustrates how different actors can enact similar roles, even while maintaining distinct positions within a particular network of relationships and resources.

Figure 21.2 makes salient the ability for actors to integrate various practices depending on the task at hand. In this view, various actors can draw on marketing and operations (and other) roles as resources to solve problems, develop relationships, and engage in exchange. By unbundling and rebundling (Normann 2001) sets of practices, actors can enact different roles depending on the social context and available resources that frame each interaction. The consideration of roles as operant resources implies that people are capable of developing creative solutions and uniquely creating value in the market. Because, in this view, roles are not fixed to particular positions, any actor can draw on a variety of roles, including marketing and operations.

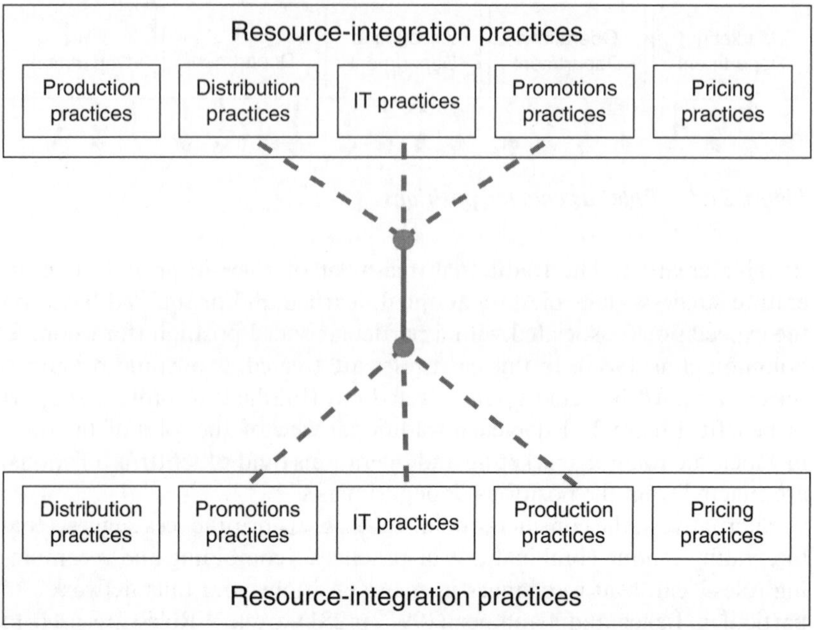

Figure 21.2 Integrating roles as resources

This is reflected in the integration of unique combinations of practices or sets of practices (that is, roles) that are increasingly evident in modern market interactions. It is important to note that, although the figure depicts a dyadic interaction, this micro-level interaction occurs within a network of a multitude of relationships and resources and overlapping and intersecting institutions. In addition, the two nodes represent "generic" actors (A2A) in value co-creation. That is, the roles that are integrated as resources can be drawn upon in business-to-business (B2B), business-to-customer (B2C), or customer-to-customer (C2C) (or any other combination) interactions.

This emphasis on roles as operant resources does not suggest that expectations are not important: they are. Expectations are established by institutions, which both enable and restrain the actions and interactions within a service ecosystem (Vargo and Lusch 2011a). However, by considering the operant nature of roles, actors can be more empowered to respond to unique situations and will be better equipped to aid in processes of value co-creation. This is especially important from the perspective of service ecosystems, in which the recombination of practices can potentially contribute to the reconfiguration of relationships and resources (systems) as well as social norms and meanings (structure) (Giddens 1984; Vargo and Akaka 2012). The interconnected and dynamic nature of service ecosystems, and the consideration of roles as sets of practices that can be drawn upon as resources by multiple stakeholders, emphasize the centrality of marketing and the ubiquity of operations, as well as marketing, in value co-creation.

The Centrality of Marketing in Value Co-creation

The S-D logic, service-ecosystems view discussed above redirects the role of the firm to focus on value creation through market interaction, rather than within the firm. This suggests that marketing, in a broad and service-centered sense, is a central driver of value co-creation and the main purpose of the firm. This is because all firm activities should be focused on developing relationships with customers and assisting them in creating value in their own lives. This falls in line with Drucker's (2003, p. 20) argument that "Because its purpose is to create the customer, the business has two – and only two – basic functions: marketing and innovation." He argues, "the aim of marketing is to know and understand the customer so well that the product or service fits him and sells itself" (ibid., p. 21). In this view, the role of marketing is to connect various actors in value co-creating processes, by establishing lines of communication and facilitating the integration of resources, with the goal of creating value for and with all parties involved in exchange. When all employees of a firm are concerned with mutually beneficial exchange relationships and helping customers to create value, the role of marketing becomes central for all jobs and all employees within a firm.

Furthermore, in a revised theatrical metaphor, the customers or "audience" might be brought on stage to participate more fully in the value creation process and even establish new expectations and rewrite the script. With the consideration of roles as resources, firms can better understand how customers and other stakeholders are integrating different practices, such as those related to marketing (for example, word-of-mouth), as well as operations (for example, product customization), to create value for themselves, and for others. With more emphasis on interaction, firms will be better able to understand and respond to (that is, innovate for) the changing needs of customers.

In this way, all firm practices can be connected to the role of marketing as long as they contribute to developing value propositions and increasing the potential of value creation for others. With the redirection of the central actor of value creation—moving from value created by the firm to value that is derived and determined by customers—internal firm departments will be more synchronized. Each actor within a firm can draw on and enact different sets of practices, and integrate a variety of roles, depending on the task at hand. Furthermore, all actors in the firm can take on the role of marketing and combine particular marketing-related practices with others related to their specialization within a firm. With the emphasis on marketing as the central role of the firm, the role of operations, then, shifts from an inward focus on production, toward an outward focus on quality as perceived by the customer (versus the engineer). Furthermore, in this view, the role of operations (and marketing) extends beyond the confines of the firm and is drawn upon through customer resource-integration practices, which contribute to the creation of value for individuals, as well as the broad social contexts through which value is derived (Edvardsson et al. 2011).

The Ubiquity of Operations and Resource Integration

According to Lovelock (2000), operations functions are generally considered to dominate most service businesses because operations departments are responsible for creating and delivering the "service product." In this production-oriented view, marketing activities are considered as supplemental but helpful in understanding customer needs and habits and identifying opportunities for new product development. However, from a service-ecosystems view, marketing activities move to the forefront of firm efforts. From a value co-creation perspective, the focus of the firm is to help others co-create value, and this is done through the (re)configuration of relationships and the development of value propositions that increase the accessibility, adaptability and integrability of resources for others (Akaka et al. 2012).

Within service ecosystems, the goal of operations is to maintain and improve the efficiency and effectiveness of firm efforts to develop compelling value propositions. However, because "all social and economic actors are resource integrators" (Vargo and Lusch 2008, p. 7), the role(s) of operations (and marketing) can be drawn upon as a resource by all actors contributing to value co-creation. Furthermore, value propositions can be developed anywhere within a particular service ecosystem (Akaka and Chandler 2011). Thus, when customers are considered as the primary resource integrators in value co-creation, the role of operations within a firm is to integrate resources in such a way that customers are able to easily integrate that firm's value propositions with other resources, to create, and sometimes propose, value.

One of the ways a firm can support customers' resource-integration practices is to help shape the configuration of resources and relationships so that resources are easily accessible, adaptable and integrable (Akaka et al. 2012). Within a service-ecosystems view, firms can develop more compelling value propositions by considering how customers uniquely integrate their offerings with other private, public, and market-facing resources. When firms make efforts to unbundle and rebundle (Normann 2001) or enable customers to rebundle its value propositions in ways that best fit with other resources, the potential for value creation to occur increases. The following section provides an example of how the roles of both marketing and operations were integrated as resources by various stakeholders and, along with a commitment to customer value and advances in technology, contributed to the co-production of one of the most compelling value propositions in the twenty-first century: the iPod.

THE INTEGRATION OF ROLES AS RESOURCES: THE CASE OF THE IPOD

In 2001, Apple Inc. launched the iPod with limited capabilities that restricted the mp3 player to Macintosh computers, which accounted for less than 4 per cent of computer sales in the U.S. at that time (Belk and Tumbat 2005). Although Apple's focus on customer usage (for example, aesthetic design, ease of use, and capacity of files space) undoubtedly helped its penetration in the digital music market, the widespread use of the iPod would probably have not been so swift, or perhaps so substantial, had it not been for several factors: (1) timely technological advancements, (2) Apple's ability to integrate resources and apply various roles (for example, designer, programmer, and music retailer) in unique ways, and (3) the development of collaborative relationships with a number of firms as well as customers (Reppel et al. 2006).

Nearly a year after the launch of the iPod (2002), Apple introduced its first Windows-compatible version. This accessibility, coupled with the enhancement of USB 2 connectivity (in 2003), exponentially increased iPod sales. Kahney (2005, p. 14) explains:

> Adding USB 2 was a subtle shift for Apple. It marked a departure from the principle of making products primarily for the Mac platform. But it also had the most dramatic impact on sales. Prior to the May 2003 switch, Apple had sold 1 million iPods but within the next six months, it had sold another million iPods, and nearly 3 million more were sold within a year. In the next 18 months 9 million more were sold.

To integrate technologies across different platforms and increase the reach of the iPod, Apple integrated sets of practices associated with the role of marketing (that is, developing relationships with other actors) as well as operations (that is, developing more efficient and effective production processes). For example, Apple collaborated with a number of firms (integrated internal and external practices) to piece together the hardware and software components of its products (Linden et al. 2007). In 2003, Apple integrated a new set of practices, by developing and launching its iTunes store, which enabled customers to legally access a variety of music online. Furthermore, Apple eventually collaborated with a conglomerate of companies from Nike to Bose, which began providing accessories that enabled customers to integrate the iPod throughout various aspects of their daily "operations" or routine practices (for example, exercising and home entertainment).

Apple's collaborative efforts also went beyond partnerships with other firms. Importantly, the company collaborated with celebrities to make a number of special edition iPods with names such as U2, Madonna and No Doubt (Kahney 2005). This ability to focus on strategically configuring relationships and resources reflects how Apple was able to draw on roles as operant resources and drive market change. Apple's collaborations with selected firms shifted the position of Apple in the market from a manufacturer of computers to the initiators of a new market for music, among others. Although Apple's collaborative efforts with established firms and celebrity brands contributed to much of the success of the iPod, the main contributors to the iPod's value propositions were less well known.

In particular, Apple was able to collaborate with individual employees and contract partners, which sparked the development of the iPod in the first place. Tony Fadell, a computer engineer from the University of Michigan, presented the iPod idea to Apple after he was rejected from a number of other companies, including Sony. Apple, under the leadership of former chief executive officer (CEO) Steve Jobs, was able to successfully integrate new practices (providing a platform for listening to music) with the company's existing practices (providing computing capabilities) through the development the iPod. Importantly, Apple's internal efforts to develop new products stayed focused on customer perspectives. In particular, Jonathan Ive, Apple's head of design, focused on connecting the customer to the value proposition.

> Ive clearly puts the customer as the central figure in the company's product development efforts. This does not necessarily mean that Apple is asking its customers for their product requirements and opinions. But it does imply that the customer's connection to the end result of the development process was identified to be central to that process.
>
> (Reppel et al. 2006, p. 240)

Ive's approach to the development of Apple's value propositions was driven by Apple's firm-wide focus on how customers use their products.

This focus on customer-use led to the development of products that were easy to use and aesthetically appealing (Reppel et al. 2006). Apple's holistic approach and the firm's relentless focus on the customer placed marketing in a central role for the firm and made its strategy "unlikely to be replicated by copying selected organizational aspects of the company" (Reppel et al. 2006, p. 240). Thus, it was largely through Apple's focus on marketing (developing relationships and reconfiguring resources), integration of resources beyond the firm and even the "computer industry," and collaboration with talented people and successful firms, that the company was able to develop and maintain the iPod, and its value proposition. However, the initial emergence and expansion of the iPod (Kahney 2005) was driven not by the suppliers of Apple, or Apple-related products, but by the customers that used them.

Ultimately, it was Apple's ability to collaborate with customers, and its customers' integration of practices related to marketing (for example, word of mouth) and operations (for example, developing applications), that propelled the brand into a "cult-like" state (Kahney 2005). As discussed above, the process of value co-creation occurred when Apple's customers (that is, beneficiaries) applied the competences of Apple in conjunction with their own competences, in the context of their lives. Although value has been universally co-created among Apple and its customers through the selection and customization of play lists and general use of the iPod (that is, operations), it was Apple's ability to facilitate value co-creation by customers in unique and extremely personal ways that grew into what has been recognized as a cultural revolution. One of the many examples of how customers have co-created value by developing relationships with their iPods can still be seen at "The iPods Around the World" gallery on iLounge.com. Here, avid iPod fans have uploaded photos of their iPods at different places around the world to connect with other fans (that is, marketing). The gallery includes iPods in a wide array of places, such as exotic beaches, baseball games, places of work and home, as well as with a variety of pets, plants and objects. This site reflects the locations and situations in which customers have used their iPods, and has allowed them to share the value that is derived through the use of their iPod with other friends and strangers, in particular contexts.

Another important way customers integrated the roles of operations was through further development of Apple's value proposition, by driving the transformation of the iPod from a simple audio player to a multipurpose digital device. According to Kahney (2005, p. 73):

> It's possible that Apple had planned from the start to make the iPod into a PDA, but it's also possible the company took its lead from iPod hackers, who, almost

> from the minute the gadget hit store shelves, were busy figuring out clever ways of making the iPod do more than just play music."

By paying attention to customer resource-integration practices (that is, operations), Apple was able to further the reach of the iPod and increase its value potential.

It is evident that Apple's central role of marketing, and collaborative capabilities with employees, firms, celebrities, and especially customers, fueled the success of the iPod. In order to develop and maintain this collaborative competence, it seems almost impossible that Apple could have operated in functional silos and truly separated the roles of marketing and operations.

The way in which Apple was able to align technical product specification (for example, design, function, aesthetics) and develop strong and loyal relationships with customers emphasizes the company's central role of marketing. This also points toward the way in which Apple's internal operations and resource-integration practices were closely interconnected with the roles of operations engaged by customers, and their resource-integration practices as well. In other words, the role of marketing was central for Apple and its development and launch of the iPod. Arguably, the centrality of marketing within Apple contributed to its customers' ability to integrate the roles of "marketers" and "operators," even "innovators," in the context of their own lives. This type of collaboration with external actors likely required the collaborative effort of everyone within the firm, focused on developing the core value proposition and helping customers to create value in their lives and in the lives of those around them.

CONCLUSION

The service-ecosystems view presented above suggests that the central role of a firm in value co-creation is to increase the ability for customers to access, adapt, and integrate resources (Akaka et al. 2012). This view shifts the role of the firm from as a value creator, to an enabler or supporter of value creation. As mentioned, within firm-level service ecosystems, there are sub-level systems (for example, functional departments) that integrate resources in order to accomplish certain tasks that contribute to the firm's ability to develop long-term exchange relationships. These necessary tasks are conducted through the integration of specialized skills and knowledge of individual employees (for example, managers, accountants, sales people, and administrative clerks) and collectively result in the proposition of value and provision of service in markets.

Owing to increasingly interconnected social systems and recent advances in technology, the traditional roles of marketing and operations have been unbundled and rebundled in various ways and integrated as resources in value co-creation. Thus, from an S-D logic, service-ecosystems view, the measure of a firm's contribution toward value creation becomes a function of how well one firm is able to integrate operant (and sometimes operand) resources, including roles, and enable others to do the same. In this view the roles of marketing and operations can be integrated by various actors within a firm, but also by customers and other stakeholders in their own value-creation processes.

Within service ecosystems, the main purpose of a firm is to enable other actors to facilitate the exchange of service and integration of resources through the development of collaborative relationships and compelling value propositions. In order to survive and thrive in complex and dynamic markets, firms need to anticipate market changes and have the ability to respond rapidly (Haeckel 1999). This process is complex and messy, dynamic and continuous. In order to succeed in this environment, firms must be able to see beyond their surrounding networks (of relationships and resources) to view those within which customers are embedded. Furthermore, managers need to be aware of the social norms and institutions that influence and are influenced by interaction and exchange.

Within an S-D logic, service-ecosystems framework, firms play a critical role in the process of value creation by integrating both operant and operand resources (that is, operations) in order to propose value in markets (that is, marketing) and help other actors (firms and people) to create, and even propose, value in the context of their own lives. This A2A view of value creation and stakeholder-oriented view of markets provides important insights for firms. From this perspective, marketing is seen as a central role of the firm (Drucker 2003) and the role of operations, as well as marketing, can be found throughout service ecosystems. This broader view of marketing and operations helps to reconcile the seemingly disparate goals of "front end" and "back end" roles by focusing on customer views on value as central to value creation. The example of the iPod illustrates how this dynamic ecosystems approach centers on customers as central actors, rather than audience members, in value creation, and the recombination of resources (including practices) as the driver of innovation as well as market formation.

REFERENCES

Akaka, M.A. and J.D. Chandler (2011), "Roles as resources: a social roles perspective of change in value networks," *Marketing Theory*, **11** (3), 243–60.

Akaka, Melissa A., Stephen L. Vargo and Robert F. Lusch (2012), "An exploration of networks in value co-creation: a service-ecosystems view," in Stephen L. Vargo and Robert F. Lusch (eds), *Special Issue – Toward a Better Understanding of the Role of Value in Markets and Marketing* (*Review of Marketing Research, Volume 9*), Bingley: Emerald Group, pp. 13–50.

Baker, Wayne E. and Robert R. Faulkner (1991), "Role as resource in the Hollywood film industry," *American Journal of Sociology*, **97** (2), 279–309.

Balasubramanian, Sridhar and Pradeep Bhardwaj (2004), "When not all conflict is bad: manufacturing-marketing conflict and strategic incentive design," *Management Science*, **50** (4), 489–502.

Belk, Russ W. and Gulnur Tumbat (2005), "The cult of Macintosh", *Consumption, Markets and Culture*, **8** (3), 205–17

Bitner, Mary Jo (2000), "The servicescape," in T.A. Swartz and D. Iacobucci (eds), *Handbook of Services Marketing and Management*, Thousand Oaks, CA: Sage Publications, pp. 37–50.

Chandler, Jennifer D. and Stephen L. Vargo (2011), "Contextualization and value-in-context: how value frames exchange," *Marketing Theory*, **11** (1), 35–49.

Chase, Richard (1978), "Where does the customer fit in a service operation?" *Harvard Business Review*, **56** (6), 137–42.

Chase, Richard B. and Ray M. Haynes (2000), "Service operations management. A field guide", in T.A. Swartz and D. Iacobucci (eds), *Handbook of Services Marketing and Management*, Thousand Oaks, CA: Sage Publications, pp. 455–72.

Christensen, Clayton M, Scott D. Anthony, Gerald Berstell and Denise Nitterhouse (2007), "Finding the right job for your product," *MIT Sloan*, **48** (3), 37–47.

Constantin, James A. and Robert F. Lusch (1994), *Understanding Resource Management*, Oxford, OH: The Planning Forum.

Drucker, Peter (2003), *The Essential Drucker: The Best Sixty Years of Peter Drucker's Essential Writings on Management*, New York: HarperCollins.

Edvardsson, Bo, Bard Tronvoll and Thorsten Gruber (2011), "Expanding understanding of service exchange and value co-creation: a social construction approach," *Journal of the Academy of Marketing Science*, **39** (2), 327–39.

Gilmore, James H. and B. Joseph Pine (1997), "The four faces of mass customization," *Harvard Business Review*, **75** (1), 91–101.

Granovetter, Mark S. (1973), "The strength of weak ties," *American Journal of Sociology*, **78** (6), 1360–80.

Grove, Stephen, Ray Fisk and Joby John (2000), "Services as theatre: guidelines and implications," in T.A. Swartz and D. Iacobucci (eds), *Handbook of Services Marketing and Management*, Thousand Oaks, CA: Sage Publications, pp. 21–36.

Gronroos, Christian (1995), "Relationship marketing: the strategy continuum," *Journal of the Academy of Marketing Science*, **23** (4), 252–4.

Gummesson, Evert (1987), "The new marketing – developing long-term interactive relationships," *Long-Range Planning*, **20** (4), 10–20.

Haeckel, Stephen (1999), *Adaptive Enterprise: Creating and Leading Sense-and-Respond Organizations*, Boston, MA: Harvard School of Business.

Kahney, Leander (2005), *The Cult of iPod*, San Francisco, CA: No Starch Press.

Karmarkar, Uday (1996), "Integrative research in marketing and operations management," *Journal of Marketing Research*, **33** (May), 125–33.

Kjellberg, Hans and Claes-Fredrik Helgesson (2006), "Multiple versions of markets: multiplicity and performativity in market practice," *Industrial Marketing Management*, **35** (7), 839–55.

Korkman, Oskar, Kaj Storbacka and Bo Harald (2010), "Practices as markets: value co-creation in e-invoicing," *Australasian Marketing Journal*, **18** (4), 236–47.

Linden, G., K.L. Kraemer and J. Dedrick (2007), "Who captures value in a global innovation system: the case of Apple's iPod,". Irvine, CA: Personal Computing Industry Center, accessed 16 September 2013 at www.signallake.com/innovation/AppleiPod.pdf.

Lovelock, Christopher (2000), "Functional integration in services: understanding the links

between marketing, operations, and human resources," in T.A. Swartz and D. Iacobucci (eds), *Handbook of Services Marketing and Management*, Thousand Oaks, CA: Sage Publications, pp. 421–39.
Lusch, Robert and Stephen L. Vargo (2006), "Service-dominant logic as a foundation for a general theory," in R.F. Lusch and S.L. Vargo (eds), *The Service-Dominant Logic of Marketing: Dialog, Debate and Directions*, Armonk: M.E: Sharpe, pp. 406–20.
Lusch, Robert and Fred Webster (2011), "A stakeholder-unifying, co-creation philosophy of marketing," *Journal of Macromarketing*, **31** (2), 129–34.
Lusch, Robert, Stephen L. Vargo and Matthew O'Brien (2007), "Competing through service: insights from service-dominant logic," *Journal of Retailing*, **83** (1), 5–18.
Lusch, R.F., Vargo, S. and Tanniru, M. (2010), 'Service, value networks and learning,' *Journal of the Academy of Marketing Science*, **38** (1), 19–31.
Malhotra, Manoj and Subhash Sharma (2002), "Spanning the continuum between marketing and operations," *Journal of Operations Management*, **20** (3), 209–19.
Meuter, Matthew L., Amy L. Ostrom, Robert I. Roundtree and Mary Jo Bitner (2000), "Self-service technologies: understanding customer satisfaction with technology-based service encounters," *Journal of Marketing*, **64** (3), 50–64.
Normann, Richard (2001), *Reframing Business: When the Map Changes the Landscape*, Chichester: John Wiley and Sons.
Ordanini, Andrea and Paolo Pasini (2008), "Service co-production and value co-creation: the case for a service-oriented architecture (SOA)," *European Management Journal*, **26** (5), 289–97.
Orsini, Joseph L. and Necmi Karagozoglu (1988), "Marketing/production interfaces in services industries," *SAM Advanced Management Journal*, **53** (3), 34.
Paul, Pallab, Richard B. Chase, Jayashree Mahajan and Asoo J. Vakharia (1994), "An exploratory investigation of the interdependence between marketing and operations functions in service firms," *International Journal of Research in Marketing*, **11** (1), 1–15.
Prahalad, C.K. and V. Ramaswamy (2000), "Co-opting customer competence," *Harvard Business Review*, **78** (January–February), 79–87.
Reppel, Alexander, Isabelle Szmigin and Thorsten Gruber (2006), "The iPod phenomenon: identifying a market leader's secrets through qualitative marketing research," *Journal of Product and Brand Management*, **15** (4), 239–49.
Schau, Hope J., Albert M. Muniz Jr. and Eric J. Arnould (2009), "How brand community practices create value," *Journal of Marketing*, **73** (September), 30–51.
Smith, Adam (1776), *The Wealth of Nations*, republished 2000, New York: The Modern Library.
Solomon, M.R., C. Surprenant, J.A. Czepiel and E.G. Gutman (1985), "A role theory perspective on dyadic interactions: the service encounter," *Journal of Marketing*, **49** (1), 99–111.
Spohrer, Jim, Paul P. Maglio, John Bailey and Daniel Gruhl (2007), "Steps toward a science of service systems," *Computer*, **40** (1), 71–7.
Vargo, Stephen L. and Melissa Archpru Akaka (2009), "Service-dominant logic as a foundation for service science: clarifications," *Service Science*, **1** (1), 32–41.
Vargo, Stephen and Melissa Archpru Akaka (2012), "Value co-creation and service systems (re)formation: a service ecosystems view," *Service Science*, **4** (3), 207–17.
Vargo, Stephen L. and Robert F. Lusch (2004a), "Evolving to a new dominant logic for marketing," *Journal of Marketing*, **68** (January), 1–17.
Vargo, Stephen L. and Robert F. Lusch (2004b), "The four service marketing myths: remnants of a goods-based manufacturing model," *Journal of Service Research*, **6** (4), 324–35.
Vargo, Stephen L. and Robert F. Lusch (2006), "Service-dominant logic: what it is, what it is not, what it might be," in R F. Lusch and S.L. Vargo (eds), *The Service-Dominant Logic of Marketing: Dialog, Debate and Directions*, Armonk: M.E. Sharpe, pp. 43–56.
Vargo, Stephen L. and Robert F. Lusch (2008), "Service-dominant logic: continuing the evolution," *Journal of the Academy of Marketing Science*, **36** (1), 1–10.

Vargo, Stephen L. and Robert F. Lusch (2011a), "It's all B2B. . .and beyond: toward a systems perspective of the market," *Industrial Marketing Management*, **40** (2), 181–7.
Vargo, Stephen L. and Robert F. Lusch (2011b), "From goods-dominant logic to service-dominant logic," invited presentation at Workshop on Service-Dominant Logic: An Evolution or Revolution in Marketing Theory and Practice?, hosted 20 October by Concordia University, Montreal.
Vargo, Stephen L., Paul Maglio and Melissa Archpru Akaka (2008), "On value and value co-creation: a service systems and service logic perspective," *European Management Journal*, **26** (3), 145–52.
Von Hippel, Eric (2009), "Democratizing innovation: the evolving phenomenon of user innovation," *International Journal of Innovation Service*, **1** (1), 29–40.
Womack, James and Daniel Jones (2005), *Lean Solutions: How Companies and Customers can Create Value and Wealth Together*, New York: Free Press
Zeithaml, Valarie A., A. Parasuraman and Leonard L. Berry (1985), "Problems and strategies in services marketing," *Journal of Marketing*, **49** (Spring), 33–46.

22 Marketing: a service science and arts perspective

Jim Spohrer, Stephen K. Kwan and Raymond P. Fisk

1 INTRODUCTION: MOTIVATIONS AND GOALS

What is marketing and what will it become? The service science and arts perspective on marketing presented in this chapter is closest in spirit to Morgan and Hunt (1994, p. 20, emphases in original): "These global dynamics have resulted in the somewhat paradoxical nature of relationship marketing: To be an effective *competitor* (in the global economy) requires one to be a trusted *cooperator* (in some network)."

For our purposes in this chapter, we define marketing as an entity "competing for collaborators" and, in turn, serving them and keeping them. How do types of entities in diverse contexts approach this competition? What rules and boundaries govern competitors and collaborators? How and why do rules and boundaries change over time? When do competitors collaborate, and when do collaborators compete? "Coopetition"[1] is real (Bengtsson and Kock 2000), but so what? What difference does a service science and arts perspective on marketing, as "competing for collaborators," make to a marketing professional? More technically, does scale (population size) and level ("knowledge burden") matter a lot or a little? Also, can a balance be struck between the science (that is, function) and the arts (that is, form) perspectives? As we will see, the significance boils down to leadership and the ability to create a compelling vision of the future that resonates with your customers and partners.

Marketing is arguably a key part of any number of evolved or designed solutions to human challenges and opportunities. Businesses and governments can be viewed as complex adaptive systems that evolve and change, but all too often with no discernable guiding purpose, instead merely reacting to unpredictable winds of change. However, unlike evolved systems, designed systems exist first often as a dream in the minds of leaders and entrepreneurs with a vision of what the future might become.

Natural ecological systems are evolved, but markets are designed systems to some degree. For example, the abundance of cars (Henry Ford), personal computers (Bill Gates), and smart phones (Steve Jobs) result from the formation of markets (designed systems) which first existed in the minds of visionaries, science fiction writers, and entrepreneurs.

Big change is shaped as much by arts as science, as much by passion as reason, and can arise from people asking seemingly little questions, such as "Should we? Can we? May we? Will we?" "May we?" is often of little concern to visionary leaders. "Can we?" is often informed by reason and science, but "Will we?" is driven most strongly by passion and art. Priorities often have a large emotional component that can flip a decision—esthetic appeal (for example, form, ease of use) can override quantitative factors (for example, function, complex capabilities).

To address these questions about marketing as entities competing for collaborators, while serving and keeping them, a broad perspective on human history and our world is needed. Service science and arts, which is an emerging transdiscipline, provides one such broad perspective. A transdiscipline borrows from existing disciplines, without replacing them.

Like any emerging science, service science provides a new way of thinking and talking about the world in terms of measurements on entities, interactions, and outcomes, but also adds diverse symbolic processes of valuing that balance reason and passion (Spohrer and Maglio 2010; Spohrer et al. 2011). Specifically, a service scientist seeks to measure the number and types of entities, interactions, and outcomes, and to advance better methods and architectures for thinking and talking about the world in terms of nested, networked service system entities and value co-creation phenomena, including their diverse processes of valuing with objective and subjective components (Spohrer et al. 2012).

These concepts (service systems, value co-creation, processes of valuing) are rooted in a worldview known as service-dominant logic or SD logic (Vargo and Lusch, 2004, 2008). In the parlance of SD logic, service systems are sometimes referred to as resource integrators, and value co-creation is often manifested in exchange. According to SD logic foundational premise (FP) 10, "Value is always uniquely and phenomenologically determined by the beneficiary," which means ultimately the action takes place in entities' processes of valuing.

In fact, all entities, whether social organizational entities (such as a nation, city, foundation, hospital, or business) or individual human entities (such as a person), have implicit processes of valuing that they are sometimes able to make explicit and empirically evaluate against other explicit processes of valuing. Formal service system entities (as opposed to informal service system entities) can be ranked by the degree to which they are governed by written (symbolic) laws and reason, and they evolve to increase the percentage of their processes that are explicit, symbolic, and rationally defensible. In contrast to the formal, early hunter-gatherer groups that existed before written language are a type of informal service system (social entity). However, today, modern nations have constitutions, written laws, regulations, policies, and create written reports evaluating their compliance, often further validated by external auditors. The age of "Big Data" shifts increasingly towards formal symbolic processes. Modern service systems use information and communications technologies (ICT) to augment their capabilities (Engelbart 1995). The augmentations create a reliance on technology (and other formal physical symbol systems), which adds to the "knowledge burden" of society (Jones 2005).

Often service science, without the arts, is framed in the context of business-to-business outsourcing services (Maglio et al. 2006; Spohrer et al. 2007). To address service design for social enterprises, refinements to the foundational concepts of service science have been proposed (Tracy, 2012; Tracy and Lyons, 2012). Some researchers also see that there is a need to balance the science of service with the artistic components of marketing (see next section). The emerging service science and arts community greatly benefits from theoretical and empirical studies done by a growing number of service researchers (see the Appendix to this chapter). Empirical studies of the economic success of businesses that adopt SD logic have begun to appear (Ordanini and Parasuraman 2011). So like all early-stage scientific communities, the language for talking about service systems and value co-creation phenomena continues to evolve.

Section 2 is a short overview of marketing from a conventional perspective, Section 3 provides background on service science and arts, Section 4 is an initial service science and arts perspective on the concept of marketing, and Section 5 concludes with future research directions.

2 OVERVIEW: MARKETING

Marketing requires understanding the needs, wants, and aspirations of others, and the way people in context balance these concerns. Marketing communicates a message about a possible future, wrapped in a value proposition. Both entities' futures will be better if they can communicate, agree, and realize that future. Entities come to realize that more win-win changes are possible working together than from either entity working alone; especially when change co-elevates capabilities in addition to co-creating value, then a positive-feedback loop is created. More capabilities lead to more possibilities, more possibilities lead to more win-win value co-creation opportunities, more opportunities lead to those that impact capabilities differentially. Great marketing creates an "upward spiral" as the aspirations of one generation become the wants or even the needs of the next generation (for example, access to the Internet or smart phones), elevating the capabilities and even the aspirations of all entities as they change over time.

From a service science and arts perspective, we will argue that marketing is "competing for collaborators," and, in turn, serving them and keeping them. Collaborators can be customers, partners, employees, suppliers, or others—really any other entities with resources that can play by mutually agreed to "rules of the game." At this complex level, marketing can be viewed as a mechanism to connect service systems with other service systems (that is, collaborators). Christopher et al. (1991) describe relationship marketing as seeking relationships across six markets: internal markets, supplier markets, recruitment markets, referral markets, influence markets, and customer markets.

Marketing must tap into the cooperative nature of entities. "The cooperative aspect of economic behavior has been relatively neglected. Economists speak of competitive theory, of pure and perfect competition. There is no corresponding development of cooperative theory, of pure and perfect cooperation" (Alderson 1965, p. 239).

Sustainable cooperation depends on trust. "One of the most salient factors in the effectiveness of our present complex social organization is the willingness of one or more individuals in a social unity to trust others. The efficiency, adjustment, and even survival of any social group depend upon the presence or absence of such trust" (Rotter 1967, p. 651).

Sustainable competition depends on a certain type of trust as well, as we quote again: "These global dynamics have resulted in the somewhat paradoxical nature of relationship marketing: To be an effective *competitor* (in the global economy) requires one to be a trusted *cooperator* (in some network)" (Morgan and Hunt 1994, p. 20, emphases in original).

The art of competition that co-elevates capabilities is fundamental in human society, from sports to business to politics.

> However competitive a particular industry may be, it always rests on a foundation of shared interests and mutually agreed-upon rules of conduct, and the competition takes place not in a jungle but in a society that it presumably both serves and depends upon. Business life, unlike the mythological jungle, is first of all fundamentally *cooperative*.
>
> (Solomon 1992, p. 26)

The society sets the law and regulations (that is, rules of conduct) which govern the validity and legality of value propositions among the competitors. This is often considered the government's "soft power" in persuading (not coercing) the players to play fairly.

So marketing as a type of human activity can be viewed as the observable phenomena of service system entities' "competing for collaborators," which rests on commitment and trust.

> If commitment and trust are key, how can such characteristics be nurtured? We posit that relationship commitment and trust develop when firms attend to relationships by (1) providing resources, opportunities, and benefits that are superior to the offerings of alternative partners; (2) maintaining high standards of corporate values and allying oneself with exchange partners having similar values; (3) communicating valuable information, including expectations, market intelligence, and evaluations of the partner's performance; and (4) avoiding malevolently taking advantage of their exchange partners.
>
> (Morgan and Hunt 1994, p. 34)

Morgan and Hunt used structural equation modeling method and data from a survey of customers of automobile tire retailers to validate their model over a competing model. They found that trust comes before commitment, and that trust derives from shared values. They also found that too much use of coercive power in a relationship can undermine trust and commitment, and lead to conflict or acquiescence. Communication was important to build trust, and opportunistic behavior was confirmed to reduce trust. Relationship termination costs and relationship benefits were confirmed to increase commitment. Trust and commitment were confirmed to increase cooperation. Commitment was confirmed to reduce propensity to leave. Trust was confirmed to increase "functional conflict," that is, amicably resolved disagreements. Trust was confirmed to decrease uncertainty.

3 BACKGROUND: SERVICE SCIENCE AND ARTS

Service science and arts draws on a great breadth of academic disciplines, without replacing them. How entities use knowledge to co-create value is intimately tied to all disciplines, which can be thought of as societal fountains of knowledge. As disciplines create knowledge, which is woven into the fabric of society and becomes essential to maintain quality of life, that knowledge becomes part of the "knowledge burden" of that society (Jones 2005).

What differentiates service science and arts from all existing disciplines is that it is a transdiscipline, drawing on all and replacing none, with a unique focus on the evolution of service systems and value co-creation phenomena. Service science and arts aspires to provide the breadth for T-shaped service innovators who have both depth *and* breadth of knowledge (for example, see Harris 2009). "Depth" can be in any existing academic discipline, while appropriate "breadth" can improve communications, teamwork, and learning rates (IBM 2011; Spohrer et al. 2010).

A "service science and arts perspective," as we will see below, is a way of looking at the world through the lens of SD logic. A physics perspective is a way of looking at the world, and "seeing" a world of things made of atoms and forces. A computer science perspective is a way of looking at the world in terms of universal computing machines (for example, physical symbol systems and Turing machines) and codes (for example, symbols as both data and algorithms). An economics perspective is a way of looking at the world in terms of actors, supply and demand, externalities, and moral hazards. As we see below, a service science and arts perspective is a way of looking at the world in terms of an ecology of nested, networked service system entities and the value co-creation phenomena that interconnect them; including "processes of valuing" based on both reason/function/science/needs/wants and passion/form/arts/aspirations/dreams.

Human endeavors, such as "sciences," build on philosophical foundations, and each science must first provide ontology (what exists, and can be categorized and counted),[2] then epistemology (how we know, and how others can replicate results), and finally praxeology (actions, and how knowing matters or makes a difference).[3] These three "ologies" explicitly or implicitly underlie all sciences. As humans, we seek knowledge of the world and of ourselves, and then work to apply that knowledge through actions to create benefits for ourselves and others by changing aspects of what exists (service), in full awareness of our human sensory, cognitive, and motor limits—yet increasingly augmented by our technologies and organizations, and scientifically and imaginatively derived knowledge of both what is and what might be. However, "all this knowing" does create a "knowledge burden" which must be carefully managed (Jones 2005).

Human endeavors, such as "arts", build on philosophical foundations, too. Aesthetics is a branch of philosophy that concerns the nature of art, beauty and taste. According to Postrel (2004, p. 6), "aesthetics is the way we communicate through the senses." Such sensory communications include sight, sound, smell, taste, and touch. Esthetics are deeply embedded in human cultural experiences and evolved with human cultures (Dutton 2010). While the arts are culturally universal, each culture has its own sense of aesthetics. It can also be said that the arts originate in the universal human urge of childhood play (Boyd 2009).

Like service science, service arts should be a foundation of modern service thought (Fisk et al. 2007). The service arts are primarily performing arts (for example, the act of service is often referred to as a performance). The arts are often grouped into the subfields of performing arts, visual arts and literary arts. The performing arts (dance, music, opera, and theater) occur and must be experienced in real time. Services, like the performing arts, involve real time human interaction and are deeply rooted in the emotional core of human experience (Fisk and Grove 2012). Though they are often poorly practiced, services are arts.

Like the sciences, the arts are concerned with systems. The counterpart to the standard systems stages of inputs, throughputs, and outputs is the structure of beginnings, middles and ends in the performing arts (dance, music, opera and theater). Service systems have three stages, too, comprising entry, experience, and exit. This parallels the perspective of service performance that demarcates the encounter between the customer and service provider (front stage) and the supporting functions (back stage) (Teboul 2006).

Augmentation layers lead to the nested, networked nature of our world—specifically, as an ecology of service system entities. Value co-creation phenomena (service-for-service exchange) form the core of our human ecology (Hawley 1986). Value co-creation phenomena are also known as win-win or non-zero-sum games (Wright 2000). "Competing for collaborators" drives the evolution of markets and institutions, and contributes to both their dynamism/stagnation as well as stability/instability (Friedman and McNeill 2013). Information technology, Internet-of-things, big data, and so on are accelerating the ability of service systems to develop and continuously evolve and refine explicit symbolic processes of valuing, which further augment service system capabilities. As Alfred North Whitehead, English mathematician and philosopher, is quoted as saying: "Civilization advances by extending the number of important operations which we can perform without thinking of them." Augmentation layers, including technological and organizational augments, contribute to the nested, networked nature of our world, and our "knowledge burden." Augmentation layers have many benefits, but they can also "hide" the extent of a society's knowledge burden.

The mature sciences of physics, chemistry, biology, and even computer science and economics can be used to tell a series of stories—overlapping and nested stories about our world and us. Physics describes the world in terms of matter, energy, space, and time, with fundamental forces well quantified across enormous scales to explain phenomena much smaller than atoms and much larger than galaxies. Physicists theorize and quantify to tell a story that stretches from before the big bang to beyond the end of time itself. Chemistry describes the world in terms of the elements, molecules, reactions, temperature, pressure, and volume. Geologists and climatologists, born of modern chemists, can tell the story of the birth and aging of our planet. Biology describes the world in terms of DNA, cells, and molecular machinery driven by diverse energy sources. Ecologists informed by modern biology tell the story of populations of diverse species shaping and being shaped by each other and their environments. Computer science describes the world in terms of physical symbol systems and other computation systems, codes, algorithms, and complexity. Cognitive scientists and neuroscientists are today working with computer scientists and others to propose stories of the birth of consciousness, communication, and culture in humans and pre-human species. Finally, economics describes the world in terms of supply, demand, externalities, principles, agents, moral hazards, and more. Economists theorize and quantify to tell the story of morals and markets, laws and economies evolving over the course of human and even pre-human history, and how the world can be in balance one moment, and then go completely out of balance the next (Friedman 2008; Friedman and MacNeill 2013).

Service science adds to these stories, and is an emerging transdiscipline that builds on these and many other academic disciplines, but does not replace any of them. Service science is enormously practical, as national economies and businesses measure an apparent growth in "services" in gross domestic product (GDP) and revenue, respectively. Getting better at service innovation is the practical purpose of service science.[4] Service science is also academic, and like the academic discipline of ecology, it is an integrative and holistic transdiscipline drawing from (and someday perhaps adding to) other disciplines without replacing them. While the basis of service is arguably division of labor and specialization, which leads to the proliferation of disciplinary, professional, and cultural silos, nevertheless service science, as an accumulating body of knowledge, can add some measure of breadth to the depth of specialists. In this sense, service science is holistic and inclusive; every individual can add to her or his breadth as she or he adopts a service science perspective and learns more about how the overlapping stories of other sciences and disciplines fit together into a whole. The nested, networked nature of our world becomes more apparent. Service scientists look for service systems entities and study their interactions.

In the remainder of this section, we explain more fully the emergence of service science as an effort to integrate the work of service researchers from many disciplines, while extending that research as well through a greater emphasis on service systems and value co-creation (see Appendix). We do this by summarizing historical service research (and the relationship to the emerging service science community, both the academic discipline(s) and professional association(s), service-dominant logic, service science foundational concepts and foundational premises, a proposed research agenda for a science of service, and some proposed extensions to that research agenda, each in turn.

3.1 Service Research History and Community

Since so many disciplines study service, there is a great need for a transdiscipline like service science. Elsewhere we have more fully elaborated the history of service research (Spohrer and Maglio 2010). Over 24 academic disciplines now study "service" from their own unique disciplinary perspective, and not surprisingly each has one or more definitions of "service."

Given that so many professional associations have a service-related special interest group (SIG), journal, or conference, so many nations and businesses have service innovation roadmaps, and so many universities have or are starting service research centers, there is a great need for a transdiscipline such as service science and an umbrella professional association such as the International Society of Service Innovation Professionals (ISSIP), which promotes service innovation professional development, education, research, practice, and policy. The ISSIP[5] is an umbrella, democratically run nonprofit professional association that tries to add value to existing professional associations with service-related SIGs, conferences and journals.

Just as service science draws on, without replacing, existing academic disciplines, the ISSIP draws on, without replacing, existing professional associations—by design. The ISSIP community is new, but growing. Professional associations are a type of service system that can be designed and evolved, within a population of other professional associations competing for collaborators.

Why are so many academic discipline and so many professional associations turning to service as an area of focus? First, since "service" is the application of knowledge to create mutual benefits, disciplines and professional associations are eager to show the way in which their body of knowledge can be applied to create real-world benefits. Sciences typically choose the path of creating engineered icons to demonstrate benefits (for example, a bridge, a new material, or a genetically-enhanced plant), and arts typically choose the path of creating cultural icons to create benefits (for example, a play, a song, or a fashion). We remember icons because they inspire awe and create value for diverse beneficiaries. Engineering is good for creating certain types of realities, and arts are good for expressing as well as inspiring possible realities. Service is the application of knowledge to create mutual benefits. Furthermore many countries recognize that the service sector (both domestic and export) is the engine for growth and are building up the capabilities of their service industries, also as an engine for tourism and the celebration of their unique culture and history.

A summary of the main branches (that is, economics, marketing, operations, engineering, computing, informatics, systems, organizations, law, and so on) that service science draws can be found in the Appendix.

3.2 Service-dominant Logic

For most people, the notion that goods have value seems obvious. Isn't that why we pay for them? However, SD logic (Vargo and Lusch 2004) challenges us to change the way we think about goods, value, and more.

Value is not an intrinsic property of goods. For example, a physicist would have a hard time measuring "the value" of a good, although "the mass" and other physical properties could be measured. On the other hand, a lawyer could quickly assess "the value" of a good (property) a client lost access to through the negligent behavior of some other actor. Common sense tells us that "the price" one pays to own or lease goods can vary depending on market conditions and context. Common sense also tells us "the price" is not "the value." A measure of "the value" runs straight into subjective customer experience. Ng (2013) talks about "worth" as a point-in-time decision about what one is willing to pay ("the price") for something, and "value" as a subjective, context-specific feeling of "goodness" at a later time. Customer knowledge and action can impact value realization. For example, buying an exotic fruit, properly harvesting, transporting, storing, preparing, and then enjoying eating it ("positive value/feeling") versus the fruit spoiling and throwing it away ("negative value/feeling") demonstrates the way the customer's actions impact their experience.

Service-dominant logic is deeply rooted in a notion of value based on customer experience and outcomes, which is in turn rooted in customer knowledge and actions. By applying knowledge (for example, eating the fruit in a timely manner, versus letting it spoil), the customer co-creates value with the provider who got the fruit to the customer just at the right time to maximize value for both of them. The customer may even store the fruit in a particular way to optimize the readiness of the fruit for a particular recipe. There is no end to how elaborate a customer's knowledge might be to realize an outcome. More and more, service innovators understand this view of "active customers" applying knowledge to co-create value directly or indirectly with provider networks versus the view of "passive consumers." Service innovators work to co-elevate both the provider and customer knowledge to realize more important and significant outcomes. Providers compete for customers, which is to say providers "compete for collaborators."

Service-dominant logic terms actors, customer and provider, "operant resources" because they can apply knowledge to co-create value. "Operand resources" are the raw materials, tools, and information that can be used by the "operant resources"—if they, the actors, have the "right" knowledge to use it appropriately. Much of service comes down to putting knowledge into action, and then the processes of valuing the resulting experience and outcomes.

Service-dominant logic makes an important distinction between "operand resources" and "operant resources." The latter interact directly or indirectly to co-create value (service-for-service exchange), and are also referred to as "actors" and "resource integrators." As we will see, in the parlance of service science, these actors are called "service system entities" and can be people, businesses, universities, cities, nations, or any other entities capable of knowledge-intensive interactions based on value-propositions and governed by rights and responsibilities ("governance mechanisms"). When "operant resources" interact directly or indirectly, it is both the experience and outcome of those interactions that concerns service innovators.

For example, a "car" is not just a type of good that can be purchased and used, but a car is an "operand resource" that came to exist only through the interactions of many people and businesses over time, and these people and businesses are the "operant resources" with the capability to apply knowledge to create benefits for others and themselves. When you buy a car, you are really buying an unimaginably long series of service-for-service exchanges throughout history that lead to the car, and the money you use to buy a car summarizes an equally unimaginably long series of service-for-service exchanges.

To use a car as intended for transportation (to gain benefits) requires an "operant resource" applying knowledge (driver). Service is the application of knowledge for the benefit of others and self. To say this somewhat differently, "operant resources" apply knowledge to create benefits with other "operant resources," directly or indirectly. All goods and money are just "operand resources" that arose as a result of "operant resources" applying knowledge. So goods (or "operand resources") have no intrinsic value. Instead, value resides in the experiences and outcomes of "operant resources" and is not something intrinsic in "operand resources." While better explanations of "applying knowledge" and "experiencing outcomes" are necessary, suffice it to say SD logic provides a way to change the way we think and talk about the world, and prepares us to think about service innovations more clearly—service innovators improve the way "operant resources apply knowledge and experience outcomes." Service innovators design better games for the players ("operant resources"), and the goods ("operand resources") are props in the game. Better games raise the bar on outcomes. Some fundamental service innovations improve our ability to compete for collaborators, co-elevating our capabilities in the process.

With this background, the ten foundational premises[6] of service-dominant logic as revised by Vargo and Lusch (2008) and Vargo and Akaka (2009) are listed below.

SDL-FP1: Service is the fundamental basis of exchange

Implicit in SDL-FP1 is a definition of service as operant resources (actors) applying knowledge and skills for mutual benefits (value co-creation experiences and outcomes). Service for service exchange is the fundamental building block of all exchange ("I'll do this for you, if you do that for me," or more precisely, "I'll put my knowledge into action for you, if you put your knowledge into action for me"). From a service science perspective, exchange is a type of knowledge-intensive value-proposition-based interaction between entities.

SDL-FP2: Indirect exchange masks the fundamental basis of exchange

Implicit in SDL-FP2 is a definition of indirect exchange. For example, exchanges involving goods and/or money (so-called operand resources, available to or derived from previous effort of operant resources) obscure the fundamental service-for-service nature of exchange. The series of questions arising from "and where did that operand resource come from?" always leads back in human history to a person (operant resource) applying knowledge for mutual benefits, in some sort of service for service exchange. From a service science perspective, operant resources such as people and businesses have rights and responsibilities, but operand resources such as technology/things or information/ideas do not have rights and responsibilities.

SDL-FP3: Goods are distribution mechanisms for service provision

Goods are operand resources. Well-designed goods incorporate a great deal of knowledge that may be the accumulation of the knowledge and practices of many people over many years.

SDL-FP4: Operant resources are the fundamental source of competitive advantage

Operant resources (that is, people) can put knowledge into action, and take responsibility for their actions. Certain people or businesses may possess unique knowledge, or capacity for safely taking on added responsibility (that is, reduced risk). Goods and information are operand resources, which, in general, are easier to copy than operant resources.

SDL-FP5: All economies are service economies

Implicit in SDL-FP5 is a definition of an economy. An economy is a population of operant resources with capabilities for exchange interactions. By SDL-FP1, service is the fundamental basis of exchange. Therefore, all economies, hunter-gatherer, agricultural, extractive, information, etc., are based on service-for-service exchange between operant resources.

SDL-FP6: The customer is always a co-creator of value
Implicit in SDL-FP6 is a definition of value co-creation. The customer is an "operant resource" and must apply knowledge in context to generate the experience and outcome. Win-win requires customer and provider to both realize benefits. It is worth noting that this confuses many people, because they think of co-production as a kind of physical work effort on the part of the customer. Work can be direct physical collaboration (co-production) or indirect cognitive/social coordination (co-creation). When I trust a cleaning service with the key to my house, and they trust me to pay them, we are co-creating value. When I stay at home, open the door, and get involved in cleaning my house with them, we are co-producing value. The value is in the experience and outcome, which can be derived from physical direct collaboration or trusted indirect coordination. That is, value can be co-created with or without co-production.

SDL-FP7: The enterprise cannot deliver value, but only offer value propositions
Implicit in SDL-FP7 is a definition of value. Providers can assess "the cost" of service provision, but only the customer can assess "the value" of the experience and outcome. The customer can make a decision about "the worth" of an offer, based on the "the price" and some mental simulation, expectation or anticipation of "the value to come" (for example, Ng 2013). For example, even when an emergency response team is trying to rescue a person in peril, if that person does not want to be rescued, and does not comply or cooperate in the rescue, then it is more likely that the emergency response team will fail. Both the customer and the provider must agree to the value-proposition, and see the mutual benefit as well as the mutual responsibility. Win-win value-propositions are at the heart of value co-creation interactions.

SDL-FP8: A service-centered view is inherently customer oriented and relational
"Provider value" depends on "customer value," which derives from experience and outcomes, and ability to apply knowledge. Win-win value-propositions are at the heart of value co-creation interactions. Repeatable mutual benefits depend on mutual knowledge, trust and coordination (for example, Morgan and Hunt 1994). Service innovators know that customer-to-customer interactions can scale value via word-of-mouth and platforms.

SDL-FP9: All economic and social actors are resource integrators
Implicit in SDL-FP9 is a definition of resource integrators. Operant resources are resource integrators, they can apply knowledge to combine

and configure ("integrate") both other operant as well as operand resources. For example, a driver must know how to drive to benefit from a car, and a student must know how to read to benefit from a book (at least for the primary intended use). All economic and social actors apply knowledge to integrate resources. Resources can be divided into three categories: market-facing resources (available for purchase to own-outright or for lease/contract), private non-market facing resources (privileged access), and public non-market facing resources (shared access). Service system entities are economic and social actors, which configure (or integrate) resources.

SDL-FP10: Value is always uniquely and phenomenologically determined by the beneficiary

Implicit in SDL-FP10 is a reference to "value determination" as a process, unique to each beneficiary. Therefore value determination is a process unique to each subject, or a subjective process. However, this does not mean that the process is random or unknowable. Culture and education can shape the process of valuing. Value realization is more than a decision (anticipatory calculation of benefits or worth). Value realization is contextual, history dependent, and uniquely determined by the beneficiary, shaped by culture and education. Building models of these processes, and the way culture and education shape them, is essential to advancing service science. Furthermore, these models could provide a foundation for theoretical service science.

Vargo and Lusch are clear that these foundational premises are only a starting point, and they have worked with many others to continue the evolution of SD logic. For example, reducing the foundational premises to a smaller number of definitions and foundational axioms has been undertaken. Four of the foundational premises (1, 6, 9, and 10) have been shown to be adequate for deriving the others (Vargo and Lusch 2008).

3.3 Service Science Foundational Concepts

The fundamental concepts of service science should facilitate the creation of a trading zone between many academic disciplines (Gorman 2010).[7] A trading zone invites individuals from different backgrounds with different vocabularies to communicate, share ideas, and engage in mutually productive interactions. The value of the concepts below, versus some other fundamental set of concepts, is in giving individuals easier access to ideas from many different disciplines. One branch of the service science community (Spohrer 2013), sometimes known as the SSME+DAPP branch, had identified ten foundational concepts (SS-FC1-10: ecology, entity, interactions, outcomes, value propositions, governance mechanisms, resources, access rights, stakeholders, and measures), plus an additional 18 foundational sub-concepts (SS-FSC1-18: holistic-service system, whole service, informal-service system entity, formal-service system entity, capabilities, constraints, identities, reputations, ISPAR, recovery, worth, value, risk, reward, processes of valuing, processes of deciding, rights, and responsibilities).

Service science as a transdiscipline aims to be holistic and integrative, borrowing from many disciplines without replacing them. The concepts and sub-concepts below are general enough to allow many disciplines to contribute to the creation of service science, and build a better understanding service systems and value co-creation phenomena.

SS-FC1: Ecology

Service science borrows from ecology (populations) as much as from economics (price). Ecology as a discipline is the study of populations of entities ("evolving," "competing," "cooperating," and so on) and their relationship to each other and their environment. Ecology as a concept is quite general, and can apply to atoms in stars (stellar neucleosynthesis), animals in a forest, or nested, networked service system entities. Measurement of the number and type of entities, interactions, and outcomes is fundamental to ecology (and the ontological foundations of a new science).

Service ecology as a concept provides the fundamental way of thinking more scientifically about service system entities—they exist as populations of entities ("evolving," "competing," "cooperating," and so on) in relationship to each other and their environment, and can be counted and classified. The population of service system entities forms the service ecology. Currently, the service ecology is based on just one foundational species, humans, which have evolved formal ("written/computational symbol-based") service system capabilities for assigning and externalizing the rights and responsibilities of service system entities as legal, economic, and social systems.

Order of magnitude observation An interesting observation about the human service ecology is that as the world population approaches 10 billion people, the estimate of the total number of formal service system entities (with legal rights and responsibilities) is less than 100 billion entities. The ten entities per person average may be tied to the structure of society. Each person plays a role in several other service system entities, for example, since over 50 per cent of the world's population lives in cities, most people are part of service systems for their nation, state, and city. If they have a job, they may be part of a business or social enterprise. It is also interesting that, to a first level of approximation, most people (individuals) are nested ten levels deep in service systems—(1) world, (2) continental union, (3) nation, (4) state, (5) county-metro, (6) city, (7) district, (8) community, (9) street, and (10) household. The rough order of magnitude relationship may have to do with human capabilities and limitations, as well as the sustainable "knowledge burden" level of augmentation with technology and governance mechanisms. The observation may also be related to the lifespan and sustainability of businesses of various scales. Some businesses are global and operate in nearly all nations, and other "businesses" are local to a street or community.

From a service science perspective, each individual human and many collectives are service system entities. Human families are hundreds of thousands of years old, cities only about 10,000 years old, universities that have survived to today are only about 1,000 years old, and modern businesses with professional managers arguable just 100 years old. Looking in order of magnitudes across time, it is clear that the scale (population size) and level (knowledge burden) of the human ecology has grown dramatically. As population size increases a society can take on a larger knowledge burden. In fact, there is archeological evidence that as human populations become isolated and shrink (for example, land bridges to islands disappear), the level of technological and other indicators of cultural complexity decrease (Kremer 1993).

A luxury cruise ship is a good example of a holistic service system (Motwani et al. 2012). Holistic service system (SS-FSC1) is a type of service system entity in the service ecology, such as nations, states, cities, universities, hospitals, cruise ships, and families/households, which provide whole service to the people inside the holistic service system (Spohrer et al. 2012). Whole service (SS-FSC2) refers to three categories of service capabilities necessary to sustain the quality of life of people inside service systems, namely, flows (transportation, water/air, food/products, energy, information/communications), development (buildings/shelter, retail/hospitality/entertainment/culture, finance, health, education), and governance (rules that make competing for collaborators co-elevating) (Spohrer 2010). Holistic service systems can remain viable for some period of time, even if disconnected from all interactions with other external service systems for some period of time.

SS-FC2: Entities

Service system entities are the fundamental abstraction of service science (Maglio et al. 2009). A formal service system entity (SS-FSC3) is a legal, economic entity with rights and responsibilities codified in written laws. An informal service system entity (SS-FSC4) uses promises, morals, and reciprocity in place of contracts, written laws, and money (Friedmand

2008). Mature, economically productive citizens of nations are formal service system entities with rights and responsibilities, but still operate as informal service systems when at home with their families. Children suing parents (or other family squabbles that require legal remedy) is an indication of the formal-informal boundary dispute/redefinition in progress.

Entity capabilities and constraints (SS-FSC5,6) change over time. Capabilities and constraints impact the ability of entities to compete for collaborators, and succeed at co-elevating forms of value co-creation. Human service system entity capabilities include physical, cognitive, and social capacity for work, including ability to augment capabilities with technology and governance mechanisms. Human service system entity constraints include finite life span, finite learning rates ("bounded rationality"), and finite social networks, though augmentations change these constraints, while introducing a "knowledge burden" (Jones 2005; Simon 1996). Capabilities and constraints also include socially constructed rights and responsibilities, and are discussed below.

Entity identities and reputations (SS-FSC7, 8) change over time. Identity and reputation impact the ability of entities to compete for collaborators, and succeed at co-elevating forms of value co-creation. Business service system entity identities and reputations contribute to brand and word-of-mouth marketing. National service system entity identities and reputations contribute to international trade in services such as emigration, international study, and tourism. Individual human service system entity identities and reputations contribute to credit ratings, marriage suitability, and social network followings.

SS-FC3: Interactions

Measuring the number and types of interactions between service system entities is complex. Service system entity interactions can be well designed or spontaneous, and then well or poorly executed. Also, interactions can be service interactions or non-service interactions. Service interactions are either value propositions based or governance mechanism based. Both service and non-service types of interactions are represented in the Interact-Service-Propose-Agree-Realize (ISPAR) model of possible outcomes for service system entity interactions (see SS-FC4 below).

SS-FC4: Outcomes

Measuring the number and types of outcomes when service systems interact is complex; nevertheless, a few first order simplifications can be made. For example, in the case of two entities interacting, a simple four-outcome model is: win-win, lose-win, win-lose, or lose-lose. Of these, only the win-win outcome is a service interaction with mutual benefits realized;

nevertheless, in a nested, networked ecology of entities, even win-lose games can serve a higher purpose.

Service science underlies service management, engineering, design, arts, and public policy (SSME+DAPP), which can be seen as entities evolving both better win-lose (zero sum) and win-win (non-zero-sum) games to play—a process of transforming zero-sum-games (competitions) that have winners and losers into "the servants" of larger non-zero-sum games (collaborations) in which every players wins; creating an incentive to play the game. This blended or balanced use of competition and collaboration to improve capabilities of entities is at the heart of value co-creation interactions and outcomes.

For example, the U.S. National Football League (NFL) has a series of weekly competitions (win-lose) and an annual draft that helps maintain competitive parity. This type of governance (system of rules, or game) helps to keep the weekly games (win-lose) exciting (passion) and maximize fan interest and engagement, increasing revenue (science) for teams, players, their management, and owners (win-win). Chess rankings pit near competitive parity players against each other (win-lose), making it hard to predict winners, but creating opportunities for incremental learning and improvement to get to the next ranking level (win-win).

For another example, the design of the European Union (EU), which won the Noble Peace Prize in 2012, created a continental scale service system entity (see "order of magnitude observation" above) with component service system entities (nations). The design of the EU is an example of blended competition and collaboration to enhance capabilities for value co-creation, intended to make the EU more competitive on the global stage, and improve the quality-of-life in all component nations.

Interact-Service-Propose-Agree-Realize (SS-FSC9) is an elaboration of the simple four-outcome model with ten-outcomes (Maglio et al. 2009). Interact-Service-Propose-Agree-Realize includes both service and non-service interactions. Non-service interactions can be either welcomed or not welcomed, legal or not legal, and result in justice or not justice. Service interactions may not be realized if the proposal is not-understood, or if not-agreed-to. Even if the proposal is understood and agreed to, the result may be not realized, and this can lead to a dispute or no-dispute, which can be resolved or not-resolved to the satisfaction of both entities.

Recovery (SS-FSC10) is a foundational sub-concept of great importance, especially when a series of outcomes is expected between entities over time and disputes arise when some outcomes are not realized to the mutual satisfaction of entities. Studies indicate that when a provider recovers well from a service failure, it can create a higher level of trust and loyalty with customers than if no failure had occurred (Magnini et al. 2007). Of course, this finding has many implications, if the motivation in optimizing provider value is seen as customer manipulation. Loyalty programs that provide enhanced benefits to customers, even when a failure has not occurred, can have a similar impact. Customer lifetime value informed investment strategies also create enhanced outcomes that pay off over the lifetime of interactions and outcomes (Rust et al. 2000).

SS-FC5: Value propositions

Value propositions are offers to play non-zero-sum games, and are at the heart of competing for collaborators. Often the value to the provider of the offer is hidden, and not accessible to the intended customer. In some cases the provider outcome is not hidden, such as in so-called "ultimatum games" where a player may refuse benefits, if a culturally determined sense of fairness in allocation is not realized (Seabright 2010). In the cases where provided benefit is unknown, the customer will evaluate the value proposition relative to similar offers from the provider's competitors. If no similar offers exist to choose from, then the offer can be viewed as competing at a higher level for the attention, time, and other resources of the customer.

The science of value proposition design is evolving rapidly (for example, see Winkler and Dosoudil 2011). The essential considerations include models of other stakeholders' capabilities, limitations, and processes of valuing. A customer must understand an offer, agree to the offer, and then contribute (co-creation, co-production) to realize the benefits of the offer. The more sophisticated the offer, the greater the customer's capabilities must be to understand, agreed to, and realize the outcome. Stakeholders include the provider, customer, competitors, and authority (Is the offer legal? Can disputes be resolved?). Competitors may include the customer (self-service), legitimate competitors (abiding by same laws and constraints), non-legitimate competitors (criminals, black or gray market), authority (government of social sector programs), and even on-line or other competitors who can play by different rules. Kwan et al. (2012) suggested a value proposition model for service system networks based on a formal model from Kwan and Müller-Gorchs (2011) that incorporates many of the attributes discussed above. Morgan and Hunt (1994) have also provided some important and necessary components of value propositions based on commitment and trust (see section 2 above).

Worth and value (SS-FSC11, 12) are different concepts (Ng, 2013). Worth is a point in time decision about what an entity is willing to pay for some anticipated future value. Value is an experience of "goodness" by an individual in context. Is an offer (value proposition) worth it? Did an offer (value proposition) become realized as anticipated, or provide superior value?

Risk and reward (SS-FSC13, 14) are unknowable in advance, and so must be estimated (Adams 2013). Every offer (value proposition) has associated risks and rewards that may be hard to anticipate and estimate. Some entities have greater risk-tolerance than other entities.

Processes of valuing and deciding (SS-FSC15, 16) are ultimately at the heart of service science. If we had a perfect model of our own processes of valuing and that of all other service system entities, and we had perfect data about the world and unlimited computational resources, then the science of service could become more objective. Unfortunately, we do not have that capability. Advances in cognitive science and the brain sciences do in fact help researchers build betters models of processes of valuing and deciding, and increasing computational capabilities can help certain well-scoped systems operate more optimally. Processes of valuing generate options and rank them. IBM's Watson supercomputer, known for its prowess in outscoring the top human Jeopardy! winners and creating diagnostic options for doctors to consider, is an example of a system with algorithmic processes of valuing (Ferrucci et al. 2010). Processes of deciding are tied to action. A decision with no action is not a true decision. Risk-tolerance often prevents individuals from taking action, even when processes of valuing suggest great potential rewards for certain options. It may be worth it to have others take the actions, but principle-agent problems may then arise, creating a different type of risk. Perhaps the order of magnitude observation (see above SS-FC1) combined with better governance mechanisms (SS-FC6) may offer a solution to many types of principle-agent problems, thus advancing the practice of value proposition design.

SS-FC6: Governance mechanisms

Governance mechanisms are based on a system of rules or laws that constrain entity interactions, with coercive power. Formal service system entities (SS-FSC1) exist as formal entities, because of their rights and the power of an authority service system entity to recognize, protect, and uphold those rights. Smart machines do not yet have rights. Businesses do have rights, because of laws. Both laws and technologies contribute to the "knowledge burden" of society. A nation without coercive powers would have to exist based purely on "voluntary value propositions," and no such nation exists. The weakest form of coercive power is banishment, or "cease existing here." The strongest form of coercive power is death of individual, family, and species with permanent erasure of historical mentions, or "cease existing everywhere for all time."

Only one set of service system entities legitimately retains rights to "coercive value propositions" that can threaten the fundamental rights including the right of refusal and right to exist, and that is government authorities. Criminal service system entities also use coercion, but they operate outside of national and international laws. All other service system entities are restricted to "voluntary value propositions," and use "coercive value proposition" only in criminal or private/non-public situations.

Rights and responsibilities (SS-FSC17, 18) go hand in hand. Rights are a privilege earned through responsible actions. Unless a service system has the capability to understand the responsibilities that accompany rights, they cannot enjoy those rights. Young children, debilitated elderly, the mentally ill, and other individuals may have restricted rights, because of their limited cognitive capacities. Imprisoned criminals could also have their rights suspended (for example, voting rights).

SS-FC7: Resources

Resources can exist in four types, exemplified by people, technology, organizations, and information. People and organizations are operant resources (actors), and technology and information are operand resources (used by actors). People augment themselves with technology and organizations to increase their capabilities and overcome constraints. This augmentation can positively impact quality of life, but can also introduce a significant "knowledge burden" on society. The size of the knowledge burden is reflected in the quantity of shared information. Shared information includes language, laws, measures, and much more.

Resources exist in context, as either as physical or not physical, and with rights or without rights. In the context known as "the real world," people are an example of a physical, with-rights resource, and businesses are an example of a not-physical, with-rights resource. Even though a business may have buildings, or component physical resources, no physical component is essential to a business, and a business can stay in existence with none of the original buildings or people that were originally part of it. However, the body of a person is an essential part of that person, and so a person is a physical, with-rights resource, even though a person as a service system entity includes far more than just the body of the individual person. A person as a service system entity is a much larger resource constellation, or configuration of component resources. For example, my car and house are component resources with the service system entity, which makes up me as an individual.

SS-FC8: Access rights

Access rights include owned-outright, leased-contracted, shared-access, and privileged access. Owning property versus leasing property comes with different rights and responsibilities. Similarly, shared access resources, such as roads and the air we breathe, come with different rights and responsibilities, compared to privileged access resources, such as one's own thoughts or family members.

SS-FC9: Stakeholder roles

Stakeholder roles include customer, provider, authority, and competitor. An employee may be viewed as both a provider to a business, a customer of the business's benefits program, an authority governing and resolving disputes associated with certain business processes, and a competitor of another employee interested in that same organizational role. Service system entities are at once customer, provider, competitor, and authority, depending on perspective.

SS-FC10: Measures

Measures include quality, productivity, compliance, and innovativeness. Many other measures and key performance indicators can be associated with service system entities or processes in which an entity participates. Measures allow ranking of service system entities. For example, universities (as service system entities) may be ranked based on the starting salaries of their graduates. Holistic service system entities may be ranked based on innovativeness, equity (competitive parity), sustainability, and resilience.

The disciplines observation The disciplines observation is a mapping of disciplines to the fundamental concepts of service science. The disciplines observation helps justify the choice of concepts. Four disciplines deal with stakeholders (types of entities): marketing (customer), operations (provider), political science/public policy (authority), and game theory/strategy (competitors). Four disciplines deal with access (types of resources): cognitive science/psychology/human factors (people), industrial engineering (technology), computer science/information systems (information), and social sciences/organization theory (organizations). Other disciplines deal with change and value (types of interactions and outcomes): history studies/economics and law as well as future studies/arts and design (outcomes). Associated with the disciplines observation is the professions observation that abstract job types map to Run-Transform-Innovate roles in organizations and society (see SS-FP6 below).

3.4 Service Science Foundational Premises

Maglio and Spohrer (2013) have been evolving foundational premises for service science. Others linking the concept of viable systems to service systems are also working on foundational premises (Barile and Polese

2010). An extension and evolution under consideration is presented below.

SS-FP1: All viable service system entities dynamically configure four types of resources: people, technologies, organizations, and information

Put another way, a service system that cannot dynamically configure resources is not viable. The application of knowledge to dynamically configure access to resources for mutual benefits is a fundamental capability of service system entities, and often access to resources (rights and responsibilities) must be earned. For example, earning a driver's license is an earned right that requires demonstrating capabilities and taking on additional responsibilities. Earning and using a driver's license in society requires access to people (for example, driving test certifier), technology (for example, a car), organizations (for example, Department of Motor Vehicles), and information (for example, rules of the road booklet and test). For example, setting up a business is an earned right that requires capabilities and taking on additional responsibilities—people (for example, hiring employees), resources (for example, capital), technology (for example, equipment or environmental resources used in the business), organizations (for example, working with suppliers), and information (for example, submitting tax forms on time).

SS-FP2: All viable service system entities compute value given the concerns of multiple stakeholders, including customer, provider, authority, and competitor

Put another way, a service system that cannot compute value given the concerns of multiple stakeholders is not viable. For example, a business must offer something of value to customers, maintain relationships with supply chain organizations (providers), obey any regulations that apply to the business (authority), and in the long-run out perform competitors.

SS-FP3: All viable service system entities reconfigure access rights associated with resources by mutually agreed-to value propositions or governance mechanisms

SDL-FP9 states that all social and economic actors are resource integrators. All economic and social actors apply knowledge to integrate resources. Resources can be divided into three categories: market-facing resources (available for purchase to own outright or for lease/contract), private nonmarket-facing resources (privileged access), and public nonmarket facing resources (shared access). Access rights fall into four categories: own outright, lease/contract, privileged access, and shared access. Ensuring that nested entities have protected rights and comply with responsibilities is work performed by a governing authority.

SS-FP4: All viable service system entities compute and coordinate actions with others through symbolic processes of valuing and symbolic processes of communicating
Written laws and contracts are relatively new innovations in human history. Computers, spreadsheets, expert decision support system, and electronic trading system are even newer innovations. The transition from purely informal promises (moral codes) to formal contracts (legal codes) speaks to the evolution of service systems from primarily informal to increasingly formal. Viewed from the perspective of computer science, artificial intelligence, and organization theory, people and organizations can be modeled as a type of physical symbol system (March and Simon 1958; Newell and Simon 1976).

SS-FP5: All viable service system entities interact to create ten types of outcomes, spanning value co-creation and value co-destruction
Interact-Service-Propose-Agree-Realize (SS-FSC9) is an elaboration of the simple four-outcome model with ten outcomes (Maglio et al. 2009). Interact-Service-Propose-Agree-Realize includes both service and non-service interactions. Non-service interactions can be either welcomed or not welcomed, legal or not legal, and result in justice or not justice. Service interactions may not be realized if the proposal is not understood, or if not agreed to. Even if the proposal is understood and agreed to, the result may be not realized, and this can lead to a dispute or no dispute, which can be resolved or not resolved to the satisfaction of both entities.

SS-FP6: All viable service system entities learn
Learning, exploitation and exploration, is fundamental to organizations (March 1991). If service systems can only apply knowledge in fixed patterns, they will not be able to compete with service systems that learn, adapt, and change to become more competitive. Run-Transform-Innovate is IBM naming for March's exploitation and exploration distinction, where exploitation (routine knowledge use) maps to run, and exploration (novel knowledge use) maps to both transform (copy from others) and innovate (invent for oneself). Abstract job types can be mapped to Run-Transform-Innovate (Spohrer and Maglio 2010).

3.5 Proposed Research Agenda for a Science of Service

The service research community has taken some steps to define a research agenda and establish research priorities to advance the science of service

(Ostrom 2010). The ten priorities include strategic, development, and execution priorities from a managerial (marketing, operations) perspective, and one pervasive priority from an engineering (computing) perspective; each priority is described briefly below.

SS-RP1: Strategic priority: fostering service infusion and growth
This research priority deals with the ability of organizations to create and improve service offerings to grow. Changing culture (customer focus, service logic, servitization), strategy, business models (outcome-based), and portfolio management are important research topics related to this priority.

SS-RP2: Strategic priority: improving well-being through transformative service
This research priority deals with the ability of governments and social enterprises to create and improve service offering to improve quality of life for citizens and the disenfranchised. Social welfare (health, education), environment (sustainability, green), democratization (open data, transparency), urbanization (smarter systems), and bottom-of-pyramid issues are important research topics related to this priority.

SS-RP3: Strategic priority: creating and maintaining a service culture
This research priority deals with ability of organizations to create and maintain a service culture. Human resources (hiring, training, incentives), globalization (diversity), mind-set (values), and learning (adaptation) are important research topics related to this priority.

SS-RP4: Development priority: stimulating service innovation
This broad research priority deals with the ability of organizations to innovate to compete. Drivers (globalization, automation), types (incremental, radical), roles and sources (employees, customers, supplier, research, managers, universities), methods (design, arts, creativity), tools (modeling, simulation), and policy (investment, measurement) are important research topics related to this priority.

SS-RP5: Development priority: enhancing service design
This research priority deals with the ability of organizations to design better customer experience and outcomes. Thinking (design, systems, processes), arts (performance, visual), challenges (economic cycles, cultural variations, market segments), and methods (collaborative, crowd sourcing) are important research topics related to this priority.

SS-RP6: Development priority: optimizing service networks and value chains
This research priority deals with the ability of networks of organizations to optimize collective performance. Supply chain, outsourcing, value migration, inter-organizational governance, globalization, productivity, and optimization algorithms are important research topics related to this priority.

SS-RA7: Execution priority: effective branding and selling of services
This research priority deals with the ability of organizations to establish brands to enhance sales. Social media, word of mouth, multichannel, consistency, assessment of brand value, sales force and employee training are important research topics related to this priority.

SS-RA8: Execution priority: enhancing service experience through co-creation
This research priority deals with the ability of organizations to fully utilize co-creation. Sharing (responsibilities, work effort, risks, rewards, information, property rights), role of actors (employee, customer, manager), role of technology (channels, complexity), customer community management, recovery, and loyalty are important research topics related to this priority.

SS-RA9: Execution priority: measuring and optimizing value of service
This research priority deals with the ability of organizations to measure and optimize processes. Self-service technologies, return on investment, instrumentation, estimation, standards, portfolio management, and optimization algorithms are important research topics related to this priority.

SS-RP10: Pervasive force: leveraging technology to advance service
This research priority deals with the ability of organizations to keep up with and incorporate disruptive technologies into service operations, and to use advanced technologies to improve service offerings and customer experience. Platforms (smart phones, cloud computing, smart systems, web services, service-oriented architectures), accelerating change (business models, acquisitions), self-service technologies, real-time decision making (cognitive computing, stream computing), security, privacy, biometrics, are important topics related to this priority.

Translating these priorities into a set of grand challenge research questions for service science remains to be done, though there have been some tentative efforts in this direction (Tang 2012).

3.6 Proposed Extensions to the Research Agenda

The ten research priorities in the previous section can be seen as priorities aimed at impacting practice with largely managerial and engineering implications. We propose three other priorities aimed at education, public policy (tooling), and theoretical research as part of the service science research agenda.

SS-RA11: Extension education priority: curriculum
Creating curriculum and best practices for teaching and learning service science is an additional research priority. A curriculum that is designed to create T-shaped service innovators with depth and breadth, who have interactional expertise across disciplines, sectors, and cultures, is being requested by leading employers to improve innovativeness, teamwork, and learning rates (IBM 2011).

Since service science is a transdiscipline and borrows from so many other disciplines, one interesting proposal for a service science curriculum is optimizing the recapitulation of history from a technological and governance perspective (Spohrer 2012). Rapidly rebuilding societal infrastructure and institutions, without the many twists and turns of history, might allow for a compressed, integrated, holistic curriculum. This is also possibly an approach to reducing the "knowledge burden," without reducing quality-of-life measures. Ultimately, service innovations must address the rising knowledge burden and the inter-generational transfer of knowledge challenges because they depend increasingly on symbolic knowledge and symbolic processes of valuing.

SS-RA12: Extension policy priority: global simulation and design tool
Creating a global simulation and design tool for evaluating alternative governance mechanisms is an additional research priority. Modeling the nested, networked service ecology could also have a profound impact on teaching and learning service science, especially if appropriate pedagogical idealizations can be developed (Spohrer and Giususa 2012).

Based on the order of magnitude observation, there is a much larger market for individuals than cities, a larger market for cities than nations. The global simulation and design tool could be used to experiment with policies intended to improve competitive parity between regions at all order of magnitude scales, while increasing the speed innovations could spread globally.

SS-RA13: Extension theory priority: foundations
To put service science on a more fundamental theoretical foundation, it might be a useful research priority to consider a nested, network service ecology based on something other than the human species. For example, a service ecology based on intelligent machines, with greatly extended life spans, much faster learning rates, and much larger and denser populations, might be useful for thinking about a service ecology in the limiting case, when constraints on the basic building block service system entity (individuals) are removed. Alternatively, a service ecology with a diversity of species with different physical, cognitive, and social constraints could open up new theoretical directions for service science. Some work on Abstract-Entity-Interaction-Outcome-Universals (AEIOU) framework has begun, and an extensive elaboration of this could be part of an expanded theoretical foundation for service science and other transdisciplines (Spohrer et al. 2011).

Understanding and characterizing the fundamental constraints on species is an important area of research for developing the theoretical foundations for service science. For example, humans have the following constraints:

1. Physical: finite life span
2. Cognitive: finite learning rate
3. Social: finite population size/density.

In the last 200 years, life spans have extended, education levels have risen, and population size/density have increased. In complex service systems, as fundamental (weakest link) constraints are removed, other constraints emerge to dominate system performance (Ricketts 2007). The mapping of fundamental constraints for other types of service system entities has not been developed yet.

4 CONTRIBUTION: BALANCING FRAMEWORK

In section 2, we introduced the notion of marketing as entities "competing for collaborators," building off a prominent article in the relationship marketing literature by Morgan and Hunt (1994). In section 3, we reviewed service science and arts, in terms of service research history and community (3.1), service-dominant logic (3.2), foundational concept (3.3), foundational propositions (3.4), research priorities (3.5), and some proposed extensions (3.6). In this section, we present a "balancing framework," which argues that the future of marketing will be the search for improved methods of "competing for collaborators" and other balancing mechanisms that sustain a healthy ecology.

Marketing is embedded in human interactions. As such, balancing the needs of the parties to the exchange has always been central to the logic. This balancing appears in human societies as a norm of reciprocity, which underlies much of the logic in the fields of economics and ethics. Gummesson (2008) proposed the concept of balanced centricity to better balance the needs of multiple stakeholders in networked service systems.

Marketing has a long history of seeking balance in other ways, too. The phrase "marketing mix" has long been used to describe the need to "mix" the various marketing tools to better serve customers. The same logic applies to the promotional mix that refers to a mix of communication tools to better reach customers.

Service science and service arts require balancing, too. Because they address different aspects of serving human needs, neither science nor arts can fully serve human need. Together, service science and service arts can more fully support human needs in their many nested, service networks—families, communities, cities, and nations.

From a service science perspective, the creation of new markets can be seen as the creation of new types of entities, new types of interactions between existing entities, or both. Within an ecology of nested, networked service system entities, both the creation of new types of entities and new types of interactions arise first as ideas about the future.

From a service science perspective, the lead thinkers would compete for collaborators with rational economic arguments, for example. Also from a service arts perspective, creating new markets still depends on lead thinkers to imagine new ideas for serving customers. The lead thinker might compete for collaborators with an emotional, instead of a rational appeal.

Some new ideas have both a scientific (more rational, for example, function) and artistic (more emotional, for example, form) appeal. When two ideas seem equally good from a scientific perspective, the artistic perspective can help us differentiate them. Even when one idea is a little better from a scientific perspective, if the other alternative is much better from an artistic perspective, it is likely that the alternative will win out over purely rational decision-making.

So in the "competition for collaborators," a service science and arts perspective suggests that the ecology of service system entities evolves to maintaining a balance. Similarly, if competition becomes too cutthroat, it may not be sustainable. If cooperation becomes too forgiving, it may not be sustainable (for example, "non-zero sum" games in Wright 2000). There is also a healthy balance between moral forces and market forces in the healthiest economies (Friedman and McNeil 2013). In policymaking, rule systems that lead to winner-take-all are often not sustainable, but those that balance improve-weakest-link are more robust (Spohrer and Giuiusa 2012; Wright 2000).

If balance is lost, the ecology of nested, network systems will not be sustainable. For marketplace behaviors to be sustainable, human-to-human relationships must also be balanced with human-to-nature relationships (Shirahada and Fisk 2011). Such balancing efforts are necessary to refresh the nested and networked systems of the planet into harmony.

5 CONCLUDING REMARKS: FUTURE DIRECTIONS

We live in a human-made ecology of nested and networked service system entities—families, businesses, universities, cities, states, and nations. Humans are unique in our ability to communicate, collaborate, compete, and realize shared dreams about the future, from start-up grand challenges (like building a social graph of the world) to national grand challenges (like landing a man on the moon) to scientific grand challenges (like mapping human DNA). Humans have evolved to compete for the cooperation of larger and larger groups of others. Many competitions are in fact mechanisms for cooperation in disguise, positively reinforcing rule-following compliance and punishing rule-violations. Balancing competition and cooperation to accelerate learning and social benefits is fundamental to human progress.

The human ecology of nested, networked service system entities has already evolved through several technical infrastructure stages, remarkable in terms of energy, transportation, and communications, which enable great cities to emerge at an accelerating pace (Hawley 1986). Designing alternative viable futures for people in an age of rapidly increasing technical and organizational capabilities presents many challenges and opportunities. For example, policymakers understand that norms and laws must co-evolve with technical capabilities created by engineers. Two important types of constraints shaping the evolution of service systems are the technical and environmental capabilities (infrastructure) and governance responsibilities (institutions). These two constraints interact with two other constraints, the education and skill levels (individuals) and quality-of-life aspirations of families (cultural information). Service is the application of knowledge for mutual benefits (value co-creation). Service innovations scale the benefits of new knowledge globally and rapidly. T-shaped professionals are professionals with depth and breadth of knowledge across academic disciplines, industry sectors and regional cultures. T-shapes balance depth and breadth to optimize abilities to compete as individuals and collaborate in teams. Appropriate breadth has the potential to improve innovativeness, teamwork, and learning rates.

In this chapter, within the context of providing a service science and arts perspective on marketing, we presented a balancing framework for analyzing the historical evolution of service system entities and exploring the design space for alternative viable futures. Surprisingly, we argue that dealing with the "knowledge burden" of society, which helps people develop the skills to rapidly rebuild societal infrastructure and institutions along alternative possible historical pathways, may open up the largest design space for alternative viable futures. We also advocate that creating a trading zone (or "big tent") for the development of service science as a transdiscipline, which borrows from disciplines without replacing them, is a useful and timely model (Gorman 2010; Rust 2004). T-shaped service innovators are on the path towards transdisciplinarity. This chapter has implication for those in academia, industry, government, and the social sector interested in a more service-oriented view that balances past, present, and future possibilities.

ACKNOWLEDGMENTS

Discussions with many colleagues at service science related conferences around the world, as well as email and social media interactions with ISSIP.org members globally have helped shape these ideas.

NOTES

1. "Coopetition" refers to enterprises which cooperate in certain businesses while competing in other businesses with the same entities.
2. New sciences may seem like "stamp collecting" or "counting stamps" to scientists in more mature sciences. For example, Lord Rutherford said, "All *science* is either physics or *stamp collecting*." Service science is still at the stage of counting and categorizing types of entities, interactions, and outcomes.
3. Thanks to Paul Lilrank (Aalto University, Finland) for this thought.
4. Service science is short for the IBM-originated name of service science, management and engineering (SSME), since service science was originally conceived to be the broad part of T-shaped professionals, that complements depth in any disciplinary area with breadth in SSME (IBM 2011). Recently service science has been referred to as short for SSME+D, adding design (Spohrer and Kwan 2009). Subsequently part of the service science community extended SSME to SSME+DAPP by adding design, art and public policy. The naming of a transdiscipline is especially challenging, and communities can endlessly debate pros and cons of names.

5. ISSIP's website is at www.issip.org.
6. The first five fundamental premises are based on macroeconomics and the second five are microeconomics based, see Kwan and Müller-Gorchs (2011).
7. Sometimes this trading zone is colloquially referred to as the "big tent" (Rust 2004, p. 211).

REFERENCES

Adams, J. (2013), *Risk*, London: Routledge.

Alderson, W. (1965), *Dynamic Marketing Behavior: A Functionalist Theory of Marketing*, Homewood, IL: R.D. Irwin.

Barile, S. and F. Polese (2010), "Smart service systems and viable service systems: applying systems theory to service science," *Service Science*, **2** (1–2), 21–40.

Bengtsson, M. and S. Kock (2000), "'Coopetition' in business networks—to cooperate and compete simultaneously," *Industrial Marketing Management*, **29** (5), 411–26.

Boyd, B. (2009), *On the Origin of Stories: Evolution, Cognition, and Fiction*. Cambridge, MA: Belknap Press of Harvard University Press.

Christopher M., A. Payne and D. Ballantyne (1991), *Relationship Marketing*, Oxford: Butterworth-Heinemann.

Dutton, D. (2010), *The Art Instinct: Beauty, Pleasure, and Human Evolution*, New York: Bloomsbury Press.

Engelbart, D.C. (1995), "Toward augmenting the human intellect and boosting our collective IQ," *Communications of the ACM*, **38** (8), 30–32.

Ferrucci, D., E. Brown, J. Chu-Carroll, J. Fan, D. Gondek, A.A. Kalyanpur, A. Lally, J.W. Murdock, E. Nyberg, J. Prager, N. Schlaefer and C. Welty (2010), "Building Watson: an overview of the DeepQA project," *AI Magazine*, **31** (3), 59–79.

Fisk, R.P. and S.J. Grove (2012), "A performing arts perspective on service design," *Touchpoint: The Journal of Service Design*, **4** (2), 20–25.

Fisk, R.P., S.J. Grove, A. Daly and W. Ganz (2007), "Service arts: broadening the services field", paper presented at the 2007 AMA Frontiers in Service Conference, San Francisco, California, 4–7 October.

Friedman, D. (2008), *Morals and Markets: An Evolutionary Account of Modern Life*, New York: Palgrave Macmillan.

Friedman, D. and D. McNeill (2013), *Morals and Markets: The Dangerous Balance*, New York: Palgrave Macmillan.

Gorman, M. (2010), *Trading Zones and Interactional Expertise: Creating New Kinds of Collaboration (Inside Technology)*, Cambridge, MA: MIT Press.

Gummesson, E. (2008), "Extending the service-dominant logic: from customer centricity to balanced centricity," *Journal of the Academy of Marketing Science*, **36**, 15–17.

Harris, P. (2009), "Help wanted: 'T-shaped' skills to meet 21st century needs", *T+D*, **63** (9), 42–7.

Hawley, A.H. (1986), *Human Ecology: A Theoretical Essay*, Chicago, IL: University of Chicago Press.

IBM (2011), "The invention of service science," accessed 19 September 2013 at www-03.ibm.com/ibm/history/ibm100/us/en/icons/servicescience/.

Jones, B.F. (2005), "The burden of knowledge and the 'death of the renaissance man': is innovation getting harder?" NBER Working Paper, No. 11360, May.

Kremer, M. (1993), "Population growth and technological change: one million BC to 1990," *Quarterly Journal of Economics*, **108** (3), 681–716.

Kwan, S.K. and M. Müller-Gorchs, M. (2011), "Constructing Effective Value Propositions for Stakeholders in Service System Networks," *Proceedings of SIGSVC Workshop. Sprouts: Working Papers on Information Systems*, **11** (160), accessed 19 September 2013 at http://sprouts.aisnet.org/11-160.

Kwan, S.K., P. Hottum and C. Kieliszewski (2012), "Moving from B2X to B2X2Y value propositions in service system networks," 1st International Conference on Human Side of Service Engineering, HSSE 2012, San Francisco, California, 20–25 July.
Maglio, P.P., S. Srinivasan, J. Kreulen and J.C. Spohrer (2006), "Service systems, service scientists, SSME, and innovation," *Communications of the ACM*, **49** (7), 81–85.
Maglio, P.P. and J.C. Spohrer (2013), "A service science perspective on business model design," *Industrial Marketing Management*, forthcoming.
Maglio, P.P., S.L. Vargo, N. Caswell and J.C. Spohrer (2009), "The service system is the basic abstraction of service science," *Information Systems and e-Business Management*, **7** (4), 395–406.
Magnini, V.P., J.B. Ford, E.P. Markowski and E.D. Honeycutt Jr. (2007), "The service recovery paradox: justifiable theory or smoldering myth?" *Journal of Services Marketing*, **21** (3), 213–25.
March, J.G. (1991), "Exploration and exploitation in organizational learning," *Organization Science*, **2** (1), 71–87.
March, J.G. and H.A. Simon (1958), *Organizations*, New York: Wiley.
Morgan R.M. and S.D. Hunt (1994), "The commitment-trust model of relationship marketing," *Journal of Marketing*, **58** (3), 20–38.
Motwani, J., R. Ptacek and R. Fleming (2012), *Lean Sigma Methods and Tools for Service Organizations: The Story of a Cruise Line Transformation*, USA: Business Expert Press.
Newell, A. and H.A. Simon (1976), "Computer science as empirical inquiry: symbols and search," *Communications of the ACM*, **19** (3), 113–26.
Ng, I.C.L. (2013), *Value and Worth: Creating New Markets in the Digital Economy*, Cambridge: Innovorsa Press.
Ordanini, A. and A. Parasuraman (2011), "Service innovation viewed through a service-dominant logic lens: a conceptual framework and empirical analysis," *Journal of Service Research*, **14** (1), 3–23.
Ostrom, A.L., M.J. Bitner, S.W. Brown, K.A. Burkhard, M. Goul, V. Smith-Daniels, H. Demirkan and E. Rabinovich (2010), "Moving forward and making a difference: research priorities for the science of service," *Journal of Service Research*, **13** (1), 4–36.
Postrel, V. (2004), *The Substance of Style: How the Rise of Aesthetic Value Is Remaking Commerce, Culture & Consciousness*, New York: Perennial.
Ricketts, J.A. (2007), *Reaching the Goal: How Managers Improve a Services Business Using Goldratt's Theory of Constraints*, Armonk, NY: IBM Press.
Rotter, J.B. (1967), "A new scale for the measurement of interpersonal trust," *Journal of Personality*, **35** (4), 651–65.
Rust, R. (2004), "A call for a wider range of service research," *Journal of Service Research*, **6** (3), 211.
Rust, R.T., V.A. Zeithaml and K.N. Lemon (2000), *Driving Customer Equity: How Customer Lifetime Value Is Reshaping Corporate Strategy*, New York: Free Press.
Seabright, P. (2010), *The Company of Strangers: A Natural History of Economic Life*, revd edn, Princeton, NJ: Princeton University Press.
Shirahada, K. and R.P. Fisk (2011), "Broadening the concept of service: a tripartite value co-creation perspective for service sustainability," in B. van der Rhee and L. Victorino (eds), *Advances in Service Quality, Innovation and Excellence*, Ithaca, NY: Cayuga Press, pp. 917–26.
Simon, H.A. (1996), *The Sciences of the Artificial*, Cambridge, MA: MIT Press.
Solomon, R.C. (1992), *Ethics and Excellence*, Oxford: Oxford University Press.
Spohrer, J.C. (2010), "Whole service," accessed 19 September 2013 at http://service-science.info/archives/1056.
Spohrer, J.C. (2012), "A new engineering-challenge discipline: rapidly rebuilding societal infrastructure," accessed 19 September 2013 at http://service-science.info/archives/2189.
Spohrer, J.C. and A. Giuiusa (2012), "Exploring the future of cities and universities: a

tentative first step," in Proceedings of Workshop on Social Design: Contribution of Engineering to Social Resilience, System Innovation, University of Tokyo, Tokyo, 12 May.
Spohrer, J. and S.K. Kwan (2009), "Service science, management, engineering, and design (SSMED): an emerging discipline – outline & references," *International Journal of Information Systems in the Service Sector (IJISSS)*, **1** (3), 1–31.
Spohrer, J.C. and P.P. Maglio (2010), "Toward a science of service systems," in J.C. Spohrer and P.P. Maglio (eds), *Handbook of Service Science*, New York: Springer, pp. 157–94.
Spohrer, J.C., H. Demirkan and V. Krishna (2011), "Service and science," in J.C. Spohrer, H. Demirkan and V. Krishna (eds), *The Science of Service Systems*, New York: Springer, pp. 325–58.
Spohrer, J.C., M. Gregory and G. Ren (2010), "The Cambridge-IBM SSME white paper revisited," in J.C. Spohrer and P.P. Maglio (eds), *Handbook of Service Science*, New York: Springer, pp. 677–706.
Spohrer, J.C., P.P. Maglio, J. Bailey and D. Gruhl (2007), "Steps toward a science of service systems," *Computer*, **40** (1), 71–7.
Spohrer, J.C., P. Piciocchi and C. Bassano (2012), "Three frameworks for service research: exploring multilevel governance in nested, networked systems," *Service Science*, **4** (2), 147–60.
Tang, V. (2012), "Survey: service science top open questions," accessed 19 September 2013 at http://service-science.info/archives/2071.
Teboul, J. (2006), *Service is Front Stage: Positioning Services for Value Advantage*, New York: Palgrave Macmillan.
Tracy, S. (2012), "Service systems and social enterprise: beyond the economics of business," Doctoral dissertation, University of Toronto.
Tracy, S. and K. Lyons (2012), "Service systems and the social enterprise," *Human Factors and Ergonomics in Manufacturing & Service Industries*, **23** (1), 28–36.
Vargo, S.L. and M.A. Akaka (2009), "Service-dominant logic as a foundation for service science: clarifications," *Service Science*, **1** (1), 32–41.
Vargo, S.L. and R.F. Lusch (2004), "Evolving to a new dominant logic for marketing," *Journal of Marketing*, **68** (1), 1–17.
Vargo, S.L. and R.F. Lusch (2008), "Service-dominant logic: continuing the evolution," *Journal of the Academy of Marketing Science*, **36** (1), 1–10.
Winkler, M. and L. Dosoudi (2011), "On formalization of the concept of value proposition," *Service Science*, **3** (3), 194–205.
Wright, R. (2000), *Nonzero – The Logic of Human Destiny*, New York: Vintage Books.

APPENDIX: CONCEPT, DISCIPLINE, RESEARCHER, AND SO ON

Researchers from many disciplines have contributed to advancing service science and the study of service systems. Based on a sampling of publications (Spohrer 2013), some disciplinary branches are partially summarized in Table 22A.1.

Table 22A.1

Concept	Discipline	Researcher	Journal	Conference	Association
Stakeholder Customer	Marketing	Rust	JSR, CACM	Frontiers	AMA, INFORMS, ASA
		Fisk	JSR	Frontiers, AMA SERVSIG	AMA
		Bitner	JSR, CACM	Frontiers	AMA
		Vargo	JM, JAMS	Frontiers	AMA
		Lusch	JM, JAMS	Frontiers	AMA
		Grönroos	JSR, JAMS	Frontiers, QUIS	FSSL
		Edvardsson	JAMS	Frontiers, QUIS	
		Gummesson	JBIM	Forum, QUIS	SSEBA, ISQA
Stakeholder Provider	Production operations	Sampson	JSR	POMS	POMS
	Operations Management	Neely	OMR	Alliance	EOMA
		Davis	IBMSysJ, OMR	ArtSci	DSI, POMS
		Metters	DS	POMS	DSI, INFORMS, POMS
		Apte	POMS	POMS	POMS, DSI
	Operations research	Larson	JoSS		INFORMS
		Badinelli	JoSS	Forum	INFORMS, ISSIP

Table 22A.1 (continued)

Concept	Discipline	Researcher	Journal	Conference	Association
Stakeholder	Governance	Piciocchi	JoSS	Forum	ISSIP
Authority		Bassano	JoSS	Forum	ISSIP
Stakeholder	Strategy	Polese	JoSS	Forum	ASVSA
Competitor		Barile	JoSS	Forum	ASVSA
Resource People	Social sciences anthropology	Baba	CACM	HSSE	AAA NAPA
	Cognitive science	Glushko	JSR, IBMSysJ	Frontiers, HSSE	CSS, OASIS
	Human factors	Freund	HFEMSI	HSSE	HF&E, IIE, ISSIP
Resource	Industrial engineering	Rouse	IBMSysJ		IIE, INCOSE
Technology	System engineering	Tien	JSSE		IEEE, NAE
		Berg	JSSE		IEEE, NAE
Resource Information	Computer science	Spohrer	CACM, JAMS, Computer	Frontiers, HSSE, AMCIS	ACM, ISSIP
		Maglio	CACM, JAMS, Computer	HICSS	ACM
	Information systems	Alter	IBMSysJ	AMCIS, ICIS	AIS, IFIP
		Demirkan	ECRA	AMCIS	AIS, ISSIP
		Kwan	IJISSS	AMCIS, ICIS, Forum, HSSE	AIS, ANSI, ISSIP
	Information management	Karmarkar	MS	BIT	INFORMS
Resource	Economic geography	Bryson	SIJ		
Organizations	Service systems	Ng	EMJ	Alliance	
	Social enterprises	Lyons	HFEMSI	HSSE	AIS, ISSIP

Notes:

Journals

CACM = *Communications of the Association for Computing Machinery*
Computer = *Institute of Electrical and Electronic Engineers Computer*
ECRA = *Electronic Commerce Research and Applications*
EMJ = *European Management Journal*
HFEMSI = *Human Factors and Ergonomics in Manufacturing & Service Industries*
IBMSysJ = *IBM Systems Journal*
IJIMA = *International Journal of Internet Marketing & Advertising*
IJSIM = *International Journal of Service Industry Management*
IJISSS = *International Journal of Information Systems in the Service Sector*
ISEBM = *Information Systems and E-Business Management*
MS = *Management Science*
JAMS = *Journal of the Academy of Marketing Sciences*
JBIM = *Journal of Business & Industrial Marketing*
JOSM = *Journal of Service Management*
JSM = *Journal of Services Marketing*
JSR = *Journal of Service Science*
JSSE = *Journal of Systems Science and Systems Engineering*
MSQ = *Managing Service Quality*
OMJ = *Operations Management Research*
SIJ = *The Service Industries Journal*

Conferences

Alliance = Cambridge Alliance Conference
AHFE = Applied Human Factors and Ergonomics Conference
AMA SERVIG = American Marketing Association SERVIG Conference
AMCIS = Americas Conference on Information Systems
ArtSci = Art & Science of Service Conference
Frontiers = Frontiers in Service Conference
HICSS = Hawaii International Conference fro Systems Sciences
HSSE = Applied Human Factors and Ergonomics Conference Human-Side of Service Engineering
Forum = Naples Service Forum
ICIS = International Conference on Information Systems

Table 22A.1 (continued)

Notes:
POMS = Production and Operations Management Society
QUIS = Quality in Services
Associations
AAA = American Anthropological Association
AAAS = American Association for the Advancement of Science
ACM = Association for Computing Machinery
AIS = Association for Information Systems
AMA = American Marketing Association
ANSI = American National Standards Institute
ASA = American Statistical Association
ASVSA = Associazione per la ricerca sui Sistemi Vitali (Viable Systems)
CSS = Cognitive Science Society
DSI = Decision Science Institute
EOMA = European Operations Management Association
FSSL = Finnish Society of Sciences and Letters
IEE = Institute of Industrial Engineers
IEEE = Institute of Electrical and Electronic Engineers
IEEE EMS = IEEE Engineering Management Society
INFORMS = Institute for Operations Research and the Management Sciences
ISQA = International Service Quality Association
ISSIP = International Society of Service Innovation Professionals
NAE = U.S. National Academy of Engineering
NAPA = AAA National Association for the Practice of Anthropology
NYAS = New York Academy of Sciences
OASIS = Advancing Open Standards for the Information Society
SSEBA = Swedish School of Economics and Business Administration

23 Hospitality marketing and branding research: insights from a specific service context

Chekitan S. Dev

INTRODUCTION: MOTIVATIONS AND GOALS

The hospitality, travel, and tourism business has in recent decades developed into a multi-trillion dollar global industry, creating many new opportunities and challenges. Whereas in the past businesses could survive and even prosper using ad hoc, trial-and-error business strategies, today firms must use better, smarter, scientifically validated, and globally relevant methods to run businesses efficiently and effectively.

Business strategy in hospitality firms once began with marketing and incorporated branding as one of its elements; today the brand drives marketing within the larger hospitality enterprise. Not only has it become the chief means of attracting customers, it has, more broadly, become the chief organizing principle for most hospitality organizations. The never-ending quest for market share follows trend after trend, from offering ever more elaborate and sophisticated amenities to the use of social media as a marketing tool—all driven by the preeminence of the brand.

Strategically, brands have become the central organizing principle for major hospitality organizations, guiding every decision and action and constituting much of the market value—the brand equity—of many successful companies. While making money is the objective of any hospitality firm, managing brands profitably has become the single most important means to that end. Most hotels and restaurants in the U.S. today are affiliated with branded chains. The hospitality industry has experienced this "branding" chiefly because of the customer's desire for a predictable product and service experience, economies of scale in advertising and distribution, and market power in negotiation with high-volume buyers.

In global terms, all the major hospitality companies are engaged in restructuring their business strategies and organizations around brands. In short, the hospitality industry offers a complex, fragmented, global, competitive context for developing an understanding of brand management. In this chapter I summarize eight studies that illustrate the ascendancy of the brand as the touchstone of success in hospitality marketing. The first two studies cover general aspects of brand management, namely, how to orient a brand strategically relative to its marketplace and how to form profitable brand marketing partnerships with brand properties, respectively. These are followed by two views on a vexing problem facing brands: opportunism on the part of individual hotels that undermine brand partnerships. The fifth study explores the extension of brands into alternative market segments, positing an ideal number of such extensions. We then move into globalization, with two studies of the best strategies for entering foreign markets. The chapter ends with a look at the latest trend in hospitality marketing—Internet-based social couponing—and considers how such marketing innovations will affect the study of hospitality marketing and branding into the future.

MARKET ORIENTATION[1]

By adopting a market orientation, a brand commits itself to satisfying its customers' needs over the long run by providing customers with superior value on a sustained basis (Kohli and Jaworski 1990; Narver and Slater 1990). This means instituting an organization-wide culture that effectively provides a brand with norms and beliefs that shape an integrated organizational strategy for sensing changing customer demand and anticipating future market conditions. The study summarized here surveyed 185 hotel general and senior managers in 56 countries (26 developed and 30 developing countries) across six continents, representing a wide variety of local conditions. The average hotel in the sample offered 365 rooms and had been operating for 23 years.

John Narver and Stanley Slater laid down the canonical view of market orientation, according to which such an orientation combines three main components: a customer orientation, whereby a brand strives to understand its target customers; a competitor orientation, whereby a brand strives to understand what its competitors are doing; and interfunctional coordination, the organizational culture that orients employees in all departments of a business unit to understanding the brand's customers and competitors in its market (Narver and Slater 1990).

The study addressed three theoretical issues pertaining to adopting a market orientation: the extent to which the efficacy of a market orientation depends on environmental factors (thereby assuming the contingency approach); whether, having adopted a market orientation, a brand should lean more towards a customer orientation or a competitor orientation; and the effects of global competition on a brand's market orientation.

In adopting the contingency approach the study tested hypotheses at the country level to reflect stages of economic development, at the local level to reflect local business conditions and resource availability, and at the consumer level to reflect variations in customer demand (we were guided in this effort by Fahy et al. 2000), thereby addressing the abovementioned theoretical issues. Interfunctional coordination served only as a control variable.

Customer versus Competitor Orientation: Four Hypotheses

The study adopted the United Nations classification scheme based on industrialization, according to which the U.S.A., Japan, and the U.K. represent developed economies, and Brazil, China, and Indonesia represent developing economies. A competitor orientation should work better in a developing country due to the cost advantages it provides in a market whose customers have low buying power, whereas a customer orientation should work better in a developed country due to its sophisticated customer base and the higher cost of learning about competitors. Therefore, the more developed an economy is, the stronger should be the effect of adopting a customer orientation on brand performance, whereas the less developed an economy is, the stronger should be the effect of a competitor orientation.

Local business conditions that favor a competitor orientation include poor infrastructure, political instability, scarcity of value chain partners and strategic factor markets, and unfamiliar legal systems (Peng and Heath 1996; Peng and Luo 2000). Such conditions require brands to rely on personal ties or networks to form constructive relationships with local politicians and business leaders. Consequently, the poorer the local business conditions, the weaker should be the effect of a customer orientation and the stronger should be the effect of a competitor orientation on brand performance.

The scarcity of local resources typically found in a poorly developed country should also favor a competitor orientation. Here again, information about a brand's competitors should help it understand how they configure their value chains and adopt procurement approaches in a given market. Moreover, with poor access to critical resources, customer information is of little use. Therefore, the greater the resource availability, the stronger should be the effect of a customer orientation on brand performance, whereas the lower the resource availability, the stronger should be the effect of a competitor orientation.

Finally, customer demandingness—the extent to which customers require superior quality and high standards—should favor a customer orientation. In a market featuring high customer demandingness a customer orientation should better position a brand to understand highly specific, specialized customer requirements and track changing requirements. Hence, the more demanding the customers, the stronger should be the effect of a customer orientation and the weaker should be the effect of a competitor orientation on brand performance.

Insights

The results of the study support the contingency approach when assessing a market orientation, as the effectiveness of such a strategic posture varies with environmental factors.

Consider first the relative level of development that a brand faces as it moves into a foreign country. A brand moving into a developed market can achieve competitive advantage if it establishes a customer orientation. On the other hand, a brand moving into a developing market should establish a competitor orientation. These two components of a market orientation both yield valuable information that should be disseminated throughout an organization. Yet the information that is typically provided through a customer orientation seems largely irrelevant in a developing country, while the reverse is true for the information that is typically provided through a competitor orientation.

Considering the local market level, brands moving into markets characterized by good local business conditions should orient themselves toward learning about and responding to customer needs, while brands moving into markets characterized by poor local business conditions should orient themselves toward learning how their key competitors operate. In a stable market a brand does not need specialized knowledge about idiosyncratic local customs or important local agents to succeed. In developing markets a brand cannot acquire the resources or institutional support it needs on the basis of customer-centered information.

Finally, then, a brand entering a market characterized by a highly demanding customer base should establish a customer orientation and seek indications of future demand. Such a strategic orientation should enable a brand to anticipate how its customers might respond to future offerings.

FRANCHISING[2]

As franchising spreads in the lodging and restaurant industries, achieving higher levels of market growth becomes more difficult for franchisors. Researchers have investigated an approach known as relationship marketing, which involves strengthening a brand's relationships with its suppliers and customers (Dwyer et al. 1987; Heide 1994). To test whether strong relationships foster higher performance and better franchisor–franchisee relationships in the hospitality industry, the study summarized here examined relationships between two major hotel franchisors and their North American hotel properties by surveying 331 of their general managers.

Franchisees are the primary customers for hotel franchisors. Local franchisees implement the plans and strategies formulated by the brand. Moreover, local operators are responsible for managing direct contact with the brand's ultimate customers, the guests.

Increasing mutual participation in the decision-making process involved in relationships between hotel franchisors and their franchised hotels gives partners an expanded stake in the success of the relationship and encourages them to work harder to ensure that success. As a result, building marketing partnerships between hotel franchisors and their franchisees should generate stronger performance. The question is: does a stronger marketing partnership between a hotel franchisor and its franchised hotel lead to higher performance, both for the hotel and for the partnership as a whole?

Discrete and Complex Exchanges

Traditional economic theory views relationships among independent businesses as short-term exchanges on simple terms—parties exchange money for a service or product and neither the seller nor the buyer has any expectations that a long-term relationship will develop. Such one-shot, arm's-length relationships between buyers and sellers are termed discrete exchanges (Dwyer et al. 1987, p. 13). The contemporary hotel marketplace typically involves exchanges of greater complexity, involving implied or express agreements and contracts (Arndt 1979). The multitude of frequent-guest programs, buyers' clubs, and affinity credit cards on the market demonstrates retailers' efforts to extend such trading beyond discrete exchanges.

Hotel brands and property owners behave more like partners and less like parties to arm's-length business transactions. Such long-term exchanges become personal as, for instance, the brand's field representative calls upon the same hotel managers time after time. This enables people in both the brand and the hotel to develop personal rapport.

Marketing Partnerships

Brands and hotels in effective marketing partnerships jointly pursue mutual objectives. Among the critical factors involved in guiding such joint planning are (a) the mutual desire to preserve the relationship, (b) role integrity, and (c) the harmonization of marketing conflict (Macneil 1980, p. 65).

In an effective marketing partnership the parties agree on the relationship's intrinsic importance and view themselves as members of the same team (Kaufmann and Stern 1988; Macneil, 1980). A contract defines the goods or services that each firm provides to the partnership and what each can expect to gain. Beyond that, roles in relational partnerships "cover a multitude of issues not directly related to any particular transaction" (Kaufmann and Stern 1988, p. 536).

Role integrity is achieved when all related parties clearly understand their respective rights and responsibilities, which makes it easier for partners to predict how each will behave and leads to smoother relations. Role integrity is critical to providing the stability necessary to allow exchange relationships to deepen (Dant and Schul 1992, p. 43).

Enduring relationships of all types experience difficulties. Relational partnerships survive these difficulties because the parties attempt to resolve their conflicts in mutually satisfying ways. In the harmonizing of relational conflict, the integrity of a partnership is placed above the separate interests of the individual parties (Macneil 1980, p. 68).

Insights

Partnership for performance

The results of the study indicate that a franchisor seeking to improve its hotels' performance should treat them more like partners than as "necessary evils" to be tolerated or, worse, as adversaries to exploit. Strong marketing partnerships yield the following benefits:

- higher overall performance for both parties;
- higher hotel occupancy rates relative to competitors' rates;
- higher average room rates relative to competitors' rates;
- higher gross operating profits relative to competitors' profits;
- higher quality assurance ratings relative to other hotels under the brand;
- higher guest satisfaction ratings relative to other hotels under the brand;
- higher gross operating profit (GOP) earnings and income before interest and taxes (in terms of available rooms) relative to hotels with weaker partnerships; and
- higher income before fixed costs (on a per employee basis) relative to hotels with weaker partnerships.

This research identifies several means for strengthening a brand's hotel partnerships. First, franchisor brands should view relationships with their hotels as intrinsically important and strive to preserve those relationships. Second, franchisor brands should behave consistently by refraining from abrupt or frequent changes in strategic direction. Third, franchisor brands and franchisees should jointly form clear expectations about what functions each is to perform and how the brand will evaluate that performance. Similarly, hotels must have clear expectations about the support that they can expect from a franchisor. Feedback programs that allow hotels to evaluate franchisor brand performance along dimensions that affect it are also important. Finally, franchisor brands and hotels should work harmoniously to resolve the inevitable conflicts that arise in any business relationship.

The growth factor

Hotel franchisors court additional franchisees as marketing partners for continued growth in sales revenue. In today's competitive climate, potential franchisees have their choice of suitors and are likely to scrutinize them carefully. Hotels affiliated with brands that forge strong partnerships are more likely to achieve superior performance. A brand that promises (and delivers) strong partnerships should enjoy greater choice regarding prospective hotel partners. Thus, developing strong partnerships can be a powerful tool with which franchisors can recruit high-quality franchisees.

MANAGING MARKETING RELATIONSHIPS[3]

This section summarizes a study of marketing relationships between hotel brands and the properties with which they do business. The section focuses on governance mechanisms that can minimize the costs of exchange by preventing or at least minimizing the impact of opportunism on partners in a business relationship. The study surveyed 368 hotel general managers to test hypotheses pertaining to relationships between individual hotels and their brand headquarters associated with two large North American hotel brands, both of which included brand-owned properties and franchised units in their portfolios.

Opportunistic behavior, which includes dishonesty and neglecting obligations, is undertaken to achieve short-term, unilateral gains, perhaps even at the expense of a trading partner. As a result, opportunism on the part of one party in a relationship can erode the long-term gains potentially accruing to both (Gassenheimer et al. 1996). Fortunately, mechanisms for managing opportunism in a marketing relationship exist (Stump and Heide 1996).

Corporate brands strive to develop and maintain broad marketing programs that reflect brand identity, while managers of individual hotel properties may be less than assiduous in fostering such an identity. Brands use a variety of mechanisms to govern individual properties' operations (Dev and Brown 1991; Lewis et al. 1995; Malley 1997).

The conceptual framework for controlling opportunistic behavior depends heavily on transaction-cost analysis, which provides a theoretical rationale for governance structures ranging from horizontal open markets to vertical hierarchies. Franchising shares characteristics with both markets and hierarchies.

Opportunism has been characterized as "a lack of candor or honesty in transactions, to include self-interest seeking with guile" (Williamson 1985, p. 9). Opportunism before the fact (adverse selection) occurs when one firm disguises its true ability to perform the functions required of an exchange. Franchise systems carefully screen potential franchisees to eliminate property owners that are unlikely to maintain the hotel brand's quality image, while franchisees attempt to verify a brand's revenue and profit projections. Parties to a prospective management agreement also conduct similar due diligence before they sign a hotel management contract.

Opportunism that occurs after a relationship launches includes withholding or distorting information so as to "mislead, distort, obfuscate, or otherwise confuse" (Williamson 1985, p. 47), or shirking duties, as in the case of "not delivering the promised action and resources" (Hardy and Magrath 1989, p. 123). Some hotel brands protect themselves against franchisee opportunism by establishing codes of ethical operation and setting up strict inspection systems.

Mitigating Opportunism

Governance mechanisms establish and structure exchange relationships. Accordingly, the study examined the efficacy of three mechanisms for mitigating opportunism in hotel-marketing channels: (a) brand headquarters' ownership of a hotel, (b) investments made by a hotel in *transaction-specific assets*, and (c) relational-exchange norms developed between a hotel and its brand headquarters.

The advantages of ownership include the potential for instituting a richer system of rewards and punishment and an organizational culture that provides common norms and values that align the parties' interests (John and Weitz 1988; Williamson 1985, pp. 56–7). Through ownership a brand can employ extensive monitoring and surveillance of its outlets. A vertically integrated brand can offer more subtle rewards for employees (desirable assignments) and more extensive sanctions (suspensions) than it could apply to independent partners (Anderson and Weitz 1986). In short, ownership weakens everyone's incentives to behave opportunistically because such behavior hurts both parties (Williamson 1975). Given these considerations, it would seem that hotel opportunism will be reduced where brand headquarters has full ownership of a hotel.

Businesses invest in transaction-specific assets (Anderson and Weitz 1986)—including specialized equipment and facilities as well as training and experience—for at least three reasons. First, such assets are more efficient and effective than generalized assets in accomplishing business objectives. Second, investing in transaction-specific assets signals a property's honorable intentions for the trading relationship (Mishra et al. 1998). Third, such investments may be required as a condition of exchange, serving essentially as performance bonds to be forfeited if a hotel behaves opportunistically. This suggests that the risk of forfeiting transaction-specific assets restrains hotel malfeasance (Stump and Heide 1996): Investment in transaction-specific assets should reduce a hotel's opportunism.

Finally, shared norms are characteristic of relational exchange (Dwyer et al. 1987; Heide and John 1992; Macneil 1980). Among these are relationship preservation, which is the extent to which parties view their relationship as more than a series of discrete transactions, see it as intrinsically valuable, and wish to preserve it (Kaufmann and Stern 1988; Macneil 1980). Role integrity reflects expectations regarding necessary future roles and suggests that roles expand to "cover a multitude of issues not directly related to any particular transaction" (Kaufmann and Stern 1988, p. 536), ensuring stability that deepens exchange relationships (Dant and Schul 1992; Kaufmann and Dant 1992). The norm of harmonization of relational conflict reflects the extent to which channel members achieve mutually satisfying conflict resolution (Heide and John 1992; Macneil 1980; Noordwier et al. 1990). The study viewed the extent of relational exchange in a marketing channel as the degree to which the norms of role integrity, relationship preservation, and harmonization of relational conflict characterize that channel. Under a relationship-preservation norm, exchange partners see a relationship as ongoing and mutually beneficial and eschew actions that jeopardize it (Heide and John 1990; Joskow 1987). Accordingly, perceived relational exchange should reduce opportunism between a hotel and its brand headquarters.

Insights

Reducing opportunism

The study's strongest finding is that brand managers should focus on building effective relationships with their hotels' general managers (GMs).

A strong relationship is the only governance mechanism that placed any significant limitation on hotel opportunism. Contrary to the predictions of transaction-cost theory, the study suggests that increased investment in specialized assets can actually increase opportunism.

Overly aggressive exercise of ownership rights can also exacerbate opportunism, perhaps because ownership pressure and sanctions provoke GMs into exerting their independence. Moreover, the extrinsic rewards of brand ownership may reduce a hotel manager's intrinsic motivation to cooperate, especially where norms of relational exchange prevail (Frey 1993). A strong relationship creates a sense of identification between a hotel and its brand. The study suggests that this effect persists even when relational exchange is used in conjunction with ownership or investment in specialized assets. Apparently top management should emphasize building strong relationships to reduce opportunistic behavior at affiliated hotels.

Relations over transactions

As noted, the study's findings conflict with transaction-cost theory. Perhaps the positive link between investment in specialized assets and opportunism is that opportunistic behavior helps hotels generate additional returns on such investments. To be sure, hotel brands may not regard transaction-specific assets as governance mechanisms, instead appreciating the operational consistency gained by ownership in fostering the hotel's critical role of maintaining and reinforcing the brand's image. Additional research would be needed to test this supposition.

It is also possible that the hotel brands involved in the study used such assets poorly. When monitoring or punishments is ineffectual, the threat of economic losses rooted in a hotel's asset investment has little effect on opportunism. Further research is needed to investigate the effectiveness with which brands monitor their hotels and sanction them for opportunistic behavior.

Finally, the results reveal that the most effective governance mechanisms combine ownership with relational exchange and asset investment with relational exchange, differing from those found in much of the channel-governance literature. Apparently channel partners should consider the extent of relational exchange before offering prescriptions based purely on transaction-cost analysis.

BRAND PARTNERSHIPS[4]

Brand partnerships in hotels typically involve an owner (often a franchisee) and an operator (not always providing a brand identity), separate business entities that contribute their respective assets to help the hotel succeed in the marketplace. The quality of such a brand partnership drives how customers, competitors, suppliers, and partners perceive the hotel. However, when the relationship is not cordial, one partner or the other might work deceptively in a self-interested pursuit of advantage. This section summarizes another study of that possibility, opportunism, and discusses strategies for successful brand partnerships, using a sample of 367 general managers of two large North American hotel brands, both of which included in their portfolios brand-owned hotels and franchised units.

Positive brand partnerships reduce opportunism and increase mutual cooperation (Dev et al. 2000). Moreover, better brand-hotel relationships lead to higher occupancy, average room rates, gross operating profits, quality assurance scores, and guest satisfaction ratings. Poor brand partnerships, on the other hand, have the opposite effect (Brown and Dev 1997).

Managing Brand Partnerships

Although parent brands can act opportunistically, the study summarized here focused primarily on how such brands can influence the behavior of hotel-owning partners. The temptation to behave opportunistically arises in an environment in which, for their part, owners and managers want their hotels to be profitable (regardless of occupancy and rate), while, for their part, brands want to preserve their brand positioning. Brands therefore try to maintain their rates (sometimes at the cost of occupancy) and top-line revenue (sometimes at the cost of profit), as they typically are paid a percentage of that revenue.

There is, then, a fundamental tension between rate and occupancy, on the one hand, and, on the other, revenue and profit (sometimes pitting the owner's interests against the brand's interests). For brand managers, understanding how to influence a partner's behavior so as to minimize opportunism not only can protect the brand's interests; it also can strengthen the hotel's business insofar as opportunism's short-term benefits often lead to long-term disadvantages for both (Wathne and Heide 2000). This study investigated whether brands can manage opportunism better by forming relationships with their partners that establish certain norms of behavior.

Studying Opportunism

Scholars generally classify influence strategies, or means of communication that are expected to produce favorable outcomes, as coercive or noncoercive (Frazier and Sheth 1985; Frazier and Summers 1984, 1986; Frazier et al. 1989). Coercive strategies are designed to control opportunism through a combination of rewards and punishments and by communicating to partners the likely consequences of guileful behavior. Here the basis for behaving cooperatively is said to be external to the target partner—the opportunistic behavior is altered not by making it less intrinsically attractive but rather by promising rewards for good behavior and threatening punishments for bad. Even if the motive to behave opportunistically remains, the behavior is suppressed. The coercive strategies considered in the study included promises, threats, and legalistic pleas.

Noncoercive strategies attempt to change a brand partner's attitudes toward the partnership by influencing the target partner internally, making that partner less disposed to opportunism. The three main categories of noncoercive influence strategies considered in the study were information exchange, recommendations, and requests (Mohr and Nevin 1990; Payan and MacFarland 2005).

Through socialization one partner hopes to avoid potential opportunism by establishing *relational norms* that induce a degree of self-governance by the second partner. This study focused on the following three norms that become especially salient in the context of close partner relationships: solidarity, role integrity, and conflict harmonization. When partners share the solidarity norm, they attach an intrinsic value to their partnership and pursue shared goals, sometimes even at the expense of self-interest. Partners that value role integrity share an interest in maintaining each other's contribution to the partnership's effectiveness. Conflict harmonization indicates the extent to which partners are consistently able to resolve potential or actual conflicts quickly to their mutual satisfaction (Dev et al. 2000; Heide and John 1992; Kaufmann and Dant 1992; Kaufmann and Stern 1988; Macneil 1980).

Conceptual Framework

Noncoercive strategies

Noncoercive strategies operate by inducing a brand partner to become more supportive and cooperative. Relational norms may support this process by enhancing reciprocal communication, making it easier for one partner to deliver a message that limits opportunism by disposing the other partner to fully and diligently process the information contained in the message. Within such an environment, a brand can apply noncoercive influence strategies more effectively to limit a partner's opportunism (Bhatnagar 1993; Falbe and Yukl 1991; Jap et al. 1999; Mohr and Sohi 1995; Payan and Nevin 2006).

Clearly such an environment should enhance the relational norms of role integrity and conflict harmonization. Effective message communication should encourage one's partner to fully process a message's content, helping to maintain the partners' respective roles. Open lines of communication allow partners to achieve conflict resolution, as their messages will be conveyed clearly, facilitating negotiations over potential disagreements. When it is difficult for partners to communicate openly, however, disputes arise over the messages themselves. This renders noncoercive strategies ineffective, as weak relational norms open communications to misinterpretation and eventually the exploitation of shared information.

Coercive strategies

In essence, coercive strategies invoke immediate rewards for complying with exchange arrangements and punishments for noncompliance. Because coercive strategies operate in the short term, they are likely to be most effective in an exchange environment in which the partners work at arm's length. If neither partner operates with long-term future outcomes in mind, imminent rewards and punishments seem more credible in the context of a relationship emphasizing short-term financial outcomes.

Indeed, in an exchange environment characterized by strong relational norms, coercive strategies seem likely to justify opportunistic behavior in reaction. It seems, therefore, that where strong relational norms prevail, norm violation is likely to be reciprocated.

Insights

Before reviewing the study's practical insights, it must be noted that the data reflected the perceptions reported by hotel managers rather than the perceptions of brand executives. Perhaps brand executives would not have perceived such partnerships precisely as their hotel managers did. The study also clearly identified an area that deserves further research, namely, the question of how relational norms are developed and preserved.

The study's results suggest that brand executives should approach opportunism on the part of hotels by carefully assessing the quality of their relationships. Those who enjoy relatively close relationships marked by strong relational norms should employ noncoercive influence strategies to limit or prevent opportunism. Brands can expect their hotels not to misuse information that they share and can rely on the information that flows back from the hotels. The study shows that the better a relationship a brand enjoys with its hotels, the more effective noncoercive influence strategies will be in limiting opportunism.

Where relational norms are weak or nonexistent, however, noncoercive strategies may encourage opportunism. Indeed, in the absence of strong relational norms, coercive influence techniques are more effective than noncoercive strategies in limiting opportunism. Nevertheless, coercive approaches must be considered only as short-term tactics, as they apparently provoke opportunism irrespective of the presence of relational norms.

BRAND EXTENSIONS AND CUSTOMER LOYALTY[5]

Brands recognize that brand equity—the brand's overall value—drives stock price and shareholder value. Consumers often base hotel stay decisions on perceptions of a specific hotel's brand name. The United States now has over 300 hotel brands, many of which are extensions of existing brand names.

Brand extension is the practice of introducing a new brand (differentiated by market segment) under a well-established brand name. Although most major hotel companies have at least one brand extension, two dangers lurk when creating multiple sub-brands. First, managing many brands can complicate and possibly overwhelm the core corporate structure. Second, having the same name on too many products can erode the parent brand's equity—this is the topic of this section. This study attempted to estimate empirically whether brand extensions encourage guests to repeat stays with a particular chain's brands.

Brand extensions allow hotel brands to penetrate a variety of market segments with differentiated products that carry a single, well-established brand name. This yields quicker acceptance of new products by consumers, economies of scale in marketing-support expenditures (Arnold 1992, p. 142), lower risk associated with new product introductions (Kapferer 1992, p. 113), and guest retention. There are, of course, disadvantages to extending a brand (Aaker 1996, p. 240; Aaker and Keller 1990; Farquhar et al. 1992; Kim and Sullivan 1998; Loken and John 1993), but a brand that knew extending its reach would increase customer loyalty would surely consider doing so.

This study posited that brand extensions can increase customer loyalty by increasing the costs of switching from a particular brand family to a competitor's brand. With extensions, firms can reach distinguishable groups of consumers with diverse needs who are more likely to patronize an extension of a brand than they are to risk choosing an unfamiliar brand (a risk that is part of switching costs). If there is an "extension effect," the probability of a customer's staying within a corporate brand family will be proportionally greater than the number of brands offered by that corporation, all other factors being equal.[6]

The data for the study were drawn from two sources: first, consumer-survey data that included only respondents who had made at least two hotel stays in consecutive months during the most recent three-month period, with information on individual prices paid, trip context, and customer characteristics. Second, lodging-firm characteristics collected from secondary sources: parent-company affiliation, member brands, advertising expenditures, and numbers of units, covering 88 brands, of which 42 had no extension, 16 had one extension, 13 had two extensions, 12 had three extensions, and 5 had four extensions. The dataset included information for 46 parent hotel brands, representing all the large hotel chains operating in the United States.

Three's a Charm

This study was the first empirical attempt to derive the ideal number of extensions beyond which switching is likely, finding that, when brands offer up to three extensions, they keep customers within their brand families by offering a choice of segments under the same name. Furthermore, offering three extensions balances the choices offered to customers against the extent to which a concept can realistically be stretched before the brand extension begins to undermine the customer's belief that one brand name can, in fact, offer a meaningful choice in widely diverse segments.

With fewer than three extensions the switching rate rises, perhaps because the limited choice of segments is inadequate to cover a wide enough set of customer needs. Moreover, consumers would rather stay with the one brand that satisfies their needs, in the absence of intervening factors, than find an almost-right brand, an effect that is likely to be magnified by frequent-user or loyalty programs. If we consider the three purposes of hotel stays—business trips, conferences, and vacations—it is plausible that travelers who find one brand that fulfills all three travel purposes might keep all their business within that one brand family. Beyond three extensions, however, the switching rate rises, due in part perhaps to the dilution of brand position. From the brand perspective, too many extensions may dilute the company's support for the individual brands in the family. Contrary to other findings in the literature, then, this study strongly suggests that there is an optimum number of hotel brands within a family—three.

Insights

The results of this study should be interpreted with caution—although the theoretical model is sound—because the data are correlational and only the direct or main effects were tested.

Hotels can favorably influence consumer choice through marketing activities that emphasize multiple brand extensions. Effective brand extensions seem likely to increase customer loyalty and promote repeat buying as customers avoid the risk of disappointment with an unknown brand. Put another way, customers who perceive that a particular brand's mainline hotel offers high quality will be more likely to patronize that brand's specialized-market hotels (and vice versa). Extending the analysis, if consumers tend toward brand loyalty to avoid switching costs, hotel firms can exercise price discrimination and charge higher prices to their loyal customers.

Corporate extensions in the lodging industry appear to be most helpful in retaining customers when extensions involve about three hotel tiers. The study suggests that brands with no extensions should undertake appropriate corporate extension in reasonable numbers of brands and in diverse geographical locations.

From a company perspective, analyzing customers' switching behavior among brands applies not only to a company's own brand family but also offers a more comprehensive understanding of the demand curves that each of its brands faces. Loyal customers are price-insensitive compared with brand-shifting patrons and may not need as substantial a price promotion to encourage purchase as would a first-time customer. Customer brand loyalty can be factored into the next generation of revenue management systems to help determine the extent of rate adjustments needed to increase revenue.

GLOBAL BRAND EXPANSION[7]

Global expansion requires hotel brands to assess their capabilities and balance their strengths and weaknesses against available local resources as they develop affiliation arrangements in foreign markets. The study summarized in this section assumed that global expansion works best when a firm's entry strategy reflects this balance (Ekeledo and Sivakumar 1998; Hwang and Kim 1990). The data drew on a sample of 124 hotel managers who had worked on at least three continents representing at least thirty globally oriented brands distributed across fifty-three countries.

Hotel firms contemplating entry in a foreign market typically make separate decisions regarding ownership and management of their foreign properties, first determining whether to own such properties and then deciding whether to manage the properties themselves, hire a management company, or seek local management. Expanding hotel companies should also make separate ownership and control decisions for business activities such as investment in physical facilities and control of operations and marketing (Dev et al. 2002). Moreover, an expanding firm's knowledge is key. Codified knowledge includes characteristic design features and signature service offerings and can be easily identified, structured, and communicated. Tacit knowledge includes firm culture, workplace routines, and business processes, and is less easily communicated.

Local Partners in Global Markets: Transfer and Absorption, Ownership and Control

To transfer codified and tacit knowledge to be absorbed by a foreign market successfully, a hotel firm must align its competitive strengths and shortcomings with the market's resources and business conditions as it develops the most advantageous local partnerships. This means finding partners who understand the local market and can leverage the firm's know-how to achieve competitive advantage while avoiding the local opportunism to which it is vulnerable if there are few suitable local partners available. It also means distinguishing those components of its knowledge that are easy to transfer to other markets, such as plant and equipment, from those that are more difficult to transfer, such as branding and marketing. The general rule has been that an entering firm should undertake high-risk activities itself while outsourcing low-risk, easy-to-transfer activities to local partners (Erramilli et al. 2002).

Four Variations on Ownership and Control

Some foreign market entrants claim an ownership stake in a local hotel while others do not. Some local hotels follow the policies and procedures of a franchise system or third-party marketing network while others develop their own policies and procedures. This yields four possible market entry strategies: chain-owned, affiliated (COA) hotels are operated as part of a franchise system or marketing network. Here the market entrant invests in the physical assets of these hotels while relying (at least in part) on the franchise system or marketing network to guide its marketing and operations activities. Management company affiliated (MCA) hotels are operated by third-party management companies and also linked with a franchise system or marketing network; the entering firm holds no equity position in the hotel facility. Management company affiliated hotels are subject to the marketing and operations policies of the system or network. Management company unaffiliated (MCU) hotels operate under management contracts but have no affiliation with franchise systems or marketing networks, instead developing an in-house approach to marketing and operations. Chain-owned, unaffiliated (COU) hotels are owned and operated under a common brand name as part of a corporate chain, independently of both third-party management companies and franchise systems. The COU entry strategy therefore offers a firm the highest level of control over the hotel's marketing and operations functions.

Insights

This study demonstrated the benefits of separating decisions about ownership from decisions about control. For example, a hotel entering a foreign market where the cost of training local employees is high should retain control over a local facility's marketing and operations but avoid owning the facility. A similar prescription applies to firms that have a competitive advantage based on superior customer service—control can be gained without ownership.

Interestingly, a hotel firm's competitive advantage based on its management and organization can be transferred to local markets using several entry modes—in particular, the COU, MCU, and MCA entry modes. This suggests that a franchising system or marketing network may hinder an entrant's ability to transfer its tacit management and organizational advantages.

The study strongly suggested that the ownership dimension of an entry decision depends on a local market's capacity to absorb an entering firm's competitive advantages. For example, when trustworthy and reliable local equity partners are available (the absorptive capacity of the local equity market is high), a firm should use a management company entry strategy rather than equity ownership. Such a strategy is also recommended when the cost of training managers and employees is high (the local market's absorptive capacity is low).

When a local market's absorptive capacity for operations is high, an entering firm can transfer its tacit competitive advantages through some form of marketing affiliation because local resources are readily available. Lower-control entry strategies are the choice when local human resources are abundant.

Finally, in seeking to transfer a competitive advantage based on codified knowledge embodied in physical facilities, chain ownership of a hotel property is the best choice, especially when the entering firm is affiliated with a franchise system or marketing network. This finding suggests that an entering firm can build hotels to its specifications more easily by retaining ownership than by opting for the management company entry strategy.

BRANDING BEYOND BORDERS[8]

The choice between franchising or management contracts for hotel brand expansion into foreign markets is critical because when brands transfer technology and deploy transaction-specific assets effectively, they maintain consistency in brand image and operations. The study summarized here, based on a survey of 139 hotel managers in foreign markets operating under either pure franchising arrangements or pure management contracts, adopted an organizational-capabilities perspective to focus on the transfer of one firm's competencies to another. More than thirty brands distributed over forty-three countries were represented.

Transferring Organizational Resources: Franchising or Management Contracts?

The capabilities-based perspective views a firm's superior performance as a consequence of its distinctive capabilities rather than of the structural properties of its industry. In this approach a firm is a bundle of resources that comprise its assets, organizational processes, attributes, information, and expertise (Barney 1991). Under franchising, a brand transfers resources and expertise across firm boundaries, whereas under management contracts it transfers such assets within the firm. The capabilities-based approach measures the value of a resource in terms of its contribution to a firm's competitive advantage (Collis and Montgomery 1995; Madhok 1997). The question then becomes whether franchising or management contracting is the better choice for transferring capabilities while preserving competitive advantage.

Answering this question depends in part on judging the reproducibility of a given capability. Some capabilities, such as quality and organizational competence, are more difficult to reproduce than others, such as entry, physical, and customer competence, due to specific historical conditions, complex social interactions, and the intangible nature of the know-how involved (Barney 1991; Hu 1995; Kogut and Zander 1993; Teece 1998). Transferring tacit knowledge is difficult, and when it involves capabilities that are deeply entrenched in company-specific routines and practices, it can be transferred only through intimate social interactions (Lam 1997; Madhok 1997).

A hotel brand that expands by transferring irreproducible capabilities should favor management contracts to avoid reducing or losing its competitive advantage. Since the influence of such irreproducible capabilities on this choice depends on the strength of that advantage, when such competencies do not generate value for a brand and are difficult to transfer, they are not likely to influence the brand's choice. On the other hand, when such capabilities are critical to the brand's advantage, they will dominate the decision-making process. It seems likely therefore that the greater is the competitive advantage generated by a brand's irreproducible competencies, the more likely it is that the brand will choose a management contract over franchising.[9]

Other Factors

Among other factors affecting the franchising–management contract decision are the availability of management capabilities in the host market, the availability of suitable partners in that market, and the level of economic development in the host market's business environment. Franchising, for example, is not conducive to exploiting a brand's advantages if a host country's franchisees cannot find competent managers in the host market (Hu 1995; Madhok 1997). On the other hand, management contracts work best when a hotel management firm can find qualified, trustworthy partners who can make the necessary capital investments in infrastructure and facilities (Contractor and Kundu 1998; Dunning 1988). Finally, franchising is more effective and franchisees are more capable in developed countries than in developing countries. We can summarize these considerations as follows: (1) the presence of irreproducible resources and capabilities favors management contracts over franchising; (2) the availability of management resources in a host market favors franchising arrangements over management contracts; (3) the availability of qualified local investment partners in a host market favors management contracts over franchising; and (4) a highly developed business environment favors franchising arrangements over management contracts.

Insights

The study's results suggest that as a hotel brand expands internationally, it must focus on two main factors in choosing between franchising and management contracts. First, such a brand should ascertain the reproducibility or irreproducibility of its key capabilities. Second, the brand should ascertain the extent to which it depends on irreproducible competencies for its competitive advantage. If irreproducible competencies support a brand's establishment and survival, that brand should expand using management contracts. On the other hand, franchising requires relatively little involvement by the entering company. Therefore, franchising suffices as long as the key aspects of a hotel brand can be codified and transferred.

The results also corroborate the contention that brands need a range of internal and external support capabilities to exploit their advantages (Hu 1995; Madhok 1997). For instance, franchising is favored in developed countries and in those with an abundance of professional managers. Moreover, physical competence and a strong brand reputation work together in a way that unambiguously favors franchising (Arora and Fosfuri 2000; Kogut and Zander 1992).

When reliable investment partners are abundant in a host market, however, management contracts become increasingly attractive. In addition, scale effects emerge when quality competence and hotel size are combined. The study's results suggest that as quality competence becomes more important as a source of competitive advantage and a brand's properties expand in size, a management contract becomes all the more necessary to transfer key capabilities (Gatignon and Anderson 1988; Shane 1998).

Management contracts are also favored when an entering firm combines high-quality competence with a service-sensitive market (Collis and Montgomery 1995). As a hotel's customers become increasingly service conscious and demand better and better amenities, hotels with a strong quality competence become increasingly committed to management contracts.

Finally, management contracts are favored when a brand has strong organizational competence and enters a highly developed market with irreproducible capabilities. The results suggest that firms with irreproducible capabilities not only shun franchise arrangements but also become strong advocates for management contracts in developed markets.

HOSPITALITY MARKETING AND THE INTERNET[10]

In the twenty-first century the hospitality industry is coming to terms with new marketing channels that run on interactive Internet platforms and seemingly promise new business and higher profits based on user-generated data and social relationships. The proliferation of smart phones and tablet computers drives the growing popularity of these new marketing channels, particularly a phenomenon known as social couponing, which offers discounts to consumers through flash sales in the form of daily deals and private sales.

This section summarizes a study based on a survey of 225 respondents from the global subscriber base of the Cornell Center for Hospitality Research aimed at shedding light on the risks and benefits of flash sales by exploring their use by hospitality brands and identifying the opportunities and challenges associated with these emerging marketing channels.

Flash Sales: Daily Deals and Private Sales in the Hospitality Market

The flash sale daily deal model features short-lived, deeply discounted promotions that typically depend on a threshold number of customers who sign on. Customers interact with firms via email or social networking websites. Private sales require customers to register for membership to receive email notification of sales as firms target select subsets of customers who value the perceived exclusivity of the promotions.

Daily deal travel websites

From August 2011, travel deals not only represented the third largest category of daily deals, they also yielded the highest revenue per deal. That revenue potential has attracted considerable interest from online travel agents such as Priceline and Travelocity as well as offshoots of general social couponing sites such as LivingSocial Escapes and Expedia's partnership with Groupon known as Groupon Getaways, which outperformed LivingSocial Escapes in its first month of operations (*Yipit* 2011).

Private sales travel websites

Private sales hospitality sites fall into three categories: travel-only sites; retail-oriented sites that include travel in their offers; and online travel agent sites that have added private sales to their offers. Most private sale sites increase membership by offering credits for referrals that lead to purchases, with regular discounts typically around 30 percent and purchase windows of no more than a week for vouchers that may remain valid for several months. Most privates sales travel deals are either nonrefundable or apply steep cancellation penalties (Perkins 2011).

Insights

The study found, on balance, that flash sales were effective marketing channels for hotel brands, yielding the following recommendations to brands that anticipate using or hope to improve their use of flash sales:

- Define your purpose: pick the right site for the right reasons.
- Study sites carefully: understand the business model.
- Accept market insights from site representatives.
- Negotiate: terms vary and some sites are willing.
- Manage cost structure: calculate profit, volume, and ancillary revenue.
- Calculate room-nights needed and determine the best available times.

- Employ unique package deals to avoid cannibalization and protect market position.
- Start small; then adjust.
- Monitor user profiles and usage continually.
- Have a strategy for converting first-time users to repeaters; encourage referrals.

Brands seeking to maximize the benefits of flash sales can frame the value proposition of such sales more effectively by learning to balance customer repurchase potential against margin potential. Brands that find it difficult to convert flash sales customers into returning guests should manage deal margins carefully, perhaps seeking cross-selling and up-selling opportunities with such guests to achieve that goal.

CONCLUSION

Hospitality marketing and branding, as the previous studies indicate, will inevitably involve further exploration of web-based marketing channels. In addition to striving to stay on top of developments in social couponing, hotel brands will unavoidably find themselves weighing the costs and benefits of harnessing a range of rapidly proliferating social media such as Facebook, Twitter, Pinterest, Tumblr, Google+, Foursquare, Instagram, and, no doubt, a host of other online marketing opportunities still to come (Nand 2012; Stokes 2012). The future is bright for both scholars and practitioners.

NOTES

1. Adapted from Dev et al. (2009).
2. Adapted from Dev et al. (2000).
3. Adapted from Brown and Dev (1997).
4. Adapted from Dev et al. (2011).
5. Adapted from Jiang et al. (2002).
6. First, assume that customers know at least something about whether a brand is an extension. Second, consider "proportional" draw: suppose a market has two corporations, one with two equivalent brands and the other with three. With no extension influence, the first will draw two-fifths of all customers and the other three-fifths. With a positive effect of extension length, the second corporation will draw more than three-fifths of all customers; with a negative effect, the second will draw less than three-fifths of all customers.
7. Adapted from Dev et al. (2007).
8. Adapted from Dev et al. (2002).
9. A brand can sustain its competitive advantage even with no irreproducible competencies

using legal means such as copyrights, trademarks, patents, and licenses, but this section concentrates on the relationship between the reproducibility of competencies and the franchising/management contract choice.
10. Adapted from Piccoli and Dev (2012).

REFERENCES

Aaker, David (1996), *Building Strong Brands*, New York: Free Press.

Aaker, David and Kevin Keller (1990), "Consumer evaluations of brand extensions," *Journal of Marketing*, **54** (1), 27–41.

Anderson, Erin and Barton A. Weitz (1986), "Make-or-buy decisions: vertical integration and marketing productivity," *Sloan Management Review*, **27** (3), 3–19.

Arndt, Johan (1979), "Toward a concept of domesticated markets," *Journal of Marketing*, **43** (4), 69–75.

Arnold, David (1992), *The Handbook of Brand Management*, Boston, MA: Addison-Wesley.

Arora, Asish and Andrea Fosfuri (2000), "Wholly owned subsidiary versus technology licensing in the worldwide chemical industry," *Journal of International Business Studies*, **3** (4), 555–72.

Barney, Jay (1991), "Firm resources and sustained competitive advantage," *Journal of Management*, **17** (1), 99–120.

Bhatnagar, Deepti (1993), "Evaluation of managerial influence tactics: a study of Indian bank managers," *Journal of Managerial Psychology*, **8** (1), 3–9.

Brown, James R. and Chekitan S. Dev (1997), "The franchisor-franchisee relationship: a key to franchise performance," *Cornell Hotel and Restaurant Administration Quarterly*, **38** (6), 30–38.

Collis, David J. and Cynthia A. Montgomery (1995), "Competing on resources: strategy in the 1990s," *Harvard Business Review*, **73** (4), 118–28.

Contractor, Farok J. and Sumit K. Kundu (1998), "Modal choice in a world of alliances," *Journal of International Business Studies*, **29** (4), 325–58.

Dant, Rajiv P. and Patrick L. Schul (1992), "Conflict resolution processes in contractual channels of distribution," *Journal of Marketing*, **56** (1), 43.

Dev, Chekitan S. and James R. Brown (1991), "Franchising and other operating arrangements in the lodging industry: a strategic comparison," *Journal of Hospitality and Tourism Research*, **14** (3), 25.

Dev, Chekitan S., James R. Brown and Dong Jin Lee (2000), "Managing marketing relationships: making sure everyone plays on the team," *Cornell Hotel and Restaurant Administration Quarterly*, **41** (4), 10–20.

Dev, Chekitan S., James R. Brown and Kevin Zheng Zhou (2007), "Global brand expansion: how to select a market entry strategy," *Cornell Hospitality Quarterly*, **48** (1), 13–27.

Dev, Chekitan S., M. Krishna Erramilli and Sanjeev Agarwal (2002), "Brands across borders: choosing between franchising and management contracts for entering international markets," *Cornell Hotel and Restaurant Administration Quarterly*, **43** (6), 91–104.

Dev, Chekitan S., Stephan Grzeskowiak and James R. Brown (2011), "Opportunism in brand partnerships: effects of coercion and relational norms," *Cornell Hospitality Quarterly*, **52** (4), 377–87.

Dev, Chekitan S., Kevin Zheng Zhou, James R. Brown and Sanjeev Agarwal (2009), "Customer orientation or competitor orientation: which marketing strategy has a higher payoff for hotel brands?" *Cornell Hospitality Quarterly*, **50** (1), 19–28.

Dunning, John H. (1988), *Explaining International Production*, London: Unwin Hyman.

Dwyer, F. Robert, Paul F. Schurr and Sejo Oh (1987), "Developing buyer-seller relationships," *Journal of Marketing*, **51** (2), 11–27

Ekeledo, Iketchi and K. Sivakumar (1998), "Foreign market entry mode choice of service

firms: a contingency perspective," *Journal of the Academy of Marketing Science*, **26** (4), 274–92.
Erramilli, M. Krishna, Sanjeev Agarwal and Chekitan S. Dev (2002), "Choice between non-equity entry modes: an organizational capability perspective," *Journal of International Business Studies*, **33** (2), 223–42.
Fahy, John, Graham Hooley, Tony Cox, Jozsef Beracs, Krzysztof Fonfara and Boris Snoj (2000), "The development and impact of marketing capabilities in Central Europe," *Journal of International Business Studies*, **31** (1), 63–81.
Falbe, Cecilia M. and Gary Yukl (1991), "Consequences for managers of using single influence tactics and combination of tactics," *Academy of Management Journal*, **35** (3), 638–52.
Farquhar, Peter H., Julia A. Han, Paul M. Herr and Yuji Ijiri (1992), "Strategies for leveraging master brands: how to bypass the risks of direct extensions," *Marketing Research*, **4** (3), 32–43.
Frazier, Gary L. and Jagdesh N. Sheth (1985), "An attitude-behavior framework for distribution channel management," *Journal of Marketing*, **49** (3), 38–48.
Frazier, Gary L. and John O. Summers (1984), "Interfirm influence strategies and their application within distribution channels," *Journal of Marketing*, **48** (3), 43–55.
Frazier, Gary L. and John O. Summers (1986), "Perceptions of interfirm power and its use within a franchise channel of distribution," *Journal of Marketing Research*, **23** (2), 169–76.
Frazier, Gary L., James D. Gill and Sudhur H. Kale (1989), "Dealer dependence levels and reciprocal actions in a channel of distribution in a developing country," *Journal of Marketing*, **53** (1), 50–69.
Frey, Bruno S. (1993), "Does monitoring increase work effort? The rivalry with trust and loyalty," *Economic Inquiry*, **31** (4), 663–70.
Gassenheimer, Jule B., David B. Baucus and Melissa S. Baucus (1996), "Cooperative arrangements among entrepreneurs: an analysis of opportunism and communication in franchise structures," *Journal of Business Research*, **36** (1), 67–79.
Gatignon, Hubert and Erin Anderson (1988), "The multinational corporations' degree of control over foreign subsidiaries: an empirical test of a transaction cost explanation," *Journal of Law, Economics, and Organization*, **4** (2), 305–36.
Hardy, Kenneth G. and Alan J. Magrath (1989), "Dealing with cheating in distribution," *European Journal of Marketing*, **23** (2), 123.
Heide, Jan B. (1994), "Interorganizational governance in marketing channels," *Journal of Marketing*, **58** (1), 71–85.
Heide, Jan B. and George John (1990), "Alliances in industrial purchasing: the determinants of joint action in buyer-supplier relationships," *Journal of Marketing Research*, **27** (1), 24–36.
Heide, Jan B. and George John (1992), "Do norms matter in marketing relationships?" *Journal of Marketing*, **56** (2), 32–44.
Hu, Yao-Su (1995), "The international transferability of the firm's advantages," *California Management Review*, **37** (4), 73–88.
Hwang, Peter and W. Chan Kim (1990), An eclectic theory of the choice of international entry mode," *Strategic Management Journal*, **11** (2), 117–28.
Jap, Sandy D., Chris Manolis and Barton A. Weitz (1999), "Relationship quality in buyer-seller interactions in channels of distribution," *Journal of Business Research*, **46** (3), 202–13.
Jiang, Weizhong, Chekitan S. Dev and Vithala R. Rao (2002), "Brand extension and customer loyalty: evidence from the lodging industry," *Cornell Hospitality Quarterly*, **43** (4): 5–16.
John, George and Barton A. Weitz (1988), "Forward integration into distribution: an empirical test of transaction cost analysis," *Journal of Law, Economics, and Organization*, **4** (2), 337–55.
Joskow, Paul L. (1987), "Contract duration and relationship-specific investments: empirical evidence from coal markets," *American Economic Review*, **77** (1), 168–85.
Kapferer, Jean-Noel (1992), *Strategic Brand Management*, New York: Free Press.

Kaufmann, Patrick. J. and Rajiv P. Dant (1992), "The dimensions of commercial exchange," *Marketing Letters*, **3** (2), 171–85.
Kaufmann, Patrick J. and Louis W. Stern (1988), "Relational exchange norms, perceptions of unfairness, and retained hostility in commercial litigation," *Journal of Conflict Resolution*, **32** (3), 534–52.
Kim, Byung-Do, and Mary W. Sullivan (1998), "The effect of parent brand experience on line extension trial and repeat purchase," *Marketing Letters*, **9** (2), 181–93.
Kogut, Bruce and Ugo Zander (1992), "Knowledge of the firm, combinative capabilities, and the replication of technology," *Organization Science*, **3** (3), 383–97.
Kogut, Bruce and Ugo Zander (1993), "Knowledge of the firm and the evolutionary theory of the multinational corporation," *Journal of International Business Studies*, **24** (4), 625–46.
Kohli, Ajay K. and Bernard Jaworski (1990), "Market orientation: the construct, research propositions, and managerial implications," *Journal of Marketing*, **54** (2), 1–18.
Lam, Alice (1997), "Embedded firms, embedded knowledge: problems of collaboration and knowledge transfer in global cooperative ventures," *Organization Studies*, **18** (6), 973–96.
Lewis, Robert C., Richard E. Chambers and Harsha E. Chacko (1995), *Marketing Leadership in Hospitality: Foundations and Practices*, 2nd edn, New York: Van Nostrand Reinhold.
Loken, Barbara and Deborah R. John (1993), "Diluting brand beliefs: when do brand extensions have a negative impact?" *Journal of Marketing*, **57** (3), 71–84.
Macneil, Ian. R. (1980), *The New Social Contract*, New Haven, CT: Yale University Press.
Madhok, Anoop (1997), "Cost, value, and foreign market entry mode: the transaction and the firm," *Strategic Management Journal*, **18** (1), 39–61.
Malley, Mike (1997), "Getting the most value out of franchising," *Hotel and Motel Management* (supplement), **212** (8), 31–2.
Mishra, Debi Pradad, Jan B. Heide and Stanton G. Cort (1998), "Information asymmetry and levels of agency relationships," *Journal of Marketing Research*, **35** (3), 277–95.
Mohr, Jakki J. and John R. Nevin (1990), "Communication strategies in marketing channels: a theoretical perspective," *Journal of Marketing*, **54** (4), 36–51.
Mohr, Jakki J. and Ravipreet S. Sohi (1995), "Communication flows in distribution channels: impact on assessments of communication quality and satisfaction," *Journal of Retailing*, **71** (4), 393–416.
Nand, Lisa Francesca (2012), "Big hotel brands get personal on social media," 12 January, *HotelNewsNow.com* website, accessed 3 October 2012) at www.hotelnewsnow.com/articles.aspx/7285/Big-hotel-brands-get-personal-on-social-media.
Narver, John C. and Slater, Stanley F. (1990), "The effect of a market orientation on business profitability," *Journal of Marketing*, **54** (4), 20–35.
Noordwier, Thomas G., George John and John R. Nevin (1990), "Performance outcomes of purchasing arrangements in industrial buyer-vendor relationships," *Journal of Marketing*, **54** (4), 80–93.
Payan, Janice M. and Richard G. McFarland (2005), "Decomposing influence strategies: argument structure and dependence as determinants of the effectiveness of influence strategies in gaining channel member compliance," *Journal of Marketing*, **69** (3), 66–79.
Payan, Janice M. and John R. Nevin (2006), "Influence strategy efficacy in supplier-distributor relationships," *Journal of Business Research*, **59** (4), 457–65.
Peng, Mike W. and Peggy Sue Heath (1996), "The growth of the firm in planned economies in transition: institutions, organizations, and strategic choice," *Academy of Management Review*, **21** (2), 492–528.
Peng, Mike W. and Y. Luo (2000), "Managerial ties and firm performance in a transition economy: the nature of a micro-macro link," *Academy of Management Journal*, **43** (3), 486–501.
Perkins, Ed (2011), "How to navigate travel flash sale sites," 25 August, *USA Today Travel*, accessed 5 September 2011) at http://travel.usatoday.com/deals/inside/story/2011–08–25/How-to-navigate-travel-flash-sale-sites/50125442/1.
Piccoli, Gabriele and Chekitan S. Dev (2012), "A global study of emerging marketing

channels in hospitality: Internet enabled flash-sales and private-sales," report, Center for Hospitality Research, **12** (5).

Shane, Scott A. (1998), "Hybrid organizational arrangements and their implications for firm growth and survival: a study of new franchisors," *Academy of Management Journal*, **39** (1), 216–34.

Stokes, Jon (2012), "How are the top hotel brands innovating on social media?" *Business 2 Community* website, accessed 23 October 2012) at www.business2community.com/social-media/how-are-the-top-hotel-brands-innovating-in-social-media-0169225.

Stump, Rodney L. and Jan B. Heide (1996), "Controlling supplier opportunism in industrial relationships," *Journal of Marketing Research*, **33** (4), 431–41.

Teece, David J. (1998), "Capturing value from knowledge assets: the new economy, markets for know-how, and intangible assets," *California Management Review*, **40** (3), 55–79.

Wathne, Kenneth H. and Jan B. Heide (2000), "Opportunism in interfirm relationships: forms, outcomes, and solutions," *Journal of Marketing*, **64** (4), 36–51.

Williamson, Oliver E. (1975), *Markets and Hierarchies: Analysis and Anti-trust Implications*, New York: Free Press.

Williamson, Oliver E. (1985), *The Economic Institutions of Capitalism—Firms, Markets, Relational Contracting*, New York: Free Press.

Yipit (2011), "Daily deal trends in North America," *Yipit Data Report*, 12 August, accessed 22 September 2011) at www.scribd.com/doc/64647590/Yipit-August-2011-Report-09-10-11-Draft-Copy-2.

PART VIII

SERVICE FOR SOCIETY

24 Transformative service research: an emerging subfield focused on service and well-being

Amy L. Ostrom, Daniele Mathras and Laurel Anderson

Consumers spend most of their lives co-creating and being affected, at least to some degree, by service, services, and service systems. From education and healthcare, to financial services and telecommunications, service processes, employees, organizations, and service systems can and do affect consumers in myriad ways that can ultimately influence their well-being (Anderson et al. 2013a). In the more than 30 years since the emergence and significant growth of the services marketing discipline (Brown et al. 1994), service research has focused significantly on understanding the drivers of service quality perceptions, customer satisfaction, loyalty, word of mouth, service recovery, and new service adoption, as well as factors related to service employees and their impact on consumers and the firm. However, service research has focused much less on how co-creating and co-producing service and being a participant in a service system influence consumer well-being. Although service-dominant logic (for example, Vargo and Lusch 2004; Vargo et al. 2010) has focused greater attention on customer roles, co-creation, and perceptions of value and there is clear recognition of the effect that the social context can have on customers' experiences (for example, Edvardsson et al. 2011), we are lacking a systematic examination of how consumer experiences with service entities affect consumer well-being at the individual and collective level (Anderson et al. 2013a).

Recently, service researchers have shown increasing interest in understanding the well-being implications of service and have called for more work in the area of transformative service research (TSR) (Anderson et al. 2013a; Ostrom et al. 2010; Rosenbaum et al. 2011). For this area to thrive, service researchers require not only a clear definition of what constitutes TSR but also a better understanding of prior research that has examined the relationship between service and well-being. A review of prior work that would be considered TSR can illustrate the progress that has been made in the marketing and service literature to date toward understanding the well-being implications of service. It can also help identify important topic areas and issues that warrant further attention.

Our goal for the chapter is to advance the emerging subfield of TSR by first providing a detailed discussion of what constitutes TSR. Second, we review research published during the past 20 years in the top marketing and service journals to identify examples of prior work in the TSR area, and organize this review by the key service-related themes on which this research has focused. Third, we highlight additional TSR that could be undertaken related to each of the themes where further focused attention by service researchers could make important contributions to both academic thought and consumer and societal well-being. Finally, we conclude with recommendations meant to spur additional TSR and grow this important, emerging subfield.

WHAT CONSTITUTES TRANSFORMATIVE SERVICE RESEARCH?

When developing any new domain of research, key tasks include defining it and describing how it relates to and differs from other similar areas. Thus, we begin by discussing the emergence of TSR, our definition of it, and how we view TSR in relation to other areas of research.

Emergence of the Subfield of TSR

Although prior research has attempted to understand the effects of service on consumer well-being (for example, Hill 1994; Kang and Ridgway 1996; Lee et al. 1999), only relatively recently has the term, transformative service research, been used in the service literature. Rosenbaum et al. (2007) were the first to mention the term transformative service research and to explicitly discuss the need for this type of work. More recently, Ostrom et al. (2010) highlighted TSR as one of the ten research priorities for the science of service. Since then, many special sessions at conferences and workshops (for example, the 2010 Association for Consumer Research Conference, the 2011 Winter American Marketing Association Conference, the 2011 Transformative Consumer Research Conference, and the 2012 Hot Topics in Service Research IV hosted by the Manchester Business School) and at least two publications (for example, Anderson et al. 2013a; Rosenbaum et al. 2011) have further discussed TSR and provided directions for future research. In addition, a special issue on TSR is due to appear in the *Journal of Service Research* in 2015.

Defining TSR: What Is It?

At a broad level, TSR focuses on the impact of service on well-being. Anderson et al. (2013b, p. 3) describe TSR as "the integration of consumer and service research that centers on creating uplifting changes and improvements in the well-being of consumer entities: individuals (consumers and employees), communities and the ecosystem."

We view TSR as residing at the intersection of service research and transformative consumer research (TCR), and thus it can draw from many disciplines, including those that inherently focus on service and well-being (for example, education policy, health policy). To better understand TSR, we examine what constitutes service research and TCR. Although no one clear definition of service research exists, by using Zeithaml et al.'s (2013, p. 3) definition of services as "deeds, processes, and performances provided or coproduced by one entity or person for another entity or person" or Lusch and Vargo's (2006, p. 283) definition of service as "the application of specialized competences (knowledge and skills), through deeds, processes, and performances for the benefit of another entity or the entity itself," any research that strives to understand these aspects related to service can be considered service research. However, in practice, research positioned as service research, especially within the marketing discipline, often focuses on common themes (for example, service quality, service encounters, service design, service recovery, new service adoption). In addition, research not specifically positioned as service research has examined issues and relationships that have important implications for service (for example, Moisio and Beruchashvili 2010; Wang et al. 2010).

Significant emphasis has been placed on the study of well-being and welfare related to consumption since David Mick's (2006) presidential remarks to the Association for Consumer Research (ACR). The ACR defines TCR as "a movement within our association that seeks to encourage, support, and publicize research that benefits consumer welfare and quality of life for all beings affected by consumption across the world" (see www.acrwebsite.org/web/section/transformative-consumer-research.aspx). Mick et al. (2012) present an in-depth discussion of TCR, its origins and qualities. Transformative service research shares many of the same qualities and commitments of TCR, especially with regard to the following tenets—"to improve well-being," "to employ rigorous theory and methods," and "to disseminate findings to relevant stakeholders" (Mick et al. 2012, p. 6)—but with an emphasis on the role of service and service systems in influencing well-being. With this understanding of TSR, we examine prior work that pertains to TSR to better understand what researchers have previously studied in relation to service and well-being.

TSR PUBLISHED IN KEY MARKETING AND SERVICE JOURNALS

Because researchers have been increasingly interested in investigating well-being implications related to service yet questions remain about what constitutes TSR, we undertook a review of prior research to identify what has been examined in the past in regards to service and well-being as well as to more fully explore what qualifies as TSR. The review was not meant to be comprehensive, but rather to serve as a catalyst for future research focused on service and well-being by delineating some of the major themes of prior research related to TSR.

Method

We conducted a review of the top three marketing journals (*Journal of Marketing*, *Journal of Consumer Research*, and *Journal of Marketing Research*) and two of the top service journals (*Journal of Service Research* and *Journal of Service Management*, formerly *International Journal of Service Industry Management*) consistent with Moussa and Touzani's (2010) ranking of marketing journals using the Google Scholar-based hg-index. We also included two other journals that are more oriented to policy and macro issues in marketing (that is, *Journal of Public Policy & Marketing* and *Journal of Macromarketing*) because TSR emphasizes both individual and collective well-being. We selected articles published from 1993 through 2012 (a 20-year span) by examining titles and then the abstract and the article itself, if necessary, to determine whether it fit the criteria. To meet our criteria for a TSR article, the researchers needed to have clearly investigated some service-related issue or service itself and examined well-being-oriented outcomes and implications. Not surprisingly, few articles were explicitly positioned as focusing on service and well-being, which required us to determine how much service focus and emphasis on well-being was necessary for our purposes. Although debate about any one article can arise, the themes that emerged from our review highlight the progress that has been made in exploring the relationship between service and well-being.

TSR Themes and Opportunities

On initial inspection we identified more than 230 articles that appeared to be examples of TSR. On closer examination, we decided that approximately 100 of them met the criteria and we categorized these articles into broad themes. Although some articles clearly pertained to TSR and were positioned as service research that aimed to enhance understanding of some aspect of well-being, as noted previously, other articles were positioned instead on well-being implications within a service setting. In the sections that follow, we describe the eight main themes that emerged and discuss opportunities for further research in those areas. The first four themes—co-creation and well-being, customer-contact employees and their well-being, the service experiences of vulnerable consumers, and service-based friendships and social support—focus on well-being influenced by the interaction between employees and customers and on the well-being of the participants themselves. The next two themes focus on service access and literacy, both of which can have an effect on consumer vulnerability. The last two themes focus on well-being related to design, one centering on service design at a more micro level and one at a more macro level concentrating on the design of service systems.

Co-creation and well-being

Research on service-dominant logic has "used the term 'co-creation of value' to convey the customer's (and others') collaborative role in value creation" (Vargo et al. 2010, p. 143). Although earlier work described the importance of understanding customer co-creation (for example, Prahalad and Ramaswamy 2000), service-dominant logic's focus on co-creation has sparked increased interest in how customers and service providers interact to create offerings that customers value. Given the roles of customers and employees in service creation, their interactions and the context in which those interactions take place can and do affect well-being. We identified a number of articles that addressed this broad issue but in slightly different ways. For example, some articles focus on the dialogical interaction that occurs within a service context. Hill (1994) investigates the interface between debtors and bill collectors, examining their perceptions of and reactions to each other. He examines the service process of debt collection, including the role of debt collectors, the response of indebted consumers, and their ensuing relationship, which often involves aggressive behaviors by both parties. Using a qualitative-based, multi-method approach, McColl-Kennedy et al. (2012) examine the role of healthcare customers in the co-creation process. They develop a typology of co-creation styles and link them to quality-of-life metrics. These dialogical studies examine on a more granular level the nature of the activities and interactions that occur within a service setting with a focus on well-being-related outcomes.

Other articles concentrate on how being embedded in a service system or culture affects the nature of the interaction and the service that customers experience. Much of this work has been done in the context of healthcare. For example, Wong and King (2008, p. 579) examine how perceived risk related to decisions concerning breast cancer screening and treatment "are influenced by the dominant illness narrative of restitution within Anglo-Western cultures." They suggest that these risk perceptions lead to usage of healthcare interventions that surpasses U.S. medical guidelines.

In their study on tragic choices in a healthcare setting, Botti et al. (2009) examine the choice parents must make to discontinue or maintain their infants' life support systems and their preferences for autonomy (that is, to make the decision themselves or have physicians make the decision). They find that parents in the United States are more autonomous and decide on their children's treatment themselves. By doing so, they ultimately experience more negative emotions than French parents, who leave the choice to their doctors. Also in a healthcare setting, Wang et al. (2010) show that consumers' lay theories of medicine (related to the nature of illness and their beliefs concerning health remedies) affect both their desire for Western- versus Eastern-based medicine and their perceptions of the importance of engaging in related healthful lifestyle behaviors.

Brennan et al. (2010, p. 8) examine the socio-cultural phenomenon of medicalization, which is the "process by which aspects of the human condition, formerly considered nonmedical, are brought within the medical realm." They present a conceptual model that links drivers of medicalization including pharmaceutical marketing strategies, mass media's reporting of medical issues, and societal trends and their interplay to medicalization and its related outcomes. Their model suggests that medicalization may affect, among other things, the patient–doctor interaction and the occurrence of iatrogenic illness that results from a medical examination and/or medical treatment. In addition, medicalization may increase the number of false positives, lead to more drug use and hence a greater number of adverse drug reactions, and an overall increase in medical service usage, all of which lead to an increase in healthcare spending. The authors also highlight a TSR-oriented research agenda focused on medicalization.

Outside of the realm of traditional healthcare but yet still health related, Moisio and Beruchashvili (2010, p. 858) examine U.S. consumers' "quest for well-being" and the role of support groups with a specific focus on Weight Watchers. They argue that the spiritual-therapeutic model helps explain members' conduct and that their behaviors center on three practices: therapeutic confession, therapeutic oversight, and autotherapeutic testimonial. Their model, a hybrid of "spiritual and therapeutic meaning systems," helps explain "how support groups emerge as irreplaceable partners in consumers' quest for well-being in the United States" (Moisio and Beruchashvili 2010, p. 870).

There is also research that has focused on how being embedded within a culture affects the service experience outside of health-related services. For example, in the context of consumers' usage and meanings surrounding financial services, Peñaloza and Barnhart (2011) identify cultural meanings that influence how consumers use credit and debt. These meanings are represented as continua that include the use of credit in relation to others (that is, to exert independence versus require social integration because others are needed to access it), self-regulation in the use of credit (that is, self-discipline versus indulgence), how credit can harm or aid users (that is, threat versus security), and the connotations of credit and debt (that is, freedom versus constraint).

Other articles pertain to co-creation but focus more on issues related to consumer involvement and power within a service context. Roth (1994) examines how consumers' values correspond to their sources for and use of information, the quality of the patient–physician relationship, and patient compliance by eliciting cognitive ladders from respondents. The results show the importance of control, trust, empowerment, and quality of life, among other values, in influencing these issues. Dellande et al. (2004) examine how service provider characteristics (that is, expertise and demographic and attitudinal homophily) and consumer attributes (that is, role clarity, motivation, and ability) influence customer compliance and goal attainment within the context of a medically-based weight loss program. Lee et al. (1999) examine the social power inequality that can exist between physicians and patients in their study of women's healthcare encounters (viewed as "a field of struggle"; ibid. p. 236) taking place in an Appalachian coal-mining community. They explore the social, economic, and cultural capital of patients and physicians and show how their interplay can influence social inequality. Schwartz et al. (2011) examine the effects of a long-term relationship between a customer and expert service provider in the context of healthcare and show that as the tenure of the relationship grows, the amount of customers' out-of-pocket costs for routine procedures increases and the desire for a second opinion decreases. Hence, while long-term relationships with expert service providers can no doubt enhance consumer well-being, there is evidence that those relationships have the potential to negatively influence well-being in important ways.

Although prior work has demonstrated that the interactions between customers and employees, the nature of the relationship between them, and the context in which service occurs can all affect aspects of well-being, much remains to be examined. For example, research could explore how the nature of the interaction, co-creation processes, and characteristics of the context can lead to negative consequences (for example, discrimination, marginalization, shame, guilt, poor mental or physical health). Research could also examine how positive outcomes, such as happiness, life satisfaction, and strong physical and mental health, can be engendered by the nature of service interactions or co-creation activities between employees and customers and those that occur between customers.

Customer-contact employees and their well-being

Another strong theme that emerged involved frontline employees and their well-being. Given the important role of contact employees in service settings, service research has striven to understand not only the factors that affect their productivity but also well-being-related issues, such as burnout and emotional exhaustion. Some of this research focuses on the effect of negative customer behaviors on frontline employees. For example, Harris and Reynolds (2003) explore the possible negative consequences of dysfunctional customer behavior on customer-contact employees, other customers, and the organization itself. Their evidence suggests that customer-contact employees can experience long-term psychological effects, such as stress disorders and persistent feelings of degradation, short-term emotional distress (for example, fear, anger, irritation), as well as behavioral and physical consequences. Goussinsky (2012) examines how frontline employees cope with customer aggression and finds that seeking emotional support is the strategy used most often (in comparison to behavioral disengagement and venting negative emotions). Her findings also indicate that experiencing customer aggression leads to employee emotional exhaustion, with a stronger negative effect for employees with low (versus high) self-efficacy.

Research also examines other factors with negative implications for contact employees. A significant body of work addresses the issue of contact-employee burnout, though in many cases the focal dependent measure is not employee well-being but employee job performance and/or customer satisfaction. Research has examined the factors that affect emotional exhaustion and burnout, including role stressors (Singh et al. 1994), work–family conflict (Yavas et al. 2008), empowerment (Yagil 2006), core self-evaluations (Yagil et al. 2008), employee optimism (Crosno et al. 2009), and organization mission fulfillment (Suh et al. 2010).

Although most of the work examining employees has focused on negative health outcomes, further research could investigate how to generate positive well-being outcomes such as greater life satisfaction or better physical health for individual employees and positive outcomes that could accrue to their families and communities. As an example, in their meta-analysis on the effect of employee well-being programs on cost reduction, Keller et al. (2009) find that cardio/heart programs and customized health feedback are associated with greater cost reduction, and that the relationship between well-being programs and cost reduction depends on the gender of the employees and the size of the firm. Although not tested in their meta-analysis, they discuss evidence suggesting that lower health costs are associated with improved employee health. Future research could not only further explore the effects of employee well-being programs on individual employee health, but also examine the positive effects that may accrue to employees' families, thus looking at such programs' impact at the collective level. In addition, research could also investigate the nature of the relationship between employee and consumer well-being.

The service experiences of vulnerable consumers

A primary focus of TCR is vulnerable consumers. Although research has conceptualized vulnerability in various ways, Baker et al. (2005, p. 134, italics in original) define consumer vulnerability as:

> a state of powerlessness that arises from an imbalance in marketplace interactions or from the consumption of marketing messages and products. It occurs when control is not in an individual's hands, creating a dependence on external factors (for example, marketers) to create fairness in the marketplace. The actual vulnerability arises from the *interaction* of individual states, individual characteristics, and external conditions within a context where consumption goals may be hindered and the experience affects personal and social perceptions of self.

Vulnerability can arise from individual characteristics (for example, biophysical and psychosocial characteristics), an individual's state (for example, grief, life transitions), and external conditions (for example, discrimination, resource distribution). In reviewing prior work, a strong theme emerged on vulnerable consumers and how they interact in service settings.

Some research focuses on service-related issues in the context of groups and individuals whose characteristics (for example, adolescence, visual impairment) may contribute to their vulnerability. Anderson and McCabe (2012) examine how adolescents' online socialization can lead to an increase in risky behaviors, such as when people who met online meet offline and when aggressive social language used online is used offline. Baker et al. (2001) investigate how independence/dependency are manifested in terms of how visually impaired consumers navigate and cope in service settings. They examine the negotiation of these service settings after enactment of the Americans with Disabilities Act in 1990. Kaufman-Scarborough and Childers (2009), who also study the experience of people who are visually impaired, focus on online services that do not fall under the purview of the Americans with Disabilities Act. They examine the technology acceptance model from the perspective of consumer normalcy and vulnerability.

Other research focuses more on vulnerability in terms of an individual's state. For example, Gentry et al. (1995) examine vulnerability arising from experiencing grief and the interactions with organizations, such as funeral homes and insurance companies, that occur after the death of a loved one. Gabel and Scott (2009) discuss life insurance settlement services (in which an investor acquires a life insurance policy of someone living, pays the premiums, and receives the payout after the person's death) and their potential to lead to consumer vulnerability.

Other articles examine the effects of more external conditions, such as poverty and emergency situations after a disaster. Bertrand et al. (2006) examine the poor from a behavioral economics perspective and identify issues related to financial services, such as low participation rates of the poor in mainstream financial services and in welfare programs. They also examine how self-identity, lack of information, and duress influence the poor's response to certain offerings. Arnould et al. (2009) investigate the well-being of poor farmers in Latin America who either participate or do not participate in the TransFair USA cooperative. Their findings show that participants used their land more productively, earned more money, and were more likely to receive needed medical attention than nonparticipants. Furthermore, farmers who were in the program longer tended to have greater access to medical services than those who participated over a shorter period of time. Varman and Vikas (2007) examine healthcare utilization by subaltern consumers in India in terms of their experiences with both government and private hospitals and the perspectives of physicians and pharmaceutical sales representatives who serve them. Their findings reveal the marginalization of these consumers due to poorly maintained government health facilities, the high costs associated with private medical services, and the pharmaceutical companies' incentive structure that rewards physicians for prescribing certain medicines. These factors all lead consumers to purchase medical services from untrained medical practitioners, resulting in incorrect diagnoses and treatment and potentially serious negative consequences. Other situations that can enhance vulnerability include disasters and emergency situations. Research on natural disasters explores the role of government and nongovernment organizations in providing resources to consumers affected by natural disasters and their experiences interacting with these organizations (Baker 2009; Baker et al. 2007; Guion et al. 2007).

Service-related research also examines vulnerable consumers' experience in a variety of service settings that affect their well-being. For example, Cornwell and Gabel (1996, p. 281) focus on the "lived experience of consumers affected by institutionalization." Interviews with key informants (for example, individuals currently or previously institutionalized, their family and friends as well as service employees who work in institutional settings) provided information about consumption-related activities of the institutionalized, including activities that were fully sanctioned (both internal and external) and those that occurred, in some settings, "underground." Ozanne et al. (1998) examine consumption-related meanings of institutionalized juveniles regarding stealing cars, money, and sensual (for example, alcohol, drugs) and status (firearms) products and the implications of these meanings for institutional reform services. Hill and Macan (1996) discuss consumers' survival on welfare and focus on both the Food Stamp Program and Medicaid. Hill and Stephens (1997, p. 40) examine consumer behavior of welfare mothers and find evidence that "in addition to feelings of deprivation, many women involved with the welfare system express anger and/or unease about welfare administrators and staff assuming the role of unwelcome and intrusive parent" and that they also experience feelings of humiliation in service settings (for example, when using food stamps or receiving medical services).

Future research could address the many remaining questions related to how service characteristics contribute to or reduce consumer vulnerability. Service offerings that are difficult to understand or service systems that are challenging to navigate may increase consumers' perceptions of powerlessness and reduce mental and physical health. Thus, service research could explore vulnerability as a well-being related outcome metric. Conversely, service offerings related to education and financial services can help reduce vulnerability and enhance well-being, as can social services and a host of other service offerings that provide support to vulnerable customers. New theories, models, and frameworks could be developed to enhance our understanding of these relationships.

Service-based friendships and social support

In our review, we identified a stream of research that investigates the role of customer–customer and customer–employee relationships (also described as commercial friendships by Price and Arnould 1999) in providing social support, which has been linked to both mental and physical health. Kang and Ridgway (1996) present a conceptual framework that depicts how commercial ties, interactions, and relationships between customers and service employees influence both mental and physical health of elderly consumers. Rosenbaum (2006) provides qualitative and quantitative evidence that customer–customer and customer–employee relationships facilitated by third places can provide social support to older customers. In addition, Rosenbaum et al. (2007) find that the extent to which customers have experienced socially supportive destructive events (for example, death, divorce, illness, retirement) influences the degree of social support facilitated by third places. Rosenbaum and Massiah (2007) show that younger consumers also receive social support from service establishments, which in turn influences the care they provide to other customers. Rosenbaum (2008) demonstrates how the social support provided by service establishments provides health-related returns to adults by reducing their health worries and despondency and increasing their feelings of personal well-being. Although social support has typically been viewed in terms of how it can help customers, other research suggests that, at times, it can affect behavior in ways that are potentially harmful. For example, participating in an online community can increase participants' risk-seeking tendencies related to financial decisions (Zhu et al. 2012). When strong ties are present in an online community, consumers expect to get help from community members if financial difficulties occur.

To date, research has examined how customer–customer and customer–employee relationships provide social support that can positively influence consumer well-being. More work could examine how service organizations can facilitate these types of interactions and provide a better understanding of the service settings that have the most profound positive impact on well-being. Note, however, that in some situations, service-based friendships can lead to reduced well-being (Schwartz et al. 2011; Zhu et al. 2012). Future research could investigate the situations in which this is likely to happen as well as the nature of the negative outcomes that might occur.

Access to service and well-being

Several articles discuss access to or the appropriate utilization of services, especially healthcare. Scammon et al. (1995) focus on public policy that affects the supply and characteristics of healthcare professionals who could successfully serve vulnerable populations. Franzak et al. (1995) explore the rural healthcare environment and describe a model for delivering cancer care to rural areas. Mason et al. (2002) find evidence that in managed healthcare plans, chronically ill patients experience more restricted access than healthy plan participants. Mittelstaedt et al. (2009, p. 97) examine the U.S. healthcare marketing system in terms of consumers' constrained consumption, which focuses on "access to assortment and appropriateness of assortment," which can contribute to greater potential consumer vulnerability.

While most of the research focuses on a lack of access to needed services, Grier et al. (2007) investigate the relationships between parents' access to and exposure to promotions for fast-food restaurants and children's fast-food consumption, with parents' attitudes toward fast food and social norms related to fast-food consumption as mediators of those relationships. Their results indicate that fast-food promotions affect children's consumption of fast-food by influencing parents' social norm perceptions.

Hispanics and African Americans both had more perceived fast-food promotional exposure and access to fast-food than whites.

Access is a key well-being metric in industries such as healthcare, education, and financial services. Thus, research could examine the antecedents and consequences of lack of access to service offerings focused on enhancing consumer well-being. For example, undocumented immigrants who give birth in the United States may have access to healthcare for that child (who is an American citizen) but not for their other children who were born outside the United States. How does this influence not only the well-being of the children involved but also that of the family collective?

Service literacy and well-being

Consumer literacy, which involves the ability to interpret and communicate meaning though socially constructed symbols and texts (Street 2001), is a central concept in the well-being literature. Another theme that emerged during our review involved research on consumer literacy, how it affects consumers in service settings, and the implications for well-being. Some research broadly examines consumer or marketplace literacy and the characteristics of educational programs or interventions (which we view as a type of service) that could help enhance consumers' understanding. For example, Adkins and Ozanne (2005a) discuss how different consumer literacy profiles (based on available social skills and resources and shame management orientation) necessitate the need for different consumer education strategies. Viswanathan et al. (2009) examine the effectiveness of literacy-based interventions aimed at enhancing marketplace literacy of poor consumers in South India.

Other research investigates how literacy interventions can be beneficial within specific service contexts. For example, Brinberg and Axelson (2002) examine how to improve the effectiveness of nutrition counseling through the use of a customized nutrition messaging intervention. Also in a nutrition-related service context, Viswanathan and Gau (2005) focus on nutritional education programs for illiterate consumers and investigate how the educational materials used can be improved. Bolton et al. (2011) examine how the marketing of debt consolidation loan services influences consumers and the extent to which interventions focused on providing loan and lender related information affect consumers' attitudes towards debt consolidation loans, the perceived importance of the amount of interest charged, and their money management intentions. Jayanti and Singh (2010) assess social learning within online communities by examining inquiry processes within six health-related threads from an open forum, electronic bulletin board (that is, mythyroid.com) and their connection with individual action.

In the future, more research could be done to examine how low literacy, whether it be functional, marketplace, or service related, can influence well-being related outcomes such as access, discrimination, and consumers' mental and physical well-being. Research can seek to learn from how low literate consumers navigate in service settings. For example, what can researchers learn from low-literate consumers and the coping strategies they use when they interact with service providers? Future TSR can examine how service literacy can be enhanced especially when functional literacy is low and the service and service system are complex. It can also investigate what can be done to mitigate negative well-being outcomes that may result when low literate consumers engage in co-creation. Recent research has investigated consumer learning in the context of resource integration (Hibbert et al. 2012). Future work can examine the implications it has for well-being.

Service design

Another theme focused on the elements of service design and how they can influence well-being. Some work examines service in regards to how the assortment of options and even the number of service options available can impact consumer well-being. For example, Morrin et al. (2012) investigate how a 401(k) plan's assortment of funds, grouping of funds, and fund information influence participation in the plan. In regards to the number of options available, research suggests that more may not always be better. When consumers are given too many options in terms of prescription drugs, healthcare, social security, and investments, well-being may be negatively affected because of the constraints in their cognitive and emotional resources (Botti and Iyengar 2006).

Both the design of the service environment and the environmental cues that are present can affect consumer well-being. For example, Tansik and Routhieaux (1999) find that individuals in a hospital waiting area (who are waiting for surgery patients or who are friends and family of patients in the intensive care unit) reported lower stress (for example, anxiety, nervousness, tenseness) and greater relaxation (for example, ease, calmness) when music was played than when it was not. Social influences triggered by environmental cues may also affect consumer well-being through environmental benefits. Goldstein et al. (2008, p. 476) found that hotel guests were more likely to reuse a bath towel when a sign in their room's bathroom indicated that "75% of the guests who stayed in this room . . . participated in our new resource savings program by using their towels more than once." That is, a descriptive norm about others' behaviors in the immediate surroundings motivated more green behaviors than descriptive norms about gender, other hotel guests in general, and more than an appeal based on the importance of protecting the environment.

Part of service design involves the organizational policies that affect consumers' experience with the service and, relevant to TSR, their well-being. Another theme that emerged was how service policy influences consumer well-being outcomes. For example, research has examined online privacy policies related to church websites (Hoy and Phelp 2003) and pharmaceutical direct-to-consumer websites (Sheehan 2005). Palmer et al. (2001) examine the effect of requiring parents to be co-obligors on a student's credit card application on the student's credit card balance. Although the research was prompted by proposed federal legislation, such requirements could also be considered an example of a potential service policy. Dority et al. (2010) examine school food policies and find that prohibiting the sale of à la carte junk food decreases the likelihood of students being overweight or obese. Navarro-Martinez et al. (2011) investigate how credit card companies' minimum payment policy and the disclosure of supplemental loan information impact debt repayment. They show that, for U.S. consumers, the presence of a minimum payment negatively affects repayment behavior and that providing additional information about interest costs and the time needed for loan repayment does not mitigate those negative effects. D'Rozario and Williams (2005, p. 176) describe types of retail redlining, defined as:

> a spatially discriminatory practice among retailers, especially chain stores, of either not serving certain areas or targeting stores operating in those areas for unfavorable treatment, based on the racial-/ethnic-minority composition of either the customers that those stores serve and/or the owners/operators of those stores, rather than on economic criteria (such as the potential profitability of operating in those areas).

They propose a method to empirically identify the practice.

Work related to service design also focuses on new service development in which the new service positively contributes to well-being. For example, Hill (2002) investigates the creation of a service delivery system for homeless teenagers. Epstein and Yuthas (2012) develop a framework of the key levers needed to successfully scale effective education in developing countries. Other research focuses on ways to include the customer in the process of new service development intended to, at least in part, improve well-being. Examples include case studies on customer orientation techniques used by the World Bank to include customers of its projects in their development (Talukdar et al. 2005) and community action research focused on customer participation in identifying local needs and solutions related to healthcare (Ozanne and Anderson 2010).

The research we highlight in this section demonstrates the diversity in work examining how design choices can influence not only customer satisfaction but also customers' well-being. However, this is only a fraction of what could be studied. For example, how can the design of service offerings, including the policies put in place, affect consumers' physical and mental health and whether consumers feel stigmatized or marginalized by participating in the service? How can new service offerings be developed in ways that maximize consumer, family, and societal well-being? How can service design and policy decisions enhance service sustainability and reduce the negative environmental effects of service provision?

Service systems and well-being

Though challenging, some recent work has examined a more macro view of how service systems affect well-being. Spohrer et al. (2007, p. 72) state that "service systems comprise service providers and service clients working together to coproduce value in complex value chains or networks. Providers and clients might be individuals, firms, government agencies, or any organization of people and technologies." This more macro focused research has examined the factors affecting sustainable energy consumption (Press and Arnould 2009); the customer, vendor, and family relationship subsystems managed by subsistence consumer-merchants (Viswanathan et al. 2010); retail sector development in emerging economies and its effect on small-scale retailing (Polsa and Fan 2011); organizations' leveraging of local economic conditions and laws to improve the well-being of poor HIV patients (Chance and Deshpandé 2009); and the network of actors that make up the food marketing system in the United States and how they have contributed to childhood obesity (Goldberg and Gunasti 2007). Though vastly different in focus, these studies take a more systems view in identifying the network of contributors that can influence consumer well-being.

Although examining service systems is challenging, we encourage more research in this area. Many negative consumer well-being outcomes result from structural issues and the interconnectedness of key stakeholders within a service system. Some service systems, especially those in healthcare (see Berry and Bendapudi 2007; Samli 2010; Scammon et al. 2011), education, and financial domains, are in need of a significant overhaul to enhance individual and collective well-being.

Limitations

As with any review of this nature, this research has some limitations. We examined only a small number of journals; thus, there likely exists research in other journals similar in theme to the articles examined, as well as the potential for additional TSR themes to emerge from a broader review of the literature. Our review was not meant to be comprehensive and, due to space constraints, not all TSR articles that we identified were discussed. Also, because the majority of the articles were not positioned as service research and variance existed across articles in terms of their emphasis on well-being, we used our own judgment to classify articles as TSR. However, despite the inherent subjectivity involved in the classification process, we believe the resulting themes help to clarify and advance TSR-related work.

IMPLICATIONS AND RECOMMENDATIONS TO FURTHER TSR

Our research review shows some of the progress made to date in examining the relationship between service and well-being. However, given the importance of well-being-related issues and service, more work can and should be done. Therefore, we encourage service researchers to continue investigating the themes we identified, with a focus both on the service settings that can significantly affect well-being and on the well-being implications of service-related constructs and relationships. In addition, we urge researchers (1) to include well-being-related questions and metrics (micro and macro when possible) in the development of new service research projects and also (2) to examine TCR projects through a service lens to identify new research questions with the potential for theory development.

To better illuminate the latter two recommendations, we take an example of each from the literature and propose ways they could have been more illustrative of TSR. This exercise is not meant to criticize these studies; rather, we chose them because of our high regard for them and their contribution to the literature.

Traditionally, research in the service literature considers the company's well-being, not consumers' well-being. Furthermore, studies that do consider consumer outcomes tend to use metrics such as satisfaction. Thus, it is important for TSR to move beyond the usual satisfaction outcome measures, which do not adequately capture well-being, to include more robust measures of well-being, such as dropout behaviors, stigmatization, power, discrimination, access, literacy, health, and happiness (Anderson et al., 2013a). For example, Grégoire et al.'s (2009) study on customer revenge discusses the phenomenon of consumers' perceived betrayal in service failures as a predictor of the desire for revenge and thus raises the issue of the amount of psychological energy needed on the part of consumers to maintain this desire. This study underscores the impact of customer revenge on the firm (and its well-being). If we add a TSR lens to this topic of customer revenge, it suggests research could focus on how customer revenge affects consumer well-being including how it might lead to consumer dropout behaviors (especially in health or education services), take an emotional toll on consumers, impact their health, negatively impact consumers' trust in subsequent service providers, and so on.

Conversely, we often find service contexts used on the TCR side. Here, the opportunity exists to integrate service concepts and issues that might provide further insights into and opportunities for well-being. For example, Adkins and Ozanne (2005b) discuss literacy as a public act that may not meet social expectations, with the low-literate person facing negative social judgment and stigmatization. The majority of public acts occur in service contexts. Considerable insights into consumer well-being with regard to negative social evaluation and stigmatization might be gleaned by considering service concepts such as service as a co-creation and dialogical process, the impact of different elements in the servicescape, and different service interaction strategies on the part of both the low-literate person and the service provider.

We would be remiss if we did not also highlight other increasingly critical areas of TCR that would benefit from adding a service perspective or component. These include sustainability, food marketing (for example, obesity, access, food deserts, social justice of food), subsistence marketplaces, and welfare systems, to name a few. All in all, TSR provides a rich opportunity for meaningful and insightful research that has repercussions for social, collective, and individual well-being.

REFERENCES

Adkins, Natalie Ross and Julie L. Ozanne (2005a), "Critical consumer education: empowering the low-literate consumer," *Journal of Macromarketing*, **25** (2), 153–62.

Adkins, Natalie Ross and Julie L Ozanne (2005b), "The low literate consumer," *Journal of Consumer Research*, **32** (June), 93–105.

Anderson, Laurel and Deborah Brown McCabe (2012), "A coconstructed world: adolescent self-socialization on the Internet," *Journal of Public Policy & Marketing*, **31** (2), 240–53.

Anderson, Laurel, Amy L. Ostrom, Canan Corus, Raymond P. Fisk, Andrew S. Gallan, Mario Giraldo, Martin Mende, Mark Mulder, Steven W. Rayburn, Mark S. Rosenbaum, Kunio Shirahada and Jerome D. Williams (2013a), "Transformative service research: an agenda for the future," *Journal of Business Research*, **66** (8), 1203–10.

Anderson, Laurel, Amy L. Ostrom, Daniele Mathras and Mary Jo Bitner (2013b), "Surrounded by services: alternative views for examining service and well-being," working paper, W.P. Carey School of Business, Arizona State University.

Arnould, Eric J., Alejandro Plastina and Dwayne Ball (2009), "Does Fair Trade deliver on its core value proposition? Effects on income, educational attainment, and health in three countries," *Journal of Public Policy & Marketing*, **28** (2), 186–201.

Baker, Stacey Menzel (2009), "Vulnerability and resilience in natural disasters: a marketing and public policy perspective," *Journal of Public Policy & Marketing*, **28** (1), 114–23.

Baker, Stacey Menzel, James W. Gentry and Terri L. Rittenburg (2005), "Building understanding of the domain of consumer vulnerability," *Journal of Macromarketing*, **25** (2), 128–39.

Baker, Stacey Menzel, David M. Hunt and Terri L. Rittenburg (2007), "Consumer vulnerability as a shared experience: tornado recovery process in Wright, Wyoming," *Journal of Public Policy & Marketing*, **26** (1), 6–19.

Baker, Stacey Menzel, Debra Lynn Stephens and Ronald Paul Hill (2001), "Marketplace experiences of consumers with visual impairments: beyond the Americans with Disabilities Act," *Journal of Public Policy & Marketing*, **20** (2), 215–24.

Berry, Leonard L. and Neeli Bendapudi (2007), "Health care: a fertile field for service research," *Journal of Service Research*, **10** (2), 111–22.

Bertrand, Marianne, Sendhil Mullainathan and Eldar Shafir (2006), "Behavioral economics and marketing in aid of decision making among the poor," *Journal of Public Policy & Marketing*, **25** (1), 8–23.

Bolton, Lisa E., Paul N. Bloom and Joel B. Cohen (2011), "Using loan plus lender literacy information to combat one-sided marketing of debt consolidation loans," *Journal of Marketing Research*, **48**, special issue, 51–9.

Botti, Simona and Sheena S. Iyengar (2006), "The dark side of choice: when choice impairs social welfare," *Journal of Public Policy & Marketing*, **25** (1), 24–38.

Botti, Simona, Kristina Orfali and Sheena S. Iyengar (2009), "Tragic choices: autonomy and emotional responses to medical decisions," *Journal of Consumer Research*, **36** (October), 337–52.

Brennan, Ross, Lynne Eagle and David Rice (2010), "Medicalization and marketing," *Journal of Macromarketing*, **30** (1), 8–22.

Brinberg, David and Marta L. Axelson (2002), "Improving the dietary status of low-income pregnant women at nutritional risk," *Journal of Public Policy & Marketing*, **21** (1), 100–104.

Brown, Stephen W., Raymond P. Fisk and Mary Jo Bitner (1994), "The development and emergence of services marketing thought," *International Journal of Service Industry Management*, **5** (1), 21–48.

Chance, Zoë and Rohit Deshpandé (2009), "Putting patients first: social marketing strategies for treating HIV in developing nations," *Journal of Macromarketing*, **29** (3), 220–32.

Cornwell, T. Bettina and Terrance G. Gabel (1996), "Out of sight, out of mind: an exploratory examination of institutionalization and consumption," *Journal of Public Policy & Marketing*, **15** (2), 278–95.

Crosno, Jody L., Shannon B. Rinaldo, Hulda G. Black and Scott W. Kelley (2009), "Half full or half empty: the role of optimism in boundary-spanning positions," *Journal of Service Research*, **11** (3), 295–309.

D'Rozario, Denver and Jerome D. Williams (2005), "Retail redlining: definition, theory, typology, and measurement," *Journal of Macromarketing*, **25** (2), 175–86.

Dellande, Stephanie, Mary C. Gilly and John L. Graham (2004), "Gaining compliance and losing weight: the role of the service provider in health care services," *Journal of Marketing*, **68** (July), 78–91.

Dority, Bree L., Mary G. McGarvey and Patricia F. Kennedy (2010), "Marketing foods and beverages in schools: the effect of school food policy on students' overweight measures," *Journal of Public Policy & Marketing*, **29** (2), 204–18.

Edvardsson, Bo, Bård Tronvoll and Thorsten Gruber (2011), "Expanding understanding of service exchange and value co-creation: a social construction approach," *Journal of the Academy of Marketing Science*, **39** (2), 327–39.

Epstein, Marc J. and Kristi Yuthas (2012), "Scaling effective education for the poor in developing countries: a report from the field," *Journal of Public Policy & Marketing*, **31** (1), 102–14.

Franzak, Frank J., Thomas J. Smith and Christopher E. Desch (1995), "Marketing cancer care to rural residents," *Journal of Public Policy & Marketing*, **14** (1), 76–82.

Gabel, Terrance G. and Clifford D. Scott (2009), "An unsettled matter of life and death: a public policy and marketing commentary on life insurance settlement," *Journal of Public Policy & Marketing*, **28** (2), 162–74.

Gentry, James W., Patricia F. Kennedy, Katherine Paul and Ronald Paul Hill (1995), "The vulnerability of those grieving the death of a loved one: implications for public policy," *Journal of Public Policy & Marketing*, **14** (1), 128–42.

Goldberg, Marvin E. and Kunter Gunasti (2007), "Creating an environment in which youths are encouraged to eat a healthier diet," *Journal of Public Policy & Marketing*, **26** (2), 162–81.

Goldstein, Noah J., Robert B. Cialdini and Vladas Griskevicius (2008), "A room with a viewpoint: using social norms to motivate environmental conservation in hotels," *Journal of Consumer Research*, **35** (October), 472–82.

Goussinsky, Ruhama (2012), "Coping with customer aggression," *Journal of Service Management*, **23** (2), 170–96.

Grégoire, Yany, Thomas M. Tripp and Renaud Legoux (2009), "When customer love turns into lasting hate: the effects of relationship strength and time on customer revenge and avoidance," *Journal of Marketing*, **73** (November), 18–32.

Grier, Sonya A., Janell Mensinger, Shirley H. Huang, Shiriki K. Kumanyika and Nicolas Stettler (2007), "Fast-food marketing and children's fast-food consumption: exploring parents' influences in an ethnically diverse sample," *Journal of Public Policy & Marketing*, **26** (2), 221–35.

Guion, Deirdre T., Debra L. Scammon and Aberdeen Leila Borders (2007), "Weathering the storm: a social marketing perspective on disaster preparedness and response with lessons from Hurricane Katrina," *Journal of Public Policy & Marketing*, **26** (1), 20–32.

Harris, Lloyd C. and Kate L. Reynolds (2003), "The consequences of dysfunctional customer behavior," *Journal of Service Research*, **6** (2), 144–61.

Hibbert, Sally, Heidi Winklhofer and Mohamed Sobhy Temerak (2012), "Customers as resource integrators: toward a model of customer learning," *Journal of Service Research*, **15** (3), 247–61.

Hill, Ronald Paul (1994), "Bill collectors and consumers: a troublesome exchange relationship," *Journal of Public Policy & Marketing*, **13** (1), 20–35.

Hill, Ronald Paul (2002), "Service provision through public-private partnerships: an ethnography of service delivery to homeless teenagers," *Journal of Service Research*, **4** (4), 278–89.

Hill, Ronald Paul and Sandi Macan (1996), "Consumer survival on welfare with an emphasis on Medicaid and the Food Stamp Program," *Journal of Public Policy & Marketing*, **15** (1), 118–27.

Hill, Ronald Paul and Debra Lynn Stephens (1997), "Impoverished consumers and consumer behavior: the case of AFDC mothers," *Journal of Macromarketing*, **17** (2), 32–48.

Hoy, Mariea Grubbs and Joseph Phelps (2003), "Consumer privacy and security protection on church web sites: reasons for concern," *Journal of Public Policy & Marketing*, **22** (1), 58–70.

Jayanti, Rama K. and Jagdip Singh (2010), "Pragmatic learning theory: an inquiry-action framework for distributed consumer learning in online communities," *Journal of Consumer Research*, **36** (April), 1058–81.

Kang, Yong-Soon and Nancy M. Ridgway (1996), "The importance of consumer market interactions as a form of social support for elderly consumers," *Journal of Public Policy & Marketing*, **15** (1), 108–17.

Kaufman-Scarborough, Carol and Terry L. Childers (2009), "Understanding markets as online public places: insights from consumers with visual impairments," *Journal of Public Policy & Marketing*, **28** (1), 16–28.

Keller, Punam Anand, Donald R. Lehmann and Katherine J. Milligan (2009), "Effectiveness of corporate well-being programs: a meta-analysis," *Journal of Macromarketing*, **29** (3), 279–302.

Lee, Renée Gravois, Julie L. Ozanne and Ronald Paul Hill (1999), "Improving service encounters through resource sensitivity: the case of health care delivery in an Appalachian community," *Journal of Public Policy & Marketing*, **18** (2), 230–48.

Lusch, Robert F. and Stephen L. Vargo (2006), "Service-dominant logic: reactions, reflections, and refinements," *Marketing Theory*, **6** (3), 281–88.

Mason, Marlys J., Debra L. Scammon and Robert P. Huefner (2002), "Does health status

matter? Examining the experiences of the chronically ill in Medicaid managed care," *Journal of Public Policy & Marketing*, **21** (1), 53–65.
McColl-Kennedy, Janet R., Stephen L. Vargo, Tracey S. Dagger, Jillian C. Sweeney and Yasmin van Kasteren (2012), "Health care customer value cocreation practice styles," *Journal of Service Research*, **15** (4), 370–89.
Mick, David Glenn (2006), "Presidential address: meaning and mattering through transformative consumer research," in Cornelia Pechmann and Linda L. Price (eds), *Advances in Consumer Research*, vol. 33, Provo, UT: Association for Consumer Research, pp. 1–4.
Mick, David Glen, Simone Pettigrew, Cornelia Pechmann and Julie L. Ozanne (2012), "Origins, qualities, and envisionments of transformative consumer research," in David Glen Mick, Simone Pettigrew, Cornelia Pechmann and Julie L. Ozanne (eds), *Transformative Consumer Research: For Personal and Collective Well-being*, New York: Routledge, pp. 3–24.
Mittelstaedt, John D., Charles R. Duke and Robert A. Mittelstaedt (2009), "Health care choices in the United States and the constrained consumer: a marketing systems perspective on access and assortment in health care," *Journal of Public Policy & Marketing*, **28** (1), 95–101.
Moisio, Risto and Mariam Beruchashvili (2010), "Questing for well-being at Weight Watchers: the role of the spiritual-therapeutic model in a support group," *Journal of Consumer Research*, **36** (February), 857–75.
Moussa, Salim and Mourad Touzani (2010), "Ranking marketing journals using the Google Scholar-based hg-index," *Journal of Informetrics*, **4** (1), 107–17.
Morrin, Maureen, Susan M. Broniarczyk and J. Jeffrey Inman (2012), "Plan format and participation in 401(k) plans: the moderating role of investor knowledge," *Journal of Public Policy & Marketing*, **31** (2), 254–68.
Navarro-Martinez, Daniel, Linda Court Salisbury, Katherine N. Lemon, Neil Stewart, William J. Matthews and Adam J.L. Harris (2011), "Minimum required payment and supplemental information disclosure effects on consumer debt repayment decisions," *Journal of Marketing Research*, **48**, special issue, 60–77.
Ostrom, Amy L., Mary Jo Bitner, Stephen W. Brown, Kevin A. Burkhard, Michael Goul, Vicki Smith-Daniels, Haluk Demirkan and Elliot Rabinovich (2010), "Moving forward and making a difference: research priorities for the science of service," *Journal of Service Research*, **13** (1), 4–36.
Ozanne, Julie L. and Laurel Anderson (2010), "Community action research," *Journal of Public Policy & Marketing*, **29** (1), 123–37.
Ozanne, Julie L., Ronald Paul Hill and Newell D. Wright (1998), "Juvenile delinquents' use of consumption as cultural resistance: implications for juvenile reform programs and public policy," *Journal of Public Policy & Marketing*, **17** (2), 185–96.
Palmer, Todd Starr, Mary Beth Pinto and Diane H. Parente (2001), "College students' credit card debt and the role of parental involvement: implications for public policy," *Journal of Public Policy & Marketing*, **20** (1), 105–13.
Peñaloza, Lisa and Michelle Barnhart (2011), "Living U.S. capitalism: the normalization of credit/debt," *Journal of Consumer Research*, **38** (December), 743–62.
Polsa, Pia and Xiucheng Fan (2011), "Globalization of local retailing: threat or opportunity?: the case of food retailing in Guilin, China," *Journal of Macromarketing*, **31** (3), 291–311.
Prahalad, C.K. and Venkatram Ramaswamy (2000), "Co-opting customer competence," *Harvard Business Review*, **78** (1), 79–87.
Press, Melea and Eric J. Arnould (2009), "Constraints on sustainable energy consumption: market system and public policy challenges and opportunities," *Journal of Public Policy & Marketing*, **28** (1), 102–13.
Price, Linda L. and Eric Arnould (1999), "Commercial friendships: service provider-client relationships in context," *Journal of Marketing*, **63** (October), 38–56.
Rosenbaum, Mark S. (2006), "Exploring the social supportive role of third places in consumers' lives," *Journal of Service Research*, **9** (1), 59–72.

Rosenbaum, Mark S. (2008), "Return on community for consumers and service establishments," *Journal of Service Research*, **11** (2), 179–96.
Rosenbaum, Mark S. and Carolyn A. Massiah (2007), "When customers receive support from other customers: exploring the influence of intercustomer social support on customer voluntary performance," *Journal of Service Research*, **9** (3), 257–70.
Rosenbaum, Mark S., Canan Corus, Amy L. Ostrom, Laurel Anderson, Raymond P. Fisk, Andrew S. Gallan, Mario Giraldo, Martin Mende, Mark Mulder, Steven W. Rayburn, Kunio Shirahada and Jerome D. Williams (2011), "Conceptualization and aspirations of transformative service research," *Journal of Research for Consumers*, **19**, 1–6.
Rosenbaum, Mark S., James Ward, Beth A. Walker and Amy L. Ostrom (2007), "A cup of coffee with a dash of love: an investigation of commercial social support and third-place attachment," *Journal of Service Research*, **10** (1), 43–59.
Roth, Martin S. (1994), "Enhancing consumer involvment in health care: the dynamics of control, empowerment, and trust," *Journal of Public Policy & Marketing*, **13** (1), 115–32.
Samli, A. Coskun (2010), "The medical services paradox in the U.S. market system: the desperate need for improvement," *Journal of Macromarketing*, **30** (4), 398–401.
Scammon, Debra L., Punam A. Keller, Pia A. Albinsson, Shalini Bahl, Jesse R. Catlin, Kelly L. Haws, Jeremy Kees, Tracey King, Elizabeth Gelfand Miller, Ann M. Mirabito, Paula C. Peter and Robert M. Schindler (2011), "Transforming consumer health, " *Journal of Public Policy & Marketing*, **30** (1), 14–22.
Scammon, Debra L., Lawrence B. Li and Scott D. Williams (1995), "Insuring the supply of providers for the medically underserved: marketing and public policy issues," *Journal of Public Policy & Marketing*, **14** (1), 35–47.
Schwartz, Janet, Mary Frances Luce and Dan Ariely (2011), "Are consumers too trusting? The effects of relationships with expert advisers," *Journal of Marketing Research*, **48**, special issue, 163–74.
Sheehan, Kim Bartel (2005), "In poor health: an assessment of privacy policies at direct-to-consumer web sites," *Journal of Public Policy & Marketing*, **24** (2), 273–83.
Singh, Jagdip, Jerry R. Goolsby and Gary K. Rhoads (1994), "Behavioral and psychological consequences of boundary spanning burnout for customer service representatives," *Journal of Marketing Research*, **31** (November), 558–69.
Spohrer Jim, Paul P. Maglio, John Bailey and Daniel Gruhl (2007), "Steps toward a science of service systems," *Computer*, **40** (1), 71–77.
Street, Brian (2001), *Literacy and Development: Ethnographic Perspectives*, London: Routledge.
Suh, Taewon, Mark B. Houston, Steven M. Barney and Ik-Whan G. Kwon (2010), "The impact of mission fulfillment on the internal audience: psychological job outcomes in a services setting," *Journal of Service Research*, **14** (1), 76–92.
Talukdar, Debabrata, Sumila Gulyani and Lawrence F. Salmen (2005), "Customer orientation in the context of development projects: insights from the World Bank," *Journal of Public Policy & Marketing*, **24** (1), 100–111.
Tansik, David A. and Robert Routhieaux (1999), "Customer stress-relaxation: the impact of music in a hospital waiting room," *International Journal of Service Industry Management*, **10** (1), 68–81.
Vargo, Stephen L. and Robert F. Lusch (2004), "Evolving to a new dominant logic for marketing," *Journal of Marketing*, **68** (January), 1–17.
Vargo, Stephen L., Robert F. Lusch and Melissa Archpru Akaka (2010), "Advancing service science with service-dominant logic: clarifications and conceptual development," in Paul P. Maglio, Cheryl A. Kieliszewski and James C. Spohrer (eds), *Handbook of Service Science: Research and Innovations in the Service Economy*, New York: Springer Science+Business Media, pp. 133–56.
Varman, Rohit and Ram Manohar Vikas (2007), "Rising markets and failing health: an inquiry into subaltern health care consumption under neoliberalism," *Journal of Macromarketing*, **27** (2), 162–72.
Viswanathan, Madhu and Roland Gau (2005), "Functional illiteracy and nutritional educa-

tion in the United States: a research-based approach to the development of nutritional education materials for functionally illiterate consumers," *Journal of Macromarketing*, **25** (2), 187–201.
Viswanathan, Madhu, José Antonio Rosa and Julie A. Ruth (2010), "Exchanges in marketing systems: the case of subsistence consumer–merchants in Chennai, India," *Journal of Marketing*, **74** (May), 1–17.
Viswanathan, Madhubalan, Srinivas Sridharan, Roland Gau and Robin Ritchie (2009), "Designing marketplace literacy education in resource-constrained contexts: implications for public policy and marketing," *Journal of Public Policy & Marketing*, **28** (1), 85–94.
Wang, Wenbo, Hean Tat Keh and Lisa E. Bolton (2010), "Lay theories of medicine and a healthy lifestyle," *Journal of Consumer Research*, **37** (June), 80–97.
Wong, Nancy and Tracey King (2008), "The cultural construction of risk understandings through illness narratives," *Journal of Consumer Research*, **34** (Februrary), 579–94.
Yagil, Dana (2006), "The relationship of service provider power motivation, empowerment and burnout to customer satisfaction," *International Journal of Service Industry Management*, **17** (3), 258–70.
Yagil, Dana, Gil Luria and Iddo Gal (2008), "Stressors and resources in customer service roles: exploring the relationship between core self-evaluations and burnout," *International Journal of Service Industry Management*, **19** (5), 575–95.
Yavas, Ugur, Emin Babakus and Osman M. Karatepe (2008), "Attitudinal and behavioral consequences of work-family conflict and family-work conflict: does gender matter?" *International Journal of Service Industry Management*, **19** (1), 7–31.
Zeithaml, Valarie A., Mary Jo Bitner and Dwayne E. Gremler (2013), *Services Marketing: Integrating Customer Focus Across the Firm*, 6th edn, New York: McGraw-Hill/Irwin.
Zhu, Rui (Juliet), Utpal M. Dholakia, Xinlei (Jack) Chen and René Algesheimer (2012), "Does online community participation foster risky financial behavior?" *Journal of Marketing Research*, **49** (June), 394–407.

25 Creating social value through citizen co-creation

P.K. Kannan

1 INTRODUCTION

Government *of the people, by the people, and for the people*, shall not perish from the earth.

(Abe Lincoln, 1863)

Consider the following reports: "Malmo, Sweden, an industrial city in which the economy crashed and burned in the 1990s, has reinvented itself as a pioneer in sustainable development as an Ekostaden, or eco-city" (Bhalla 2011). This initiative involved "widespread solicitation and implementation of citizens' unique ideas," "government-encouraged innovation from architects and planners to enable 100% renewable energy" with citizens taking initiatives to insulate their own homes, plant herb and vegetable gardens to make their environment better. Similarly, the city of Curitiba in Brazil has developed a holistic urban plan to impact the environment in the area's green space, city transportation and recycling, which relies significantly on citizens taking their own initiatives (Green 2011). Finally, parents at Burning Tree Elementary School in Bethesda, Maryland, contribute hundreds of hours every year to help teachers and administrators in the school in co-creating and implementing lessons, not only for their own school but also for a sister school, Broad Acres Elementary, located in an economically disadvantaged neighborhood where parents do not have the time or resources to volunteer. These illustrations all make the above statement of Lincoln come alive. Citizens all over the world want to get more involved in co-producing and co-creating services, regardless of whether these are services provided by governments or others, in setting the objectives, defining the outcomes, and shaping the services to their own and fellow citizens' needs and wants.

As the above examples highlight, citizens do not view such initiatives as one-time, feel-good volunteering events, rather they want to get involved in co-creating social value on an ongoing basis and being presented with the opportunity to shape government services and social value on a continual basis. This desire on the part of citizens has become stronger with the advent of Web 2.0+ technologies, social networks, network-based service provision by government, ubiquitous, on-demand access to communication channels to interact with the government, and an overall increase in education levels and training opportunities for citizens. So, the central question this chapter examines is, "How can citizens create value through co-creation of services so that they are able to leverage this process for social welfare and service efficiency?" This is a particularly timely question to ask as governments at all levels are increasingly facing budget cuts and financial crises, as the economy struggles to move on after the recessionary impact.

The world is interconnected much more than ever before, with geographical and social boundaries rapidly disappearing. These changes have been fueled by rapid advancement in information and communication technology (ICT), opening up new possibilities and opportunities for active participation in Web communities, social networks, and increasing the awareness of issues facing societies, and providing a channel for action to change societies and the political landscape. Citizens want greater transparency and control over governance and service provision from governing agencies. The trend of providing self-service options by firms in both public and private sectors by taking advantage of these developments in ICT has, in part, led to this desire on the part of citizens and customers for greater control. However, at the same time, the greater connectivity, awareness of economic disparity, and changing social landscape has led to increased interest in social value creation, working for altruistic causes, doing good for others, all with a nonprofit motive. Social value creation has become more popular across societies, and citizens have been examining creative ways to implement it. Citizens now want to be more frequently involved and treated as active partners in initiatives that are focused on helping specific communities and citizen groups—especially in initiatives that affect their families, communities, and societies. There is also an increased perception among citizen groups that government agencies typically underestimate their willingness to help others. While they see other nonprofit, nongovernmental agencies taking an active role in leveraging public effort in causes that benefit communities, there is a perception that government could do more in similar ways.

Governments all over the world are under increasing budget pressures, which has made the possibilities of designing creative solutions for service provision using input from citizens all the more important. Designing such solutions that leverage citizens' desire for control over how service decisions are made (à la self-service) and how resources are allocated can lead to citizen empowerment. This could, in turn, lead to them contributing more of their own resources across many dimensions—expertise, effort, money, time, and motivation. There is increasing evidence and realization based on private sector experiences that such co-creation initiatives can lead to improved outcomes. In the public sector, in the case of health services, crime prevention and social programs, it can be argued that the intended benefits of such initiatives can never be fully achieved without co-creation processes. The value that citizens can bring to co-creation processes can be significant, which is often not measured or recognized by service providers. Additionally, the outcome is not just in economic terms but also in social dimension. Input of citizen resources through co-creation processes can often have a leveraging impact on the resources that government agencies put in, leading to improved social and economic value for money invested in such initiatives.

Realizing the potential value of co-creation, businesses and governments have already started many initiatives to leverage customer/citizen input in various ways. Customers provide design ideas for products and services; citizens are actively involved in designing educational policies and schools for their cities and regions; citizens help improve their neighborhoods through the use of online tools to create community awareness and create neighborhood watch programs. Some of these efforts can be considered pilots and experimental, but these are clear indications that co-creation is taking root in both public and private sectors. So, the time is right for understanding in a more nuanced manner the nature of co-creation activities and their suitability for various governmental applications. Understanding how such initiatives can lead to strengthening the bond between citizens and governments can lead to increased trust in the government. It is also important to understand the perceptions that citizens have regarding their involvement in co-creation initiatives and how to take these insights into account in designing co-creation initiatives. Such an understanding can help leverage the emerging social trends by citizens, leading to increased civic engagement in such citizen groups and making governments more relevant.

Organizations in both private and public sectors face a challenge in how they can effectively harness the potential of co-creation amid an environment that is constantly evolving. This evolution is not just limited to the technology dimension, where the changes are very fast paced indeed, but is also in the organizational and social dimensions.

It is clear that in all dimensions there is a shift of control from firms and institutions to citizens and customers. Thus, co-creation initiatives would necessarily have to address this shift in control from agencies to users. This shift may be accomplished using intermediaries. The design of services and the model for allocation of resources, measurement and accountability models have to be transformed. Collectively, this is a challenging problem to take on for government, quasi-government and nonprofit agencies. This chapter aims to address this issue through two specific objectives:

1. Understanding co-creation as a concept, process, and strategy and the implications for its use in public and private sectors; and,
2. Developing a framework for applications of co-creation in the government and nonprofit contexts, and identifying co-creation technologies and processes and measurement issues.

Successful implementation of co-creation initiatives requires an understanding of the concept and process of co-creation and differentiating it from other related concepts such as co-production, which I discuss in the next section. Since technological development plays a crucial role in enabling the co-creation process, I also examine the opportunities created by technology.

In Section 3, I propose a framework for identifying the most fertile application areas for co-creation, based on a risk versus value assessment, as well as nature of service co-creation process versus time frame for service outcome. Examples of co-creation initiatives will be discussed, along with co-creation processes and technologies required for implementation. In Section 4, I conclude with a discussion on challenges in designing co-creation and in developing metrics for evaluating progress on such initiatives.

2 UNDERSTANDING CO-CREATION

The term "co-creation" evolved in the last decade of the twentieth century with a realization that the value that is created in a firm–customer interaction is largely a "shared" value creation, where both the firm and the customer are actively involved in the value-creation process. This was contrasted with the model of value creation where the firm created value through a product or service and the customer was a passive user of the product or service provided by the firm. There is an explicit recognition in the co-creation of value perspective that the customer has competence that can contribute to the value that is being co-created, and the higher the level of competence the more the contribution of the customer to the co-creation process and the value that is generated (Prahalad and Ramaswamy 2000). This perspective can be easily understood through an example of self-service systems, although the notion of co-creation goes much further than self-service. The value that is created in the vehicle registration process at the Department of Motor Vehicles (DMV) can be accomplished through an employee providing service at a counter in a face-to-face setting, with the customer being largely passive in this process. There is the usual wait time for the customer, as efficiency considerations dictate that the employee be busy at all times. However, in a self-service kiosk a customer can cut down the wait time and self-process the registration without the need for a DMV employee to oversee the process. This, of course, calls for competence on the part of the customer to operate the kiosk independently and perform the process. More value is created in the self-service encounter as the customer's wait time is reduced and the process rendered more efficient, while the DMV benefits through elimination of the more expensive effort of a DMV employee—the value co-created benefits both parties in the transaction. Thus, the co-creation value perspective would suggest that value will be increasingly co-created by an organization and the customer rather than being created entirely within the organization.

While the notion of co-creation of value is more easily understood in the context of service provision, it applies equally to the goods and products context. For example, Vargo and Lusch (2004), using a service-dominant perspective, view goods and products as just the means of transferring the opportunity to create value to customers, and it is customers who create the value they derive from the product. That is, customers are always co-creators of value, irrespective of whether the exchange involves products or services. This is a stark shift from a goods-dominant perspective, which views customers as totally separated from the value-offering process because goods and products creation requires maximum efficiency, and this precludes involvement of customers in the goods creation stage. Vargo and Lusch (2004) argue that the service-dominant perspective leads to more opportunities for value creation, and customers play a central role in this value co-creation process. Gronroos (2011) and Edvardsson et al. (2011) have extended their own arguments for a slightly different perspective. In the following sections, we discuss the notion of co-creation of value, differentiating it from self-service and co-production, and how technology plays a key role in creating opportunities for co-creation. In the discussion, it will become clear what the key characteristics of co-creation are as well as the implications for implementation in the public sector context.

2.1 Self-service versus Co-creation

The standard model of self-service is one where the customer or the citizen inputs his or her own effort in a setting that allows the service to be performed with minimal intervention from the service provider. Thus, the self-service checkout in a grocery store or a self-service kiosk for motor vehicle registration allows customers to input their own effort for the service they receive (creation of value). Self-service in a standard mode can be considered as co-creation of value with customers providing their own effort along with the effort input by the firm (usually through technological means), a setting where the potential of co-creation is limited. Specifically, there is limited opportunity for customization in the design of the self-service. Recently, there have been efforts to include a customization component in the design of the service or product. In the realm of product, mass customization is a trend that allows customers to create the design of the product they would like to purchase. For example, Nike was one of the first product companies to offer a highly visual application called Nike ID, a "build-your-own shoe" application on its website, which surpassed $100 million in sales for 2010. Messenger bag and carry-on bag marketer Timbuk2 (www.timbuk2.com) allows customers to design their own bags and order them online.

The realm of self-service, therefore, is characterized by customers and citizens providing input to the value creation process in terms of effort or design suggestions, and the benefit derived is entirely for the individual interacting with the organization in the self-service setting, as shown in Figure 25.1.

As seen in Figure 25.1, the realm of self-service is limited to the customer/citizen and organization interaction. It does not extend beyond to

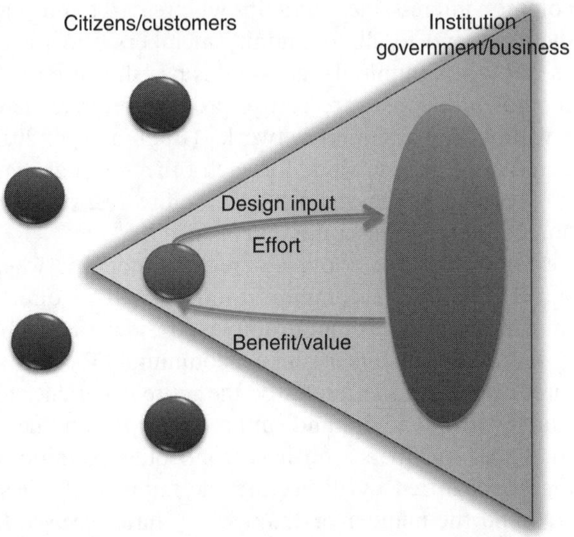

Figure 25.1 Realm of self-service

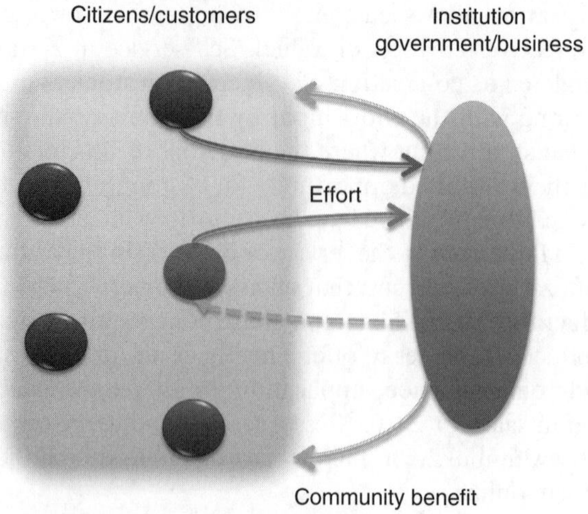

Figure 25.2 Customer/citizen service for common good

other customers or citizens. The co-creation notion extends these benefits to community members. Take, for example, Proctor & Gamble's (P&G) Vocalpoint community, a network of influential mothers. In this community, mothers share their experiences using P&G's new products with other members of the community who are also mothers. Members share information of common interest, ideas and tips with regard to the new products and the benefits extend to all community members. Proctor & Gamble, too, benefits from the community, as analysis has shown that "in markets where Vocalpoint influencers are active, product revenues have reached twice those without a Vocalpoint network" (Bughin et al. 2010). In this example, customers co-create value for each other through a mechanism (community) provided by the organization. Figure 25.2 captures this idea of co-creation of value for the community.

Another extension of the above co-creation model is when customers contribute effort for the common good as well as directly helping other community members. As an example, consider the TurboTax Live Community of Intuit, a customer support community for its financial and tax return products. In this community, the more experienced customers co-create value by giving advice and support to those who need help (see Figure 25.3). Those members who have contributed significantly to the community get recognized by displaying the number of questions they have answered and the number of thanks they have received from other members. McKinsey's estimates that when customer communities handle an issue, the per-contact cost can be as low as 10 percent of the cost to

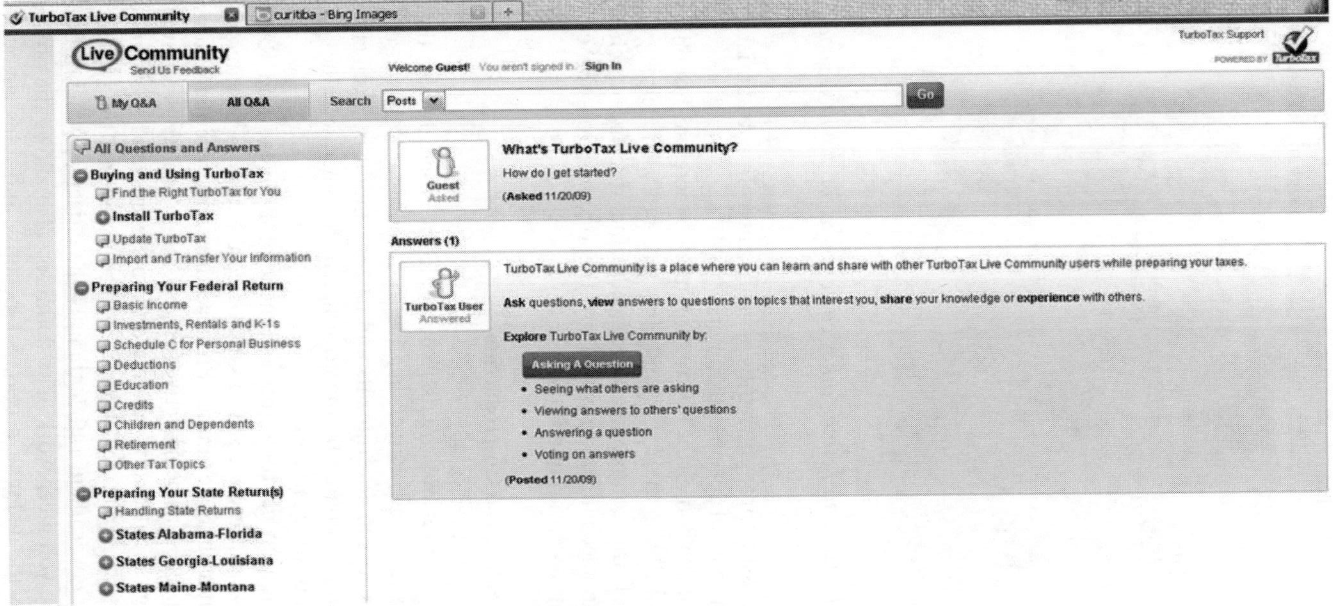

Figure 25.3 TurboTax Live Community

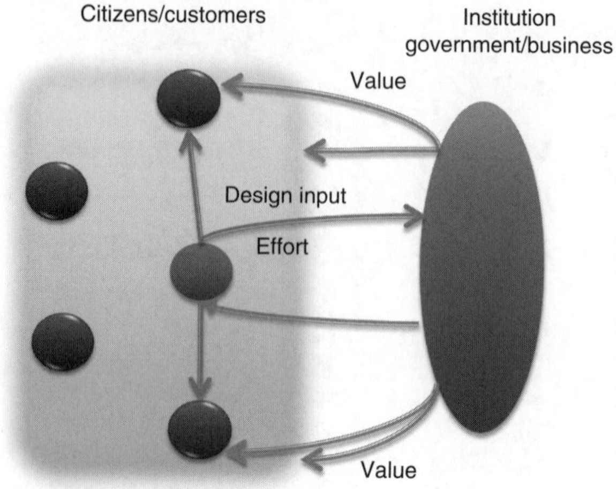

Figure 25.4 Citizens helping other citizens and for common good

resolve the issue through traditional call centers, a substantial saving for Intuit in the cost of serving customers.

The full extension of the co-creation model, therefore, not only includes customers helping the community overall, but also helping individual members of the community specifically and directly, which could be beyond the mechanism provided by the organization for community service. This is captured in Figure 25.4.

2.2 Co-creation and Co-production

In light of the previous discussions, we define co-creation in the government context as: an active, creative and social process, based on collaboration between governments and citizens and/or between citizens and citizens, that is initiated by the government to generate value for citizens through innovative services.

This definition captures the sentiment of Prahalad and Ramaswamy (2000, 2004) and the latest thinking of co-creation in private-sector, for-profit businesses (for example, Promisecorp.com). The definition characterizes the process as being active (as opposed to passive), creative in terms of the design input that is generated from citizens, and social in terms of citizen-citizen interactions. Also, it is to be noted that the process is initiated by the government rather than by the citizens—which differentiates it from pure volunteer work. The definition also allows the process to be governed by the dialogue, access, risk-benefits, and transparency (DART) model of Prahalad and Ramaswamy. This model specifies that dialogue between customers/citizens and firm/government is a necessary precondition for any co-creation process to be initiated. This dialogue not only encourages sharing of views but also could lead to "new levels of understanding" between the citizens and the government, which is necessary for the creative component of the process to take hold. Dialogue cannot occur without access and transparency, while co-creation involves sharing of not only the benefits between the citizens and governments, but also the risks involved. This has important implications in the context of government-citizen interactions, and we will focus on this later in the chapter. The important point to take away here is that co-creation, although initiated by the government, is a two-way process.

It is useful to distinguish between co-creation and another related concept of "co-production," which has gained much traction in the U.K., especially in public sector applications. In the context of government services, an excellent report by Boyle and Harris (2009) defines co-production as a "new way of thinking about public services and which has the potential to deliver a paradigm shift in providing services such as health, education, policing, etc., to make them more effective, efficient, and sustainable." The notion of co-production puts the emphasis on "production," and the resources need to enable the production of services. Obviously, part of the input—resources—comes from the citizens and for the service contexts that Boyle and Harris focus on—social, education, and health services—the resource input from citizens plays an important role in improving efficiency and the outcome of these services. In a recent article Lehrer et al. (2012) provide a contingent view of co-production within the framework of co-creation.

The relationship between co-creation and co-production can be explained using Figure 25.5. The production of product/service focused on customers or citizens requires effort. This effort can be shared between the firm/organization and the customer/citizen. Co-production assumes that effort is shared, which is the case with many of the social and health service initiatives in the government context. Co-creation focuses on the value that is created and stresses that the customer/citizen is always a

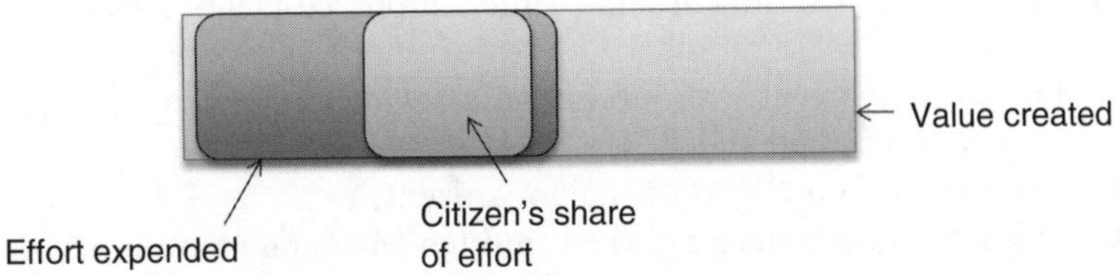

Figure 25.5 Relationship between value and effort in co-creation

co-creator of value, even if co-production is absent (that is, the customer does not provide any input in the production of the product/service). For example, consider Lego blocks produced by the manufacturer and sold to customers. Customers may not input any effort in producing the toy, yet the value in use of the product is co-created. Depending on the competence and creativity of the user, the value derived by the customer could be different among customers.

The relationship between value and effort highlights the characteristics of the co-creation process on which we are focusing:

- The extent of value derived by citizens and the community depends on their competence to some extent, even if a firm or a government entity expends all the effort in creating a citizen service. Value is defined from the perspective of citizens and is outcome-based.
- When citizens expend their own effort in creating value along with the government entity, there is an opportunity for reducing the input by the government entity. This could lead to efficiency gains as compared to regular citizen service provision. This is similar to the gains experienced by Intuit when they host the TurboTax Live Community.

It might be very tempting for a government entity to focus on the efficiency gains and reduction in input resources; however, the above also implies that efficiency does not automatically mean effectiveness. This is because value is defined from the citizens' perspective and not from the perspective of resources expended. Too much focus on resources and co-production might take attention away from the outcome, or value. As Boyle and Harris (2009) explain, the focus of the co-production should be on maximizing positive outcomes, which are defined in terms of public value, rather than focusing on reducing costs. Also, in many public service contexts such as welfare, health, and citizen safety, prevention is a greater value, which can be attained at much lower effort levels both on the part of the government entity and citizens.

A recent article by Hoyer et al. (2010) highlights the benefits and value realized by both firms and customers in their co-creation initiatives. Extending the analogy to the government-citizen interactions, co-creation views:

- citizens as partners, resources and assets who can provide input to service provision;
- value is based on the outcome for citizens;
- value creation is accomplished through leveraging citizen networks; and,
- value creation is accomplished through citizen reciprocal relationships.

2.3 Impact of Technology on Co-creation

With technological advances, the power of the traditional models of co-creation increases significantly. Take a very simple service application that citizens face frequently, for instance—the toll charged for using certain roads. The traditional model of service—the manned toll booth—requires vehicles to stop and pay the toll to the person in the booth. This is the most expensive form of service, because it is labor intensive, and the speed of service depends on how well trained the service personnel are. The value for the citizens based on the outcome is a quick transaction with minimum wait time. The self-service form of this toll collection process is the traditional hopper system for dropping the coins or a credit-card swipe system which requires drivers to pay the toll themselves without the help of service personnel. This reduces both the resources and effort on the part of the service provider, as the effort is now co-produced; however, the value for a driver—service speed—depends on the efficiency of the other drivers ahead in line. In the traditional manned booth the variability in service due to the service provider's efficiency and the drivers' efficiency is now replaced by just the efficiency of the other drivers in the self-service lane. The self-service model assumes that the drivers are competent enough to perform the self-service task efficiently. However, if a driver is not competent enough in a self-service lane he could delay and inconvenience others in the lane. Thus, the success of self-service technology depends on how it is designed and also on how the process is set up in such a way that the competent citizens/customers self-select themselves for self-service. If the process is not able to do this, the value proposition for citizens does not improve, even though the service provider is able to reduce their costs.

Technological advances can provide paradigm shifts in self-service situations. The self-service example in the above case can be vastly improved by the use of radio frequency identification (RFID) systems, on which EZ-Pass systems work. By having the chips installed on vehicles, drivers no longer have to stop to pay tolls, they are charged electronically, the effort on the part of service provider is minimized, and the effort on the part of the driver is negligible, other than putting the sticker with the chip on the vehicle or ensuring the EZ-Pass transmitter is in the vehicle. In this situation, there is no wait time, drivers are the not at the mercy of other drivers who may be less competent in using self-service, congestion is minimized, and all drivers in the community benefit (that is, value is created not just for the self but also for others in the whole community). Thus, technology creates a "super-service" (Campbell et al. 2011) by completely transforming a service situation. This paradigm shift is significant.

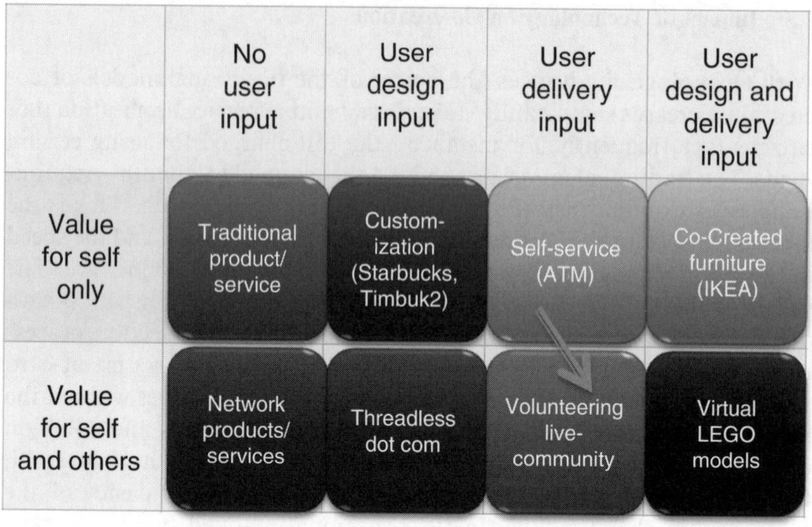

Figure 25.6 Co-creation matrix and impact of technology

In going from a self-service to a super-service context, the variability is that the service provider is eliminated, variability in customer competence or skill-level is no longer an issue, co-production efforts are minimal on the part of customers, and the whole community derives value. It is on such technological advances that the future potential of co-creation rests. By making use of technology in a creative way, this potential can be made a reality.

Figure 25.6 presents the co-creation matrix, which highlights the two important dimensions on which co-creation initiatives can be classified: focus on value creation (self versus self and others), degree of user input (no input to design input, delivery input, and design and delivery input).

The top row of the matrix is characterized by value creation for self only. The case of no user input corresponds to the traditional product/service transaction model, where input is only from the firm or service provider. Input of use design leads to the customization model—the example of Timbuk2, where users can create their own design, or in Starbucks where users can create their own designer drink. When the user inputs just effort and no design, this corresponds to a pure self-service situation—a bank automated teller machine (ATM), for example. Finally, when the user inputs both design and delivery, as in the case of co-created IKEA furniture, we have a very significant involvement of the user in creating value (see Ford et al. 2012).

The second row of the matrix is characterized by value creation for self and others. The no user input corresponds to the network products/services case—as in a web-based video game service where, as new users enter the network, the value for existing users increase, or a telephone network where the value of network increases as more users join in. Threadless.com is a perfect example of a co-creation model where users can create new designs on T-shirts and purchase them for themselves as well as make the designs available for others to use. When users input their own designs, the variety and assortment of products increases, which creates additional value for all customers. When users input service delivery (without any design input) it corresponds to a volunteering situation (TurboTax Live Community, for example, or a parent volunteering at an elementary school) where value is co-created and it benefits all in the community. Finally, when users input both design and delivery (Virtual Lego models created online by customers that benefits all customers), we have the highest form of co-creation.

The impact of technology on co-creation is to move the co-creation model from benefiting only the self to benefiting both self and others in the community. The super-service example in the case of toll roads exemplifies it. With the EZ-Pass system, not only does the individual driver derive the benefit of a superior service, but also all drivers benefit as wait time is eliminated in such a system. Thus, technology moves the co-creation for self (self-service toll booth) to co-creation for all. It is powerful advances such as these examples that can make the potential of co-creation become a reality.

It is also important to note that for the above potential of co-creation to become reality there need to be catalysts. In the toll collection example, the greater the number of people to adopt the EZ Pass system, the more all motorists will benefit. However, if the number of motorists adopting the EZ Pass system is low, then the service provider still has to have the regular coin-based system and manned booths, as is the case with many toll systems. In this case, segmenting the motorists and providing special lanes for them to pass through provides superior service to those who are willing to adopt the technology-based system. In using technology to enable co-creation opportunities in the governmental context, this insight needs to be accounted for in the design of the initiatives. The performance of the initiative and the advantages derived is a function of the number of citizens adopting technology. So appropriate incentives for adoption need to be made available, and processes to segment citizens based on their needs and wants should be put in place. The coming sections will focus on these issues in more detail.

3 LEVERAGING CO-CREATION FOR SOCIAL VALUE

In order to understand how co-creation might work and create social value in public sector and non-profit settings, let us consider some real examples of co-creation initiatives that create social value. These examples will help us to better understand the proposed framework for co-creation and utilize it effectively for designing such initiatives.

- *The Library of Congress* is using co-creation to classify and categorize content to help in appropriate retrieval of information for all users. It is in the process of implementing several pilot projects which would allow users of its information to tag the content and provide metadata information using "social bookmarking." The pilot projects have three specific goals: (1) to provide the library's public domain content in user community environments; (2) to encourage users to co-create by generating tags for the content they read, which helps other users as well as the library; and (3) to create folksonomy to supplement expert-generated taxonomy. After verification procedures to ensure the integrity of the content, the library plans to display such user-generated content on its website so other users may take advantage of it (Novak and Springer 2007).
- *The Youth Court of Washington*, in the District of Columbia (www.youthcourtofdc.org), has put co-creation into action by designating first-time non-violent offenders between the ages of 12 and 17 to serve as the jury in the Youth Court, who then try other offenders that come up before them (Rosenberg 2011). This keeps the first-time offenders out of the formal juvenile justice system and puts them to work, making the co-creation (of justice) experience into something positive and helping them to get back on the right track. The co-creation experience lowers the probability of recidivism, helps the offenders to negotiate and communicate better, and makes them more responsible for their actions. The Youth Court system has been fairly successful. A recent survey showed that 77 percent of the youth graduated from high school and 43 percent of those went on to study in colleges, and the recidivism rate of 11 percent was much lower than that of the formal juvenile system (Rosenberg 2011).
- *Keyring*, a U.K.-based community organization (www.keyring.org), helps citizens with mental and physical disabilities to share their skills and talents for the benefit of everyone in the community. The focus is on ensuring that the community members have the right to live independently and enabling them to make choices about how

and where they live their lives. The community members are organized into networks, with each network consisting of a volunteer who lives in the community, knows the members, sees them regularly and helps them to make useful links with other members in the community. The members work on varied projects that involve helping to save lives of people in emergency situations to running campaigns for street lights and neighborhood improvements. The member networks are also supported by community support workers and supported live-in managers, funded by Keyring.

- *Expert Patient Program* is another U.K.-based co-creation initiative (www.expertpatients.co.uk), which provides peer support that enables patients to contribute their expertise to one another. The aim of the program is to help patients with chronic or long-term health conditions to build self-confidence in themselves through a series of six-week courses. The topics of these courses range from healthy eating to dealing with pain and feelings of depression and self-help techniques. The courses are delivered by trained tutors who have the same conditions as the patients. The aim of the program is to help patients to take more responsibility for managing their own health and to cooperate with healthcare professionals, which leads to positive, manageable outcomes. The program covers about 17.5 million patients with long-term health conditions such as arthritis, asthma, diabetes and multiple sclerosis (Horne and Shirley 2009).
- *Consulting Canadians*: the Canadian Government provides an online single-point access to its citizens wishing to provide their input on any matter of government policy and any actions being contemplated by the any government agency or department. These "consultations," as they are called, are listed by each agency or department at the www.consultingcanadians.gc.ca website indicating the dates of consultation—when citizens can provide their input—and the progress on each consultation. The consultations are updated on a regular basis by each agency and department and provide easy access to citizens to provide their "design" input on any action listed at the website.
- *The New South Wales Education Department* in Australia undertook a strategic planning exercise in 2007 for the design of its education services for the Tamworth region that exemplifies a co-creation exercise by soliciting significant input from the stakeholders such as teachers, students and parents, and local government planners (Holmes 2011). The interaction among stakeholders was facilitated by a third-party independent agent, who ensured the inclusiveness and deliberation of all stakeholders in the process. The process

itself involved multiple sessions with students, parents and teachers, workshops, deliberation forums with citizens acting as a jury, briefings with interest groups and the Education Department, with the output of the engagement communicated through varied local media. The process resulted in 58 recommendations being made to the Education Department, with consensus on a significant number of them. This was accomplished through a process that ensured the local community had an active and significant input in the design of the education initiative that would impact the local community for years to come.

- *The United States Small Business Administration*'s website and community www.business.gov features online tools and resources to engage and facilitate conversation between the small business community and all levels of government.

> The small business community benefits from expanded access to other small business owners and experts who can help answer their questions. The community facilitates and expedites the exchange of information between a business owner and a wide range of resources including other small business owners, intermediaries representing small business, and federal, state, and local government employees. Additionally, the government gains very valuable input from the customers it serves so that resources and policy can best help the small business community thrive and grow.
>
> (www.whitehouse.gov/open/innovations/Business)

- *The United States Patent and Trademark Office (USPTO)* has embarked on a co-creation initiative by enlisting public help in reviewing patent applications and allowing the public to examine the patent applications and provide input of prior examples. This initiative is called Peer-to-Patent: Community Patent Review Pilot, and was launched in 2007 to allow the USPTO to reduce its backlog of reviews through community involvement in the patent examination process. It is an excellent example of how co-creation through a community network can help government agencies be more efficient and effective (Deloitte 2008).
- *The Harlem Children's Zone* (HCZ) program in New York City is an excellent example of a sustained co-creation effort in a social application arena focusing on the well-being and development of children. The two guiding principles of the program are: (1) to help children "in a sustained way, starting as early in their lives as possible, and (2) to create a critical mass of adults around them who understand what it takes to help children succeed" (www.hcz.org/about-us/the-hcz-

project). The co-creation effort involves professionals, volunteers, public servants and working local citizens—who are parents and adults—to impact the health and educational outcomes for children living in Harlem in a positive manner.

> Harlem Children's Zone Project is a unique, holistic approach to rebuilding a community so that its children can stay on track through college and go on to the job market. The goal is to create a "tipping point" in the neighborhood so that children are surrounded by an enriching environment of college-oriented peers and supportive adults, a counterweight to "the street" and a toxic popular culture that glorifies misogyny and anti-social behavior.

The program supports parents' classes, prenatal care, schools, and university preparation classes. The impact of the program has been very positive and hailed as a miracle in a *New York Times* article (Brooks 2009).

3.1 A Framework for Co-creation

The examples in the preceding sections provide the breadth of co-creation initiatives that are possible within the public sector settings. They cover diverse programs—services for businesses, social service, health service, crime prevention, information service—focusing on individual citizens to small and large businesses. The nature of service co-creation process also varies from being purely transaction oriented (for example, Small Business Administration business.gov)—where citizens co-create service that has a short-term and immediate outcome—to relational oriented (for example, Keyring's community for disabled members or the Harlem Children's Zone) where the co-created service outcome is long-term oriented, with the service value derived going well into the future. The other examples fall somewhere within the spectrum.

Figure 25.7 identifies the opportunity space for co-creation in the public sector using two main dimensions—the nature of service co-creation process and the time frame for service outcome. Two other variables are included in the figure—risks and value. Both variables are functions of service outcome and service process. Those co-creation opportunities that are relational in nature (for example, Keyring and Harlem Children's Zone) also tend to have higher risks in terms of service outcomes. Since the relational co-creation process involves significant input from players other than the government entity, it is also characterized by relatively lower control by the government entity. This could lead to higher risks for negative outcomes. However, the relational co-creation opportunities also tend to be longer term, which affords the time for appropriate evaluation of the process, which is inclined to bring down the risks. Nevertheless,

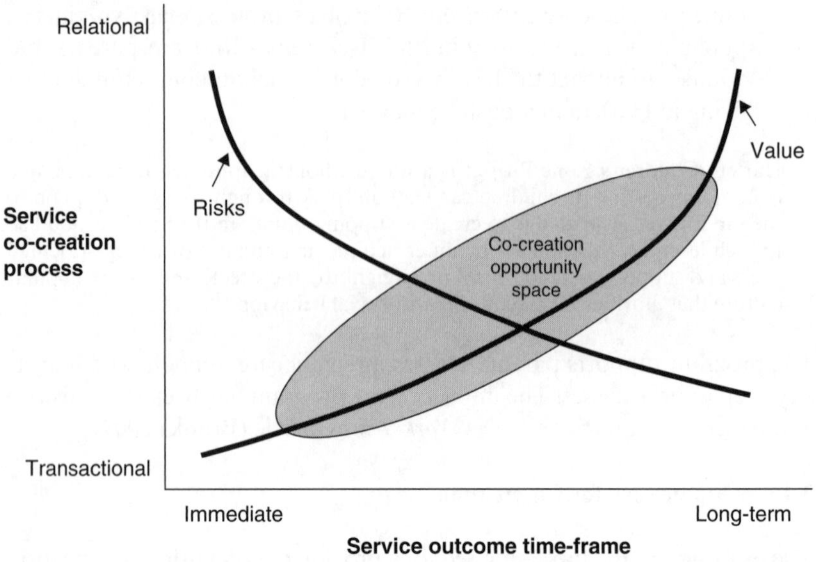

Figure 25.7 Identifying the opportunity for co-creation

as compared to transactional co-creation processes, relational processes always involve higher risks. On other hand, the value associated with service outcomes under relational co-creation processes is much higher as compared to the transactional co-creation processes. Thus, for relational co-creation opportunities, it is a trade-off between value and risks. If the risks outweigh the value derived, then such processes should not be undertaken. Transactional co-creation processes, on the other hand, are characterized by lower risks and lower value.

In Figure 25.7, the diagonal elliptical region in the middle characterizes the viable opportunity space for public sector initiatives. The transactional oriented co-creation processes generally are characterized by short time-frame service outcomes, with the relative values and risks being smaller. As the service co-creation processes become more relational, the time frames for service outcome become long term, with increasing values and risks.

The trade-off between value of the service outcome and risks associated with the outcome needs some discussion. It can be argued that in many applications that require a relational approach, value cannot be realized without taking the necessary risks. For example, initiatives such as Youth Court of Washington for crime prevention and minimizing recidivism are fraught with risks of the system becoming farcical, with minimal positive outcome. Similarly, the Harlem Children's Zone initiative has high risks of failure with an associated waste of resources. In both cases, however, the value of a positive outcome can be highly significant. Such benefits cannot be derived without taking the risks. It can also be argued that such values cannot be derived otherwise—that is, without a co-creation approach. While such claims may be arguable, it is clear that values and risks in such initiatives come with the territory.

3.2 Co-creation Process and Technologies

The processes and technologies for co-creation are functions of the service-outcome time frame and the nature of applications. The service co-creation processes that are transactional in nature with immediate service outcomes (for example, the EZ Pass system) are mainly technology driven (Figure 25.8). Innovations in digital and network technologies are likely to provide many opportunities for co-creation initiatives such as the Library of Congress example and the many examples discussed in this section. These technology-driven opportunities are the low-hanging fruit. As Figure 25.9 shows, developments in mobile and social media technologies, self-service applications, and other related technologies will hasten co-creation initiatives that are transactional based.

The technology platforms as shown in Figure 25.9 help organizations to harness citizens' motivation to benefit both their own selves and to

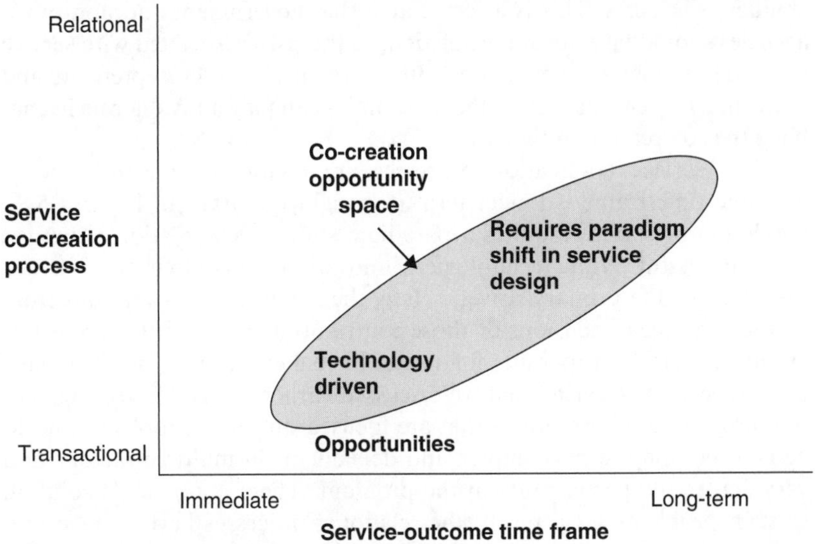

Figure 25.8 Drivers of opportunities

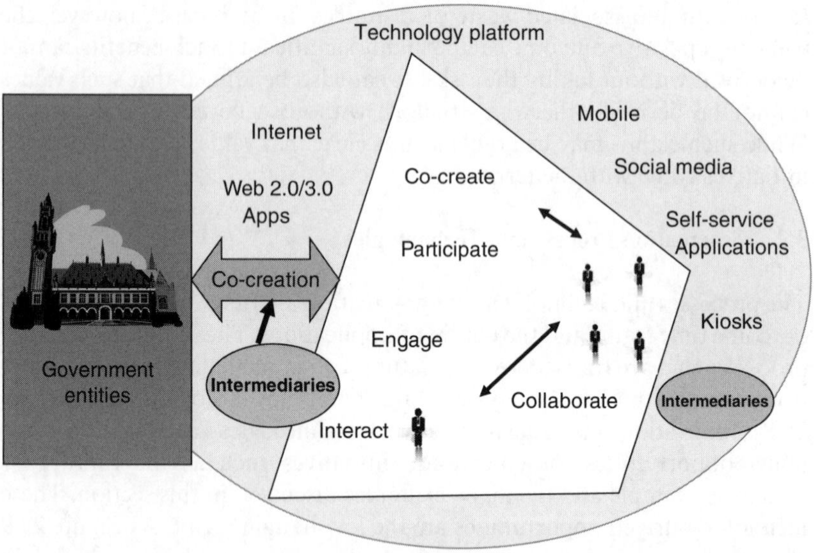

Figure 25.9 Technology platform for transactional co-creation initiatives

benefit the community. The EZ Pass system primarily benefits those who adopt the system, but as more people adopt it, the benefits increase and flow across to all. Designing such co-creation activities leads to high probabilities of success. This is a fertile area that government and non-profit agencies should take advantage of first, as the risks associated with service outcome are low. Intermediaries (other organizations, entrepreneurs and individual citizens) as seen in these examples can play a pivotal role in enabling the co-creation initiatives.

When service co-creation processes are relational and the service-outcome time frame is longer term (top right quadrant in Figure 25.8), the design of service requires a paradigm shift for co-creation initiatives to be successful. While technological innovations can help in this process, they are not the primary drivers. Here, the extent of contributions from citizens and the dimensions of those contributions play a critical role. For example, consider programs for mentally challenged and disadvantaged citizens, such as Keyring that we discussed earlier, or the family intervention projects. Such programs that are focused on social problems tend to be chronic, long term, complex and dependent on multiple factors, and vary across the participants in the program. There is no single solution to such problems; as a result, the relational processes have to take into account the customization required for each participant in the program. Since the service-outcome time frame is long term, there will be a tendency on the part of the participant, as well as the service provider, to be present-biased—that is, prefer short-term, positive outcomes to long-term, consistently successful outcomes. Accordingly, long-term outcomes tend to be discounted (Horne and Shirley 2009).

The successful outcome in those programs focused on social, crime prevention, medical, addiction, and educational disciplines depends on to what extent citizens contribute their resources to solve the problems. These resources are not just time, skill, knowledge or effort on the part of the citizens, but more importantly their self-control, motivations, social relationships with their family and desire to volunteer which play a critical role in the outcome. These resources cannot be substituted by other resources and cannot be made up by more money and time invested by the government agencies. Government can bring in resources, such as money, expertise, case workers and professional service providers, plans, and expectations, but unless citizens contribute significantly in the above-mentioned dimensions, successful outcomes cannot occur. In this regard the risks of service outcome need to be shared between the government agencies and the participants in the program (Horne and Shirley 2009). Successful outcome hinges not only on contribution of resources from both parties—government agencies and participants—and sharing of risks, but also sharing of control over how the resources are used. Government needs to cede some control to case workers and participants so that customization in service provision is achieved. The relational aspects of service provision become significant because the participants need to trust the government agencies and professional workers focusing on better outcomes to these problems. A paradigm shift in service provision based on mutual trust, participants having more control and using their own non-substitutable resources, is necessary for successful outcomes. When such a framework is implemented, it also reduces the risks of bad outcomes while reducing the need for more monetary resources from the government agencies. This realization of the nature of co-creation processes is necessary for designing creative new service programs in the social domain.

4 DESIGN AND MEASUREMENT CHALLENGES AND CONCLUSION

Based on the content discussed in previous sections, we now identify the key issues that need to be tackled by firms and government agencies as they contemplate initiating co-creation processes to create social value. Some of the identified issues may not have easy answers, but a careful consideration of them at the design phase can help eliminate potential problems down the road and increase the probability of success of these initiatives. First, we discuss issues and challenges in the domain of designing co-creation initiatives and then move on to discuss measurement issues.

4.1 Designing Co-creation

Co-creation is based on equality of participants in creating value. Thus, the design of the process has to "foster equal partnership between providers and users of service, afford equal value of different kinds of knowledge and skills, and acknowledge that everyone has something to contribute" (Boyle and Harris 2009). As we pointed out earlier, this means a paradigm shift as far as design is concerned and completely changing the expectations and approach of both service professionals and users.

Co-creation of social value has service innovation at its heart. While this is possible in the service design stage, ceding control to the users of services to innovate the process is essential. When citizens are involved in designing and delivering services for themselves and for others in their community, local innovations will flourish. Thus, the service design and the service professionals have to be flexible enough to let such innovations emerge. Getting the incentives right in the design stage is important. It is essential to understand the citizen groups targeted from their motivational viewpoint. Is it their own benefits they value most, or is it their reputation in the community or their altruistic goals? Since motivations can be different, the designs can be made flexible enough to let citizens with different motivation co-create and thrive. This certainly calls for creativity and experimentation in the design process.

Focusing on the appropriate citizens to target for co-creation initiatives is important. Citizens who have the right skill set and motivation to participate in the value creation initiative over a longer term are critical for the success of the initiatives. It is important to keep the citizens engaged, providing feedback to encourage their continued participation and commitment. Targeting and interacting with the right segment for a co-creation initiative is essential for its continued success. Co-creation of social value calls for effort and time from citizens. In the context of transactional oriented co-creation processes, some citizens may not have the time to use the co-created service channel, but rather may want to use full-service. (This is similar to self-service versus full-service in a grocery checkout.) The issue is how to deal with the heterogeneity in needs over time. This calls for design of multiple channels of service provision which might increase overall costs and reduce the benefits of co-creation.

Nonprofit, nongovernmental organizations (NGOs) and government agencies have to be particularly careful in setting boundaries in the co-creation space to delineate separation between the tasks performed by employees and professionals and tasks performed by citizens. An ill-structured design of tasks could risk participants stepping on each other's toes, leading to conflicts and dissatisfaction with the process. A too rigid separation, on the other hand, could stifle the innovations that could potentially arise in co-creation processes. Agencies need to monitor the process carefully on a continual basis to learn what works and what does not and refine the design over time. Co-creation initiatives require education and training of both sets of participants—citizens as well as employees and professionals—to set expectations, guidelines and rules of engagement. While emphasis is generally always put on citizens, preparing the staff for co-creation is absolutely essential for its success. The design of the initiative should include this component. In addition, in order to ensure that the momentum of these initiatives is sustained beyond their initial novelty period, periodic feedback to participants and staff is necessary to keep participants motivated. Creative ideas from participants and staff are to be appropriately channeled for consideration and implementation. Transparency of service operations is touted as an advantage of co-creation. However, from the agency viewpoint, being completely transparent may not be the best strategy. Depending on the application areas, appropriate levels of transparency should be included in the design. This calls for a careful review of tasks involved in the process, especially in the context of transactional services.

What level of risk is appropriate for a co-creation process? This is a key decision that needs to be made at the design stage. Programs such as Youth Court may be deemed too risky, and yet without taking such risks, successful outcomes are not achievable. It is necessary to tackle the fear of reasonable risk at the design stage of the co-creation process. Undertaking pilots on a smaller scale may be a viable way to reduce such risks.

Technology, in and of itself, cannot lead to a successful co-creation process. However, faulty design of technology for supporting the co-creation process can certainly lead to failures, especially in the case of transactional service processes. Appropriate on-line and off-line technology should be considered in the context of an application, with funding and support commensurate with the scale of the initiative.

Finally, co-creation initiatives need to be marketed to the citizens in the right way to set the intended expectations and rules of engagement. Nothing succeeds like success for marketing such initiatives and thus a small successful pilot should always be the first step.

4.2 Measuring the Success of Co-creation Initiatives

When it comes to measurement, there is clear demarcation between transactional-oriented service co-creation processes and relational-oriented service co-creation processes. In the former case, there is a generally clear and more tangible service outcome that is immediate as compared to relational service processes. The nature of the service outcome also tends to be more standard and measurable using standard service quality metrics (Zeithaml et al. 1990). However, in the case of relational service processes, the service outcome is much more diffused over time, less tangible and very customized and "contested." This makes the measurement of outcome all the more difficult. Following are key points on how to measure success in these two types of co-creation initiatives.

The transactional-oriented co-creation processes generally need to have some emphasis on the relative input of government agencies versus citizens in terms of all kinds of resources, and clear standards of operations. The initiatives need to have multiple targets—an overall goal with a number of intermediate targets, so that a clear message can be sent out to citizen participants on how the initiative is meeting goals and making a difference. Achievement of the intermediate targets needs to be communicated to the participants so that they remain motivated to engage in the initiatives. In addition to measuring the outcome quality and participant (both citizens' and employee staff) input, in terms of the government agency, the resources should be measured so that return on investment (ROI) of the initiative can be quantified. Participant growth and retention rates vis-à-vis other channels can be compared to highlight the efficacy of the co-creation strategy.

There are two schools of thought on relational-oriented co-creation processes. One perspective calls for less emphasis on the process per se and stresses looking outward to increasing the social networks to aid in successful outcomes (Horne and Shirley 2009). The reasoning here is that inward-looking measures such as meeting targets, rigid standards, and process milestones may stifle innovation and creativity that are sorely needed for successful outcomes. Since the definition of success varies from case to case, the heterogeneity may not lend itself to rigid processes and standards. Thus, as the reasoning goes, a spirit of experimentation is needed to allow out-of-the-box thinking that may lead to successful outcomes. Another perspective that we offer is to have process milestones and milestones for resources expended, but experiment with different mixes of levels of control between participants and staff. The mix of control is customized to a particular situation to maximize chances of a successful outcome. For example, depending on the skill level of a participant in the Expert Patient program, some patients will have more control as to how they allocate their resources while some will have less. However, there is accountability in terms of the resources spent and the outcome is measured intermittently to determine progress based on which subsequent decisions on control and resources are made. Both perspectives still need to grapple with metrics such as measuring quality of life, convenience and service quality improvements. These are likely to be more intangible than in the transactional co-creation processes.

A measurement issue that is common to both processes is "tackling the accounting problem" (Boyle and Harris 2009). In many cases, co-creation initiatives could lead to costs accruing in one department or agency while the savings and benefit accrue in another agency. For example, one of the results of family intervention programs could be reduced unemployment and result in less food stamps being distributed. If the accounting of these programs is in "silo" systems that do not reconcile with each other, then benefits may be underestimated. This highlights a need for a systems approach in measuring the benefits of such co-creation programs.

It needs to be stressed that measurement at the individual co-creation initiative level is only the beginning of understanding how the initiatives can be improved and made more successful. The knowledge that is created in a collective analysis of all initiatives, each with different business models, with different experiences across different geographical and service contexts, will be of significant help in improving co-creation processes. This calls for a meta-analysis across a number of co-creation initiatives spanning transactional and relational processes, which will help identify common factors—participant and staff skill, contexts and applications—that lead to successful co-creation programs. Knowledge management systems that record specifics of each initiative—design, implementation, experience, and measurement—and function as case repositories, can be of significant help in providing support and advice to others. Similarly, technological developments and technology tools used to support co-creation can be shared across agencies to foster the adoption of these models for citizen service.

In conclusion, it is important to point out that we are in a period of enormous potential for citizen engagement and social value creation, but also at a time of great risk. The potential is that we can harness the power of a crowd 300 million strong—a crowd of highly educated, highly motivated, and highly connected individuals. The risk is that engagement, if not designed appropriately, will become both the means and the end. We may be engaging for the sake of engagement and feel-good factors, which might quickly sour people when they begin to feel that offering their voice and effort is little more than lip service. If the agencies—both government and

NGOs and private sector entities—are to reap the greatest rewards from citizen engagement in value creation—in terms of lower operating costs and more efficient operations and creating social value—they need to be transparent and open in their orientation towards citizens and customers.

REFERENCES

Bhalla, Gaurav (2011), *Collaboration and Co-delivery: New Platforms for Marketing and Innovation*, New York: Springer.

Boyle, David and Michael Harris (2009), "The challenge of co-production," discussion paper, NESTA, London, December, accessed on 11 November 2011 at www.nesta.org.uk/publications/reports/assets/features/the_challenge_of_co-production.

Brooks, David (2009), 'The Harlem miracle', *New York Times*, 7 May, accessed 6 July 2011 at www.nytimes.com/2009/05/08/opinion/08brooks.html.

Bughin, Jacques, Michael Chui and James Manyika (2010), "Clouds, big data, and smart assets: ten tech-enabled business trends to watch," *McKinsey Quarterly*, August, accessed 10 November 2011 at www.mckinseyquarterly.com/Clouds_big_data_and_smart_assets_Ten_tech-enabled_business_trends_to_watch_2647.

Campbell, Christopher, Paul Maglio and Mark Davis (2011), "From self-service to super-service: a resource mapping framework for co-creating value by shifting the boundary between provider and customer," *Information Systems and E-Business Management*, **9** (2), 173–91.

Deloitte Report (2008), "Change your world or the world will change you: the future of collaborative government and Web 2.0," Deloitte, Washington, DC.

Edvardsson, Bo, Bard Tronvoll and Thirsten Gruber (2011), "Expanding understanding of service exchange and value co-creation: a social construction approach," *Journal of the Academy of Marketing Science*, **39** (2), 327–39.

Ford, Robert, Bo Edvardsson, Duncan Dickson and Bo Enquist (2012), "Managing the innovation co-creation challenge: lessons from service exemplars: Disney and IKEA," *Organizational Dynamics*, **41** (4), 281–90.

Green, J. (2011), "The dirt: uniting the built and natural enviornments – an interview with Jaime Lerner," accessed 11 November 2011 at http://dirt.asla.org/2011/03/07/interview-with-jaime-lerner/.

Gronroos, Christian (2011), "Value co-creation in service logic: a critical analysis," *Marketing Theory*, **11** (3), 279–301.

Holmes, Brenton (2011), "Citizens' engagement in policymaking and the design of public Services," Research Paper no. 1 2011–12, Politics and Public Administration Section, July, accessed 21 February 2012 at www.aph.gov.au/library/pubs/rp/2011-12/12rp01.htm.

Horne, Matthew and Tom Shirley (2009), "Co-production in public services: a new partnership with citizens," discussion paper, London: Cabinet Office, The Strategy Unit, accessed 10 November 2011 at http://webarchive.nationalarchives.gov.uk/+/http://www.cabinetoffice.gov.uk/media/207033/public_services_co-production.pdf.

Hoyer, Wayne D., Rajesh Chandy, Matilda Dorotic, Manfred Krafft and Siddharth Singh (2010), "Consumer co-creation in new product development," *Journal of Service Research*, **13** (3), 283–96.

Lehrer, Mark, Andrea Ordanini, Robert DeFillippi and Marcela Miozzo (2012), "Challenging the orthodoxy of value co-creation theory: a contingent view of co-production in design-intensive business services," *European Management Journal*, **30** (6), 499–509.

Novak, Kevin and Michelle Springer (2007), "Government as a participant in social networks: adding authority to conversation," paper presented at the Toward More Transparent Government Workshop on eGovernment and the Web Conference, 18–19 June, United States National Academy of Sciences, Washington, DC.

Prahalad, C.K. and V. Ramaswamy (2000), "Co-opting customer experience," *Harvard Business Review*, **78** (1), 79–87.
Prahalad, C.K and V. Ramaswamy (2004), *The Future of Competition: Co-creating Unique Value with Customers*, Cambridge, MA: Harvard Business School Press.
Rosenberg, Tina (2011), "Where teenagers find the jury isn't rigged," accessed 21 February 2012 at http://opinionator.blogs.nytimes.com/2011/10/18/where-teens-find-the-jury-isnt-rigged/.
Vargo, Stephen L. and Robert F. Lusch (2004), "Evolving to a new dominant logic for marketing," *Journal of Marketing*, **68** (1), 1–17.
Zeithaml, V., A. Parasuraman and L. Berry (1990), *Delivering Quality Service; Balancing Customer Perceptions and Expectations*, New York: Free Press.

Index